Corporate Vaastu
Applied Indian Architecture for Righteous Earning

ॐ
श्रीं गं सौम्याय गणपतये वरवरद।
सर्वजनं मे वशमानय स्वाहा।।

(May we get the grace and blessings of Ma Lakshmi and Lord Ganesha in every birth! May they bless us to lead a healthy and prosperous life! May they bless us with good luck and remove all our obstacles!)

LAKSHMI GANESHA

Goddess Lakshmi is the Goddess of all wealth, money, fortune and prosperity, while Lord Ganesha is the God of intelligence, wisdom, and success. They are worshipped together often by the merchant community on the auspicious day of *Diwali* which is believed to bring prosperity and peace in our life. The *pooja* place is also marked with the written words "*Shubh-Laabh*" (Righteous Gain) – which points out that we should aim for profits which are through fair means only. Lakshmi Ganesha also remind us that we don't have to aim for material wealth only but have also to aim for prudence and wisdom.

Corporate Vaastu
Applied Indian Architecture for Righteous Earning

Er. Ashwini Kumar Bansal

STERLING PUBLISHERS (P) LTD.
Regd. Office: A1/256 Safdarjung Enclave,
New Delhi-110029. CIN: U22110DL1964PTC211907
Tel: 26387070, 26386209
E-mail: mail@sterlingpublishers.in
www.sterlingpublishers.in

Corporate Vaastu: Applied Indian Architecture for Righteous Earning
© 2018, Er. Ashwini Kumar Bansal
ISBN 978 93 86245 24 3
First Edition 2018

All rights are reserved. No part of this publication may be reproduced, stored in a retrieval system or transmitted, in any form or by any means, mechanical, photocopying, recording or otherwise, without prior written permission of the original publisher.

Note from the Publishers

The author and publisher cannot accept any responsibility for any misadventure resulting from the practice of any of the principles and therapies set out in this book. Any information given in this book is not intended to be taken as an alternative for expert medical advice. Any person with a condition requiring medical attention should consult a qualified practitioner or therapist.

Printed and Published in India by

Sterling Publishers Pvt. Ltd.,
Plot No. 13, Ecotech-III, Greater Noida - 201306, U. P. India

Dedicated

To the Memory of

My Parents

Smt Vidya Devi & Sri Mahabir Prashad

Steady Seller!

Unfolding the Veil of Mystery – Vaastu: The Art & Science of Living is an intelligent amalgamation of the ancient practice of Vaastu living and modern technologies of house building and architecture. It offers an introduction to Vaastu Shaastra, systematising and standardising its techniques and methodologies.

The book has been divided into three sections. The first section has been devoted to the understanding of the key concepts, principles and forces of Vaastu that exert an influence on any given space. The second section of the book reveals how to create heaven on earth; right in your home. It shows how we can achieve internal peace by first achieving external peace in the house. The third section is related to the day-to-day use of Vaastu.

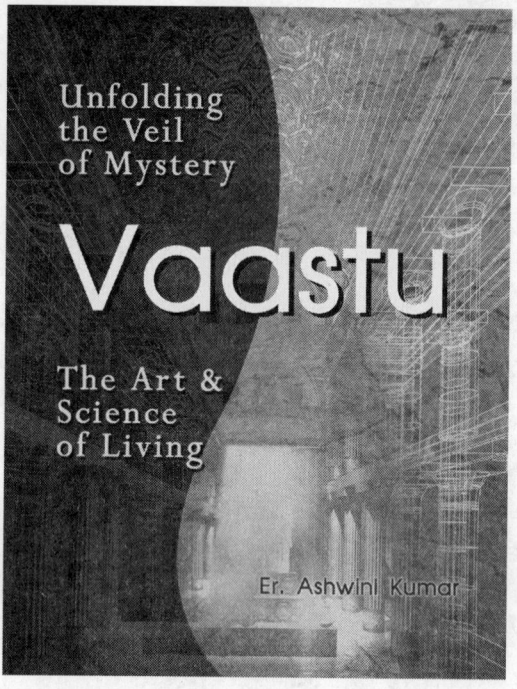

Society for Study of Mystique Sciences
(Registered with the Govt. of NCT of Delhi)
Courses and Consultancy Services

Society for Study of Mystique Sciences is conducting specialized courses in Vaastu Shastra, Feng Shui, Tarot Card Reading, Remedial Astrology, Gemmology & Colour Therapy, Mantra Shaastra, Lal Kitab System of Astrology, Graphology (Handwriting Analysis), Palmistry, Numerology and other allied subjects. The classes of these courses are held during the weekends or holidays around Connaught Place, New Delhi. The society also awards Certificate(s) of Participation after successful completions of the course(s).

The author is honorary chief guide and professor at the Society and honorary guide and professor of Vaastu Shastra and Palmistry at the Centre of Indology, Bhartiya Vidya Bhavan, New Delhi. He is also available for private consultation, assistance and advice in Vaastu Shaastra and Feng Shui. If you wish to contact the author or would like more information about the courses or this book, please contact:

Ashwini Kumar Bansal
Phone Number: 91-9968718607
WhatsApp Number: 91-9958167853
Facebook ID: ashwinibansal@yahoo.com
E Mail: ashwinikumarbansal1@gmail.com, akbdelhi@yahoo.com

Foreword

Vaastu - a mystery or a science? The debate is on between the believers and the non-believers. For me it is a MYSTIC SCIENCE. My own experiences with implied Vaastu force me to believe that it is a science but a lot of dedicated and honest research needs to be done to raise the curtain from over the Mystic part of Vaastu.

As an Architect, I see Vaastu as a climatic science. It is also a social science and a science that has the potential of altering the behavior of humans. Vaastu is truly a science of living and growing in cohesion with the forces of nature.

Business is one of the most important karma of life. Your work place is sacred. It is from this place you earn name, fame and money. And it is good to earn money and live a life that one desires.

A number of texts have been written on Vaastu of temples, forts, cities and homes but hardly does one find something on Vaastu of work places and that too well researched.

I am sure this book will fill in the vacuum of availability of such texts for professionals, researchers, students and anyone who has a fascination for Vaastu. As I read the book, I realized a great effort has been made. An in-depth study has been undertaken, references have been taken from various scriptures after a lot of research. Inferences and their implication as explained in the book have been drawn after a thorough analysis.

Truly, a new Vaastu has been evolved – Corporate Vaastu. Apt to the name, 'Corporate Vaastu' deals with various principles of Vaastu for the workplace as researched by Shri Ashwini Kumar Bansal. This book, as I understand is the outcome of his research for over two decades.

I have had the privilege of knowing him for over a decade. A great master of Vaastu, he strongly believes that Vaastu if implemented with proper knowledge has the potential of changing our lives and fortunes. A passionate researcher, he writes or speaks with conviction and only after a thorough study and analysis.

I am very sure the readers will find the book very informative and captivating. The principles of Corporate Vaastu have been explained in a very simple, systematic and organized manner.

My heartiest thanks to Shri Ashwini Kumar Bansal to have done this herculean effort of understanding and sharing the mysticism of Vaastu through this book.

Architect Atul Gupta *

*An expert of Implied Vaastu, Architect Atul Gupta is a leading practicing Architect. A thinker and a motivator. Ar. Atul Gupta is the Principal Architect of Spatium Architects. He is the past president of Uttar Pradesh Architects Association.

Acknowledgements

The production of this work, "**Corporate Vaastu: Applied Indian Architecture for Righteous Earning**" has only been possible with the help of following:

- Highly intelligent faculty at the Institute of Astrology; Bhartiya Vidya Bhavan; New Delhi for gaining formal knowledge in Astrology, Indian Council of Astrological Sciences' Research Classes conducted by Sri A. B. Shukla at Pusa Road; New Delhi for in depth knowledge of astro-vaastu remedies and faculty members at the Department of Astrology; Lal Bahadur Shastri Sanskrit Vidyapeeth, New Delhi for in depth knowledge of Remedies through Mantra Shaastra.
- Architect Sri Atul Gupta; former Chairman of UP Architects Association and my Vaastu student, special thanks for writing the foreword, readily offering all his office support for drawing most of the figures on Auto CAD, for providing encouragement and giving innovative ideas from time to time.
- My soul-friends—Sri Hem Raj Singhal, Sri Kamal Kishore Aggarwal, Sri Subodh Kumar Goyal, Sri Suneet Kumar Aggarwal, and Sri Tanmaya Behera—whom I find ever ready to unload my heavy thoughts and feelings with their timely help, individual support, love, encouragement, and wise advice. I feel blessed having these angelic souls in my life!
- My students of Vaastu Shaastra & Feng Shui—Ms Anubha Jain, Ms Hema Dhingra, Sri P K Mittal, Ms Preeti Sharma, Ms Priyanka Goenka, Ms Shubhani Sharma, Ms Taruna Gupta, and Ms Vijeta for their willing assistance and co-operation in different capacities in the preparation of this book.
- Mr Deepak Singh and Mr Raunaq Jain, both B Arch students for their unending enthusiasm and meticulous attention to detail while drawing the intricate figures in this book on Auto CAD.
- Hundreds of my students of Vaastu Shaastra and Feng Shui, Palmistry, Vedic and Lal Kitab Astrology, Gemology and Colour Therapy, Tarot Card Reading, Handwriting Analysis (Graphology) and Numerology at the Institute of Mystique Sciences (IMS), New Delhi and Centre of Indology, Bhartiya Vidya Bhavan, New Delhi whose queries and feedback has been a constant source of inspiration for me.
- My wife Dr Jhilmil who has been a perennial source of strength, inspiration and support.
- My nephew Piyush Bansal for helping me overcome various computer-related technical issues in connection with the production of this book and my adolescent nephews; Dhruv Bansal and Lakshay Bansal whose naughty activities kept me entertaining during the long hours of deep studies and research.
- My family members, friends and well wishers who all contributed through their patience, constant encouragement, love and blessings to help me succeed in my project.
- Many clients over the years, too numerous to mention, I acknowledge everyone for his / her support.
- The planetary lords Jupiter and Mercury for granting me the will power and strength to complete this book in their running major and sub-periods as it became much more ambitious than initially conceived.
- My publishers, who made it possible for you to read it, and enjoy a happy and contented long life through righteous earning.

Preface

Vaastu Shastra is the classical art and science of constructing houses, palaces, temples, monuments, wells and step wells, pools, stadiums, and theatres—virtually all types of constructions. Sound knowledge of construction engineering is the first basic requirement for becoming a vaastu expert (*Mayamatam* 5.15a & 5.18a):

स्थपति: स्थापनार्ह: स्यात् सर्वशास्त्र विशारद:
सुनामा दृढबुद्धिश्च वास्तु विद्याब्धि पारग:।

"The architect is a man of quality; he must know how to establish buildings and must be well versed in all the sciences. Of good name and persevering, he must have crossed the ocean of the science of architecture."

Except having in depth knowledge of building construction, vaastu requires thorough knowledge of Physics (at least laws of magnetism, heat, sound and optics), Astronomy, Astrology, Mythology, History, Geography, Human Psychology, local socio-cultural and religious practices, and a deep attunement with the Mother Nature. Knowledge of the Sanskrit language is an added advantage as most of the original classical texts of vaastu shastra are available in Sanskrit only. The available English translations of the classical texts of vaastu shastra, even the standard ones like Mayamatam and *Samaranganasutradhar*, have discrepancies.

It is surprising that in contrast to the above recommendations of Mayamatam, most of the new age vaastu books have been written by the so called *Vaastu Shaastris* (vaastu experts) who don't even have the basic knowledge of building science, leave aside having formal academic qualification in Civil Engineering or Architecture. Astrologers (Jyotishis), traditional *Karmakandi Pandits* and translators of Sanskrit texts of vaastu shastra are posing themselves as expert vaastu *shastris*.

Some architects and interior designers too - without having in depth knowledge of the principles of classical vaastu - claim their clients that they have included "vaastu" in their design. Mere knowledge of the so called auspicious directions for the main door, slope of the floor, flow of water and position of our head while sleeping does not make one a vaastu expert. Such types of claims only bring a bad name to this time-tested classical science.

Talking astrologically, building construction is seen from the fourth *bhava* (house) of the horoscope. A person desirous of becoming an expert in Vaastu Shastra should have a strong fourth bhava in his / her horoscope. Fourth bhava is considered strong when auspicious classical combinations (yogas) are formed here. It also becomes strong when it is occupied and / or aspected by its own lord and / or benefic planets, when flanked by benefics and when its lord participates in benefic planetary combinations (*yogas*).

Saturn, the significator of building material and construction, should also be strongly placed in the horoscope of a person desirous of becoming an expert in Vaastu Shastra. Saturn is considered strong when it forms auspicious combinations in the horoscope (for example

Shash, *Mahabhagya*, *Shrikanth*, *Shridaam*, *Vairinchi* etc), when it is in its own or exaltation sign, or when it is *vargottama* (the same sign in *navamsha* as in the natal horoscope) etc. Strong Saturn also gives an acute touching sense.

Mars is the significator of construction activities. Its overall strength and beneficence also gives active interest in construction and property business. When Mars is also strong in the horoscope and is strongly related with the 4th *bhava*, 4th lord and Saturn, vaastu expert will not only plan the building but will also be actively involved in the construction activities. Strongly placed Mercury in the horoscope makes one an expert in sketching, drawing and calculation work.

Vaastu, when judged from the 'Time' factor, is of three types – static (*sthira*), dynamic (*chara*) and daily (*nitya*). Static vaastu assumes a static position of *vaastu purush* throughout the year – head with face down in the north-east and feet in the south-west. As per the dynamic aspect of vaastu, vaastu purush goes on changing his position every three months. North direction is auspicious mainly during the summers. Otherwise; east, south and west are also auspicious during the rainy season, early winters and harsh winters respectively. No direction is completely auspicious or inauspicious for all the seasons. The same rule applies for different people involved in different businesses working from different places on the earth.

We also read about daily vaastu (*Nitya Vaastu*) in the classical vaastu texts. Vaastu goes on changing on daily basis. The golden rule of daily vaastu is:

पृष्ठतः सेव्येदर्कं जठरेण हुताशनम्।

(Take sunrays from your back's side and fire from your front side).

Following this classical rule, while sitting in an open area during the mid-day, facing north is best to avoid the scorching sunrays when Sun becomes a fireball in the south direction. On the contrary, keeping head towards south is best during midnight for enjoying the sound sleep.

South, the direction of Yama - though inauspicious during the noontime - becomes auspicious at night. Likewise, south delivers worst results only during the scorching summers, worse during the moderate summers, bad during the rainy season but good during the winters. For inhabitants of the south facing houses, winters are virtually a party time. On the contrary, people living in the north or east facing houses (with closed south and west) suffer in winters on account of non-availability of the direct solar heat. Consequently, senior citizens, patients, housewives and children are the main victims.

Now, I will like to discuss application of vaastu in trade, commerce, industry and business - all the activities except the residential one. For residential vaastu, readers are advised to refer my earlier book, *Unfolding the Veil of Mystery Vaastu The Art & Science of Living*. Here, in the present book, my main concern is on the Vaastu principles regarding earning; may be money, kinds, health, knowledge, power, position, service or reputation. It will be worthwhile to point out here once again that most of the modern vaastu experts have wrongly put the business vaastu in the same category i.e., fixed (*sthira*) vaastu. Principles of fixed vaastu are used for constructing permanent residential buildings which are meant for performing different types of activities.

In *sthira* (fixed) vaastu, construction is allowed only on around 50 percent of the total plot area, with offsets all around (*paishach-sthan*) and in the middle (*braham-sthan*). Principles of fixed vaastu have been designed to accommodate the needs of movable (*chara*) vaastu and daily (*nitya*) vaastu. These principles were carved during the ancient golden era when plenty of land was available free of cost. Even during the reign of Mughal emperor Akbar (1556 to 1605 AD), sufficient land was available free of cost for agriculture and housing purposes in the sixteenth and early seventeenth centuries. In our modern times, at least in the smaller and medium size constructions, it is generally not possible to keep the ideal offsets of one ninth on all the four sides.

A business premise is much different from a residential building. Different recommendations are found for the main door meant for a residence and for other purposes in the classical vaastu texts. According to *Mayamatam* 16.50; "There is no error placing the door of a building meant for gods, *brahmins* or kings in the middle of the facade, but for all the other categories an auspicious door is placed to one side of the middle of the facade". Buildings meant for Gods here means religious buildings, buildings meant for Brahmins means places of learning and buildings meant for kings means the modern government, judicial and public buildings.

The door of a residence opens inside while door of a shop opens outside or upwards. A roller shutter fixed at the entry of any room normally indicates that it is being used for commercial purposes. Shutter, which is larger in size than a common door, makes it lion faced (*sher mukhi*). On the contrary, a simple small door opening inside makes the premises cow faced (*gau mukhi*). A larger opening not only invites more clients and more shoppers, it also advertises your goods and services as well. A smaller door, on the contrary, is good for the residential premises as it helps in maintaining privacy, safety, security and sanctity of the house and its inhabitants.

A wider plot or construction at the entry does not always mean wider dimensions of the front side than the backside. Likewise a narrow entry does not mean smaller dimensions of front side than the backside. The plot becomes trapezoidal in shape in such a case, which is never considered good in vaastu. Trapezoidal plots always need rectification before construction.

Residence is mainly meant for sleeping at night. This activity of sleeping is of inactive nature (*tamasic*) and is best recommended in the south-west (*nairritya*) direction. The second most important activity in the household is cooking and it should be performed during the daytime only. For this purpose, south-east is the best direction. Likewise, the daytime activities - the business activities - are best in the south-east facing premises. This area is called the "Wealth Zone" in Feng Shui; Chinese equivalent of the Indian Vaastu Shastra.

As north-east is the ideal direction for all types of residences, south-east is normally the ideal direction for all types of business activities. Otherwise, different directions are auspicious for different businesses activities, as different sectors in the house are auspicious for different purposes. These recommendations are based on the daily movement of sun and degree of absorption of heat by the different directions. Vaastu Shastra talks about the suitability of different directions for different purposes; though in the mythological language of the nine ruling planets (*grahas*), ten directional lords (*dikpalas*) and forty-five demi-gods.

During my vaastu visits, I visited a factory in an industrial area in Delhi. This factory was manufacturing leaf bearings which are generally used in the trucks and other HTVs. The factory was north facing with a small offset in the south direction, the backside of the factory. East and west sides were completely closed because of the adjacent buildings. The owner wanted to close the existing small offset in the south direction so as to make more working space inside. As the factory was already not running well, he was not sure of his step. So, he contacted me for proper guidance. I predicted that the factory was a sick unit. The owner confirmed that the overall output is very less and factory remains virtually closed during the winters.

The work in this factory was related to the heavy metals, heat and fire. All these are ruled by the fiery Mars, the lord of the south direction. This factory should have been south facing or having more openings in the south. A blacksmith cannot be supposed to work efficiently in an air-conditioned space. Likewise, printing and publishing work – for which north is most auspicious – cannot efficiently be done in the south. The owner told me that earlier he was running this factory in another industrial area. His factory was south facing in the earlier location. There, he was never short of orders and was well known for timely completion of the job. As polluting industries had to shift in non-residential areas due to court orders, the present owner had to leave that place. He had chosen the present north facing premises by consulting some so called vaastu expert who applied the same principles as are considered good for the residence! The result was before him!

Factory vaastu can't ever be equalized with that of the residential vaastu. Even vaastu of two factories, manufacturing different things, will be different. All the ten directions are auspicious but only for certain activities, for certain time period of the year and for certain people. These directions, at the same time, become inauspicious for certain other activities, time period and people. Ultimately *graha* (planetary lord), *dikpal* (directional lord) and demi-god(dess) of any direction decide the type(s) of auspicious and inauspicious activities for it. An individual's horoscope, in turn, will decide auspicious directions for him or her.

Corporate Vaastu: Applied Indian Architecture for Righteous Earning offers an introduction to the principles of business Vaastu - including the vaastu of offices, factories, educational and religious premises, resorts, housing societies – virtually all the aspects of public related Vaastu. This book is intended to systematise and standardise the techniques and methodologies of the corporate use and office vaastu. Whole of the book has been divided into nine chapters.

Chapter 1 of the book explains the key concepts and forces of Vaastu Shastra that exert influence on any given space. The skeleton of Vaastu Shastra stands mainly on the ten directions. Certain planets, directional lords, thermal & optical qualities, elements, shapes, *gunas*, weight and energies are allotted to all of these ten directions. All these aspects have been discussed and efforts have been made to clarify the underlying deep philosophy. For detailed study of the same, readers are advised to refer my book, *Vaastu: The Art & Science of Living*.

Traditional Vaastu is expressed in terms of myths and symbols. Forty-five gods, demi-gods and goddesses occupy the body of *vaastu purush* - ranging from single to nine squares in an eighty-one square grid. Though familiar with some names like Indra, Surya, Yama, Varuna, Soma etc, most of the present day readers are completely ignorant of the names of most of these demi-gods. Neither the Vaastu classics nor the modern authors of the vaastu books have paid serious thought for deciphering their deep meanings. All the possible efforts have been made here to decode the deep meanings of these demi-gods and goddesses in Chapter 2.

Most auspicious business or professional activities for all the eight directions have been discussed at length in Chapter 3. Location of business, its building, entrance, sitting arrangement, name and logo of the business, advertising strategies, and wealth management have been discussed in details. Business-related classical Hindu gods and goddesses, events and festivals have also been described in the modern day context.

Different classical texts of vaastu recommend specific directions and squares not only for the residential purposes but also for different types of commercial, professional, administrative and religious activities. Recommendations of mainly the four popular classical texts of vaastu shastra - "*Mayamatam*" written by the great *Vaastushilpi Maya*, "*Vaastumandanam*" written by *Sutradhara Mandana Bhardwaj*, "*Aparajitaprichchha*" written by *Bhuvan Devacharya* and "*Samaranganasutradhara*" written by the great king *Bhoja Deva* – have been discussed at length in Chapter 4. Efforts have been made to discuss the individual as well as the comparative statement of the auspicious directions and squares recommended for different public activities in all of these four classical texts.

Chapter 5 is exclusively devoted to the principles of office and workplace vaastu. The principles of vaastu shastra, used creatively in the home and office, can greatly contribute in career success. The energies of home and workplace are interdependent. Something wrong with the one will affect the other. Unhappy relationships at home could be because of a problem in the office or vice versa. Likewise, problems in the office could be caused by a lack of harmonious relation between the co-workers or blockage of *prana* due to the bad position of your working table.

Principles of vaastu, along with the residences like the modern apartments and pent houses, may equally be applied to all the places related with the masses e.g., temples, institutions of learning, service apartments, agricultural land, farmhouses, resorts, hotels and restaurants, shopping malls etc. These places may include not only the religious, industrial, commercial, and public buildings but all the other types of constructions. I have discussed some peculiar areas of mass appeal in Chapter 6. After going through the earlier chapters and this chapter conscientiously, intelligent readers would virtually be able to apply the vaastu principles to each and every type of vaastu.

Modern Architect's view about vaastu is based on the strong scientific principles, climatic conditions and human behaviour. There is no place for mystical vaastu recommendations in the modern architecture. Location of plot and various rooms in any house are based on the pragmatic fundamentals like the direction of sunrise with respect to the plot, and the direction of wind. In the old days, the wise learned people had to "mystify" these principles. They had to make it sound like real bad luck would fall upon the house owner in case he did not follow these principles. Chapter 7 has been introduced to explain how these ultra modern building practices like eco-friendly buildings and water harvesting are in reality the changed or modified versions of the age old established principles of the classical vaastu shastra.

Varied aspects of vaastu have been discussed in Chapter 8. Intelligent readers may use this information for further enriching their minds. Some aspects, though discussed at length in the earlier chapters, have been added here to provide additional knowledge of vaastu from the classical, modern, personal or practical point of view.

Actual case studies regarding some particular areas have been discussed in Chapter 9. Readers are advised to first go through the general principles of vaastu shastra - residential and commercial both - before giving a study to these cases. Also, these cases should not be applied in the similar manner to all the similar cases. Always apply the *Desh* (place), *Kaal* (time) and *Paatra* (person) factors.

The present book mainly deals with the principles of commercial and public Vaastu, in tune with the necessities of modern technology and practical usage. This work is meant primarily for those who want to learn the principles of business and office vaastu from the very beginning and pursue it seriously in a scientific manner. The present book is also aimed to help those who intend to indulge in the hitherto unexplored areas of Vaastu Shaastra e.g., suitability of certain directions for certain activities and hidden meanings of the forty-five types of energy systems.

We have ventured to establish the "Society for Study of Mystique Sciences" in Delhi which is now registered with the Govt. of NCT of Delhi. The society is conducting workshops and courses in Vaastu Shaastra and Feng Shui, Palmistry, Gemology and Colour Therapy, Lal Kitab Astrology, Mantra Shastra, Handwriting Analysis (Graphology), Tarot Card Reading and allied subjects in New Delhi.

The society is acting as initiator of a radical method of teaching these Mystic Sciences in co-relation with the Human Physiognomy, Human Psychology, Sanskrit, Science, Spirituality and Engineering. The Society is following the sacred tradition of distributing the long accumulated knowledge of these divine *vidyas* to the people who are worthy of receiving it. The members of SSMS (Regd) in Delhi wish all readers a grand success in understanding the art and science of Vaastu Shaastra and in acquiring the expertise by themselves.

Most of the classical texts were written in a male-dominated society. In the modern day context 'son' should be understood as 'child'. Everywhere in this book, 'He' is equally applicable on male and female, unless specifically pointed out otherwise.

All kinds of suggestions from the intelligent readers are most welcome with thanks for the improvement of this book and science. My efforts will be more than rewarded if this work fulfils its intended aims.

Ashwini Kumar Bansal
Narela, Delhi,
4th April 2018,
Facebook ID: ashwinibansal@yahoo.com
E Mail: ashwinikumarbansal1@gmail.com

Contents

Foreword	vii
Acknowledgements	viii
Preface	ix

Chapter 1
Principles of Vaastu Shastra — 1

Introduction	1
What is Vaastu Shastra?	3
Directions	4-7
Four Directions and Four Castes	7
Shapes	7-10
Shurpa and Laangal Shapes	10-11
Dimensions	11
Pada-Vinyas and their Usage	12
Vaastu Purush (Space Personified)	12
Marma-sthanas (Vulnerable points)	13
Types of Vaastu	13
Prana	13-14
Trigunas	14-16
Panchmahabhootas and Related Businesses	16-22
Sunlight	22-23
Lighting	23
Colours	23-25
Astrology (Jyotish)	25-26
Electional Astrology (Muhoorta)	26

Chapter 2
Vaastu Gods and Goddesses — 27

Introduction 27-32

• 1. Vahni (32-33) • 2. Parjanya (33-34) • 3. Jayant (34-35) • 4. Mahendra (35-36) • 5. Aaditya (36-38) • 6. Satya (38-39) • 7. Bhrish (39-41) • 8. Antariksh (41) • 9. Maarut (41-43) • 10. Poosha (43-45) • 11. Vitath (45) • 12. Grihakshat (45-46) • 13. Yam (46-48) • 14. Gandharv (48-49) • 15. Bhringraaj (49-50) • 16. Mrig (50-51) • 17. Pitar (51-53) • 18. Dauvaarik (53) • 19. Sugreev (53-54) • 20. Pushpdant (55-56) • 21. Varun (56-57) • 22. Asur (57-58) • 23. Shosh (58-59) • 24. Paapyakshama (59-60) • 25. Rog (60-61) • 26. Naag (62-63) • 27. Mukhya (64-65) • 28. Bhallaat (65-66) • 29. Som (66-68) • 30. Charak (68-69) • 31. Aditi (69-70) • 32. Diti (70) • 33. Aap (71-72) • 34. Aapvats (72-73) • 35. Aryama (73-74) • 36. Savita (74-75) • 37. Saavitr (75-76) • 38. Vivasvaan (76-77) • 39. Indra (77-78) • 40. Jaya (78-79) • 41. Mitra (79-80) • 42. Rudra (80-81) • 43. Raajyakshma (82-83) • 44. Kshitidhar (83-84) • 45. Brahma (84-85)

Chapter 3
Principles of Business Vaastu — 86

Residential Versus Business Vaastu	86-88
Directions and Corresponding Business Activities	88-93
Location of Business	93-96
Commercial Building	96-100
Main Entrance	100-104
Lobby	104-105
Reception	105-107
Name of Your Business	107-108
Business Logo or Emblem	108
Signboards	108-110
Advertising your Goods and Services	110

Wealth Management — 110-127

Kuber	112
Alakshmi: The Goddess of Misfortune	112-113
Lakshmi: The Wealth Goddess	113-119
Diwali: The Festival of Goddess Lakshmi	119-125
Clutter	125-126
Cash Counter	126-127
Treasury	127

Chapter 4
Classical Principles of Administrative, Business, Professional, Public, and Religious Vaastu   128

- **Mayamatam**   128-152

Space Allocation for Residence of People of Different Professions   128-130
Different Activities and the Related Squares   130-131
Vaastu of Bazaars Described in Mayamatam   131-133
Classification of Residences for People of Four Varnas (Castes or Classes of Ancient Indian Society)   133-134
Kayabhara Dwellings for Vaishyas   134-136
Activities and the Relevant Auspicious Squares in a Three Enclosure Palace   136-141
Direction wise commercial, public, administrative and religious activities recommended in Mayamatam, Vaastumandanam, Aparajitaprichchha and Samaranganasutradhara and their equivalent activities in the modern context   142-144
Activities and the Relevant Auspicious Squares in a Saubala Palace (Palace with Five Enclosures) as per Mayamatam   144-146
Guard's place   146
The council chamber   146
Vaastu Purush   146-147
Marma-Sthanas or Vulnerable Points of the site   147-148
Auspicious Shapes   148-149
Propitious Objects   149-151
Gateways and Doors   151
Additions and alterations   151
Palace   151-152
Other Useful Recommendations   152

- **Vaastumandanam**   152-160

Dwara Vedha (Obstruction to the door)   153
Importance of the direction of Main Door over the direction of Sunrise   153-154
Exceptions in Vaastu   154-155
Secular Nature of Vaastu   155
Auspicious Pillar Shapes   155
Pictures and Paintings   155
Forty-five Squares and Auspicious Activities   155-156
Comparative statement of auspicious squares recommended for different administrative, commercial, professional, public, and religious activities as per Vaastumandanam, Aparajitaprichchha and Samaranganasutradhara   156-160

- **Samaranganasutradhara**   160
- **Aparajitaprichchha**   161

Chapter 5
Workplace Vaastu   162

Layout and Decoration   164
Space Management   164-166
Office Layouts   166-167
Head's Office   167-170
Other Staff and Departments   170-171
Cellular Office   171
Open Plan Offices   171-172
Cubicles   172-174
Hot Desking Office   174-175
Personalising Your Office   175
Boardrooms   175-176
Meeting Etiquettes   176-177
Office Hardware   177-178
Working Table/Desk   178-180
Good Placements of Working Table   180-181
Bad Placements of Desk   182
Computers   182-183
Home Office   183-188

Vaastu in Career Building   188-192

Examining the home   188-190
Examining the Workplace   190-192

Chapter 6
Applied Vaastu of the Masses   193

Temples   193-199
Institutions of Learning   199
Skyscrapers   200-201
Apartment Living   201-203
Penthouses   203-204
Parking Norms   204
Gates of Townships   204-205
Pre-Fabricated Structures   205
Service Apartments   205-206
Agriculture Vaastu   206-207
Vaastu of Farmhouses / Holiday Homes / Resorts   207-209

Hotel and Restaurant Vaastu	209-210
Restaurants	210
Liquor Bars and Gambling	210
Shopping Malls	210-216
Good Modern Practices of Mall Management	214-215
Retail Store in a Mall	215-216
Markets and Shopping Complexes	216-217
Real Estate	217
Money Transactions and Gold Loans	217-218
Gems and Jewellery	218
Wood Working	218
Call Centres	218-219
Hospital Vaastu	219-230
Factory Vaastu	230-235
Monasteries (Viharshala)	235

Chapter 7
Modern Perspective of Vaastu 236

Magnetic Declination	236-238
Sun-Responsive Design	238-245
Building Orientation	245-246
Window Orientation and Shading	246-248
Exterior Window Shading	248
Interior Window Shading Strategy	248-249
Sunlight	249-251
Atrium (Light Well)	251
Skylights	251-252
Clerestory window	252
Awnings	252-253
Artificial Lights	253
Colours	253-254
Trees and Plants	254-255
Energy Efficient Design	255-256
Solar Geysers	256-257
Geothermal Energy	257-258
Natural Methods of Cooling	258-259
"Cool Roof" Techniques	259-260
Water Conservation	260-261
Rainwater Harvesting (RWH)	261
Physical Work	261-262
Sleep Patterns	262
Study Timings	262263
Sick Building Syndrome (SBS)	263-266
Green buildings or Intelligent Buildings (Automation within commercial buildings)	266-272
City and Town Planning	272-274
Planning, Designing and Construction of Buildings	274
Functional Homes	274-275
Cellars	275-276
Building Materials	276-277
Glass as building material	277-278
Wooden Flooring	278-279
Contemporary Workplace Design	279-280
Ergonomically Designed Office Furniture	280-281
Earthquake Resistance of Buildings	281-286
Precautions before, during and after an earthquake	284-285
Retrofitting	285-286
Fire Safety	286-287
Termite Problem	287-288
Noise Pollution	288-289
Electrosmog	289
Facilities Management (FM)	289-290

Chapter 8
Diminutive Vaastu 291

History of Vaastu	291
Vaastu and its Four Types (Maansaar)	291-292
Origin of Vaastu (Maansaar)	292
Sources of Vaastu (Maansaar)	292
Pada-Vinyaas or Site Plan (Maansaar)	292-293
Foundation (Maansaar)	293
Graam-Lakshan-Vidhaan or Villages (Maansaar)	293
Nagar-Vidhaan or Towns (Maansaar)	294
Forts (Maansaar)	294
Bhumi-Lamba-Vidhaan or Height of Buildings (Maansaar)	294
Building Materials (Maansaar)	294
Classifications of Buildings (Maansaar)	295
The Dwelling Houses (Maansaar)	295
Ratha-Lakshan-Vidhaan or Cars and Chariots (Maansaar)	295
Shayan-Vidhaan or (Couches) (Maansaar)	295
Rangashala Vaastu (Maansaar)	295-296
The Measurements (Maansaar)	296
Marcus Vitruvius Pollio (Maansaar)	297
Marma-Sthanas or Vulnerable Points	297
Shalya	297-298
Directions	298
Five Elements	298-299
Simplicity of Design	299

Synchronicity with Surroundings	299-300
Openings	300
Entrance	300
Door	300
Female Goddesses	300-301
Jyeshtha Devi (Alakshmi or Sheetala Mata)	301-303
Shayan Vaastu (Vaastu of Rest and Sleep)	303
Retirement	304
Phone Etiquette	304
Interiors	304
Mirrors	304
Wall Paintings	304
Furniture	304
Lighting	305-306
Summer Interiors	306-307
Greenery	307
Television (TV) versus Music	307-308
Water Vaastu	308
Auspicious Trees	308
Brahamsthan	308-309
Basements	309
Staircases	309
Art of Living the Vaastu Way	309-311
Changing the Home	311
Domestic Help	311
Offices	311-313
Staff welfare	313-314
Expanding your office	314
Stability	314
Cleanliness	314
Vaastu Friendly Workplace	314-315
Home Office	315-316
Career	316
Web Vaastu	316
Libraries and Museums	316
Hospitals	316-317
Vaastu in Muslim Architecture	317
Astro-Vaastu	317-318
Dynamic Vaastu	318
Ayadi Formulae	318
Muhoorta (Auspicious Time) for starting a business	318-319
Auspicious Days for Business Travel	319
Trees and Plants as Remedy	319-320
Mirrors as Remedy	320
Building at the Top of a T-Junction	320
Kona Vedha (Cutting Corner)	321
Classical views on earning, human karmas, destiny, and desires	321-322

Chapter 9
Case Studies   323

1. Publishing House in Sector 63, NOIDA, Uttar Pradesh	324-325
2. Footwear Factory in Narela Industrial Area	325-326
3. Electronic Parts Manufacturing Unit at Okhla, Delhi	326-327
4. Advertising Agency in Chandni Chowk, Delhi	327-328
5. A Public School in Gurgaon	328-330
6. Wheat Flour Mill in Bawana Industrial Area, Delhi	330-332
7. Selection of Commercial Space for Renowned Plywood Company in Netaji Subhash Place, Pitampura, New Delhi	332-333
8. Three Star Hotel on Haridwar Rishikesh Highway	333-334
9. Gems and Jewellery showroom in the main market of sector 18, NOIDA	334-336
10. Akshardham Temple Complex in Delhi	336-337
11. Vaastu of Shakuntalam Theatre in Pragati Maidan, New Delhi	337-338
12. Vaastu of a Bank of India branch in Delhi	338-339
13. Green Office of an Indian Software Company at Gurugram	339-340
14. Office of Multinational Software Company	340-341
15. Government Buildings at Bhopal and Delhi	341

Reference Books and Other Sources   342

Chapter 1
Principles of Vaastu Shastra

यदेव तीव्रसंवेगाद् दृढं कर्म कृतं पुरा।
तदेव दैवशब्देन पर्यायेणेह कथ्यते।।
यथा यथा प्रयत्न: स्याद्भवेदासु फलं तथा।
इति पौरुषमेवास्ति दैवमस्तु तदेव च।।

The keen and firm resolution with which an act was done in a former state of life is truly termed destiny in the successive births. As are one's exertions, so are the rewards. Therefore, only human exertions are true and destiny is nothing but the same (human efforts).

Yoga Vaashistha (2/9/16, 2/6/2)

Introduction

Most of the working people spend nearly one third to half of their lives working outside their homes. Hence the working place should be as nurturing as possible. The role of business in our lives is different to that of our homes. Business *vaastu* requires a large scale of energy management. Good energies can be harnessed by arranging our working environment. It requires creating the potent wealth energy without compromising the health energy. Principles of *Vaastu Shastra* make spaces valuable for the work environment. It ensures constant success during the slow business periods also. Vaastu acknowledges individual needs of the different employees without compromising a company's needs. Vaastu also leads us to happiness and success in our chosen careers.

There is a great revival of interest in vaastu shaastra in the current times. All over India, business people are increasingly consulting expert vaastu practitioners (vaastu shastris) and astrologers for ensuring workers' happiness as well as corporate stability. Proper use of principles of vaastu shastra gives them an extra edge in their businesses. Many would not make any structural changes without consulting a vaastu shastri. Many western-educated new generation scions, who manage inherited businesses, have also acknowledged the potency of this ancient science of vaastu shastra.

I personally, know of many businessmen who have made changes to their work environment. As a result, they have become happier and more successful. If your business is also failing, consult a vaastu expert. A couple of vaastu-based changes may turn your business around. You can also become a wealthy and successful businessman.

Vaastu shastra can be used in several ways as a tool to enhance the business success. Auspicious directions can be chosen for arranging the office positions to improve prosperity of your business. There are methods aimed at increasing turnover at retail establishments such as general stores, boutiques, restaurants and franchise outlets. The productivity of the employees can be improved by introducing principles of vaastu shastra in the factories.

The wisdom of this ancient science can easily be tapped. The practice of vaastu shastra requires relatively insignificant investment in monetary terms. Moreover, it does not require any major compromise of social or religious beliefs. We have little control over our destiny but we can greatly influence the quality of our lives by applying the rules of vaastu shastra. Principles of vaastu shastra help in creating an environment that will support us and enable us to make quick progress.

The internal layout can make a great difference to the way people feel, behave and act. Some buildings are termed as 'sick buildings' due to stagnation of energies within their envelope. Keen awareness and rectification of such causes can improve the life of people working there. Wise application of vaastu principles can assist movement of stagnant energies in the environment of any office. The *prana* (life force) of an office depends on the people working there and their mutual relationships. Environment of an office can dramatically be improved if its occupants cooperate with one another in a positive way. Paints, plants and images also help in improving an unsatisfactory office environment. These things can make it a better place to work in.

Today, few people are able to choose an ideal site that is completely as per the strict guidelines of vaastu shastra. For an ideal living, ancient vaastu texts recommend that the back of the construction should be protected by gentle hills and the front should have gently flowing fresh water stream. Hills towards the backside give protection, while water or roads in the front invite prosperity. In the modern context, high-rise or taller buildings represent hills and broad roads with moderate traffic represent rivers.

Ideally, perfect direction for facing any business premises is south-east or south of south-east. Otherwise, there are different auspicious directions for different business activities. However, effects of any direction may be increased by following any of the following means:

1. Orienting the building towards the chosen direction.
2. Open areas like road, river, open ground, lawn, park, garden, etc., towards the chosen direction.
3. More offsets towards the chosen direction and less towards the opposite one.
4. More openings in the form of doors, windows, ventilators, balconies, etc., towards the chosen direction.
5. Thin walls and smaller sunshades and overhead balconies in the chosen direction.
6. Slope of ground towards the chosen direction.
7. No high and heavy constructions and big trees towards the chosen direction.

To decide the ideal work suitable for your business premises, you need to find out the compass direction that the main door of your premises faces. Take into consideration all the above given seven factors. Combining these with the individual's horoscope will indicate the auspicious business for an individual in the existing premises.

The success of any business depends mainly on owner's luck, and the overall vaastu of the business, along with many other factors. Owner's luck can be read by referring to his or her horoscope or palm. A person has very little control on his or her luck. Lucky business can be decided in advance through astrology or palmistry. The overall vaastu of a business also determines its degree of success. The ultimate goal of any commercial business is profit. It is the main criteria of success in any business.

Customers are the source of earning profit. They are the prana of any successful business. Success of any business depends on attracting and retaining more and more customers. For attracting customers, following factors should seriously be considered in vaastu:

- Location and surroundings of the business
- Orientation and construction of the building
- Exterior and interior design and decoration of the building
- Design of the front door
- Layout of CEO's office
- Layout of different departments
- Proper placement of treasury or safe

All these aspects, including many others, will be discussed in detail in this book. Some other factors responsible for success of any business include the product quality, customer service, marketing skills and pricing strategy.

What is Vaastu Shastra?

The word 'Vaastu' literally means 'to live', while 'Shastra' means 'a science having well-defined rules and regulations'. Thus Vaastu Shastra means 'the scientific knowledge and way of living'. According to the vaastu classic Mayamatam (2.1-3):

अमर्त्याश्चैव मर्त्याश्च यत्र यत्र वसन्ति हि।
तद् वस्त्विति मतं तज्ज्ञैस्तद्भेदं च वदाम्यहम्॥
भूमि प्रासादयानानि शयनं च चतुर्विधम्।
भूरेव मुख्यवस्तु स्यात् तत्र जातानि यानि हि॥
प्रासादादीनि वास्तूनि वस्तुत्वाद् वस्तुसंश्रयात्।
वस्तून्येव हि तान्येव प्रोक्तान्यस्मिन् पुरातनैः॥

(Experts call all places where immortals and mortals dwell 'Vaastu or 'dwelling sites'. I present their four varieties: earth, temples (*prasada*), conveyances and seats. The Earth is the principal dwelling place because it is on Her that vaastu such as temples have appeared. It is because of Her nature as site and because of the temples' union with this site that the ancients called them 'Vaastu' in this world).

The term 'prasada' used in the above-mentioned verses is applied not only to temples but also to all kinds of buildings where Gods or men may inhabit. Vaastu is an intriguing mixture of science of construction, astrology, human anatomy and psychology, social and religious values, beliefs, myths, legends and many more. The myths and beliefs surrounding this subject are charming. Useful knowledge is gained through their scientific interpretations.

Vaastu Shastra is the art and science of living in perfect harmony with Mother Nature. Indian people of Vedic Age (nearly 5,000 years back) had discovered the secret of leading happy, contented and long lives by placing their homes facing north or east with gentle hills behind them and gently flowing waters in the front. They noticed hot scorching sunrays entering from the south, south-west and the west directions. Hills towards these directions of their homes protected them from these malignant rays. Flowing water in the north, north-east and east allowed the crops to grow and created the positive *pranic* energy.

This was based on the intelligent management of gifts of nature – sunlight, fresh air, rains, solid earth, etc., in an enclosed space – in tune with the time, place and person. All the human constructions meant for temporary or permanent living or working purposes or of architectural; monumental; historical or religious importance are included under the subject of Vaastu Shastra.

According to another opinion, Vaastu originated from the word 'Vastu', i.e., 'article'. Hence, Vaastu Shastra is the science dealing with articles too – their shape, size, colour, material, weight, design, visual effect, utility, their placement and many more.

Directions

Vaastu Shastra considers ten directions for every space — four cardinal, four angular, upward and the downward. These directions have been assigned with their directional lords (*dikpalas*), planetary lords (*grahas*) and other peculiar characteristics. Different demi-gods, total forty-five in number, also occupy these directions. Depending upon their lords, demi-gods and other characteristics, different directions become auspicious for different activities, for different periods of time in the year. In a residential Vaastu, if north is auspicious during summer, south becomes auspicious during winters. Likewise, if south-east (*aagneya*) is good for a restaurant, north-west (*vaayavya*) is best for a pet's shop.

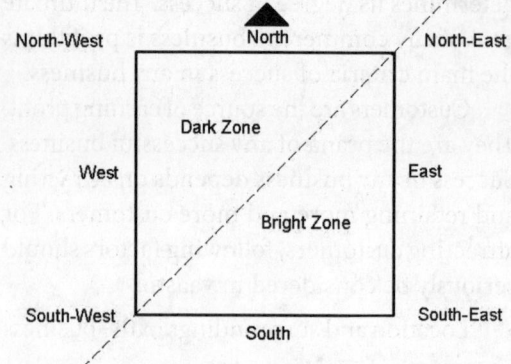

Fig. 1.2: Bright and Dark Zones in a Square Plot

Luckiest directions for a particular person may be ascertained by referring to his horoscope. Certain directions are also considered lucky for certain business activities, discussed at length in the following pages. When you are relocating your old business or setting up a new one, try to choose a building with an entrance towards your luckiest direction(s). Maximum openings should be towards your lucky direction(s) in the form of windows, ventilators or balconies. After occupying the premises, ensure that your desk faces one of your lucky directions.

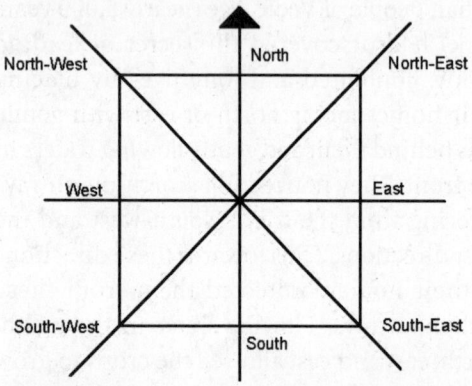

Fig. 1.1: Eight Directions in a Square Plot

Vaastu is the arrangement of space based on different directions. So, directions shall seriously be taken into account while setting up a new business or moving an existing one to another place. The entrance of an office or business should ideally face one of the owner's most auspicious directions. If you are working for others, try to arrange your desk to face a lucky direction, if possible.

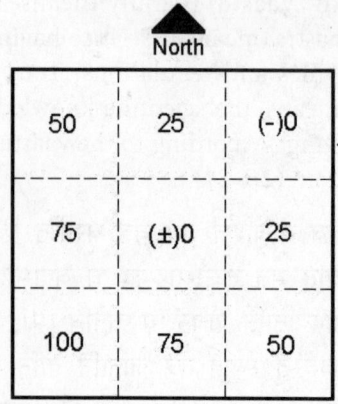

Fig. 1.3: Load Distribution in Nine Sector Vaastu

1. North-east (*Ishaan*)

Its ruling planet is Jupiter, the most benefic planet. Jupiter signifies sound judgment, meditation, *sattva* and *dharma*. *Isha* or Shiva is the directional Lord of north-east. It is the lightest as well as the coolest direction. Ishaan is the ending point of darkness as well as the starting point of sun's light. Benefic solar and magnetic radiations enter from Ishaan. Normally, slope towards north-east is considered most auspicious.

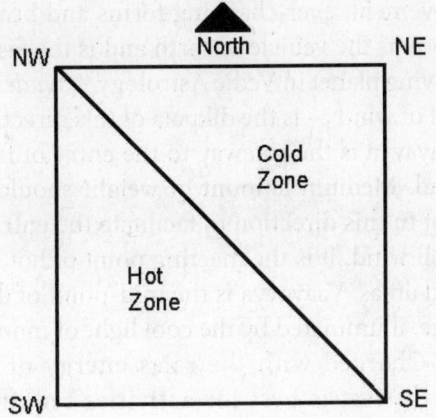

Fig. 1.4: Cold and Hot Zones in a Square Plot

North-east is best for places of worship, yoga, pranayama, meditation, arbitration and other courts of law, for industries dealing in drinking water and life saving drugs, etc. Ice and ice-cream factories should harness the energies of north-east for maximum benefits.

2. East (*Poorva*)

East direction is the entry point for the positive solar rays. Its ruling planet is sun being the direction of the rising sun. A new tithi, day and life, according to the Indian astrological tradition, starts with the rising sun. Indra (the king of gods) is dikpala of east. Objects with light weight should be kept in this direction to facilitate the entry of benefic morning sunrays. It is comparatively cool and lighted direction. Ground slope towards east is considered good. This direction is best for achieving power, position, leadership, dignity, name and fame.

East direction is best for kings and rulers, number one people, heads of institutions, political party in power or aspiring for power, worldwide organisations, businessmen in entertainment, swimming pools and sea beaches, public baths, etc.

3. South-east (*Aagnaya*)

Its ruling planet is Venus, the significator of taste, sense, water, vitality and the eyesight. Venus is called morning as well as the evening star. *Agni* — which cooks food and makes it soft, tasty and digestive — is the directional lord of south-east. This direction receives maximum daylight, – neither too hot nor too cold. It is the meeting point of sun's cold and hot rays. It is kept lighter than south-west but heavier than the other directions.

This direction is best for those business activities where natural light and normal amount of heat are the main considerations like restaurants, dhabas, confectionary shops, food processing industries, kitchens, coffee homes, antique shops, fancy light showrooms, inverter and generator showrooms, gems and jewellery shops and industries dealing in lights and colours. A woman organisation will progress faster when it harnesses the energy of south-east.

4. South (*Dakshin*)

Its ruling planet is Mars, the significator of bodily heat, self-efforts (*purusharth*) and courage. Mars governs our physical activities (*karmas*). The dikpala of south is *Yama*, the God of death. South is a very hot direction and shall therefore be kept heavy for avoiding the entry of noon time scorching sun rays. Its level should be higher than all the other cardinal directions, but lower than the angular direction south-west.

South is ideal for physical labour, heat and fire-related works, arms and ammunition manufacturing and testing. It is also best for industries using heat, electricity, fire and metals on a large commercial scale. Stadiums meant for violent games – boxing, archery, football, shooting, karate – should be south facing.

5. South-west (*Nairritya*)

Its ruling planet is *Rahu* as it is the direction of harmful infrared rays of sun. Rahu – a poisonous snake in Hindu mythology – governs these radioactive radiations. *Nirriti* (a demon goddess of malefic nature who haunts the cremation grounds at night) is the directional lord of nairritya. It is an extremely hot direction. It should normally be loaded with heavy weights to stop the entry of poisonous sunrays. Normally, its level should be highest than all the other directions. Nairritya brings lethargy, sleep, death and destruction.

South-west is best for processing of dead things or the things causing death. It is most suitable for industries dealing in poisonous drugs and chemicals like herbicides, germicides, pesticides and insecticides. Stone, wood and leather processing related industries are also good in this direction. According to vaastu, even a piece of stone is a living being till extracted from the earth. Likewise, an uncut tree is considered to have life. Stone and wood, including leather, are dead when removed from their origin. Mortuary in the hospital and night shelter in any town should also be located in nairritya.

6. West (*Pashchim*)

Its ruling planet is Saturn, the significator of darkness. West is the direction of setting sun. It signifies the end of a useful day. Dikpala of west is Varuna, the ruler of mystical worlds and large sheets of water. Heavy weights are preferred in the west to stop the entry of harmful evening radiations of sun. It is a hot and dark direction. Its level should comparatively be lower than nairritya; nearly equal to south but higher than rest of the directions. Natural light is available in the west till late hours in summers.

West is best for libraries, research institutes, laboratories, detective agencies, petroleum and mining industries, fast food shops, dining and banquet halls operating in the evening, overhead water tanks, etc.

7. North-west (*Vaayavya*)

Its ruling planet is Moon, the significator of movement, ever-changing forms and beauty. Moon is the vehicle of earth and is the fastest moving planet in Vedic Astrology. *Vayudeva* – god of winds – is the dikpala of this direction. Vaayavya is the gateway to the entry of fresh wind. Medium amount of weight should be kept in this direction to facilitate the entry of fresh wind. It is the meeting point of hot and cold areas. Vaayavya is the mid-point of dark zone, illuminated by the cool light of moon.

Charged with the rajas energy of air, north-west is best for activities requiring coolness and calmness of nature. Accordingly, it is most suitable for showrooms, car parking areas, vehicle workshops and service centers, pet animals, dairy farms, shops dealing in air-coolers and air-conditioners, beauty salons, music parlours, spa's, etc.

8. North (*Uttar*)

Its ruling planet is Mercury, the neutral planet. Mercury signifies speech, writing, printing, publishing and communication. *Kubera* – the lord of wealth – is the directional lord of north direction. North receives cold diffused sunlight during the daytime. It should be kept light in weight to receive the benefic magnetic radiation, which enters from north. Ground sloping towards north is also good.

North is best for skin and speech therapy clinics, educational institutes, money lending and banking institutions. It is also best for the people involved in reading, writing, printing, publishing and selling of the books and other study material. Studios of TV and radio channels should be north facing for better communication with their viewers and listeners.

9 & 10. Upward and Downward Directions

Upward direction means sufficient working height and height of different storeys. Client-based businesses should be located slightly higher than the existing road level. More than the required height of business place from the existing ground level means lesser the number of clients. A business located below the existing ground level results in sharp degradation with the passage of time. *Brahamasthan* of a business should be open to the sky. It may be kept higher than the rest of the building for this purpose. There should not be any depression in this area.

It is important to feel confident and comfortable at work. Favorable position and facing of your desk help in strengthening your position in a business. In this highly competitive financial world, using principles of vaastu for your sitting gives you an extra advantage.

Four Directions and Four Castes

Vaastu recommends that North, East, South and West directions are respectively the best directions for *Brahmins, Kshatriyas, Vaishyas* and *Shudras*. According to Mayamatam (27.12), 'The *sukhalaya* (or *saukhya*) is the principal main building intended for brahmins; it is placed in the north. In the same way, the *annalaya* (or *mahanasa*) is the principal main building for the kshatriya and is placed in the east; the *dhaanyalaya* placed to the south is for vaishya; and the *dhanalaya* placed to the west for shudra'.

Kaamika (1.35.156) also recommends house for brahmins in the north, for kings in the east, for vaishyas in the south and for shudras in the west. It perfectly synchronises with the recommendations of Vedic Astrology where brahmin, khatriya, vaishya and shudra *rashis* (signs) are respectively related with north, east, south and west directions.

Osho (Gita Darshan, Chapter 9-10) has beautifully described these four categories of people mentioned in the classical Indian tradition. According to Osho, shudra is the person who lives within the boundaries of his physical body, for whom this human body is the ultimate truth and the only God. Once the demands of the body are met with, all his desires get fulfilled. Shudra is the person who considers 'I am the body only', who identifies himself only with his physical body. Shudra is lowest because it is the base, the foundation of the higher aspects of life – mind, soul and the supreme soul.

Vaishya is the person who lives on the level of *mana* – the logical and emotional mind. His search is for name and fame, power and position, money and material possessions. Above the level of mind is the human soul, *atma* – the human consciousness. At this level, purification and enlightenment of soul is the main theme. Lord Rama, Lord Krishna, Mahavir Swami, Gautam Buddha, Guru Nanak and other Sikh Gurus – all were born in Kshatriya families. A true Brahmin is the one who has known the ultimate, the Supreme Soul, *Braham janati brahmnah*. A particular direction can accordingly be chosen suiting one's ultimate life purpose, irrespective of one's caste, colour or creed.

Shapes

Vaastu shastra is the extension of human body in regular shape plots and buildings. Vaastu recommends regular shapes for all types of plots and constructions. The most preferred shapes for residential areas are square and rectangular. According to Mayamatam, the length of plot should never be greater than 1.25

times of its width. Square, made of four equal sides, is the sign of stability and is long lasting. Preference for a circle is supposed to suggest someone who is calm and balanced while a person liking square shape is considered a confident and clear-thinking person. One shall remember that classical square and rectangular shapes have stood the test of time.

As the human body is beautifully proportioned, so shall be the vaastu of any space or design. That's why a rectangular space having length more than two times the width looks odd. It is like one hand being too longer than the other. A circular shape is representative of death in Hindu philosophy. Circular shapes are best for wells, stadiums and boundary walls of fortified cities. Square, circular and octagonal shapes are most auspicious for public, monumental, historical, religious and commercial activities. These shapes have extensively been used in the *Akshardham* monument in Delhi.

According to the vaastu text Vaastu Mandanam (3.18-19, 31-32):

'Chosen area for different type of vaastu can be hexagonal, octagonal and circular but for residential purpose it should always be like a square.

Square area must be selected for kings and brahmins but not for other classes like kshatriyas and vaishyas.

Circular, square, octagonal, leaf-shaped, barley grain-shaped, *swastic*-shaped and shaped like a human body – forts of these shapes provide comfort to the inhabitants.

Single and double cart shaped, triangular, hexagonal, thunderbolt-shaped, trident shaped, snake-shaped and much angular city shall be discarded'.

All the irregular shapes like triangular, trapezoidal, pentagonal, hexagonal, elliptical etc., should be discarded. Triangular shapes are too rajas (pinching). No matter where we sit, we are pressed in a corner. The word 'cornered' means 'being trapped'. Triangular shape for a small space is its shear wastage. In the triangular shaped areas, inner as well as the outer space can't be utilised properly. Consequently, lot of precious space goes waste. Trapezoidal buildings become unsymmetrical. They invite problems regarding good workmanship and proper utilisation of space.

Pentagon shape is equally inauspicious. According to Hindu mythology, Brahma – the lord creator – had five heads in the beginning. Later on, he had to lose his fifth head as it had sexual feeling towards his own daughter. Presently, he has four heads only. In Numerology, along with other characteristics, number 5 also represents love of freedom and change, sexuality and quickness of mind. You can 'expect the unexpected' from a number 5 person. Thus 5 is an extremely unpredictable number. The shape of American defense headquarter 'Pentagon' is pentagonal. Was it the pentagonal shape of this building that invited the 9/11 terrorist attack on it?

The corners of a hexagonal building don't give a soothing look and pinch the viewer's eyes. It seems as if something is lacking in this shape. Elliptical shapes, denoting an egg, do not encourage much activity.

While circular shape is completely blind regarding the directions, octagonal shape clearly identifies all the eight directions. The theory of eight directions is considered highly auspicious in Indian as well as Chinese traditions. The number 8 itself is symmetrical when cut in two halves – horizontally, as well as vertically. In Hindu religion, an eight petal lotus has commonly been used as the seat for all the Gods. Usually Lord *Brahma* and Goddess *Lakshmi* are shown seated on it. Octagonal shape feels soothing to the eyes.

In geometry, sum of all the angles of a regular geometrical figure can be known by applying the formula; $(2n - 4) \times 90°$, where 'n' is the number of sides.

So, in an octagon, sum of all the inner angles will be = (2 x 8 – 4) x 90° = 1080°

Therefore one inner angle = 1080° / 8 = 135°

Likewise, inner angle for a 16-side polygon will be = (2 x 16 – 4) 90° / 16 = 157.5°

And, for a 32-side polygon = (2 x 32 – 4) x 90° / 32 = 168.75°

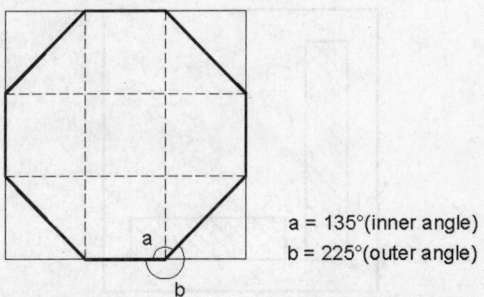

Fig. 1.5: Inner and Outer Angles in an Octagon

From the above calculations, it is clear that the inner angle increases with the increase in the number of sides. On a straight line, inner and outer angles at any point are of 180° each. In a circle, inner angle at any point on its periphery is slightly less than 180° while the outer angle is slightly more than 180°.

A polygon behaves like a circle as we increase its sides from 8 to 16, 16 to 32, and 32 to 64 and so on. A polygon has definite directions too which are absent in a circle. People sitting around a circular table can't stay for long hours. Circle spins away anything put near to it. Also, its outer surface acts like a cutter's edge.

The matter becomes different with the octagon. People feel easy and comfortable while occupying their definite direction around an octagonal table. The angles in an octagon are also not the eye sores as in the hexagonal, pentagonal, and triangular shapes. Octagonal shape balances the dual requirements of well-marked directions and soothing visual effect. The protruded angles become more and more bearable as we go for further multiples of 8 i.e., 16, 32, 64 and so on.

Circular shape is also not always good, though good for enclosures due to the least perimeter. A circular plot needs minimum length of boundary wall. Circular shape is much useful in design of buckets, storage, kitchen equipments, utensils and cutlery. Otherwise, circular shape does not give any sense of definite direction. Inhabitants of circular shaped buildings become directionless. Parliament house in New Delhi is of circular shape. Ours is the largest constitution in the world and we, within half a century of getting freedom, have already scored a century of constitutional amendments! Is it because of the circular shape of our Sansad Bhawan?

Don't go for fancy shapes just for the sake of originality or doing something different. Zigzag plots, walls and furniture mould our

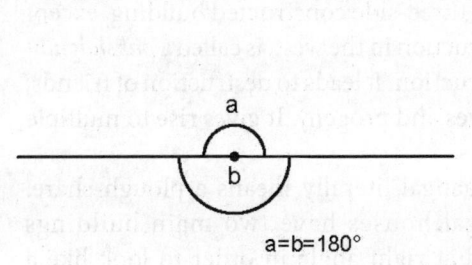
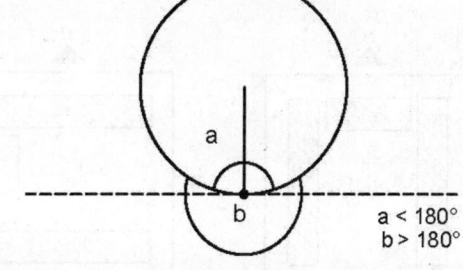

Fig. 1.6: Inner and Outer Angles on a Straight Line and Any Point on a Circle

lives in the same manner. It is a usual practice in the rural areas to deliberately cut off a corner of the letter when the news of someone's death is to be conveyed. A postman knows this very well. Likewise, sooner or later, a cut off corner in any room brings bad news. Corners are sacred. These are ruled by different directional lords. Don't waste them with the construction of bathrooms and toilets. Multi-cornered rooms are generally considered bad.

Shurpa and Laangal Shapes

Mayamatam (26.18-21) describes two special shapes for specific public or business activities. These are the *Shurpa* and *Laangal* houses. Shurpa literally means a winnowing basket. A shurpa house consists of three main buildings. When these three buildings are positioned to the east, south, and west of the plot (i.e., without construction in the north), the shurpa house brings prosperity. When these are positioned to the south, west and north of the plot (i.e., without construction in the east), it brings victory.

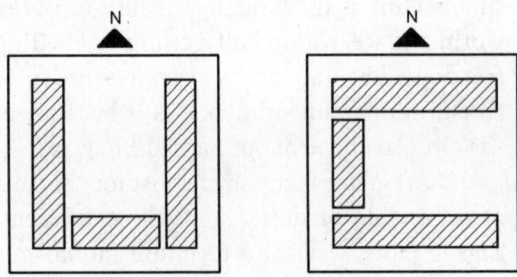

Fig. 1.7: Auspicious Shurpa Houses (Two cases)

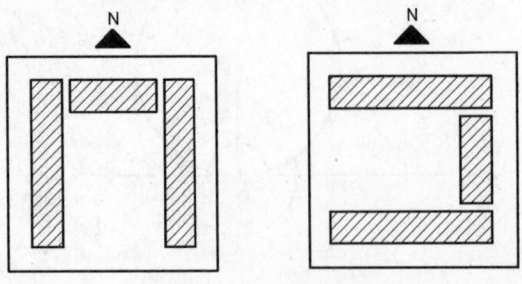

Fig. 1.8: Inauspicious Shurpa Houses (Two cases)

Shurpa houses without the main building to the south or west are nothing but mistakes. Shurpa houses are suitable for *ugropajivin* (who live on violence or extreme physical activities). In modern day context, this shape is best for military and police training grounds, boxing rings and playgrounds for games requiring excessive physical stamina and the like.

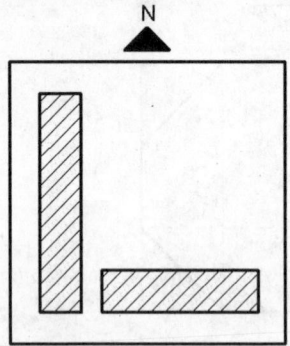

Fig. 1.9: Auspicious Laangal House (One case)

According to Vaastu Mandanam (6.115), and Matsya Purana (254.4-8):

'A three-side constructed building, except construction in the north, is called a *dhanyaka* construction. It bestows peace, prosperity and progeny.

A three-side constructed building, except construction in the east, is known as *sukshetra* construction. It bestows riches, fame and longevity on one side and destroys sorrows, and distraction on the other.

A three-side constructed building, except construction in the south, is called a *vishal* construction. It leads to destruction of family line and causes all types of diseases and fears.

A three-side constructed building, except construction in the west, is called a *pakshaghan* construction. It leads to destruction of friends, relatives and progeny. It gives rise to multiple fears'.

Laangal literally means a plough-share. Laangal houses have two main buildings joined at right angle in order to look like a plough-share. If the two main buildings of a

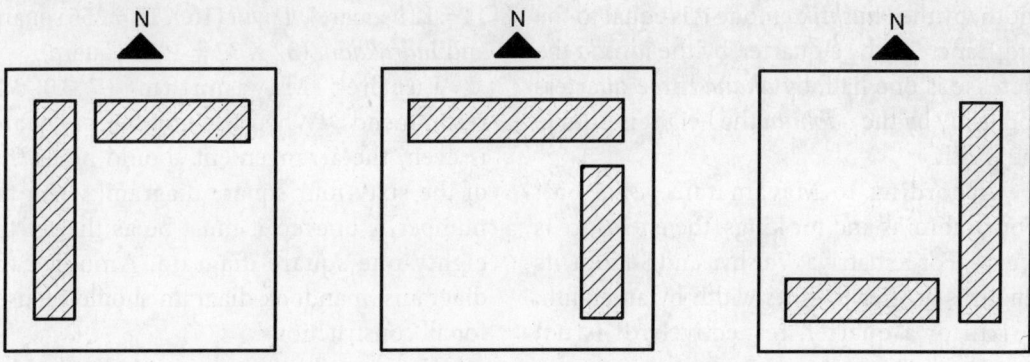

Fig. 1.10: Inauspicious Laangal Houses (Three cases)

laangal house are to the east and south, or to east and north or to west and north, this will bring about the owner's death. They have to be placed to the south and to the west if good fortune is desired.

Laangal houses are suitable for courtesans (a harlot, prostitute) and people of that ilk. In the modern day context, Laangal shape is best for theatres, open air theatres, amphitheatres, exhibitions and places meant for public performances.

Dimensions

Human body is considered the height of God's creation. Everything in it is perfectly proportioned. Vaastu is extension of the human body. That's why an elongated building with its length more than thrice the width is not good. Such a building is like a long corridor. One has ample freedom to go forward or backward but is restricted to walk sideways here. Likewise it becomes the life path of a person inhabiting such a place where his lateral movement gets restricted. He is not able to take up multiple jobs in hand.

Vaastu emphasises on balancing the three dimensions. A very high ceiling overpowers us and makes us disoriented while a low ceiling suppresses us. Very high ceilings are good in public, religious and monumental buildings. These buildings can be grand and have ornamental carvings. But our homes should be simple as we need normalcy to retain our sanity. We need order and routine in our life.

It seems ridiculous if the head of an organisation has a working table of 20 feet x 8 feet. Likewise any office, commercial or residential space occupied by a particular person should be in accordance with his needs, not as per his wants. We should remember that excess of everything is bad. Objects should be in proportion to their immediate environment and their intended usage.

Mayamatam (26.6b-9a) describes eight ways of calculating the length from the width. According to it, the length is one and a quarter, one and a half, one and three quarters or twice the width. Otherwise it is equal to double the width increased by a quarter, half or three quarters. Or it is equal to three times the width, this being the maximum.

All these lengths are appropriate for gods. For ordinary people the length must not be more than double the width. For the inhabitants of monasteries and hermitages, all length equal to or more than double the width are appropriate. In a house where all such inhabitants dwell together, the length must be equal to, or at the most double the width.

Mayamatam (26.9b-10) also describes five ways to calculate the height from the width. By the *shantika* mode the height is equal to the width, by the *paushtika* mode it is equal to the width increase by a quarter, by the *jayada* the increase is one half, by *dhana* three quarters and lastly by the *adbhuta* the height is double the width.

According to Mayamatam (27.5-6a): 'For Brahmins and for kings, the enclosure is square. For Kshatriya, Vaishya and Shudra, its length is greater than its width by an eighth, a sixth or a quarter, respectively. It is not appropriate to construct a house the enclosure of which measures less than sixteen cubits'.

Enclosure here means the plot of ground. The building is constructed on a part of it, the rest being occupied by courtyards as well as various appurtenances.

Mayamatam (27.5) has clearly made distinction between 'kings' and 'kshatriya'. Characteristics of dwelling sites are given in Chapter 2 of Mayamatam. Here, the site is said to be square for brahmins only. It is said to be rectangular for 'kings', which clearly includes all the kshatriyas.

Further, according to Mayamatam (27.14-15a): 'It is said that small dimensions are for lesser people and large ones for the great. Large dimensions shall never be used for people of little substance. However, everything that is fitting with respect to dimensions which suit lesser people is fitted as well for the great'.

Pada-Vinyas and their Usage

Mayamatam (Chapter 7) describes thirty-two types of diagrams (pada-vinyas) suitable for all sites, ranging from *Sakal* (one square) to *Indrakaant* (1024 square). Out of these thirty-two diagrams, mostly *Paramshayin* (9 X 9 = 81 square) diagram and secondarily *Mandook* (8 x 8 = 64 square) diagram have been used in this book. Other diagrams used here and there for explaining the peculiar points are: Sakal (single square), *Pechak* (2 X 2 = 4 square), *Peeth* (3 X 3 = 9 square), *Upapeeth* (5 X 5 = 25 square), *Sthandil* (7 X 7 = 49 square), *Sthaaniya* (11 X 11 = 121 square), *Triyut* (16 X 16 = 256 square) and *Indrakaant* (32 X 32 = 1024 square).

Further Mayamatam (7.30-31) recommends: 'When the number of squares is even, the arrangement should be as that of the sixty-four square diagram; when the number is uneven it must be as that of the eighty-one square diagram. Amongst the diagrams, mandook diagram should be used for all constructions'.

However, Samaranganasutradhara (13.3-5) recommends sixty-four square diagram for layout of king's *shivir* (royal camp), village and city; eighty-one square diagram for designing residence of *varnin* (all four varnas i.e., brahmins, kshatriyas, vaishyas and shudras), king's palace and Indra-sthaan (place of Indra) and hundred square vaastu for construction of God's temple, peculiar (strange) pavilions and other similar constructions.

Vaastu Purush (Space Personified)

Vaastu Shastra considers that every vaastu is occupied by a vaastu purush. He lies with his face downwards in the north-east, his right elbow and right knee in the south-east, left elbow and left knee in the north-west and both of his feet in the south-west. He is the personification of each and every space, design or construction. Thus every construction is thought to behave like a living human being and shall accordingly be designed.

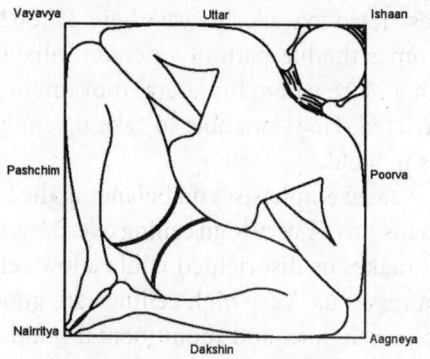

Fig. 1.11: Vaastu Purush

Marma-sthanas (Vulnerable points)

The most vulnerable points (ati-marma-sthanas) of vaastu purush are his heart and navel (braham-sthan) and his face (north-east), shown here in figure 1.12. Readers are advised to refer Chapter 4 for a detailed note regarding marma-sthanas.

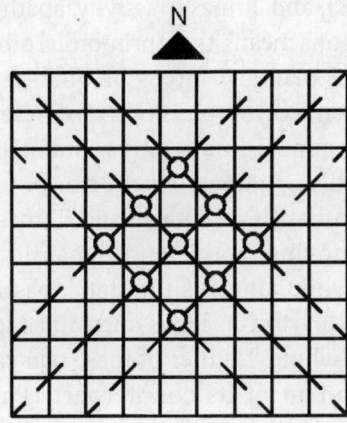

Fig. 1.12: Marma Sthanas on Vaastu Purush

These should not be loaded at any cost. It is better to keep these organ-areas open to the sky. Heavy load can be placed on his thighs and back (south-west, south and west directions). Right and left hands (south-east and north-west) can safely bear the medium loads. In this way we can appease vaastu purush. In turn, he promotes our lives, wealth and comforts. He guards our vaastu and showers his blessings on us.

Types of Vaastu

Vaastu Purush occupies every space, design and construction. He is the vibrant energy of the material substance. He has three positions. His permanent position (sthir vaastu) is along the northeast–southwest axis. He lies along this axis with his face down in the northeast. This position is taken into account for designing residences of permanent nature.

His second position is his moving body according to the changing seasons (chara vaastu). He keeps on rotating in a clockwise direction. His face is towards the north from mid-March to mid-June; towards the east from mid-June to mid-September; towards the south from mid-September to mid-December; and towards the west from mid-December to mid-March. Starting and ending time given here are the approximate time periods. This distribution of months is based on the change of seasons in North Indian region. It is evident that east is auspicious during the rainy season while west is best during the harsh winters. Thus malefic or benefic nature of a particular direction depends on the seasons and the desired activity.

The third position of vaastu purush is his daily movement (nitya vaastu). He keeps on changing his position every three hours (one prahar) until he covers all the eight directions in one full day. At sunrise, his face is towards west, during mid day towards north and during midnight towards the south. In the same manner, our body and mind also experience ups and downs during the whole day. Our energy and alertness is highest during the midday and lowest when we go to sleep. So, different directions are suitable for different activities at different intervals of time.

Prana

Prana, equivalent to Ch'i in the Chinese tradition, is the universal life force. It is infrequently mentioned in the classical texts of Ayurveda. Prana is found in all the living beings. It strings body, mind and spirit together like beads on a strand of breath. Prana is the life force, which is carried in the water we drink, the food we take and the air we breathe in. Prana is not air though life-giving oxygen is one of its vehicles. *Vaat* is the unstable or reactive form of prana. Prana is grosser than vaat and is the essence of air element. Nerve impulses etc., are the physical vehicles of prana. It is the force that keeps living beings alive. Its creation and dissipation continues all the time.

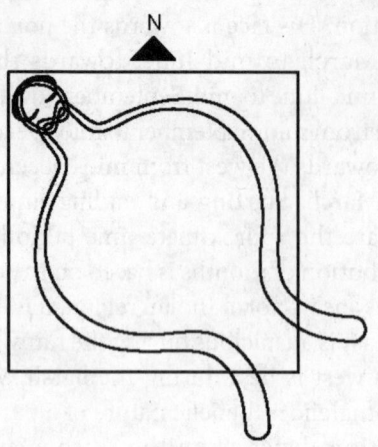

Fig. 1.13: Movement of Prana in General Business

The presence of prana gives a feeling of sweet smell. Everything goes according to your own sweet will. Prana is created whenever anything is done perfectly. An architect who designs a beautiful building is creating prana and a cook preparing a dish perfectly is also creating prana. Clean corners, properly whitewashed walls, healthy potted plants and well-designed furniture create prana. Try to attract more and more prana into your workplace. Presence of plenty of prana makes us feel happy and contented.

Good circulation of prana in an office helps in encouraging job satisfaction and harmonious working relationship. Prana moves in the physical environment and influences our mind and emotions in a subtle manner. Whenever movement of prana is slow or becomes struck in or around the building, it greatly affects our performance and sense of well being. In such a situation, our dealings with our colleagues and clients are affected badly.

Trigunas

Guna literally means 'Merit', 'Quality' or 'Primordial property'. Philosophically, *gunas* are the qualities or conditions of existence which make up the nature. When the qualities are in perfect equilibrium, they are in a state of rest and in a state of evolution when one or more of them prevail over the others. According to the *Samkhya* philosophy, these qualities are composed of three natural 'materials' – Sattva (representing kindness, the pure essence of things), Rajas (active energy, passions), and Tamas (passivity, apathy).

Triguna means 'three primordial properties' or 'three primary forces or qualities'. This symbolism corresponds to the representation of the group Vishnu – sattva, Brahma – rajas and Rudra – tamas. Prana can be divided into two halves i.e., Rajas and Tamas. Rajas is the moving, active and dynamic part of prana, while tamas is the static, passive and stagnant part of it. Rajas and tamas together create a whole. Neither of these two can exist independent of its counterpart. The right combination of these two – depending on the accepted requirements of particular time, place and person – is sattva. Arrangement of *trigunas* in a Pechak (2 x 2) Vaastu is shown in the figure.

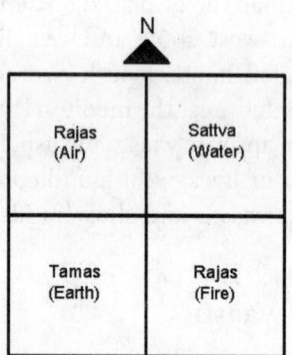

Fig. 1.14: Trigunas in Pechak Vaastu

Chapter 14 of Srimadbhagwad Geeta has been completely devoted to trigunas. Its fifth verse reads as:

सत्वं रजस्तम इति गुणाः प्रकृतिसम्भवाः।
निबध्नन्ति महाबाहो देहे देहिनमव्ययम्।।

(Purity, passion and inertia—these qualities, O mighty-armed Arjuna, born of Nature, bind fast in the body, the embodied, the indestructible!)

According to it, three gunas are present in all the human beings. None is free from the operation of any one of the three qualities. They are not constant. Sometimes sattwa predominates and at other times rajas or tamas predominates. One should analyse and stand as a witness of these three qualities.

The rajas and tamas of Vaastu Shastra may be equalised with Yang and Yin of Feng Shui (the Chinese counterpart of Indian Vaastu Shastra). Yin and yang are represented by a very interesting symbol with deep meaning. This symbol is a circle which consists of two tadpole like shapes – one black (yin) with a white circle (yang) inside; the other white (yang) with a black circle (yin) inside.

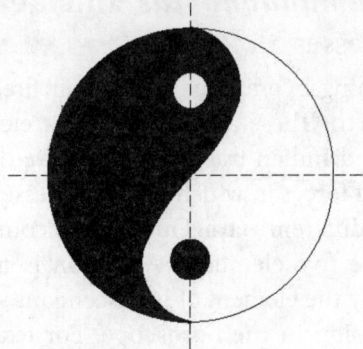

Fig. 1.15: Yin-Yang Diagram

Circle symbolises the infinite space. Yin-yang symbol shows that world may broadly be divided into two categories – black and white – the boundary between the two goes on changing constantly. There is nothing in this world which is perfectly black or white. A greater part of white is always combined with a smaller part of black and vice versa. Everything is grey in this existence – the combination of black and white. Only the proportion may vary.

Rajas represents creation, initiative, creative heat, light, hot colours (red, orange, yellow), angular shapes, brisk movement and the like. The activities involving heat, light, fire, electricity and metals on a large scale are rajas activities. In vaastu, south-east and north-west are the rajas areas. These are full of rajas energy of fire and air respectively.

Tamas represents destruction, inertia, coldness, darkness, cold colours (violet, indigo and blue), too much heat or cold leading to destruction, circular shapes, and the like. The activities mainly involving poisons, leather, earth, stones, dead bodies etc., are tamas activities. In any vaastu, south-west is the tamas area which is full of tamas energy of earth. The forces of rajas and tamas can be combined in varied proportions to get the desired results in any given situation. They balance any environment.

In the offices, rajas and tamas can also be related to the layout and decoration. Mostly, workplaces tend to be more rajas than tamas. Angles and straight lines of the furniture, blinds, bright lights, plastic paints, smooth and shining floor tiles, active computer screens, metal cabinets, photocopiers, fax machines, ringing phones, people traffic, conversation, light decor – all these are indicative of a rajas environment. On the contrary papers, carpets, curtains, round-cornered desks, art works, dark coloured furniture, wooden cabinets, wall papers, textured surfaces and single person occupying the space create more tamas environment. Soft colours and fabrics may soften the straight lines and the reflective surfaces.

Office activities can also be divided in rajas and tamas categories. Decision-making and implementation of policies are mainly rajas. These activities also include brainstorming meetings, advertising, marketing and selling products. On the other side, day-to-day administrative tasks and putting the ideas into practice, is largely a tamas activity. Creating, producing, packaging and reviewing etc., are also tamas activities. Tamas and rajas always co-exist. Boardroom and CEO's room should be remote from the daily hectic routine. These should have a more tamas decor in the form of art works or other pleasing things, which reflect a company's wealth.

Use good quality plants in a busy office. Plants have the ability to soften the harshness of a rajas environment. A water feature kept near the business's entrance or the reception area is very auspicious. It symbolically draws wealth in the business. Moving water is better than still water. Stagnant water stops circulation of money. Water is must for our existence, growth and prosperity. Remember, *Lakshmi* – the Goddess of Wealth – arose from the *ksheersagar* (ocean of milk like pure water) during its churning.

Metallic furniture, straight lines and shining surfaces of the office are too rajas. Excessive rajas energy often results in the staff becoming over-stressed. This can be toned down with plants, pictures and wooden surfaced furniture. Dark-coloured furniture, thick carpet, decorative paintings and a general air of calmness make it a tamas space. Boardroom or the room in which decisions are made should be very functional. There should not be any distractions or uncomfortable chairs.

People can also be divided in rajas and tamas categories. Rajas people are energetic, enthusiastic, quick thinking and precise while tamas people are receptive, creative, imaginative and methodical. Rajas people are high-powered decision makers. They often need people who work in a calm and efficient manner to put their ideas into practice. One shall balance the rajas with tamas for smooth running of any organisation. A too rajas office creates a too stressful environment. Jobs will not be completed in time here. Contrarily, productivity falls in an extremely tamasic environment. The business would remain static, failing to move forward.

Sattwa is the harmonious stage or the right combination of rajas and tamas. It represents growth, continuity, survival, peace and balance. Preaching; courts of law; religious, social, research and educational institutions, meditation and yoga centers, religious places, places of eating etc., are rich in sattwa. In any vaastu, north-east is the sattwa area. It is full of *sattwic* energy of water.

These trigunas should also be made use of while selecting an auspicious direction for a particular activity. For example, tamas of south-west is best utilised as a saw-mill, marble-cutting industry or leather-tanning industry. Rajas energy of south-east and north-west is best utilised in restaurants and vehicle workshops respectively. Sattwa of north-east will be best for an arbitration chamber or yoga and meditation centre.

Panchmahabhootas and Related Businesses

Everything is composed of space, air, fire, water and earth. These are the five great elements of sacred Indian tradition. These are the five types of forces in which prana expresses itself in five different ways. Our body is composed of these five elements. A person is mainly ruled by the element of his ascendant sign or Moon sign in the horoscope. For example, a person with Aries ascendant and Moon in Scorpio will be fiery in nature and will be best suited for a business governed by Mars e.g., industries dealing in heat, metals and chemicals, land development, building construction, armaments and the like.

Vaastu principles are based on the cycles of nature. Vaastu considers that certain directions are suitable for certain type of activities only, because these directions are rich in certain elements (*mahabhootas*) only. Energies of water, fire, earth and air emanate from the north-east, south-east, south-west and north-west, respectively. These four elements, associated with the four directions, are shown in the following figure.

Principles of Vaastu Shastra

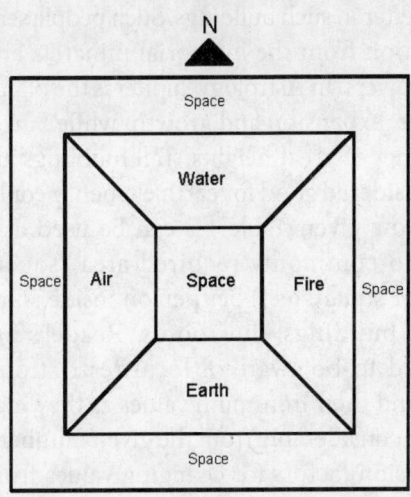

Fig. 1.16: The Five Elements
(Cardinal Direction Wise)

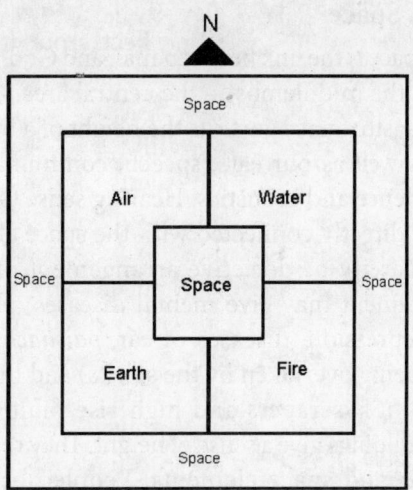

Fig. 1.17: The Five Elements
(Angular Direction Wise)

The energy of any business is primarily determined by the direction of its main entrance. For instance, energy of the east represents the rising sun, spring, birth, fresh and young growth. Energy of the east will thus be suitable for new companies. The energy of south, i.e., fire would be suitable for dynamic activities such as marketing. The extreme static energy of west, i.e., earth is good for storage and consolidation activities. The cool but vibrant energy of north, i.e., air can best be harnessed for counseling. Libraries and archives, symbolising communication activities, are ideal in the north.

Correlate the dominating element of a business with the direction of its main entrance.

Choice of right direction can help any store – for instance groceries, auto parts, clothes, hardware, cosmetics etc., – shall sell more of it. It also ensures a business's profitability, efficiency and employee's loyalty. Retail stores, restaurants, corporations and home offices – all can benefit from the implementation of these principles.

These five elements are seriously taken care of in vaastu shastra. The table below shows the relationship of four elements. These four elements exist in space, the fifth element. This table can be used to strengthen or weaken an element. For balancing an environment, we can use the shape, material, colour or article related to the particular element.

Table 1.1: Relationship of Four Elements

Element	Helping Element	Weakening Element	Inimical Element
Fire	Air	Earth	Water
Earth	Water	Fire	Air
Air	Fire	Water	Earth
Water	Earth	Air	Fire

1. Space

Space is the link between man and God. Its area is the middlemost – the central area – in any vaastu. Space governs the height of a building as well as our ears, speech, communication, silence and acoustics. Hearing sense (*shabda*) is directly connected with the space element. Scarcity or defective arrangement of space element may give mental diseases, phobias, depression, diseases of ear, *paishach badha* (being overtaken by the spirits) and the like.

Skyscrapers and high rise multi-storey buildings give a sense of height. They represent air and space elements. People born with strong and benefic Jupiter and / or Sun can work better in such buildings. Such people seek inspiration from the memorial minarets and watch towers. In Astrology, Jupiter is the planet of space, expansion and growth, while Sun is the planet of great heights. Tall buildings are not considered good for earth element people.

Below given Table 1.2 can be used as a guide to commonly required area (square metre or square feet) per person inside some typical buildings and rooms. Readers are required to be aware of local restrictions, codes and their minimum values as they may diverge considerably from the given numbers. Conversion factors for changing values from one system to the other have also been given in the end of table.

Table 1.2: Area Required Per Person in Some Typical Buildings

Type of Building	Type of Room	Area per Person	
		(m^2)	(ft^2)
Apartments			100-400
Assembly building	Lecture room	0.6	
	Library	5	
	Cinema	0.6	
	Concert hall	0.6	
	Theater	0.6	
Banks			50 - 150
Bars			15 - 50
Cafeterias			10 - 50
Churches			5 - 20
Clubhouses			15 - 50
Cocktail Lounges			15 - 50
Computer Rooms			80 - 150
Court Houses			50 - 150
Dental Centers	Clinic and Offices		50 - 150
Department Stores			15 - 75
Dining Halls			10 - 50
Drug Store			15 - 50
Factories	Assembly hall	2 - 5	
Factories	Light manufacturing	10 - 20	
Factories	Heavy manufacturing	20 - 30	
Fire Stations			100 - 500

Hotels	Rooms	5	
	Lobby	0.6	
	Assembly room	1.5	
Hospitals	General Areas		50 - 150
	Patient Rooms		80 - 150
Kindergarten		2 - 3	
Kitchens			50 - 150
Libraries			30 - 100
Luncheonettes			10 - 50
Lunch Rooms			10 - 50
Malls			50 - 100
Medical Centers	Clinic and Offices		50 - 150
Motels, Dormitories	Public Spaces		100 - 200
	Guest Rooms, Dormitories		100 - 200
Municipal Buildings			50 - 150
Museums			30 - 100
Nightclubs			15 - 50
Nursing Home Patient Rooms			80 - 150
Offices	Single office	10	
	Meeting room	1.5	
Police Stations			100 - 500
Post Offices			100 - 500
Precision Manufacturing			100 - 300
Residential			200 - 600
Restaurant	With service	1.5	
	Without service	1	
Retail Stores			15 - 75
Schools	Lecture rooms	0.6	
	Class rooms	2	
	Corridors	2	
	Laboratory	3	
Shops	Retail	2	
	Supermarkets	2	
Sports	Gymnasium	1.5	
	Swimming pools	4	
Supermarkets			50 - 100
Taverns			15 - 50
Town Halls			50 - 150

$1\ m^2 = 1550\ in^2 = 10.764\ ft^2 = 1.196\ yd^2$
$1\ ft^2 = 0.0929\ m^2 = 144\ in^2 = 0.1111\ yd^2$

2. Air

Air is must for life sustenance. It contains oxygen, which is vital for the human body. In any vaastu, air is prevalent in the north-west direction. Air element governs the air temperature, pressure and humidity, skin, hands, work, climate and air-conditioning. Touching sense (*sparsh*) is directly connected with the air element. Scarcity or defective arrangement of air may cause air-borne diseases, and the like.

Air is related to the north-west and north directions. Circular and round shapes and shapes that are a combination of angles and curves create a strong air environment. Air rounds off the irregular shapes. Sports cars, bullet trains and airplanes are designed with rounded front so as to penetrate the air with least resistance. Buildings having domes, curved roofs and arches belong to the air element. These buildings are constructed for social, religious, historical, monumental, scientific or political purposes. Parliament House and Lotus Temple in New Delhi and Taj Mahal in Agra are excellent examples of air shape buildings. A perfectly designed dome has made Taj Mahal the most active and attractive building in India.

Air is often known as 'The Arousing' in the rajas form. It signifies growth and movement. The dynamic air suggests brainstorming new ideas and snap decisions. Air strongly relates to mental activities, freshness, cross-ventilation, pranic force and life. Air is often referred to as 'The Penetrating' in the tamas form. Tamasic air helps to carry forward and execute the plans. The ideas are turned into designs.

Air environment is inauspicious for earth element people, but is excellent for fire element people. If you are an earth element person and have to work in an air environment, you need to increase some water element in your working area. The most effective remedy will be to keep an aquarium, a small fountain or anything that looks clear like a crystal in your working area.

Airy professions are related with air communications, violet colours, curved shapes and airy seasons. Some of the airy professions, for instance are the garment stores, travel agencies, stationary stores, book stores, florists, publishing houses, auto shops, car rentals, paper manufacturing industries, advertising companies, newspapers, notary public etc.

3. Fire

Fire includes both heat and light. The right amount of fire is must for our survival on earth. In the residential vaastu, desirable fire resides in the south-east direction. Fire governs our eyes, feet, mobility, lights, colour therapy, and physical along with mental and spiritual energy too. Sight sense (*roopa*) is directly connected with the fire element. Scarcity or defective arrangement of fire may cause eye diseases, decreased mobility and various physical, mental and spiritual abnormalities.

Fire is related to south and south-east directions. Angular and pyramidal shapes, sharp angles, pointed roofs or spires, intense heat, red colour and pungent taste – all these create a strong fire environment. Fire is purely rajas. It is also known as 'The Clinging'. Fire suggests activities concerned with bringing and promoting ideas and production to fruition. Some of the fire activities are publishing, public relations and laboratories.

If you belong to the water element and have to work in a fire environment, you need a cure representing water or earth element. Water extinguishes fire while earth has a dampening effect. A water feature or a small porcelain object will serve this purpose. Anything that is grey, green or soil colour is equally good.

Fiery professions are related with heat, chemicals, electricity, bright light, hot colours like red; orange and yellow, triangular; angular and conical shapes and summer season. Some of the fiery activities are: restaurants, barber shops, beauty salons, video and electronic stores, optical shops, goldsmiths, jewellery manufacturing stores, computer firms and stores, engineering firms, metal fabrication, and martial art schools.

4. Water

Drinking water is a scarce and shy element. For site selection of any vaastu, availability of water is the main criteria. In vaastu, the ideal position of water is considered in the north-east sector. Water governs our tongue and anus, as well as the plumbing work and water supply arrangement. Its connected sense is taste (rasa). Scarcity or defective arrangement of water may give diseases related to mouth and discarding organs.

Water symbolises money. It is the most important asset of mankind, of earth and its creatures. Water flowing behind the business premises means losing the financial opportunities. On the opposite, its flow in front of the workplace symbolises financial opportunities, which can easily be grasped. If there is no water feature in front of your business premises, create an artificial one in the form of a well-maintained water pond or a water fountain. A water fountain creates and circulates prana. It also attracts money to your premises. Water attracts human beings. Moving water creates prana. It is always better than the stagnant water.

Water is related to the north-east and east directions, wavy and meandering patterns, mixed shapes and watery features. These things create a strong water environment. Water can assume any shape. Its effect is sattwic – combination of rajasic and tamasic in the right proportion. Water is also known as 'The Abysmal'. Water environment suggests an area with a regular flow of energy. The energy is not much active here. Water element buildings undulate and often appear to be a mixture of other three elements. These buildings are ideal for storage, warehousing and production lines.

Water environment is not good for fire element people but is excellent for earth element people. A fire element person working in a water environment must introduce extra fire or air. A beautiful red or yellow colour piece of art may serve as an effective remedy. Air dancing objects, wind chimes, or soothing instrumental music are good examples of air objects.

Watery professions are related with water supply, caring industry, money transactions, orange and indigo colours, wavy and undefined shapes and rainy season. Some of the watery professions are fisheries, stores of aquatic product, laundries, seafood stores, banks, hospitals, clinics, pharmacy, insurance companies, crèches, child care centers, nursery and kindergarten schools, stock brokers, cleaning business, etc.

5. Earth

Earth bears the load of all types of vaastu situated on it. The soil available at the building site should be dense, compact and non-porous. Only then will it be able to bear the load safely. In vaastu, earth resides in nairritya (south-west) direction. Earth governs our nose, genital organs, procreation, landscape, flora and building materials. Locally available building materials are considered the best. They make the building eco-friendly i.e., in tune with Mother Nature. Earth element governs our smelling sense (gandha). Foul smelling earth may lead to problems in child birth and diseases of the genital organs. Foundation on loose non-compacted soil shall lead to collapse of structure.

Earth is related to the south-west and west directions. Square, rectangular and flat shapes, solid and stable forms, grey and earthy colours – all these create a strong earth environment.

Earth element is mainly tamas and thus indicates stillness. Activities like sowing seeds, preparing and providing support are related to tamas. Earth, in its rajas form, is often referred to as 'The Receptive'. It is productive, i.e., its output is turned into goods. It includes activities like quarrying, pottery and food production.

A square shape building with pointed roof is a combination of earth and fire elements. Earth buildings are ideal for people born under the influence of water element. Earth and water enjoy a harmonious relationship. Earth buildings are not good for the people born under the influence of air element. If an air element person has to work in an earth element building, it will be a good idea to introduce something fiery in the work environment. Anything representing heat, angular shape, fire or a red colour object may act as a remedy.

Earthy professions are related with earth, clay, ceramics, solid and stable things, grey and earthy colours, square and rectangular shapes and all the seasons. Some examples of earthy businesses are: architectural and civil engineering firms, farms, farming equipment, pawn shops, cement plants, grocery store, departmental store, fruit stores, mining plants, hardware stores, ceramic factories, brick kilns, auto manufacturers, furniture stores, jewellery sale stores, bank's lockers, rice or grain stores, accounting firms, construction firms, real estate, cosmetics and antique shops, funeral homes, mortuaries, horticulture, gardening, agricultural stores, sawmills, timber mills, packaging companies, carpenters, sculptors, employment services, financial services, legal firms, crematoriums, machinery manufacturing and retail.

If you are constructing your own building, try and make good use of vaastu principles during the planning stage itself. First of all, determine the location, direction and type of the building that is in harmonious relation to your lucky business. After its selection, evaluate it further for different activities. Divide the floor plan in accordance with the three gunas, five elements, nine planets and ten directional lords.

Most important functions of your business shall be located in the most suitable sectors. For instance, you would not want a toilet in the north-east sector. Likewise, sales people working in the south-west will not be able to produce the desired results. South-west rules tamasic energy of inactivity. They shall perform best when occupying the north-west, the direction of active wind energy.

Sunlight

Morning time sun rouses hope while the afternoon sun or setting sun rouses despair. We are most productive in the morning. See most of the schools in India have only the morning shift! Study, play or plan your day's work in the morning. Fix your most important meetings in the early hours because as the day advances, certain dullness sets in our mind and body. Light of afternoon sun received inside the premises shall be diffused and not the direct one. We get nectar like ultra-violet colour from the sunrays in the morning which turns out to be the radioactive infra-red colour in the afternoon.

When we live in a well-lighted room, our chances of going astray are meager. A person's view of reality gets distorted in the absence of light. Light gives us the perspective because we see the world in its true sense. Grey colour on the walls is not good for attracting pure natural light. No one can be happy in a dark room. Dark surfaces absorb light while the light coloured surfaces reflect it. White or off-white colour makes us cheerful.

There is an easy way to admit natural light in your premise. It can be achieved by breaking a portion of the roof and putting transparent or translucent fiberglass sheet there. This is a common practice in vehicle workshops where we get our car regularly serviced.

Lighting

Human beings can work only in the presence of light. That is why tenth *bhava* (house) in the horoscope, representing midday time in the North Indian system of Vedic Astrology, is considered the place of physical karmas (activities). In Indian tradition, light is equivalent to Lakshmi, the goddess of wealth. When sun sets in the evening in north India, businessmen usually greet the electric light with their folded hands. Adequate lighting is must in the workplace. It ensures health, safety and maximum efficiency. Working areas should be well lit. Variety of lighting can be introduced to support the various functions going on there.

The best form of light in any workplace is the natural daylight. Natural light not only enables us to see the things but also supplies vitamin D to our body. It increases our immunisation power. People living in cold areas, receiving comparatively lesser amount of sunlight during the winters, may suffer from the disease called Seasonal Affective Disorder (SAD). This disease is brought about by an excess of melatonin, a hormone produced by our brain during the long hours of darkness. Depression and high suicidal rate is also common in such areas.

People working in natural light are certainly healthier than the people working in artificially lit houses. Recent studies have shown that artificial lights, especially the fluorescent light, cause depression and lethargy. Other probable problems are headache, nausea, poor eyesight, stress, fatigue and many more. Keeping this in view, some multinationals are now designing their offices where staff can work in the natural daylight, at least during the day hours.

Though natural daylight is best, strong sunshine causes too much glare on the highly reflective glass surfaces. Sun's glare can also create problems where computer screens and desks are close to the windows. Take precautions to filter the light through the vertical blinds, plants and movable screens. Use tilted reading stands. They can be ingeniously designed to make the light fall on the page at a right angle.

Quality of light should seriously be considered. Full spectrum artificial lighting was designed to copy the natural daylight. It contained slightly higher levels of harmful radiation than the other ordinary light sources. Fluorescent lights are still the primary source of artificial light in the offices. They are easy to install and cheap to run. But these lights emit higher electromagnetic fields than the other sources, which can be detrimental for the workers. Flickering fluorescent lights can cause stress and headaches. These can even bring on fits in a person suffering from epilepsy.

Incandescent light bulbs give an even light throughout the office. They are also used for a particular task on the desks. Light source shall always be positioned on the non-working hand side to prevent shadows falling across the works. Uplighters are also useful in low ceiling offices. They are also used when it is not desirable to have spot lighting on the desks. Uplighters are directed onto the walls and ceilings. Consequently the reflected light offers an additional source of light. Low-voltage tungsten and halogen lamps are useful for this purpose. They give white light like natural daylight. These bulbs are also energy efficient.

Colours

Colours are the vibrations of light. Colour usage means working with the light. We respond to colours – consciously or unconsciously. The auspicious colour for a residence is one which is compatible with the spirit of its inmates. On the contrary, a commercial office is open to a large group of people. Thus some natural colour suitable to the taste of masses should be preferred. However, one can use his most liked colour(s) in a private office. This colour shall make him feel comfortable and encouraging. Colours can be introduced in the form of furniture and furnishings, paintings, stationery items, storage boxes and the like.

Normally offices are rajasic in nature. Using rajasic colours – red, orange, bright yellow and their tints and tones – will add to the rajas energy of any working place. Tamasic colours – violet, indigo, blue and black – will create a less dynamic field. Colours in the public areas should be neutral. The accent colours must reflect the nature of the company or the colours of the company's logo.

Availability of natural daylight and artificial lighting affect the use of colours in any workplace. Materials used have a great role in the overall effect of a business. Too dark coloured walls in your home or office are not good. Dark coloured curtains and upholstered chairs have a tamasic effect. Too gaudy a home or office meant for general purpose is also not good. Light coloured walls spread cleanliness and purity. Light, smooth, hard and metallic surfaces have rajasic attributes. Materials used in the furnishings and decorations also absorb or transmit light. Their colours also affect the office energy. Plenty of natural light and lively colours can make any area an energetic space. Homes having too many things with too many colours look like museums.

In commercial vaastu, auspicious colours of the building are determined by the nature of the business and which of the four elements (i.e., fire, earth, air or water) it corresponds to. The colours associated with the four elements evoke the energy of each element. These colours can be used in the office to highlight the nature of the business. They also enhance the qualities we wish to invoke there. For example, auspicious colours for the business of a fire nature e.g., a restaurant or a bakery will be red, orange or yellow being the fiery colours. Bright fire colours in shades of red and orange are most appropriate for any dynamic business e.g., an advertising agency or a TV studio.

For an earth nature business, say the real estate or a money exchange company, best colour choices are golden and yellow. Yellow is the native colour of earth, while golden is the basic colour of money. For a furniture showroom, green, golden brown or other wooden colours are the most auspicious ones. For a hardware store – all earth colours e.g., grey, sandy, yellow, white etc., will be good. If the business is of water nature, e.g., fishery or cleaning related business, the auspicious colours are glass, white and indigo. Glass colour represents clear water while white and indigo are respectively the colours of Moon and Venus. Moon and Venus both signify water.

For individual performances, blue is a good colour. It is the colour of Jupiter, the planet of inner development. Red colour is good for public performance. It is the colour of Sun, the king ruling the public. Black is not a good colour in the Indian tradition. But it can be used to highlight the lighter colours. Black and white colours are the problem-solving colours. That's why black and white are the colours of courts of law in India. White is revealed better in a black background and vice versa. If God is white, Satan is black. If Sun is white, Saturn is black. Red and black together are the colours of magic and of casinos. People in media and the people who want to become the centre of attraction generally wear these colours in combination. Combination of golden and red colours suits a boudoir (dressing-room).

The colours corresponding to the five elements should be balanced in any office. A dominating or lacking element may prove disastrous to the balance of energies at work. If walls are painted in strong colours, choose neutral colours for the furnishings or blend the colours. Clashing colours may also be used as a way of energy movement. In solar spectrum, a colour in the fifth position from a particular colour is its clashing colour. So red-blue, orange-indigo, and yellow-violet are mutually clashing colours. White-black are the specially clashing colours. Clashing colours are useful especially in businesses where quick decisions are called for. For instance, red-blue combination is used in police department in Delhi and surrounding states.

Astrology (Jyotish)

Jyotish or Astrology literally means the science of stars, the source of celestial light. It is the study of effect of heavenly bodies of the solar system on us. These heavenly bodies are called *grahas* in Vedic Astrology. Graha literally means 'to catch hold of'. The nine grahas – Sun, Moon, Mars, Mercury, Jupiter, Venus, Saturn, Rahu and Ketu capture our body, mind and spirit through their optical and magnetic rays. We are deeply connected with the Sun, our primal father. He is *amshi* (whole) and we are His *amsha* (fraction). An astrologer does not take into account the effect of Earth, the planet right under our feet. This effect of earth is the main subject matter of Vaastu Shastra, though it also includes the time tested principles of Astrology.

Astrology uses personified form of time (*Kaal Purush*) while Vaastu Shastra uses the personified form of space (*Vaastu Purush*). The main stress of Jyotish and Vaastu Shastra is respectively on time and space. Combined together, they spin the web of spacio-time, i.e., space and time. Vaastu Shastra, when combined with Jyotish becomes a complete tantra, i.e., system where we study the effect of all the planets of solar system including mother earth. Astrology stresses on planetary periods (*dashas*) while Vaastu Shastra stresses on directions (*dishas*).

Astrology and Vaastu go hand in hand. A bad planetary period, combined with a good vaastu or a bad vaastu combined with a good planetary period will deliver only the moderate results. Sometimes, the problem lies with one's bad time only, not with the vaastu and vice versa. Once the bad phase is over or the vaastu defects are rectified, the good results start pouring in. See, you are far freer in selecting your business premises than changing or modifying your planetary period.

Most auspicious business direction(s) for a person can be decided by looking at his or her horoscope. The direction of the lord of the ascendant, if strong and un-afflicted, is the luckiest direction for an individual. The other lucky directions are the directions of strong and un-afflicted 10th, 9th or 5th House Lords and of planets involved in benefic classical planetary combinations (*yogas*). For example, if Ruchaka Yoga is formed in the 10th House of someone's horoscope, particularly in the Capricorn sign, it will bring him good luck from the South direction. Directions of all the planets have already been given under the heading 'Directions'.

Analyse the 10th house of your horoscope for deciding your luckiest profession(s). More the number of planets connected with the 10th house and its lord, more the number of businesses / activities one pursues. The type will depend on overall synthesis of the horoscope and the current planetary period. If most of the planets are posted in the bright half, i.e., between 7th to 12th houses without any malefic influence of Saturn, the person may be a workaholic.

Broadly, karmas are of three types, i.e., of body, mind and speech. Physical work is best in the south direction (equivalent to 10th bhava in the horoscope). Mental karmas will be more fruitful in the north of northwest (equivalent to 5th bhava in the horoscope).

Karmas related to speech are auspicious in the east of north-east (equivalent to 2nd bhava in the horoscope). Otherwise, normally one shall select the direction compatible with the related planet and the chosen activity.

Electional Astrology (Muhoorta)

Muhoorta literally means an auspicious time slot of two *ghatis* i.e., 48 minutes. An auspicious time is chosen for starting any desired activity to ensure success of any business. There is a popular saying in English, 'Well begun is half done'. Good starting is the pre-requirement for success of any work. When we move into a new building for residential or business purposes, or start an important travel, muhoorta is considered crucial to its success. In muhoorta we consider the effect of transit of Vedic planets on the doer's (*karta*) horoscope. Muhoorta ensures the doer's positive attitude, peaceful mind, and the whole hearted readiness for the work / activity in question.

Business owner should pay close attention to the timing, because timing refers both to the owner's personal life and the mundane aspect. From personal point of view, it is inauspicious to open a business when there is some serious illness in the family, immediately after a loved one's death, when one is financially weak, when there is instability in marriage or when one is facing some other tough situation that has weakened his personal energy.

Timing also refers to the mundane aspect i.e., *tithi* (lunar dates), *vaara* (weekdays), *nakshatra* (constellations), yoga (combinations) and *karna* (half of a tithi). When starting a new business, it is common for devout Indian business people to consult a *pandita* (learned person) who is well versed in Electional Astrology (Muhoorta). He refers his locally published ephemeris (*panchaang* or *patra*) for deciding the auspicious starting date and time of business.

Panchanga is a detailed yearly calendar that rates each day according to its auspiciousness. It is available at many book stores and stationary shops. Panchaang helps determine best days and time to start a new business, construction of buildings, planting crops, making money-related decisions, filing a law suit, purchasing a property, performing marriage, travelling and other occasions. After an auspicious date and time is chosen, all the pending work of building is scheduled to finish in time for the designated opening day.

Chapter 2
Vaastu Gods and Goddesses

श्रीमङ्गलात् प्रभवति प्रागल्भ्यात् सम्प्रवर्धते।
दाक्ष्यात् तु कुरुते मूलं संयमात् प्रतितिष्ठति।।

Sree (prosperity) takes its birth in good deeds, grows in consequence of boldness, drives its roots deep in consequence of dexterity and acquires stability owing to self-control.

Mahabharata, 5/35/51

Introduction

Paramshayin Vaastu consists of eighty-one squares. Forty-five gods, demi-gods and goddesses occupy these eighty-one squares – ranging from single to nine squares. Arrangement of these fourty-five gods and goddesses in Paramshayin diagram is shown in figure 2.1. Numbers shown against the respective Gods in this figure correspond with the respective God in Table 2.1 and also with the gods discussed later in the following pages.

According to Mayamatam, outer thirty-two of these gods from Ishaan to Diti (1 to 32), occupy one square (pada) each (forming Paishach Sthan). Eight of the remaining thirteen – Aap, Aapvatsa, Savita, Saavitr, Indra, Jaya, Rudra and Rudraaj (33, 34, 36, 37, 39, 40, 42 and 43) – occupy two squares each. The four demi-gods – Aryama, Vivasvaan, Mitra and Bhudhar (35, 38, 41 and 44) – occupy six squares each. Brahma (45) occupies the middle nine squares forming Brahamsthan.

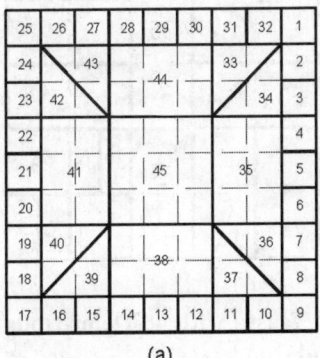
(a)

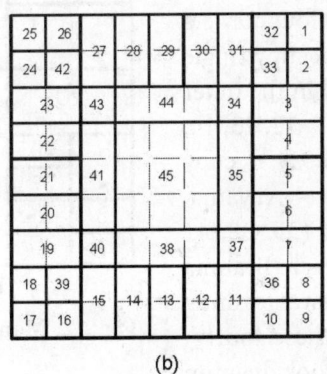
(b)

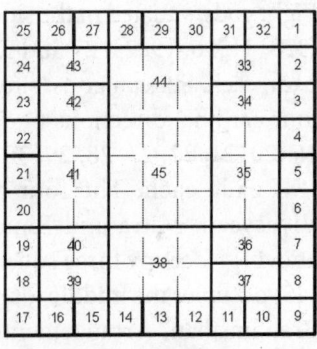
(c)

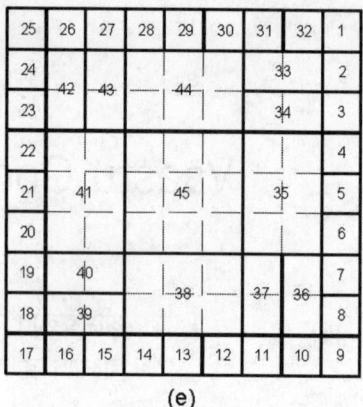

1.Vahni 2. Parjanya 3. Jayant 4. Mahendra 5. Aaditya 6. Satya 7.Bhrish 8 . Antariksh 9. Maarut 10. Poosha 11. Vitath 12. Grihakshat 13. Yam 14. Gandharv 15. Bhringraaj 16. Mrig 17. Pitar 18. Dauvaarik 19.Sugreev 20. Pushpdant 21. Varun 22. Asur 23. Shosh 24. Paapyakshama 25. Rog 26. Naag 27. Mukhya 28. Bhallaat 29. Som 30. Charak 31.Aditi 32.Diti 33. Aap 34. Aapvats 35.Aryama 36. Savita 37. Saavitr 38. Vivasvaan 39. Indra 40.Jaya 41. Mitra 42.Rudra 43.Raajyakshama 44. Kshitidhar 45. Brahma

Fig. 2.1 (a) : Paramshayin Vaastu with 45 Demi-Gods and Goddesses
{(b),(c),(d) and (e) are Alternate Arrangements of Squares}

Another space arrangement 'Mandook Vaastu' consists of sixty-four squares. Forty-five gods, demi-gods and goddesses occupy these sixty-four squares – ranging from half to four squares. According to Mayamatam, sixteen of these gods, situated in the four corners (1, 2, 9, 10, 17, 18, 25, 26, 33, 34, 36, 37, 39, 40, 42 and 43), occupy half pada each. Eight gods, situated in the sides of four corners (3, 8, 11, 16, 19, 24, 27 and 32), occupy single pada each. Sixteen gods, situated in the outer four cardinal directions (4, 5, 6, 7, 12, 13, 14, 15, 20, 21, 22, 23, 28, 29, 30 and 31), occupy two pada each. The four gods – Aryama, Vivasvaan, Mitra and Bhudhar (35, 38, 41 and 44) – occupy three squares each. Brahma (45) occupies the middle four squares forming Brahamsthan. Arrangement of these forty-five gods and goddesses in Mandook diagram is shown in figure 2.2.

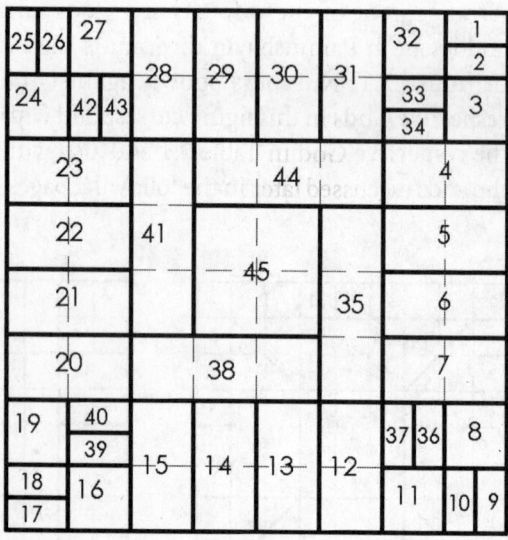

Fig 2.2: Mandook Vaastu with 45 Demi-Gods and Goddesses

Recommendations of other classical texts of vaastu vary to some extent while allotting number of squares to these gods and demi-gods. For the same demi-god(s), different names are also found in different classical texts.

Though familiar with some names like Indra, Surya, Yama, Varuna, Soma, etc., most of the present day readers are completely ignorant of the names of most of these demi-gods. Neither the Vaastu classics nor the modern authors of vaastu books have paid serious thought for deciphering their deep meanings. Glossary of these vaastu gods and goddesses is found in the popular vaastu classic *Samaranganasutradhara* (14.14-31) under the heading *Vaastudevanam Nighantu*. Another classical text on vaastu *Aparajitaprichchha* (56.1-17) mainly follows the recommendations of Samaranganasutradhara with minor deviations. Meanings of these forty-five demi-gods have been given in these two classical texts in just one or two words. The same are being given below in a tabular form. Author has not found interpretation and application of these demi-gods in any of the available classical texts of vaastu.

Table 2.1: Glossary of Vaastu Gods and Goddesses available as 'Vaastudevanam Nighantu' in Samaranganasutradhara (14.14 – 31) and Aparajitaprichchha (56.1 – 17)

S No	Name of Door	Meaning as per Samaranganasutradhara	Meaning as per Aparajitaprichchha
1	Vahni / Agni / Ish	Har-Lord Shiva, Sarvabhuta-Har,	Shankardeva
2	Parjanya	Rain cloud, lord of rain-clouds (Vrishtimaan, Ambudadhip)	Vrishtikaraka
3	Jayant	Lord Kashyap rishi, Dual name (dwinama)	Kashyapa Deva, Rain God
4	Mahendra / Kulishayudh / Indra	King of gods, demon-killer	Indra, the king of gods
5	Aaditya / Ravi	Ruler of the day time, Vivasvaan (Ahaskar)	Prabhakar (Sun)
6	Satya	Welfare-oriented dharma of all the Beings	Dharma, Dharmaraaj
7	Bhrish	Kamadeva, (Manmatha)	Manmatha
8	Antariksh / Nabha / Ambar	Sky-lord, (Nabhodeva, Antarikshadeva)	Antariksha, Akash
9	Maarut / Anil / Agni	Lord of Air	Teja samudbhava
10	Poosha	Group of mothers (Matrigana)	Matrigana
11	Vitath	The excellent son of Kaliyuga 'Adharma'	Adharma
12	Grihakshat	Son of Moon i.e., 'Mercury' (Chandratanaya)	Budha

13	Yam / Yama	Son of Vaivasvat, Lord of the dead (Pretas)	Pretadhipa
14	Gandharv	Lord Narada (Celestial Singer)	Narada
15	Bhringraaj	Son of demon-goddess Nirriti	Son of Nirriti
16	Mrig	Endless (Ananta) self-originated Brahma and Dharma	Ananta, self-originated and Dharma
17	Pitar / Pitrigan	Gods inhabiting Pitriloka	Vishvedev
18	Dauvaarik	Head of the soldiers of Shiva (Pramath) 'Nandi'	Nandi
19	Sugreev	Creator 'Manu', Adi Prajapati Manu	Manu
20	Pushpdant	Son of Vinata, very quick in action (Mahajava)	Mahajav
21	Varun	Lord of the oceans, Water-lord, Lokapal	Saliladhip
22	Asur	Rahu, Son of demon-goddess 'Simhika', devourer of Sun and Moon, Arkendumardan	Rahu
23	Shosh	Son of Sun i.e., 'Saturn'	Sauri or Shanishchara
24	Paapyakshama	Disease (Kshaya), destruction, decreasing	Kshaya
25	Rog / Jvara / Vyadhi /	Fever	Roga and dooshaka
26	Naag / Ahirbudhnya	King of snakes 'Vasuki'	Vasuki
27	Mukhya	Vishvakarma, Tvashtra	Tvashta or Vishvakrita
28	Bhallaat	Moon	Chandra
29	Som / Saumya	Kuber	Kuber
30	Charak / Giri	Business (Vyavasaya)	Himvaan, Shail
31	Aditi	Mother of Adityas, Shri, Lakshmi	Shri
32	Diti / Daityamata	Trident bearer bull-flagged Lord Shankara (Shulabhrida)	Vrish-dhwaja Sharva
33	Aap	Himvaan, the Himalaya mountain	Ocean on the earth (Dhararnava)
34	Aapvats	Uma	Uma-pati
35	Aryama	Aditya	Bhaskara
36	Savita / Savitr	Goddess Ganges	Jahanvi Ganga
37	Saavitr / Savitri	Mother of Vedas 'Gayatri'	Ved-mata

Vaastu Gods and Goddesses

38	Vivasvaan / Vaivasvat	Death which takes away this physical body	Mrityu
39	Indra / Vibudhanpati	Mighty Hari	Amaradhipa, lord of gods
40	Jaya / Indrajaya	Vajri, Holder of Vajra	Kalanala
41	Mitra	Gardener, plough-holder	Balabhadraka
42	Rudra / Raudra	Maheshwar	Ishvara
43	Raajyakshama / Rudradaas / Rudraj	Guh (to conceal, to keep secret) or Karttikeya	Son of Rudra
44	Kshitidhar / Bhudhar / Prithvidhar / Amitaujas	Ananta, Sheshnaga	Vishnu
45	Brahma / Hemgarbha	Creator, lord of all the worlds, thousand-headed, (achintaya-vibhava, abjasambhavah),	Pitamaha

In addition to the above discussed forty-five demi-gods and goddesses, eight malefic beings have been mentioned which rule the directions beyond the boundary of the premises. Their respective directions and probable literal meanings are given in Table 2.2. They work as servants to the gods. They do not own any square on the vaastu purush and are born under the demon lineages.

Table 2.2: Eight Demi-Goddesses, their Directions and Probable Meanings

S No	Demi-Goddess	Direction Ruled	Probable Meanings
1	Charaki	North-east	Kind of venomous fish
2	Pilipichchha	East	Inciting venomous saliva of a snake
3	Vidari	South-east	Swelling in the groin
4	Jambha	South	Opening of the mouth
5	Pootna	South-west	Kind of disease in a child
6	Skanda	West	Causing destruction
7	Paap-raakshashi	North-west	Witch, evil female demon
8	Aryama	North	Milkweed plant

Vaastumandanam (1.126-127) describes eight outer Bhairavas – Hetuk, Vetaal, Agni, Dwijak, Kaal, Karal, Ekahni and Bhima. These should be worshipped starting with Ishaan. Names of eight bhairavas given in *Mantramahodadhi* (1.54) are, Asitanga, Ruru-bhairava, Chanda-bhairava or Kaal-bhairava, Krodh-bhairava, Unmatt-bhairava, Kapali-bhairava, Bhishan-bhairava and Samhar-bhairava. Mention of eight demi-goddesses or Bhairvas in the vaastu classics indicate the need to protect the inner constructed space from the surrounding ferocious (asuri or negative) forces, to tame the unruly forces in the neighborhood and to take care of the four corners as well as the four sides outside the premises.

All the possible efforts have been made here to decode the deep meanings of these demi-gods and goddesses. If you refer to the Sanskrit-English dictionary, all the relevant meanings of these seemingly strange words / terms have been given there. Literal meanings of the names of these demi-gods and their classical as well as the possible modern interpretations have also been indicated. Care has been taken to mention only those qualities, characteristics, myths, excerpts, references and stories related to these demi-gods which could directly or indirectly be useful in vaastu.

For example, Shiva ruling the Ishana square is an omniscient Yogi living an ascetic life on Mount Kailash. Thus Ishana is best for running a Yoga and Meditation centre successfully. One can achieve ultimate wisdom here easily, if so inclined. Ishana is best for living an ascetic life. Like Mount Kailash, it is the coldest area in any vaastu. Considering another example, Nirriti literally means "absence of *Rta* or lawless or that which is beyond the order". Thus the square of Nirriti can be best utilised for production and selling of liquor, running a brothel, a slaughter house, gobar gas plant in a farm house or an operation theatre in a hospital. This square invites and encourages illegal, immoral, unethical and anti-social activities)

1. Vahni (Ishana, Ish, Isha, Ishah, Ishan, Ishanah, Eashan, Ishaan, Ishaka, Ishdeva, Ishvara, Hiranyaretas, Agni, Shikhi, Shikh, Shikhin, etc.)

As per the Sanskrit–English dictionary, 'Ishana' means, Shiva, the Sun as a form of Shiva-Rudra, capable of, to govern, to be powerful, reigning, one who is completely master of anything, supreme, king, ruler, god, lord, master, possessing, wealth, owing, sharing, light, splendor, number eleven (11), etc.

Ishana is the name of God Shiva. It means the one from whom the universe emanates. The name Ishana is also mentioned in *Shiva Mahapurana* as one of five names of the god. Ishana has its roots in the word 'Ish', which means the invisible power that governs the universe. Ish is the shortened form of Ishana, one of the names of Rudra, the symbolic value of which is eleven. This power itself or the wielder of this power is 'Ishana'. It is synonymous with Ishvara, which means 'The Lord'. Ishvara is one of the attributes of Shiva, who is an emanation of Rudra. Ishvara means 'Lord of the universe' or 'The Supreme divinity'.

Panchanana

The Sanskrit word 'Shiva' means 'The Auspicious One'. According to Yajurveda, God Rudra-Shiva has two contrary sets of attributes. He is malignant or terrific (Rudra) as well as benign or auspicious (Shiva). The benign part rules the north-east while the terrific part rules the north-west. In His benevolent aspects, Shiva is not only an omniscient Yogi living an ascetic life on the Mount Kailash, but also a householder with wife Parvati and his two children, Ganesha and Karttikeya.

The consort of Shiva represents the dynamic extension of Shiva onto this universe. Ganesha is worshipped throughout India as the Lord of Beginnings, Lord of the Obstacles and also Remover of the Obstacles. He rules chaturthi tithi, the fourth lunar date of bright as well as the dark half.

Shiva is also regarded as the patron god of yoga and arts. When depicted as a yogi, he may be shown sitting and meditating. His epithet Mahayogi (the great Yogi: *Maha* = 'great', *Yogi* = 'one who is master of Yoga') refers to his association with yoga. Shiva is also depicted as a corpse below the Goddess Kali. It represents that Shiva is a corpse without Shakti. He remains inert here. While Shiva is the static form, Mahakali or Shakti is the dynamic aspect without whom Shiva is powerless.

In contrast to Rudra, His name Shankara, 'beneficent' or 'conferring happiness' reflects his benign form. This name 'Shankara' was adopted by the great Vedanta philosopher Adi Shankara (788-820 AD), who is also known as Shankaracharya. Adi Shankara, in his interpretation of the name Shiva, the 27th and 600th name of *Vishnu Sahasranama* (the thousand names of Vishnu) interprets Shiva to have multiple meanings: 'The Pure One' or 'the One who is not affected by three Gunas of Prakriti'. His name Shambhu, 'causing happiness', also reflects his benign aspect.

Shiva is one of the three major deities of Hinduism. He is *Anant*, one who is neither found born nor found dead. At the highest level, Shiva is regarded as limitless, transcendent, unchanging and formless. Other popular names associated with Shiva are Mahadeva (The Great God), Mahesha, Maheshvara, Rudra (Grumbling, The Lord of tears, Violent), Rishikesha (Man of knowledge), Hara (One who captivates), Trilochan, (One having three eyes), Devendra (Chief of the gods), Neelakantha (One having blue throat), Shulin (The Master of the animals) and Trilokinatha (Lord of the three realms).

Shiva has six heads, of which only five (*Isana, Tatpurusha, Vamadeva, Aghora* and *Sadyojata*) are visible while the sixth (*Adhomukh*) can be seen only by the enlightened one. Each of the five heads denotes one of the five elements:

1. Isana – internal aspect that conceals – associated with all that exist – represents ether.
2. Vamadeva – north aspect that sustains manifest Brahman – associated with Vishnu – represents water.
3. Tatpurusha – east aspect Rishi, Muni, Jnani and Yogi – represents air.
4. Aghora – south aspect that rejuvenates manifest Brahman – associated with Rudra – represents fire.
5. Sadyojata – west aspect that propagates manifest Brahman – associated with Brahma – represents earth.

Ether is also called the sky-element that makes up the universe. This fifth head of Shiva faces the upward direction, towards the sky. Ishana signifies the subtle ethereal form of Shiva that represents the transcendental knowledge. This dimension is reinforced by Vaastu Shastra, which says that north-east direction represents prosperity and knowledge. In Hindu customs, north represents wealth and happiness while the east symbolises knowledge and peace. Ishana is the right combination of both. It is also the name of the god of Vaastu Shastra. The square of Ishana governs the right brain, eyes and the central nervous system of the Vaastu Purush. It rules our ideas and bestows us peace and serenity.

2. Parjanya (Vrishtimaan, Ambudadhip)

According to the Sanskrit–English dictionary, 'Parjanya' means, rain personified or the god of rain; a cloud in general, rain-cloud, thunder-cloud, muttering or roaring of the clouds, rain, etc.

Parjanya is the sky god of rains in Vedic literature. He was also one of the *Sapta-rishis* (Seven Great Sages) in the fifth Manvantara and is one of the 12 Adityas. According to the Vishnu Purana, he is guardian of the month of Kartik. He is called a Gandharva and a Rishi in the Harivamsa Purana. According to Shrimadbhagvadgita (3.14), "all living beings are created and find their source in food and food is created by the rainfall. Parjanya gives us the material blessings of rainfall and thus abundance in the material world by the creation of food and other crops".

The square of Parjanya bestows refreshment and governs insights, evolution, fertile thoughts and fertility in women. Two hymns of the Rigveda (5.83, 7.101) are dedicated to Parjanya to invoke the blessings of the rains:

"Sing forth and laud Parjanya, son of Heaven, who sends the gift of rain. May he provide our pasturage! Parjanya is the God who forms in kine, in mares, in plants of earth and womankind, the germ of life. Offer and pour into his mouth oblation rich in savoury juice. May he forever give us food!"

Parjanya is a ferocious rain god who made the desert places fit for travel probably by bringing the rains. When Parjanya fills the sky with rain-clouds, winds burst forth, lightning flashes, plants shoot up, food springs abundantly for all creatures and earth bows low before him. At his command cattle fly in terror, plants assume all colours and floods descend in torrents. Parjanya is also the upholder of law who punishes the sinners and protects the pious people.

3. Jayant (Jayanta, Jaya, Aindra)

According to the the Sanskrit-English dictionary, 'Jayanta' means the name of Indra's son, victorious, Durga, etc. In Hindu mythology, Jayanta means 'victorious'. The square of Jayanta bestows courage and is the success maker. Jayanta is the son of Indra, the king of the gods and his consort Shachi. He has a sister called Jayanti. He resides in the heaven governed by Indra. He fought many wars on behalf of the gods and his father.

A pot of *amrita* (elixir of life) emerged from churning of the ocean of milk by gods and demons. The demons seised the pot but Jayanta took it from them in the guise of a crow. Pursued by the demons, he flew for 12 years without rest. He stopped at four locations on earth – Prayag, Haridwar, Ujjain and Nashik – where the Kumbha Mela is celebrated every 12 years in remembrance of the incident. It indicates that the square of Jayanta has amrita like quality. The *Vayu Purana* narrates a tale wherein Jayanta is cursed and turns into a bamboo.

Samaranganasutradhara (14.15) identifies Jayant as Bhagwan Kashyapa Rishi, "Jayantastu dvinamakhyah kashyapo bhagvan rishih". Rishi Kashyapa was an ancient sage who is counted as one of the *Saptarishis* (the Seven Seers) of Divine Truth or Wisdom in the present *manvantara*. Legend says that Kashyapa shone so brilliantly with inner light that his contemporaries called him a human Sun. It indicates that qualities like wisdom, divine truth and inner light can easily be achieved here. Kashyapa is a manas-putra (wish-born-son) of Lord Brahma. Kashyapa had many wives; thirteen of them were the daughters of Daksha Prajapati.

Kashyapa with His Thirteen Wives

Kashyapa is considered the father of all of humanity including the Adityas, Devas, Daityas, Nagas (snakes), Aruna (Charioteer of Lord Sun's chariot – time right before sunrise), Garuda (vehicle of Vishnu), Daanavas (who are generally considered part of the Asuras), Yakshas, Gandharvas, Pishachas (flesh eating monsters), Apsaras, Jatayu, Sampati, Bali and Sugreeva. Kashyapa had a wife named Surabhi who gave birth to the Rudras. It can safely be assumed that there were many Kashyapas and this name indicates a status and not just an individual. However, the square of Kashyapa becomes an extremely fertile place for planning and preview meetings resulting in all-round multiple growth.

Kashyapa is considered a great discoverer of Mantras. So this square is also best for mantra-siddhi (mastering mantra). Kashyapa is said to have written the treatise *Kashyapa Samhita* or *Jivakiya Tantra*. It is considered a classical reference book on Ayurveda especially in the fields of Ayurvedic pediatrics, gynecology and obstetrics. All these fields are related to the well-being of child and mother. Kashyapa Sutra describes the concept of enlightenment as well as the method of its attainment.

4. Mahendra (Indra, Surendra, Kulishayudh, Pakshashan)

According to the Sanskrit-English dictionary, 'Mahendra' means, God of the atmosphere and sky, king of gods, king, god, chief, prince, best or first or excellent, pupil of the right eye, human soul, Earth, number fourteen (14), etc.

Mahendra or Indra is the embodiment of strength, courage and power. He is one of the principal gods of the Vedic times and of the Brahmanic pantheon. He represents the source of cosmic life that he transmits to the earth through rains. His strength lies in the seminal fluid of all beings. Indra is said to be 'made of all the gods put together'. He is eternally young, because he rejuvenates himself at the start of each manvantara, which means each of the fourteen 'ages' of our world which make up a 'kalpa'.

In the Rigveda, Indra or Shakra (the mighty-one) is the god of thunder and rain and a great warrior. He is lord of the heavens. He is most popular and powerful of the Vedic deities.

Indra Mounted on Airavata

He is described as god of the blue sky. He rides a white elephant called Airavata and wields the dazzling weapon of lightening called Vajra made by another god Tvashtra. Rigveda (1.65) reads that Shakra is wonderful, well-skilled in horses and the purifier of his worshippers. Indra is the golden-bodied dancing god who, clothed in perfumed garments, rides his golden cart. The rainbow is called 'Indra-dhanush' (Indra's Bow).

He is the god of war, smashing the stone fortresses of the Dasyus. Indra fought many battles to drive the demons away and ensure victory to the gods. He also destroyed many cities of his enemies. As the god of war, he is also regarded as guardian of the east direction. His most famous achievement was slaying of Vratrasur. The word *vrtra* means 'obstacle'. Thus, he is the 'smiter of resistance'. He killed demon of the dark skies (symbolically the clouds) with his weapon (the lightning) and released the cows (waters) that were held in captivity by Vratrasur.

He is prone to drinking soma, a stimulant and often losing control over himself. He is mighty and sensuous, always concerned about his survival and status as the leader. He also commits many kinds of mischief for which he is sometimes punished. He has a spiritual side too. According to the Kena Upanishad, he is the only god to have gone nearest to Brahman and was able to know Him as Brahman. This act of him earned him the right to become the ruler of the heavens. According to the Chhandogya Upanishad he studied under Prajapati Brahma and learned the secrets of immortality. Indra is the lord of Jyeshtha and Vishakha (first half) Nakshatras.

Indra wields the power of thunderbolt and is a friend to Vayu, the wind god. They work together. Also, it is Agni, Indra and Surya who represent the three forms of fire in its earthly state, its electrical charge and the sun globe. Indra, along with Varuna and Mitra, is one of the twelve Adityas, the chief gods of the Rigveda. In the Vedic period, the number of gods was assumed to be thirty-three and Indra was their lord. These thirty-three gods are; the eight Vasus, the eleven Rudras, the twelve Adityas, Indra and Prajapati.

Indra is also the prototype for all the lords and thus a king is called Indra or lord of men. Lord Rama, hero of the great epic Ramayana, is referred to as Raghavendra (Indra of the clan of Raghu). The original Indra was also referred to as Devendra (Indra of the Devas). In Shrimadbhagvad Geeta (10.22), Lord Krishna says; "Of the demigods I am Indra, the king of heaven". The square of Mahendra is related to administration and organising.

5. Aaditya (Ravi, Surya, Bhaskara, Marici)

According to the Sanskrit–English dictionary, 'Surya' means, son of Aditi or Sun, a student of the four vedas up to his forty-eighth year having control over his senses, solar, drug, bitter gourd, new bride, symbolic expression of the number twelve (12), etc.

The Adityas, meaning 'of Aditi', are the twelve sons of Aditi (wife of Kashyapa). In Brahman and Vedic cosmogony, Aditi is the infinite sky, the original space. The Adityas are its children. In Vedic times, they were five, then they became seven and finally twelve. They were consequently identified by the twelve months of the year and the 'course' of the sun during this period of time. Adityas together are considered the eternal gods of light or the beings that manifest luminous life throughout the universe. In each month of the year, it is a different Aditya (Sun-God) who shines.

The Adityas have been described in the Rig Veda as bright and pure as streams of water, free from all guile and falsehood, blameless and perfect. Adityas are beneficent gods who act as protectors of all beings, who are provident and guard the world of spirits and protect the world. They are personification or embodiment of the universal laws. They regulate the behavior of humans among themselves in conjunction with the natural forces. In Shrimadbhagvad Geeta (10.21), Lord Krishna says; "Of lights I am the blazing Sun".

Different names for 12 Adityas found in Rigveda, Bhagavata Purana, *Chhandogaya Upanishad*, Shatapatha Brahmana and other Vedic literature are: Amsha or Amshuman (one who is munificent), Aryaman (one who eliminates foes), Bhaga (one who bestows), Daksha (one who is skilled in ritual and magic), Mitra (friend), Pushya or Pusha or Pushan (one who nurtures), Savitr or Savitri (one who activates), Indra or Shakra (the forceful), Tvashta or Tvashtr or Tvashtri (one who designs), Varuna (one who surrounds or restrains), Vishnu (Head of all the Adityas but different from Lord Vishnu; the omniscient maintainer) and *Vivasvat* or Vivsvan (the brilliant or the sun, Surya). In the same order, they also refer to the universal principles known as: the share given by the gods, chivalry and honor, that which is inherited, skill in rituals, solidarity in friendship, prosperity, potency in the language, courage, skill in crafts, laws of providence as directed by the gods, universal law and morality and social order.

Other names available for the twelve Adityas are: Indra, Dhatri or Dhata or Dhatr or Dhuti, Vayu or Maartanda, Vaaman, Yama, Khaga, Hiranyagarbha, Marichi, Bhaskar, Ravi, etc. Surya, as Indra, destroys the enemies of the gods. As Dhata, he creates the living beings. As Parjanya, he showers down rain. As Tvashta, he lives in the trees and the herbs. As Pusha, he makes food grains grow. As Aryama, he is in the wind. As Bhaga, he is in the body of all the living beings. As Vivasvana, he is in the fire and helps to cook food. As Vishnu, he destroys the enemies of the gods. As Amshumana, he is again in the wind. As Varuna, Surya is in the waters and as Mitra he is in the Moon and in the oceans. Adityas are true to the eternal Law and act as the exactors of debt in the form of Mitra-Varuna.

Aditya, in the present day usage in Sanskrit, has been made singular in contrast to the Vedic Adityas and is being used synonymously with Surya, the Sun. Surya, the blazing sun, is the nearest and most easily recognised form of divinity. He is thus accepted as a form or representation of the Supreme God. It is through his rays that he puts life into all the beings. However, he also gives death because of his extreme heat. He perpetually creates, supports and then destroys all the life. He is the bestower of power and strength, as well as the destroyer of laziness and darkness. With bright light radiating from him, he knows all that lives. Like Varuna, he is ever watchful. He is the provider of good health, removes heart disease and takes away the yellow hue (jaundice). In Vedic theology, the sun represents the highest and the best. He is eulogised as the source of prana, who keeps the world alive by bringing light and vigour.

His other names that relate to his peculiar abilities and character are: Aditya (source of the world), Ahar-pati (lord of the day), Jagat-chakshu (eye of the universe), Karma-sakshin (witness of actions), Graha-rajan (king of planets), Sahasrakiran (one with a thousand rays) and Dyumani (jewel of the sky). Surya 'the Supreme Light' is also known as Bhanu or Ravi-Vivasvana in Sanskrit. Surya is worshiped in the 'Arka' form mostly in the Northern and Eastern parts of India. Surya is also known as 'Mitra' (friend) for his life-nourishing properties.

Lord Sun Riding His Chariot

Surya rides a chariot harnessed by seven horses which might represent the seven colours of the rainbow or the seven chakras in the human body. Surya's sons, Shani and Yama, are responsible for the judgment of human life. Shani provides the results of one's deeds during one's life through appropriate punishments and rewards while Yama grants the results of one's deeds after death. In the Vedas, Surya is frequently referred to as 'the eye of Mitra, Varuna and Agni'. In the Ramayana, Surya is described as the father of king Sugreeva, who helped Rama and Lakshmana in defeating the demon king Ravana. Surya also trains Hanuman. The Suryavanshi dynasty of kings, Lord Rama being one of them, also claims descent from Surya. Lord Surya is also considered to be the eye of the Viraat Purush (Lord Sri Krishna's Universal Form).

Surya is chief of the Navagrahas, the nine classical Indian planets and important elements of Vedic Astrology. He is also the presiding deity of Sunday. In Vedic astrology, Surya is considered a mild malefic on account of his hot and dry nature. Surya represents soul, will-power, fame, eyes, general vitality, courage, kingship, father, highly placed persons and authority. He is exalted in the Aries sign, is in *mooltrikon* in the sign Leo and is in debilitation in the sign Libra. Surya is lord of three nakshatras or lunar mansions: Krittika, Uttara Phalguni and Uttara Ashadha. Sun is the lord of Saptami tithi (seventh lunar date).

The Gayatri Mantra is associated with Surya. Another hymn associated with Surya is the Aditya Hridaya Stotra, recited by the great sage Agastya to Rama on the war field before the fight with demon king Ravana. Twelve mantras, having twelve different names of Surya, are chanted during the practice of twelve postures of surya namaskar yoga. Surya has the following associations: the colors – golden or red, the metals – gold or copper, the gemstone – ruby, the direction – east and the season of summer. The food grain associated with Him is wheat. The square of Surya is related to influence. He is the observer and the controller.

6. Satya (Satyaka, Dharma, Rta, Ritah)

According to the Sanskrit–English dictionary, 'Satya' means, ratification of a bargain, true, truth, genuine, reality, quality of goodness or purity or knowledge, *ashvattha* tree, water, etc. Samaranganasutradhara (14.16) identifies Satya as the 'welfare-oriented dharma of all the beings'. Dharma is the general law, the Duty, the thing which is permanently fixed, the ensemble of rules and natural phenomena which rule the order of things and of men.

Satya is the Sanskrit word for truth. In Vedas and the later sutras, meaning of the word Satya evolves into an ethical concept about truthfulness and is considered an important virtue. It means being true and consistent with reality in one's thought, speech and action. A related concept 'sattwa' which is also derived from 'sat', means nature, character, true essence and the spiritual essence. Sattwa is also a guna, a psychology concept in the Samkhya School of Philosophy. It means goodness, purity, clean, positive and the one that advances good true nature of the self.

Satya (truth) is equated to 'Rta' in the Vedas. Rta means that which is properly joined, order, rule, nature, balance and harmony. Rta results from 'Satya' in the Vedas as it regulates and enables operation of the universe and everything within it. Satya is considered essential. Without Satya, the universe and reality falls apart and cannot function. In Rigveda, opposed to 'Rta' and 'Satya' are 'Anrita' and 'Asatya' (falsehood). Truth and truthfulness is considered a form of reverence for the divine, while falsehood a form of sin.

The Lion Seal of Indian Government

According to Rigveda (Book 1, 4, 6, 7, 9 and 10), Satya includes action and speech that is factual, real, true and reverent to Rta. However, Satya isn't merely about one's past that is in context in the Vedas. It has one's current and future contexts as well. Satya is the modality of acting in the world of Sat, as the truth to be built, formed or established. Truth is sought and praised in the hymns of Upanishadas. It is held as one that always prevails ultimately. For example, Mundaka Upanishad (3.1.6) states, *Satyamevajayate Naanritam*. (Truth alone triumphs, not falsehood).

This magical excerpt has also been accepted as the motto of the Republic of India's emblem. In Yoga Sutra of Patanjali, Satya is one of the five Yamas or virtuous restraints, along with *ahimsa* (restraint from violence or injury to any living being); *asteya* (restraint from stealing); *brahmacharya* (celibacy or restraint from sexually cheating on one's partner); and *aparigraha* (restraint from covetousness and craving). According to the Yoga Sutras of Patanjali, "When one is firmly established in speaking truth, the fruits of action become subservient to him."

Patanjali considers satya as the restraint from falsehood in one's action (body), words (speech, writing) and thoughts as well as feelings (mana or mind). In Patanjali's teachings, one may not always know the truth or the whole truth, but one knows as if one is creating, sustaining or expressing falsehood, exaggeration, distortion, fabrication or deception. In Patanjali's Yoga, Satya is the virtue of restraint from such falsehood, either through silence or through stating the truth without any form of distortion. The square of Satya is goodwill creator and is related to the energies of commitment and ego.

7. Bhrish (Bhrsh, Bhrisha, Kamadeva, Manmatha)

According to the Sanskrit-English dictionary, 'Bhrish' means, to fall down, severely, harshly, violently, strongly, frequently, often, abundant, etc. Bhrish means a particular tutelary (who is a guardian, patron or protector of a particular place, geographic feature, person, lineage, nation, culture or occupation) deity or spirit, number thirteen (13), etc. The square of Bhrish is related to the energies of analysis, gravity, honing or poor implementation of the plan and delay or hastiness in decisions.

Samaranganasutradhara (14.16) identifies Bhrish as the demigod 'Kamadeva or Manmatha'. Kamadeva is generally considered the Hindu divinity of Cosmic Desire and carnal love whose actions decides the laws of the reincarnation of the living beings (samsara). Kamadeva (God of sex) is the lord of Trayodashi tithi (thirteenth lunar date) which is Jaya-prada or one giving victory. He is the god of love, attraction and sexuality. Kama literally means *trishna*, i.e., desire or thirst or longing, especially in the sensual or sexual love while *Deva* means heavenly or divine or just a lord. Kamadeva is in-charge of inciting the lusty desires, the cause of generation. In Shrimadbhagvad Geeta (10.28), Lord Krishna says, "I am Kandarpa (Cupid or Kamadeva), the motivation of procreation for begetting progeny".

Other names for Kamadeva include, Manmatha (churner of hearts), Atanu (one without a body), Ragavrinta (stalk of passion), Ananga (incorporeal), Kandarpa (inflamer even of a god), Manasija (he who is born of mind), Madana (intoxicating), Ratikanta (lord of Rati), Pushpavan (flower-garden) and Kusumakshara (one with arrow of flowers). Kamadeva is said to be the son of Hindu goddess Sri. Lord Krishna himself and his son Pradyumna are also considered the incarnations of Kamadeva. Kama often took part in Puranic battles with his troops of soldiers.

gentle breeze. All of these are the symbols of spring season, when his festival is celebrated as Vasanta, Holi or Holika. Holi, a Spring New Year festival in India, is called Madanotsava or Kama-Mahotsava in Sanskrit.

Kamadeva Mounted on a Parrot

Lord Krishna as an Incarnation of Kamadeva

Kamadeva is represented as a young, handsome winged man with green skin who wields a bow and arrows. His bow is made of sugarcane with a string of honeybees and his arrows are decorated with five kinds of fragrant flowers. These five flowers are of Ashoka tree, white and blue Lotus, of Mallika (Jasmine) plant and flowers of Mango tree. All these significations make this square the best place for developing a garden with flowering trees and plants as well as for a small zoological park. Kamadeva is wed to Rati, the daughter of Daksha, created from his sweat. His companions are a cuckoo, a parrot, humming bees, the season of spring and the

The religious rituals addressed to Kamadeva offer a means of purification and re-entry into the community. Devotion to Kamadeva keeps desires within the framework of the religious tradition. No images of Kamadeva are sold in the market place for worship at home. A temple dedicated to Kama in North India is the Kameshvara Temple in Kamyavan, one of the twelve forests of Vrindavana, the sacred place related to Lord Krishna.

Blessings of Kamadeva are sought by the people seeking health, physical beauty, husband or wife and progeny. He is generally invoked in marriage ceremonies. Believers of Vedic Astrology generally avoid marriage during the combustion of Venus, the planet signifying Kamadeva. Marriage solemnised during the combustion of Venus is thought to invite problems related with the seminal fluids, sexual satisfaction, fertility and conception.

8. Antariksh (Nabh, Nabho-deva, Kha, Aja, Akash, Gagan, Vyoman, Panktika)

According to the Sanskrit-English dictionary, 'Antariksha' means, atmosphere, air, sky, intermediate space between heaven and earth, middle of the three regions of life, talc, numeric value Zero (0), etc. Kha, the other name of Antariksha, also means 'space'. Zero symbolism of Kha is explained by the fact that space is nothing but a 'void'. Kha is the empty space which marks the absence of units of a given order in positional numeration. The square of Antariksha is related to the qualities of initiative, allowing and the inner space.

Samaranganasutradhara (14.17) identifies Antariksh as the demigod 'Nabhodeva or The Sky-God'. The ancient Sky-God of Vedic pantheon is Dyaus Pita or literally the 'Sky Father'. He impregnated Prithvi, the earth and mother, in the form of rains. He is the father of Indra (future king of the Gods and the lord of rain), Agni (fire) and Usha (the dawn). The name Dyaus Pita is closely related to Latin Jupiter. Jupiter is considered the planet of vast expanse of sky in Indian Vedic Astrology. Later, Indra replaced Dyaus as the chief god while Prthivi still survives as a Hindu goddess.

The word Dyaus means 'sky or heaven' and occurs frequently in the Rigveda as a mythological entity. In Rigveda (1.89, 1.90, 1.164, 1.191, 4.01), Dyaus is given the title of 'Heaven, the father'. Dyaus is mentioned in Rigveda in hymns dedicated to agni, water, grass and the sun. His mention is also found in a selection of hymns dedicated to the Visvedevas, who are a regiment of gods dedicated to multiple universal functions, including – time, speech, dawn and winds. Dyaus Pita is also said to have caused subsequent growth of flora and fauna on the earth. He is identified as the Sire, the Begetter and one who showers true blessings. Thus this square can be used as a small garden or for keeping the potted plants.

9. Maarut (Anil, Agni, Jvalan, Vayu, Anila, Vahni, Anala, Pavaka, Shikhi, Shikhin)

According to the Sanskrit-English dictionary, 'Agni' means, God of fire, fire, sacrificial fire, digestive faculty, gastric fluid, bile or fire of the stomach, gold, number three (3), etc. In some vaastu texts, this square is also called as Shikhi or Shikhin, which according to the Sanskrit-English dictionary, means, having flame, lamp, fire or the fire god, God of love, a mountain, bull, peacock, cultivated, Brahman, religious mendicant, kind of magic, having a lock of hair on the top of head, proud, one who has reached the summit of knowledge, etc. The square of Agni is related to the energies of uplifting, awakening and taking the things further. In Shrimadbhagvad Geeta (10.23), Lord Krishna says, "Of the Vasus I am Agni".

Agni is the first word of the first hymn of the Rig Veda. With this mantra the Rig Veda begins with a prayer to Agni, the receiver, holder and distributor of energy, who leads the *devtas* (gods) to victory in their battles against the *asuras* (demons). Agni is the envoy, the carrier of offerings to the gods. He is called ever-young, because the fire is re-lit every day and is immortal. His vehicle is ram, a typical sacrificial animal. His association with it denotes his connection with the sacrificial rituals. His banner (*dhoomaketu*) is smoke. At times he is viewed riding a chariot, in which case it is drawn by red horses and the seven winds are its wheels. Agni rules the south-east direction. Agni denotes *tejas*, bodily heat and knowledge and is the prime cause of birth.

Agni has been called the eldest son of Brahma. In Vishnu Purana, Agni (Abhimani) is said to have sprung from the mouth of the Viraat Purush, the Cosmic Man. According to another version, Agni is the son of Dharma

(Eternal Law) and Vasubharya (daughter of Light). His other names depicting his peculiar qualities include: Jvalana (burning), Pavaka (purifier), Vibhavasu (abundant in light), Chitrabhanu (multi-coloured), Bhuritejas (resplendent), Shikhin (flaming) and Plavanga (flickering). Agni has been given the status of a supreme god in some of the hymns.

Agnideva Mounted on a Ram

Agni is also said to have two mothers or has two parts of the fire-drill used to start the fire and ten servant maids (ten fingers of man lighting the fire or the ten undisclosed powers that nourish Agni). Agni is called 'Madhujivham' meaning the sweet-tongued. Agni is addressed as Atithi (guest) and 'Jaatvedsam' (one who knows all the things that are born, created or produced). He married Svaha (invocation) and Svadha (offering) and fathered three sons – Pavaka (purifier), Pavamana (purifying) and Shuchi (purity) who in turn had forty-five children, all different aspects of fire. Abhimani (Agni), his three sons and their 45 grandsons constitute the 49 mystic fires of the Puranas and Hindu Theosophy. The daughter of Agni is Agneya, the Hindu Goddess of Fire.

Agni is represented as a man with three bearded heads who appears in three different forms: in the sky as the sun, in the air as lightning and on the earth as fire. Hence the numeric value of fire is three. The word Agni is derived from the three verbs – from 'going', from 'shining or burning' and from 'leading'. The fire-god is called Agni because he is Agrani; the forward leader who is ever awake as disseminator of knowledge and the first principle of thought which manifests as speech.

Agni thus represents great learning and enlightening wisdom which ought to be sought, located and humbly approached. Agni-rahasya (the secret of fire) is the key to all the knowledge because Agni is the power of inner as well as outer illumination. Medha (intelligence) is Agni's sister. Agni excites Buddhi (reason and intellect) and makes one understand and comprehend the truth by illuminating one's mind (Rig Veda I.xliv.7). In Rig Veda, Agni is addressed as Rudra, the one who makes the evil persons weep.

Agni is more closely connected with the human life than any other god. He is often identified with the other gods, especially with Varuna and Mitra. He becomes Mitra when he rises in the morning, while in the evening he becomes Varuna. He is often invoked along with Indra, with whom he shares the passion for soma drink. He is also invoked along with Marutas probably to ward off the dangers of forest fires.

Indra is the celestial fire represented by Sun and Agni is the bodily fire which is represented by Mars. Both reside in the human body the former as prana and the latter as the body warmth. Agni is not only the power of heat and light but also the will-power united with wisdom. Human will-power is a feeble projection of the power of Agni which could be strengthened by the Vedic chants to Agni. Offended by Agni, sage Bhrigu had cursed him to become the devourer of all the things on earth. Brahma modified that curse and made Agni the purifier of all things he touched.

Agni lavishes wealth and dispels the darkness. He is truthful, the Radiant One and the guard of the eternal law rta. Agni is the Lord of Red Steeds, one who loves songs. Agni is the kind and bountiful giver of gifts, of wondrous fame, friend of all and loved by many in their homes. Agni is present in many phases of life such as honouring of a birth (diva lamp), prayers (diva lamp), at weddings (the yajna where the bride and groom circle the fire seven times) and at death (cremation).

Agni is also sometimes represented as a two-faced, red-coloured divine being. He has long flowing hair, a pot belly, six eyes, seven hands, four horns and three legs. His two faces suggest both his destructive and beneficent qualities. His pot belly denotes his love for rich oily food. His seven hands represent the seven flames and the three legs represent the three worlds which he reigns. One of his names is Saptajihva, 'the one having seven tongues', with which he licks the sacrificial butter.

Agni is worshipped as the symbol of piety and purity. As expression of two kinds of energy, i.e., light and heat, he is the symbol of life and activity. When Agni is worshipped, all gods (who are symbols of life) lend their powers to this deity. The ancient seers had divided Agni into three parts — garhapatya (for general domestic usage), ahavaniya (for inviting and welcoming a personage or deity) and dakshinagni (for fighting against all the evil). In Vedic Astrology, persons born in the fiery signs ruled by Agni are enthusiastic and energetic but accident prone. Agni rules Krittika nakshatra and Pratipada tithi (first lunar date), which is called vriddhi-prada or one giving rise.

Ayurveda attributes special healing powers to 'water' and 'fire'. Agni is considered the fiery metabolic energy of digestion in Ayurveda. It allows assimilation of food while ridding the body of wastes and toxins. It also transforms dense physical matter into subtle forms of energy the body needs. In Shrimadbhagvad Geeta (15.14), digestion of the food is referred to as Vaishvanara Agni. Jathar-agni determines the production of hydrochloric acid in the stomach, Bhuta-agni determines the production of bile in the liver, Kloma-agni determines the production of sugar-digesting pancreatic enzymes and so forth. The nature and quality of these agnis depend on one's prominent dosha which can be — vata, pitta or kapha.

10. Poosha (Pushan, Pusha, Matrigana)

According to the Sanskrit-English dictionary, 'Pushan' means, Sun, Earth, growth, nourishing, cherishing, increasing, flame lily plant, etc. The square of Pushan is related to the qualities of elderly, strength, blocked payment and the power to recover from losses.

Pushan is a Vedic solar deity and one of the twelve Adityas. His name literally means, 'One who causes people to thrive'. He represents sun as a pastoral god, the guardian of the flocks and herds. In the Rig Veda, Pushan is appealed to feed, guard and find the lost livestock. He is lord of the paths, who protects people from the wild animals and makes their paths pleasant to tread in solitary places. He was also responsible for marriages, journeys, roads and feeding of the cattle. He protected travelers from the bandits and wild beasts. He also protected men from being exploited by the other men. He was a supportive guide, a 'good' god, leading his adherents towards rich pastures and wealth. He carried a golden lance, the symbol of activity.

He is described variously as a cloud-born god, lord of the path, wonder worker and lord of all prosperity. He is often associated with Soma, both being protectors of the whole world – one from the above and other from below. Pusan stirs our thoughts, drives away enemies and inspiresthe miserly to make generous donations. He helped Indra to generate ripe warm milk from the young raw cows. His chariot is pulled by goats. He himself is also described as the goat borne. Pusha's connection with cows and goats makes it an ideal place for a cowshed. Pusha travels across the oceans in golden ships to meet the Sun. Pusha rules the Revati nakshatra in Vedic Astrology.

Samaranganasutradhara (14.17) identifies Pusha as the demi goddesses, 'Maatrigan'. Maatrigan (mothers) or Saptamatrikas (seven mothers) is a group of seven Hindu goddesses who are always depicted together. They are sometimes called Ashtamatrikas (eight mothers) or sometimes even sixteen. The Ashtamatrikas are: Brahmani, Vaishnavi, Maheshvari, Indrani, Kaumari, Varahi, Chamunda and Narasimhi. They assist great Shakti Devi (goddess) in her fight with the demons. They represent the prodigiously fertile as well as the destructive aspect of nature. According to Rig Veda (IX 102.4), Matrikas control the preparation of Soma.

These Sapta-Matrikas are also associated with Skanda (Kumara), his father Shiva, *Yakshas* and Kubera. Their worship is related to conception, birth, diseases and protection of children. These goddesses are considered as personification of perils related to children and are thus pacified by worship. Matrikas were permitted to torment children as long as they are younger than 16 years and afterwards act as their protectors. The infant Skanda was also worshipped with the Matrikas. In the sculptures, Matrikas are depicted as protectors and benevolent mothers only.

In the epic Mahabharata, all the seven mothers are described as fatal or they serve as threats to fetuses or infants. They are dark in colour, speaking foreign languages and live in 'peripheral areas' away from the human settlements like crossroads, caves, mountains, springs, forests, riverbanks and the cremation grounds. Saptamatrika shrines are generally located in 'the wilderness', usually near the lakes or rivers and are made of seven vermilion smeared stones. Pregnant women and nursing mothers worship them. When these goddesses are angry, they make women barren and strike newborns with fatal fevers. When they are appeased, they ensure health and happiness of the children.

Matrikas are also the goddesses of the battlefield. They are considered as giver of powers to defeat enemies. As per Nitisara, Matrikas acted as king's tangible Shaktis (powers) and conferred power to conquer and rule. They are described as assistants of Durga, having sinister as well as propitious characteristics. Matrikas function both as city protectors and individual protectors.

Devi Purana mentions that Matrikas should be worshipped for Mukti (liberation) by all, but particularly by the kings for powers of domination. Saptamatrika are worshipped for 'personal and spiritual renewal' with Mukti

The Nine Matrikas

as the ultimate goal as well as for powers to control and rule the earthly desires (Bhukti). The banners or attributes of the Saptamatrikas are: swan, bull, peacock, conch, discus, elephant and skeleton. A king installing these banners is believed to get mukti and bhukti both.

The Natya Shastra (13.66) recommends worship to Matrikas before setting up the stage and before starting the dance performances. Matrikas are said to be worshipped on all the occasions with Navagraha (the nine planets) and the Dikpalas (Guardians of the directions). Matsya Purana and Devi Purana prescribe that Matrika shrines should be north-facing and be placed in the northern part of a temple-complex. Durga (Goddess of power) rules Navami tithi, which is Ugra or one giving aggression.

11. Vitath (Vitatha, Anrita, Adharma)

According to the Sanskrit-English dictionary, 'Vitatha' means, false, unreal, untrue, incorrect, vain, futile or free from. Samaranganasutradhara (14.18) identifies Vitath as the demigod 'Adharma, the extraordinary son of Kaliyuga'. In Hindu mythology, Anrita (the falsehood) is the son of Adharma (unrighteousness or vice).

Adharma is the Sanskrit antonym of Dharma. It means 'that which is not in accord with the Dharma' or which is opposite of Dharma. Adharma literally means 'unrighteousness'. 'Dharma' is 'that which supports and sustains'. Adharma means all that attempts to destroy or oppose or reverse the process of supporting and sustaining. If dharma is the straight path leading to well-being, prosperity and spiritual perfection, adharma is the crooked path that leads away from these. Adharma means the sense of unrighteous deeds and conduct resulting in sin.

For instance, telling lies, stealing, cheating, adultery and committing such other forbidden acts and crimes is Adharma. Dereliction of duty and not discharging the responsibilities one is entrusted with is adharma. Adharma means chaos, evil, vice, disorder, non-harmony, immoral, sinful, wrong, wicked, unjust, imbalanced or unnatural.

Sometimes Adharma does not mean absolutely unethical or exactly opposite of Dharma. Its meaning depends on a specific circumstance, purpose and context being just like dharma. Anrita is also the name of one of the mystical weapons delivered to Rama by sage Viswamitra, as mentioned in the Ramayana. Vishnu Purana (Chapter 7) recites a legend that includes Dharma and Adharma as mythical characters. The personified adharma is said to be a descendant of Brahma, have Hinsa (violence) as his wife, Anrita (falsehood) as his son and Nikriti (deceit) as his daughter. Other off-springs in this lineage are Maya (delusion), Bhaya (fear), Vedana (torment), Naraka (hell), Dukha (sorrow) and Mrityu (death).

The children of Mrityu are Vyadhi (disease), Jara (old age), Shoka (sorrow), Trishna (desires) and Krodha (wrath). They are all without wives, without posterity and without the faculty to procreate. They perpetually operate as causes of the destruction of this world. Thus Adharma is at the root of all our fears, troubles and sufferings. The square of Vitatha is related to the qualities of pretention, action, good packaging and presentation of things.

12. Grihakshat (Rakshasha, Brihatkshat, Brihatkshati)

According to the Sanskrit-English dictionary, 'Grihakshata' means a kind of divine being. Different meanings of 'Rakshasha' are: type of demi-god, infested by demons, an evil or malignant demon, night, demoniacal, etc. 'Brihat' means large, great, big or extended, while 'kshat' means injury, or wound. Samaranganasutradhara (14.18) identifies Grihakshat as 'Chandratanaya, i.e., Mercury, the son of Moon'.

Mercury or Budha is called Saumya, that is, 'Son of Soma (Moon).' He is the Hindu god of merchandise and protector of merchants. Budha is said to be the son of Sage Brihaspati and Tara. But he was fathered by the lunar god Moon. Thus the intellect is born of the mind. *Lord Budha* is the awakened discriminating intellect (buddhi) and the part of us that knows. Mercury is described as an inconstant, vivacious and curious planet.

Budha is endowed with an attractive physique and the capacity to use words with many meanings. Budha learned all the Vedas and the arts with Vishnu's blessings. Budha is mythological messenger of the gods. He is noted for his speed and swiftness. He is the planet of day-to-day expressions and practical relationships. Budha's work is to take things apart and put them back together again. He is an opportunistic planet, decidedly unemotional and curious.

Lord Budha

Astrologically speaking, Budha represents the principles of communication, mentality, thinking patterns, rationality, reasoning, adaptability and variability. He governs schooling and education in general, the immediate environment of neighbors, siblings and cousins, transport over short distances, messages and forms of communication such as post, e-mail, newspapers, journalism and writing, information gathering skills and physical dexterity. Mercury is also a karaka or indicator of the smelling sense, science, mathematics, business and commerce, self-confidence, humour, wit, books, scholars, thieves, astrologers, writers, lecturers, artists, teachers and traders. Telephone, radio, television and computers are the products of Mercurial needs aligned with the engineering capacity of Mars.

In Vedic astrology, Budha is friendly with Sun and Venus, hostile to the Moon and neutral towards the other planets. The relationship of enmity between Moon and Budha belies a deep truth. Moon is innocent in its observation, while Mercury is evaluative and discriminating in its observation. As Budha is nearest to the Sun he is restless, which also makes him quick-changing and fickle. In medicine, Budha is associated with the nervous system, brain, respiratory system, thyroid, mental perception, intestines and the smelling sense.

Budha is considered as the greatest among the wise. He bestows wisdom and wealth on his devotees. He removes evil thoughts from their minds. A prayer to Him, especially on Wednesdays brings in manifold benefits like removal of all the obstacles, helps one to get a progeny and possession of fertile lands. The square of Grihakshata is the definer and governs limitation.

13. Yam (Yama, Pitripati, Dharmaraja, Dharma, Pretadhipa)

According to the Sanskrit-English dictionary, 'Yama' means, God of death, couple or twins, any rule or observance, five deeds of yoga (ahimsa, satya, asteya, brahamcharya, aparigraha), to control or self-control or to restraint, forbearance, rein, controlling of the mind, to give, driver, charioteer, bad horse, planet Pluto, number two (2), Primordial couple, etc. The square of Yama governs morals and discipline. It is the maintainer. In Shrimadbhagavad Geeta (10.29), Lord Krishna says, "Of chastisers I am Yama".

Yama is god of ultimate justice, controller of the human karmas, ruler of the dead and spirits of the departed. The word yama means to arrest or to restrain. Yama's name can also be interpreted to mean 'twin'. He is paired with Yami, his twin sister, wife and his feminine energy (Shakti). Yami later became the river goddess Yamuna. According to the Vishnu Purana, his parents are the sun-god Vivasvan and Sanjna, the daughter of Tvashtra. He is also called Dharmaraja or the king of Dharma, the principles of duty and law upon which the world is supported. This law is what gives balance to the society. Yama is lokapala of the south direction. His earthly counterparts in the great epic Mahabharata were Yudhishthira and Vidura.

His assistants who help him in doing his work are Kaal (time), Jwara (fever), Vyadhi (disease), Krodha (anger) and Asuya (jealousy). He has two dogs with four eyes and wide nostrils guarding the road to his abode. They are said to wander about among the people as his messengers. Agni, who is a conductor of the dead, has close relation with Yama. In Rigveda (10.21.5) Agni is said to be the friend (kamya) of Yama. Agni is Yama's priest, serving as the burner of the dead (Rigveda 10.52).

Yama is the great master of knowledge. In the Katha Upanishad, Yama is portrayed as a teacher to Nachiketa; the legendary little boy. Their conversation evolves to a discussion of the nature of humans, knowledge, *Atman* (soul, self), Brahman, immortality and moksha (liberation). In other texts, Yama is also called Kaal (time).

According to Rigveda, he helped humankind to find a place to dwell. He gave every individual the power to tread any path he or she wanted to. In the Vedas, Yama is said to have been the first mortal who died. By virtue of precedence, he became the ruler of the departed, called 'Lord of the Pitrs'. Yama, though one of the most powerful controllers, is subordinate to Shiva and Vishnu.

Image of Yama is usually of dark color resembling the rain-cloud, with two arms, fire-coloured eyes and sharp side-tusks. He is depicted with red or black clothes and seated either on a he-buffalo or a lion throne. Vishnudharmottara Purana depicts him with four arms and wearing golden yellow garments. Yama is shown carrying a mace as his weapon and holding a loop of rope in his left hand with which he pulls the soul from the corpse.

Sitting on his throne (vicharabhu), he gives the judgment of rewards or punishments to all who have died and sends them to the *naraka* (hell) or *swarga* (heaven) for the results of

Lord Yamraaj

their life's actions. Naraka holds many hells and Yama directs the departed souls to the appropriate one. Naraka serves only as a temporary purgatory where the soul is purified of the sin by its suffering. Yama is aided in this task by Chitragupta who keeps an account of the deeds of the mortals when they were alive on earth. Yama (God of death) is the lord of Bharani Nakshatra and Dashmi tithi (tenth lunar date), which is considered Saumya or sober.

14. Gandharv

According to the Sanskrit-English dictionary, 'Gandharva' means, Celestial musician or singer, a skilled singer in general, etc. Gandharva is a name used for distinct heavenly beings. They have superb musical skills and are frequently depicted as singers in the court of Gods. Gandharvas are male nature spirits and husbands of the Apsaras. Some of them are part animal, usually a bird or horse. They guarded the Soma and made beautiful music for the gods in their palaces. Gandharva is also a term for skilled singers in Indian classical music. The square of Gandharva governs trance and is the preserver.

Gandharvas act as messengers between the gods and humans. In Hindu law, a gandharva marriage is the one contracted by mutual consent and without following the formal rituals. According to the epic Mahabharata, Gandharvas are associated with the gods as dancers and singers and with the yakshas as formidable warriors. Gandharvas are variously called the creatures of Prajapati, of Brahma, of Kasyapa, of the Munis, of Arishta, or of Vach. The word Gandharva is also used in reference to a being (or, strictly speaking, part of the causal continuum of consciousness) in a luminal state between death and rebirth.

Samaranganasutradhara (14.19) identifies Gandharv as 'Lord Narada'. Narada literally means the one who gives or spreads the name of the God Narayana. He is generally regarded as one of the great masters of the celestial music. He is depicted carrying a *khartal* and a *veena* known as 'mahathi'. He uses his veena for singing hymns, prayers and mantras as an act of devotion to Lord Vishnu. Narada is described as both wise and mischievous. In Shrimadbhagvad Geeta (10.26), Lord Krishna says, "Of celestial sages I am Narada. Amongst Gandharvas I am Citraratha".

In his previous birth Narada was a Gandharva (angelic being) who was cursed to be born on earth. He is probably the most travelled Vedic sage with the ability to visit the distant worlds and realms (lokas). He was the primary source of information among Gods and is believed to be the first journalist on Earth. His square is thus fit for studio of a news channel or film and TV division. Department of journalism in an institute should preferably be located in this square. Vaishnav enthusiasts depict Narada as a pure elevated soul who glorifies Vishnu through his devotional songs, singing the names Hari and Narayana and therein demonstrating bhakti yoga. The Narada Bhakti Sutra is attributed to him.

Narada Muni

Narada was a thorough master of every branch of learning. He was fond of war and music and was incapable of being repulsed by any science or any course of action. He was conversant with the Vedas and the Upanishadas and was acquainted with history and Puranas. He is termed to be conversant with *nyaya* (logic) and the truth of moral science. He was the master of Sankhya and Yoga systems of philosophy. He was also conversant with the sciences of war and treaty and proficient in drawing conclusions of judging things not within the direct knowledge.

15. Bhringraaj

According to the Sanskrit-English dictionary, 'Bhringraja' means, the bumble-bee king, kind of oblation or sacrifice, name of an Ayurvedic medicinal plant, fork-tailed shrike (butcher-bird), false daisy (wild flower), etc. The Sanskrit root 'Bhrj', from which this word it seems originated, means 'to roast' or 'to fry'. Samaranganasutradhara (14.20) identifies Bhringraaj as 'Rakshasha who is Son of the demon-goddess Nirriti'. The square of Bhringraja governs the qualities of let-go, discrimination and power.

Rakshasa, in Hindu mythology, is a type of demonic being or goblin. The female equivalent of a rakshasa is *rakshasi*. Translated to English, Rakshasa means injurer. Some sources credit Rishi Kashyapa with the origin of rakshasas. His sons with Diti, one of the thirteen daughters of Daksha married to Kashyapa, are the Daityas or Rakshasas. There were both good and evil rakshasas and as warriors they fought alongside the armies of both good and evil. Some were more akin to yakshas (nature spirits), while others were similar to asuras, the traditional opponents of the gods. Rakshasa rules the Moola Nakshatra.

The term rakshasa, however, generally applies to those demons that haunt cemeteries, eat the flesh of men and drink the milk of cows dry as if by magic. They are ugly, fierce-looking and enormous creatures. They have two fangs protruding down from the top of the mouth and have sharp, claw-like fingernails. They are mean, growling like beasts and as insatiable cannibals who could smell the scent of flesh. Some of the more ferocious ones are shown with flaming red eyes and hair, drinking blood with their palms or from a human skull.

Rakshasa

They are most powerful in the evening, particularly during the dark period of the new moon, but are dispelled by the rising sun. They especially detest sacrifices and prayers. Most powerful among them is their king, the ten-headed Ravana. Putana, a female demon, is well known for her attempt to kill the infant Krishna by offering him milk from her poisoned breast. She was, however, sucked to death by the God.

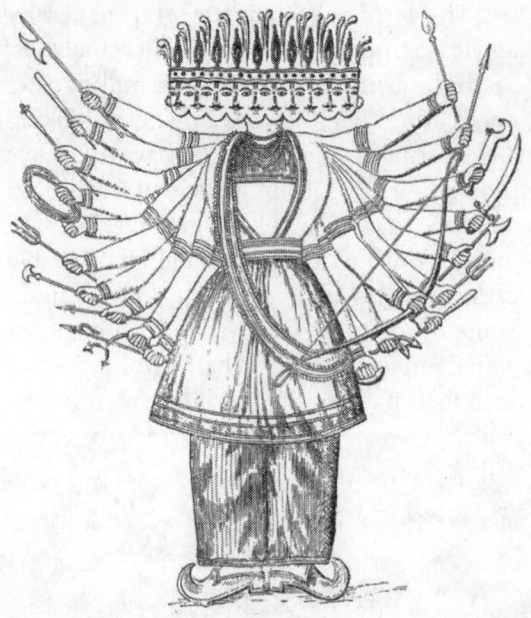
Ravana

Rakshasas are possessors of superhuman strength and of heightened senses. They have the power to fly, vanish and possess *Maya* (magical powers of illusion), which enables them to change their shape at will. They can appear in the forms of humans, large birds, animals, monsters, or as in the case of the female demons, in the appearance of beautiful women. As great shape-changers, it was not always clear whether they had a true or natural form. This quality of Rakshasas can be utilised by using this square for locating a theatre, stage shows, plays, performances, make-up and shooting for movies.

16. Mrig (Mriga, Mrsa, Mrish, Mrisha)

According to the Sanskrit–English dictionary, 'Mrig' means, to search or to investigate, an antelope, deer, any beast or animal, lion, etc. Mrisha means, to touch or to touch mentally, to consult, suffer, seize, grasp, stroke, to bear patiently, to forgive, deliberate, disregard, sprinkle, pour out, to permit, not heed or mind, etc. Mrsa means endurance, forbearance or patience. Samaranganasutradhara (14.20) identifies Mrig as *ananta* (endless), *svayambhu* (self-originated) and *dharma*. The square of *Mriga* governs curiosity and helps in attaining skills.

Ananta is a Sanskrit term which means 'endless', 'limitless', 'eternal' or 'infinite'. In Hindu mythology, Ananta denotes a huge serpent representing eternity and the immensity of space. As 'space' = 0, the name of the serpent became a synonym of zero. It is the name given to the number ten to the power thirteen which is equal to ten billion. It also means infinitude or an unending expansion or without limit. Ananta is shown resting on the primordial waters of original chaos. Vishnu is lying on the serpent, between the two creations of the world, floating on the 'ocean of unconsciousness'. Ananta is also an epithet of Brahma, Vishnu, Shiva, Skanda, Krishna, Balarama, Earth and the letter 'A'.

Ananta

The serpent is always represented as coiled up, in a sort of a figure eight on its side (like the infinity symbol) and theoretically has a thousand heads. He is considered to be the great king of the Nagas and the lord of Patala. Each time the serpent opens its mouth it produces an earthquake because there is a belief that the serpent supports the world on its back. He is the serpent that at the end of each kalpa spits the destructive fire over the whole of creation. Rudra, who consumes the three worlds, is believed to have emanated from the face of Ananta. By the grace of Ananta, sage Garga was able to master the sciences of astronomy and causation.

Ananta denotes the infinite causal energy of the Creator, the energy in the form of *chaitanya* that has no end. There exist four types of objects or categories – 1) *Nitya*, which has no beginning or an end, 2) *Anitya*, which has a beginning and end, 3) *Anadi*, which has no beginning but has an end and 4) *Ananta*, which has a beginning but no end. Brahman has no initial cause and is known as *anadikarana*, the uncreated who is not a product, which means Brahman has no material cause and is not the material cause of anything. Ananta is the infinite space and the infinite space is Brahman.

Ananta is without destruction because it is not subject to the six modifications such as birth, growth, death, etc. According to the Vedanta School, the term Ananta refers to the Infinite, the single non-dual reality. According to the Yoga School, Ananta was sentenced by Lord Shiva to teach Yoga on earth. He assumed the human form and was called Patanjali because he desired to teach Yoga to human beings. In his Yoga Sutras, Patanjali stresses upon the use of breath to achieve perfection in posture which entails steadiness and comfort. The effort of breathing has been highlighted by the term 'Ananta' in Sutra 2.47.

Swayambhu or Svayambhu means 'self-manifested' or 'that which is created on its own accord'. The word 'Svayambhu' is derived from two Sanskrit words – '*Svayam*' which means 'self' or 'voluntarily' and '*bhu*' which means 'springing' or 'arising'. So the definition of the word is 'arising on its own'. Based on details in Bhagavata Purana and Matsya Purana, Narayana or Krishna is said to be the self-manifested Swayambhu form of Brahman as the first cause of creation.

17. Pitar (Pitrigan, Nirriti, Nirhity, Pitriganadhish)

According to the Sanskrit–English dictionary, 'Pitar' means, ancestors or forefathers. Samaranganasutradhara (14.21) identifies Pitar as, 'Gods inhabiting Pitriloka'. *Pitriloka*, according to Vedas, is governed by Nirriti. It has been said that, "Those who are condemned to the realm of Nirriti do not receive nourishment from the offerings of their descendents nor from their own accumulated merit".

Nirriti is the demonic or destructive goddess of poverty and corruption. Nirriti is that *nir* means 'to go out', 'to be deprived of' or 'dissolution' and rta refers to 'that which is right' or 'the law' or the 'natural order'. Thus Nirriti means 'absence of rta or lawless or that which is beyond the order'. She is the Lokapala (guardian or regent) of the south-west. A statue of Nirrti controlling the south-west direction is found on the Rajarani temple outside Bhubaneshwar in Orissa where she is depicted holding a sword and a severed head and standing over a prostrate body.

Nirriti is much feared and is mentioned in a few hymns of the Rig Veda, mostly to seek protection from her or imploring for her departure to distant places so that no calamity may befall. Rig Veda (7.104.1, 9-11) describes the 'realm' of Nirriti as an endless pit without light or warmth – a place reserved for those who act against the basic ideals of Vedic society. Nirriti is representative of the dark side to Vedic vision of feminine divinity.

She manifests herself in decay, dissolution, need, anger, old age, cowardice and death. Nirriti is the personification of calamity, misfortune, death (particularly untimely death), poverty and infertility in the Rig Veda. According to some indications she is also associated with stealing children. Nirriti is the mother of Rakshasis and Rakshasas. The Rakshasas – with whom she is associated – are related to disrupting the sacrificial rituals.

Nirriti is both the 'goddess of misfortune' as well as the 'remover of misfortune'. In the Vedas, Nirrti is also described as the daughter of Surabhi (the cow goddess), the wife of Adharma (Destroyer of All Things) and also as the Goddess of Disease and Death. Nirriti means 'misery' and she is worshipped in order to dismiss diseases. She is also considered the goddess who punishes the sinners. However, she also protects those borne into crime as long as they remain ethical.

Shitala Mata

She is often linked to Alakshmi, Kali or Dhumavati. When the ocean of milk was churned to get ambrosia, a goddess was born known as Alakshmi or Nirriti. Lakshmi, the goddess of wealth was born after Alakshmi. So Nirriti is considered as elder sister of Lakshmi. Lakshmi presides on wealth and Nirriti presides on poverty that is why she is called Alakshmi (Non-Lakshmi). Alakshmi adorns a black dress and iron ornaments. She uses a donkey as her vehicle and holds a scimitar and broom.

In the Taittiriya Brahmana (I.6.1.4), Nirriti is described as of dark black complexion, often unkempt hair and her sacrificial shares are dark husks. In the Shatapatha Brahmana (X.1.2.9), she is associated with pain. As the south-west quarter is her region, pain is associated with the south-west. Relation with pain makes it an ideal place for delivery or operation theatre in a hospital. But elsewhere in the same text (V.2.3.3), Nirriti is mentioned as living in the south, the direction of the kingdom of the dead.

In the epic Mahabharata, Nirriti is called the wife of Nirrita (Adharma or unrighteousness) and the mother of three sons i.e., Bhaya (fear), Maha-Bhaya (great fear) and Mrityu (death incarnate). Another version of this text says that she is the daughter of Adharma and Hinsa (violence or injury). Her birth in Bhagavatam is given as, 'Nirriti plunked out of Brahma's anus'. According to the Agni Purana, spirit of the 'doer of bad deeds' leaves the body through the anus. The implication is that if soul leaves the body through the lower orifices (rather than, for example, the head) then the future of the jivatma (soul) is bound to the lower worlds. It indicates fitness of this square for toilet area in any organisation, enema room in a naturopathy centre, garbage dumping ground or sewage treatment plant in a city, gobar gas plant in a farm house, mortuary in a hospital and the like.

In Taittiriya Samhita, the pigeon, owl and the hare are listed as being sacrifices to Nirriti. In Atharva Veda, owls and pigeons are said to be her messengers. Owls are considered as harbingers of death and pigeons as bringers of misfortune. The cry of an owl is generally considered an inauspicious sign. Owls are believed to be the spirits of those who have suffered untimely deaths. Later, the owl became the vehicle of Lakshmi. She conquered and tamed the animal associated with misfortune or delusion and took it as her vehicle.

Nirriti is believed to dwell in desolate places, always on the look-out for hungry people or aggrieved people in mourning. Offerings to Nirriti are often black in colour – black grain, iron and stones, or diseased and malformed animals with an intention to keep her away from rituals rather than to invite her to join in. It means a slaughter house or a butcher's shop should be operated from this square, if so required. Nirriti, through tradition, was endowed with both the male and female attributes thus giving her another manifestation as a Goddess for the 'third sex' and transgender people. Her association with swamp and wild asses is also well known. The square of Pitar is related to the energies of bonding, security and comforts. Pitrigana (ancestors) are the lord of Amavasya tithi and Magha Nakshatra.

18. Dauvaarik (Dauvarika, Nandi)

According to the Sanskrit–English dictionary, 'Dauvaarik' means, kind of demon or genius, porter, warder or a door keeper. Samaranganasutradhara (14.21) identifies Dauvaarik as, 'Nandi – the head of the soldiers (Pramathas) of Shiva'. The square of Dauvarika is the door keeper and governs the energies of bonding, retention of knowledge, learning and the memory of children.

The Sanskrit word 'Nandi' in English translates as happy, joyous or happy person. The bull Nandi is Shiva's primary vehicle and his principal *gana* (follower). Nandi was one of Shiva's two door-keepers, the other being Mahakaal. Temples venerating Shiva display stone images of a seated Nandi, generally facing the main shrine. Nandi is also Shiva's foremost disciple. According to some puranas, Nandi was born to sage Shilada who got him by the grace of Shiva. Brahmavaivartta Purana mentions Krishna himself to have taken the form of a bull as no one else in the Universe can bear Shiva.

Nandi

In Sanskrit, a bull is called *vrisha*, which has another connotation — that of righteousness or Dharma. It is important to seek the blessings of Nandi before proceeding to worship Lord Shiva. Some Puranas mention that Nandi is the chief in Shiva's army. He leads Shiva's Ganas or attendants. In the Natha and Siddha tradition, Nandi is the chief guru of eighteen masters (Siddhas) including Patanjali and Thirumular. From the yogic perspective, Nandi is the mind dedicated to Lord Siva, the Absolute. Spiritually, Nandi represents an individual *jiva* (soul) and the message that the jiva should always be focused on the Atman (Paramatman).

During the churning of the ocean by the gods and demons, poison (*halahala*) was also produced. Shiva took the poison into his hand and drank it and is therefore known as Nilakantha (the blue-throated one). Nandi saw some of the poison spill out of Shiva's mouth and immediately drank it off the ground. Nothing ill happened to Nandi. This episode confirms that Nandi had so completely surrendered into Shiva that he had all His powers and His protection.

19. Sugreev (Sukantha, Sugala)

According to the Sanskrit–English dictionary, 'Sugreev' means, beautiful-necked, hero, sort of weapon, of a divine being, body of water, conch, countenance (facial expression) of a friend, kind of pavilion, serpent of paataal, name of one of the four horses of Krishna or Vishnu. Samaranganasutradhara (14.21) identifies Sugreev as, 'Adi Prajapati Creator Manu'.

Sugreev

The name Manu is similar to the Indo-European 'man'. It also has an etymological connection with the Sanskrit verb *man*, meaning 'to think'. Manu, literally meaning 'human', is the name given in the traditional legends to the Progenitor of the human race as a symbol of the thinking being. He is considered as the intermediary between the creator and the human race. According to the Vedas, the Manus constituted the first divine legislators who fixed the rules of religious ceremonies and ritual sacrifices.

According to the Puranas, fourteen Manus appear in each *kalpa (aeon)*, sovereigns living in the ethereal worlds where they are meant to direct the conscious life of humankind and its ability to think. Thus, the numerical value of manu = 14. The period of each Manu is called Manvantara. The current world is that of Vaivasvata Manu (born of the sun), the seventh Manu of the aeon of the white boar (*sveta varaha kalpa*), a part of the Kali Yuga. Manu is the first man in the mythology of India. Manu appears in the Vedas as the performer of the first sacrifice. He is also known as the first king.

Vaivasvata, also known as Sraddhadeva or Satyavrata, was the king of Dravida who preserved life from extinction in a great flood. He was warned of the flood by Matsyavatar of Vishnu that a flood would destroy the whole of humanity. He therefore built a boat, as the fish advised. When the flood came, he tied this boat to the fish's horn and was safely steered to a resting place on a mountain top. When the flood receded, the sole human survivor Manu performed a sacrifice, pouring oblations of butter and sour milk into the waters. After a year, a woman was born from the waters who announced herself as 'the daughter of Manu.' These two then became the ancestors of a new human race to replenish the earth.

Manu is the legendary author of an important Sanskrit law code, the *Manu-smriti* (*Laws of Manu*). Vaivasvata Manu was also the writer of five *riks* (stotras) in Rigveda (8:27-31). In these riks, he performed his prayers to some named devas and devis (e.g., Marutas, Brahmanaspati, Agni, Adityas, Varuna, Aditi, Mitra, Indra, Pusha, Ajarma, Asuras, etc.,) and to some un-named deva-devis e.g., 33 devas). The square of Sugreeva is receptive and governs receiving power, knowledge and grasping power, retention and saving.

20. Pushpdant (Pushpadanta, Kusumdant or Pushpa)

According to the Sanskrit–English dictionary, 'Pushpdant' means, flower-toothed. Samaranganasutradhara (14.21) identifies Pushpdant as, 'Son of Vinata, very quick in action'. The square of Pushpadanta is related to the assistance power and exploring.

Vinata, one of the sixty daughters of Daksha Prajapati, was married to Rishi Kashyapa along with her 12 sisters. She bore him two sons, named Aruna and Garuda. Aruna became a charioteer and herald for the sun god and creator of the red sky at dawn. Vinata's second son Garuda was born in the form of a huge bird with immense power. According to the great epic Mahabharata, when Garuda first burst forth from his egg, he appeared like a cosmic fire that consumes the world at the end of every age. Garuda is said to be massive, large enough to block out the sun. He was so brilliant that he was mistaken for Agni, the fire god. Frightened, the gods begged him for mercy. Garuda, hearing their plea, reduced himself in size and energy.

Garuda brought the elixir of immortality (also called amrita) from the Gods to liberate his mother from the serpents. In another version, Garuda spilled the amrita four times at the four places where the Kumbha festival is now held. His journey took twelve days, equaling twelve years for mortals. Garuda plays an important role in Krishna Avatar in which Krishna and Satyabhama ride on Garuda to kill Narakasura. On another occasion, Lord Hari rides on Garuda to save the devotee elephant Gajendra. It is also said that Garuda's wings when flying will chant the Vedas. Importance of Garuda is also found in Shrimadbhagvad Geeta (10.30), where Lord Krishna says, "Of the birds I am Vainteya, the son of Vinata".

Various names have been attributed to Garuda – Tarkshya, Suparna, Gaganeshvara, Kashyapi, Khageshvara, Vishnuratha and others. According to Vedas and Puranas, the mighty bird Shyena (Sanskrit for eagle) brought nectar to earth from heaven. One of the faces of Sri Panchamukha Hanuman is Mahavira Garuda. This face points towards the west. The image of Garuda is often used as the charm or amulet to protect the bearer from snake attack and its poison. Worship of Garuda is believed to remove the effects of poison from one's body. Garuda Vidya is the mantra against snake poison to remove all kinds of evils. Garuda Vyuha is worshipped in Tantra for Abhichara and for protection against Abhichara.

Garuda is one of the three principal animal deities in the Hindu Mythology. The other two are: Ganesha, the elephant-headed god and Hanuman, the monkey god. Garuda is the king of birds and often acts as a messenger between the gods and men. Garuda is depicted as having the golden body of a strong man with a white face, red wings, an eagle's beak and a crown on his head. He was the ally of the gods. He mocks the wind with the speed of his flight. Garudopanishada and Garuda Purana are devoted to him.

Garuda

Garuda is also well-known for feeding exclusively on snakes. Garuda was very hungry right at the time of his birth. His father advised him to spare the cows and Brahmins. As Lord Vishnu only was able to satisfy his hunger, he became the trusted mount (vahana) of Vishnu. This story reveals that the square of Pushpadanta can be utilised as dining room. As the appointed charger of Vishnu, Garuda is venerated by all, including the humans. Garuda is much revered for his ethics and his strength to correct the evil-doers. He was born with a great hatred for the evil and he is supposed to roam about the universe devouring the bad.

Garuda is also considered as the bearer of knowledge. He carries a pot of Amrita, the water of eternity which symbolises eternal knowledge. Garuda is considered the Sankarshana form of the lord who primarily possesses the knowledge aspect of the lord during creation. This square is thus considered ideal for studies. Garuda represents the five vayus within us: prana, apana, vyana, udana and samana through his five forms Satya, Suparna, Garuda, Tarkshya and Vihageshwara respectively. These five vayus can be controlled through yoga and Pranayama which can lead to Kundalini awakening, leading to higher levels of consciousness.

Throughout the epic Mahabharata, Garuda is invoked as a symbol of impetuous violent force, of speed and of martial prowess. Powerful warriors advancing rapidly on doomed foes are likened to Garuda swooping down on a serpent. Defeated warriors are like snakes beaten down by Garuda. The field marshal Drona in Mahabharata uses a military formation named after Garuda. Lord Krishna also carries the image of Garuda on his banner.

21. Varun (Varuna, Jalaadhip or Jaladheesh)

According to the Sanskrit–English dictionary, 'Varun' means, God of the sea or water, oceanic, aquatic, marine, fish, aquatic animal, western, the west, God, a king, etc. The square of Varuna is related to the observational power and gains. Varuna is the Vedic god of water, oceans, Celestial Ocean and the night sky (space). Importance of Varuna as waterlord is also found in Shrimadbhagvad Geeta (10.29), where Lord Krishna says, "Amongst the inhabitants of the water I am Varuna".

Varuna rules over the rivers and their spirit beings, as well as the serpent gods called nagas. Varuna is the lord of Shatabhisha Nakshatra. His relation with nagas and Shatabhisha (hundred doctors) Nakshatra makes it a good place for medication and recovery. It is considered that those who drown go to Him as he is the God of the underwater world. Thus, Varuna is also a God of the dead and can grant immortality. He can also ward off any bad effects related to water. He is Guardian deity of the west direction. Varuna is also depicted as a lunar deity, as a yellow man wearing a golden armour and holding a noose or lasso made from a snake. His consort is Varuni and he rides a crocodile (*Makara*) suggestive of his lordship over the aquatic life.

Originally, Varuna was chief of the twelve Adityas. The Rig Veda and Atharva Veda portray Varuna as an omniscient, omnipresent, omnipotent and compassionate God. He is the ruler of the worlds, the ordainer and enforcer of law and upholder of the world order. He is the supreme God capable of controlling and dispensing justice. Varuna is concerned mostly with moral and societal affairs than being a deification of nature. Varuna is the knower and controller of all. His spies (rays of light) are spread everywhere acting as his eyes and ears. Aided with these innumerable spies, he knows all that goes on in this world. This square is thus best for locating the courts of justice or running a private detective agency.

Varuna

Varuna and Mitra (agreement) are Adityas, the deities connected with the Sun. They are the gods of the societal affairs including the oath and are often twinned Mitra-Varuna. Varuna is associated with the night and Mitra with the daylight. Varuna is the protector, the Holy One, helper of all mankind, the law maker whose holy laws remain unweakened. Together with Mitra, he controls Rta (the world order). When people transgress the moral order and commit sin, he knows and punishes them. But if they repent and seek forgiveness, he forgives them too.

He causes the rains to come down and the sun to travel. He makes the rivers flow. The rivers that flow because of him know no weariness, nor they cease flowing. Varuna gradually lost much of his importance as an omnipotent and omnipresent god after Indra assumed more prominence in Vedic literature.

22. Asur (Nishachar, Rahu)

According to the Sanskrit–English dictionary, 'Asur' generally means, anti-god, incorporeal, opponent of the gods, demon, evil spirit, chief of the evil spirits, ghost, a name of Rahu, zodiacal sign, mustard leaf, etc. It is the name given to the Titans of Indian mythology. In Vedic literature, sometimes it has also been used in the good sense. Samaranganasutradhara (14.22) identifies Asur as, 'Rahu, the devourer of Sun and Moon and son of the demon-goddess Simhika'.

The Symbol of Rahu

In Hindu mythological and cosmological tradition, Rahu is the severed head of an asura that caused eclipses by 'devouring' the sun or the moon due to a privilege conferred on him by Brahma. He is depicted in art as a serpent without the lower body and riding a chariot drawn by the eight black horses. In Vedic Astrology, Rahu is considered to be a rogue planet. According to the legend of *Samudra-manthan* (churning of the ocean), asura Svarbhanu drank some of the amrita (divine nectar). The sun and moon realised it and alerted Mohini (the female avatar of Vishnu). Mohini cut off Svarbhanu's head before the nectar could pass his throat. The head, however, remained immortal due to the effect of amrita and was called Rahu. It is believed that this immortal head from time to time swallows the Sun causing eclipses.

Lion Mounted Rahu

Rahu is seen as an asura or demon that can plunge any area of life he controls into chaos, mystery and cruelty. Various names are assigned to Rahu in the Vedic texts including; the chief, the advisor or minister of the demons, ever-angry, the tormentor, bitter enemy of the luminaries, lord of illusions, one who frightens the Sun, the one who makes the Moon lustreless, the peacemaker, the immortal, bestower of prosperity and wealth and ultimate knowledge.

Rahu is one of the nine planets in Vedic Astrology and is paired with Ketu. Rahu dasha can either be the best time of any person's life or plunge him into deep trouble depending on other factors. Rahu dasha gives immense scope for obtaining spectacular results through worship or dhyana. He is associated with the world of material manifestation and worldly desires as well as random and uncontrolled growth without wisdom or understanding. Mining of petroleum also falls under the significations of Rahu. Asura Rahu is magical and an illusionist.

Rahu is associated with dualities resulting from its *mayavi* (illusory) nature. It is a legendary master of deception who signifies cheaters, pleasure seekers, operators in foreign lands, drug and poison dealers and insincere and immoral acts. Rahu is the symbol of an irreligious person, an outcaste, harsh speech, falsehood, uncleanliness, abdominal ulcers and transmigration. Sudden changes in luck and fame are also linked to Rahu. He is also considered instrumental in strengthening one's power and converting even an enemy into a friend.

The astrological text *Lal Kitab* notes that if Saturn and Mars are conjunct, they can together be considered as Rahu (exalted), while if Saturn and Venus are conjunct, they can together be treated as Rahu (debilitated). Rahu is lord of three nakshatras or lunar mansions in Vedic astrology: Ardra, Svati and Shatabhisha. It is said that Rahu is at His apex of power when operating through Shatabhisha nakshatra. Rahu is associated with the following: its color is smoky, metal is lead and its gemstone is honey-coloured hessonite. Its element is air and its direction is south-west. Articles that are donated in order to mitigate the negative effects of Rahu include mustard, radishes, blankets, sesame, lead, saffron, *satnaja* (a mixture of seven grains) and coal.

23. Shosh (Shosha, Shani)

According to the Sanskrit-English dictionary, 'Shosh' means, desiccating, drying up, dryness, sucking, breath, pulmonary consumption, vital energy, etc. Shosha means the dryer, one who detoxifies the emotions. Samaranganasutradhara (14.23) identifies Shosh as, 'Saturn, the Son of God Sun'.

Saturn or Shani dev (Shanaishchara) is one of the Navgrahas of *Jyotish* (the nine primary Celestial Beings in Vedic Astrology). Shani dev is embodied in the planet Saturn and is the Lord of Saturday. The word *Shani* also denotes the seventh day or Saturday in most Indian languages. The word Shani comes from *Shanaye Kramati Sah*, the one who moves slowly, because Saturn takes about 30 years to revolve around the Sun. Shani dev is depicted dark in colour, clothed in black, holding a sword, arrows and two daggers and is mounted on a vulture or a crow. In Hindu mythology, vultures and crows represent harmful and inauspicious characteristics, both of which Shani possesses.

Lord Saturn

Shani is a *deva* (god) and son of Surya and his wife Chhaya, hence also known as Chhayaputra. He is the elder brother of Yama, the Hindu god of death and deliverer of justice. Surya's two sons, Shani dev and Yama are great judges of human karmas. Shani dev gives results of one's deeds throughout one's life through appropriate punishments and rewards. Yama grants results of one's deeds only after death. Saturn is known as the greatest teacher and well wisher for the righteous as well the greatest punisher for those who follow the path of evil, betrayal, back-stabbing and unjust revenge.

It is said that when Shani dev opened his eyes as a baby for the very first time, the sun went into an eclipse, which clearly denotes the impact of Shani dev on the astrological charts. Shani is lord of the masses and his blessings are thus considered very important in an individual's horoscope for bestowing him with mass following and popularity e.g., in politics, show-business and public-oriented businesses. Hindu traditions often include the worship of Shani dev in order to dispel dangerous ghosts and other supernatural beings. This square is related to transparency.

24. Paapyakshama (Paap, Yakshama, Raajyakshama, Kshaya, Rog, Shosh)

According to the Sanskrit–English dictionary, 'Paapyakshama' means, an evil disease or consumption or a diseased spot, breaking up of strength, infirmity, variegated ginger, etc. Rajayakshama generally means suffering from consumption or consumptive disease. This square is related to disease, drug addiction, feeling of loneliness and fault-finding nature. Samaranganasutradhara (14.22) identifies Paapyakshama as 'Kshaya'. Kshaya has also been called Kshaya-roga, Ati-roga and Roga-raaj.

Kshaya-roga or Yakshma (TB or tuberculosis) is a disease which can be traced back to the time of man's origin. It is a disease that leads to diminish or restrict the internal as well as the external activities of the human body. It is called pulomonary tuberculosis in the modern medical science. Kshaya is called Rajayakshma as Ayurveda considers it the king of diseases. Even modern medicines have not been very effective in tackling this dreadful disease. It is also called Shosha as it leads to depletion of the body tissues.

Ancient Ayurvedic Acharyas have given four causes of Rajyakshma:

1. *Sahas:* When physically weak person does physical work much more than his capacity.
2. *Sandharan:* When a person supperesses his urges.
3. *Kshaya:* When a physically weak person suffering from anxiety, tension and depression takes meal much less than the requirement of his body, takes dry diet and keeps fast.
4. *Visham Bhojan:* When person takes diet against the eight laws of diet as discussed by Acharya Charak in Charak Samhita.

A Kshaya Patient

Astrology can tell us in advance whether a particular person has any consumptive tendencies. In such a case, Ascendant and Moon will be badly afflicted, diminishing the physical and mental vitality. Saturn, the planet of consumption, is mainly associated with the kshaya-roga. Tendency to suffer from this disease is usually seen in the chart in which Saturn and Mars are in the sixth house with powerful aspect of Rahu and Sun.

The presence of Rahu or Ketu in the sixth house also indicates tendency towards tuberculosis. Weak Moon aspected by Mars or Saturn also gives rise to pulmonary consumption. If Venus is badly afflicted by Rahu and Mars, the native may experience consumption after marriage. If 6th or 8th lord is with Rahu, then also the native is likely to suffer from tuberculosis. All these symptoms may indicate death due to tuberculosis in the time period of malefic planets.

25. Rog (Roga, Vayu, Samirana, Marut, Vyadhi, Jvar)

According to the Sanskrit–English dictionary, 'Vayu' means, Marutas, god of the wind, wind as a kind of demon producing madness, vital air, gas, wind of the body, desired by the appetite, greedy, number Fourty-nine (49), etc. This square is a drainer and a weakener, related to the immune system and timely support. Samaranganasutradhara (14.23) identifies 'Rog' as 'Jvara or Fever'.

Vayu is lord of the winds. Vayu is described in Rig Veda as having 'exceptional beauty', ideally the first partaker of soma juice which he seems to be especially fond of. The name Vayu comes from the root, 'Va', which means 'to blow'. He is also known as Marut (Immortal), Anila (Breath of life), Vata (Wandering, He who is in perpetual movement), Pavana ('the Purifier') and sometimes Prana ('the breath'). Importance of Vayu as purifier is also found in Shrimadbhagvad Geeta (10.31), where Lord Krishna says, "Of purifiers I am the wind".

Vayu is the 'deity of Life', who is sometimes referred to as 'Mukhya-Vayu' (the chief Vayu) or 'Mukhya Prana' (the chief of Life) for clarity. Invisible, Vayu moves in the heavens as well as in the human body as the vital breath (prana).

Vaastu Gods and Goddesses

Vata, an additional name for Vayu, is the root of Sanskrit and Hindi term for atmosphere i.e., 'Vatavaran' meaning atmosphere. His task is to guard the north-west 'horizon'. Vayu is the lord of Swati Nakshatra.

Vayudeva

Vayu is a trusted friend of Indra and a hero who shares glory of victory with the latter. He is swift as mind, thousand-eyed and the Lord of thought. He is praised in Vedic hymns as the Intelligence, who illumines the earth and heaven and makes the dawn to shine. Vayu is described as moving noisily in his shining coach, driven by two or fourty-nine or one-thousand white and purple horses. His main attribute is a white banner. Like other atmospheric deities, he is a fighter and destroyer, powerful and heroic.

Like Rudra, Vayu also brings medicines to cure people. Having medicinal qualities, this square is thus suitable for doctor's clinic and medication. It has been said that cows yield milk for Vayu's sake. As vayu is related to milch cows, cowshed is also auspicious in this square. Vayu is a protector of people.

Cowards pray to him for luck and strength. Vayu removes cowardice and bestows vitality. He is the father of Hanumana and Bhima, both symbols of immense strength, loyalty and brotherhood. Blue in colour, he is depicted with four hands. He holds a fan and a flag in two hands while the other two are held in *abhaya* and *varada* mudras (postures). The Chhaandogya Upanishad states that one can't know Brahman except by knowing Vayu as the Udgeet (the mantric syllable Aum).

In Hinduism, Marutas, Marut-gana or Rudraj, are considered the storm deities and sons of Rudra. Generally, number of Marutas is forty-nine, though it also varies from twenty-seven to sixty. They are very violent and aggressive, described as armed with golden weapons i.e., lightning and thunderbolts, as having iron teeth and roaring like lions, as residing in the north and as riding in golden chariots drawn by ruddy horses. This square can be utilised as goldsmith shop or for training horses. Marutas, the troop of young warriors, are Indra's companions. According to the Rig Veda, they wore golden helmets and breastplates and used their axes to split the clouds so that rain could fall. They were widely regarded as clouds, capable of shaking the mountains and destroying the forests.

Mighty and well-armed, impetuous in their haste, Marutas send their windless rain even on the desert places. Loud roarers, devourers of the foe and restless shakers; they drain the udders of the sky and fill the earth full with milk. The Marutas are positively destructive forces of the heaven, ferocious but not wicked. They are divine beings, who work for the welfare of the world and men, though they do it in their quite noisy way. Marutas give strength to the worshippers to make them invincible in battle, bring wealth to the people, increase their progeny and prolong the life. Thus couples desiring a child should perform sexual intercourse in this square for positive results.

26. Naag (Gotranaag, Ahi, Ahirbudhnya)

According to the Sanskrit–English dictionary, 'Naag' means, cobra, serpent, an elephant, shark, lead, tin, one of the five airs of the human body, best or most excellent of any kind, cloud, kind of sexual intercourse, kind of talc, cruel man, etc. This square is also related to craving and lusty graving. Samaranganasutradhara (14.24) identifies 'Naag' as, 'Vasuki, the king of snakes'. Importance of Naga is also found in Shrimadbhagvad Geeta (10.28), where Lord Krishna says, "Of sarpas (snakes) I am Vasuki".

Naga or *sarpa* is a Sanskrit word for an Indian cobra. Naga is a deity or class of entity or being, taking the form of a very great snake. Hindu texts refer to three prominent naga deities – Shesha, Vasuki and Takshaka. Nagas are the children of rishi Kashyapa and Kadru. Nagas live in Patala, the seventh of the nether dimensions or realms. They are said to live with the females; the nagini (renowned for their beauty). They are the masters of poetry and the art of poetic metric. They are the princes of Arithmetic. Due to their considerable fertility, the nagas represent the incalculable.

Just as metric involves the regulation of rhythm, they are also associated with rhythm of the seasons and weather cycles. They are susceptible to mankind's disrespectful actions in relation to the environment. Nagas are the nature spirits and the protectors of springs, rivers, lakes, seas and wells. They bring rain and thus fertility, but are also thought to bring disasters such as flood and drought. Thus Vayu and Naga squares combined together govern fertility and are considered best for sexual intercourse for getting children.

Their relation with flood, drought and nature may mean that this square should never be concretised. It should be left kachcha (porous) and is best utilised for water harvesting and gardening with small water features. Naga are generally regarded as guardians of the underground treasure. Naga is the lord of panchami tithi (fifth lunar date), which is Lakshmi-prada or one giving wealth. Ajcharan (Ajaikpaad) and Ahirbudhnya (serpent or dragon of the deep) are considered the lords of Poorva Bhadrapada and Uttar Bhadrapada Nakshatras respectively.

Nagas as Village Deities

Nagas are worshipped through offerings of milk and food at the beginning of rain season in Rajasthan, Bengal, Tamil Nadu and many other states in India. In popular religion, cobras are to be found adoring stones called 'grama-devata' or 'divinities of the village', which are placed under the banyan trees. These may also be in the form of an anthill or a snake that lives inside an anthill. Hindu women make offerings to the female snake goddesses. These goddesses are believed to make women fertile, protect them and their family and bring prosperity to them. Hindus believe that a person who harms or kills a snake will be inflicted with a condition known as 'naga dosha' which causes infertility and delays in marriage. Naga dosha can only be reversed through varying degrees of worship to naga.

Nagas are snakes that may take the human form. They tend to be very curious. According to traditions nagas are only malevolent to humans when they have been mistreated. Mahabharata calls nagas as the 'persecutors of all creatures'. It tells us that the snakes were of virulent poison, having great prowess and excess of strength and ever bent on biting the other creatures (Adi Parva, Section 20). In the Mahabharata, the great nemesis of the nagas is the gigantic eagle-king Garuda.

Nagas also carry the elixir of life and immortality (medicine). Garuda once brought the cup with elixir to the Nagas. Though it was taken away by Indra, some part of it got spilled on the kusha grass and nagas licked the kusha grass. But in doing so nagas cut their tongues on the grass and since then their tongues have been forked. Takshaka represents the dangerous aspect of snakes, as they are feared by all due to their venom. Shesha represent the friendly aspect of snakes, as they save food from the rodents.

Lord Vishnu is described in Hindu scriptures as always on continuous meditation (Yoga-nidra) with Ananta forming a bed for him. Brahma entrusted Shesha with the duty of carrying the world on his head (Adi Parva, Section 36). The serpent is also a common feature in Ganesha iconography and appears in many forms: around the neck, sacred thread wrapped around the stomach as a belt, held in a hand, coiled at the ankles, or as a throne.

Manasa

Vasuki is the great king of nagas and has a gem (Nagamani) on his head. Manasa, another naga, is his sister. Vasuki is famous for coiling around the neck of Lord Shiva. Lord Shiva blessed Vasuki and wore him as an ornament. Vasuki also took part in the incident of Samudra-manthan, the churning of the ocean of milk. He allowed devas (gods) and asuras (anti-gods or demons) to bind him to Mount Mandara and use him as their churning rope to extract the ambrosia of immortality from the ocean of milk. As this square is deeply related to Yoga-nidra and Samudra-manthan, it becomes the right place to review one's daily karmas, performing deep meditation, introspection and self-development too.

27. Mukhya

According to the Sanskrit–English dictionary, 'Mukhya' means, guide, leader, commander, main, first, chief, most excellent, face, head, moustache, being in or coming from or belonging to the mouth or face, reading or teaching the vedas, essential rite, month reckoned from new moon to new moon, etc. Samaranganasutradhara (14.24) identifies Mukhya as, 'Tvashta or Vishvakarma'.

According to the *Rig Veda*, Vishwakarma (all-accomplishing, maker of all and all-doer) is the personification of creation and abstract form of the Supreme God. He is the presiding deity of all vishwakarma (caste), artisans, engineers and the architects. He is believed to be the 'Principal Architect of the Universe '. Vishwakarma is visualised in the Rig Veda as the Ultimate Reality (later developed as 'Brahman'), from whose navel (Hiranyagarbha) all visible things emanate. Vishvakarma (sometimes Indra) is considered the lord of Chitra Nakshatra. Vishwakarma is also used as an epithet of Indra, Surya and Agni in Vedic literature.

Vishwakarma (the invisible creative power) is the unborn (Aja) creator. He helps Tvashtar (the visible creative power of viswakarma) in producing all the Heavenly, Earthly and other Celestial realms and preserves them through the exercise of his arms and wings. His attributes like Vachaspati connect him with Brihaspati (the Guru of Gods). He is also called Brahma, Prajapati, Pashupati and Rudra-shiva, the one who is dwelling in all the living forms.

As per the Rig Veda, Tvashtar belongs to the clan of Bhrigus. According to the Yajur Veda *purusha sukta*, the divine smith Tvashtar emerged from Vishwakarma. Tvashtar is sometimes associated or identified with the similar deities, such as Savitra, Prajapati and Pushan. Tvashtar is a solar deity in the *Mahabharata* and the *Harivamsha*. He is mentioned as the son of Kashyapa and Aditi. He is the father of Saranyu, who bears Yama and Yami twins to Surya (Rigveda 10.17.1). Mahabharata mentions Tvashtar as Shukra's son. He is called *garbha-pati* or the lord of the womb and is invoked when desiring offspring. He is the designer of the bodies of men and animals. Tvashtar is the guardian of Soma.

Vishvakarma

Tvashtar revealed the Sthapatya Veda / Vaastu Shastra (fourth Upa-veda) and presides over the sixty-four mechanical arts. Shilpi Vishwakarma is the designer of all the flying chariots of the gods, all their weapons and divine attributes. Tvashtar also created *Vajra* (the sacred weapon of Lord Indra) from the bones of sage Dadhichi. He is regarded as the supreme worker, the very essence of excellence and quality in craftsmanship. Thus, this square may be best utilised for locating workshops where creativity is the main criterion e.g., designing a fuel-efficient bike or car, designing a vehicle running on bio-fuel, designing a new age aeroplane, designing clothes or jewellery, etc.

Tvashtar or Tvashta is the heavenly builder. He is said to have made the three worlds with pieces of the Sun god, Surya. He built Svarga (Heaven) in the Satya Yuga, Lanka in the Treta Yuga and Dwarka (Krishna's capital) in the Dwapara Yuga. Since Vishwakarma is the divine engineer of the world, he is not only worshiped by the engineering and architectural community but also by all the professionals as a mark of reverence. It is customary for craftsmen to worship their tools in his name. This square is the natural care taker and is related to one's resources.

28. Bhallaat (Chandra)

According to the Sanskrit–English dictionary, 'Bhallaat' means, bear, the marking nut plant, marking nut, etc. The root 'bhall' means, to kill, to take or to talk; while 'bhal' means 'to see'. This square abounds in the qualities of expansion, abundance and creation. Samaranganasutradhara (14.25) identifies Bhallaat as, 'Chandra or Moon'.

Chandra is one of the gods of fertility. Chandra is a lunar god and a Graha (planet) in Vedic Astrology. Chandra is a Sanskrit name meaning 'illustrious'. According to the Rig Veda, Chandra was born from the mind of Viraat Purush (God symbolised as the entire universe); 'Chandrama manasojaatah'. Another opinion says that Chandra was born of the Ocean of Milk in the form of elixir of life (Amrita or Soma) and was raised to the status of a planet. Importance of Chandra is also found in Shrimadbhagvad Geeta (10.21), where Lord Krishna says, "Of celestial bodies I am the Moon (Shashi)". Chandra is described as young, beautiful, fair, having a club and a lotus in his two arms. He rides his chariot across the sky every night, pulled by ten white horses or an antelope.

Chandra

Chandra is also identified with the Vedic lunar deity *Soma*. It was the name of an intoxicating drink made from the juice or sap of a climbing plant. It was used in Vedic times for religious ceremonies and sacrifices. Relation of Soma with the plants made Moon the lord of plants and vegetation. Soma was capable of conferring supernatural powers and was worshipped as though it were a god. It was also called the wine of immortality (amrita). It symbolises transition from the ordinary sensual pleasures to the divine happiness (ananda).

In Indian thought, Soma also represents the source of all life and symbolises fertility. It is thus the sperm, the receptacle of the seeds of cyclic rebirth. In this respect, Soma is connected to the symbolism of the moon. This is why Soma is also the lunar star, a masculine entity compared with a full goblet of the drink of immortality. He is also called Rajanipati (lord of the night) and Kshupakara (one who illuminates the night) and *Indu* (the bright drop). There is a similarity between the waxing and waning of the moon and vacillation of mind between experiences of grief and happiness. Soma is connected with dew and his numerical value is one. As Soma, he presides over *Somvar* or Monday.

In Vedic astrology Chandra represents the brain and mind, emotions, sensitivity, softness, imagination, queen and the mother. Chandra rules over the sign Karkataka (Cancer). Moon is considered to be one of the best planets to be born under as it promises wealth and happiness. Indians, who suffer from the excessive heat of Sun, prefer the Moon sign. It is said that Lord Rama was born under the Cancer ascendant, with conjunction of Moon and Jupiter. In Lord Krisna's horoscope Taurus rises and the Ascendant is graced by the presence of exalted Moon, in Rohini.

The bright moon is considered a benefic, while the dark moon is considered a malefic. Chandra is lord of Mrigshira Nakshatra and Poornima tithi (full Moon), which is saumya (sober). He has the following associations: the color white and orange, the metal silver and the gemstones white pearl and moonstone. His element is water, direction is north-west and season is winter. The foodgrain associated with him is rice (one of Nava Dhanyas i.e., nine grains).

According to Hindu mythology, Chandra has not been very fortunate in life. He is known for having a series of disastrous love affairs. Budha (Mercury) is considered his illegitimate son from Tara, the wife of Brihaspati (the planet Jupiter). Chandra married twenty-seven daughters of Daksha on the condition that he will not favour any single daughter over the others. Chandra failed to do this and Daksha placed a curse on him, which accounts for the moon's waxing and waning. When Indra was trying to rape Ahilya, wife of rishi Gautama, Chandra was present in the form of a peacock to alert Indra on Gautama's arrival. It is said that the dark spots on the moon are the result of the curse of rishi Gautama.

Moon is usually called Chanda-mama, the maternal uncle. Mothers address their handsome brother Chandra while feeding their children, requesting him to bring milk, butter and curd for his sister's child. Chandra is also addressed by various other names depending on his attributes. He is called Vidhu, Indu, Himansu, Subhranshu (whose rays are cool and clean), Rajneesh or Rakesh (Lord of the night), Rajanikar or Nishakar (maker of the night), Shashi, Sudha-nidhi or Sudhamaya (one who is full of nectar), Kumudesh (lover of the white water lily) and Kunda Pushpojjwala (as bright as the jasmine flower).

Chandra is the most favourite topic of songs sung by the lovers. Moon is also a symbol of beauty in Indian literature. The beautiful face of a woman has been compared to the moon by almost all the Indian poets as Chandra literally means 'luminous'. Chandra is a common surname in North India. Full name of Lord Sri Ram and Lord Krishna is Ramachandra and Krishnachandra respectively. Lord Shiva is called Chandrashekhar because he wears a crescent moon on his forehead. The crescent moon with a star is also a sacred symbol of Islam.

29. Som (Soma, Kuber)

According to the Sanskrit–English dictionary, 'Som' means, the soma plant, drug of supposed medical properties, nectar, extract, substance, essence, camphor, Moon or Moon god, heaven, ether, sky, air, water, rice water or rice gruel, particular class of pitars, particular mountain or mountainous range, etc. The square of Soma governs the qualities of transformation and treasure.

Soma, one of the most popular gods of the Rigvedic hymns, is the god of inspiration. He rules the intoxicant that stirs the minds, lures the gods and brings them to the place of worship. Also known as Indu or Soma Pavamana, he brings joy into the lives of people, cures them from diseases and leads them to the world of bliss and immortality. He gives strength not only to the mortals, but to the gods as well. It is because of him that Agni maintains his sway and Indra was able to slay Vratrasura (Vratra, the demon).

He is also known as Lord of speech (Vachaspati), because of his intoxicating influence on the movement of speech. On the physical plane, Soma is a kind of intoxicating juice and a magical energy drink full of medicinal qualities. In the prayers dedicated to Soma, emphasis is on the need for the purity of juice for Indra's happiness. Due to these qualities, this square becomes the best place for preparing drugs in the liquid or semi-liquid form. Cold drinks, extracting and packing juices, mineral water and soda water units will also flourish in this square.

Samaranganasutradhara (14.25) identifies 'Som' as, 'Kuber'. In Hindu mythology, Kubera (Kuber, Kuver) is considered as Dikpala (the regent and protector) of the North direction. He is god-king of the semi-divine Yakshas, the Guhyakas, Kinnaras and Gandharvas, who act as his assistants and protectors of the jewels of the earth as well as the guardians of his city. He is owner of all the treasures of the world.

Importance of Kuber is also found in the Shrimadbhagvad Geeta (10.23), where Lord Krishna says, "Of the Yakshas and Rakshasas I am Kuvera". Vishnudharmottara Purana describes Kubera as the embodiment of both Artha (wealth, prosperity, glory) and Arthashastras, the treatises related to it. Kubera is described as born from a cow. Puranas describe him as grandson of sage Pulastya, son of Vishrava and half brother of demon king Ravana.

His city is usually called Alka or Alkapuri (girl-city), but also Prabha (splendour), Vasudhara (bejewelled) and Vasu-sthali (abode of treasures). It was situated on the Gandhamadan mountain in the Himalayas, near Mount Kailash — the cosmological abode of Lord Shiva. Here, Kubera had a grove where the leaves were jewels and the fruits were girls of heaven. There was also a charming lake called Nalini in the grove. A description of Kubera's magnificent court appears in the epic Mahabharata as well as in poet Kalidasa's Meghaduta where Gandharvas and Apsaras entertain Kubera. Shiva and his wife Parvati often frequent Kubera's court, which is also attended by the semi-divine beings like the Vidyadharas; Kimpurushas; Rakshasas; Pishachas; and personified treasures (nidhis).

Kubera

Kubera is often depicted as a dwarf with big belly and of fair complexion. He is adorned in golden clothes and ornaments, symbolising his wealth. Kubera holds a mace, a pomegranate or a money bag in his hand. He may also carry a sheaf of jewels or a mongoose with him. Mongoose is considered a symbol of Kubera's victory over Nagas — the guardians of treasures. Kubera is usually drawn by the spirits or men, so he is called *Nara-vahana* (one who mounts a man). Kubera also rides the elephant as a *loka-pala*. *Agni Purana* describes Kubera as seated on a goat. Jain texts depict Kubera as a drunkard, signified by the 'nectar vessel' in his hand.

'Kubera' literally means deformed or monstrous or ill-shaped one, indicating his deformities. Kubera may be derived from the verb root *kumba*, meaning to conceal. Kubera is also called *Guhyadhipa* (Lord of the hidden). *Atharva Veda* calls him the 'God of hiding'. Originally, Vedic texts like Atharva Veda and Shatapatha Brahmana describe him as the Lord of thieves, criminals and the spirits of darkness. He acquired the status of a god only in the *Puranas* and the Hindu epics. In the *Manusmriti*, he became a respectable loka-pala and the patron of merchants.

As the son of *Vishrava* (fame), Kubera is called *Vaisravana*. He is called *Ekaksipingala* (one who has one yellow eye) as he has only the left eye. His face is also inclined to the left. He is also called *Bhutesha* (Lord of spirits) like Shiva. His other names are: 'king of the whole world', 'king of kings' (*Rajaraja*), 'Lord of wealth' (*Dhanadhipati*), 'giver of wealth' (*Dhanada*), 'king of Yakshas' (*Yaksharajan*), 'Lord of Rakshasas' (*Rakshasadhipati*), 'Lord of Guhyakas' (*Guhyakadhipa*), 'king of Kinnaras' (*Kinnararaja*), 'king of animals resembling men' (*Mayuraja*) and 'king of men' (*Nararaja*).

The Mahabharata says that Brahma conferred upon Kubera the lordship of wealth (*nidhis*), equality with the gods and status as a world-protector, the Pushpaka Vimana (a flying chariot) and lordship of the *Nairrata* demons. Kubera is often described as a friend of Shiva in the epics. The Padma Purana says that Kubera prayed to Shiva for many years and Shiva granted him the kingship of Yakshas. Puranas and the Mahabharata record that Kubera married Bhadra (auspicious), also called *Yakshi* – a female Yaksha and *Charvi* (splendour). They had three sons: Nalakubara (reed-axle), Manigriva (bejewlled-neck) or Varna-kavi (colourful poet) and Mayuraja (king of animals resembling men); and a daughter called Minakshi (fish-eyed).

In contrast to Indra (the god-king of heaven), Kubera is generally considered the king of earthly kings. Though still described as an *asura* (demon), Kubera is offered prayers at the end of all ritual sacrifices. Offerings of meat, sesame seeds and flowers are made to Kubera. He is also the guardian of travellers and the giver of wealth to individuals, who please him. Kubera also developed as minor marriage-divinity. He is invoked with Shiva at weddings and is described as *Kameshvara* (Lord of *Kama* – pleasure, desire, etc). He is associated with fertility of the aquatic type.

Kubera is prescribed to be worshipped as the treasurer of the riches of the world. Kubera also credited money to the God Venkateshwara (a form of the Lord Vishnu) for his marriage with Padmavati. In remembrance of this, the reason devotees go to Tirupati to donate money in Venkateshwara's *Hundi* (donation pot), so that he can pay it back to Kubera. While Kubera still enjoys prayers as the god of wealth, his role is now largely taken by the god of wisdom, fortune and obstacle-remover, Ganesha, with whom he is generally associated.

30. Charak (Sarpa, Bhujag, Shail, Giri, Mrga, Mriga, Mrig)

According to the Sanskrit–English dictionary, 'Charak' means, kind of medicinal plant, kind of ascetic, wanderer or wandering religious student, spy, to search or to investigate, beast, etc. Shail means 'sort of lotion or wash for eyes'. This square governs immunity, core strength and kundalini of the inhabitants. Samaranganasutradhara (14.25) identifies Charak as, *Vyavasaya* (business).

Sarpa or serpent represents the dual expressions of good and evil. Historically, serpents represent fertility or the creative life force. As snakes shed their skin through sloughing, they are symbols of death, rebirth, transformation, immortality, continual renewal of life and healing. The serpent also represents the sexual desire. In Yoga Shastra, Kundalini is equated to a coiled serpent, the residual power of pure desire. Serpents are represented as the potent guardians of temples, treasures of sacred sites and sacred spaces. Snakes represented freedom in Hindu mythology because they can't be tamed.

Serpents are also connected with vengefulness and vindictiveness.

Serpents are connected with poison and medicine as well. Snake's venom is associated with the chemicals of plants and fungi that have the power to either heal or poison or to provide the expanded consciousness (and even the elixir of life and immortality) through divine intoxication. Snake was often considered as one of the wisest animals, connected to the after-life and immortality. The serpent, when forming a ring with its tail in its mouth, is a clear and widespread symbol of the 'All-in-All', the totality of existence, infinity and the cyclic nature of the cosmos. Sarpa (serpent) is the lord of Ashlesha Nakshatra, which has appearance like a wheel.

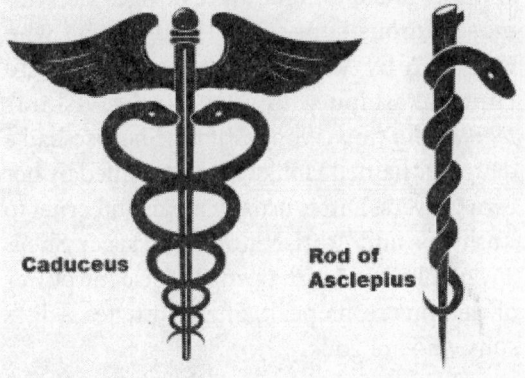

Snakes are an integral part of the symbol of modern medicine and also deeply related with the areas of business and commerce. In western mythology, a single snake entwined the rough staff of Asclepius, the Greco-Roman god of medicine and healing. On the caduceus of Hermes, the Roman Mercury, the snakes were not merely duplicated for symmetry, they were also paired opposites. The wings at the head of the staff identified it as belonging to Hermes, the winged messenger. Hermes was the god of magic, diplomacy and rhetoric, inventions and discoveries, protector of both of merchants and the allied occupations and also of thieves. Hermes was also the escort of newly deceased souls to the afterlife. Mercury was also considered the protector of alchemy and of arcane or occult Hermetic information.

Later on, Chemistry and medicine linked the rod of Hermes with the staff of healer Asclepius (which was conflated with Mercury's rod). Consequently, modern medical symbol which should simply be the rod of Asclepius often became Mercury's wand of commerce. Art historian Walter J. Friedlander, in *The Golden Wand of Medicine: A History of the Caduceus Symbol in Medicine* (1992) collected hundreds of examples of the caduceus and the rod of Asclepius and found that professional associations were just somewhat more likely to use the staff of Asclepius, while commercial organisations in the medical field were more likely to use the caduceus.

31. Aditi

According to the Sanskrit–English dictionary, 'Aditi' means, mother of gods, entire, not tied, boundless, free, inexhaustible, abundance, perfection, happy, creative power, heaven and earth, unbroken, unimpaired, speech, safety, freedom, security, destitution, devourer i.e., death, cow, milk, etc. Samaranganasutradhara (14.25) identifies Aditi as 'Sri or Lakshmi', which has been described in detail in chapter 3.

According to Rigveda, Aditi (limitless) is mother of the gods and all the twelve zodiacal spirits. As celestial mother of every existing form and being, the synthesis of all things, she is associated with space (*akasha*) and with mystic speech (*vach*). In Vedanta, she is seen as a feminised form of Brahma and associated with the primal substance (*mulaprakriti*). Shiva Purana and Bhagavata Purana suggest that Aditi is wife of sage Kashyapa. Aditi was regarded as both the sky goddess and the earth goddess. She was attributed the status of *first deity* in the Vedic culture. She flies across the boundless sky on a rooster (cock), which symbolises strength and honour. Her weapons include the famous Trishul (Trident) and a sword. Aditi rules the Punarvasu Nakshatra.

Aditi

Aditi is said to be the mother of great god Indra, the mother of kings (Mandala 2.27) and the mother of gods (Mandala 1.113.19). Aditi is mentioned in Vedas as mother of Surya (Sun) and other celestial bodies or the twelve Adityas (meaning sons of Aditi): Vivasvan, Aryama, Pusha, Tvashta, Savita, Bhaga, Dhata, Vidhata, Varuna, Mitra, Shakra and Urukrama (Vishnu was born as Urukrama). She is also the mother of Vamana avatar of Vishnu.

In the Rig Veda, Aditi is often asked to guard the one who petitions her (1.106.7, 8.18.6) or to provide him or her with wealth, safety and abundance (10.100; 1.94.15). The name Aditi includes the root 'da' (to bind or yoke) and suggests another attribute of her character. As A-diti, she is un-bound, free one and it is evident in the hymns addressed to her that she is often called to free the petitioner from varied hindrances, especially sin and sickness (Rigveda 2.27.14, 8.67.14). She also unbinds like her son Varuna, the guardian of *Rta*, the cosmic moral order. She has also been called the supporter of creatures (Rigveda 1.136).

32. Diti (Uditi, Daityamata)

According to the Sanskrit–English dictionary, Diti means, distributing, cutting, dividing, splitting, liberality, king, tej or brilliance or idea, etc. Samaranganasutradhara (14.26) identifies 'Diti' as, 'Lord Shankara: Trident-bearer (Shulabhrida) with an image of a bull on his flag'.

Diti, the mother of Daityas, is an earth goddess. She was one of the sixty daughters of Daksha-Prajapati. He was one of the grandfathers of creation, a son of Brahma, the god of ritual skills and a king. Diti was one of the thirteen wives of Kashyapa, another prajapati and a great sage. Her two most famous sons were Hiranyaksha who was slain by Vishnu's *Varaha* avatara and Hiranyakashipu who was slain by Vishnu's *Narasimha* (man-lion) avatara. She also had a daughter named Holika who was killed by her own powers. Diti is usually mean and cruel to Kashyapa and Aditi, her own real sister. She is always obsessed with trying to raise the power of demons to its peak. She also hates Aditi's sons who are gods.

Diti wanted to have a son who would be more powerful than Indra (who had killed her previous children) and so she practiced magic and kept herself pregnant for one year. Indra, disguised as a mendicant, entered her womb. He sliced up her embryo into seven pieces with his weapon, the Vajra. When the foetus began to cry, Indra tried to silence the child by saying "Ma Ruda" (don't cry), but the baby continued to cry. In anger, Indra sliced the seven pieces into forty-nine parts. Diti gave birth to the forty-nine Marutas, who were given that name due to the words addressed to them by Indra in their mother's womb. Marutas rule the north-west direction and are generally described as ferocious in nature.

33. Aap (Aapah)

According to the Sanskrit-English dictionary, 'Aap' means, water, quantity of water, to get or to be obtained, to spread, to get, etc. Aap is the Vedic Sanskrit term meaning 'water'. The Indo-Iranian word for Aap also survives as the Persian word for water, Aab, i.e., 'water'.

In the Rig Veda, several hymns (7.49, 10.9, 10.30 and 10.47) are dedicated to 'the waters'. In the oldest of these (7.49), the waters are connected with the drought of Indra. Agni, the god of fire, has a close association with water and is often referred to as *Apam Napat* or the 'offspring of the waters'. The female deity Apah is the presiding deity of *Purva Ashadha* (the former invincible one) asterism (*nakshatra*) in Vedic Astrology. In Hindu philosophy, water as an element is one of the *Panchamahabhutas* or 'five great elements'. In Hinduism, it is also the name of the Varuna Deva (God), a personification of water.

Samaranganasutradhara (14.26) identifies 'Aap' as, 'Himvaan'. Himavaan (snowy) or *Himavat* (frosty) or *Himavant* (icy) or *Himaraja* (king of snow) or *Parvateshwara* (lord of mountains) is a personification of the Himalayan Mountains. According to the epic Mahabharata, Himvan was ruler of the himalayan kingdom of ancient india. His story also finds mention in *Devi Bhagawatam*, *Brahmanda Purana* and *Kena Upanishad*.

Devi Bhagawata Purana and Shiva Purana tell tales of Sati's marriage to Shiva against her father Daksha's wishes. The conflict between Daksha and Shiva gets to a point where Daksha does not invite Shiva to his *yajna* (fire-sacrifice). Daksha insults Shiva when Sati comes on her own. She self-immolates herself at the ceremony. This shocks Shiva, who is so grief-stricken that he loses interest in the worldly affairs, retires and isolates himself in the mountains, in meditation and austerity.

Kailash-Mansarovar

Mount Himalaya and his wife Mainavati appease goddess Adi Shakti. Pleased, Adi Shakti (Sati) herself is reborn as their daughter Uma-Parvati. Sati is named Parvati, or 'she from the mountains', after her father Himvan who is also called god of the great Himalayas or king Parvat or personification of the Himalayas. Importance of Himalaya is also found in Shrimadbhagvad Geeta (10.25), where Lord Krishna says, "Of immovable things I am the Himalayas".

In the Nava Durga pantheon, Parvati is referred to as Shailaputri. The first form of the mother Goddess Durga among her nine forms is Shailaputri. 'Shail' means mountains and 'Putri' means daughter. As such, she is the 'Daughter of the Mountains', popularly known as Uma-Parvati in the Puranic mythology. Some communities also believe her as the sister of Lord Vishnu as well as the river-goddess Ganga (the Ganges). She is said to be the embodiment of the power of Hindu Gods Brahma, Vishnu and Shiva.

34. Aapvats

Aapvats literally means, descendent of Aap or child of Aap. Samaranganasutradhara (14.26) identifies 'Aapvats' as, 'Uma'. In Sanskrit, the word uma also mean 'tranquillity', 'splendour', 'fame' and 'light'. Uma is another name of Hindu goddess Parvati. Goddess Uma came to earth from her heavenly abode Kailasha. The name Uma or Parvati is used for Sati (Shiva's first wife, who was reborn as Parvati).

In the *Harivamsa Purana*, Parvati is referred to as Aparna (one who took no sustenance) and then addressed as Uma, who was dissuaded by her mother from severe austerity by saying "u ma" (oh, don't). Other names which associate her with mountains are *Shailaja* (daughter of the mountains), *Adrija* or *Nagaja* or *Shailaputri* (daughter of mountains), 'Haimavathi' (daughter of Himavan) and 'Girija' or 'Girijaputri' (daughter of king of the mountains). *Kena Upanishad* (3.12) calls her Uma-Haimavati.

Lord Shiva and Goddess Parvati with Family

Parvati is the embodiment of divine knowledge and mother of the world. She appears as the *shakti* (essential power) of the Supreme Brahman. Her primary role is as a mediator in the conflicts of heaven. Along with Lakshmi (goddess of wealth and prosperity) and Saraswati (goddess of knowledge and learning), she forms the trinity of Hindu Goddesses (Tridevi).

Uma-Parvati is the wife of Lord Shiva – the destroyer, recycler and regenerator of the universe and all its life. Uma is the recreative energy and power of Shiva. Parvati and Shiva are often symbolised respectively by a yoni (*argha*) and a linga in the temples dedicated to her and Shiva. Yoni means womb and place of gestation, the yoni-linga metaphor represents 'origin, source or regenerative power'. The icon represents the interdependence and union of the feminine and masculine energies in recreation and regeneration of all life.

Parvati is the mother goddess and has many attributes and aspects. Each of her aspects is expressed with a different name. She is called Annapurna (abundance and food),

Kamakshi (goddess of love and devotion), Ambika (dear mother), Shakti (power), Durga (invincible), Bhavani (fertility and birthing), Shivaradni (Queen of Shiva), Lalita (the playful Goddess of the Universe) and Bhairavi (ferocious). As a calm and placid wife, Parvati is usually represented as Gauri (the fair one), beautiful and benevolent. Gauri (wife of Lord Shiva) is the lord of *tritiya tithi* (third lunar date), which is *bala-prada* or one giving power and strength. She is Kali or Shyama as a goddess who destroys the evil.

Parvati is sometimes shown with golden or yellow colour skin, particularly as goddess Gauri, symbolising her as the goddess of fertility and ripened harvests. In her benevolent manifestation such as Kamakshi or Meenakshi (goddess with eyes shaped like a fish), a parrot sits near her right shoulder symbolising cheerful love talk, seeds and fertility. Parvati is thus a mixture of the Vedic goddesses Aditi and Nirriti.

Annapurna

Parvati typically wears a red dress (often a sari) and may have a head-band. When depicted alongside Shiva, she generally appears with two arms, but when alone, she may be depicted having four. Parvati's right hand in Abhaya mudra symbolises 'do not fear anyone or anything', while her Varada mudra symbolises 'wish fulfilling'. These hands may hold a conch, crown, mirror, rosary, bell, dish, farming tool such as goad, sugarcane stalk or flowers such as lotus. Her younger child Ganesha is on her knee, while her elder son Skanda may be playing near her in her watch. Parvati's sculpture is often depicted near a calf or cow – a source of food.

Parvati is expressed both in nurturing and benevolent aspects, as well as destructive and ferocious aspects. She is the voice of encouragement, reason, freedom and strength, as well as of resistance, power, action and retributive justice. She identifies and destroys evil to protect (Durga), as well as creates food and abundance to nourish (Annapurna). Parvati symbolises different virtues like fertility, marital felicity and devotion to the spouse, asceticism and power. Parvati is the embodiment of an ideal wife, mother and householder in the Indian legends. She manifests in every activity; from water to mountains, from arts to inspiring warriors and from agriculture to dance.

35. Aryama (Aryaman, Aaryaka, Aaryak, Aarya)

According to the Sanskrit–English dictionary, 'Aryaman' means, companion, bosom friend or play-fellow, friend who asks a woman in marriage for another, milk weed plant, etc. Aaryak means a respectable woman or man, a superior man, grandfather, ceremony performed to the manes, vessel used in sacrifices made to the manes. Manes means souls of the departed ancestors. Aryama means, the sun, the judge, controller and god.

His name signifies 'close friend', 'play-fellow' or 'companion'. Samaranganasutradhara (14.27) identifies Aryama as, 'Aditya'.

Aryama is the third son of Aditi, mother of the twelve Adityas. After creating Prajapati, Sun divides itself into twelve forms each representing a month of the year. Aryama represents the Vaishakha month and is the ruler of Uttara Phalguni nakshatra in Vedic Astrology. In the Rig Veda, Aryaman is described as the protector of mares and Milky Way is said to be his path. Aryaman is commonly invoked together with Varuna-Mitra, Bhaga, Brihaspati and other Adityas and Asuras. In Rig Veda, Aryaman is a supreme deity alongside Mitra and Varuna. According to the Rig Veda, Indra who is traditionally considered the most important deity in the Rig Veda is asked to obtain boons and gifts from Aryamaan.

Aryama is Sun's unfailing nature of following dharma constantly and of keeping contracts and oaths (in which capacity he is invoked at Hindu weddings). Aryaman, like Pusha, promotes prosperity and concord in marriages. Agni is addressed as Aryaman who makes 'wife and lord one-minded.' Together with Varuna and Mitra, this harmonious order in marriage and family is the reflection of Aryaman's role as guardian of the cosmic order rta.

The name Aryama itself contains the notion of order and harmony. He, along with Mitra, is associated with friendship. In the case of Aryama, perhaps this association recognises the true friendship that may be offered by one who is trustworthy and dependable. Aryaman is god of harmony and reconciliation and of the unbroken path. Associated with pathways like other demigods Bhaga and Pushan, he is called 'The Companion on the Path, or the harmoniser'.

According to David Frawley, "Aryaman is very auspicious. He bestows riches, affluence and material prosperity. The people whom he protects are victorious over their adversaries". Aryama is also described as the chief of Pitraloka where the souls of our ancestors rest before taking rebirth. Importance of Aryama in this form is also found in Shrimadbhagvad Geeta (10.29), where Lord Krishna says, "Amongst the forefathers I am Aryama". Aryama is considered the lord of Uttar Phalguni (sometimes Poorva Phalguni) nakshatra, pairing with Bhaga (an Aditya, the incarnation of Sun).

36. Savita (Savitr, Savitar, Savitra, Savindra)

According to the Sanskrit–English dictionary, 'Savitr' means, Sun, orb of the sun or its god, vivifier, stimulator, rouser, crown flower plant, instrument of production, cause of generation, etc. Samaranganasutradhara (14.27) identifies 'Savita' as, 'Goddess Ganga'. In Shrimadbhagvad Geeta (10.31), Lord Krishna says, "Of rivers I am the Ganga".

Savitr (stem) or Savita (nominative singular) is a solar deity in the Rigveda and one of the twelve Adityas. In the Vedas, Savita is a symbol of the Divine. Savita means God on the plane of Eternity. It means sun on the physical plane, it means intelligence on the psychic plane and it means vitality on the biological plane. Savitr is a beneficent God who acts as protector of all the beings, who are provident and guards the world of spirits. Savitr is considered the lord of Hasta Nakshatra.

Savitr is an Aditya who is described as golden eyed, golden handed and golden tongued. He is generally regarded as the golden sun of the morning, but sometimes also distinguished from the sun. From far away he comes, looking on everyone, chasing away all the distress and sorrow and illumines the worlds. The Gayatri Mantra is addressed to Savitr of adorable splendor for the enlightenment of human consciousness.

Goddess Ganga

Drawing the gold-yoked car with his white footed bays, he manifests light to all the people. He goes to darksome regions to illumine them. Far-seeing Savitr goes on his way between the earth and the heaven, drives away sickness, bids the Sun approach us and spreads the bright sky through the darksome regions. Like other Adityas, he is an upholder of the eternal law. Sometimes he is described as superior to all the other gods, whose statutes none disobey.

Humans too have Shakti (power) of Savita, but only in limited amount. This power acts as an impetus in humans and brings about the requirement for them to do something. They cannot sit idle and are constantly searching for something to do. This is what is commonly known as the 'creative urge'. It is through this Shakti that mankind has created art and scientific advances are made. The gift of Savita also gives creatures the ability of procreation. Hence, Savita can be thought of as meaning Father (or Mother) also.

Savitr is the most adorable, mysterious and effulgent god of mystic realms. He is considered to be the goal, the purpose and the object of meditation. When he descends into the consciousness, a golden disc with bright pointed rays, the inner world is lit up with the splendor of God and indescribable beauty. It is the power of Savita that enables mankind to distinguish the right from the wrong and vice from the virtue. Through this ability, we are able to direct our own selves and thus, Savita imparts us a certain self-guiding ability. Thus, by using this word in the mantra, we demonstrate that we are also making efforts ourselves, since God will not help us unless we are willing to help ourselves.

Savitr bestows immortality on the gods as well as length of life on the mortals. Like other gods, Savitr is a supporter of the sky. Also, he supports the whole world, a role which has been assigned to Lord Vishnu. Like Surya, Savitr is implored to remove the evil dreams and to make men sinless. Savitr drives away evil spirits and sorcerers. He observes the fixed laws. The waters and the wind are subject to his ordinance. He leads the waters and by his propulsion they flow broadly. He is lord of all the desirable things and sends blessings from heaven to air and earth.

37. Saavitr (Saavitra, Saavindra)

According to the Sanskrit–English dictionary, 'Saavitr' means, Sun, ray of light, solar ray, particular form of the Gayatri metre, verse of prayer addressed to Sun accompanied or effected by the Savitri verse, initiation as a member of the three twice-born classes (dvija) by reciting the above verse and investing with the sacred thread, ring finger, belonging to the solar dynasty, derived or descended from the Sun, related to Karna, particular fire of oblation, Brahman, particular kind of ladleful, etc.

Samaranganasutradhara (14.27) identifies Saavitr as, 'Gayatri, the mother of Vedas'.

Goddess Gayatri is considered the Vedamata, mother of all the Vedas. She is Saraswati, mother and source of all the knowledge and the embodiment of pure knowledge. Gayatri is the feminine form of *gayatra*, a Sanskrit word for a song or a hymn. Gayatri is the name applied to the most sacred Vedic hymn consisting of twenty-four syllables. Importance of Gayatri is also found in Shrimadbhagvad Geeta (10.35), where Lord Krishna says, "Of Vedic rhythms I am the Gayatri". This hymn is addressed to god Surya (Sun) as the supreme generative force. On translation this hymn means, 'We meditate on that glorious light of the divine Surya (Sun); may He, the lord of light, illuminate our minds'. It is ordained that repeating this hymn again and again leads to salvation.

and sky. The four heads of Gayatri represent the four Vedas and the remaining one represents the Almighty Lord himself. In her ten hands she holds all the weapons of Lord Shiva, Lord Vishnu and Lord Brahma. She is also accompanied by a white swan, holding a book to portray knowledge in one hand and a cure in the other as the Goddess of education.

She is another consort of Brahma. She is a form of Adi Shakti, an aspect of Mata (mother) Saraswati, Mata Lakshmi and Mata Parvati, all three in one form. She possesses the Rajasi Guna and, hence, is the source of Brahma's power. Without her, Brahma remains dormant or unable to create. One of the sacred texts explicitly reads, 'The Gayatri is Brahma, the Gayatri is Vishnu, the Gayatri is Shiva, the Gayatri is Vedas'. In Hindu mythology, there is only one creation who can withstand the brilliance of Aditya and that is Gayatri.

The term 'Gayatri Mantra' might be translated as, "a prayer of praise that awakens the vital energies and gives liberation". Gayatri is impregnable spiritual armour, a veritable fortress that guards and protects its votary. She transforms him into the divine and blesses him with the brilliant light of the highest spiritual illumination. It is universally applicable, for it is nothing but an earnest prayer for Light, addressed to the Supreme Almighty Spirit. This single mantra repeated sincerely and with clear conscience brings the supreme good.

It is said that whenever and wherever the Gayatri mantra is uttered with devotion and sincerity, the entire atmosphere and aura of the people participating in the chanting lights up in a splendorous manner by the golden rays that descend from above.

Goddess Gayatri

Goddess Gayatri is the Gayatri mantra personified. She is seated on a red lotus, signifying wealth. She has five heads (Mukta, Vidruma, Hema, Neela and Dhavala) with ten eyes looking in eight directions plus the earth

38. Vivasvaan (Vivasvat, Vivasvant, Martanda, Marttanda, Martamda, Surya, Savitri)

According to the Sanskrit-English dictionary, 'Vivasvan' means 'The Sun'.

Samaranganasutradhara (14.28) identifies Vivasvaan as, 'Death which takes away this physical body'. In some references, Vivasvan is identified as Vivasvat, Vivasvant, Martanda, Marttanda, Martamda, Surya and Savitri. Vivasvat and *Martanda* are often used interchangeably. Vivasvan is the God of midday and the lord of fire.

Martanda is etymologically derived from *Marta* meaning 'dead or undeveloped'. The word Martanda is connected with mrita, the past participle of 'mri' i.e., 'to die' and anda, an egg or a bird. Thus his name literally means 'dead-egg'. It denotes a dead sun, or a sun that has sunk below the horizon or the sun causing death due to its scorching rays in the south direction.

According to the Rigveda (10.72), Aditi originally had only seven sons but later gave birth to an eighth son named Martanda, who she cast away (presumably because he was dead). She brought Martanda thitherward to spring to life and die again. The Taittiriya Aranyaka reads: *tat para Martandam a abharat* (she set aside Martanda for birth and death). In the post-Vedic period, when number of Adityas increased to twelve, another name Vivasvat and Martanda are often used interchangeably. Martanda is exclusively identified with Surya and Vivasvant in Mahabharata.

The energy and life that we get from Vivasvan is used to nourish plants and fruits that are later consumed as food. Jatharagni (the digestive fire in our digestive system) is also a form of the Agni of Vivasvan. Vivasvan is the husband of Saranyu and father of the twin Aswins, Vaivasvata Manu (the eighth Manu), Yama and Yami.

39. Indra (Shakra, Vibudhadhip, Vibudhanpati)

Samaranganasutradhara (14.28) identifies 'Indra' as, 'Mighty Hari'. Hari is the Supreme God in Hinduism. Hari is derived from the verbal root *hra,* meaning 'to take away or remove evil or sin'. He is also known as Vishnu and Narayana. Vishnu made Indra's success possible. Traditional explanation of the name *Vishnu* involves the root *vish,* meaning 'to settle' or also (in the Rigveda) 'to enter into, to pervade'. Thus, Vishnu means 'the All-Pervading One'. He is not limited by space, time or substance. According to the Nirukta, Vishnu is the 'one who enters everywhere' and 'that which is free from fetters and bondages'. Indra's other name 'Shakra', also means 'powerful' or 'having strength'.

In the Rigvedic texts, the deity or god referred to as Vishnu is the Sun God, who also bears the name 'Suryanarayana'. The word 'Vishnu' referred to in 'Vishnu Purana', 'Vishnu Sahasranamam' and 'Purusha Sooktam' is Lord Narayana, the Consort of Lakshmi. Aitareya Brahmana declares, 'Agni is the lowest or youngest god and Vishnu is the greatest and the highest God'. Vishnu as Sun God is also found in Shrimadbhagvad Geeta (10.21), where Lord Krishna says, "Of the Adityas I am Vishnu". Vishnu is the only God called upon to save the good beings by defeating or killing the asuras.

Indra

The word Hari appears as 650th name of Vishnu in the Vishnu Sahasranama of the Mahabharata. Vishnu is 'He who destroys samsara', along with ignorance as its cause. Samsara is the entanglement in the cycle of birth and death. Vishnu is usually described as having dark complexion of water-filled clouds and having four arms. He is also depicted as a pale blue being, as are his incarnations Rama and Krishna. He holds a padma (lotus flower), the Kaumodaki Gada (mace), the Paanchjanya Shankha (conch) and the Sudarshana Chakra (discus) in his four hands.

Lord Narayana is the 'Paramam Padam', which literally mean 'highest post' and may be understood as the 'supreme abode for all the souls' (Yajur Veda, Taittiriya Aranyaka; 10-13-1, Rig Veda 1:22:20a). He is also known as Param Dhama, or Vaikuntha. Vishnu is called 'Preserver of the universe' as he preserves, supports, sustains and governs the universe. Lord Vishnu takes his incarnations or avatars to the Earth to save humanity from evil beings, demons or Asuras. Rig Veda describes Vishnu as close friend of Indra. Brahma emerged from Vishnu's navel.

Vishnu occupies the highest place. Vishnu is the Supreme God who lives in the highest celestial region, contrasted against those who live in the atmospheric or terrestrial regions. It indicates that this square is best for the most important person in any premises. Vishnu is considered as resident in the direction of 'Makara Rashi' (the 'Shravana Nakshatra'), coincident with the Capricorn constellation. In the horoscope of Kaal Purush (time personified), Capricorn sign falls in the tenth *bhava* (house) which corresponds with the South direction. Tenth house reveals our physical activities and success in the business. Vishnu rules *dwadashi tithi* (twelfth lunar date), which is considered *yash-prada* (one giving fame and good qualities). It has also been considered the most auspicious lunar date; 'Na tithirdwadashi sama'. Vishnu's eye is considered to be aimed at the infinitely distant Southern Celestial Pole.

40. Jaya (Indrajaya, Indraraja)

According to the Sanskrit–English dictionary, 'Jaya' means, Indra, Sun, Arjuna, banner, one of the seven flag-sticks of Indra's banner, conquering, victory, triumph, kind of flute, kind of measure, Arani tree, black gram, yellow myrobalan, etc. Indra has already been discussed under the heading 'Mahendra'. 'Indraj' means descended from Indra. As Samaranganasutradhara (14.28) identifies Indra as 'Mighty Hari', Indraja may also mean the 'descendents of Hari'. Vayu Purana (28.2) lists two named sons of Vishnu and Lakshmi, 'Bala (strength) and Utsaha (energy)'. The square of Jaya bestows strength and energy to the occupants.

Samaranganasutradhara (14.28) identifies 'Jaya' as, 'Vajri, Holder of Vajra'. Vajra is described as the weapon of Indra, the god of heaven and chief deity of the Rigvedic pantheon. Indra is described as using vajra to kill the sinners and ignorant persons. Vajra is considered the ultimate weapon of gods. It indicates that this square was reserved for the king's armoury. Any weapon of self-defense in the house should also be kept here.

Rigveda states that the weapon Vajra was made for Indra by Tvastar, the maker of divine instruments. The associated story describes Indra using the vajra, which he held in his hand, to slay the asura Vritra, who took the form of a serpent. On account of his skill in wielding the vajra, some epithets used for Indra in the Rigveda are *Vajrabhrit* (bearing the vajra), *Vajrivat* or *Vajrin* (armed with the vajra), *Vajradaksina* (holding the vajra in his right hand) and *Vajrabahu* or *Vajrahasta* (holding the vajra in his hand). There have been instances where the war god Skanda (Murugan) also is described as holding a vajra.

Vajra is a Sanskrit word meaning both thunderbolt and diamond. Additionally, it is a weapon which is used as a ritual object to symbolise both the properties of a diamond (indestructibility) and a thunderbolt (irresistible force). Vajra is essentially a type of club with a ribbed spherical head. The ribs may meet in a ball-shaped top, or they may be separate and end in sharp points with which to stab. The vajra often represent firmness of spirit and spiritual power. In Shrimadbhagvad Geeta (10.28), Lord Krishna while describing seventy-five of his common manifestations, declares, 'aayudhanam aham vajram'. It means 'Of all weapons, I am the Vajra (thunderbolt)'.

Vajra

Many later Puranas describe the vajra, with the story modified from the Rigvedic original. One major addition involves the role of the sage Dadhichi. Sage Dadhichi, on the request of gods, is said to have given up his life by the art of yoga after which the gods fashioned *vajrayudha* (vajra-weapon) from his spine. Another version of the story exists where sage Dadhichi was asked to safeguard the weapons of the gods as they were unable to match the arcane arts being employed by the asura to obtain them. Dadhichi is said to have kept at the task for a very long time and finally tiring of the job, he is said to have dissolved the weapons in sacred water which he drank. Brahma is then said to have fashioned a large number of weapons from Dadhichi's bones, including the vajrayudha.

41. Mitra

According to the Sanskrit–English dictionary, 'Mitra' means, Sun, friend, ally, etc. Surya is also known as Mitra for his life nourishing properties. The Mitra form of 'Surya' had been worshiped mostly in Gujarat, where a clan of Suryavanshi kings was known as Mitravanshi kshatriyas, also known by its derivative name 'Maitrakas'.

Mitra, along with Varuna, is lord of the heaven. They are guardians of the world, who sit in a gold hued chariot from day break and behold the infinity. Mitra is associated with the morning light, while Varuna with the night sky. Together they uphold the law, cause the cows to stream and the plants to flourish. They scatter the swift drops and send down the rain-flood. Mitra and Varuna rule *Anuradha* and *Shatabhisha* Nakshatras respectively.

Both Mitra and Varuna are Adityas, the sons of Aditi. They are mostly invoked together, probably because of their close friendship. The watchful twains, most potent, together uphold Rta or the moral order. Home of Mitra, Aryaman and Varuna is firmly set in the heaven. They give forth great vital strength which merits praise, high power of life that men shall praise. Mitra stirs men to action and sustains both earth and heaven.

Samaranganasutradhara (14.29) identifies Mitra as, 'Haldhar; the plough bearer' and 'Mali, the Gardener'. Balaram, also known as Baladeva, Balabhadra and Halayudha, may have originated in the Vedic times as a deity of agriculture and fertility. Narratives of Balarama are found in the Mahabharata, Harivamsha Purana, Bhagavata Purana and other Puranas. He is considered an avatar of Aadishesh in Dwapara Yuga, as Lakshman in Tretayuga and as Patanjali (original practitioner who wrote the first book on Yoga Shastra and writer of Mahabhashya to Panini's grammar) in Kaliyuga.

Balarama

Balarama is the elder brother of Krishna (an avatar of God Vishnu). He spent his childhood as a cow herder with his brother Krishna. He was born under the Shravana nakshatra on Shravana Purnima or Raksha Bandhan. At birth, Krishna had a darker complexion, while Balarama was born fair. According to *Bhagavata Purana (10.8.12)*, "Because Balarama, the son of Rohini, increases the transcendental bliss of others, His name is Rama and because of His extraordinary strength, He is called Baladeva. He attracts the Yadus to follow His instructions and therefore His name is Sankarshana".

Balarama is known for his strength. He killed an asura Dhenuka as well as the wrestlers Pralamba and Mushtika sent by Kansa. After the death of evil king Kansa, Balarama and Krishna went to the ashrama of sage Sandipani at Ujjayini for study. Balarama taught both Duryodhana of the Kauravas and Bhima of the Pandavas the art of fighting with a mace. He often wears blue garments and a garland of forest flowers. He is often depicted with a drinking cup, pitcher, shield and sword. His weapons are the plough (hala) and the mace (gada).

42. Rudra (Randhra)

According to the Sanskrit–English dictionary, 'Rudra' means, God Shiva, abbreviated name for the texts or hymns addressed to Rudra, horrible, rumbling, howling, crying, roaring, terrible, dreadful, water or tears, lord of tears, violent, kind of stringed instrument, eleventh or number Eleven (11). Samaranganasutradhara (14.29) identifies Rudra as 'Maheshwar'.

Rudra is the personification of vital breaths, which came from Brahma's forehead, of which there were eleven. The name Rudra reflects Shiva's fearsome aspect. According to Yajurveda, God Rudra-Shiva has two contrary sets of attributes. He is malignant or terrific (Rudra) as well as benign or auspicious (Shiva). Terrific part rules the north-west while benign part rules the north-east. Rudra is father of the eleven Marutas or Rudras and a militant god of storms and lightening. Intelligent and benevolent, he protects people from their enemies. He was worshipped for happiness, his saving help and not to disturb the cattle in the cow pans. In His fierce aspects, he is often depicted slaying the demons.

The epithet Rudra originated from the verb root *rud* or *ru* and means howler, roarer, shouter, rumbler, violent or Lord of the tears. Rudra is name of the ancient Vedic divinity of the tempest. *Rudra* also means 'wild, of rudra nature', 'the wild one', 'the fierce god', or 'terrible'. Hara, another name of Shiva means, 'one who captivates', 'one who consolidates', 'one who destroys' and 'the ravisher'. Another of Shiva's fearsome forms is as Kaal 'time'

Vaastu Gods and Goddesses

and Mahakaal 'great time', which ultimately destroys all things. Hanuman is popularly known as 'Rudravtaar', the eleventh avatar of Rudra-Shiva. He is also called 'Pavanputra', the son of the God of air.

The *Vishnu Purana* narrates that Rudra – here identified with Shiva – was born from the anger of the creator-god Brahma. The furious Rudra was in *Ardhanari* form, half his body was male and the other half female. The male form then split itself into eleven, forming the eleven Rudras. Some of them were white and gentle, while others were dark and fierce. *Vamana Purana* describes Rudras as the sons of Kashyapa and Aditi. Marutas are described distinct from the Rudras as 49 sons of Diti.

Brahma allotted Rudras eleven positions of the heart and five sensory organs, the five organs of action and the mind. In the *Brihadaranyaka Upanishad*, the eleven Rudras are represented by the ten vital energies (*rudra-prana*) in the body and the eleventh one being the Atman (the soul). Rudra has the ability to bring medicines to the people to prolong their lives. *Chhandogya Upanishad* prescribes that Rudras be propitiated in case of sickness. They become the cause of tears on departing the body, the meaning of the name Rudra being the 'one who makes people cry'. The Brihadaranyaka Upanishad explicitly states the fact that since the Rudras leaving the body – causing death – makes people cry, they are Rudras. Rudra's relation with medicines makes it an auspicious place for doctor's clinic.

In Shrimadbhagvad Geeta (Chapter 10, verse 23), Shri Krishna while describing seventy-five of his common manifestations, declares, "Of the Rudras I am Shankara". Shiva (Lord of destruction) rules *ashtami tithi* (eighth lunar date), which is called 'dwindva' (one giving conflicts). He also rules *chaturdashi* tithi (fourteenth lunar date), which is called *ugra* (aggressive). Rudra is the lord of Ardra Nakshatra.

Rudra

Rudras are described as loyal friends and messengers. The *Shatapatha Brahmana* mentions that Rudra is the prince, while Rudras are his subjects. They are considered as attendants of Shiva in later mythology. According to the Rig Veda and Krishna Yajur Veda, Rudras are gods of the middle world situated between earth and heaven i.e., the atmosphere. So, Rudras represent life-breath as the wind-gods.

The *Mahabharata* describes Rudras as companions of Indra, servants of Shiva and his son Skanda and companions of Yama, who is surrounded by them. They have immense power, wear golden necklaces and are 'like lighting-illuminated clouds'. These qualities of Rudra can be utilised by a beauty parlour in this square or keeping the dressing table at home. The *Bhagavata Purana* prescribes the worship of Rudras to gain virile power.

43. Raajyakshma (Rudrajaya, Rudraraja, Rudraj, Rudradaas)

According to the Sanskrit–English dictionary, 'Rudraj' means, produced from rudra or quick silver. Samaranganasutradhara (14.29) identifies 'Raajyakshma' as, 'Guh or Karttikeya'. Guh or Guha is another name for the Hindu deity Karttikeya.

The Upanishadas constantly make a reference to a Supreme Being called Guh, the indweller. Guha means the resident of the 'cave of the heart'. According to the Hindu Philosophy, it means that the ultimate truth or reality is God. He is ever present in the hearts of all the living beings and is also cause of the life force. It is said that he never hesitates to come to the aid of a devotee when called upon. Guh is accessible to all who worship and love him, regardless of their birth or heritage. Guh appears in the 'Ramayana' as a boatsman. He assists Lord Rama to cross the river during Rama's exile to the forests and is revered for his high-standing honourable qualities.

Karttikeya or Kumar is the Hindu god of war and the planet Mars. He is the Commander-in-Chief of the army of devas. Before Karttikeya, Indra and Agni were considered to be the gods of battles. Karttikeya is the only single-minded defender of the gods than any of his predecessors. He is interested in nothing but battles and warlike adventures. One of the major Puranas, the *Skanda Purana* is dedicated to him. In Shrimadbhagvad Geeta (Chapter 10, Verse 24), Krishna, while explaining his omnipresence, names the most perfect being, mortal or divine, in each of the several categories. While doing so, he says: "Among military generals, I am Skanda, the lord of war."

The *Atharvaveda* calls Kumar as *Agnibhu* because he is a form of Agni. Agni held him in his hands when Kumar was born. The *Shatapatha Brahmana* refers to him as the son of Rudra (Rudraj). He was first spotted and cared for by six women representing the Pleiades — Krittika in Sanskrit. He thus gets named Karttikeya. His other names include Kumaran (prince, child, young one), Svaminath (smart, clever), Dandapani (god with a club) and Skanda (attacker). The Chhandogya Upanishad refers to Skanda as 'the way that leads to wisdom'. Baudhayana's *Dharmasutra* calls Skanda *Mahasena* 'having a great army' and *Subramanya* 'beloved of Brahmins'.

According to the most popular version, Karttikeya is the eldest son of Shiva and Parvati. The birth of Karttikeya was very purposeful. He was born to fulfill the gods' mission of killing the tyrannous asura Taraka. Many of the major events in Murugan's life took place during his youth. So Murugan is also worshipped as a child-God in south India, very similar to the worship of Baal (child) Krishna in north India. Goddess Skandamata, with son Skanda or Karttikeya on her lap, is worshipped as fifth form of Navadurga. Each Tuesday of the Tamil month of Adi is also dedicated to the worship of Murugan. Tuesday in the Hindu tradition connotes Mangal, the god of wars and the planet Mars. Karttikeya is the lord of *shashthi* tithi (sixth lunar date), which is called *yash-prada* (one giving fame).

Karttikeya

Karttikeya is usually dressed simply in white clothes without any other embellishments, as befits an austere warrior. His symbols are based on the weapons. He is depicted wielding a *shakti* or spear, symbolising his purification of the human ills. His javelin symbolises his far reaching protection, his discus symbolises his knowledge of the truth, his mace represents his strength and his bow shows his ability to defeat all the ills. His peacock mount symbolises his destruction of the ego.

He is reputed to be not interested in women. During His bachelorhood, Lord Murugan is also regarded as Kumaraswami (Bachelor God), *Kumara* meaning a bachelor and *Swami* meaning God. His youth, beauty and bravery are much celebrated in the Sanskrit works like the Kathasaritsagara. As a young lad, he destroyed Tarakasur. The temples dedicated to Him in the towns of Pehowa in Haryana and Panchavati region of Nasik in Maharashtra celebrate the *Brahmachari* form of Karttikeya. Women are not allowed anywhere close to these temples.

His six heads represent the six *siddhis* bestowed upon yogis over the course of their spiritual development. This corresponds to his role as the *bestower of siddhis*. As described above, Karttikeya is interested in warlike adventures. So, in ancient India, he was also regarded as the patron deity of thieves, as may be inferred from the *Mrichchhkatikam*, a Sanskrit play by Shudraka and in the *Vetalapanchvimshati*, a medieval collection of tales.

44. Kshitidhar (Prithvidhar, Bhudhar, Mahidhara, Amitaujas)

According to the Sanskrit–English dictionary, 'Kshitidhar' or 'Bhudhar' means, dwelling in the earth, earth supporting, kind of chemical or medical apparatus, mountain, king, number seven (7), etc. Bhudhar is an allusion to mount Meru, a sacred mountain. According to the ancient Indian cosmological representation, it was situated at the centre of the universe and thus constituted the axis of the world. It was a dwelling, meeting and resting place for the gods. The pole star, situated directly above this mountain, is the *Sudrishti*, the divinity 'who never moves'.

Samaranganasutradhara (14.29) identifies Kshitidhar as, 'Ananta'. Ananta (endless) or *Shesha* (Sesha, the serpent) is also known as *Sheshanaga* or *Adishesha* (the first Sesha). He is the nagaraja or king of all the nagas and one of the primal beings of creation. Naga also means mountain or 'That which does not move'. 'Shesha' in Sanskrit texts, especially those relating to mathematical calculation, also implies the 'remainder' – that which remains when all else ceases to exist because when the world is destroyed at the end of the kalpa, Shesha remains as he is. It is said that when Adishesa uncoils, time moves forward and creation takes place and when he coils back, the universe ceases to exist.

In Shrimadbhagvad Geeta (Chapter 10, verse 29), Shri Krishna while describing seventy-five of his common manifestations, declares, 'anantashchasmi naganaam'. It means 'of the nagas, I am Ananta'. In the Puranas, Shesha is said to hold all the planets of the universe on his hoods and to constantly sing the glories of the god Vishnu from all his mouths. Vishnu is often depicted as resting on Shesha. Shesha is also considered a servant as well as a manifestation of Vishnu.

As per the Mahabharata (Adi Parva), Shesha was born to sage Kashyap and his wife Kadru. Kadru gave birth to a thousand snakes, of which Shesha was the eldest. Shesha, disgusted by the cruel acts of his mother and brothers, left his mother and kin and took to austere penances. Brahma, convinced of Shesha's will, asked Shesha to request a boon. Shesha asked that he be able to keep his mind under control so that he could continue to perform ascetic penances. Brahma gladly accepted the request and asked a favour of Shesha, that of to go beneath the unstable earth and stabilise it. Shesha agreed and went to the netherworld and stabilised her with his hood. He is known to support her even today, thus making Patala his perennial residence.

Lord Vishnu Resting on Shesha

Brahma

In the Bhagavata shesha is also named Sankarshana, the tamasic energy of Lord Narayana Himself and is said to live deep within the inner layers of patala, where Sankarshana is the ruler. He is said to live even before the creation of the universe and when the universe is towards its end he creates eleven Rudras from him to destroy the universe for a new one to be created. He also expands himself as *garbhodakshayi-vishnu* in the beginning of the universe to create Brahma. The city of Thiruvananthapuram is named after him as the 'City of Lord Ananta.'

45. Brahma (Sah, Ka, Braham-man, Vidhi, Asana, Brahmasana)

According to the Sanskrit–English dictionary, 'Brahma' means, God, creator of the world, hymns, vedas, scholar of four vedas, main priest in a sacrifice, wealth, edible, etc.

Samaranganasutradhara (14.13) identifies Brahma as, 'Lotus-born, lord of all the worlds, thousand-headed, achintaya-vibhava'.

Brahma is the god of creation in Hinduism. He is different from the genderless Brahman, the Supreme Being in the Hindu philosophy of Vedanta. According to the Puranas, Brahma is self-born in the lotus flower. According to the *Bhagavata Purana*, Brahma was born through a lotus growing from Vishnu's navel. Brahma is often identified with Prajapati, a Rigvedic deity. He is the 'Director of the sky', the 'Master of the horizons' and the 'One' amongst the diversity.

In the Ramayana and the Mahabharata, he is often referred to as the progenitor or great grandsire of all the human beings. According to the *Brahma Purana*, he is the father of Manu, from whom all human beings are descended. Brahma's wife is Saraswati, also known by names such as Saavitri and Gayatri. As the husband of Saraswati or *Vagdevi* (goddess of the vach, 'speech'), Brahma is also known as *Vagish* (Lord of Speech).

The golden face of Brahma indicates that He is actively involved in the process of creating the Universe. He is clad in red clothes. Brahma uses the swan as his vahana (carrier or vehicle). Swan is the symbol of grace and discernment. Brahma's crown indicates His supreme authority. The lotus symbolises nature, and the living essence of all things and beings in the Universe. Brahma's black or white beard denotes wisdom and the eternal process of creation. Brahma holds no weapons. One of his hands holds a scepter, while the other holds a book symbolising knowledge. Brahma also holds a string of prayer beads called the 'akshmala' (literally 'garland of eyes'), which He uses to keep track of the Universe's time.

Brahma is traditionally depicted with four heads, four faces and four arms. With each head, He continually recites one of the four Vedas. There is a story of a fifth head of Brahma. This head came when Shatrupa started flying away from him upwards and the head came on top of the four heads – symbolising lust and ego. This head was decapitated by Lord Shiva returning Brahma to his four-head avatar which gave birth to the four Vedas. The fifth head stayed with Shiva hence Shiva got the name Kampala.

Humans cannot afford to lose the blessings of Brahma and Sarasvati, without whom the populace would lack creativity and knowledge to solve mankind's woes. Within Vedic and Puranic scripture, Brahma is described as interfering in the affairs of the other devas (gods) only occasionally and even more rarely in the mortal affairs. Lord Brahma is reverentially addressed as Pitamaha (great ancestor, grandfather or first father) by devas, demons and humans. Since Brahma is also a Prajapati, all these people used to visit him and Brahma used to teach the Vedas and importance of virtue to these people.

Lord Brahma is also called as Vidhi, Dhata and Vidhata. Vidhi means the Ordainer. Vidhata means disposer, ordainer, arranger or law-maker. Vidhata also means the governor of nature's Laws relating to the journey of the soul. He is also known as Twashta and Viswadeva. Lord Brahma is not only the creator as mentioned in the Purusha Sukta, but also the decider of the destiny or fate of the beings that are going to be born. Brahma is the lord of Rohini and Abhijeet Nakshatras and *dwitiya* tithi (second lunar date), which is called *mangal-prada* (one giving auspicious events).

Chapter 3
Principles of Business Vaastu

काममय एवायं पुरुष इति
स यथाकामो भवति तत्क्रतुर्भवति।
यत्क्रतुर्भवति तत्कर्म कुरुते
यत्कर्म कुरुते तदभिसंपद्यते।।

Human being is the desire personified (sum total of his desires). As are his desires, so is his determination. As is his determination, so are his deeds. As are his deeds, so is his destiny.

Brihadaranyakopanishada, 4.4.5

Residential Versus Business Vaastu

The principles of residential and commercial vaastu are not always the same. Rather, most of the common principles of business vaastu are completely opposite of the residential vaastu. All types of activities – *rajasic, tamasic* and *satvik* are performed at home. If cooking is rajasic and sleeping is tamasic then, offering prayers is satvik. On the contrary, commercial vaastu shastra is the area that mainly utilises the *rajas* energies of nature or the combination of rajas and *sattva*. There is nearly no place for *tamas* in business. Tamas represents lethargy, sleepiness, inactivity and postponing tendency.

The main goals of residential vaastu are peace and privacy. Requirements of business vaastu are very different. Stores and corporate office buildings are included in the commercial buildings. Commercial Vaastu needs no privacy. What it needs is an active and energetic environment, which is full of customers. Attracting maximum number of customers means attracting maximum success. Calm and quite areas are ideal for residential vaastu while busy areas are suitable for business vaastu. 'Business' literally means 'busy-ness'.

Go mukhi plots (cow faced i.e., front width lesser than the depth) are considered good for the residential purposes while *Sher rmukhi* plots (lion faced i.e. front width larger than the depth) are considered good for the business purposes. Residences are fitted with comparatively smaller doors, opening inside. Inside opening doors are in complete control of the house dwellers. Inhabitants can open or shut the door from inside according to their own sweet will. In any residence, only the chosen one are allowed to enter the inside premises.

Principles of Business Vaastu

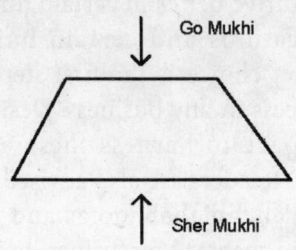

Fig 3.1: Sher Mukhi Vs Go Mukhi Plot (Wrong Perception)

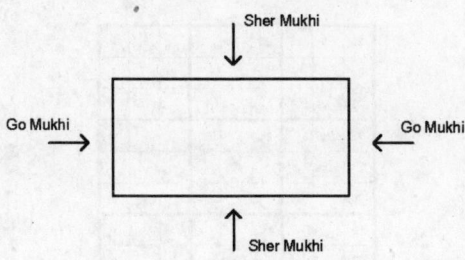

Fig 3.2 (a): Sher Mukhi Vs Go Mukhi Plot (Right Perception)

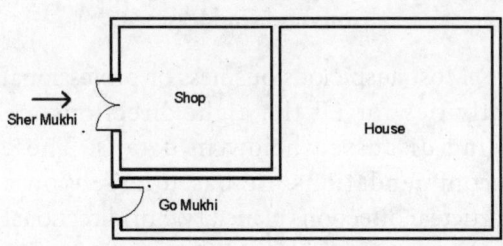

Fig 3.2 (b): Sher Mukhi Vs Go Mukhi Plot (Right Perception)

On the contrary, business premises are fitted with larger and bigger doors, opening outwards or upwards like shutters. There is little or no control of the entry from the inside. Bigger and transparent doors attract more and more customers by advertising the products. Transparent door projects an image of fair dealing. A business door is never locked from inside. It is open to public at large, though sometimes; minor restrictions are imposed to allow only the genuine customers.

Astrologically, residence is seen from the fourth *bhava* (house) of horoscope. It corresponds with the cardinal North direction in the North Indian system of horoscope casting. North, being a cool direction, is ideal for residence in the North Indian plains.

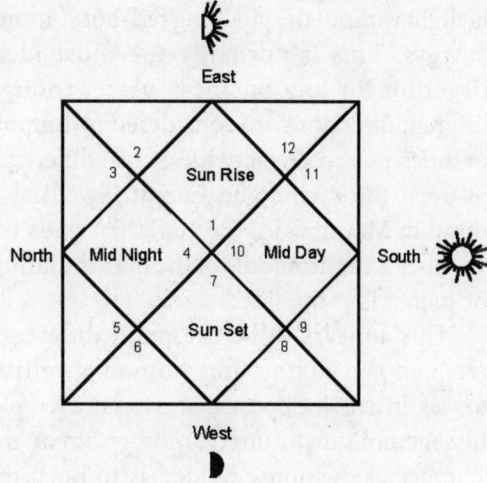

Fig 3.3 (a): Horoscope and Directions

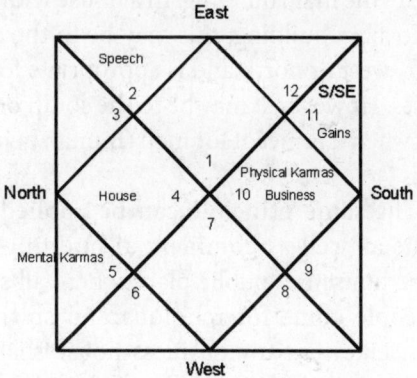

Fig 3.3 (b): Horoscope and our Karmas

Business, source of earning, vocations and physical activities are considered from the tenth house of horoscope, which corresponds with the south direction. South, being a hot and lighted direction, is ideal for the business activities. Eleventh bhava, corresponding with the south of south-east, is considered the bhava related to gains and fulfilment of desires. Second bhava is called *dhan-sthan* i.e., place of money. Eleventh bhava, being the second bhava from the tenth, represents business's money. This is the best place for earning money through business.

South of south-east receives maximum daylight without the pinching red-hot summer sunrays. This is normally the most ideal direction for any business place, though different directions are considered favourable for different business activities. Clear difference between the divine and human dwelling is found in Mayamatam (26.16a); 'For gods the chamber is in the middle of the main building, for men it is at the side'.

This appears to be the main difference between the divine and human dwelling houses. In a divine house that is to say a temple, the sanctum sanctorum (*garbha-griha*) or 'the chamber of the house holder' is to be at the centre while in human houses that chamber is always placed off-centre, in one of the side parts of the main building. In a house with one single main building, this may be to the east, south, west or north and is appropriate for all classes. However, it may be to the south or the west when it is meant for men (human beings) only.

The same principle can be applied for public as well as commercial buildings. A divine house is a public place where all sorts of people come for religious and spiritual gains. Likewise, any business house shall be constructed in the middle of the plot and its main door shall be in the middle of the façade. Heart of any business activity or the public place shall generally be visible to the prospective customers or the visitors.

Directions and Corresponding Business Activities

Vaastu shastra admits that different directions are rich in different energies. Certain types of businesses thrive better in certain directions, certain locations and certain buildings. Their correct choice is the first step on the path to success in any business. Design your business space to harness these energies accordingly. Readers are also advised to refer the topic 'Panchmahabhootas and Related Businesses' in chapter 1 for further short listing a particular business. Eight sectors based on eight directions and their corresponding demi-gods are shown in the figure.

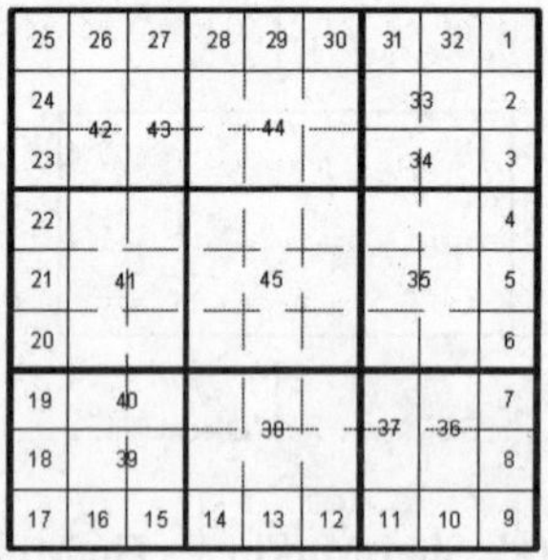

Fig 3.4: Eight Sectors in Vaastu with their Demi-Gods and Goddesses

Most auspicious business or professional activities for all the eight directions are being discussed below in details. These recommendations are based largely on a particular direction's planetary lord, directional lord, occupying demi-gods, its energies and its elements.

1. North direction

Planetary lord: Mercury (*Budha, Saumya*)

Directional lord: *Kubera*

Demi Gods: *Bhallata, Soma,* Giri, *Kshitidhara*

Energy: Sattvic rajas (of air)

Element(s): Air and Water

Professional and commercial activities: Mercury governs places of trade and commerce (stock exchanges, malls, swap meets, etc.), places of communication (publishing houses, photocopy stores, press rooms, conference rooms, post offices, etc.), places of learning and knowledge (schools, colleges, libraries, bookstores, etc.), places of short distance travel (local airports, bus & train stations, etc.).

North direction is related to work with language & speech (public speakers, speech writers, speech therapists, linguists, etymologists, etc.), work with education (teachers, educators, etc.), work with business & merchandise (economists, marketing, networking, commerce, trade, merchants, importers, etc.), work with communication systems (internet, computers, phone industry, etc.), work with writing & publishing (journalists, editors, writers, publishers, etc.), work with numbers (mathematicians, accountants, data entry operators, etc.), work with performing (storytellers, actors / actresses, entertainers, etc.), astrologers, astronomers, athletes, yoga teachers, etc.

Businesses governed by Mercury are communications, objects used for speaking or communicating (telephones, microphones, speakers, etc.), telecommunications, aviation, printing & publishing industry, media, FMGC, IT, internet services, insurance, computer, software, electronic media, objects that store information (books, computers, tapes, CD's, etc.), objects of trade or commerce (money, currency, wallets), shops of clothes and dress materials, mobile shops, books & stationary shops, institutes imparting academic education, agricultural production and related business activities, vegetable shops, guest houses and *dharma-shalas* (charitable places of stay), businesses related to escalators and lifts, businesses related to trees and plants; lawns and parks, gardens and orchards, playgrounds, stadiums where non-violent games are played, libraries and reading rooms, exhibition grounds, recreation rooms, amusement parks, dormitories, drawing & painting exhibitions, large store houses of grains and pulses, halls & *pandals*, new or youthful objects, green objects, commission agents, consultation chambers of astrologers and palmists, home offices, offices of CAs; architects and lawyers, etc.

Business activities related to Kubera are banking & money-lending, finance, money exchanging, gold loan & other loan related activities, businesses of precious stones and metals, etc .

In a hospital or clinic, north is related to the departments of skin, speech therapy, ENT, nervous system, respiratory system (lungs, nose, throat, etc.), frontal brain, hips, intestines, etc.

2. *Ishana* (North-east) direction

Planetary lord: Jupiter (*Guru*)

Directional lord: *Ish*

Demi Gods: *Ish, Parjanya, Jayanta, Aditi, Diti, Aap, Aapvatsa*

Energy: Sattva

Element(s): Water

Professional and commercial activities: Objects related to Jupiter are the sacred or pure objects (holy water, *puja* or worship utensils, etc.), objects storing spiritual knowledge (books, CD's of scriptures, sacred texts), objects storing legal information (books, CD's of law books, legal documents of law, etc.), valuable objects representing wealth (treasures, gems, family heirlooms, bank account statements, status symbols, etc.), gold coloured objects, etc.

Businesses related to the north-east are water purification, storage, packing & supply, meditation centres & shrines, yoga & spiritual study centres, healing centres, storage of Ayurvedic medicines and lifesaving drugs, sweet herbs, storage of high quality wines and liquors, judiciary and legislation, arbitration chambers, preaching, religious institutions, places of worship, shops selling religious books and materials, shops of fruits and dry fruits, businesses of fatty but pure foods such as butter; ghee; olive oil and cream, business of sweet foods like sugarcane; dates; honey and sweets, departments of philosophy, psychology and management in an educational institution, money lending, planning department, humanitarian and charitable organisations, treasury, place for *hawan* and recitation of mantras, dwellings of sages and aristocratic people, residences of teachers; preachers; judges and religious leaders, worship room in an organisation, Banking and Finance (PSU Banks), insurance and investment, FMGC, textile, garments, gold, bronze, edible oils, jewellers, etc.

Other professions and works related to Jupiter are the dignified jobs, professions with degrees, gurus, teachers, scholars, business administrators, philanthropists, psychologists, counsellors, advisors, consultants, priests, ministers, healers, astrologers, travel industry, etc. Jupiter also governs work related to the prestigious and dignified places, financial institutions (banks, treasuries, vaults), charitable institutions, institutions of higher learning (universities), places of religious rites and ceremony (monasteries, temples, altars, sacred fire pits), places of long distance travel (international airports).

All the activities related to *Ketu* are also permitted in the north-east. Ketu – the secondary planetary ruler of north-east – signifies the monks, nuns, scholars, linguists, foreign languages, philosophers, doctors especially of alternative medicines, healers, priests, shamans, magicians, software programmers, religious / occult organisations, astrologers, secret occupations – spies, thieves, terrorists, etc.

In a hospital or clinic, Jupiter rules the liver, gall bladder, spleen, phlegm, fatty tissues, blood circulation, etc. Ketu governs the pineal gland and pituitary gland.

3. East direction

Planetary lord: Sun

Directional lord: *Indra*

Demi Gods: *Mahendra, Aditya, Satya, Aryama*

Energy: Sattvic rajas (of fire)

Element(s): Water and fire

Professional and commercial activities: Political party office, activities of authority and leadership, governmental institutions (palaces), governmental or administrative positions (politicians, diplomats, ambassadors, etc.), multinational organisations, business tycoons, managers, organisational ability, planning the future, authoritative and decisive actions, taking charge, dynamic and expressive actions, using conscious will, public sector / activity.

Professions and activities related to the mountainous regions, and forests, temples (places of worship), fire (especially sacred fire), swimming pools and public baths, hot sunny open places (deserts, sea beaches for taking sunbath, etc.), banking industry (bankers, financiers), atomic energy, power sector, PSU units, stock exchanges and stock brokers, wheat, honey, gold, goldsmiths, copper, bronze, and precious stones.

Professional activities related to medicines, physicists, body trainers, physical therapists, athletes, general health & vitality, medical field (doctors, physicians, optometrists, pharmacists, chiropractors, etc.), trees in general, wood, wool, stones, red objects, hot objects, teachers, creative self-expression, following one's vision, film makers and artists, performers (actors / actresses, entertainers, etc.), drama, etc.

In a hospital or clinic, Sun governs the departments of heart, head, bones, stomach, and eyes, etc.

4. *Aagneya* (South-east) direction

Planetary lord: Venus

Directional lord: *Agni*

Demi Gods: *Bhrisha, Antariksha, Agni, Pusha, Vitatha, Savitra, Saavitra*

Energy: Rajas (of fire)

Element(s): Fire

Professional and commercial activities: Women organisations, industries working in the field of light and energy, antique shops, food processing industries, coffee shops, FMGC, entertainment, banking and finance, media, sugar, hotels, insurance, investment companies, paints and paint industries, travel and tourism. Venus rules the places of art and beauty (flower gardens, art galleries, scenic natural areas, and beauty salons, etc.), comfortable places, places of sexual pleasure (bed rooms, couches, brothels, etc.), shopping malls, places of amusement and entertainment (dance halls, theatres, symphony halls, night clubs, etc.), elegant and refined places, extravagant and posh places, restaurants, etc.

Objects and substances connected with Venus are adornments (stitched / designer garments, jewellery, perfumes, cosmetics, essential oils, etc.), reproductive fluids, valuable possessions (gems, money, treasures, etc.), artistic objects (paintings, sculptures, poetry books, musical instruments, etc.), and fine luxury vehicles, etc. Venus governs the activities like connecting socially and / or romantically, buying and selling valuables, social manners, festivities, parties, etc.

Other professions related to Venus are the work in design (graphic, fashion, interior decorators, software, etc.), fine and visual artists of all kinds (singers, musicians, artists, potters, photographers, poets, writers, actors / actresses, dancers, etc.), entertainers of all kinds, models, sexual work (prostitutes), work in beautification (aestheticians, hair dressers, makeup artists, etc.), work with flowers (florists), work with adornments (clothes, jewellery, cosmetics, textiles), work with food and sweets (cooks, bakers, candy makers, etc.), work with restaurants or hotels, massage therapists, botanists etc.

Activities governed by the directional lord Agni and fire element are offices in general, fancy lights, electrical equipments and gadgets, electrical shops, office of cooking gas supply company, utensil shops, grocery shops, oil mills, mega kitchens, restaurants serving freshly cooked food, bakeries, industries requiring medium amount of heat, etc..

In a hospital or clinic, Venus governs the reproductive system (uterus, genitals, seminal fluid, etc.), pelvis, urinary system (bladder, kidneys), chin, cheeks, etc.

5. South direction

Planetary lord: Mars

Directional lord: *Yama*

Demi Gods: *Grihakshata, Yama, Gandharva, Vivasvan*

Energy: Rajasic tamas (of fire)

Element(s): Fire and earth

Professional and commercial activities: Industries using heat and / or metals on a large scale, heavy automobiles, weapons, explosives, poisons, acids and harsh chemicals, cement, iron and steel, capital goods, pharmaceuticals, infrastructure, medical and surgical equipments, health care, railways, petro-products, military personnel, policeman, martial artists, uniformed jobs, competitive businessmen, scientists, engineers etc.

Mars governs work with fire (fire-fighters, welders, industrial jobs), places for violent actions (military installations, slaughter-houses, butcher shops, battlefields, etc.), athletes, places of violent athletic games (archery, karate, free style boxing and wrestling rings, football stadiums, etc.), courageous actions using strength and will, violent and aggressive actions (litigations, arguments, combats, competitions, etc.), impulsive and rash actions, taking risks, striking and cutting actions, etc..

South is also fit for work with tools (surgeons, mechanics, technicians, handymen, construction workers, machine operators, heavy equipment operators, etc.), management & administrative positions, politicians, places near fire, places using tools (machine shops, mechanic shops, etc.), physical activity, property / buildings, metal objects, sharp objects, cutting objects, red objects, copper, gram etc. South, the direction of Yama, can also be used for all the activities related to the last rites of a dead person.

In a hospital or a clinic, Mars governs departments related to the treatment of muscles, bone marrow, head, gall bladder, blood, arms, chest, sexual organs, etc.

6. *Nairritya* (South-west) direction

Planetary lord: *Rahu*

Directional lord: *Nirriti*

Demi Gods: *Bhringraja, Mriga, Pitrigana, Dauvarika, Sugreeva, Indra, Jaya*

Energy: Tamas

Element(s): Earth

Professional and commercial activities: Actions related to Rahu are the materialistic pursuits, pioneering new territory, immigrating to the foreign country, travelling, going on adventures, hunting, invasions, addictions (alcoholism, drug abuse, etc.), illegal actions (terrorism, murder, stealing, cheating, gambling, etc.), cruel actions (rioting, assault, litigation, punishment, harsh speech, lying, etc.), separating actions (abandonment, exile, divorce, etc.), changing religion or spiritual paths, hallucinations etc.

Objects and substances related to Rahu are poisons, toxic substances, lead, hazardous chemicals, technology of mass communication (computers, internet, radio etc).

Industries manufacturing poisonous drugs and chemicals, leather industries, stone sculptures, seasoning of wood and stone, wood work, ivory work, mortuary and items required for performing the last rites, places of rest such as night shelters, etc. are good in the south-west. Professions related to Rahu are computer engineering, scientists, inventors, explorers, magicians, travel industry, foreign service, foreign languages, politicians, secret occupations (spies, undercover agents, thieves, terrorists) etc.

Rahu governs diseases which are difficult to diagnose, and chronic ailments. Places governed by Rahu are the space, cremation grounds, barren places, and underground places (graveyards, tombs, and tunnels, etc).

7. West direction

Planetary lord: Saturn

Directional lord: *Varuna*

Demi Gods: *Pushpadant, Varuna, Asura, Mitra*

Energy: Rajasic tamas (of air)

Element(s): Earth and air

Professional and commercial activities: West direction is an ideal place for laboratories, research institutes, offices of detective agencies, petroleum and mining industries, eating plazas, antique shops, leather and leather made items, realty, crude, coal, cement, iron and steel, lead, infrastructure, mining, oil and gas, and heavy metals.

The actions related to Saturn are working hard, being responsible and disciplined, austere actions, cold, bitter & ruthless actions (cruelty, bondage, torture), negative actions, self-destructive actions (drug addictions, overwork, self-mutilation, etc.), laziness, humiliation, disorganisation, procrastination, illegal actions, imprisonment, and gambling etc.

Objects and substances connected with Saturn are anything old or dirty, ashes, structures, agriculture or agricultural tools, toxic chemicals etc. Saturn governs dark or dirty places (sewers, gutters, ruins, slums and ghettos), lowly places, garbage dumps, subterranean places (basements, mines, graves, archaeological digs, etc.), cemeteries, places of isolation (prisons, monasteries, hermitages, retreats, etc.).

Professions related to Saturn are manual labour jobs, tedious repetitive work, humble professions, servants, agricultural jobs, industrial jobs, work with the elderly and death (hospice care, coroners, morticians, funeral homes, etc.), underground work (miners, excavators, archaeologists, etc.), work with building structures (construction workers, carpenters, masons, architects, plumbers, etc.), work with suffering (relief & aid, humanitarian work, psychologists, crisis and trauma centres, etc.), and illegal work (thieves, gamblers, drug dealers, etc.).

Parts of the body governed by Saturn are structural support systems (skeletal system, bones, teeth, etc.), knees, calves, legs, feet, lymphatic system, and rectum, etc.

8. *Vaayavya* (North-west) direction

Planetary lord: Moon

Directional lord: *Vayu*

Demi Gods: Shosh, Papayakshama, Jvara, Naag, Mukhya, Rudra, Rudraj

Energy: Rajas (air)

Element(s): Air

Professional and commercial activities: Audio and music parlours, beauty culture saloons, pet animals, car showrooms, vehicle service centres, air-conditioning and air-cooling, oils and gas, petroleum, salt, white objects, helping professions in general (nurses, healers, etc.), activities requiring dependence, vulnerability and support etc.

North-west is best for work related to the fluids (water, purified water, mineral water, milk and its products, cold drinks, wine, alcohol, distilleries, blood, tears, essential oils, soft chemicals, chemists, etc.), work with the sea (shipping, sailors, fishermen, sea products), work with hospitality (hotels, B&B's, etc.), work with females, work with the birthing process (conception, fertility clinics, delivery room doctors, midwives), work with the early childhood (pre-school teachers, nannies, etc.), work with the cold objects and cold snowy places.

Other activities are the work with food consumption (cooks, bakers, chefs, waiters, caterers, etc.), work within homes (housewives, home decorators, house cleaners, cottage industries etc.), work with the mind (psychologists & therapists esp. family therapists, hypno-therapists, PLR), work with the general happiness & peace of mind, work with charities (non-profits, humanitarian, aid & relief work, etc.), work with the plants (herbalist, agriculturist, vegetables, farming & esp. livestock, landscaping, gardening, etc.), work with the dairy industry, gems & jewellery, fashion & clothing, travel industry, any place near water (beaches, rivers, lakes, etc.), items of comfort (silks, soft cushions, etc.), silver, jewels etc.

Moon governs hospitals and healing centres in general. It rules the bodily fluids & secretions (blood, urine, saliva, etc.), lymphatic system, breasts, lungs, stomach, brain, face, and left eye etc.

Location of Business

The maxim, 'Location is everything' applies equally to residential and commercial vaastu. The location plays an important role in the success or failure of any business. The location can make or mar a business. Best urban planners make separate provision for residential and business premises. When you are searching for your future business premises, reconnaissance survey of such area would be very helpful. Take a slow walk on foot around this area and you will be able to know if it is thriving or not. You will also be familiar with the type and expanse of activities going on there.

Market research plays a vital role in the success of many businesses. The organisation setting up the business must be sure that the area really needs the service(s) it intends to offer. It would be impractical to setup a business or open a shop offering services or products which the area does not need. A little initial research may prevent big problems later.

The most important criterion for a good location is visibility. A favourably located business becomes its own form of advertising. Busy traffic is beneficial for business buildings. People passing the business see it repeatedly. They consciously or sub- consciously remember the business's name, though they may not enter it. They may enter the business in future. On the contrary, few people walk past a poorly located business. It means few people will enter the business or remember it. It will be worthwhile to mention here that Pragati Maidan, New Delhi's exhibition grounds - has most of the entry points in the south and west directions. Both side roads are full of traffic throughout the day. Sunlight is available till late evening hours. No doubt, it attracts million of people every year.

The business should be easily accessible. Keep all the possible communication channels of your business open. Roads, rivers, railways, website, Facebook, and telephone are very effective modes of communication. Nature of the business, number of customers and many other factors decide the choice of an effective access system. For instance, an organisation using technology as its main communication channels will not be much dependent on road or rail links. For example, success of a stock exchange entirely depends on efficient communication channels.

People working in an office also want easy access and proper parking. The office need not be the busiest and noisiest part of the town. A quieter location may be perfect. In an inappropriate workplace, the workers might find their work extremely stressful. They may suffer from continual headaches. There is a 'psychology of spaces'. It means particular places are suitable for particular persons. The right choice of a working place leads to an easier, happier and more successful life.

A business situated on busy highway should have proper parking facilities for visitors and deliveries. If parking in the business is restricted, the prana will become stuck. A garden, park or a large open space in front of the main entrance of your business accumulates prana. This prana gathers potency before entering the premises. It helps in making your business prosperous. Retail stores should be located where many people pass by.

The business should be visible from the road. Busy intersections are the perfect places for the retailers to set up their businesses. Sufficient space shall be reserved for horizontal and vertical expansion in future. Factories are best in an industrial area. Large trucks can easily make pickups and deliveries in the open locations. There are also fewer problems with noise, waste and traffic.

In the walled city area of old Delhi, many specialist retailers are known for their extremely good quality services for many generations. They are located in the side streets, narrow passages, bazaars, *kuchas* and *chhattas*. Their customers travel hundreds of kilometres to see them. Their businesses flourish because of their products, workmanship and fair dealing. They can locate themselves almost anywhere and can be successful. However, a businessman trying to establish a completely new business needs an open but busy location.

It is said that fortune of locations run in cycles. Vaastu does not recommend a business area; which is full of darkness, where vegetation does not thrive, and where there are many abandoned or vandalised buildings. A business location shall be full of rajas energy of solar heat, natural light, meandering water and freely moving fresh air. A favourable location fosters auspicious prana. Customers are the prana of any business.

A corner location is ideal for business. Corners attract traffic from different directions. This spot is continually recharged by fresh, strong beneficial energy. A business located near a subway entrance is also auspicious. The great rajas energy created by public transit benefits the business.

Consider the flow of roads and traffic moving around the business place. They indicate flow of prana in the vicinity. Several roads leading obliquely towards the business are considered good. These roads must have a gentle downward slope towards the business premises. The lucky prana, the customers, is channelled towards the business in this way. Too steep a slope makes the prana move too faster. As a result, it becomes inauspicious. .

Businesses facing a roundabout are example of good vaastu. The traffic brings circulating prana flowing towards the building. The effect gives positive results when several roads are connected to the roundabout. One of the greatest examples of such business places is Connaught Place, which is situated in the heart of New Delhi. Many radial roads connect it will different parts of Delhi.

Businesses exactly at the T-junction are bad. The incoming traffic travelling straight towards them poses a great threat. It is called *marga vedha* or *veethi shool* (road arrow). The oncoming street acts like a sharp arrow for the business. In the beginning, your business may get benefits of the increased exposure to the passing people. However, marga vedha is a disaster waiting to happen. Eventually, it will damage your business in the long run. A marga vedha heading directly towards your main entrance gives extremely bad results. In such a case, change the placement of your store's entrance so that it no longer faces a path directly.

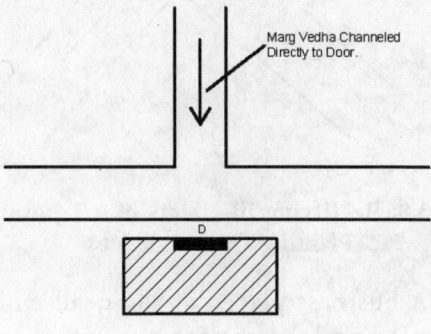

Fig 3.5: Business at T - Junction

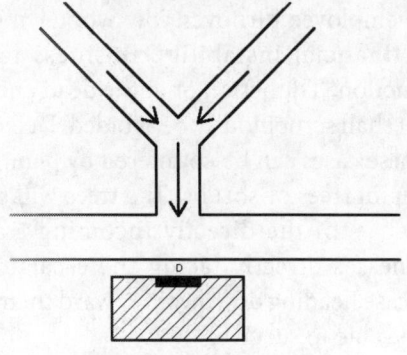

Fig 3.6: Business at Y - Junction

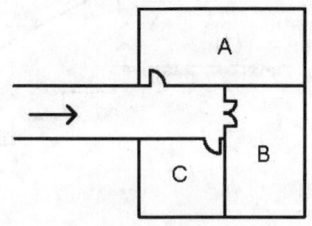

Fig 3.7: Business A, B and C at Dead End

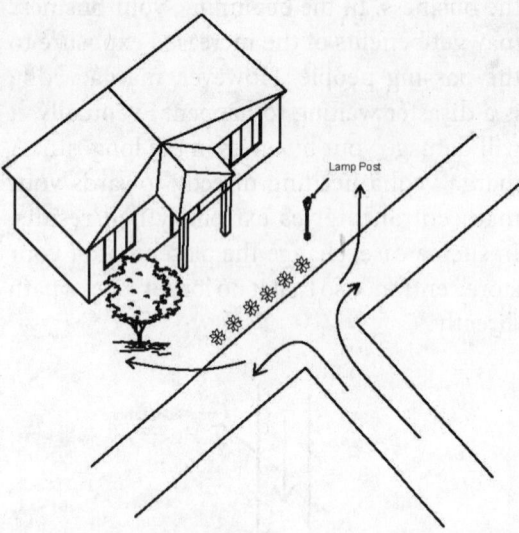

Fig 3.8: Rectifying ill-effects of a T-point by Planting Trees or Shrubs

A business placed at the dead end of a street or a long passage also suffers from veethi shool. Such a site traps poisonous energies. These stagnant energies lead to high employee turnover, low worker morale and financial instability. Business facing Y-junction, T-junction or at the dead end of a street shall scrupulously be avoided. Defects in all these cases can be countered by planting a clump of trees or shrubs. The trees will block off views of the directly incoming traffic. Businesses directly facing the escalator or staircase heading downward toward them will not be able to survive.

Flyovers and bridges are inauspicious business locations. Flyovers are serious threat to a business. They act like sharp knives. It is better to leave this place, if so possible. Bridges encourage pranic energy to travel rapidly. This fast moving traffic energy finds hard to slow down. Businesses located next to or under a bridge will die from a lack of prana. Businesses in subways also face many difficulties. Heavy traffic all around a business premises creates oppressive energy weakening it.

Any religious building, like temple, mosque, *gurudwara*, church or synagogue, creates a strong spiritual energy. This can overtake the active prana needed to nourish the business. The sattvic spiritual energy of a religious building is not in harmony with the rajasic energy of a commercial building.

Commercial Building

The building we inhabit is part of a wider environment. This environment has a great effect on how we operate within it. The location, surroundings and shape of the building has a great impact on us and our clients. It can make us feel comfortable or uncomfortable. If you have freedom to choose a site to build on, choose it as per the principles of vaastu. Design it according to your own birth element. Ideally, your personal element shall be in harmony with the element of building you work in. Arrange this site according to the landscape and surrounding buildings. There should be

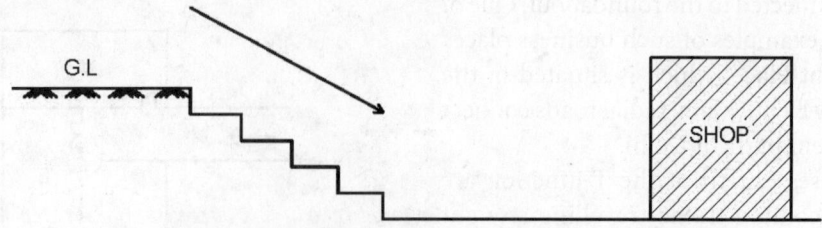

Fig 3.9: Staircase Heading Downward Towards the Business

more open space towards the front side. High rise buildings and narrow lanes are preferred towards the backside. Create a proper balance of rajas and tamas energies.

A business location should be properly supported. The back of your building should be heavy. Your building's back should preferably have hills, higher land, high structures or heavy trees. This strong backing will support you and your business. A strong backing makes you feel safe, secure and confident. Your work or business suffers if you are working in a high-rise building with no solid backing. Taller buildings or a hillock in the rear protect your back. Buildings on either side of your workplace are also considered good. Standing inside your premises and facing its main entrance, the building to your left should be higher than the building to your right. The inactive left side needs greater protection. Trees, walls or fences can also effectively support the lower buildings. A workplace, hemmed in by larger and taller buildings, is most inauspicious.

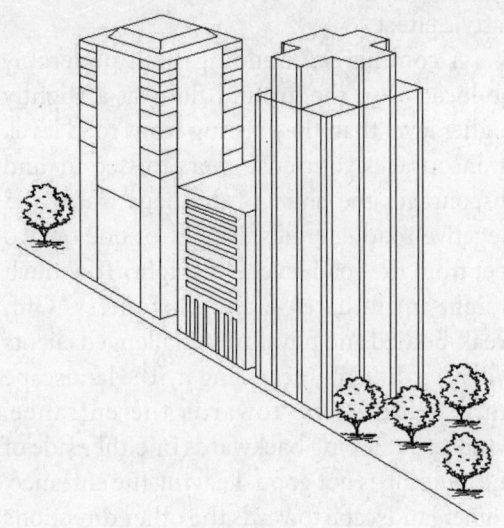

Fig 3.11: Building Not in Harmony

No building can be assessed as an independent entity. Your commercial building must fit in with the other surrounding buildings. Sky-scrapers, because of their overpowering sizes, can destroy the positive vaastu of neighbouring buildings. They must be designed to blend in with the surrounding landscape and structures.

High rise buildings or hills, towards the front side of your business, deprive you of good luck. Your venture is likely to stagnate. It will hardly move ahead. Ideally, the front should have a glimpse of a garden, park, wide road, gently flowing water, harbour or a beach. An artificial pond, fountain or stream can also be very useful as they signify abundance. Meandering water is preferable than water flowing in a straight line. Straight lines create shoolas (arrows / spikes). Make sure that any water channel, path or walkway also meanders. The natural movement in this world is curved, not linear. Traffic engineers design curved roads in all the three dimensions to break the monotony of drivers. Jumping or flowing water is better than the stagnant water. Stagnant water needs time bound cleaning and

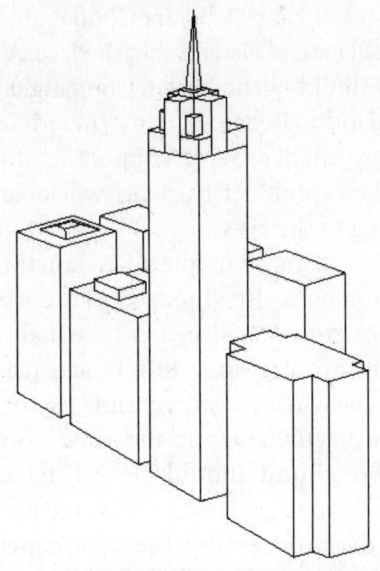

Fig 3.10: An Unprotected Building

replacement. Gently flowing water creates a sattvic effect.

A commercial building shall preferably be located on the ground floor at a slightly higher level than the existing front road level. It encourages your customers to step in, and discourages the entry of drainage water and negative road energies. Height of one or two feet from the road level is all right. Too much height intimidates many customers. Old, weak-bodied and physically challenged clients will have difficulty accessing it. The landscape must gently slope towards the entrance. Landscape sloping backwards or either side of the building is not good. Leaving the entrance, higher landscape towards the other directions gives safety, security and stability to your business.

Study the traffic directions. Examine the shapes, s, heights and dimensions of neighbouring buildings. Search for any auspicious features such as rivers, waterways and hills. Businesses gently embraced by roads with slow moving traffic are examples of good vaastu. Round-edged neighbouring buildings are more sociable than square-edged buildings.

Try to read the energy patterns of the building you wish to purchase. For instance, a business won't thrive in a building that has had a fire in the past. Look at for vedhas (poison arrows), obstacles and inauspicious positions. Investigate the past history of the business premises before committing yourself to it. Try to know the fortunes, successes and failures of its previous occupants. If they were in a similar line of business and were running in loss, it poses a serious warning. Building and its environment can be one of the possible causes of business failure.

Corners of adjacent or opposing buildings, glare from buildings fitted with float glass and dish antennas, flag poles or decorative features pointing at the office – all these can create shoolas (arrows). They appear to attack us like poisoned arrows. When a certain building is subjected to a shoola, all the offices situated within the entire building are adversely affected, though in varying degree. Normally, the deeper or higher up the building one goes, the more the negative effect diminishes.

Sharp corners and severe rooflines create trouble to the neighbouring people. Avoid them. The ideal of vaastu is, 'live and let live'. Balance the building with the already existing buildings. It is considered bad vaastu to work in a building that is much larger or smaller than its neighbouring ones. The twin towers of New York, much larger and higher than the surroundings buildings, repeatedly invited terrorist attacks. A high rise single building may however be considered good as a historical or monumental building like Qutub Minar in Delhi. Such single buildings are also prone to suffer badly under thunderbolt or earthquake.

A single high rise building in an area is not good for doing business successfully. Other high-rise buildings shall support it. This trend can be seen in the busy commercial areas of modern metropolitan cities. Some striking examples in New Delhi are Connaught Place, Nehru Place and Netaji Subhash Place. A single NDMC building, highest in Connaught Place, looked odd. Recently constructed second building shall provide support to the first one. Their combined existence will look much soothing to the eyes.

Apply the principle of balance to the road frontages also. The face width of all the adjacent stores shall nearly be equal. Equal sizes ensure harmony in a block. It is also applicable when you are running two or more than two activities from the same store. The neighbourhood should be well balanced. Wide open spaces, lawns, parks, and greenery attract the *pranic* energy. The tamasic greenery, combined with the rajasic building, creates a sattvic effect. Open drainage pipes on the outside of a building are not good. These are likely to drain away company's good fortune.

Business plot as well as its construction shall preferably be of regular shapes eg square, rectangular, circular, and octagonal. These shapes are economical, long lasting and user friendly. Irregular shapes eg triangular, cross, T, Y, etc are considered bad. Make your plot a regular one before starting the construction. The building should be aesthetically pleasing. An upward soaring arrow shape building denotes growth.

Top heavy buildings, like the building of Science Academy, at ITO, New Delhi denote imbalance. Ill planned commercial buildings of varying sizes, shapes and forms create an imbalance. Neutralise the ill effects of this kind of landscape by generous planting of trees. The swaying leaves and branches of the trees will dissipate the imbalance.

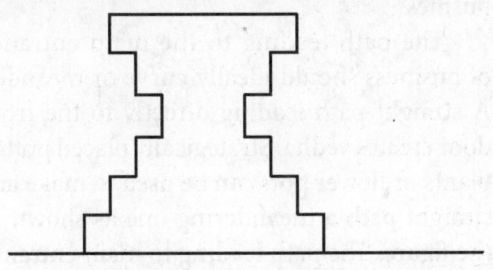

Fig 3.12: Indian National Science Academy Building at ITO, New Delhi

To attract customers, improve the environmental landscape of your business place. Include nature in your working area. Try to create a small garden around the business, if possible. Stunning foliage has a good impression on the workers and customers alike. Plant some bamboos, *ashoka* trees, palms, evergreens or flowers around the building. A bamboo signifies rapid growth. Auspicious plants generate comfortable feelings. They attract heavenly pranic energy to the business. The result is - increased number of customers and increased income.

Green area around the business premises acts as a barrier between the office and the busy highway. A well-maintained moving water feature provides a vibrant energy for any organisation. Create a spring pool in front of the building to beautify the landscape around it. A very large fountain in the central park of Connaught Place, New Delhi had a very positive effect on hundreds of commercial premises in this area. Before the construction of underground metro station, it played a great role in attracting pranic energy and wealth to this area.

Water, after oxygen rich air, is the richest asset of all the living beings on the mother earth. Water symbolises money. The main aim of a business is to earn money. So, if you want to earn money, have water near the business. Flowing water facing the main entrance is considered good. Owner is able to take advantage of the business opportunities. Water flowing behind your building is not so good. The owner won't be able to take advantages of financial opportunities. Slow moving or meandering water is considered better. One must be able to see as much of water as possible while sitting in the building.

A well maintained water pool in front of the building, not only beautifies the business environment, but also helps in accumulating the prana and consequently boosting the business. A very good example of such a business environment is the Pragati Maidan, the exhibition grounds of New Delhi. This area, having clear water lakes with water springs, lush green lawns and beautifully dressed auspicious trees, attracts millions of visitors every year.

Mark the boundary of your business to separate it from the other properties. If you have open space around your business, this area will become an attractive recreation place for the staff during their breaks and visitors alike. The boundary can be in the form of a low wall, a fence or a sign carrying the company name. Railings are far better than a solid wall, if a tall barrier is must for security reasons. A solid wall restricts view from the building, whereas railings allow the same. Railings enable your customers to see in, as well as offer security against break-ins.

The base of building should be solid or should look so. If a building is built on stilts, there is a strong likelihood that the occupants will experience a lack of foundation and a lack of money. Parking directly under the commercial building is considered bad in vaastu shastra. The energies emitted by the automobiles will gradually weaken your business.

Most of the people are not lucky enough to design or choose their own workplace. The principles of vaastu shastra help to create more pleasant and enjoyable working environment. For instance, try to sit with your back towards a solid wall while working. It makes you feel confident. Complete glass walls are inauspicious. Money trickles away easily through them. Curtain or blinds on the large windows can be used to adjust the amount of light. .

Main Entrance

The overall look of the main entrance of any business is always important. It may be a retail establishment with many visitors or a factory where rarely any customer visits. The front entrance of any business is like human face while main door is the mouth. We want maximum positive prana to enter our business's mouth.

Different businesses want to attract different type of customers. Many businesses limit the entry of people. For instance, a wholesaler may not allow the general public inside. Some businesses see people by appointment only. Retailers want to attract as many people inside as possible. Irrespective of your customer choice, your main door needs to be properly looked after. It will encourage positive prana and your customers inside.

When customers visit your place of business, the actual building and its surrounding environment create the first impression. The entrance should have a lovely view. Create a pleasing environment in the immediate front of the main entrance. Lawns and gardens outside your business place need proper care. They should look attractive. Auspicious trees and plants, bushes, creepers and flowers create prana, which can benefit your business. Small trees can be very helpful in protecting your business from any vedha coming from any neighbouring business. A fountain, pond, cascade or waterfall in front of your business's main entrance creates positive prana. A well maintained water source stimulates prosperity and success of your business.

The path leading to the main entrance of business should ideally curve or meander. A straight path leading directly to the front door creates vedha. Strategically placed potted plants or flower pots can be used to make any straight path a meandering one as shown in the figure. The path leading to main entrance should be kept neat and clean.

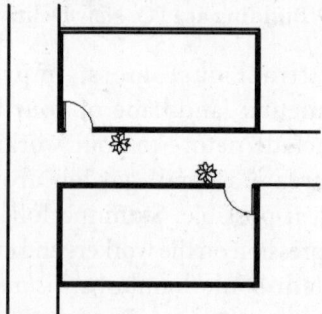

Fig 3.13: Vedha-Free Entrance

The entrance door is considered a business's mouth from the traditional Indian perspective. It is the most important place for prana to enter your retail store, restaurant or other business. The main door of a human being is his mouth through which he eats, drinks and receives most of the nutrients required for the body. Main entrance sets the tone for any business company. Main entrance helps to hold auspicious energy within a building while blocking the entrance of negative energy. It must keep the stale energy out, and allow the fresh energy in. The entrance should look inviting.

The front door projects the outer appearance of a business. A front door, designed in accordance with the principles of Vaastu Shastra, attracts customers and hence wealth. Customers are the real prana of any business. A clearly marked, clean, bright and welcoming front door will also create a positive atmosphere for the people working there. On the contrary, a dark and scruffy area indicates a failing company to the clients. It also depletes the energy of employees. What the people see each day is important.

The main entry of a business shall generally be larger than a residential main door. When a store and a house are of same size, the main door of a store shall proportionally be larger. Privacy is the main consideration for a residence and the right of admission is reserved. On the other side, for a business, the more the customers visiting the store, the better. Convenience of movement is thus the prime consideration in designing the main entrance of any business.

An effective main entrance should be in proportion to the business. Too small doors constrict the amount of entering prana, creating a stagnant environment. Eventually, it will make the business starve to death. On the contrary, too large an entrance allows prana to seep out of the business premises causing loss of profitability. The business itself will eat up all the profits. Practically, too large an opening is difficult to guard properly, inviting thefts and article lifting.

In case of double doors, keep both the doors open. A closed door creates a dark and stale area behind it. It restricts the flow of prana in the building. Revolving doors are auspicious for business buildings. They help to circulate pranic energy at the entrance and constantly supply refreshed prana to the interior. They do not cause vedha to the neighbouring business and are also excellent for deflecting any vedha that may be hurting the main door. However, these are only suited to large office buildings. For attracting good luck, a business's entrance should not be smaller than that of the neighbouring businesses. If a business's entrance is smaller, it can be increased with the help of an awning, which extends the entrance into the sidewalk.

The main door of your business shall preferably face an auspicious direction. The rules, which govern the positioning of commercial buildings, are very much different to residential buildings. The luckiest direction for any business is the south-east followed by south and east. South of south-east governs the wealth. The sun radiates with its full strength in the south and it becomes the direction of great activity. However, if you have the liberty to design your company's office building, the main entrance shall suit your horoscope or that of your head's. An entrance gives auspicious results, when facing any of the favourable directions of the owner or company's chief executive.

Your business will progress rapidly if you check out the main entrances of potential places of business before purchasing the land / constructed premises. Certain directions give auspicious results for certain businesses. These have already been discussed at length in this chapter. Chosen direction will be the luckiest direction of your business's front door. For instance, if your business is related to the fire element used for preparing eatables, the entrance is best in the south-east or south of south-east. But when fire is used for pure industrial processes using fire on a large scale, south direction is best. An air element business, for instance automobile workshop and air-conditioning, might get an extra boost from the north-west facing door. Use the vaastu guidelines on general positioning of the main entrance if yours is a rented office space within a building.

Locate the entrance of your business to the left side and exit on the right, when seen from the inside of your premises. When seen from the outside, the main door will be towards right of the entering customers. The main entry will be easily visible to the customer as most of the people are right handed. Side parking area or underground parking may lead customers to a side entrance rather than the main one. This is a good provision if your visitors have no problems in finding the lobby after entering the side door.

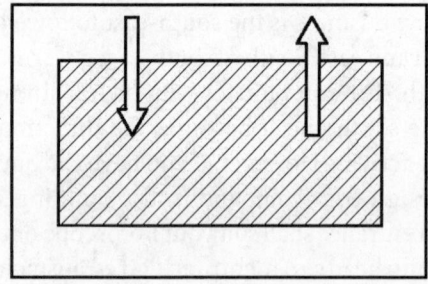

It is very auspicious to place an entrance on a store's left and exit to the right

Fig 3.14: Ideal Entry and Exit Points

This auspicious location allows prana to enter the space, circulate the premises and leave when it gets tired. Customers are the prana of any business. Many shopkeepers in North India paste a sticker near their cash counter with the writing '*grahak mera bhagwan*' which means 'customer is our God'. For different theories of location of main door, readers are advised to refer my book 'Unfolding the Veil of Mystery Vaastu the Art & Science of Living'.

The main entrance should be well lit and easily detectable. The front door of a store may be transparent. People will be able to know the products being sold in the store. This is the best way to advertise your products. It also gives an impression of fair dealing. This trend is becoming very popular among fast food restaurants, shopping malls, multinational banks and retail stores. A translucent or opaque glass of main entrance arouses confusion and suspicion in the customer's mind about your business. The customer will most likely walk away from your store due to lack of proper information.

The colour of main entrance shall be in harmony with your business. For instance, to make the entrance of a restaurant inviting to the potential diners, orange-red colour is a good choice. It is the colour of fire and ripe fruits. Fire element is associated with the food industry. Ripe fruits are the ideal food of saintly people. Coloured glass entrance door creates a wonderful energy. It gives impression of a successful company.

The entrance door should be impressive. It should be designed carefully in proportion to the building and its surroundings. The traditional Indian entrance prefers guardians on either side. A pair of stone or metal lions or elephants symbolically protects the main entrance of a business building. They also promote good luck. Lions or elephants symbolise power and security. Bronze lion idols are best to guard the main entrance of an established bank. An idol or replica of Lord *Ganesha* is equally good. He is the guardian deity, remover of obstacles and bestower of wisdom.

Keep a pair of green plants or potted flower plants on both sides of the door. The entrance space should be kept clear of any uncollected mail or other clutter to let the positive energies flow smoothly inside. Make someone responsible for regular maintenance of this area. Positive environment encourages the staff. They feel good as they arrive and leave every day.

An open and clear walkway attracts customers. Waste bins near the entrance are bad. Deliveries should be put away immediately after their arrival. The main door should not open directly onto a toilet. Doors within an office should be staggered so as to allow pranic energy 'to meander'.

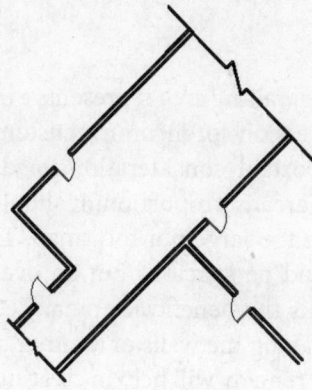

Fig 3.15: Staggered Arrangement of Doors

The main door should not directly face another door. Two or more doors in a straight line cause prana to move too swiftly through the office. Back door or open windows directly opposite the main door are not good. They encourage the vital energy to fly out swiftly. In such a situation, place one or two plants between the two. Ideally, the prana shall circulate smoothly around the building.

Doors should open easily. They should not be too heavy or they will deplete your personal energy. There should be no vedha attacking the main entrance of your business. Any obstacle placed across an entrance is believed to hamper the smooth passage of prana.

Roof lines of neighbouring buildings, sharp angles, trees or poles in front of the main door may be a vedha. Trees symbolise growth. However, they are negative when located directly opposite to an entrance. It is called 'Vriksha Vedha' or a cutting arrow sent by a tree. They block the prana trying to enter your store or restaurant. A tree, taller than a business and when its branches are draping down onto the business roof, is especially inauspicious. It symbolises overweight on one's shoulders. This situation is believed to lead the business to financial difficulties. The smaller the tree, the lesser the ill effects it has.

A street lamp post, a telephone pole, or a pointed corner of another building directly opposite the main entrance to a store also has a tree like effect. It can block the propitious prana from entering your business premises. Avoid them. A toilet or garbage bin outside the store, directly lined up with the front door, is bad vaastu. They represent tamas and have a dampening effect on the rajas business activities. Sewer pipes flowing through the main entrance or beneath the business are considered bad. Dirty water drains flowing in front of your store may lead to financial trouble. Cover them properly. The toilet should not be located directly above the front door when there is a residence above the commercial store.

A utility box placed in front of or against a business also creates vedha (obstruction). Large electricity boxes situated against the neighbouring buildings are not good. Such boxes control large amount of electromagnetic energy, which can impair the smooth flow of prana in the business. The bigger the box, and the closer it is to a business premises, the worse its impact.

Elevators, escalators or staircases directly facing the main entrance are not good. The luck treads upwards. The person entering the business won't stay at ground floor and will prefer to go upwards. Elevators and staircases are better when located at an angle to the main entrance. Main door at the end of a long corridor is inauspicious. This acts like a marga vedha (cutting arrow sent by a straight path).

It sends harmful energies directly into your office. Your business may get hurt badly. In a restaurant business, the front entrance should not directly face the kitchen. This Rahu-Mars combination may invite fire hazards. Standing in the doorway, customers shall not be able to see the kitchen.

If main entrance of your business faces another business's main entrance, the two doors shall be in perfect alignment. Slight misalignment may result in frequent quarrelling with your neighbour.

Correct the vedha, which you can. For example, you can make a straight path look gently curving. Any vedha ceases to exist for you if you are unable to see it or hear the unwanted sound. You can eliminate the problems caused by a visible vedha by using a hedge, screen or a row of plants. A vedha-free main entrance is better than an entrance facing an auspicious direction but threatened by vedha. Sometimes, entrances are set at an angle to the road to ensure favourable direction to the business's owner.

The front door of any commercial activity shall open outside or in upward direction like rolling shutters. This arrangement provides larger open areas in the front. There is no privacy required in the public oriented business premises as required in the residential premises. Doors are controlled from inside in the houses, while from outside in the businesses.

A business may have two doors – one in the front and one in the back. Front door is meant for doing the business while back door is meant for stock replenishment and garbage removal. The back door shall never be in direct line with the main door. Otherwise the wealth entering the premises will immediately be lost through the back door. It is called air draught in the architectural language. When facing such a problem, the simple remedy is to put up a screen so that the back door is not visible from the main entrance.

Location of main and other doors in business premises shall be decided by following the classical recommendations. Mayamatam (16.50) clarifies that there is no error placing the door of a building meant for gods, brahmins or kings in the middle of the façade. It means religious (gods), public (kings), and educational (brahmins) buildings may have door in the middle of the façade. Being a public activity, the same principle also holds true for all the business premises.

Lobby

A lobby or waiting area represents a business's 'first impression' for incoming customers. The most important consideration for designing a waiting area is proportion. It should ideally be neither too large nor too small. The lobby area should be spacious but an overly large lobby leaks the beneficial prana. Keep a row of plants along the walls of a rather big lobby area. This remedy will help in creating a cosier and smaller-seeming space. Too small a lobby creates a claustrophobic environment. In such a situation, a strategically placed large mirror can make it appear symbolically twice its actual size. . However, mirrors shall not directly face the entrance. The walls, perpendicular to the entrance door, are best for this purpose.

Common sense is another criterion for designing the lobby area. A smaller waiting area is required in a buffet restaurant where people are constantly up and moving around. On the contrary, a family-style sit-down restaurant, where several parties may be waiting for the availability of a table, will naturally require larger waiting area.

The entrance lobby should be well lit so that it appears spacious. Poor lighting causes prana to stagnate or die. The lobby shall appear welcoming. If the lobby is dark or gloomy, increase the amount of light to encourage more prana inside. Customers are the prana of any business. If the entrance area is more welcoming, there are more chances of customers entering the business. The lobby accumulates positive prana before sending it around the building. This positive prana also prevents negative pranic energy from coming in. If there is a receptionist stationed in the lobby area, he or she should not directly face the main entrance. Otherwise, it can prove intimidating to the incoming visitors. A wall divider in the lobby can effectively conceal the inside office.

Lobby area gives your visitors the first information about your business. The design of lobby, colour scheme, arrangement of light and sound, furniture and furnishings, plants and flowerpots and water features – all give information to your prospective clients. According to psychologists, we human beings are vulnerable to receive information all the time subconsciously without realizing it consciously. A dim lighted gloomy lobby gives a negative impression than a bright, spacious and well-lit lobby. Foul-smelling dingy surroundings distract your prospective customers. No one likes to visit a place having a depressing effect.

Different businesses need different methods of attracting customers. A petrol pump shall be able to project an impression of purity, quality and right quantity of fuel to the customers as they drive in. An industry shall convey the impression of activity and success and so on.

Reception

Some large corporations occupy an entire building but most of the companies own or rent one or more floors / part of floor area(s) of existing office building. Your office may or may not have a separate reception area, but here we will assume that you are setting up a reception area in a separate space. A separate reception area plays a vital role in creating a beneficial environment of any company.

If a business occupies an entire floor of an office building it must have an enclosed reception area, from where no elevator, staircase or lift is directly visible. If the entire floor is an open plan, every time a person comes to your floor, vaastu of the area is disturbed. When the lift stops at the floor, everyone in the office will turn to see who has arrived. The visitors will also become self-conscious and gradually their number will diminish. Continued distractions caused by the elevator can play a major role in the failure of this business.

A company's reception area is usually the first place that the incoming prana (visitors) encounters. The flow of prana is very important in the reception area. A scrupulously clean, well-lit and properly ventilated reception area, free from clutter and fussy decorating details, entice good prana to stick around. The employees should be able to move quickly through to their working areas using staircases or lifts. It is an area where your temporary staff can come in and sit in comfort while they are waiting to see you. Make sure that the reception area looks fresh and welcoming and gives a good impression of your business.

Ideally reception area should be spacious. Poor lighting kills the benefic prana. If it looks cramped, try using mirrors as they give the feeling of space. However, mirrors should not be directly opposite the entrance, as they are believed to reflect back the prana through the door. A screen placed opposite the door will force prana entering the office to meander and encourages it to enter the rest of the premises in a slow motion.

The receptionist should be well groomed and normally look pleasant to see the visitors. After all, he or she has to monitor the coming or going of persons in the organisation. Visitors should be able to see the receptionist from the entrance. The receptionist's desk should not be too close or directly opposite the entrance.

Otherwise, the receptionist will get exhausted by the activity there. Receptionist should be out of the path of prana entering the office.

The receptionist should be in sight of the elevator area. Negative energy is generated when receptionist is unable to see the persons coming in and going out. Receptionist must sit with his or her back to a solid, strong, and tall wall. The wall acts like a supportive or protective mountain. He or she won't be startled from the behind. A strong backing makes one feel safe, secure and confident. A receptionist sitting in an open area should, at least, be backed with a screen.

Sofas or other seats shall not be directly opposite the main entrance while entering. A reception area, separate from the main office, creates a feeling of privacy and security for the office workers. It also shields them from the constant distraction of entrance doors and opening elevators. A cut off reception is also not good. Beams over the reception are considered bad due to their suppressive effect.

The reception area shall adequately be equipped. Choose a comparatively large and heavy reception desk, made of some auspicious hard wood, with deep drawers suitable for keeping your records. Install a personal computer and printer together with audio equipment. This can also be used for training on different software programs and for testing each of your prospective temporaries. The receptionist shall sit in a comfortable chair. A winged chair is fully adjustable for him or her. A well padded chair is ideal for sitting in for long periods of time as one expects to do.

As a receptionist you may keep a portrait of your loved one in one corner of the desk. It adds you a homely touch. Walls can be lined with flowery prints you have collected over a number of years. The reception desk shall always be kept uncluttered. Comfortable chairs for visitors, an upright chair for someone who cannot easily get out of a comfortable chair, a round tea or coffee table, drinking water, one or two appealing pictures on the walls - all add a welcoming touch to this area.

Telephone and intercom, book-shelf for keeping reference books and telephone directories, waste paper bin(s), tea / coffee making machine or a vending machine if other refreshment facilities are not available, newspapers and magazines of general interest, information about your organisation are other requirements of an ideal reception area. A computer possibly with a printer, a fax machine and a photocopier may also be required in some cases. All these gadgets are best in the south-east or north-west of the reception desk.

Arrange the furniture and other items depending on the size of the room and the person(s) using it. A clean, tidy, well furnished and attractively decorated reception room, with welcoming staff, provides the right image in the eyes of your visitors. The right image can be projected by pastel colours on the walls, a decent carpet on the floor and an efficient air-conditioning system.

A tropical fish tank, placed in the reception area in the cold directions, enhances the desired effect still further. Fishes symbolise wealth. Often nine fishes are considered auspicious in the tank. Tiny, darting fishes create rajas, the active energy useful in commercial companies. Larger and slow-moving species create a calm atmosphere, which can be useful in health practices. The aquarium should create a natural environment in miniature. It should be large enough to enable the fish to swim freely.

Plants symbolise growth. Reception area can be decorated with a vase of fresh flowers. Fan, plants and water features play a useful role in air circulation. A water feature outside the building can be reflected in the reception area by a strategically placed mirror. Stained glass doors in the reception area add interest. Each door can be recognised by a different design and colours.

Principles of Business Vaastu

Properly train the receptionist to put visitor's need before the employees. While receiving visitors, make them feel welcome and comfortable. First impression matters much. Welcome visitors are likely to make future customers. Prepare well in advance for dealing with the visitors. Show that you know your job well. A successful business relates to creating a good impression of yourself and of the organisation.

Offer your visitor at least the drinking water free of cost. You can also offer a cup of tea or coffee. Manually prepared tea of coffee is always better than made by a vending machine. Your visitor might have travelled long distance. Providing basic refreshment is the least you can do. Indian tradition considers guest like a god (*atithi devo bhava*). If you run your own office, it is up to you to decide how much you can afford to spend on entertaining your guests. Be selective and tough. Entertain the people who are likely to pay you back in terms of business in the future.

An ideal reception area is shown in the figure. A visitor entering the business premises finds a water feature with a fountain and decorative plants to the left. It lifts prana in the reception area. The reception desk is well designed. It is so positioned that the receptionist is in contact with both the employees and the visitors. Plants symbolise growth and help to keep the air fresh. They also help in reducing the ill effects of vedha caused by depressing corners and sharp cutting edges. A round table in the waiting area helps the energy to spin around quickly.

The visitors will not be kept waiting long. Company's logo directly opposite the entrance adds prestige to the reception area. Employees and visitors pass through this pleasant area on their way to the staircases or lifts. The delivery area is also located close to the lifts for convenience. It helps to keep the area clear.

Name of Your Business

The success of any business or retail premises is directly related with its name. Carefully evaluate your business's name. A name formed from an even numbers of alphabets / words is tamasic, while odd number of alphabets /

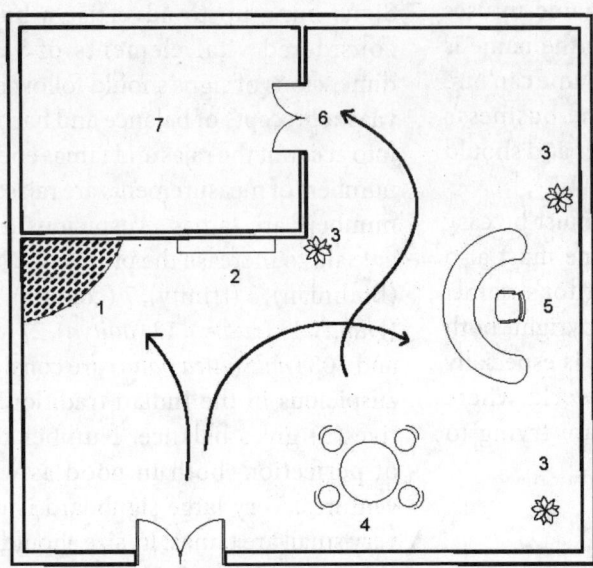

1. A water feature
2. The Company Logo
3. Plants
4. Visitor's seat
5. Reception Desk
6. Energized Passage
7. Delivery Area

Figure 3.16: An ideal reception

words is rajasic. Odd signs (*rashi*) are called the male and cruel signs in Vedic Astrology. These are considered very good for forward-looking attitude. In your car too, you have 1st, 3rd, and 5th gear – all odd ones in the forward direction.

Avoid any inauspicious, unethical, irreligious, anti-social or controversial words in your business's name. Positive words ensure positive consumer attention. Auspicious words attract the auspicious energies of nature. Any word related to death, destruction, illness or violence should resolutely be avoided. Such negative terms burden a business with their negative energies. In Vedic Astrology, eighth house of the horoscope signifies death, but, in the modern time, it is termed as house of longevity. Go for using a diplomatic positive language.

The business name should reflect the type of business and fair dealing. A name that does not conjure images of corresponding business confuses the public. It creates muddled prana. For instance, a shoe store's name should refer to shoes in some way. The business's name shall suit the taste of people. Choose a name that sounds attractive to as many people as possible. An often-mentioned business name infuses a business with prana each time the name is repeated. A frequently repeated name can lure customers to your business. The business's name and logo work well together and should be clearly visible.

The name of your business must be easy to remember. A memorable name must also be different from your competitor's name. Your identity and sanctity of copyright, both are maintained in this way. This is especially important in today's Internet world where thousands of similar websites are trying to attract the people.

Business Logo or Emblem

Many signs include the business's logo. It should be used with care. There are no hard and fast rules for choosing the shape of logo. However, some shapes are considered more auspicious than the others. Circular, square, rectangular, octagonal and other regular shapes are considered good. Images denoting upward energy are also good. Upward pointing arrows symbolise growth.

Appropriate animal symbolism can be auspicious. Most commonly used birds and animals by the Indian businessman in their logos are swan, peacock, parrot, partridge, cock, horse, tiger, elephant, bull, cow, camel, etc. Swan symbolises purity and fair dealing, horse represents power, tiger represent authority, elephant represents great strength, cow represent material wealth, peacock represents beauty and enjoyment, bull represents vitality and perseverance, and camel represents survival in the odd situations.

Don't portray unpleasant and sharp images on a logo. Avoid imbalanced, incomplete or inauspicious symbols. Leave crosses, points and arrows that point downwards. Use balanced colours only.

Signboards

Signs hung up to advertise a business are considered vital elements of vaastu. The dimensions of signs should follow the general vaastu precepts of balance and harmony. Take into account the rajas and tamas energies. Odd numbers of measurements are rajas while even numbers are tamas. Auspicious dimensions are said to increase the prosperity. Numbers 1 (Brahman), 3 (trinity), 7 (colours), 8 (*vasu*), 9 (*graha*), 11 (*rudra*), 12 (*aditya*), 27 (*nakshatra*) and 108 (*nakshatra pada*) are considered very auspicious in the Indian tradition. Numbers five (5) gives balance. Number ten (10) is of perfection, both in good as well as bad ventures. Very large signboard is rajas while very small are tamas. Its size should be sattvic, neither too large nor too small in relation to the size of the building to which it is attached.

Sign should be of a regular shape. Square, rectangular octagonal or round shapes are best. Discard triangular or other irregular shapes. Triangle symbolises fire. There will be constant danger of fire to your business. It will be even worse if triangular sign points downwards. It acts like a sharp vedha. It symbolises a dagger thrust on the head of your business. Triangular signs are best when used as traffic signals to alert the passengers. Write legible message in the sign. Use the language which can easily be understood by most of your prospective customers.

The sign should be pleasant to look at. Its alignment should be perfect and not tilted. It should not block the natural light or cast shadow on any door or window. An undesirable shadow brings in bad effect of Rahu, the shadowy planet. The sign should draw attention of the customers. Colours are very important. Analyze your element and the type of business to select the auspicious colour(s) for signs. Most successful combinations of colours for various elements are:

Fire: red, orange, yellow, bright and electrifying colours

Earth: green, and all the earth tones

Air: violet

Water: indigo, colourless or transparent like clear glass

Space: blue

Use your luckiest colour that is compatible to you and your business. Any other colour(s) should harmonise with this colour. For instance, if the proprietor is dealing in wood, then green and natural wooden colours would be good. Signs using odd number of colours are considered good. The preferred number of colours is 3 or 5. Number 3 is ruled by Jupiter and represents expansion. Number 5, ruled by Mercury, represent growth. A sign containing an even number of colours is not so effective in attracting customers. Balance the colours according to the five elements. In the solar spectrum, fifth colour from any colour is its inimical colour. The third colour from any colour is its helpful colour.

If owner is occupying the business premises, his personal colour should inevitably be represented. Colours can also be chosen according to the eight directions which the signboard could face. Colours related to the eight directions are given here:

North: green (Mercury), and black (Kuber)

North-east: blue (Jupiter / Shiva), and orange (Soma)

East: golden (Sun), and red (Indra)

South-east: indigo / white / pink (Venus), and orange (Agni)

South: red / yellow (Mars), and black or red (Yama)

South-west: smoky black (Rahu), and dark (Nirriti)

West: violet / black (Saturn), and greenish black (Varuna)

North-west: white / orange (Moon), and violet (Vaayu)

With the passage of time, some colours have now become strongly attached with certain businesses. For example, nurseries are associated with green colour. Green signifies growth and youthfulness. It is the colour of nature. Orange is frequently associated with the Indian fruit shops and the restaurants. It is the colour of naturally ripe food. It also signifies well-cooked food. Many jewellery stores use pink, silver white and golden colours. These colours are related with the precious as well as auspicious metals, i.e., silver, platinum and gold.

Vertical signs, which jut out into the street at right angles to the business building, are very eye catching. They are extremely useful for drawing people in. They are visible to every passer by without turning his or her head sideways. They are visible from a very far off distance too. These signs should be eye-catching and firmly attached to a wall or some other solid surface. Signs should be in proportion to the size of the building.

Lights attract pranic energy. Brightly coloured neon signs promote activity in the evening time. In the beginning, electricity was used in the static signs so that they were visible in the darkness. It remained in the 'on' position throughout. Later on, it was discovered that it is far more effective to put it on and off repeatedly. A man passing by will read the sign only once if the light remains static. If the light changes, goes on and off again and again, the person will have read it at least five to seven times by the time he passes it even in a running car. This repeated reading goes deeper in the subconscious mind. This subconscious mind, in future, directs the conscious mind to select the same product seen already. The person is going to purchase only your product in the near future.

Advertising your Goods and Services

Advertising can make the difference between success and failure in the present day's competitive markets. Many good businesses fail due to a lack of proper advertising. If no one knows about you, how can he do business with you? It is, therefore, very important to advertise your goods or services well in advance of starting up a new venture or business.

There are many modes of advertisement like newspapers, magazines, attractive contents, special reports, local radio broadcasts, cable TVs and TV channels, internet, Facebook, SMSs on the mobile phones, cinema halls, leaflet drops, cards in shop windows, bills, banners and letters to different companies or prospective clients / consumers. In short, try to use any lawful method that helps to spread the word about your new venture.

Write to all the companies you come across within the area which you are going to cover in the immediate future. Tell them about your new venture and ask to make an appointment to visit them. Mention very good opening rates to 'tempt' them away from their present agencies. To start with, advertise in the local papers. The most successful approach is to directly reach the companies and the prospective customers. Newspaper advertisements provide the necessary back up only.

The most important rule of advertising is, 'go on repeating, and go on advertising'. Repetition pays in the long run. Adolf Hitler in his autobiography 'Mein Kampf' has written, 'There is not much difference between truth and a lie. The only difference is that a truth is a lie repeated so often that you have forgotten that it is a lie'. That's what advertising experts recommend! Don't be worried, if people are not paying any attention to your advertisement.

People normally don't look at advertisements very consciously. They just pass through them in the movie on TV, in the newspaper or on the signboard. You go on repeating your advertisement. Just a glance of it makes an imprint in people's minds. This imprint is repeated again and again. Their subliminal minds are listening, their deepest core is being impressed, and that goes deeper. Sooner or later, they become impressed.

Extensive advertising compelled with good service and quality public dealing spell success for any business venture.

Wealth Management

Wealth is among a business's greatest concerns. A deep understanding and application of Vaastu principles will lead to increased inflow of wealth. Any business activity, that involves cash and profitability, gives best results when located in the south-east sector of the building. South-east is the money sector or wealth sector of any business.

Southeast receives maximum sunlight (see figure 1.3). Light represents life while darkness represents death. Light is divine. The words like 'day', 'divine', 'divinity', etc. have originated from the word 'div' which literally means, 'to shine' or 'light'. Gods are the luminous beings. All the right activities of our body, mind and speech are possible only in the presence of sattvik light. The light received in the south-east is sattvik – neither too hot nor too cold. South-east is the meeting point of cold and hot zones (see figure 1.4). Heat and light are the two main components of sunrays. South-east receives larger proportion of light but smaller proportion of heat in comparison to hot south and south-west.

Astrologically, south of south-east corresponds to the eleventh bhava (house) of horoscope in the North Indian system of horoscope casting. Eleventh bhava is called '*aaya-sthana*' or the house of gains, while tenth house is the house of physical activities (sharirik karmas). Tenth house, which corresponds to the south direction, receives maximum heat and light of Sun (see figure 3.3). Brisk physical activities are possible only during the mid day when sun shines with its full strength. Only right physical labour (tenth house) leads to fruitful gains (eleventh house). Auspicious deeds performed during the daytime only will earn Shubha Labha (righteous gains).

Venus - the planet of reproduction, charm and beauty - rules the south-east. Lakshmi, the goddess of wealth, is also the goddess of exceptional beauty. The directional lord of south-east is Agni. He is invoked in almost all the auspicious Hindu ceremonies. No auspicious activity is possible without his presence, i.e., without the presence of light and desirable heat. It is a common practice among devout Hindu people to fold their hands when a lamp is lighted or an electric light is switched on after the sunset. Light is considered equivalent to Lakshmi. In this way, people greeting light actually greet Lakshmi. Auspicious business activities, leading to great gains, are possible only in the presence of proper light which is neither too dim nor too bright.

Activities performed in clear light indicate money earned through fair means, while the activities performed in darkness indicate money earned through unfair means. Moreover, during the daytime, larger proportion of oxygen is available in the environment. Green plants, in the presence of sunlight, absorb carbon dioxide and let out oxygen. This process is called photosynthesis which gets reversed during the night. Plant leaves absorb oxygen and liberate carbon dioxide during night. Greater proportion of oxygen and sunlight during the daytime makes all the living beings active. Hence daytime is best for earning. On the contrary, nights are dark, comparatively cool and with larger proportion of carbon dioxide in the environment. Thus north, the cold and dark direction, is considered best for residential purposes.

The wealth of a business could be activated by introducing water into the area. Water symbolises money and prosperity. Money is said to flow like water. Lakshmi, the wealth goddess, was born from *ksheer-sagar* (sea of milk) churned for getting ambrosia of life. Milk here means pure water. She is standing on a lotus in the water. She is called *chanchala* (the fickle one), like water. To activate water, focus on its flow near your business premises.

Make sure that any auspicious water source e.g., river, pond, stream or beach is in full view of the main entrance. Water flowing past the back of your premises suggests missed opportunities. Water flowing past the front door should be in the auspicious direction. Water flowing in the north or east of your premises is considered to produce auspicious results. If you are running business from a mall, the flow of water relates to the whole building.

A fountain in the centre of a business area has a good influence on all the businesses located around it. For instance, a big inward flowing fountain in the Central Park of Connaught Place, New Delhi had a very positive influence on all the shops around it before the construction of underground metro station. The water feature for an independent single business can be in the form of an aquarium or a small revolving fountain. Live fishes symbolise steady growth while a revolving fountain represents continuous turnover. Fresh flowing water energises the workplace and brings prosperity.

Kuber

Kuber is also called a *Yaksha*, symbolising the stagnant money. Yakshas have been called protectors of the wealth, not enjoying the riches. A person hoarding money without using it or investing it further is like carrying its load on his head and shoulders. Kuber is depicted as mounted on a man in such form.

Kuber Mounted on a Man

Kuber as a *dikpala* also fortifies his role as the guard and protector of the riches. His idols on the outside of the ancient temples also reveal that he was widely accepted as the guardian deity of temple's wealth. Kautilya (Chanakya) has written that Kuber's idol shall be kept as protector of treasury. Kuber's money is black money, which is not used for any good purpose. His residence is said to be a banyan tree which are generally found outside the village. He represents a village moneylender; his money is all materialistic and solid.

Alakshmi: The Goddess of Misfortune

Alakshmi, the anti-thesis of Lakshmi, is the demi-goddess of misfortune. She is the embodiment of inactivity, lethargy and dullness. *Brahamvaivartta Purana* (1.8), and *Linga Purana* (2.67) describe her as the goddess of poverty;

'Alakshmi or misfortune grabs a lethargic person'.

Alakshmi

Her other name is *Jyestha*, the elder one. She is the elder sister of Lakshmi. During the churning of ksheersaagar (ocean of milk) by gods and demons, Alakshmi arose before Lakshmi. Alakshmi, as elder sister, means she is the first to rule us human beings. When Alakshmi arose from the ocean, neither the gods nor the asuras (demons) were willing to accept her. But a very courageous sage named Duhsaha (over-bearing) took her as his wife. It means that Alakshmi (i.e., inactivity and lethargy) can be courted by the extraordinarily active people only.

Her complexion is black. Black colour is considered an inauspicious, cold and tamasic colour in Indian tradition. It represents dark night and death. Alakshmi has two arms, representing her limited physical activity. In Hindu tradition, very active gods and goddesses are shown having four or more arms. Alakshmi wears iron ornaments. Iron is considered an inauspicious, cold and tamasic metal in the Indian tradition. Alakshmi has an ass as her vehicle. Ass is considered an inauspicious, inactive, dull and foolish animal.

Unwelcome developments take place in Alakshmi's presence – flowers and fruit laden trees suddenly wither, the trees become bare, lakes dry, standing crops in the field die and the milch cows become barren. Avoid things related with Alakshmi in your work environment. Dispel darkness and dullness. Become active and alert. In this way, we can invite Lakshmi in our life and business.

Lakshmi: The Wealth Goddess

According to the Sanatana Dharma (which is generally called the Hindu Religion), the ultimate aim of any human being is to be one with Narayana (Lord Vishnu). Lakshmi is the means to achieve this noble goal. She is the goddess of decency, fortune, wealth and prosperity. She is regarded as the goddess of exceptional charm, beauty and grace. Lakshmi bears a spotless character. She is the Shakti (active energy) of Vishnu. She is the model of constancy and wifely devotion. She often accompanies her husband, Lord Vishnu; the preserver.

The son of Vishnu and Lakshmi is Kama-deva, the god of love. Kama-deva literally means 'god of desires'. Lakshmi, the goddess of all the human virtues, is the mother or root cause of all the material desires. Lord Vishnu, representing the force of survival, maintains human life filled with justice and peace. This symbolism implies that wealth and prosperity is coupled with maintenance of life, justice, and peace. Survival needs action. Courage and constant efforts bring money. The result is – only active human beings are able to enjoy the company of Lakshmi. It is said that: 'Poverty is removed by work, sins are expunged by prayers, quarrels are avoided by keeping silence, and fears are dispelled by wakefulness'.

Lakshmi Sitting on Lotus

Lakshmi is the kindred mark or sign of auspicious fortune and prosperity in Rig Veda (x.71.2). In Atharva Veda, Lakshmi connotes an auspicious sign, good luck, good fortune, prosperity, success, and happiness. In the Epic Mahabharata, Lakshmi personifies wealth, riches, beauty, happiness, loveliness, grace, charm and splendour. She is a major goddess in the *Puranas* and *Itihasa* of Hinduism. In ancient scriptures of India, all women are declared to be the embodiments of Lakshmi.

The account of Lakshmi's birth is given in the great epic Ramayana. According to the Vishnu Purana, the universe was created when the *Devas* (good) and *Asuras* (evil) churned the cosmic ocean of milk (ksheera sagara). Lakshmi came out of the ocean bearing lotus, along with the divine cow *Kamadhenu, Varuni*, the heavenly tree *Parijat*, the *Apsaras*, the *Chandra* (the moon), and *Rishi Dhanvantari* holding the pot of *Amrita* (nectar of immortality). When she appeared, she chose to be with *Vishnu*. Importance of Shri is also found in *Shrimadbhagvad Geeta* (10.34), where Lord Krishna says, 'Of women I am *Kirti, Shri, Vak, Smriti, Medha, Dhriti* and *Kshama*'.

Lakshmi is generally equated with Sri – the goddess of decency, beauty and prosperity. In the following lines from the 'Vishnu Purana' (Indian Wisdom p. 499, Sir Monier Williams), Sri has been equated with Lakshmi:

'Then seated on a lotus,

Beauty's bright goddess, peerless Sri, arose,

Out of the waves; and with her robed in white,

Came forth Dhanvantari, the god's physician,

High in his hand he bore the cup of nectar

Life-giving draught – longed for by gods and demons'.

Sri (also spelled *Shri*, pronounced as shree), is commonly used as an honorific prefix or suffix in cultural discourse and human relationships in India. Affixed to the names of distinguished persons, the honorifics 'Shri' (also 'Sri,' 'Shree') and 'Shrimati' (also 'Srimati,' 'Shreemati') imply beauty, wealth, prosperity and auspiciousness.

Lakshmi is the embodiment of all the good human qualities. It is said that gods also took their gifts from her. Shatapatha Brahmana (xi. 4, 3) describes Sri as a goddess born with and personifying a diverse range of talents and powers. Sri was beautiful, resplendent and trembling woman at her birth with immense energy and powers. The gods then approach Lakshmi, Agni gets food from her, Soma gets kingly authority, Varuna gets imperial authority, *Mitra* acquires martial energy, *Indra* gets force, *Brihaspati* gets priestly authority, *Savitri* acquires dominion, *Pushan* gets splendour, *Saraswati* takes nourishment and *Tvashtri* gets forms.

Lakshmi is shown as a lady of bright golden colour with two or more arms, either sitting or standing on a lotus and typically carrying a lotus in one or two hands. She typically wears a red dress embroidered with golden threads, symbolism for beauty and wealth. In some representations, money pours out from one of her hands or she simply holds a jar of money. Money manifested through Lakshmi means both the material as well as spiritual wealth. Her face and open hands are in a *mudra* (gesture) that signifies compassion, giving, or *daana* (charity).

She is very closely associated with the lotus, and her many epithets are connected to the flower. The lotus, a flower that blossoms in clean or dirty water, also symbolises purity and beauty regardless of the good or bad circumstances in which it grows. It is a reminder that good and prosperity can bloom and not be affected by evil in one's surrounding. Her names include: *Padma, Kamala, Vishnupriya, Mohini, Aishwarya, Indira, Kalyani, Samruddhi, Sridevi, Tulasi, Kriyalakshmi, Gayatri, Aditi*, Smriti and Sri. She is also referred to as *Jaganmaatha* ('Mother of the Universe') in *Shri Mahalakshmi Ashtakam*.

Goddess Lakshmi is also called Rama and Chanchala. It means that she is temperamental and liable to desert anybody. She is called

Principles of Business Vaastu

Eight Forms of Lakshmi

Chanchala as her wealth is not stable. She is also called *Loka-mata* because she is a distributor of prosperity. Wealth related to Goddess Lakshmi comes with all its positivity (*shubh laabh*). She is bestowal of wealth. She doesn't hoard wealth like Kuber but showers it on others.

Her four arms are symbolic of the four goals of humanity that are considered good in Hinduism, *dharma* (pursuit of ethical, moral life), *artha* (pursuit of wealth, means of life), *kama* (pursuit of love, emotional fulfilment) and *moksha* (pursuit of self-knowledge, liberation).

Lakshmi is sometimes shown with one or two elephants below, behind, or on her sides, and occasionally with an owl. Elephants symbolise work, activity, and strength, as well as water, rain, and fertility for abundant prosperity. Her mount owl signifies the patient striving to observe, see, and discover knowledge particularly when surrounded by darkness. The owl, a bird that becomes blind in the daylight, is also a symbolic reminder to refrain from blindness and greed after knowledge and wealth has been acquired.

Eight forms of Lakshmi, of varied description, are also found in various classical texts. *Ashta Lakshmi* is a group of eight Hindu goddesses, secondary manifestations of Shri-Lakshmi, the Hindu goddess of wealth. Ashta Lakshmis preside over the eight forms of wealth, the eight great *siddhis* (*ashta* siddhis) of spiritual knowledge. 'Wealth' in the context of Ashta-Lakshmi includes material prosperity, good health, knowledge, strength, progeny and power. The prayer *Shri Ashta Lakshmi Stotram* lists the Ashta Lakshmis as follows:

1. *Aadi* Lakshmi (Primeval Lakshmi) or *Maha* Lakshmi (Great Lakshmi)

She is an ancient form of Lakshmi as daughter of the sage *Bhrigu*. Aadi Lakshmi is the deep spiritual knowledge of our roots, our base, and our primal origin. It is the knowledge of our inner self. It is the pious knowledge of one's soul – its origin, life purpose and final destination. Such a knowledgeable person becomes fearless. He feels deeply contented. He finds 'ananda'. Aadi Lakshmi comes to reside only with the Buddhas (the enlightened people). It may be equated with the planet Jupiter in Vedic Astrology.

Aadi lakshmi is depicted as four-armed, carries a lotus and a white flag in her two hands; other two arms are in *Abhaya mudra* (fearless posture) and *Varada mudra* (boon posture). Lotus is the symbol of knowledge and wisdom. It helps in the emancipation of the soul.

2. Dhana Lakshmi (Money Lakshmi)

Dhana Lakshmi means gold, money, wealth, and all types of material assets. People without the company of Dhana Lakshmi cannot be religious. They get involved in illegal, unethical, anti-social and irreligious activities. Lakshmi earned through unfair means does not last long. Money earned through fair means brings all round health, happiness and beauty. Money earned through unfair means invites regret and misery in the end. Dhana Lakshmi may be equated with the planet Venus in Vedic Astrology.

In India, business people write 'Shubh Laabh' on their account books and on the main entrance of their business premises. 'Shubh' means fair and 'Laabh' means gains. All types of our gains shall be through fair means only. Only then, Lakshmi will be stable in our business. Otherwise, standing on a lotus seat in the water, she is very unstable. Dhana should be properly used and invested in good ventures. Money is good when in circulation.

Dhana Lakshmi is depicted as six-armed, in red garments, carries *chakra* (discus), *shankha* (conch), *kalasha* (water pitcher with mango leaves and a coconut on it) or *Amrita kumbha* (a pitcher containing *Amrita*; the elixir of life), bow-arrow, a lotus and an arm in *abhaya mudra* with gold coins falling from it.

3. Dhaanya Lakshmi (Lakshmi as goddess of food)

She is the giver of agricultural wealth. Dhaanya Lakshmi means nutrition, including oxygen rich air, palatable water and all types of eatables. Food is must for our survival. Dhaanya Lakshmi also includes our physical ability to eat and digest the food. Some people are rich in Dhana Lakshmi but poor in Dhaanya Lakshmi. Dhaanya Lakshmi may be equated with the planets Sun and Moon in Vedic Astrology.

Though possessing huge amount of money, some people are unable to eat salt, sugar, purified butter (desi ghee), dry fruits, sweets or rich fried food due to certain health problems or bad digestion. Unable to enjoy the rich and tasty food means that such people are poor in Dhaanya Lakshmi. On the contrary, villagers are generally rich in Dhaanya Lakshmi. They have plenty of fresh food to eat with a good digestive power. To regard Dhaanya Lakshmi, do not waste food. Consume the food properly.

Dhaanya Lakshmi is depicted as an eight-armed, in green garments, carries two lotuses, *gada* (mace), paddy crop, sugarcane, bananas, other two hands in abhaya mudra and *varada* mudra.

4. *Gaja Lakshmi* (Elephant Lakshmi) or *Bhaagya Lakshmi* or *Raaj Lakshmi*

Gaja Lakshmi is the giver of animal wealth, like cattle and elephants. In the modern context, cattle also mean all types of vehicles including the luxury vehicles and vehicles of transportation. Gaja Lakshmi is also the giver of power of royalty. Bhaagya Lakshmi means luck or fortune. She is also called Raja Lakshmi or power to rule others. People rich in Raja Lakshmi control others. It is the power to pass orders on others. Others carry out their orders. Powerful people enjoy the company of Raja Lakshmi. Gaja Lakshmi may be equated with the planet Sun in Vedic Astrology.

Gaja Lakshmi is depicted as four-armed, wearing red garments, carries two lotuses, other two arms in abhaya mudra and varada mudra, surrounded by two elephants bathing her with water pots.

5. *Santaan Lakshmi* (Progeny or children Lakshmi)

Santaana Lakshmi means the bestower of children. Healthy, obedient and helpful children are the greatest assets of any family. Children, who help in bringing the fame and prosperity to the family, are the real Santaan Lakshmi. She may be equated with the planets Venus and Jupiter in Vedic Astrology.

Santaan Lakshmi is depicted as six-armed, carries two *kalashas* (water pitcher with mango leaves and a coconut on it), sword, shield, a child on her lap, a hand in abhaya mudra and the other holding the child. The child holds a lotus.

6. *Veer Lakshmi* (valourous Lakshmi) or *Dhairya Lakshmi* (patience Lakshmi)

Veera Lakshmi is the bestowal of valour in battles and courage and strength for overcoming the difficulties in life. Dhairya Lakshmi means the great human quality of having deep patience and self-confidence. A confident person never gets frightened in odd situations. He has great inner strength; the strength of soul. A bold and fearless personality is a great asset of any person leading one to success in life. Veer Lakshmi may be equated with the planet Mars in Vedic Astrology while her Dhairya Lakshmi form may be equated with planet Saturn.

Lakshmi, lack in Vijaya Lakshmi. They are not successful in any work. Vijaya Lakshmi makes a person successful in his ventures. She may be equated with the planets Sun and Mars in Vedic Astrology.

The teachings of Sai Baba of Shirdi can mainly be summarised in two words: *Shraddha* (unconditional trust) and *Saboori* (sabra or patience). Patience and total acceptability of anything and everything going on in our life are the keys for attaining the ultimate wealth of life.

Veera Lakshmi is depicted as an eight-armed, in red garments, carries chakra, shankh, bow, arrow, trishul (or sword), a bundle of palm leaf scriptures, other two hands in abhaya mudra and varada mudra.

7. *Vijaya Lakshmi* or *Jaya Lakshmi* (victorious Lakshmi)

She is the giver of victory, not only in battles but also in conquering the hurdles in order to beget success. Vijaya Lakshmi means the spirit to win. It is the fighting spirit, the spirit to be victorious. Many people, though rich in one or more of the above six types of

Vijaya Lakshmi is depicted as an eight-armed, wearing red garments, carries chakra, shankh, sword, shield, lotus, pasha (noose), other two hands in abhaya mudra and varada mudra.

8. *Vidya Lakshmi* (knowledge Lakshmi)

Vidya Lakshmi means the bestower of knowledge. She is shown seated on a swan in clear water. Thus, her seat is comparatively stable than that of Dhana Lakshmi. It clearly shows the greatness of knowledge over material assets. One should aspire to get complete knowledge. One shall use the accumulated knowledge but shall not misuse it. She may be equated with the planet Mercury in Vedic Astrology.

Vidya Lakshmi is somewhat similar to that of Saraswati. She is draped in a white sari but, unlike Saraswati, she is adorned with gold

jewellery. There is a gold headdress over her head, which increases her beauty four-fold. Vidya Lakshmi is a four-armed goddess with lotus in each of the upper hands. The other two hands are in Varada and Abhaya mudra. The representation of the Goddess in a white sari with gold ornament has a special significance. The underlying fact behind is that wealth is important for the survival of human being. By putting the knowledge to good use, one can generate wealth for the family. Thus, unlike Saraswati, the goddess Vidya Lakshmi is not bereft of the ornaments.

These are eight forms of Lakshmi or eight types of assets. Every human being enjoys the company of these eight Lakshmi in lesser or larger proportions. In some *Ashta* Lakshmi lists, other forms of Lakshmi included are: *Aishwarya Lakshmi* (prosperity Lakshmi), *Saubhagya Lakshmi* (giver of good fortune), and *Vara Lakshmi* (boon Lakshmi), etc.

Sharada Tilak, a *tantrik* text, mentions a different list of eight forms of Lakshmi. These are *Vibhuti* (riches, wealth), *Kanti* (beauty, brightness, glow), *Srishti* (creation), *Kirti* (fame, glory), *Sannati* (politeness, humility), *Pushti* (nourishing, strength, steadiness), *Utkrishti* (extraordinariness), and *Riddhi* (prosperity, growth, increase).

When a man grows rich, it is said that Lakshmi has come to live with him. When a man loses his wealth, he is spoken of as 'forsaken by Lakshmi'. Goddess Lakshmi has no independent temples. She is more invoked for increase of prosperity than Yaksha Kuber, the god of wealth himself. Kuber, literally meaning 'vile body', is described to have a badly deformed & dwarf body. Having greedy eyes, he is a selfish being of disagreeable countenance. It is said that the man who is merely absorbed in worldly possessions will become a *Yaksha* after death.

Gaja Lakshmi Puja is an autumn festival celebrated on *Sharad Purnima* in many parts of India on the full-moon day in the lunar month of *Ashvin* (September–October). On Sharad Purnima night, Goddess Lakshmi is thanked and worshipped for the harvests. Countless hymns, prayers, *shlokas*, *stotras*, songs, sutras, and legends dedicated to Mahalakshmi are recited during the ritual worship of Lakshmi. However, the main festival celebrated in honour of Goddess Lakshmi is *Diwali*.

Diwali: The Festival of Goddess Lakshmi

The most popular festival of India, 'Diwali' or 'Deepawali', is chiefly celebrated in the honour of Lakshmi, the goddess of wealth, prosperity and fertility. Diwali festival is connected mainly with the vaishyas (agriculturalists, cattle-rearing, money-lenders, landowners, trade and commerce class) in the same way as the festival of Dussehra is connected with Kshatriyas (ruling and military elite class), the festival of Holi is connected with Shudras (serving class) and the festival of Guru Poornima (Vyaas Pooja) and Kartika Poornima are connected with Brahmins (priests of sacred learning class).

Diwali festival is mainly associated with the worshipping of money, wealth and prosperity in many ways. The festival of 'Dhanteras' ('*dhan*' = wealth; '*teras*' = 13th) is celebrated two days before the festival of lights. Diwali is one of the biggest shopping seasons in India and Nepal, since Lakshmi connotes auspiciousness. Investment, spending and purchases are considered auspicious during Diwali. It is a peak buying season for major sweets, candy and fireworks in India. In terms of consumer purchases and economic activity, Diwali is the equivalent of Christmas in the west. At retail level, about US$800 million (INR 5,000 crores) worth of firecrackers only are consumed in India over the Diwali season.

Diwali coincides with the darkest *Amavasya* (new moon night) of the Hindu Luni-solar month of Karttika (Octtober-November). Thus, this festival is the starting point of winter season, the prime business time in Northern Indian plains. Normal activities virtually come to a stop here during the hot summer season. Indian winters are equivalent to Europe's springs. Most of the Indian festivals fall during winters. Different fairs of village, state, national and international levels are held mainly during the winters. Diwali is traditionally a time when households purchase new clothing for themselves and their families. People buy appliances, kitchen utensils, home refurbishments, even expensive items such as cars and gold jewellery. They also buy gifts for family members, friends and business partners which typically include sweets, dry fruits, and seasonal specialties depending on regional harvest and customs.

Deepawali, meaning 'Feast of lamps', is celebrated with great piety and enthusiasm. Certainly the biggest and the brightest of all the Hindu festivals, it is the festival of lights (*deep* = light and *avali*= a row of lights). King Harsha in the 7th century Sanskrit play Nagananda mentions Deepavali as *Deepa-pratipada-utsava* (*Deepa* = light, *pratipada* = first day, *utsava* = festival), where lamps were lit and newly engaged brides and grooms were given gifts. Diwali spiritually signifies the victory of light over darkness, good over evil, knowledge over ignorance, and hope over despair. Its celebration includes millions of lights, home decoration, shopping, fireworks, *pooja* (prayers), gifts, performing religious rituals, feast and sweets.

It is also the period when children listen to ancient stories, legends about battles between good and evil or light and darkness from their parents and elders.

The events connected with Diwali are all symbolic. Diwali is nowhere mentioned in the Vedas. The festival is mentioned in Sanskrit texts such as the *Padma Purana* and the *Skanda Purana* both completed in second half of 1st millennium AD. The *diyas* (lamps) are mentioned in Skanda Purana to symbolically represent parts of sun, the cosmic giver of light and energy to all life, who seasonally transitions in the Hindu calendar month of *Karttika*. Hindus in some regions of India associate Diwali with the legend of Yama and *Nachiketa* on Karttika *amavasya* (Diwali night). The Nachiketa story about right versus wrong, true wealth versus transient wealth, knowledge versus ignorance is recorded in

Katha Upanishad composed in 1st millennium BC.

Historically, the origin of Diwali can be traced back to ancient India, when it was probably an important harvest festival. Diwali falls in the time of the *kharif* crop; a time when rich rice cultivation gives its fruits. India being an agro-economic society, the significance of a rich harvest gives a new meaning to the celebrations. However, there are various mythical and historical legends pointing to the origin of Diwali and almost every region of India has its own reason to observe the occasion.

Diwali is mainly celebrated in the honour of Goddess Lakshmi to seek her blessings for fulfilling the wishes of her devotees for the coming year. The five-day festival of Diwali begins on the day Goddess Lakshmi was born from the churning of the cosmic ocean of milk by the *Devas* (gods) and the *Asuras* (demons). She was subsequently married to Lord Vishnu on Diwali; the darkest night of the year and brilliant lamps were illuminated and placed in rows to mark this holy occasion.

Along with Lakshmi, devotees in most Hindu homes on this day make offerings to Lord Ganesh (the elephant-headed God who symbolises auspiciousness, wisdom, ethical beginnings and fearless removal of obstacles), Saraswati (who embodies music, literature and learning) and Kuber (who symbolises book-keeping, treasury and wealth management). Other Hindus believe that Diwali is the day Vishnu came back to Lakshmi and their abode in the *Vaikuntha*. So, those who worship Lakshmi receive the benefit of her most benevolent mood, and therefore are blessed with mental, physical and material well-being during the year ahead.

The Bhaagavat Purana (also known as Shrimad Bhaagavatam) reveals how on a Diwali day Lord Vishnu, in his fifth incarnation as *Vaaman-avtaar*, rescued Lakshmi from the prison of King Bali during the *Treta Yuga*. King Bali (or Mahabali), was tricked into giving up his kingship and wealth (of which Lakshmi is said to be the Goddess). Bali was allowed to return to earth once a year, to light millions of lamps to dispel the darkness and ignorance, and spread the radiance of love and wisdom. It is on the next day of Deepawali — *Karttika Shukla Pratipada* that Bali steps out of hell and rules the earth according to the boon given by Lord Vishnu. In Kerala, the festival of 'Onam' is celebrated around the month of August to mark this legend.

The Bhaagavat Purana also tells us about Narakasura, an evil demon king who had managed to acquire awesome powers and was tyrannical in his reign. When Lord Vishnu was incarnated as Krishna in the Dwapara Yuga, he killed Narakasura on the day preceding Diwali and rescued 16,000 women whom the demon had imprisoned in his palace. The deliverance from the terrible Narakasura was celebrated with much grandeur, a tradition that continues to this day. Another version of the story credits Lord Krishna's wife Satyabhama as the one who eliminated Narakasura. It is said that Narakasura could only be killed by his mother *Bhoodevi* and as Satyabhama was an incarnation of the same Bhoodevi, she only could kill him. Before death, however, Narakasura realised his mistake and requested a boon from Satyabhama that everyone should celebrate his death with colourful light. To commemorate his death, the event is celebrated in some parts of India as *Naraka Chaturdasi*, the day before Diwali.

Hindus also celebrate Diwali in honour of the return of Lord Rama from his fourteen year-long exile, along with his wife Sita and his brother *Lakshmana*, after Rama defeated the demon-king Ravana in Sri Lanka. In joyous celebration of their return and to celebrate the triumph of good over evil, people of Ayodhya (the capital city of Rama) illuminated the path of Lord Rama with earthen *diyas* (oil lamps) and burst crackers.

The great Hindu epic 'Mahabharata' reveals that it was '*Karttika Amavashya*' (the new moon day of the Karttika month) when Pandavas appeared from their 12 years of banishment (*vanvaas*) and one year of living in hiding (*agyaatvaas*) as a result of their defeat in the hands of the Kauravas at the game of dice (gambling). The five Pandava brothers, their mother and their wife Draupadi were kind, gentle, honest and caring in their ways and were loved by all their subjects.

In India's eastern region like West Bengal and Orissa, the festival is dedicated to the worship of Mother Goddess Kali (the dark goddess of strength), instead of Lakshmi and is called the festival *Kali Pooja*. Kali, also called *Shyama Kali*, is the first of the 10 avatars (incarnations) of Goddess Durga, Lord Shiva's consort. According to the legend, long ago after the gods lost in a battle with the demons, Goddess Kali was born as *Kaal Bhoi Nashini* from the forehead of Goddess Durga. Said to be a personification of Nari Shakti (female power), Kali was born to save heaven and earth from the growing cruelty of the demons.

After killing all the devils, Kali lost her control and started killing anyone who came her way which stopped only when Lord Shiva intervened. The well-known picture of Ma Kali, with her tongue hanging out, actually depicts the moment when she steps on Lord Shiva and repents. That momentous day has been commemorated ever since and the main purpose of celebrating Kali Puja is to seek help of the goddess in destroying evil (both external and internal to us) as also to get her blessings for general happiness, health, wealth and peace.

Diwali has special significance in Jainism. Lord *Mahavira* (twenty-fourth and the last *Tirthankaras* of the Jains and the founder of modern Jainism) attained eternal bliss of Nirvana on this day at Pavapuri on 15 October 527 BCE, on *Karttika Krishna Amavasya*. According to the *Kalpasutra* by Acharya Bhadrabahu, 3rd century BCE, many gods were present there, illuminating the darkness. Therefore, Jains celebrate Diwali as a day of remembering Mahavira. Later, Gautam Gandhar Swami, the chief disciple of Mahavira achieved omniscience (*Kaivalya Gyan*) the same day. *Newar* Buddhists in the Nepal valleys celebrate Diwali festival (called Tihar festival) over five days, in the same way and on the same days as the Hindu Diwali.

Diwali holds a special significance for Sikhs too. The third Sikh Guru Amar Das institutionalised the festival of lights as an occasion when all Sikhs would gather to receive the Gurus blessings. Foundation stone of the Golden Temple at Amritsar was laid on the auspicious occasion of Diwali in 1577. Diwali marks the '*Bandi Chhor Divas*' (releasing the imprisoned) for Sikhs as it was on a Diwali day in 1619 that the sixth Guru Hargobind, who was held by the Mughal emperor Jahangir in the Gwalior fort, was freed from imprisonment along with other fifty-two Hindu Kings (political prisoners). Ever since then, Sikhs celebrate that occasion with the annual lighting up of Golden Temple, fireworks and other festivities. In the post Guru Gobind Singh era, *Sarbat Khalsa* used to meet on Diwali and Baisakhi to discuss important issues concerning the Sikh community.

Diwali also marks the beginning of New Year in the Western and certain Northern parts of India, where the Hindu *Vikram Samvat* calendar is popular. In ancient India, winter season was considered the ideal time period for business activities. For businessmen, new financial year starts with Diwali. It is at this time that Hindu businessmen offer their pooja, close out their old year and start a new fiscal year with blessings from Goddess Lakshmi and other deities. They start new books of accounts, and pay off all debts to start a new year afresh, a good enough reason alone to indulge in the festivities. Everyone will light hundreds and thousands of lamps to dispel darkness. Often, these lights are placed in the dark corners, and in the fields to guard crops from demonic forces of darkness.

Diwali is a five-day festival in many regions of India, starting with the thirteenth lunar date of *Ashvin* month. But in the *Braja* region, Diwali starts with *Govatsa Dwadashi*. 'Go' means 'cow' and '*vatsa*' means 'calf'. *Dwadashi* means the 12th day. The story associated with this day is that of King Prithu, son of the tyrant King Vena. Because of the ill rule of Vena, there was a terrible famine and earth stopped being fruitful. Prithu chased the earth, usually represented as a cow, and 'milked' her, meaning that he brought prosperity to the land. Each of the five days in the festival of Diwali is separated by a different tradition. Rituals and significance of each day are discussed here.

Dhanteras

Day one 'Dhanteras', celebrated in Northern and Western part of India, starts off the five day festival. This day celebrates the churning of cosmic ocean of milk between the forces of good and forces of evil. This day marks the birthday of Lakshmi – the Goddess of Wealth and Prosperity, and the birthday of Dhanvantari – the God of Health and Healing. Starting days before and through Dhanteras, houses and business premises are cleaned, renovated and decorated. Women and children decorate entrances with *Rangoli* (creative colourful floor designs), both inside and in the walkways of their homes or offices. Boys and men get busy with external lighting arrangements and completing all renovation work in progress.

Dhanteras is also a major shopping day, particularly for utensils, clothes, gold and silver articles and other items of household use. Merchants, traders and retailers stock up, put articles on sale, and prepare for this day. People decorate their shops, workplace or items symbolising their source of sustenance and prosperity. On the night of Dhanteras, diyas (earthen lamps) are ritually kept burning all through the night in honour of Lakshmi and Dhanvantari. Dhanteras usually falls 18 days after Dussehra.

Narak Chaturdasi

Narak Chaturdasi is the second day of festivities, and is also called *Chhoti Diwali*. The Hindu literature narrates that the evil *asura* (demon) Narakasura was killed on this day by Krishna or his wife Satyabhama during the *Dwapara Yuga*. It signifies the victory of good over evil and light over darkness. The day is celebrated with pooja, fireworks, and feast. This day is commonly celebrated as Diwali in Tamil Nadu, Goa and Karnataka. Typically, house decoration and colourful floor patterns called rangoli are made on or before Narak Chaturdasi. Special bathing rituals such as fragrant oil bath are held in some regions, followed by minor poojas. Women decorate their hands with henna designs. Families are also busy preparing homemade sweets for main Diwali.

Maha Lakshmi Pooja

The third day is the main festive day. People wear their best outfits as the evening approaches. Then *diyas* are lit, poojas are offered to Lakshmi, and to one or more additional deities depending on the region of India; typically Ganesh, Saraswati, and Kuber. The Diwali prayers vary widely by region of India. An example Vedic prayer from Brhadaranyaka Upanishad celebrating lights is:

असतो मा सद्गमय
From untruth lead us to Truth.

तमसो मा ज्योतिर्गमय
From darkness lead us to Light.

मृत्योर्मा अमृतं गमय
From death lead us to Immortality.

ॐ शान्ति: शान्ति: शान्ति:
Om Peace, Peace, Peace.

Lakshmi is believed to roam the earth on Diwali night. On the evening of Diwali, people open their doors and windows to welcome Lakshmi, and place diyas on their window sills and balcony ledges to invite her in. On this day, mothers working hard all the year are recognised by the family. They are seen to embody a part of Lakshmi, the good fortune and prosperity of the household. Some set diyas adrift on rivers and streams. Important relationships and friendships are also recognised during the day, by visiting relatives and friends, exchanging gifts and sweets. Diwali lights illuminate every corner of India and the scent of incense sticks hangs in the air, mingled with the sounds of fire-crackers, joy, togetherness and hope.

After the pooja, people go outside and celebrate by lighting up *patakhas* (fireworks). The fireworks signify celebration of Diwali as well a way to chase away evil spirits. According to one belief, the sound of fire-crackers is an indication of the joy of the people living on earth, making the gods aware of their plentiful state. Still another possible reason has a more scientific basis: the fumes produced by the crackers kill a lot of insects and mosquitoes, found in plenty after the rains. The illumination of homes with lights and the skies with firecrackers is an expression of obeisance to the heavens for the attainment of health, wealth, knowledge, peace and prosperity. After fireworks, people head back to a family feast, conversations and *mithai* (sweets, desserts).

Padwa, Bali-pratipada

The day after Diwali, is celebrated as *Padwa* (*prathama*). This day ritually celebrates the love and mutual devotion between the wife and husband. The husbands give thoughtful gifts, or elaborate ones to respective spouses. In many regions, newly married daughters with their husbands are invited for special meals. Sometimes brothers go and pick up their sisters from their in-laws home for this important day. The day is also a special day for the married couple, in a manner similar to anniversaries elsewhere in the world.

Lord Krishna Holding Up Mount Govardhan

The day after Diwali is *Govardhan Puja*, celebrated as the day Lord Krishna defeated Indra by the lifting of *Govardhan Parvat* (mountain) to save his kinsmen and cattle from rain and floods. 'Govardhan' literally means; 'increasing or growing the cows'. Devotees perform Govardhan pooja (or *Annakoot*) in honour of Lord Krishna on this day. Symbolic mountains of food with 56 or 108 different cuisines representing the Govardhan Parvat are prepared, offered to Lord Krishna, and then shared in the community. Devotees prepare symbolic Govardhan Parvat at their home with cow-dung, offer it cooked rice (from new harvest) with *arhar* pulse, and circumambulate it seven times after sunset. Govardhan Pooja symbolises the importance of human efforts and community togetherness.

Bhai Dooj, Bhaiya Dooj, Yama Dwitiya

The last day is *Yama Dwitiya*, Bhai dooj (brother's second) or bhai teeka in Nepal. Brothers and sisters meet to mark their lifelong bond, love and affection for each other on this day. It is a day when women and girls get together, perform a pooja with prayers for the well-being of their brothers, then return to a ritual of food-sharing, gift-giving and conversations. In historic times, this was a day in autumn when brothers would travel to meet their married sister's place living in distant areas and usually have a meal there or bring over their sisters to their village homes to celebrate the sister-brother bond with the bounty of seasonal harvests. The brothers also bring and give gifts to their sisters.

Much gambling takes place at this festival because present generation believes that Lakshmi can be propitiated by gambling. The tradition of gambling on Diwali also has a legend behind it. It is believed that on this day, Goddess Parvati played dice with her husband Lord Shiva, and she decreed that whosoever gambled on Diwali night would prosper throughout the ensuing year. Gambling, in reality, represents a courageous spirit, a risk-taking ability. After Diwali, farmers used to sow seeds and businessmen used to invest money in new businesses. These were the risky ventures for them. On the eve of Diwali, people were encouraged to take calculated risks for increased earning in agriculture or in business.

Risks, when taken properly, win favour. Activity of a person generally reduces with the increased safety and security in life. Really active life exists in challenges, in crises and in insecurity. A successful life grows in the soil of insecurity. An insecure person becomes more alive, and more alert. Progress is provoked by challenges. 'No risk no gains' is the way of life. Risks taken wisely are directly proportion to the chances of gains. Gradually, promoting risk-taking ability on Diwali converted into the social evil of gambling. Otherwise, Diwali has nothing to do with it.

On Diwali night, no alms must be given away, nor any money lost or wasted; otherwise Lakshmi becomes angry. Lakshmi also becomes angry with lethargic and unclean people. Lakshmi likes fair public dealing, personal hygiene, healthy food habits and active work life. It is said that; 'A person, who wears dirty clothes, shows unclean teeth, is gluttonous, bitter in speech, remains in slumber at sunrise and sunset – turns away Lakshmi even if he is the disc bearer Vishnu'.

Clutter (*kabaar*)

Lakshmi likes cleanliness and light. So Diwali serves a vaastu cause that the home gets rid of its rubbish and junk. Consequently, the living space is increased. Urban space is very expensive. Too many non-useful objects in the house or working place suck away our energy. They make us feel uncomfortable and vulnerable. People feel frightened in such a packed space. There is a direct connection between rubbish and poverty (*daridra*). Poverty is attracted to darkness and dimly lighted areas, foul smelling places which are full of rubbish, and unventilated areas having low ceiling levels.

Don't clutter your space with the stuff you don't need. Vaastu is dead against clutter in home, factory, office or any work-station. Unused things are equated to dead things because of their non-use in any space, excess of which deplete our energy. They create 'deadness' in us and suck our energy by consuming the valuable space around us. Cluttering the home with unnecessary articles leads to exhaustion. Only two kinds of things are considered auspicious in any premises – either it should be beautiful or be useful. Throw away any articles if it is none of the two.

Cash Counter

South-east, due to its close relation to money and finance, is the right location for your cash counter or accounts office. In this way, a business's turnover can be enhanced. Cash counter should easily be visible from all areas of a store or retail business. It should be slightly curved. A curved surface symbolises smoothness and harmony with the customers. The cash counter should be at the right height. The right height is when most of the customers are able to rest their arms on the counter easily. Too high a counter tends to push customers away. It rejects any wealth enhancing energy that enters in. On the contrary, a very lowly placed cash counter will not be able to effectively hold any wealth enhancing prana. Too low a counter also threatens privacy and security of the cash as well as of the cashier. A cash counter placed below customer's waistline is particularly bad.

Cash counter should only be used to collect money from the customers. A toilet above the cash counter is not good. Make sure that the cash counter is not located facing a toilet or a kitchen. Ideally it should be near the main entrance but not directly facing it. Don't ever set up the wealth area under a beam. In the long run, it will be harmful to your financial success. A solid wall towards the backside of cash counter gives protection. You can install a mirror on the side wall so that it reflects the cash register. It symbolises doubling of your turnover. It also gives a feeling of transparency and fair dealing in business in your client's mind.

Lighting in this area should be as natural as possible. Too dim light causes stagnant energy (tamas) while too bright light causes aggressive energy (rajas). Keep this area clean and clear. Goddess Lakshmi visits only well-lighted and uncluttered areas. A healthy potted flower plant kept in the wealth area brings lucky prana.

Decorate the cash counter area with symbols of prosperity to activate the wealth energy. Use old Indian coins to activate the wealth. Old coins represent wealth and prosperity with long lasting stability. Goddess Lakshmi is shown with gold coins dropping from her hands. Coins, with images of Lakshmi and Ganesh, are worshipped on Diwali (festival of lights). Old and antique coins are used as amulets till today.

Ancient Indian coins are mainly round shaped with or without a round hole in the centre. Tie three or seven of these old coins together with a golden or yellow or orange silk thread. Tie them to the cash counter to attract excellent business and wealth. Golden colour represents gold. Yellow and orange colours are the colours of ripe fruits and grains. These are rajasic colours and fill you with active energy. Coins represent application of this active rajas energy in money making.

There are several variations of this practice. You can use nine or eleven coins to magnify the effect. You can display coins on your desk. A yellow metal bowl containing antique coins also helps in activating wealth of a business. You can also hang replica coins on the wall of your sales manager's office. If you are unable to find the old coins, modern coins can also be helpful. Attach them to some golden yellow material and display above your cash box or counter. You can also replace the real coins with a photograph or image of coins as a substitute. Keep small change in a metal bowl.

Some Symbols of Prosperity of Different Faiths

Many religious Hindu people visit Vaishno Devi Shrine or other holy places and receive *prashad* (grace) in the form of *khajana* (small silver coins). It is believed that this khajana should be kept in the cash box. In this way, God's / Goddess's blessings will always be with you in the form of coins. Presence of such auspicious (*shubha*) coins will encourage you to earn more money, but through fair means only. A photo or painting of Goddess Lakshmi, the beautiful goddess of wealth, is best in the wealth area. She comes to reside in clear, well-lighted and beautifully decorated places. Some other symbols of prosperity are: Aum; Swastika; Shubha Laabh; Mangala Ghata (auspicious pitcher); human hand print; holy symbols of different religions, etc.

Treasury

Location of treasury is one of the most important considerations in a business. Large sums of money shall be kept out of the sight of the outsiders. The treasury or the safe shall be in a safe, secure, and least visible distant part of the building. The safe shall be appropriately concealed to ensure its proper privacy and security. The heavy treasury is best in the back corner of the store. South-west, the heaviest direction is most appropriate direction; though west and south are also suitable. It will be still better if safe is kept in a separate room with a lock and safety device. Place the safe against a wall. There would not be any access to the back of the treasury in this way. It shall preferably face north. North-east and east facing is also good. Close and cover any window behind the treasury permanently. Otherwise, the wealth will escape through the window.

Chapter 4
Classical Principles of Administrative, Business, Professional, Public and Religious Vaastu

द्वौ हुडाविव युध्येते पुरुषार्थौ परस्परम्।
य एव बलवान्स्तत्र स एव जयति क्षणात्।।
ह्यस्तनी दुष्क्रियाभ्येति शोभां सत्क्रियया यथा।
अद्यैव प्राक्तनीं तस्मात् यत्नात् सत्कार्यवान्भव।।

Both the human exertions (earlier exertions called destiny and the present time exertions) fight each other like the two fighting rams, the stronger of the two only winning. As a good deed of today can correct an ill-deed done yesterday, present human exertions can correct the earlier deeds (destiny) likewise.

Yogavaashishtha, 2.6.10, 6(2).157.29

Different classical texts of vaastu recommend specific directions and squares not only for residential purposes but also for different types of commercial, professional, administrative and religious activities. Here, I am considering recommendations of mainly the four popular classical texts of vaastu shastra ie "Mayamatam" written by the great Vaastushilpi Maya, "Vaastumandanam" written by Sutradhara Mandana Bhardwaj, "Aparajitaprichchha" written by Bhuvan Devacharya and "Samaranganasutradhara" written by the great king Bhoja Deva. Efforts have been made here to discuss individual as well as the comparative statement of auspicious directions and squares recommended for different public activities in all of these four classical texts.

Readers may please note that activities prescribed by these texts are not complete. Some of the square(s) or direction(s) have been left unattended by authors of one or the other text. Also, recommendations of these four texts are not always the same for a particular direction or a square, sometimes differing altogether. Intelligent readers are advised to use their discriminating power. One should always keep in mind that vaastu is an art and science of living based on time, place and person factors.

Mayamatam

Space Allocation for Residence of People of Different Professions

According to Mayamatam (9.63); "The dwellings of people who live on their work i.e. craftsmen should be in paishacha zone".

Mayamatam (10.90) says; "Huts of chandala and kolika must be two hundred

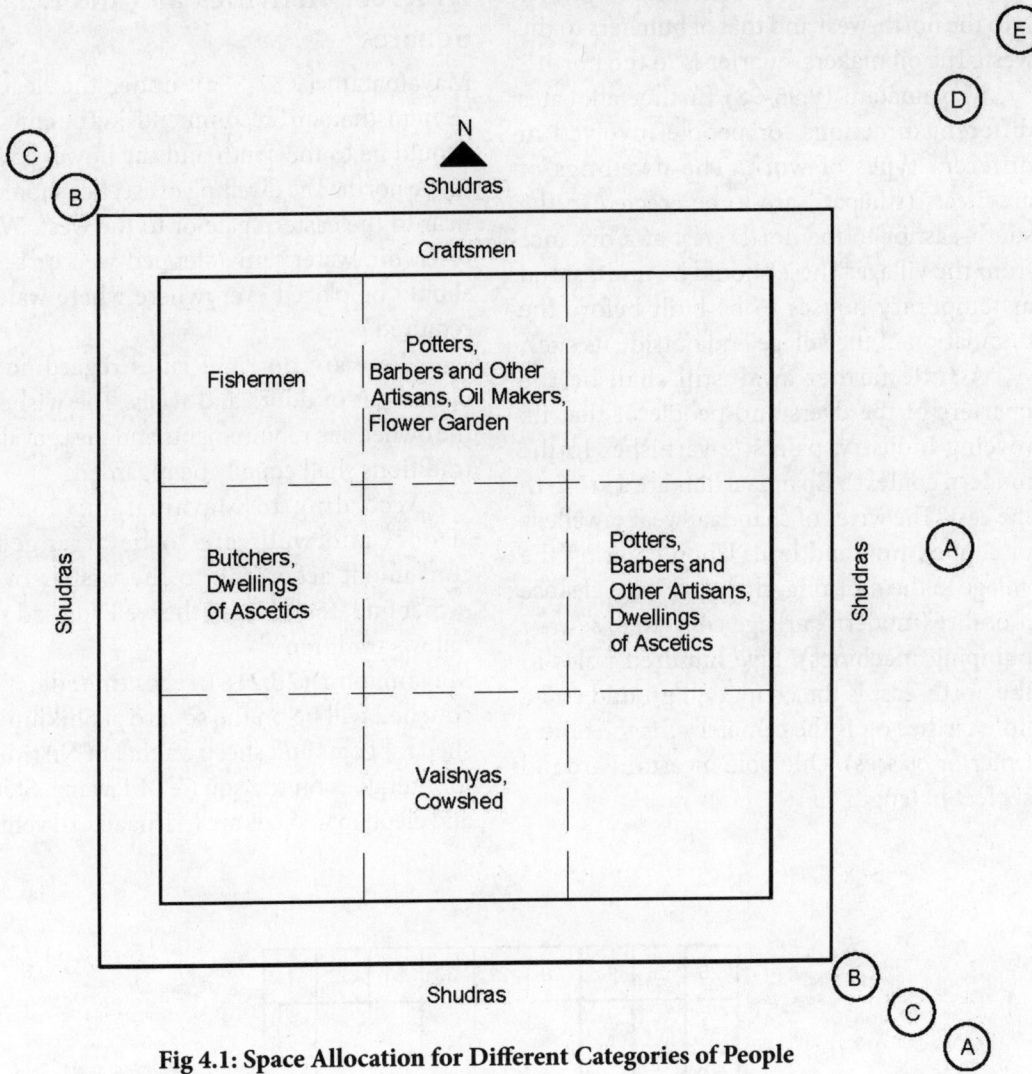

Fig 4.1: Space Allocation for Different Categories of People

A Chaandaal and Kolika Huts (200 Poles Beyond the Town)
B Sthapati Dwellings
C Quarters of Dyers and Similar People
D Cremation Ground (500 Poles Beyond the Town)
E Cemetery for Inferior Classes (Beyond D)

poles beyond the town to the east and south-east".

Chandala had to collect the refuse every morning. Kols used to collect firewood and leaves from the forest and sell these at the local markets.

Mayamatam (9.88b-91a), under the heading "Shrenisthanam", recommends; "The quarters for vaishyas are to the south and that for shudras on the periphery. The houses of potters, barbers and other artisans are either to the east or to the north. Fisherman's quarter is to the north-west and that of butchers to the west. The oil makers' quarter is to the north".

Mayamatam (9.95-98) further allocates different directions for people involved in different types of work. The dwellings of architects (sthapati) are to be erected to the south-east or to the north-west at a distance from the village. These should be understood as temporary houses to be built before the foundation of the village and outside its site.

A little farther away still shall be the quarters of the dyers and people of that ilk (dyeing industry, paints & varnishes in the modern context). Chandaal huts are a krosh to the east. The wives of chandaal wear jewellery in copper, iron and lead. Upon entering the village in the morning, chandaal must cleanse it of dirt (modern garbage collectors, sewage pumping machines). Five hundred poles to the north-east is the cremation ground and a little farther on is the cemetery for the others (inferior classes). One pole measures around six feet in length.

Different Activities and the Related Squares

Mayamatam (9.87-88a), under the heading "Shrenisthanam", recommends; "The cowshed should be to the south and the flower garden to the north. The dwelling of ascetics should be near to the eastern gate or to the west. Water reservoir, water tank, stepped well or a well should be placed everywhere where water is required".

There are no rigid rules regarding the placement of doors and walls. The wishes of the owner, site requirements and the prevailing traditions shall equally be regarded.

According to Mayamatam (26.217); "Doors and walls are to be arranged as convenient according to the wishes of the owner and, for the rest, the well advised man follows tradition".

Mayamatam (26.218) recommends; "The cowshed will be on the square of Shikhin, the shed for goats and sheep on that of Nirriti and for buffaloes on the square of Pavana. Stables and elephants' sheds are in Ishaan. All vehicles

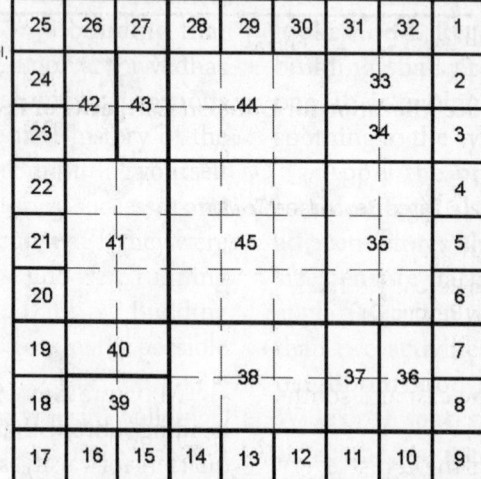

(1) Stables and Elephant Shed, Cult Ceremonies, Well, Kanji Vessel, Salted Water, Oven
(4) Annaprashan, Mill Stone
(6) Mortar
(8) Hearth, Condiments
(9) Granary, Cowshed, Byre
(13) Dinning Hall
(17) Accounts, Goats & Sheep Shed
(18) Accounts
(19) Maternity Room
(20) Maternity Room
(21) Accounts
(25) Buffalo Shed, Reception hall, Hair-cutting

(28) Reception Hall
(29) Reception Hall, Storage of Money
(32) Bath
(33) Maid's Apartments, Tank
(34) Cistern
(35) Annaprashan
(36) Annaprashan
(38) Study
(40) Hair-cutting
(41) Marriage
(44) Grind Stone
(45) Central Platform (Vedi)

Fig 4.2: Square Wise Space Allocation for Different Activities

are to the left of the doors placed at the cardinal points".

Mayamatam (26.11-12a) recommends; "Houses with single main building are appropriate for women who live by their charms (Rupopajivin)". Rupopajivin were independent courtesans which were not in the state service.

Mayamatam (26.215-216) recommends; "The dining hall is situated where Yama is, money is stored on the square of Soma, Agni has the granary, and condiments for cooking are stored on the square of Kha (Antariksha). The worship room is on the square of Isa and the well is there too. Baths are on the square of Sun. As far as other parts of the dwelling are concerned, they should each be put in a suitable position".

Mayamatam (27.24) recommends; "Only for brahmins, kings and vaishyas is there a platform in the centre of the house. Offerings are made there three times a day and it is honoured with flowers and perfumes".

Mayamatam (27.100) recommends; "The vessel for the salted water (Kanchi / kanji) is placed at the northeast; the hearth is to be on the square of Antariksha, mortar (Ukhala) on that of Satya, an oven (pachanasthana) on the square of Isha is fitting for all".

According to Kamika (1.35.177-178), the oven is at the northeast for Brahmins, at the southeast for Kshatriyas, at southwest for Vaishyas and at northwest for Shudras. All these places are next to the side of the corresponding principal main building.

According to Mayamatam (27.103); "For a king, the hearth is like a human head (probably a round form), for gods and brahmins it is square, for vaishyas it is rectangular and the other form are all fitting for the other classes".

Mayamatam (27.105-108) recommends that annaprashan (a ceremony in which the baby is fed rice for the first time) is on the square of Arya, Mahendra and Savindra. The study of the Vedas (Shravanam) takes place on the square of Vivasvant and marriage on that of Mitra. Hair-cutting is done on the square of Indrajaya, Vayu and Soma. Accounts are done on the squares of Pitr, Dauvarika and Jala. It is desirable that maternity chamber (Delivery room / Prasutigraha) is on the squares of Sugala (Sugriva) and Pushpadanta. The water tank (Jalakosham) is on that of Apvatsa, the small water tank (Kund) on that of Apa, the mill-stone on that of Mahendra and the grindstone (Chakki) on that of Mahidhara.

Mayamatam (27.123b-125a) recommends; "The reception hall is to be on the squares of Vayu, Bhallata and Soma, mortar is on Mukhya's square, harlot's (whore / courtesan / maid / ganika) apartment on Aap, the chariot is at the front and to the left of the door. All else is to be arranged there as desired".

According to Mayamatam (29.227); "If the king so desires, an underground apartment may be built for the queen and princes. It should be built under the ground at the end of a malika or where the imagination dictates".

Such type of underground construction was done so that the same can be used later during emergency for protection of life. In the modern context, the same may be used for storage and parking.

Vaastu of Bazaars Described in Mayamatam

Mayamatam (10.91) describes a 'pattana' having one straight road where no bazaars are to be found. For all other towns, the bazaars should be established according to each specific case. A detailed account regarding the placement of various types of markets (antarapanam) is given in Mayamatam in relation to the directions and squares of the Vaastu Purush. Bazaars appropriate to all types of towns have been described in chapters nine and ten of Mayamatam. A layout of Bazaar as per the details given in Mayamatam is shown here in figure 4.3.

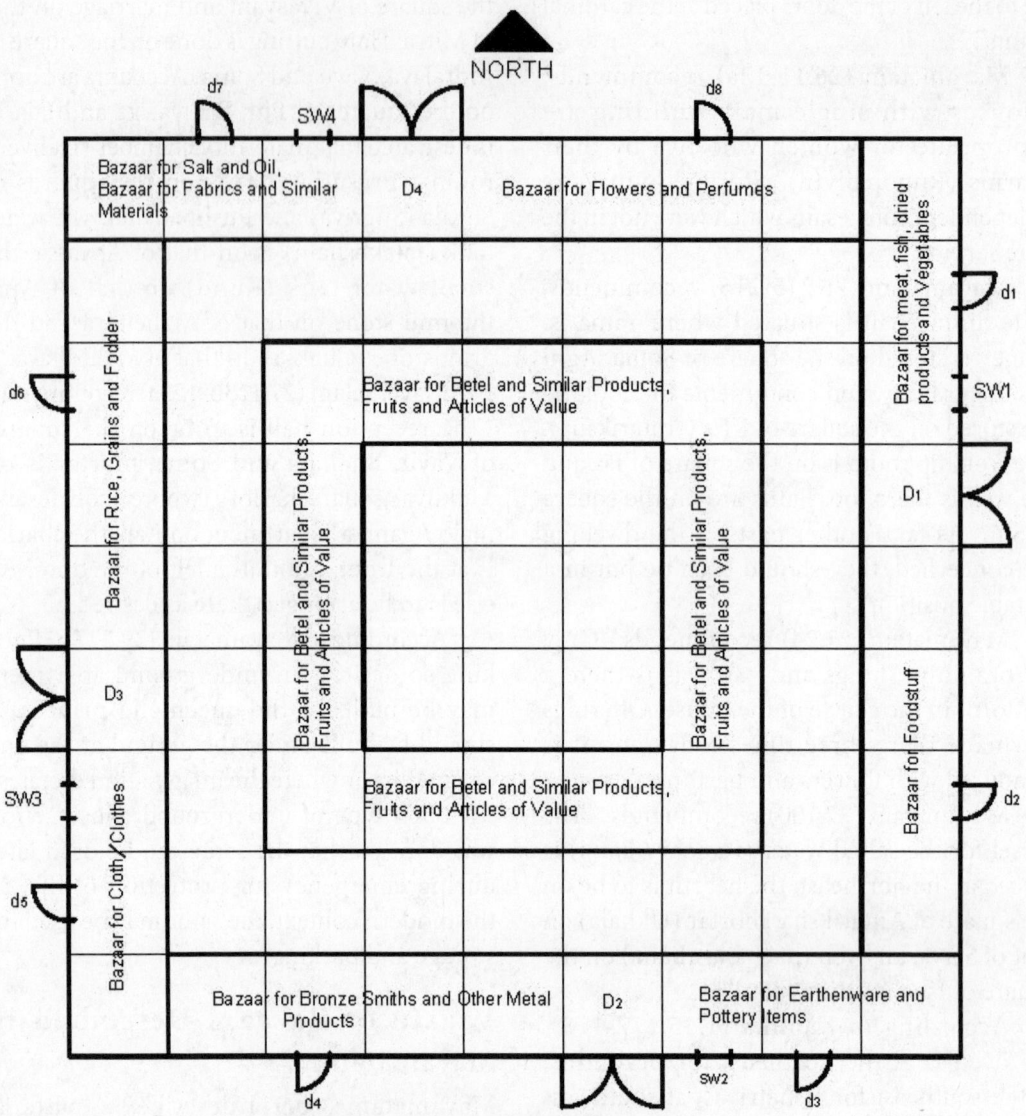

Fig 4.3: Layout of Bazaars as per the Description of Mayamatam

Mayamatam (9.57-59a) describes main gates, secondary gates and sewage outlets; "The gateways are established on the squares of Mahendra, Rakshsha, Pushpadanta and Bhallata. The four sewage outlets are on the squares of Jayanta, Vitatha, Sugriva and Mukhya. The eight secondary gates are on the squares of Parjanya, Bhrisha, Pushan, Bhringaraja, Dauvarika, Shosha, Naga, and Aditi". Based on these recommendations of Mayamatam; position of main gates, secondary gates and sewage outlets is shown here in table 4.1.

Table 4.1: Position of main gates, secondary gates and sewage outlets

S No	Direction	Main Gate	Secondary Gate	Sewage Outlet
1	East	Mahendra (4)	Parjanya (2), Bhrisha (7)	Jayanta (3)
2	South	Rakshsha (12)	Pushan (10), Bhringaraja (15)	Vitatha (11)
3	West	Pushpadanta (20)	Dauvarika (18), Shosha (23)	Sugriva (19)
4	North	Bhallata (28)	Naag (26), Aditi (31)	Mukhya (27)

Mayamatam (10.78-87) recommends different bazaar for different articles on different squares; "On the periphery is the chariot road. Houses of merchants are on the inner side of this peripheral road. Bazaar for betel and similar products, for fruits and for valuable articles should be installed in the street encircling the Brahma-sthana. Between the square of Ish and Mahendra gate is the bazaar for meat, fish, dried (products) and for vegetables. Between the Mahendra gate and the square of Agni is the bazaar for ready to eat food (restaurants and bakery etc). Potters are between the Agni square and that of Grihatkshata.

Between Grihatkshata and Nirriti are the coppersmiths and blacksmiths. Between the square of Pitar and that of Pushpadanta is the bazaar for clothing. Between Pushpadanta and Vayu is the bazaar for rice, grains and fodder. Between the squares of Vayu and that of Bhallata is the bazaar for fabrics and related material of that kind and also foodstuffs like salt and oil. Between Bhallata and the square of Ish is the bazaar for perfumes and flowers. Along the street leading to the Brahma-sthana is the bazaar for gems, gold, clothes, madder (manjishtha), black pepper, pippali, haridra, honey, ghee, oil and medicaments".

Classification of Residences for People of Four Varnas (Castes or Classes of Ancient Indian Society)

Mayamatam (27.40-54) gives rules for the habitation of four classes. These four classes are the ancient *Varnas* based on their profession or work. These four categories of people have also been explained in details under the topic "Four Directions and Four Castes" in chapter 1.

1. Sukhalaya

The saukhya dwelling of brahmins is to be built on the squares of Mahidhara, Indu, Bhallata, Mrga and Aditi as per the Mandook Diagram (8X8 = 64 pada vaastu). All these squares pertain to the northern part of the diagram. The site for brahmins slopes towards the north. Its width and length are (5 cubit x 9 cubit) or (5.5 cubit x 10 cubit) or (7 cubit x 11 cubit). The door is on the square of Mahendra and the drain pipe on that of Mukhya. A dwelling like this invariably brings success to Brahmins.

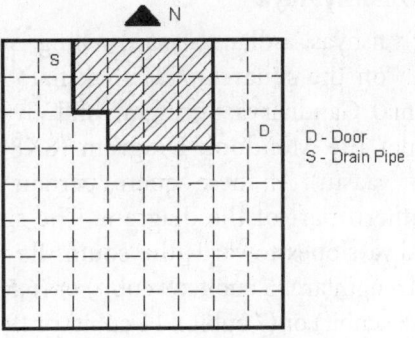

Fig 4.4: Sukhalaya as per Mandook Diagram

2. Annalaya

For kings, a mahanasa dwelling is to be built on the squares of Mahendra, Arka, Aryaka, Satya and Bhrsha as per the Mandook Diagram (8X8

= 64 pada vaastu). All these squares pertain to the eastern part of the diagram. The site for kings slopes towards the east. Its width and length are (3 cubit x 5 cubit) or (3.5 cubit x 6.5 cubit) or (4 cubit x 7 cubit) or (4.5 cubit x 8.5 cubit) or (5 cubit x 9 cubit). The door is on the square of Grahakshat and the drain pipe on that of Jayanta. A dwelling like this situated in the east is fitting for the king. It will bring an increase of treasure for him.

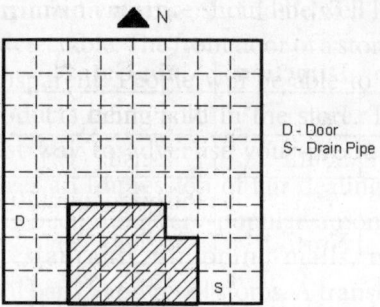

Fig 4.6: Dhaanyalaya as per Mandook Diagram

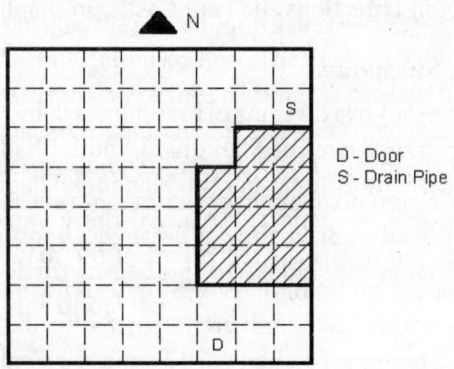

Fig 4.5: Annalaya as per Mandook Diagram

3. Dhaanyalaya

For vaishyas, a dhanyalaya dwelling is to be built on the squares of Grihakshat, Arkin (Yama), Gandharva, Bhringraja and Vivasvant as per the Mandook Diagram (8X8 = 64 pada vaastu). All these squares pertain to the southern part of the diagram. The site for vaishya slopes towards the south. Its width and length are (5 cubit x 9 cubit) or (6.5 cubit x 10.5 cubit) or (7 cubit x 11 cubit) or (9 cubit x 13 cubit) or (11 cubit x 15 cubit). The houses intended for vaishya have the biggest principal main building. The door is on the square of Pushpadanta and the drain course on that of Vitatha. A dwelling like this situated in the south brings wealth, rewards and good fortune to vaishyas.

4. Dhanalaya

A dhanalaya dwelling is to be built on the squares of Pushpadanta, Asura, Shosha, Varuna and Mitra as per the Mandook Diagram (8X8 = 64 pada vaastu). All these squares pertain to the western part of the diagram. Its width and length are similar to a dhaanyalaya but a little smaller. The door is on the square of Bhallata and its drain course on that of Sugriva. A dwelling like this situated in the west brings good fortune to shudras.

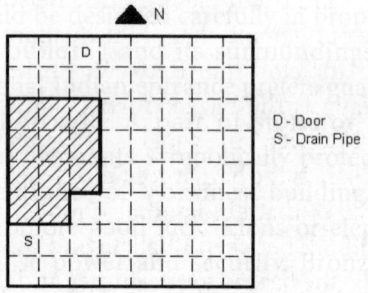

Fig 4.7: Dhanalaya as per Mandook Diagram

Kayabhara Dwellings for Vaishyas

Mayamatam (27.112-120) further prescribes vaastu rules regarding a residence meant for those powerful amongst vaishyas. This dwelling is called Kayabhara when it comprises all that is peculiar to vaishya and when the western part is unoccupied.

The total length of the site is double its width. The length is to be divided into five parts. Two parts are left in the west. Rest of the plot is divided according to the Mandook diagram (sixty-four squares).

All the elements of this dwelling are to be arranged beginning with the median pavilion. The principal main building being placed to the south (Pradhanam dakshinavasam) is a dhaanyalaya and the house is intended for vaishyas. The rest of the house is the domain of the appurtenances.

The women's quarters are on the squares of Bhringaraj, Dauvarik, Sugriva and Pitar. So these are located in the southwest corner, between the principal main building and the entrance which is on the square of Pushpadanta. Danashala or charity room too is located on the side of the entrance. The house keeping equipment is also installed on these squares. The chariot is to the left of the door. The room where alms are given is on the square of Varuna. The granary is to be on the square of Asura and the Armoury on that of Indraraj. The guest chamber is on Mitra's square and mortar (Lukhal Yantrakam) on Roga's. The treasure is to be on the square of Bhudhar. Clarified butter (ghee) and the medicines (Aushdham / simples) are on the square of Naga.

Poison, antidote, well and the shrine are on the squares of Jayanta, Apvatsa, Parjanya and Shiva respectively. The kitchen and storeroom for condiments, together, occupy the squares

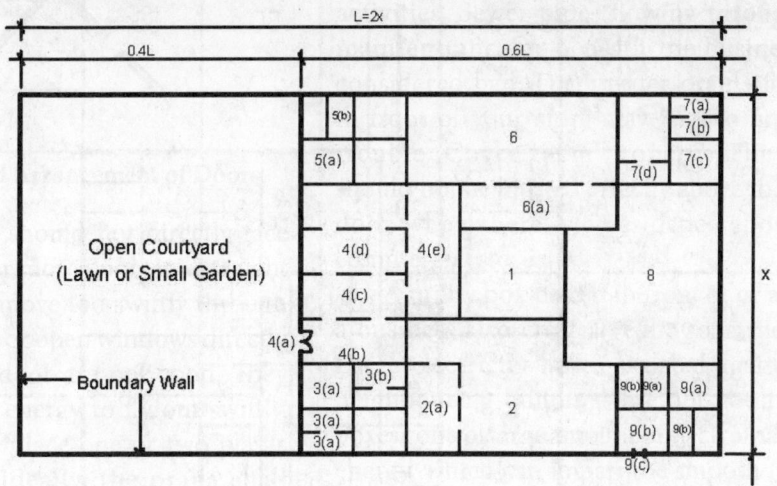

Fig 4.8: Kayabhar Dwelling for Vaishyas as per Mayamatam

1. Central Pavilion and Place of Brahma
2. Principal Main Building (Dhaanyalaya); 2(a). Women's Quarters
3. South-west appurtenances: 3(a). Women's quarters and house keeping equipments; 3(b). Armoury
4. Western Main Building: 4(a). Main Door; 4(b). Chariot Shed; 4(c). Alms Giving Room; 4(d). Granary; 4(e). Guest Chamber
5. North-West Appurtenances: 5(a). Mortar; 5(b). Clarified Butter and Simples
6. Northern Main Building: 6(a). Treasure Room
7. North-East Appurtenances: 7(a). Shrine; 7(b). Well; 7(c). Poisons; 7(d). Antidotes
8. Eastern Main Building.
9. South-East Appurtenances: 9(a). Kitchen and its Store; 9(b). Dining Room; 9(c). Drain Pipe

of Savitr and Antariksha. The pavilion which serves as dining room is best on the squares of Vitatha, Pushan and Saavindra.

Activities and the Relevant Auspicious Squares in a Three Enclosure Palace

Chapter 29 of Mayamatam (verses 12b to 86a) is consecrated to the royal palaces. It gives a general description of various kinds of palaces intended for rulers of different status.

The royal palace has the form of a cluster of buildings with many large free spaces. The ensemble was situated within a town or a fortified camp. It was arranged in concentric zones separated from each other by three or five enclosure walls. Plan for a small palace is described in verses 12 to 86 in Mandook diagram. This smallest palace comprises only three enclosures, to whose the town wall is to be added.

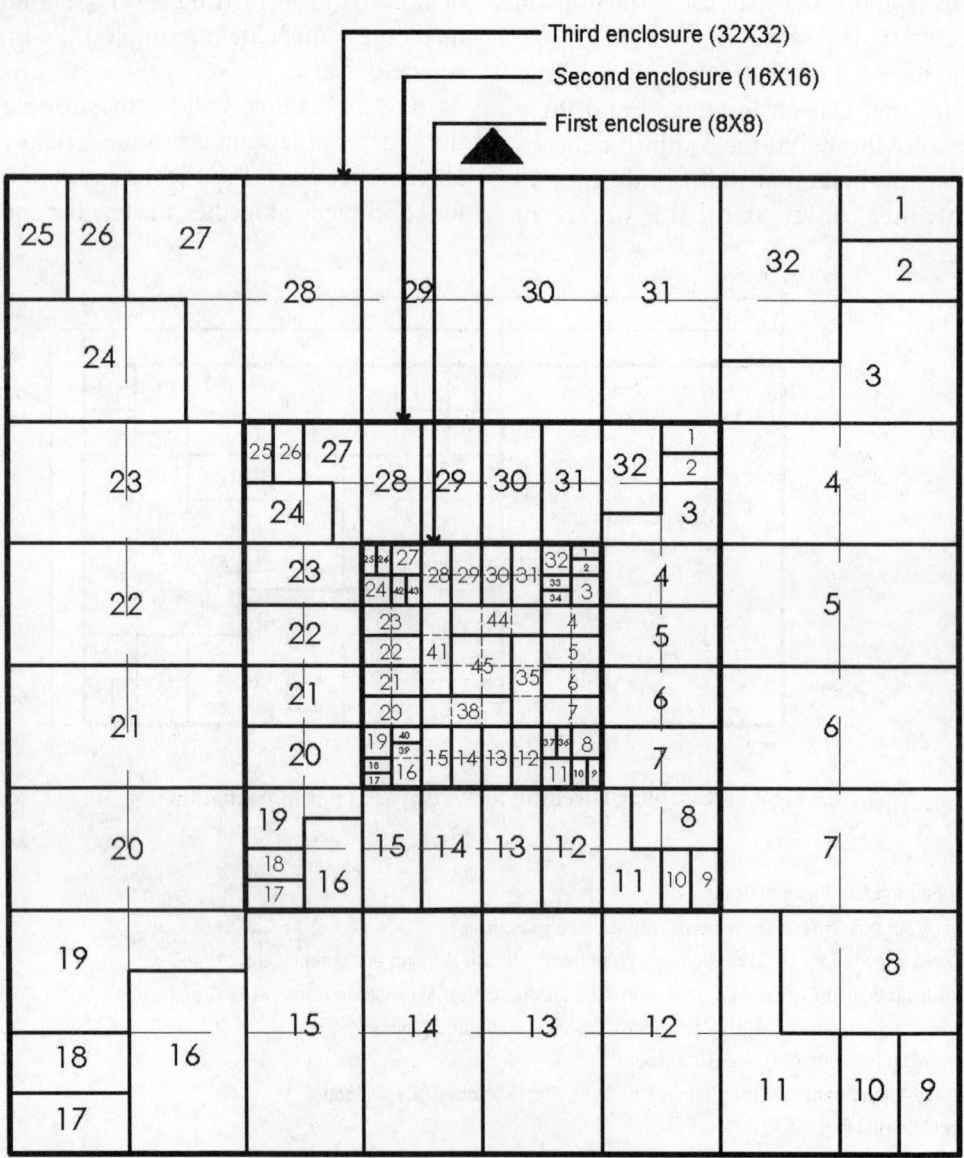

Fig 4.9: Activities in a Three Enclosure Palace

Numerous types of activities have been recommended at different squares in the three enclosures which are given below in a tabular form (see Table 4.2). The same have also been shown in figure 4.9 in three different enclosures. Readers may please note that only 1 to 32 gods are shown in the second enclosure. The rest of the gods (33 to 45) form part of the first enclosure, explained in the Table 4.3. For example; Aap (33) of second enclosure governs (occupies) the squares occupied by Ish (1), Parjanya (2) and Diti (32) of the first enclosure. Likewise shall be understood for the gods (33 to 54) of the third enclosure.

Readers are advised to refer the Figure 4.9 and Table 4.3 simultaneously. For example; "1" marked at the north-east corner of all the three enclosures is the place of "Ish" which is recommended for "king's chosen deity" in the first enclosure. In the second enclosure, "Foster mothers (dhatri)" are recommended on Ish (1), along with on Uditi (32) and Parjanya (2). In the third enclosure "pleasure-ground, lake and other water features of similar nature, orchard, pleasure gardens, large assembly hall with a courtyard, hall with women" is recommended on Ish (1), along with on Mriga (30), Aditi (31), Uditi (32), and Jayanta (3).

Table 4.2: Squares occupied by gods (33 to 45) of second enclosure

S No	Gods of Second Enclosure	Comprises of the equivalent squares occupied by the gods of First Enclosure
1	33 (Aap)	1, 2 and 32
2	34 (Aapvats)	3, 33 and 34
3	35 (Aryama)	4, 5, 6 and 7
4	36 (Savita)	8, 9 and 10
5	37 (Saavitr)	11, 36 and 37
6	38 (Vivasvaan)	12, 13, 14 and 15
7	39 (Indra)	16, 17 and 18
8	40 (Jaya)	19, 39 and 40
9	41 (Mitra)	20, 21, 22 and 23
10	42 (Rudra)	24, 25 and 26
11	43 (Rudraj)	27, 42 and 43
12	44 (Bhudhar)	28, 29, 30 and 31
13	45 (Brahma)	35, 38, 41 and 45

Table 4.3: Activities at 45 Squares in a Three Enclosure Palace

1. Ish or Ishan or Ishaana or Ishaka or Ishdeva or Shikhi or Shikh or Shikhin

First enclosure: King's chosen deity,

Second enclosure: Foster mothers (dhatri) on Uditi, Ish and Parjanya,

Third enclosure: Pleasure-ground on Mriga, Aditi, Uditi, Ishan and Jayanta, lake and other water features of similar nature, orchard, pleasure gardens, large assembly hall with a courtyard, hall with women

2. Parjanya

Second enclosure: Foster mothers (dhatri) on Uditi, Ish and Parjanya

3. Jayanta or Aindra or Jaya

First enclosure: King's chosen Deity

Second enclosure: Distribution of honoraria (dakshinashala); say social welfare department,

Third enclosure: Pleasure-ground on Mriga, Aditi, Uditi, Ishan and Jayanta, lake and other water features of similar nature, orchard, pleasure gardens, large assembly hall with a courtyard, hall with women

4. Indra or Mahendra or Surendra

First enclosure: Large courtyard, dining room

Second enclosure: Chhatra (parasols), bheri (big drums), conches, kahala drums, turahi and other musical instruments, distribution of alms

Third enclosure: Teaching the treatises (shastras)

5. Surya or Bhaskara or Marici

First enclosure: Large courtyard, dining room

Second enclosure: Chhatra (parasols), bheri (big drums), conches, kahala drums, turahi and other musical instruments.

Third enclosure: Learning mathematics (Ganam may also mean singing)

6. Satya or Satyak

Second enclosure: Room for alms giving,

Third enclosure: Learning (adhyayan)

7. Bhrish or Bhrsh

First enclosure: A kind of circular edifice for the bull,

Second enclosure: Free drinking water (charity) for travellers and visitors,

Third enclosure: Learning (adhyayan)

8. Antariksh or Gagan or Akash or Vyoman or Panktika

First enclosure: A kind of circular edifice for the bull,

Second enclosure: Grinding stone and storehouse for fuel,

Third enclosure: Main kitchen

9. Agni or Anila or Vahni (Anala, Jwalan) or Pavaka

Second enclosure: Grinding stone and storehouse for fuel,

Third enclosure: Cows with their calves

10. Pushan

First enclosure: Gold for honoraria,

Second enclosure: Stable for horses,

Third enclosure: Cows with their calves

11. Vitatha

First enclosure: Second possible location for the big courtyard,

Second enclosure: Stable for horses, Second possible location for the big courtyard, Third enclosure: Salt for (preserving) dried meat, gut and skins, second possible location for the big courtyard

12. Brihatkshat or Brihatkshati or Grihatkshat or Rakshasha

First enclosure: Second possible location for the big courtyard,

Second enclosure: Armoury, Second possible location for the big courtyard,

Third enclosure: Elephants' stable, Second possible location for the big courtyard

13. Yama or Dharmaraja or Dharma

First enclosure: Entrance building, greatly elevated and occupied by a guard,

Second enclosure: Preparation of food and drinks (food factory), covered courtyard of buildings,

Third enclosure: Building for painting, shilpa and other entertainment arts and is of dandaka, shurpa or langala plan (It means it is a building with one, two or three main buildings)

14. Gandharva

First enclosure: Building in the shape of a niche. It has a stage and is suitable for the dance. It may be a vimanamandira, a shala or a harmya,

Second enclosure: Commander-in-chief,

Third enclosure: All type of rasa (any liquid/fluid, gold, poison, resin, liquor, metals and minerals, syrup, drink, melted butter etc), store for condiments and such commodities

15. Bhringraja

First enclosure: Stable for horses,

Second enclosure: Commander-in-chief,

Third enclosure: All type of rasa (any liquid/fluid, gold, poison, resin, liquor, metals and minerals, syrup, drink, melted butter etc), store for condiments and such commodities

16. Mrsa or Mrish (Mrig)

First enclosure: Maternity chamber for the woman, who has given birth recently

Second enclosure: Snake (animals in general)-charmers, conjurors (magicians, performers) and others of the kind,

Third enclosure: Fuel

17. Pitar or Nirriti

First enclosure: Harmya or reception pavilion,

Second enclosure: Buffaloes' stable,

Third enclosure: Alms

18. Dauvarika

First enclosure: Queen's dwelling, Jalaleela (water sports) or a room for ablutions,

Second enclosure: Buffaloes' stable,

Third enclosure: Alms

19. Sugriva or Sukantha or Sugala

First enclosure: Queen's dwelling, Jalaleela or a room for ablutions,

Second enclosure: Buffaloes' stable,

Third enclosure: Wrestlers' house

20. Pushpadant or Kusumdant or Pushpa

First enclosure: Queen's dwelling, Annexe where salt and chilly are stored,

Second enclosure: Room for alms, a reception hall and baths,

Third enclosure: Four main building house

21. Varuna or Jaladhip

First enclosure: Sankaralaya or a meeting room for women of all sorts,

Second enclosure: Room for alms, a reception hall and baths,

Third enclosure: House or a maalika for the crown prince, stable for horses and elephants, residence of the purohit (priest).

22. Asura

First enclosure: Sankaralaya or a meeting room for women of all sorts,

Second enclosure: Room for alms, a reception hall and baths,

Third enclosure: Assembly room or Indrashala

23. Shosha

First enclosure: Sankaralaya or a meeting room for women of all sorts,

Second enclosure: Room for alms, a reception hall and baths,

Third enclosure: Deer shed

24. Roga or Papayakshama

First enclosure: Garbhagaar (maternity ward), an entirely closed residential house,

Second enclosure: Room for alms, a reception hall and baths,

Third enclosure: Donkey and camel shed, Infirmary (hospital / sanatorium, treatment of patients)

25. Vayu or Roga / Samirana

First enclosure: Garbhagaar (maternity ward), an entirely closed residential house,

Second enclosure: Room for alms, a reception hall and baths,

Third enclosure: Step well

26. Naga or Gotranaga or Ahi

First enclosure: Maid-servants, foster-mothers, nurses, chambermaids,

Second enclosure: Elongated tank on Naga and Rudra,

Third enclosure: Water pool or lotus pool

27. Mukhya

First enclosure: Young girls (maidens),

Second enclosure: Young (maiden) girls, foster-mothers or nurses, wet-nurses (dhatri).

Separate place at Mukhya for Kanchuki (old aged male attendants of the women's apartments), and madgu (members of a mixed caste who know medicine or they proclaim orders and, thus, may be amongst king's servants),

Third enclosure: Stable for elephants

28. Bhallata

First enclosure: Medical treatment, infirmary (hospital),

Second enclosure: Painters and artists of that kind,

Third enclosure: Stable for horses

29. Soma (Kuber)

Second enclosure: Painters and artists of that kind,

Third enclosure: Maternity chamber (Prasutika) and initiations (upaneetika)

30. Mrga or Mriga or Bhujaga or Shail or Giri

First enclosure: Masseuses' house,

Second enclosure: Painters and artists of that kind,

Third enclosure: Pleasure-ground on Mriga, Aditi, Uditi, Ishan and Jayanta, Long lake and other water features of similar nature, orchard, pleasure gardens, large assembly hall with a courtyard

31. Aditi

Second enclosure: Hunchbacked, dwarf and female eunuchs (barren women),

Third enclosure: Pleasure-ground on Mriga, Aditi, Uditi, Ishan and Jayanta, Lake and other water features of similar nature, orchard, pleasure gardens, large assembly hall with a courtyard, hall with women

32. Uditi or Diti

Second enclosure: Foster mothers on Uditi, Ish and Parjanya (dhatri),

Third enclosure: Pleasure-ground on Mriga, Aditi, Uditi, Ishan and Jayanta, Lake and other water features of similar nature, orchard, pleasure gardens, large assembly hall with a courtyard, hall with women

33. Apah or Aap

First enclosure: Baths with hot water (for baths) and cold water (drinking), place is like a temple,

Second enclosure: Step well, well, long lake, drinking water, flowers and garden

34. Apvatsa

First enclosure: Baths with hot water (for baths) and cold water (drinking), place is like a temple,

Second enclosure: Step well, well, long lake, drinking water, flowers and garden

35. Aryama or Aaryaka or Aarya

First enclosure: Dwarharmya gateway

37. Saavindra or Saavitra

Second enclosure: Stable for horses

41. Mitra

First enclosure: Sankaralaya or a meeting room for women of all sorts, Room for dance and theatre and the also the store room for the properties necessary to these two arts

42. Rudra

Second enclosure: Elongated tank on Rudra and Naga

44. Bhudhara or Prithvidhara or Mahidhara

First enclosure: Dining room

Similar type of activities have also been indicated here and there. Accordingly, the relevant business or public activity shall be performed.

Mayamatam (29.30a) recommends; "A building outside the first enclosure is to be placed in relation to the position of one of the gods of the site".

According to Mayamatam (29.55b); "All these building of second and third enclosures, meant for different purposes, are to face towards the centre of the palace (main building)". One of the striking similarities in the modern context is the layout plan of king's palace of Jaipur.

Mayamatam (29.65-66) further recommends; "The barracks for a portion of the royal army are in the front and on the sides of the palace. The quarter of the merchants and such inhabitants is there as well. To the west of the palace is a large elongated tank, step well, well etc, residence for royal ladies and hereditary servants of the palace".

Mayamatam (29.100b-107a, 29.190a-c) also recommends different commercial, administrative, religious, public and private activities according to the eight major directions. These are given below in a tabular form (Table 4.2), along with a comparative study of the recommendations of Vaastumandanam, Aparajitaprichchha and Samaranganasutradhara (wherever available). In the present time, these recommendations can easily be moulded according to the specific requirement. For example, Mayamatam recommends dwelling of singers and other performers in the northwest. Accordingly, northwest can be utilized for live performances, light and sound shows, musical fountain shows, dance shows and the like.

Table 4.4: Direction wise commercial, public, administrative and religious activities recommended in Mayamatam (29.100b-107a, 29.190a-c), Vaastumandanam (3.14-26), Aparajitaprichchha (72.28-48) and Samaranganasutradhara (10.89-102, 15.19-46) and their equivalent activities in the modern context

1. Northeast

Mayamatam: water, baths and the shrine in front of it, the place for sacrifices, place for water sports, and a hall for eating and drinking with all that is necessary

Vaastumandanam: craftsmen and dyers, temple

Aparajitaprichchha: cloth merchants, jean and other accessories required for horses (now car and automobile accessory shops)

Samaranganasutradhara: people selling clarified butter and fruits

The modern business and commercial activities equivalent to those mentioned in the Samaranganasutradhara can be; fruits and vegetable shops, shops selling perishable eatables like milk, curd, cheese, eggs, bread, butter, jams and fresh bakery items, general stores and the like.

2. East

Mayamatam: courtyard and a merugopura consecrated to goddess Durga in the exterior enclosure

Vaastumandanam: residence of brahmins, big verandah, main door

Aparajitaprichchha: dance-hall in front of the God's temple in the east, southeast, northwest or west, traders dealing in white cloths

Samaranganasutradhara: head of army, political head and other heads of departments

The modern public activities (including professional and administrative activities) equivalent to those mentioned in Samaranganasutradhara can be; headquarters and top level hierarchy concerning the political, army, police, judicial, bureaucratic, media and the like.

3. Southeast

Mayamatam: terraced building or a rostrum (platform) for review of the troops, hall with median courtyard, jewels including gold and raiment are kept here

Vaastumandanam: fire-related workers, people of the lowest castes, cowshed, buffalo-shed, kitchen, kitchen-store

Aparajitaprichchha: dance-hall in front of the God's temple in the east, southeast, northwest or west, open halls with altar for sacrifice (yajna) in a *Matha* (religious place generally inhabited by ascetics), shops of smaller size cloth, tie and dye shops, tailor shops

Samaranganasutradhara: goldsmiths and other workers earning their livelihood through fire related activities, different types of army-men

The modern business activities (including the public, professional, and administrative activities) equivalent to those mentioned in Samaranganasutradhara can be; restaurants, fancy lights, electricity, welding, metallurgy, blacksmithing, jewelry show-rooms and the like, police stations, check posts of different government agencies

4. South

Mayamatam: an aviary (place for keeping birds, monkeys, peacocks, other animals) in a convenient place to the south

Vaastumandanam: kshatriyas and king's employees, room for water (jalghar), dance room, place for dining, lamp

Aparajitaprichchha: residential quarters of ascetics performing yajnas for a *Matha*, appliances; utensils and armaments made of iron, shops of traders of fans, umbrellas, and different types of chowries (Chamar), dyeing with black colour

Samaranganasutradhara: vaishyas, richest businessmen (nagara-seth), other prominent business people (mahattar), dice-gamblers, people working with wheels, actors, dancers, crematorium, watermen (kahar),

The modern business activities (including the public, professional, and religious activities) equivalent to those mentioned in Samaranganasutradhara can be; general stores selling different items, retail stores, casinos, vehicle workshops, wheel & rim balancing workshops, oil-extracting mills, potter's workshops, all factories where circular wheels are used in machinery, acting and dancing schools, theatres and amphitheatres, dance shows, traditional and electric crematoriums in any city, mortuary and the like.

5. Southwest

Mayamatam: hall for music and dance recitals and other entertainments, hall with median courtyard and the private apartments of the concubines are around this hall, garden with residences and places for sport and for water

Vaastumandanam: distillers and vendors of spirituous liquors, prostitutes, people of the lowest castes (Rajavallabha), bath room for ladies of maternity chamber

Samaranganasutradhara: people involved in rearing and killing pig; sheep and deer, fishermen, manufacturers of sharp smelling (hard) liquor, boating, horse-trainers and other animal trainers, law-enforcement officials

The modern business activities (including the public, professional, and administrative activities) equivalent to those mentioned in Samaranganasutradhara can be; medium size animal husbandry, slaughter house, butcher's shop, fisheries, leather industry, country made (desi) liquor units and shops, boat and ship-building industry, dog-training, horse-training, police stations, army cantonment and the like.

6. West

Vaastumandanam: water features like water tank, stepped well and well

Aparajitaprichchha: dance-hall in front of the God's temple in the east, south-east, north-west or west

Samaranganasutradhara: chariot making, weapons and munitions making, people involved in reformative activities, treasurer (koshpal), head of ministers, high officials, trained workers (shilpi), exporters (through boats and ships)

The modern business activities (including the public, professional, administrative and religious activities) equivalent to those mentioned in Samaranganasutradhara can be; heavy industries, heavy vehicle and car manufacturing industries, ordinance factories, shops selling guns and fire-arms, reform organizations (social, religious, political, regional, caste-based, national etc), head office of any bank, organizations involved in money keeping and big transactions of money, treasury of any organization, upper level of bureaucrats and technocrats, schools imparting expert technical knowledge, engineering colleges, heads of different organizations, companies and people related to foreign trade, transporters and the like.

7. Northwest

Mayamatam: dwelling of singers and other performers, lodging in the form of a hall occupied by women of all sorts

Vaastumandanam: hunters, body massage, granary

Aparajitaprichchha: dance-hall in front of the God's temple in the east, southeast, northwest or west

Samaranganasutradhara: labourers, workers, servants and their associates, people involved in making and selling liquor, law enforcement officials

The modern business activities (including the public, professional, and administrative activities) equivalent to those mentioned in Samaranganasutradhara can be; companies providing unskilled and semi-skilled manpower to the local and overseas organizations, distilleries, wine and liquor shops, police check posts, government agencies with flying squads (Vigilance Department, CBI, CID, ACB etc), officials involved in outdoor activities, worker's or servant's room in any organization and the like.

8. North

Vaastumandanam: vaishyas, shudras, valuable objects (treasury), verandah, garden, cloth-room (wardrobe), worship of idols, medicine room

Aparajitaprichchha: dyers using Indian madder, dyeing with red colour, coconut traders, all types of articles of household used for dharma, artha and kama purposes

Samaranganasutradhara: ashrams for ascetics, assemblies of people with great wisdom (brahamvats or brahamgyanis), free water stall (prapa or piao), punyashala, dharmashala, priests, astrologer

The modern public activities (including the business, professional, and religious activities) equivalent to those mentioned in Samaranganasutradhara can be; all type of activities where the ultimate aim to be one with 'Brahm' – the Ultimate one, religious and charitable organizations, alms-giving, providing free of cost food to the needy people, religious preaching (Bhaagvat Katha, Ram Katha, Shiv Purana etc), place for free drinking water, bottling of drinking water, office of Astrologer or Astro-Palmist or Vaastu expert and the like.

9. Centre

Vaastumandanam: king's palace with extensions towards the right and left sides, beautiful residential quarters for businessmen involved in the import of fruits, betel leaves, variegated flowers, clothes, and precious gems like pearls from different countries.

10. Outside

Vaastumandanam: wrath-room or room for stress release outside of the southwest

Activities and the Relevant Auspicious Squares in a Saubala Palace (Palace with Five Enclosures) as per Mayamatam (29.108 -129)

According to Mayamatam (29.108 -129), this palace is most probably that of the chakravartin kings. The plan is laid out according to five concentric diagrams shown in figure 4.10. Starting from the centre they are the sakala (with one square) and the pitha (9 squares) for the first enclosure, then the upapitha (25 squares, second enclosure), sthandila (49 squares, third enclosure), paramshayin (81 squares, fourth enclosure) and sthaniya (121 squares, fifth enclosure).

Intelligent readers can get clues from the squares prescribed for different activities. For example, tank for water sports is recommended on the square of Vayu in the second enclosure. This space may be utilized now a day exclusively as a Water Park or water sports area in an amusement park.

Classical Principles of Administrative, Business, Professional, Public and Religious Vaastu

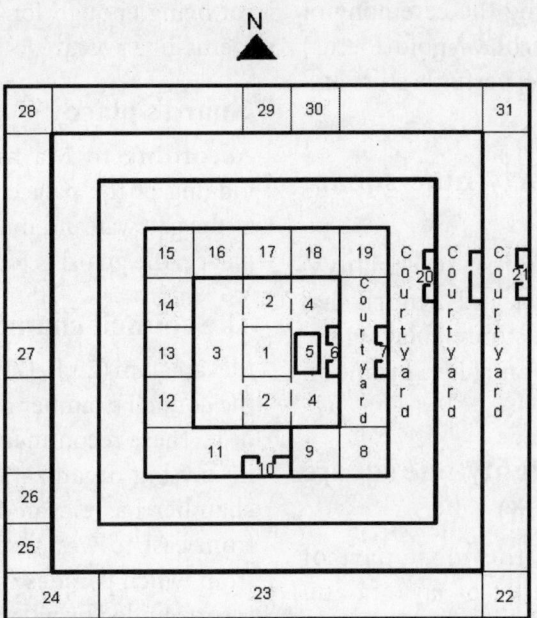

Fig 4.10: Activities at 45 Squares in a Saubala Palace

First enclosure: 1. Central pavilion and altar of Brahma; 2. Queen's apartments; 3. King's apartments; 4. Courtyard; 5. Coronation pavilion; 6. Gateway
Second enclosure: 7. Gateway; 8. Kitchen; 9. Treasury; 10. Gateway; 11. Women's lodgings; 12. Theatre; 13. King's lodgings; 14. Antahpur (purdah quarters); 15. Tank for water sports; 16. Queen's lodging; 17. Tulabhar and hemgarbh ceremony; 18. Store (gold and jewels, perfume) and elephant's stable; 19. Tank, latrines and hydraulic machine
Third enclosure: 20. Gateway
Fourth enclosure: May be a gateway opposite the gateway at third and fifth enclosure
Fifth enclosure: 21. Main gateway and Goddess Durga temple; 22. Offices and main kitchen; 23. Exercise place; 24. King's dwellings; 25. Annexes; 26. Women's house; 27. Sankaralaya; 28. Tank, garden and hermitage; 29. Tulabhar ceremony; 30. Hemgarbh ceremony; 31. Temple of Lord Shiva

First enclosure (Nine square pitha diagram)

Altar of Brahma placed on a single square in the centre which rests on a platform in a pavilion, queen's apartment in the north and the south, house of the emperor with several storeys in the west, courtyard in the east which is embellished in the centre by a dvarashobha gateway, a coronation pavilion just west of the gateway,

Second enclosure (Twenty-five square upapitha diagram)

Tank and a well, recitations, and hydraulic machines on the square of Ish, Courtyard on the squares of Jayanta, Bhanu and Bhrisha with a dvaraharmya gateway of at least three storeys, kitchen on the square of Agni, family treasure on the square of Vitatha, women's lodgings on the squares of Yama, Bhringnripa and Pitar, theatre on the square of Sugriva, lodging for the king on the square of Varuna, purdah quarters (antahpur) on the square of Shosha, tank for water sports on Vayu,

House or a malika for the queen on Mukhya (malika are rows of buildings of different sorts linked together in order to form a garland; they house attendants shrines as well as other annexes), ritual weighing (tulabhara or gift of gold, or anything else like rice or even straw equal to a man's weight) on

Soma (Kuber), performing the ceremony of gold embryo (hiranyagarbha / gold foetus) on Mriga, gold and jewels, perfume store and elephant's stable on Diti.

Third enclosure (Forty-nine square sthandila diagram)

Courtyard on the squares of Parjanya, Mahendra, Bhanu, Satya and Antariksha, gateway with four or five storeys, playing the instruments like conches and bheri drums on Mahendra,

Fourth enclosure (Eighty-one square paramshayin diagram)

Courtyard occupying the most part of the squares between those of Jayanta and Antariksha

Fifth enclosure (Hundred and twenty-one square sthaniya diagram)

Shiva's dwelling on Ish, exterior gateway and temple of Durga on Surya, main kitchen, scribes and those who work in the administration of the palace on the square of Agni, a huge closed courtyard occupies eight squares in the south of the 11x11 diagram and is meant for exercising horses or elephants and also a rostrum (stage) on Yama, king's dwelling on Pitar, annexe on Dauvarika, women's house on Sugriva, sankaralaya with a hall or malika for water sport and a residential building on Varuna, tank and place reserved for a garden and a hermitage on Vayu, ritual weighing on Soma, performing the ceremony of gold embryo (hiranyagarbha / gold foetus) on Mriga.

Tulabhara and hiranyagarbha were placed amongst the 'big gifts' (mahadana). For tulabhara the gift was that of gold (or anything else such as rice, or even straw) of which the weight is equal to that of the donor. In the case of hiranyagarbha, the donor is to maka a gold vat being enough for him to get into it, in a foetus-like posture.

Guard's place

According to Mayamatam (29.226), the lodging of the palace guard is twice as high as the gateway and must be solid. Outside the palace, the guard is to be secured by patrols.

The council chamber

Mayamatam (29.191-194a) gives an account of the council chamber and sitting arrangement in it. These recommendations can be utilized in any big organization. The king's council chamber has elevated walls. It is elongated from east to west and is pleasant. The hall, from which parades can be seen from far off, is surrounded by pillars and not by walls. That last may also be a rostrum (a platform for public speaking).

The royal throne-of-lions is to be installed in the western section of the council chamber in accordance with the rules and facing the east. The minister's seat is to the south-east of this throne, that of the ambassador (envoy) to the north-east, that of the prashastra (administrator / chief magistrate) to the north and that of the commander-in-chief to the south. All these seats are separated from one another by intervals which are both equal and narrow.

Vaastu Purush

Mayamatam (7.50-54) describes the Vaastu Purush, considering his head in the east; "It is said that the divinity named Aarya is his head, that Savindra is his right arm and Saavindra his right hand, that Apa and Apavatsa are his left arm and left hand, that Vivasvant is his right side and Mahidhara his left, that in the middle his trunk is Brahma, that his testicles are Mitra, and his right foot and leg are Indra and Indraraja and his left foot and leg are Rudra and Rudrajaya.

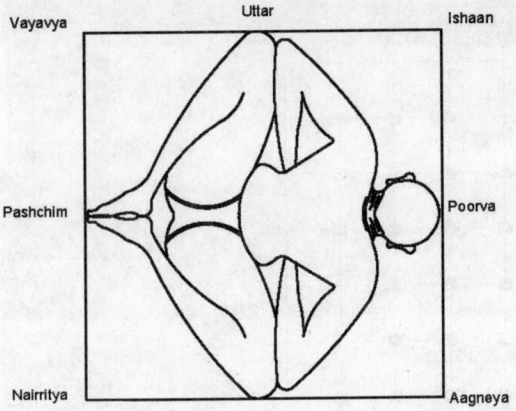

Fig 4.11: East Oriented Vaastu Purush

He rests with his face to the ground; his six bones, orientated to the east and north, are in the middle of the (central) parts of the site. In the centre of the site are found the vulnerable points and the heart which is Brahma and it is from there that the veins (or diagonals) start. Thus the spirit is described".

Marma-Sthanas or Vulnerable Points of the site (MM, 6.16-17, 7.49, 7.55-56, 9.86, 27.15b-19)

Whether the house be small or large, a line delimiting it must first be drawn, called seemasutra or paryantasutra. Those knowledgeable in the subject of building are to take care to avoid wounding the marma sthanas. A wound inflicted by the 'limbs' of the house on the lines or other vulnerable points, causes the complete destruction of the house. Care must also be taken to avoid touching the lines and other vulnerable points (MM, 27.15b-19).

In mandook pada vaastu (64 pada vaastu), vaastu purush (the spirit of the building) has six bones (vamsha or north-south line of the diagram), a single heart, four vulnerable points (marma) and four vessels (shira or diagonal) and that he lies upon the ground, his head towards the east. However, according to Prasada-Mandana, the head of vaastu purush is often placed towards the north-east (MM, 7.49).

These are the six places where there should be no temples or buildings of that kind: the heart of the spirit of the site, its bones, the stakes, the lines of the diagram, their intersections, and the diagonals and parallels (MM, 9.86). The stakes (shoola) must be the khatashanku used in the laying out operations. Khatashanku or the 'buried stakes' are used at the time of the laying out to mark the place of different parts of the building and will remain in the ground afterwards. (MM, 6.16-17)

Vaastu Purush is responsible for good and bad fortune in every human dwelling. Therefore the wise must avoid tormenting his limbs with the limbs of the house. Otherwise, innumerable sorrows will fall upon the limbs of the owner of the house. Thus the sage must always spare the body of the spirit in the course of construction (MM, 7.55-56).

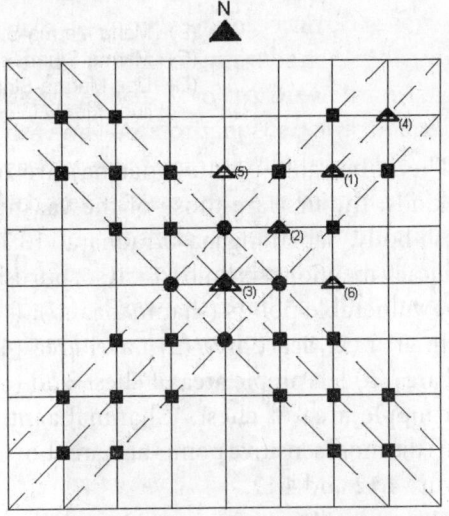

Fig. 4.12: Marma Sthanas in Mandook Vaastu

(A) Shan-Mahaanti : (1) Mouth Area
                  (2) Heart Area
                  (3) Navel Area
                  (4) Head Area
                  (5) Left Nipple Area
                  (6) Right Nipple Area
(B) Maha Marma-Sthanas (5) : ●
(C) Marma-Sthanas (25) : ■
(D) Upa-Marma-Sthanas: All Other Points where 2,3 or 4 lines Meet / Intersect.

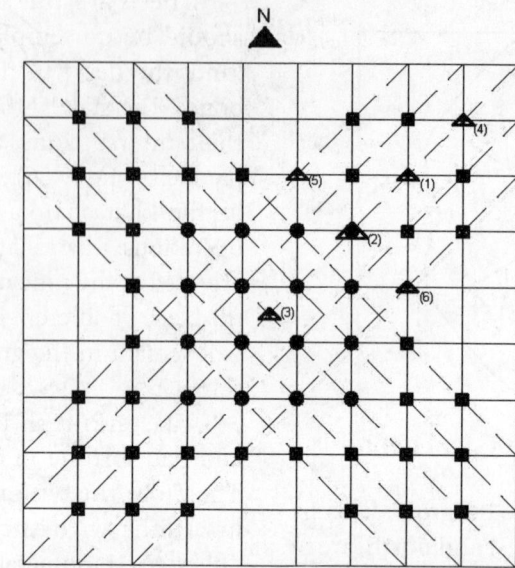

Fig. 4.13: Marma Sthanas in Paramshayin Vaastu
(A) Shan-mahaanti : (1) Mouth Area
                 (2) Heart Area
                 (3) Navel Area
                 (4) Head Area
                 (5) Left Nipple Area
                 (6) Right Nipple Area
(B) Maha Marma-Sthanas (16): ●
(C) Marma-Sthanas (36) : ■
(D) Upa-Marma-Sthanas: All other points where 2,3 or 4 lines Meet / Intersect.

The vulnerable points (marma) are of two kinds; the first are those of the vaastu-purush body. Samaranganasutradhara (13.7) specifically mentions six limbs of vaastu purush as the vulnerable points (shanmahaanti): (1) mouth area (2) heart area (3) navel area (4) head area (5) left nipple area of chest, and (6) right nipple area of chest. "Shanmahaanti" means the most sensitive points and are shown in figure 4.12 and 4.13.

The second kind of vulnerable points are the intersection points of the lines making up the diagram with the two diagonals as well as with other lines parallel to the diagonals. Each of the two diagonals gets two parallels when the diagram has sixty-four squares, clarified in the figure 4.12 and four parallels when the diagram comprises eighty-one squares, clarified in the figure 4.13. The second kind of vulnerable points are again divided in two categories based on their gravity: marma sthanas (also called maha-marma or ati-marma sthanas); where five, six or eight lines intersect and upa-marma sthanas; where two, three or four lines meet. These Marma sthanas are shown here in Mandook Vaastu (64 squares) as well as in Paramshayin Vaastu (81 squares).

Auspicious Shapes

Mayamatam (10.42b-43, 29.8b-9) describes auspicious shapes meant for enclosure of royal palace which include; square, square with curved sides, circular, semi-circular, rectangular, elliptical, triangular, octagonal, svastika shaped, chariot-shaped (shakata), nandyavarta shaped, shaped like a cock, shaped like the upper part of the forehead of an elephant, like a coiled snake, convex like a mridanga, and concave.

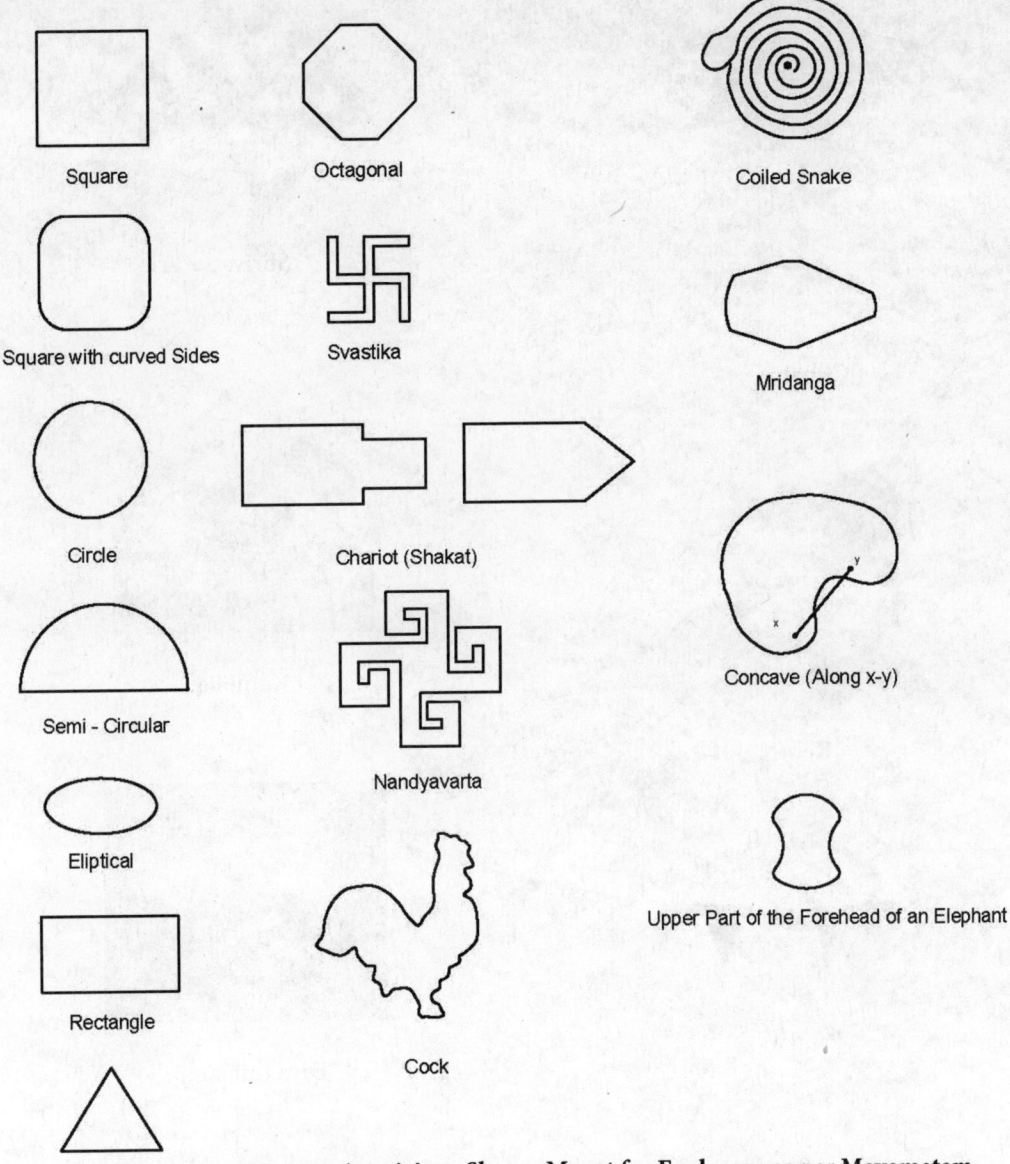

Fig 4.14: Auspicious Shapes Meant for Enclosure as per Mayamatam

Twelve types of these shapes shall deliver auspicious results when any of these is used as an enclosure for any commercial or factory premises, farm-house, hospital, educational institute or any other type of large premises; including a city.

Propitious Objects

According to Mayamatam (27.79, 29.225); "The eight propitious objects are on the fillets and other mouldings of the crossbeam of the arch which rests on the top of the pillars. The series of eight propitious objects fitting for all is: parasol (chhatra), flag (Ketu), standard (pataka or small flags in a row), Bheri (an Indian musical instrument), shri (-vatsa), vase (Kumbha), lamp and the nandyavarta".

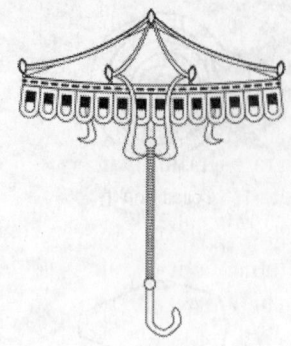
Chhatra

Shrivatsa

Ketu

Kumbha

Pataka

Diya (oil lamp)

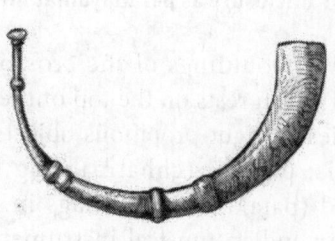
Bheri

Nandyavarta

Fig 4.15: Eight Propitious Objects

The signs mentioned above are considered very auspicious in Hindu religious traditions, Hindu Palmistry and Hindu Lakshana Shastra (Omenology).

Gateways and Doors

There should be four gateways to the city of small status. The main gateway is to be the most elevated, the western gateway the least. The main gateway faces east or south since it is not auspicious to orientate it to the north or west. (Mayamatam, 29.22-24a)

A main entrance to the north does not suit 'kings'. It is not suitable for kings to have five entrances (Mayamatam, 26.109a, 137a).

It is the privilege of narendra kings to have the largest gate on the square of Mahendra but it may also be on that of Rakshasha and have five or three storeys. The gates on the squares of Pushpadanta and Bhallata have fewer storeys (Mayamatam 29.75-76a).

There are also to be one or two storeyed side gates on the squares of Sugriva, Mukhya, Jayanta and Vitatha (Mayamatam 29.76b-77a).

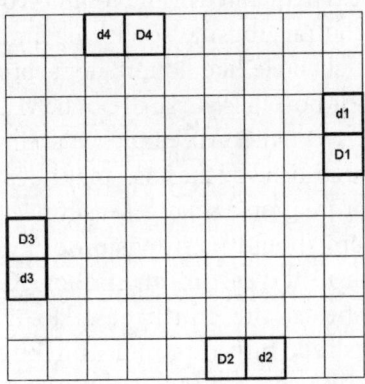

D1, D2, D3 and D4 - Main Gates   d1, d2, d3 and d4 - Side Gates

Fig 4.16: Gateways' Location

According to the learned, the way to calculate the proportions of the door of a house intended for men is: the height of the pillars of that house being divided into eight parts, the door takes up six and a half. Half the height of the door being divided into nine parts, a half part is reserved and the remainder is the width of the door (Mayamatam, 27.128).

It is auspicious when main entrance of the house is on the square of Rakshasha, Pushpadanta, Bhallata or Mahendra. It is known that there is an increase in wealth, lineage and cattle for the owner, the entrance of whose house is of auspicious proportions and is placed between a pillar and a wall (Mayamatam, 27.132).

Additions and alterations

If, when the house is finished, it is found to be smaller than envisaged for whatever reason, that will be inauspicious and will cause the inhabitant endless misfortune (Mayamatam, 29.11).

If the enlargement of a house built by the ancients is desired, it is best to enlarge it to the north or east but it is not forbidden to extend it to all directions on the periphery (Mayamatam, 29.11b-12a).

When it is desired that a ruined building be reconstructed in an existing sanctuary in another place, he who has knowledge of architecture avoids making it at the cardinal points or outside the sanctuary. A transgression of this rule brings bad luck. Thus the procedure should be carried out according to the appropriate mode. A building should be re-erected without the foundation rituals as these have already been accomplished for the destroyed monument (Mayamatam, 35.12b-14).

Palace

It is the narendra's privilege to have their palace on Indra's square ie in the southwest. (Mayamatam 29.78)

A palace adjoining to Brahma's square is a source of good fortune and of complete success. It is probably in relation to the town diagram.

King's dwelling is in a place selected, south of the place of Brahma, and that of senior queen is to the north. (Mayamatam 29.98a-99b)

Other Useful Recommendations

The man of sensible mind proceeds according to the specific circumstances in all cases where there is no prescription. (Mayamatam 29.85b)

If water falls on the wall around the house this brings ruin to the family. Thus, edge of the roof of the house shall not abut onto this wall. If it happens, then all chance of success is spoiled, no matter for what class the house is intended. (Mayamatam, 27.125b-126)

It is auspicious if the height of the house is calculated in relation to its width and length. It causes death if done otherwise. (Mayamatam, 27.127)

The main building is oriented towards the interior. Where the site is concerned, the orientation must be towards the exterior. (Mayamatam, 27.39b)

Shasta (auspicious, knowledge), Durga, Gajamukha and Lakshmi should respectively be worshipped at the places of Arya, Vivasvant, Mitra and Prithidhara. Beyond this the temples are placed all around as in a village. Houses for all castes are installed a little farther away. (Mayamatam, 10.88-89)

Vaastumandanam

"King must arrange for shops, bazaars, boundary wall, city gates, palace, public gardens, victory tower and water tank in the city and thus beautify it". (Vaastumandanam, 3.33)

"In the heart of king's city, beautiful residential quarters shall be constructed for businessmen involved in the import of fruits, betel leaves, variegated flowers, clothes, and precious gems like pearls from different countries. Brahmins shall inhabit the front part of king's palace". (Vaastumandanam, 3.15)

"The residence of Brahmins shall be in the eastern part of the city. Kshatriyas and king's employees shall be in the south and vaishyas in the north. Water features like water tank, stepped well and well shall be in the west and shudras in the north". (Vaastumandanam, 3.24)

"Craftsmen and dyers shall be in the northeast, fire-related workers (goldsmiths, blacksmiths etc) and people of the lowest castes shall be in the southeast, distillers and vendors of spirituous liquors, and prostitutes in the southwest and hunters in the northwest". (Vaastumandanam 3.25)

Mandana recommends southwest for people of the lowest castes in his another text "Rajavallabha".

"People residing in the corners of a city, village or house suffer. It is a vaastu defect. However, people of the lowest castes (Chamaar, Chaandaal, Dom, Shvpach (dog keeper / feeder / eater etc) progress when residing in the corners". (Vaastumandanam 3.26)

It can be interpreted from the above that businesses of mass appeal, which are generally considered auspicious, are not good in the corners. Auspicious type of businesses shall be in the areas frequented by the common people. On the contrary, businesses having limited or selective clientele like liquor shops, brothels, casinos, or hospitals etc shall not be visible to the general public. An employee sitting in a corner, unnoticed by the boss, may not receive his due promotion or may get easily neglected.

"There should be provision of a bigger verandah in the east of main door. Kitchen should be in the south-east. Provision for cowshed, buffalo-shed and kitchen-store shall also be done in the south-east". (Vastumandanam 5. 3)

"Room for water, dance room and place for dining shall be in the south. Bath room for ladies of maternity chamber shall be in the south-west. Wrath-room or room for stress release shall be outside". (Vaastumandanam 3.4)

"Water tank shall be in the west, body massage and granary in the northwest, valuable objects (treasury), verandah and garden in the north and temple in the north-east". (Vaastumandanam 5.5)

"House of the owner shall be in the middle which can be used as a bedroom, if so desired. Cloth-room, worship of idols and medicine room shall be in the left side of house i.e. towards the north and lamp in the south at a proper square". (Vastumandanam 5.8)

Dwara Vedha (Obstruction to the door)

Vastumandanam (4.70) recommends that door shall not be obstructed by a passage. It should not be obstructed by a raised platform or a cross-way, place where three roads meet, temple, God's idol, flag, stepped well, well, drain, water pond or still water. Obstruction caused by a wall, corner, tree, pillar, opposite door, grinding stone, balance (height equal to pillar), weapons and tools, thorny creeper, mud, nail, trap, deception and web shall also be avoided.

If door is in the middle or there is a door opposite the main door, it will invite diseases, sufferings to the family-line and loss of money. The result will also be the same when door is obstructed by any material object, balance, pillar, window and peg in the wall to hang things upon.

Importance of the direction of Main Door over the direction of Sunrise

Most of the classical vaastu texts – including Maansaar, Mayamatam and Samaranganasutradhara – have given a detailed account of finding directions based on the movement of Sun. Only after finding the eight directions, proper space allocation is done for different activities.

According to Vaastumandanam (5.1); "Consider the direction of existing main door of any residence as east. Accordingly, find out all the directions and allocate space for various activities including dining and sleeping, done otherwise may invite destruction."

Mandana has thus tried to break the old established tradition. It must be kept in mind that vaastu rules date back to the times of Vedas. During those days sufficient land for construction purposes was easily available free of cost and it was easy to construct as per the principles of ideal vaastu. Later on, with the sharp increase in population and consequent space scarcity, it became near to impossible for a common person to purchase a vaastu friendly ideal plot in a city. Most of the time, the end user is destined to purchase a builder flat, having no relation with the principles of ideal vastu. In such a situation, one can take advantage of the recommendation of Mandana. However, principles of ideal vaastu shall always rule supreme.

Recommendation of Mandana helps us in space allocation for different activities where ideal facing is not available. For example; as per the ideal vaastu, bed room shall be in the southwest. Also main door is ideally located towards the northeast or east. In this way, bed-room in the southwest is farthest from the northeast when counted from the face of Vaastu Purush throughout the year (fixed vaastu). When east is considered the entry of ideal vastu, the bed-room in the southwest falls in the left extreme corner.

Accordingly, applying the recommendations of Mandana, the bed-room shall be remotest area from the main door (while entering) or it shall be the farthest corner towards the left from the main door. Space for other activities like kitchen, dining, drawing, storage, studies, children, and prayers are also allocated. Following the recommendations of Mandana, probable space allocation for different activities in a flat or house having main entry in the southwest is shown in figure 4.17 here.

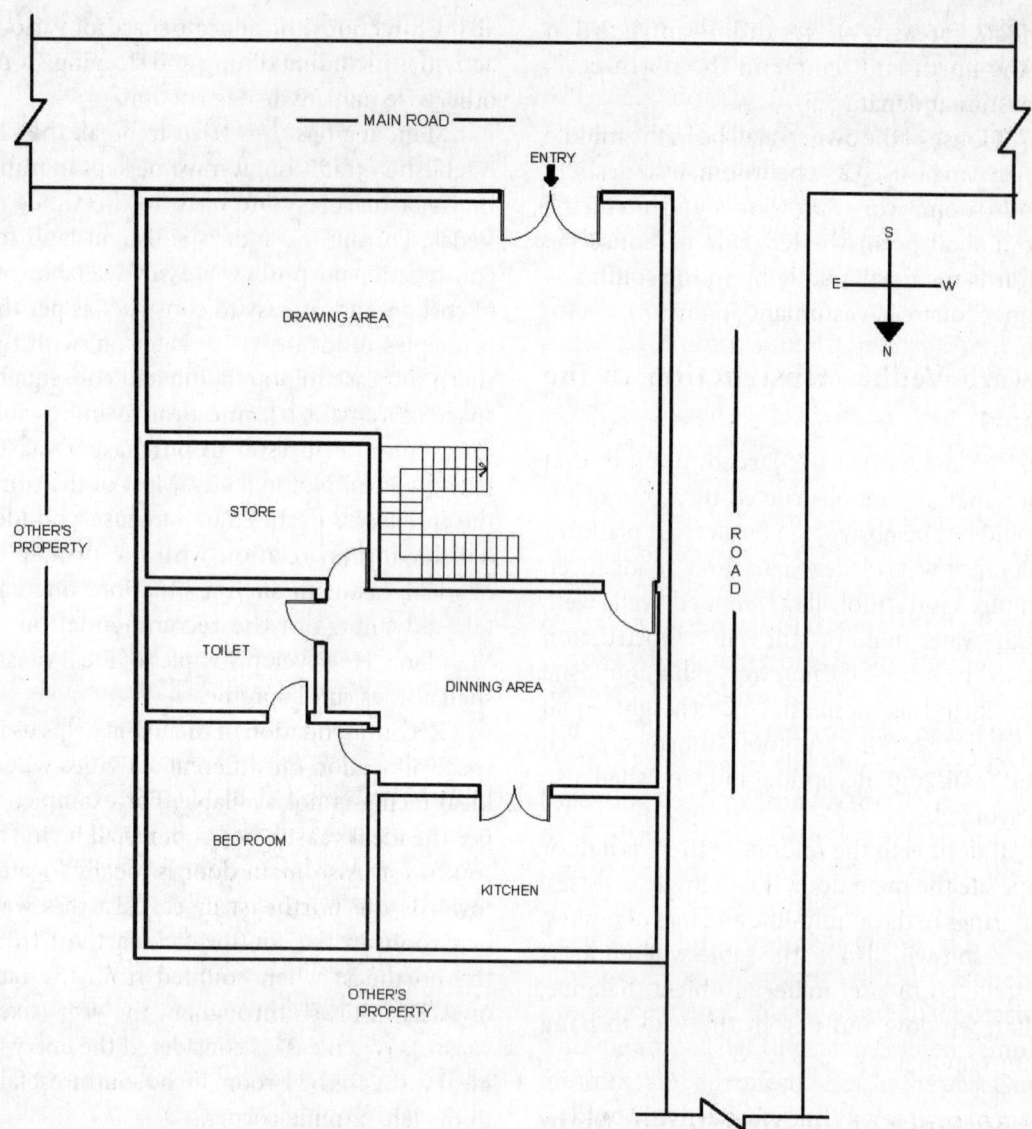

Fig 4.17: Space Allocation Considering Main Door in the South-west Zone

In Chinese Feng Shui system, the equivalent of Indian Vaastu Shastra, it is an established practice to decide the eight sectors of any premises based on the direction of main door. With the mega increase in population and unavailability of ideal locations recommended by the ancient texts of Feng Shui, some Feng Shui schools consider main door as the direction of dragon and allocate the different activities accordingly.

For Muslims throughout the world, the direction of holy Mecca is the most desirable direction, irrespective of the geographical directions. In India it is west while for Egyptian Muslims it is east. Door of any vaastu may be equalized with one's deity.

Exceptions in Vaastu

According to Vaastumandanam (1.89); "There is nothing anti-vaastu, when without considering the directions, any vaastu related work is done on the riverside, on the confluence of rivers, in a Teertha (a holy place for bathing in a river or a water tank), as a fort, Siddhashram (an accomplished hermitage) or on a mountain. However, it is always better to follow the rules of vaastu".

River banks, mountains and holy places are thought to automatically fulfill the vaastu requirements to a large extent. Shilpa Ratnakar (2.76) considers these places fit for construction of a temple.

Secular Nature of Vaastu

Vaastu is not related to vegetarianism or particular sect or religion. It has been said in Vaastumandanam (1.128) that, "The eight evil goddesses residing in eight directions outside the constructed premises and cruel gods like Yama shall be worshipped with non-vegetarian food, liquor and meat. Rest of the gods shall be worshipped with the things like ghee (clarified butter), cooked vegetarian food, scents and gold."

Worst types of evil-goddesses have been kept outside the premises. We can equate it with the example of the temples of Khajuraho where sculptures depicting sexual postures are shown only on the outer periphery.

Auspicious Pillar Shapes

Only circular, hexagonal, octagonal, twelve sided and sixteen sided pillars are considered auspicious in the residence. (Vaastumandanam, 7.8)

Pictures and Paintings

Pictures, paintings and photographs depicting mythological events and stories are inauspicious in the residence but are considered auspicious in the temples. (Vaastumandanam, 7.10)

Forty-five Squares and Auspicious Activities

Vaastumandanam (3.14-26) recommends specific directions for different business, commercial and public activities while describing vaastu of town and city. Recommendations of Vaastumandanam and equivalent modern business activities are given in table 4.4, along with a comparative study of the recommendations available in Mayamatam, Aparajitaprichchha and Samaranganasutradhara

Readers are advised to use their discretionary powers and interpret the meanings in a particular context. For example, southeast is said to be the place for 'fire-related workers'. 'Fire related workers' in the modern context can be interpreted as goldsmiths, blacksmiths, bakery owners, restaurateurs, electricians, welders, chemists dealing in harsh chemicals, stunts men, dare-devils, formula-one racers and the like.

Vaastumandanam (5.1-29) - while discussing vaastu of a king's palace - also gives a detailed account of auspicious squares for different personal and public activities, administrative departments and king's officials. Forty-five demigods' wise recommendations of Vaastumandanam are given below in Table 4.5, with a comparative analysis of the recommendations available in Samaranganasutradhara and Aparajitaprichchha. These can easily be interpreted in the modern days' changed context. For example, an 'anxiety room outside of Mriga square may mean 'releasing place for concern, worry, and tensions'. Thus it becomes the best place for location of a psychiatric chamber and / or the department of Psychiatry in a super specialty hospital.

'Wrestling ground' recommended at the square of Sugreeva may be utilized as a gymnasium, or an exercising hall. The square of 'Pushpadant' is said to be the 'parade ground'. It can be the parade ground for routine police and military exercises. Asura, which is considered good for the 'art of magic', may be utilized for construction of an amusement park. Readers may refer chapter 2 "Vaastu

Gods and Goddesses" for gaining further insights in this regard.

According to the Vaastumandanam (5.18); "The official who strictly enforces the laws shall be on the square of Satya which is equally good for the study room. Granary and Vyapar (trade) shall be on Bhrisha and kitchen on the square of Agni. 'Bhrisha' has been recommended for 'granary and businesses'. The word "Vyapar" used here in the shloka may also be interpreted as business, workplace, profession, performance, job, action, activity and the like. The square of Bhrisha falls in the east of south-east which receives the benefic sunrays throughout the daytime. These sunrays are considered vital for righteous earning.

Auspicious squares prescribed in Vaastumandanam (5.1-29), Aparajitaprichchha (76.3-40) and Samaranganasutradhara (15.19-50) are given below. Readers may please note that activities prescribed by these texts are not complete and some of the squares have been left unattended. Recommendations of Mayamatam have already been discussed at length in this chapter under the heading "Activities and the relevant auspicious squares in a three enclosure palace according to Mayamatam (29.12b-86a)" and "Activities and the Relevant Auspicious Squares in a Saubala Palace (Palace with Five Enclosures) as per Mayamatam (29.108 -129)".

Table 4.5: Comparative statement of auspicious squares recommended for different administrative, commercial, professional, public, and religious activities as per Vaastumandanam (5.1-29), Aparajitaprichchha (76.3-40) and Samaranganasutradhara (15.19-50)

1. Ish or Ishan or Ishaana or Ishaka or Ishdeva, Shikhi or Shikh or Shikhin

Vaastumandanam: temple of God
Aparajitaprichchha: big store house
Samaranganasutradhara: worship or place for the family-god (Kuldevta)

2. Parjanya

Vaastumandanam: king's court of justice (magistracy) towards the back of Parjanya,
Aparajitaprichchha: king's court of justice (magistracy) towards the back of parjanya
Samaranganasutradhara: king's astrologer or soothsayer

3. Jayanta or Aindra or Jaya

Vaastumandanam: place of bhagwati Lakshmi, abhyas-mandap (effort of the mind to remain in its unmodified condition of purity) and water pond

Aparajitaprichchha: head administrative office, Jail

4. Indra or Mahendra or Surendra

Aparajitaprichchha: beautiful step well, temple of Goddess Katyayani

5. Surya or Bhaskara or Marici

Vaastumandanam: disbursement room and verandah, hot water bath tub and massage
Aparajitaprichchha: treasurer, registrar office, archive, accountant general (now CAG), announcing sentence to the culprits

6. Satya or Satyak

Vaastumandanam: place for the official who enforces the law ruthlessly, school
Aparajitaprichchha: administration or court of justice

Samaranganasutradhara: courts of law, law enforcement agencies like police and army, other agencies controlling the public behavior

7. Bhrish or Bhrsh

Vaastumandanam: granary, business (vyapar)
Aparajitaprichchha: fodder-house on Savitra, Agni, Bhritya, and Antariksha
Samaranganasutradhara: granary, store-room

8. Antariksh or Gagan or Akash or Vyoman or Panktika or Nabha or Ambar

Aparajitaprichchha: fodder-house on Savitra, Agni, Bhritya, and Antariksha
Samaranganasutradhara: deer-house (zoo) and bird's house (bird sanctuary, aviary or a nest)

9. Agni or Anila or Vahni (Anala, Jwalan) or Pavaka or Marut

Vaastumandanam: kitchen, grains, cowshed
Aparajitaprichchha: fodder-house on Savitra, Agni, Bhritya, and Antariksha
Samaranganasutradhara: kitchen

10. Pushan

Vaastumandanam: military practice (Abhyasalaya / exercise, drill)
Samaranganasutradhara: durbar hall, assembly hall for prominent people (In modern context Sansad Bhavan and Vidhan Sabha Bhavan), dining hall / room

11. Vitatha

Vaastumandanam: arsenal of army men wearing defensive armors or army barracks or their dining room
Aparajitaprichchha: chariot-place, offices of water supply department for water conservation
Samaranganasutradhara: leather (leather made jackets, shields, jeans), accordingly leather made arms and armaments

12. Brihatkshat or Brihatkshati or Grihatkshat or Rakshasha

Vaastumandanam: barracks for city-guards

Aparajitaprichchha: chariot-place, fuel (wood) store
Samaranganasutradhara: goldsmiths and silversmiths

13. Yama or Dharmaraja or Dharma

Vaastumandanam: army settlement
Aparajitaprichchha: wilderness, cluster of blossoms, garden with big trees & creepers, forest area in the south
Samaranganasutradhara: hidden / secret store-room

14. Gandharva

Vaastumandanam: pleasure-house and dancing-room
Samaranganasutradhara: theatre for plays, dance and drama, music concert, clothes use in theatrical and musical activities

15. Bhringraja

Vaastumandanam: carriage-shed
Aparajitaprichchha: big store house
Samaranganasutradhara: palace and playground, sea-saws, swings and other recreational activities for the princesses

16. Mrsa or Mrish (Mriga)

Vaastumandanam: anxiety room outside of the Mriga square
Aparajitaprichchha: big store house
Samaranganasutradhara: king's palace, harem gynaeceum

17. Pitar or Pitrigana or Nirriti

Vaastumandanam: bathroom and gambling room
Aparajitaprichchha: big store house
Samaranganasutradhara: garbage, night-soil

18. Dauvarika

Vaastumandanam: water sports
Samaranganasutradhara: beautifully designed and attractive garden having Ashoka trees and place for taking bath (on part of Dauvarika and Sugreeva)

19. Sugriva or Sukantha or Sugala
Vaastumandanam: wrestling ground
Samaranganasutradhara: women's apartment with a separate boundary wall, maternity chamber (lying-in chamber), beautifully designed and attractive garden having Ashoka trees and place for taking bath (on part of Dauvarika and Sugreeva)

20. Pushpadant or Kusumdant or Pushpa
Vaastumandanam: parade ground
Samaranganasutradhara: water related machines (Jalyantra), other instruments and their operators, gardener's place, flower-house

21. Varuna or Jaladhip
Vaastumandanam: prince's place
Samaranganasutradhara: stepped well, place for drinking water (prapa or piao)

22. Asura
Vaastumandanam: granary and art of magic
Samaranganasutradhara: treasury (koshthagaar)

23. Shosha
Vaastumandanam: arsenal and venomous ladies (vish-kanya)
Aparajitaprichchha: big store house
Samaranganasutradhara: arsenal, armoury

24. Roga or Papayakshama
Aparajitaprichchha: big store house
Samaranganasutradhara: mortar for removing husk from rice (ulukhal or okhli), mill-stone for preparing flour, stepped well in the northwest

25. Vayu or Vyadhi or Roga or Samirana
Vaastumandanam: hanankarta (slayer or hunter, art of striking or hitting, drum-stick), mule-shed and camel-shed
Aparajitaprichchha: big store house
Samaranganasutradhara: dispensary

26. Naga or Naag or Gotranaga or Ahi
Vaastumandanam: foster-mothers (midwives, wet-nurses) and maid-servants in the women's apartments (also confidante and female messengers)
Samaranganasutradhara: snakes

27. Mukhya
Vaastumandanam: maiden's apartment (kanyagriha)
Aparajitaprichchha: elephant's shed
Samaranganasutradhara: gymnasium, wrestler's ring, theatre, art gallery

28. Bhallata
Vaastumandanam: shvebh and doctor
Aparajitaprichchha: elephant's shed
Samaranganasutradhara: cow-house or cattle refuse in general, milk-place (doodhghar)

29. Soma or Saumya or Kuber
Vaastumandanam: conductors or shampooers (massage or rubbing the limbs)
Aparajitaprichchha: elephant's shed
Samaranganasutradhara: place for family priest / spiritual advisor (purohit), place for king's coronation ceremony, also place for charity, studies and achieving peace

30. Mrga or Mriga or Bhujaga or Shail or Giri or Charak
Vaastumandanam: toilet and menstruating women
Samaranganasutradhara: residence of princes including arrangement for their studies

31. Aditi
Vaastumandanam: bath room
Aparajitaprichchha: big store house
Samaranganasutradhara: king's mother, separate place for palanquins, beds and seats for taking rest, place for refuse or as a resort

32. Uditi or Diti

Vaastumandanam: charioteers, attendants, singers, wandering actors, spy, confederate
Aparajitaprichchha: big store house
Samaranganasutradhara: residences of close relatives like paternal and maternal uncles, also residences of ministers, vassals, feudatory princes and courtesans

33. Apah or Aap

Aparajitaprichchha: flower-house
Samaranganasutradhara: place for king's elephants, place for bathing of elephants and horned animals

34. Apvatsa

Vaastumandanam: storage for cloths
Samaranganasutradhara: pure water pond full of lotus flowers, chirping voices of water birds like swans, ducks, curlew (osprey), heron and the like

35. Aryama or Aaryaka or Aarya

Samaranganasutradhara: residence of head of army (army general), east or south facing residences of armed forces, army employees, police and people involved in handling and administration of arms

36. Savitra or Savita or Savindra

Vaastumandanam: kitchen-store (vyanjanashala) and kitchen
Aparajitaprichchha: fodder-house on Savitra, Agni, Bhritya, and Antariksha
Samaranganasutradhara: vocal music room (vandinsthana)

37. Savitri or Saavitra or Saavindra

Vaastumandanam: dining room
Samaranganasutradhara: instrumental music room (vadyashala)

38. Vivasvan or Vaivasvata or Martanda

Vaastumandanam: coronation place
Samaranganasutradhara: chariot-house (carriage-shed, coach-house), elephant-house

39. Indra

Vaastumandanam: king's mother, armoury
Aparajitaprichchha: king's mother
Samaranganasutradhara: second place for king's wives

40. Jaya or Indrajaya

Vaastumandanam: store for articles of household use
Aparajitaprichchha: king's mother
Samaranganasutradhara: north facing door to women's apartment (placed on Sugreeva and also facing the king's palace)

41. Mitra

Vaastumandanam: main house

42. Rudra or Raudra

Vaastumandanam: second place for king's mother and other ladies of the royal family
Aparajitaprichchha: store room for dressing tables (boxes), bags and baskets
Samaranganasutradhara: granary, store-room

43. Rajayakshama or Rudradasa or Rudraj

Aparajitaprichchha: store room for dressing tables (boxes), bags and baskets
Samaranganasutradhara: carpenters

44. Bhudhara or Prithvidhara or Mahidhara or Kshitidhara or Amitaujas

Vaastumandanam: assembly room and treasury nearby
Samaranganasutradhara: place for articles like chowrie (chamar), umbrella (chhatra) and the like used in king's procession, place for king's counsel, place for king to review working of his subordinates, south facing stable for horses (It shall be towards the right hand side of the king while entering his palace while place of horned animals' (including the elephants) shall fall towards his left.

45. Brahma or Hemgarbha

Vaastumandanam: temple of God (Female apartments and bedrooms in the central part of the palace)

Samaranganasutradhara: flag of Indra (Indra-dwaja), otherwise vacant

Samaranganasutradhara

Samaranganasutradhara (10.89-102, 15.19-46), written by the renowned king Bhoja Deva, recommends different directions for residences of people involved in different activities or professions. Recommendations of Samaranganasutradhara and the equivalent modern business activities are given in Table 4.4, along with a comparative study of the recommendations available in Mayamatam, Vaastumandanam, and Aparajitaprichchha.

Residence given in Samaranganasutradhara also includes the workplace or place for production and / or commercial activities. During those days, people used to work usually from their residence itself. In a single storey residence, the front portion was normally used for commercial activities while the rear one was used for living. Part of the back portion or sometimes the front portion itself was used for the production activities as per the specific requirements.

In double or multi-storey buildings, whole of the ground floor was used for commercial activities, production of articles and storage purposes. Thus, whatever is recommended for residences of people involved in different commercial or production activities during those days, equally applies to shops and commercial complexes in the modern days. Some of the relevant recommendations from Samaranganasutradhara are given here.

"In any city, residences of brahmins should be in the north, kshatriyas in the east, vaishyas in the south and shudras in the west". (Samaranganasutradhara, 10.100)

"Traders and merchants, doctors, and heads of all sorts of organizations shall inhabit all the directions. Army-men or guards shall guard the city from all the directions". (Samaranganasutradhara, 10.101)

"Linga-sthana shall be outside the city in the east direction. Crematorium shall always be in the south of the city". (Samaranganasutradhara, 10.102)

Samaranganasutradhara (15.19-50) - while discussing vaastu of a king's palace - also gives a detailed account of auspicious squares for different activities, administrative departments and king's officials. Forty-five demigods' wise recommendations of Samaranganasutradhara are given in Table 4.5, with a comparative analysis of the recommendations available in Vaastumandanam and Aparajitaprichchha.

These recommendations are indicative only. Intelligent readers can interpret them in their own way with the wise application of time, place and person factors. For example, Ish is the place for 'worship or place for the family-god (Kuldevata)'. It can be interpreted as the best square for locating the main temple of any housing society, community, locality, town, city or the mega city.

Further, the square of 'Pitrigana or Nirriti' has been said the place of 'garbage and night-soil'. This square can be best utilized as garbage land fill site of any city, solid waste treatment plant of any locality, incineration unit for processing of the medical waste in any hospital, sewage treatment plant of any organization or city, gobar gas or bio-gas plant in the farm house and so on. Readers may refer chapter 2 "Vaastu Gods and Goddesses" for gaining further insights in this regard.

It has been said that the king who lives in such a vaastu-friendly palace – equivalent to the place of gods – enjoys kingdom extending the boundaries of seven seas and becomes victorious over his enemies. King's palace at that time was generally a fortified city of varying size. It was a small world in itself having all sorts of business and public activities.

Aparajitaprichchha

Recommendations regarding town planning, and other public activities - commercial, professional, administrative, religious and others - found in Aparajitaprichchha are being reproduced here. Comments have also been given as and when so required.

"Markets should be arranged at the places frequented by people, where people usually visit for sale and purchase of goods". (Aparajitaprichchha, 72.32)

Thus the law of economics ie the principle of demand and supply, and foot-fall of the prospective buyers has been given due consideration while arranging the markets.

"In front of the main gate of city, which is the most crowded place, a combined commercial area shall be established for betel leaf shops, fruit and vegetable sellers, florists and other articles used fresh on daily basis". (Aparajitaprichchha, 72.34)

The above recommendation is without consideration of any direction. Fresh perishable articles of daily use shall be available nearby, within walking distance of most of the inhabitants.

"Shops for sale and purchase of eighteen types of grains for the residents shall be everywhere, in all the directions. Shops of betel leaf and betel nut sellers shall be in the bazaars opposite the temples". (Aparajitaprichchha, 72.39)

Again this recommendation is based on the feasibility of the end users, irrespective of the specific directions. Betel leaf and betel nut has long been used in Hindu religious rites and also as mouth fresheners.

"The residence of brahmins shall be towards the east, Kshatriyas in the south, shudras in the north and vaishyas shall be in the crowded middle part of the city". (Aparajitaprichchha, 72.41)

In this shloka, Aparajitaprichchha recommends vaishyas in the crowded middle part of the city. Such a practical recommendation is available in this text only. According to the Sanskrit–English dictionary, the word 'Vaishya' means; "Person of the Vaishya class, peasant, working man, man who settles on the soil, vassalage, dependence etc". Vaishyas here means the business caste among the Hindus. Hindu religious texts assigned vaishyas to traditional roles in agriculture and cattle-rearing but over time they came to be landowners, traders and money-lenders.

"Water tank shall be towards the west". (Aparajitaprichchha, 72.46)

West is the direction of Varuna, who governs the large sheets of water.

"Shops, markets, roads and squares are auspicious towards, east, south and north. Residences of all sorts of artisans, washer-men, and dyers are auspicious in the northeast". (Aparajitaprichchha, 72.47)

"Residences of cobblers, leather workers, and outcastes shall be in the southeast. Residences of distillers and vendors of spirituous liquors, as well as of weavers shall be in the southwest". (Aparajitaprichchha, 72.48)

Chapter 5
Workplace Vaastu

यादृशै: संनिविशते यादृशांश्चोपसेवते।
यादृगिच्छेच्च भवितुं तादृग्भवति पुरुष:॥

A person becomes exactly like him with whom he lives, like him whom he regards and like him who he wishes to be.

Mahabharata, Udyogaparva 4.13

We enjoy three kinds of luck in our personal and work life. First is the heaven luck; the sum total of our karmas done in our previous births. It is revealed by one's horoscope in Astrology, by the passive hand in Palmistry, date of birth and name given at the moment of birth in Numerology or other similar methods. The second is luck generated from the space where one lives or works i.e., vaastu. The third luck comes from our present karmas, the dedicated hard work. Lord Krishna in Shrimadbhagwadgeeta (3.8) says, "One must perform his prescribed karmas (activities) since actions are better than renouncing them; by ceasing activity even your bodily maintenance will not be possible".

After determining lucky directions of your business, which have already been discussed in Chapters 1 and 3 of the present book, look at the internal design and layout of the office space. The eight compass directions are associated with certain types of energies and activities. Try to design your office space accordingly. In any organisation, various departments should be positioned in directions where the energy supports the activities they perform. To find out eight directions and corresponding eight sectors, you will need the following items:

- A good quality lensatic compass.
- A protractor – a circular one is best
- A ruler
- A lead pencil
- Coloured pencils of your choice
- A scale plan of your business space.

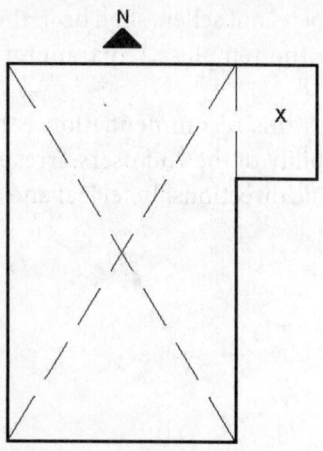

Fig. 5.1: When extension 'X' is less than 50%

Find the centre of the plan by drawing diagonal lines. This is the navel of Vaastu Purush residing in your workspace. If your office is not of a regular shape, treat any extension less than 50% of the length or width (here 'X') as an extension of that particular direction (Figure 5.1).

If the extension is more than 50% of the length or width (here 'X'), treat the remainder (here 'Y') as the missing part of that direction (Figure 5.2).

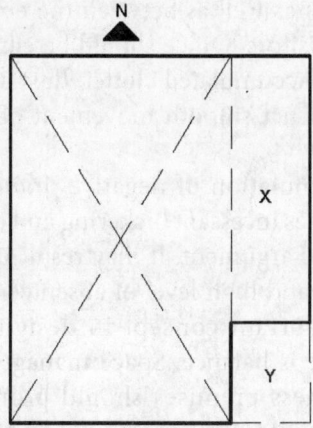

Fig. 5.2: When extension 'X' is more than 50%

After finding navel (here O) of the Vaastu Purush, select any known point (here A) on the middle of the wall towards your face. While standing at the navel point O, place the lensatic compass on your palm and note the exact compass reading of A. You can also mount this compass on a tripod or on a flat stool exactly above the navel point O. In our example, 'A' is 60° towards the right hand side from the North. Note it in your diary for future reference.

Take measurement of the external and internal walls, alcoves, staircases, doors, windows, ventilators, permanent fixtures and other important details. Fibreglass tape is considered best for this purpose. These measurements are required to design the final layout of desks, furniture and individual working areas that will benefit those working there.

Use a circular protractor and mark the north direction. Afterwards, mark the eight directions and eight sectors on the plan. Find the compass reading for the sector in which you are working. Check that you have the luckiest direction.

Mark the position of the entrance. Once the sectors are marked over the plan, we can see the direction of each room. Different rooms can now be allocated accordingly. When visitors enter the office, they should not be able to see the working area directly. Every organisation has its own times of stress. Heated conversations taking place in the office win a bad name for the organisation. Your potential customers should not be aware of such daily traumas of office life.

The visitors should receive the overall impression of an efficient, calm and congenial environment. A well-designed reception works as a buffer between the outer world and the office workplace. Doors should be so positioned that the inner working area remains out of the line of sight of visitors. The main entrance should give the widest possible view for people entering your business.

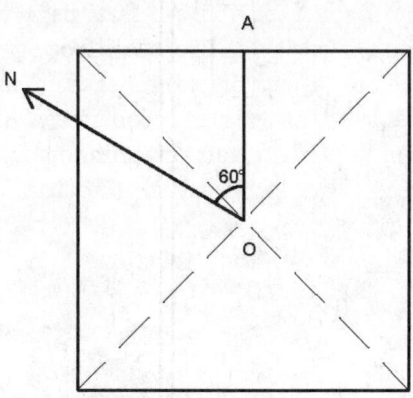

Fig. 5.3: Finding directions

Layout and Decoration

Space Management

A business premise should allow smooth functioning of all the related activities. Inter-related activities should be performed in the adjacent places. Flow of work, when taken into account, will not only increase convenience but saves labour and time too. Different directions should be earmarked for different activities. For instance, kitchen and dining areas should be separate in a restaurant. Creative workers normally feel happy to have their own separate working area.

One should be crystal clear of what he or she intends to achieve. With proper planning and forethought, it is possible to create a pleasant, comfortable and practical working environment even in a limited budget. First important consideration is the layout of each office. Plan the layout of individual offices and design features to be incorporated or avoided. Seriously consider the traffic flow in open areas, shapes and dimensions of different rooms, position of CEO's office, ideal most locations for various other departments, arrangement of working tables and other furniture.

Start the office layout with the front door. There should not be any *vedha* (obstruction) to the main entrance. All sorts of pointed and hostile structures may cause these vedhas. Protect the business premises from the effects of killing vedhas.

Space arrangement should promote good relationship between the manager and the employees as well as between the employees and the visitors. Office should be clutter-free and airy. Accumulated clutter, dust and dark areas obstruct smooth movement of benefic energies.

Accumulation of negative *prana* in the office causes incessant bickering and counter-productive argument. It may result in health problems and high level of absenteeism. The most important concept in design of any workplace is balance. Space management of any business premises should promote an environment of co-operation, enhance its productivity and attract the good fortune.

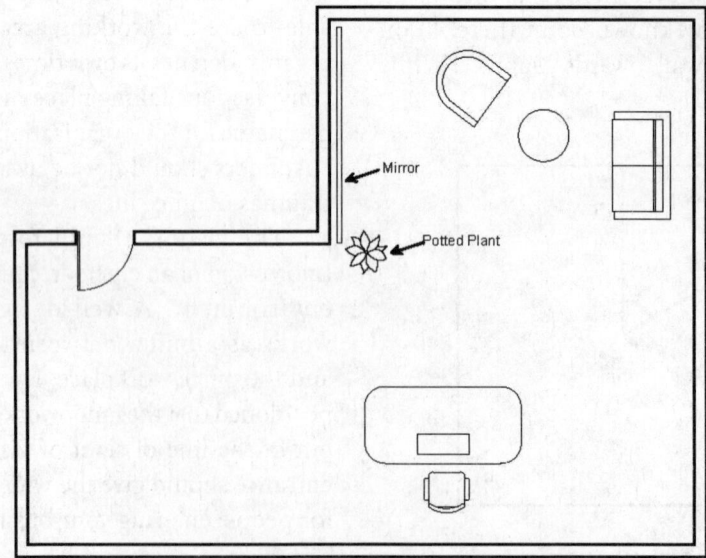

Fig 5.4: Protruding corner and its rectification

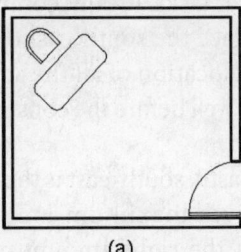 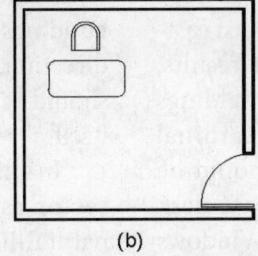 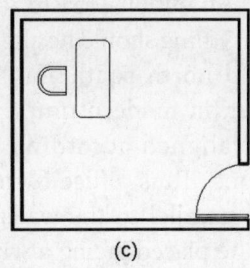

Fig 5.5: Good placement of desk

Combine the central meeting area with the individual spaces to create a harmonious working environment. Our relationships with our colleagues greatly influence our happiness and our overall performance at work. Vedic Astrology helps a lot in determining anyone's characteristics, provided his or her birth data is available. Many local companies as well as the multinational corporations select their future employees only after a thorough astrological or chirological or graphological analysis. One can also take help of these sciences to select his or her lucky business partner.

The layout should facilitate the auspicious flow of prana. Protruding corners are inauspicious. They are like sharp knives or hostile index fingers pointing directly at the person they hit. Working tables should be placed in such a manner so that nobody faces a sharp corner directly. Corner directed at the filing cabinets or the door of the CEO's office is equally bad. Plants can successfully be used to cover such sharp corners (Figure 5.4). They disguise poison arrows (vedha) sent by the sharp corners and reduce their ill effects. They bring nature into an artificial manmade environment. They create a balance of *rajas* and *tamas* energies.

Don't place working tables or chairs directly under the overhead beams. Their lower part transmit huge amount of tensile forces. These adverse forces may cause headache or undue tensions. It will also severely affect the flow of prana within the office. Immediately treat such beams in a manager's room, otherwise his entire office people might suffer. Try to avoid beams at all costs. If you are going to build your own office building, prefer inverted beams. They are not visible while sitting under them. The best way to deal with the already existing exposed beams in the office is to camouflage them with false ceilings.

In the modern times many offices are not built as per the strict requirements of vaastu. Hence, your table may look awkward if you intend to follow the above suggestions rigidly. A commanding location is preferable than facing a particular vaastu direction. A desk placed in a strange position negatively influences your room. It can also affect the flow of prana. A comfortable look and feel of your office is much more desirable. It should also reflect something of the owner's personality.

 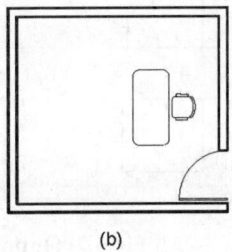 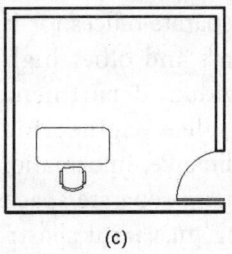 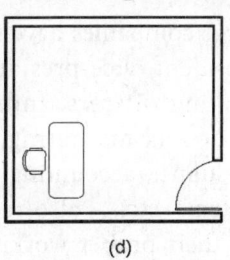

Fig 5.6: Bad placement of desk

In the traditional vaastu, it is recommended that everything should be aligned against east-west and north-south axis for best results. However, in modern times, many buildings are not aligned according to the cardinal directions. Thus, office furniture should be aligned parallel to the walls. Ideally, a desk should be placed facing a window. Windows let in natural sunlight and fresh air, which is considered a form of highly auspicious prana. We look out of the window for seeking inspiration.

Windows should be fitted with such glass that only allows people to look out but not in. A beautiful outside view is good. Glaring light from the windows is not good for effective working. You can use blinds or drapes to eliminate the problem of glaring light. Keep all the electrical and telephone cables out of sight, if possible. A toilet or bathroom directly opposite your office is bad vaastu. Negative energies generate their flow into the office affecting everyone in it.

The office should be well-lighted and well-ventilated. Natural lighting is best, should be plentiful and evenly distributed. Artificial lighting should not cause glare to anyone else. Ceiling light is best. Light coming from a worker's left side is also good. Use subtle colours in general offices. Dark, bright, electrifying and stimulating colours in ordinary offices may cause discord among the colleagues. Colours are the children of light, having substantial effect on visitor's mood and should thus be chosen wisely.

Office Layouts

Large companies have separate offices for its president, vice-presidents and other high-ranking officers. Individual departments – such as marketing, sales, engineering, personnel, accounting, finance, information systems, etc., – also require separate spaces for their proper working. In vaastu shastra certain directions are considered to give better results for particular tasks. Ideally, commercial buildings should face the south-east or south direction. Correct location of all the activities should be decided well before the construction itself.

In business vaastu, south-east is the wealth sector as it receives maximum amount of natural light with the right amount of heat. Consequently, south-east sector of the business is a good location for the accountant. It will be still better if he is located in the north of this south-east sector. Human resources manager should be in the east (new growth). Newly recruited staff should also sit in the east. Research and development staff should be in the west. The advertising and promotional staff should be in the south (limelight). Staff training should be conducted in the north-east.

The door to the office(s) should be protected from any vedhas coming from outside the office. Anything that points towards the door in a straight line is called vedha (pinching). This acts like an arrow and needs to be remedied. Use potted plants or something else to hide this vedha at its source itself.

If there are offices on both sides of a hallway, the doors of opposite offices should be similar in size. Preferably, the doors should not face each other or should be directly opposite to each other. Slightly offsetting doors are not good. The occupants are likely to have disagreements (Figure 5.7). To rectify this defect, place a mirror on the wall next to both the doors (Figure 5.8).

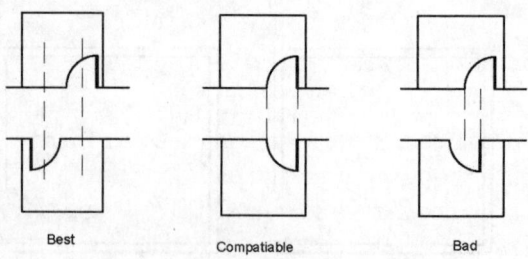

Fig 5.7: Opposing doors in a hallway

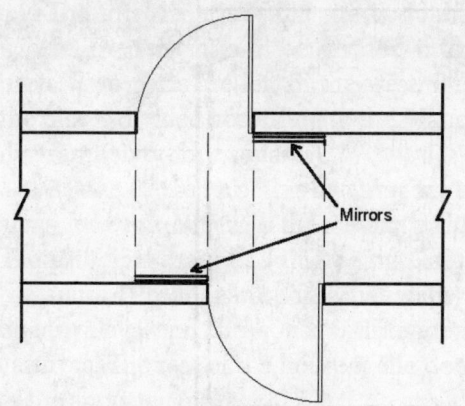

Fig 5.8: Rectifying opposing doors in a hallway

Long straight hallways create vedha. Pranic energy rushes swiftly through them. If there is a window at the end of such a hallway, the prana will leave through it. Consequently people working in such an environment will lack the required pranic energy. The pranic energy can be slowed down by placing potted plants at regular intervals along the hallway in opposite directions. Such an arrangement not only remedies the vedha, but also looks attractive.

These potted plants result in meandering and slowing down of pranic energy. It gives workers in the rooms a degree of privacy. Alternatively, murals or attractive wall paintings can also be used to attract and slow down the prana. It is a bad vaastu if your office door is at the end of a descending staircase (Figure 3.9). Every time you go to your office, you will have to go downstairs. Going downwards for business purpose will gradually lead to falling fortunes. Most of the shops located in the subways in the Connaught Place area of New Delhi are a failure. On the contrary, an office door at the top of a flight of stairs is much better. Going upwards for business represents the rising fortunes. The rising prana fills you with positive energy and vitality.

Head's Office

In any business, chief executive officer (CEO), managing director (MD), president or manager is the head. CEO is directly responsible for the performance of any organisation. His office vaastu heavily influences the company's fortune. Hence a CEO must have his own separate office in the corporation. CEO's office must provide him a private, safe, secure, peaceful and comfortable working environment. This environment will not only enhance his prestige but will also strengthen his decision-making process.

The best location for head of the company is farthest from the main entry, preferably towards the south-west. In an organisation running from all the floors of a multi-storey complex, the head may occupy the first floor but not the upper floors. Ground floor keeps one's feet grounded to the earth. First floor provides the additional security and privacy with easy accessibility. Upper floors adversely affect head's control over the business.

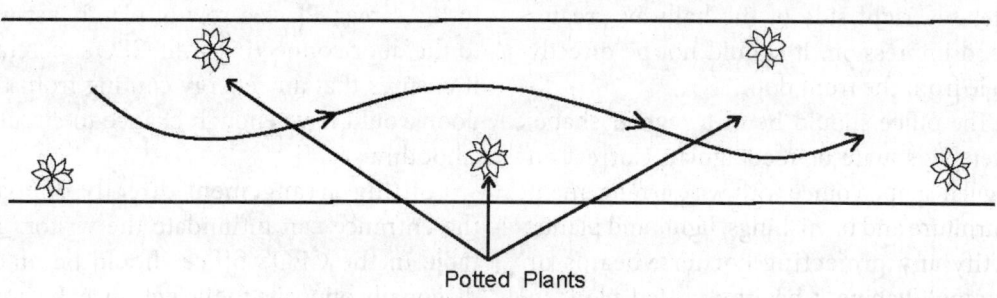

Fig 5.9: Rectifying a long straight hallway

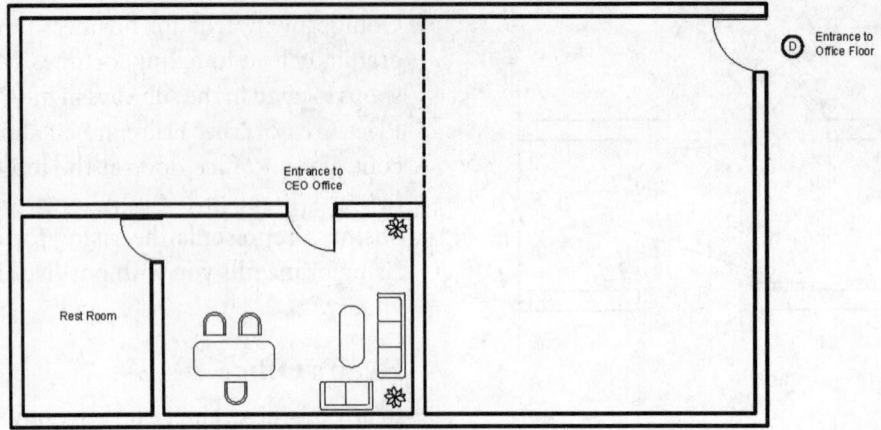

Fig 5.10: Head's office in an organisation

Top manager's office should ideally be located deep inside the building, farthest away from the receptionist's seat. Here company's president will be able to concentrate on making the corporation financially successful. CEO's office located at the back of an organisation's building creates a sense of importance and privacy for its key figure. The sense of importance is created when visitors are led to see him. Visitors have to go through a series of offices before they finally reach the CEO's office.

It should not be at the end of a long hallway. A long corridor creates *marga vedha*, which acts like a poisonous arrow heading directly to the entrance. Health and wealth of the occupier gets affected in the long run. Any staircase, elevator, lift or escalator directly facing the office is equally bad. They carry the wealth away. CEO's office on one side, preferably right side of the hallway, creates a good impression. It should not be directly visible from the front door.

The office should be of a regular shape, preferably square or rectangular. Correct an irregular shaped office with wise arrangement of furniture and furnishings, lights and plants. Rectify any projecting corners, beams or columns. Placing a healthy potted plant in front of the vedha can mitigate its ill effects. CEO's office should be larger than all the other offices as the size of space occupied also decides a person's position in any organisation.

The entrance to the office should not face a toilet. A toilet will constantly send negative energies towards your office. If unavoidable, a simple remedy is to keep your door shut as much as possible. Healthy green plants kept near your entrance as well as near the toilet may also reduce ill effects of this vedha to a large extent. A toilet right above the CEO's office is equally bad. Avoid it strictly.

Placement of working table is very important. CEO's desk should be in the most commanding position in the room. Normally, most commanding position is the farthest corner from the room's entrance as shown in Figure 5.9. This may be called the power position. Anyone sitting here will progress in his career. Place a row of plants just next to the door connecting with CEO's secretary. It ensures that any energy coming from that door would have enough chance to circulate smoothly.

Sitting arrangement directly opposite the entrance can intimidate the visitor. The table in the CEO's office should be placed diagonally opposite to the entrance. It should

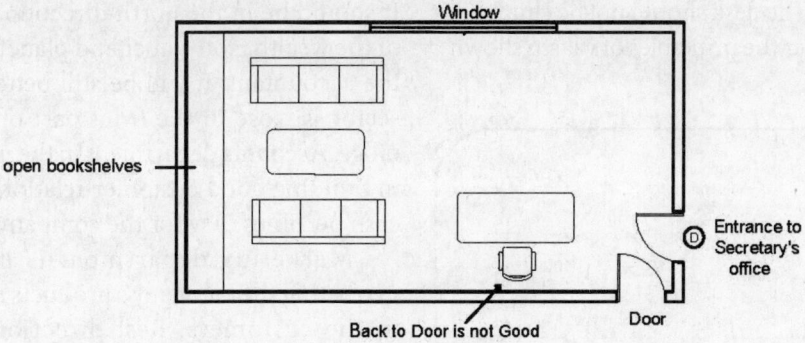

Fig 5.11: Head's office (Before changing the layout)

be in the farthest corner, preferably on the right hand side of the room, when viewed from the entrance. The CEO's chair should be so located that he is easily able to see the new entrant by turning his face to an angle of not more than 45 degrees. This position gives him a commanding view of the office as well as the door. If head is not able to see the entrance clearly from his seat, put up a looking glass at a strategic location. It will give him a better view of the door.

CEO should sit backed by a solid wall. People sitting with their backs to the door feel insecure and uncomfortable. Also, there should not be any window or passageway behind his chair. Any such opening will undermine his position, make him weak and under-confident. Nobody should be able to work behind the CEO's seat. It can be ensured by placing his desk close to the wall. At the same time, there should be enough space around the front desk for his movement. A mirror directly in front of or behind the desk is not good.

The size of desk should be appropriate to accommodate the stationary, laptop/desktop computer, drinking water and other personal belongings. A potted plant or cut flowers on the working desk improves the working

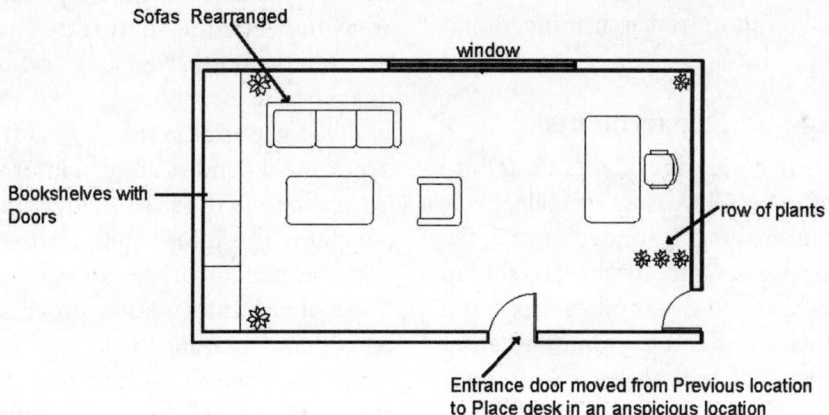

Fig 5.12: Head's office (After changing the layout)

environment. The desk should not be cluttered. Arrange it as per the principles of vaastu shown in Figure 5.13.

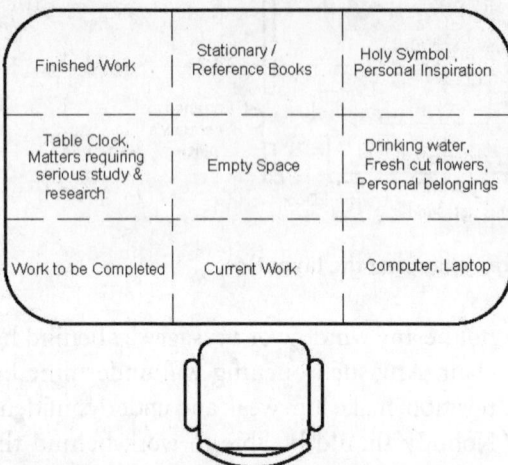

Fig 5.13: **Arranging the working/study desk**

The CEO, while seated in the office, should face an auspicious direction. One's luckiest direction can be determined by referring his horoscope and the position of office entrance. Ancient Vaastu proponents believed that one will be able to earn more when the working desk faces north. If the desk faces east, you will be dynamic and inspirational. You will earn money and fame when facing the north-east. Facing south makes you overactive. Facing west makes you more research minded and rich in serious ideas.

Other Staff and Departments

In any company, vice presidents (VPs) are important after the CEO. They are collectively responsible for making major decisions of the company's business. Offices of the VP's should be located next to the CEO's office. It will not only facilitate an effective communication between them but will also assure higher privacy levels.

Accounts department handles money collection, billing and other related activities. It should be in the north direction, direction of the wealth God Kuber and planet Mercury; the accountant. It will be still better if north sector is close to the front part of company office. Accounts department in the north helps in building good customer relations. Flow of cash becomes easy for the company.

Marketing department is meant for marketing the company's products or services to the customers. Best direction for this department is the north-west. If it is not feasible, right hand side of the entrance (from outside) is also a good choice. It should be close to the potential customers.

Business's treasury or finance department is much more a private department than the accounting and marketing departments. It primarily has internal functions and is not directly linked to the customer services. Thus, treasury should be located in a private area, preferably the south-west or west of the premises.

Personnel department is responsible for handling all the issues and benefits of the employees, as well as interviewing and hiring the new work force. Their functions are credential by nature. As this department is not linked directly with the customers, it should be situated in a more private area. The areas between the south-east and south or between the north-west and west are good for this purpose.

Data processing or information department handles all such information that is necessary to the smooth functioning of any company. This information forms the basis of decision-making process of top management. Most of the information processed here is considered private to the company. Thus, for privacy reasons, information department should be located close to the offices of CEO and Vice Presidents. It should, otherwise, be in the inner part of any organisation. This safe and secure place helps in guarding the internal information which never gets lost. It helps the top management in making future strategies.

Cellular Office

A traditional office is known as cellular office (Figure 5.10, 5.11, 5.12). It is normally a square or rectangular room with doors, windows and ventilators. A cellular office can accommodate one person or a small number of people. It gives a fair degree of privacy and peace to the people working inside.

Open Plan Offices

Open plan office is a modern idea. This is a hall or a big room divided up in small sections with or without partitions. An open plan office can house many people, all working in their own little sections. One large single office can accommodate more people than the two smaller ones. Staff working in an open plan office has more freedom to interact with their colleagues. Contrarily, biggest disadvantage of an open plan office is higher noise level and lack of privacy.

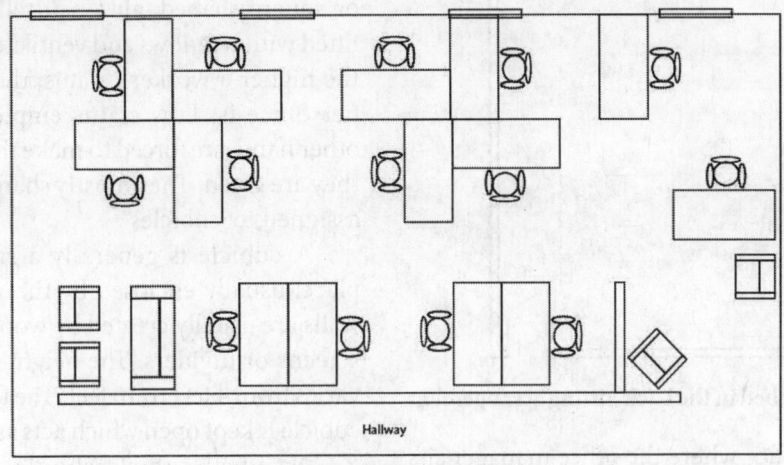

An Open Plan Office (Plan)

Actual View of an Open Plan Office

In the open plan offices, furniture and specialist equipment are arranged to give maximum space and light. Desks are often arranged in small booths. The worst position is to have your back to any door, as you risk being 'stabbed in the back' (Figure 5.14). It is also very bad position to work with one's back towards an unprotected open area. Working person is surprised when someone approaches from behind. The simple remedy is to place a looking glass on the front wall, somewhat shifted towards your active side.

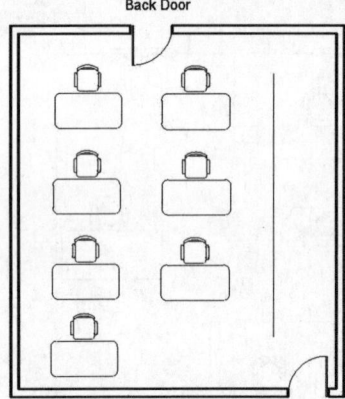

Fig 5.14: 'Stabbed in the back' sitting arrangement

A general office where the office manager sits in a position facing the other staff is much like a teacher would face his pupils at school (Figure 5.15). This is the worst position from morale point of view and is almost always confrontational.

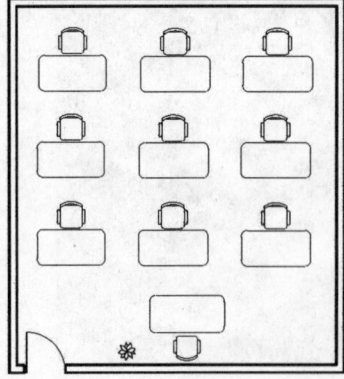

Fig 5.15: 'Classroom style' sitting arrangement

In a modern office, the planning is centred mainly on the placing of computers and their cables. Everything should be arranged in such a way as to make the working environment as safe and comfortable as possible. Secure the trailing wires in some way or run them in channels. Sitting, while facing the back of a computer monitor, is detrimental to health. Design the office in such a way that it doesn't occur.

Cubicles

There is great competition in companies for 'good' offices. These good offices are rectangular or square shaped, airy, naturally lighted and fitted with windows and ventilators. Moreover, the higher a worker's status, the larger his or her office is. Low status employees, on the other hand, are forced to make the best of what they are given. They mostly share offices or are assigned to 'cubicles'

A cubicle is generally a small working place, usually enclosed by three walls. These walls are usually created by wooden or plastic screens or dividers. The height of these walls varies from 4 feet to 10 feet. The fourth side of a cubicle is kept open which acts as the entrance.

An ideal cubicle should fulfil all the requirements of a Vaastu friendly office. The occupant should sit with his or her back towards a wall/partition and not towards the entrance. Keeping a healthy potted plant can protect the entrance. It increases the amount of prana coming in. In Figure 4 sitting arrangements are shown.

In the first case, a wall supports the back and the passive left hand side. Entrance is towards the right side of the sitting person. This arrangement gives a lot of confidence to the worker.

In the second case, a wall supports the back but active right side is also obstructed. The entrance is towards the left side of the working person. An open left, being the passive side, gives lesser self-confidence. However, it is good for a worker working primarily with his left hand.

Workplace Vaastu

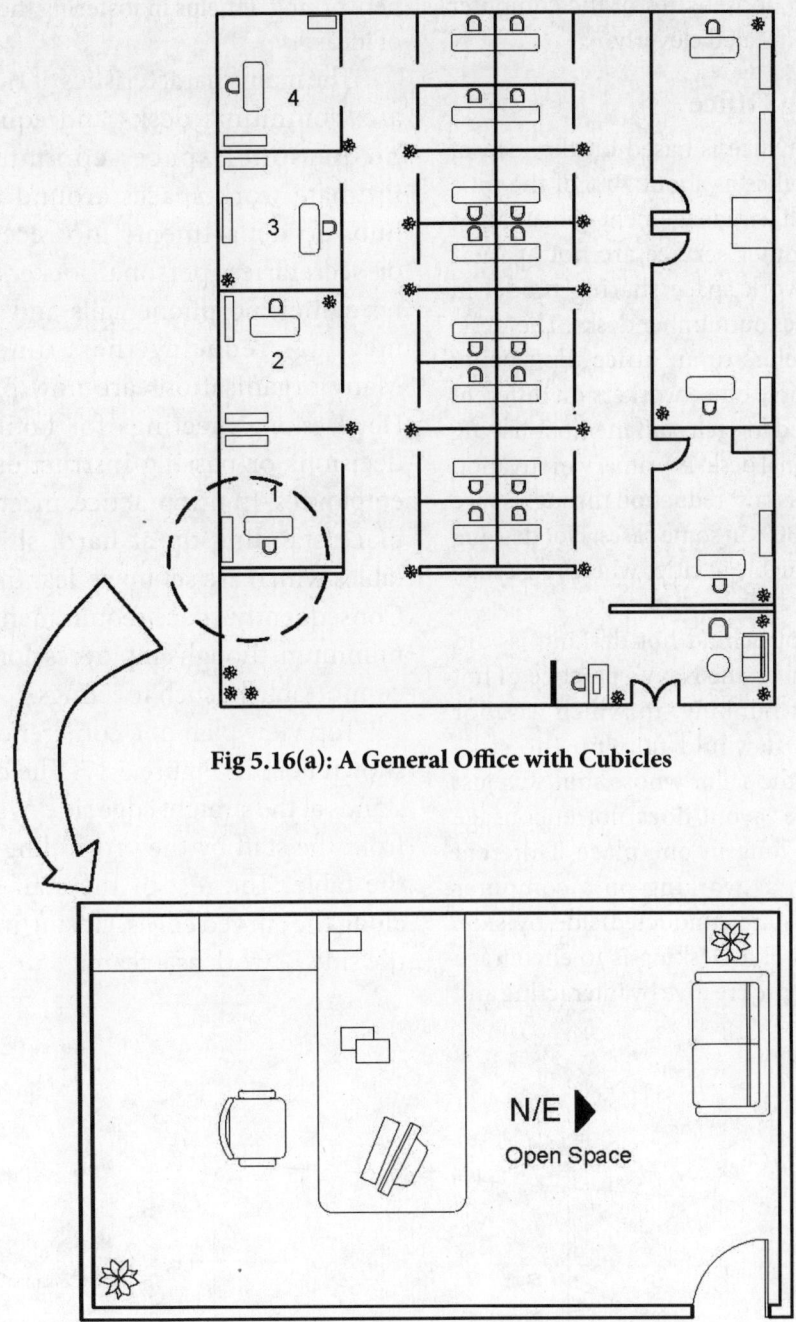

Fig 5.16(a): A General Office with Cubicles

Fig 5.16(b): Arranging a Typical Cubicle

In the third case, the employee's back is towards the entrance. This is the worst possible sitting arrangement. The person is not able to concentrate on his work.

The sitting arrangement in the fourth case makes one's position very powerful but his concentration may continually get disturbed due to people's movement outside the cabin.

In this position, loose wires of the computer shall also be concealed cleverly.

Hot Desking Office

'Hot Desking' Office is based on the idea of an open-plan office as about 70% of the time people in jobs like management consultancy, sales and customer service are not at their desks. It is a work space sharing model in which employees outnumber desks. The 'desk' in the name refers to an office desk being shared by multiple office workers on different shifts as opposed to each staff member having their own personal desk. A primary motivation for hot desking is cost reduction through space savings – up to 30% in some cases. Hot desking is especially valuable in cities where real estate prices are high.

The concept behind hot desking is said to have come from the Navy's practice of hot racking or hot bunking, in which a sailor finishing a shift would take up the still-warm bunk of the sailor whose shift was just beginning. The layout does not encourage people to stay long in one place. Different activities, such as working on a computer and discussions are conducted side by side. The purpose of Hot Desking is to encourage workers to be more creative by interacting and networking. It helps in fostering the exchange of ideas.

The main characteristics of Hot Desking are: communal desks and equipments, no personal space, communal and intimate work-spaces around a central hub, no departments, no receptionists or secretaries, personal lockers of staff, no clutter, no phone calls and stand up meetings reducing their time length. Many organisations are now practicing Hot Desking meetings for taking quick decisions or passing instructions to the employees. In this practice, meetings take place standing up at hard, shiny, rajas tables which are set up at 'leaning height'. Consequently, space requirements are the minimum, though employees don't get too comfortable in such meetings.

Top view plan of a conference table is shown here in Figure 5.17. The chairman stands at the straight edge side A, separated from the staff by the protruding edges of the table. The rest of the staff standing along the curved edges, closing in towards the side B, work as a team.

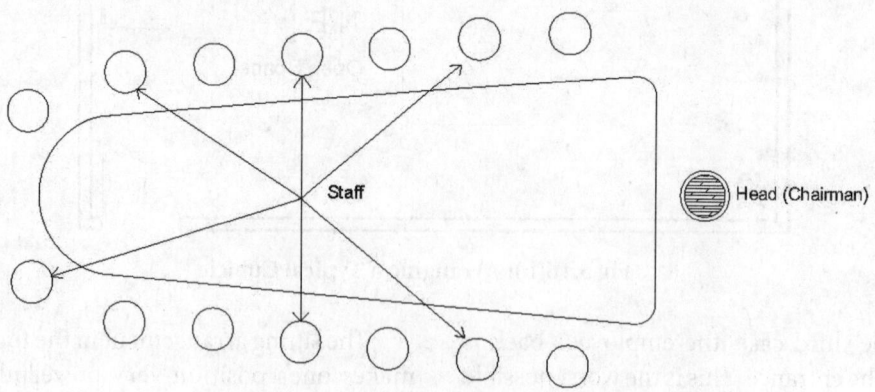

Fig 5.17: Table for Stand Up Meetings

In these offices, all staff can do all jobs. Several companies involved in more rajasic activities, for instance advertising and PR companies have already adopted this system. Their staff tends to be young and dynamic and work under pressure. Young people who are attracted to fast pace media type jobs are mainly attracted to Hot Desking. Astrologically, people born under the influence of movable signs or fiery signs or rajasic planets feel more comfortable in such offices.

Hot desking makes it harder to set up a workstation for an employee's particular needs which can be detrimental to hygiene and can be psychologically damaging. The issues like adjusting a chair/changing keyboard everyday will waste time and be a source of stress or even minor injury. Phones in particular become less appealing when shared with 100 coughing co-workers. There is sharp increase in the number of sick days taken. Employees like leaving things in drawers or in a neat pile and don't like having to pack-horse it from home or from a locker every morning. They can't personalise their desks in hot desking arrangement.

Whether done universally or specifically, hot desking can be disruptive to the hierarchy or may cause resentment. If performed in a truly egalitarian way, then you lose something of a structure. If it's not, then you lose all sense of camaraderie. Hot desking makes it harder to form something lasting and can mean trekking off to go find a desk somewhere in the wilderness. Part-timers are the ones who suffer most from hot desking as it damages their morale and makes them feel like lesser workers. A tidy desk policy becomes harder to enforce when you can't be certain whose **mess** it is.

In the long run, open plan offices are bad for businesses of stable nature. Noise here can affect the staff, reducing their performance. Workers may feel pressured in this very rajasic environment. Hot Desking is a hard way to live for very long. The staff may eventually burn out. Include some tamasic energy in such offices as a remedy by simple adjustment of furniture, furnishings, lights, colours and plants.

Personalising Your Office

All living beings mark their territory. Marking territories is one of our old habits. Scientific studies conducted on wild animals like tigers, elephants and bears reveal that all these animals scent their space to lay claim to it. Similarly, we human beings, including the office workers also tend to personalise our space in one or other manner. It can be through the peculiar choice of photographs, calendars, ornaments, plants, bunch of flowers, computer screen savers or such other items. These items not only personalise an office space but also make it attractive as per the needs of an individual. As a result, workers feel more stable and committed.

It has been found that people personalising their working places stay for a long duration in an organisation. A personalised space gives a strong sense of attachment. A successful business manager shall take into account the different working styles of his employees. Accordingly, he should provide space for different activities and approaches. He should encourage employees to make their own area a pleasant place to work in. The result will be a happier, less stressed and more stable work force.

Boardrooms

Meeting means people gathering together for discussion. Meeting rooms are the spaces meant for such discussions, ranging from a small area to the large boardrooms. These are best in the eastern sector of an organisation, when used in the early hours and in the western sector when used for review meetings during the late evening hours. Small meeting

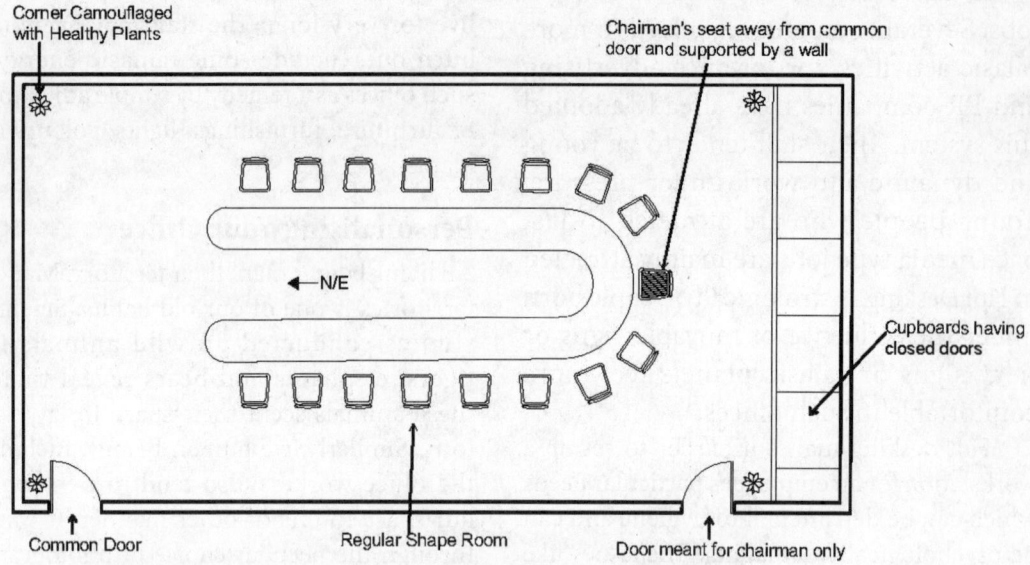

Fig 5.18: Vaastu Friendly Boardroom

rooms are useful for two or more people where they can meet to discuss a specific issue.

Meeting rooms should be of auspicious regular shapes. Cut corners cause vedhas. Corners can effectively be camouflaged with healthy potted plants. Shape of table also influences any meeting. Rectangular shape tables are good for meetings with a leader who sits at the head. Round tables are useful for brain-storming sessions. Oval tables are best in the boardroom.

Chairman's position is more important in the boardroom. The most prestigious position of head is preferably the farthest from the main entrance. The chairman can use a separate side door. Too many doors opening into the boardroom are not conducive to harmony, leading to quarrels and misunderstandings. The chairman should have a view of the entrance. Chairman's back, properly supported by a solid wall, gives a feeling of protection. Chairman's seat should be larger than the rest of all. Preferably ergonomically designed, it must have provision for hand rest and head rest. Vice-chairman and other important personnel should occupy seats to the immediate right and left of the chairman. Right side is considered active, while left side is relatively passive.

Boardrooms are used for taking important decisions. Hence, chairman should face his most auspicious direction. Everyone else should also try to sit facing his or her best direction. The boardroom then will be a source of luck for the business. Find out the luckiest element of the chairman by referring his horoscope. Introduce something related to his element in the meeting room. For instance, if his lucky element is water, install a well-maintained water feature. Design its location in a way that merges with the decoration.

Meeting Etiquettes

Hold any meeting whenever it is really necessary. Every meeting should have a definite purpose. Show consideration and tolerance for others in a meeting. Public dealing is a skill that needs to be practiced. Greet your visitors with a warm welcome. Speak clearly. Use such words that are easy to understand by everyone. Speak at the appropriate time. Don't speak when someone else is speaking.

Develop the skill of listening carefully to other people's ideas. It gives us valuable information; we have two ears but only one mouth. Be interested in what is being said. The information might not seem useful now but it could be later on. Aim to feel part of your team. Everyone leaving the meeting shall know what is exactly going to happen next and who is going to be responsible for taking action on the points made.

If you want to run your office efficiently, maintain an office diary. Keep it up to date. Make a note of all your appointments, meetings, days off, holiday's, etc. Incorporate birthdays, important occasions, following up an ongoing business matter, etc., into your diary under the appropriate dates. If you have a receptionist, make sure that he or she is informed of your appointments and movements. Carry a small pocket diary with you when you are away from the office. It will act as a double check.

Office Hardware

Usually desks, chairs of varying types for the staff, seating for guests, filing cabinets, cupboards or drawers for keeping stationary, personal computers, printers, fax machines, telephones & intercoms, dustbins, photocopiers, fire extinguishers, reference books, etc., are considered essential in modern offices.

Actual choice of desks, chairs and other furniture depend on particular requirements. Choose purpose designed furniture for your office even if it costs a little more. Discard the cheap imitations. There is a well known saying in North India – a person buying a costly item is in tears only once, while a person buying a cheaper one is always in tears. Don't prefer pre-owned furniture as it may have negative energy of its previous owner(s).

Office furniture should be well designed and ergonomically correct. Stuck doors in confined spaces can become a daily trouble. Sitting on chairs with wobbly seats and no back support or typing on keyboards at the wrong height can cause physical harm. Choose chairs of proper height for the desks, otherwise physical problems like backache shall appear with the passage of time.

Office furniture is often neglected in the offices without public dealing. Minimum storage cupboards and filing cabinets should be provided in small offices. Pointed corners of the furniture are uncomfortable. Catching a limb on the corner of a working table every time one goes to a cupboard will be frustrating which may lead to tensions. Rounded corners, on the other side, does not point at anyone close by and helps in safe movement of people around it.

People spend long hours performing the same task, which may cause great discomfort. The result is Repetitive Strain Injury (RSI). Wrist supporters, along with many other methods, are available to ease such an unwanted condition. Use suitable furniture and equipment to alleviate the problem. Try to prevent it occurring in the first place itself as the saying goes: "Prevention is better than cure".

The height of storage units should be suitable to the staff so that they can reach it easily without any expensive bending or stretching. People bend and stretch in studios. An efficient workplace has furniture of the right height and tools to hand. Shelves above the head can be oppressive and may create insecurity. Edges of shelves near a chair can create *kona vedha* (pinching angles). This vedha can cause discomfort to those sitting nearby. Floor to ceiling shelves overwhelm a smaller office room.

Prefer cupboards to open shelves near the sitting. The office looks less cluttered in this way. Open shelves, with the passage of time, get filled with unwanted things. Good quality and strategically placed mirrors can create an illusion of space in small offices. Do not place mirrors where people can see themselves while working. Mirrors may make them feel uncomfortable.

Size of the desk should be in proportion to one's position in the company. The chairman should have the largest desk. He won't be able to retain much credibility if he has a smaller desk in the office. A larger chair of the manager than his visitors, preferably with a strong high back and hand rests, gives him the edge in negotiations.

Shapes of the desk are very important. Square and rectangular shapes, with rounded corners are most suitable. Round desks are ideal for short meetings. Round shape desks do not encourage anyone to sit and work at them for long. L-shape desks resemble the meat cleavers, shorter side representing the blade. An L-shape desk cuts off useful communication and authority. It is sometimes used to provide an extra support when passive side is otherwise unprotected. The remedy for an L-shape desk is to separate the two parts, if possible. The smaller part can be used as a computer table.

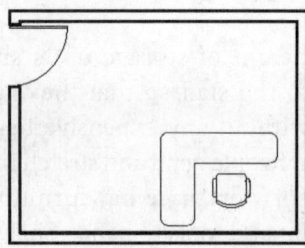

Fig 5.19 (a): L-shape desk (before remedy)

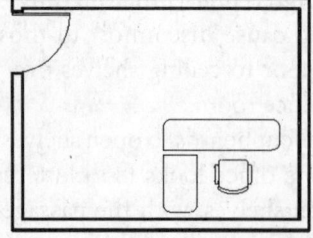

Fig 5.19 (b): L-shape desk (after remedy)

Desk drawers harbour considerable amount of rubbish. Any type of unwanted material creates *tamas*. Throw away old stationary which do not work. Make special places for all pins, paper clips and tags. Your precious time spent on searching for such things is saved. Consequently, you will feel more efficient. At the end of each day, in-tray must be completely empty, giving a feeling of deep satisfaction. A tidy desk at the end of your day's work gives the impression that all is under control. No one will like to start a new day with the debris from the past day. Pending work may deplete your energy level. Clear the day's mail daily. A well organised and tidy desk leads to a relaxed mind and clear vision.

Working Table/Desk

We spend a considerable amount of time at work. The chosen space should feel comfortable. The direction should be supportive where we can tap into the beneficial energies. The sole occupant of an office can easily achieve a favourable space (Figure 5.12). If possible, try to find a supportive space for you where an office is shared by many people.

The best place for the working table is diagonally opposite the door, where we can see anyone entering the room (Figure 5.5). If a room is occupied by several people, the farthest area from the entrance is the best place for the senior person in the room. He will be least bothered by day-to-day tasks than those closer to the door. Cabin positions marked 1 and 2 in Figure 5.16 (a) are the farthest.

Closely check the dimensions of your desk. The size of your desk in your office reveals your power and status in the organisation. Correct design and position of your desk are the key points in career advancement. A desk of favourable dimensions attracts good fortune. Wide desk ensure that people are not sitting too close to the computer screens.

An ideal desk size for the CEO would be 60" (Length) x 37" (Width) x 29" to 31"

(Height). These dimensions are excellent for MDs, senior managers, presidents or heads of organisations who have to work harmoniously with their staff. This size is very conducive to attract the career prospects. If you are a senior executive but your desk is much smaller than mentioned here, your status will also get diminished. As a result, you will be less effective and less powerful.

Auspicious dimensions for a smaller desk suitable for a mid-level executive would be 48" (Length) x 33" (Width) x 29" (Height). The desk should be a symmetrical shape rectangular table with slightly rounded corners. L-shape tables, though not preferred, are sometimes used to provide extra support on the passive left side. Round off their corners in such situations.

A secretary is usually required to handle several different tasks at the same time. Thus, his desk can be of any size. The longer the desk, the better are the results. A two to three feet wide desk is sufficient. Least dimension of a secretary's desk is 68" (Length) x 26" (Width) x 33" (Height). A desk of 33 inches height is higher than most conventional desks. To achieve a comfortable working height, you can raise the level by placing a small platform underneath your chair. Chairs with adjustable height can also be used. If your desk is unusually larger for your particular job, you will progress faster in your career.

One must feel comfortable while working. Ideally, a desk should be supported by a solid wall. The wall will protect the person by figuratively 'watching his back'. In this position the desk is highly exposed to the auspicious prana in the room. Any opening (like window or door) behind you indicates that you are lacking in solid support. It makes you feel uneasy and nervous. You may not be able to get the desired help when you need it the most. If there is no alternative position for your table, keep the window or door shut, if possible.

Sun glare through a window onto the computer screen leads to poor visibility and can cause headache. An effective remedy is to place healthy plants on the window sill or alternatively, position a piece of furniture there. These should not restrict our space at the same time. You can also keep the blinds or curtains drawn. Don't situate the edge of your desk directly against a window. Position your desk so that you can look out from a distance. Windows let in auspicious prana in the form of natural light and fresh air. They broaden our horizon too.

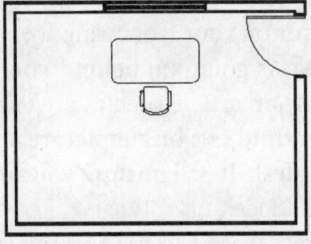

Fig 5.20 (a): **Wrong Position of desk with reference to window**

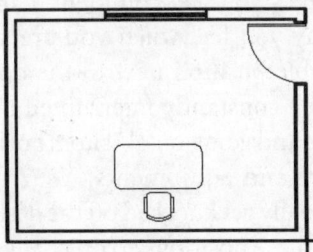

Fig 5.20 (b): **Right Position of desk with reference to window**

There should be sufficient room around your desk to get in and out of your chair easily. Pranic energy should be able to flow in and around them. If you feel confined, the pranic energy will also feel so. Ultimately, you will feel confined in your work, with restricted future prospects. It is better if everyone in the office has an indirect view of the entrance from his desk. Desks having a view of the entrance give plenty of time to see someone approaching.

Computer tables are generally placed against a blank wall because it allows all the cords and wires to get hidden. Of course, loose wires should not be visible as per the ideal vaastu conditions but placement of your table against a blank wall is also not good. It restricts one's vision and forward looking attitude. Moreover, sitting person runs the psychological risk of being stabbed in the back. Having your back to an open area which people continually use as a passage is also bad. You will not be able to see what is going on at your back. It creates nervousness and frustration. If you are unable to change your desk, hang a large mirror on your front wall. It enables you to see what is going on behind you. You can also choose an article such as a *yantra*, globe, crystal pyramid or a bright picture for placing it on your desk. It will nurture you and fill you with confidence.

Workers closest to the entrance will have less job satisfaction than those farther away. Sitting in a position that allows a view of the room makes you feel confident. Compare it to the way you feel when you are sitting in a vulnerable position next to the door. Your seat will be constantly interrupted by people coming in and going out. Visitors borrow your stationary and equipments. Your files and papers usually get knocked off the desk. People sitting in these positions go on changing their job constantly. They rarely stay long in a job. Consequently, people sitting here will not be interested in serious work. They will be clock watchers and will try to leave the office as quickly as they can.

Desks facing each other are not good. This is a confrontational position. Arrangement of desks in U-shape fashion is almost equally bad. People sitting along the two long sides will be opposite to each other. It will generate friction and discord among the staff. The manager sitting in a position directly facing the other staff is the worst position. It resembles teacher-students sitting arrangement in a classroom. It is almost always confrontational and bad from morale point of view too. L-shape arrangement of desks is believed to encourage some staff member's gang up against the other staff members. Consequently, absentee rate will increase in the office.

Desks can diagonally be placed to each other but their angles should not cause vedha to the other desks. Columns and overhead beams can also create vedha. They need to be remedied. A column can partially be concealed with potted plants or creepers. Overhead beams can be concealed with the help of false ceiling. Their ill-effect can also be mitigated by a partition wall directly under them.

For best results, position your table at an angle to the entrance. Different angular positions produce different feelings. You yourself can make experiment with different positions and feel the outcome. Some good and bad placements of working desk with reference to the entry have been shown in Figures 5.5 and 5.6.

Good Placements of Working Table

The best vaastu position of the working table is the corner diagonally opposite the entrance (see Figure 5.5). Right corner position is more dominating than the left one, when seen from the entrance. Two solid walls – one towards the back and another towards the side – act as a protector. A solid wall on the left hand side is much better than one on the right hand side. Left side, being a passive side for most of the people, needs more protection than the right one. Make sure that nothing is causing vedha (obstruction) to your door. Don't face the entrance directly. The incoming prana could be overpowering otherwise.

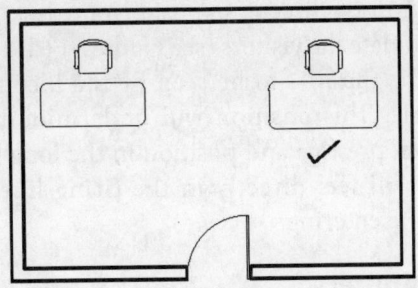

Fig 5.21: Right hand side position is better for promotion

Try to sit facing the door at an angle of your choice. Make sure that none of the corners are causing vedha. Any protruding sharp corner can be concealed effectively by keeping a healthy plotted plant near it (see Figure 5.4). If clear view of any vedha is clearly visible from the window, keep it shut and blinds closed.

The desk should face your lucky direction. The direction you face, while working in the office, greatly influences your career. Try to sit facing your favourable direction, whenever possible. Many people take their important decisions only when they are facing a fortunate direction. Vedic astrology can help you in finding out your luckiest direction(s). The direction(s) governed by the most benefic planet(s) in one's horoscope is his luckiest direction(s). Ideal vaastu for someone is when main entrance to the building as well as doorway to his office is in his luckiest direction.

People should be able to see you while working in your office. You need to be visible to your superiors. If no one is able to see you sitting in your office, you are likely to be ignored for important assignments, foreign tours, promotions and other special benefits.

Nine sector (*navpada* or *peeth*) vaastu can also be useful in determining the most suitable positions for you. South-east and south sectors or areas nearest to the main entrance of your business are the most active directions. These are usually the most favourable positions for occupying your desk if you are required to be the first to deal with the visitors.

If you are not facing your luckiest direction, use *panch-mahabhootas* and *trigunas* to attract the desired qualities. For example, a lush green healthy plant on or near your working table will give you the effect of facing north though you are facing a completely different direction. North is ruled by Mercury, the ruler of greenery. A small table lamp, a crystal artefact or a vase of fresh cut flowers, gives you the effect of facing east. East is ruled by Sun, the ruler of light, glamour and life.

Something red or angular shaped, such as a small pyramid on your table or a well maintained cactus plant (though it is considered inauspicious in home), activates the fire element. It will give you the effect of facing south. An antique piece – made of heavy materials such as earth, stone, china clay, metal, wood, etc., – activates the west direction. Heavy items, painted in black or earthy colours, also give you the advantage of facing west.

Different articles, elements, energies and colours are related with different directions; choose them as per your lucky direction and personal taste. Different combinations may result in completely different outcome. For instance, sweet smelling fresh flowers enhance the earth element but give you the feeling of facing east.

Working table as well as the office should be kept tidy, neat and clean. Your life will go much more smoothly. Avoid clutter in the office. A heap of pending files and papers on your table will make you feel frustrated and disorganised. *Lakshami*, the wealth goddess, likes neat and clean beautiful spaces to reside in. Sitting chair should be comfortable with the right height. A person is able to produce much more productive work from a comfortable chair of right height than from an uncomfortable chair of the wrong height. He will also feel happier and enjoy sitting behind his table.

Bad Placements of Desk

Sitting too close to the door makes you distracted continually (see Figure 5.6(a) and (b)). You are not able to concentrate on your work for long. The person sitting near the door will be more disturbed than the person sitting farther. Many are clock watchers and try to leave office as early as possible. A door beside you affects your concentration (see Figure 5.6(c)). It undermines your authority. It is not a commanding position.

Sitting with your back towards an open door or window makes you feel lacking in solid support (see Figure 5.14). Considered as one of the worst positions, it makes you feel extremely uncomfortable. A colleague can betray you or stab you in the back. An open door or a passage behind your chair acts like a sharp vedha. It leaves you vulnerable to office politics. A window behind the back is disconcerting. A healthy plant on the window sill may help as a barrier. Many modern offices have glass behind the executives. Fixed glass is less harmful than the movable one. It can be remedied by using blinds.

Fig 5.22 (a): Wrong Placement of Desk

A door directly opposite your desk may intimidate the visitors (see Figure 5.6(d)). You will be the first to be seen by the incoming people. This position will undermine your power, prestige and position in the long run. You will feel directly in the firing line for anyone entering.

Computers

Computers, in the modern times, have developed to such an extent that virtually every office uses at least one. Apart from the Central Processing Unit (CPU) which usually looks like a box, computers also have a Visual Display Unit (VDU) or monitor and keyboard. They have a printer and other attached devices too. Many offices have network of computers, all linked to a Central Control Unit (CCU).

Computers store a huge amount of information. They are used for preparing the accounts, charts, diagrams, designs, presentations and everyday letters. Files holding masses of information can be stored on the hard disc and compact discs. Keep your hard disc clear of out-of-date files. Such files create stagnant energy. Remove the old files to a storeroom elsewhere. Regularly back-up your working files. It helps in rapid access to the data you need.

Today electronic mail is very important for businesses. We can forget time differences between different countries. Postal delays can be forgotten. Urgent messages can reach their destination within seconds. Computer provides endless possibilities. Initially, setting up databases to print labels for e-mails is time consuming but time saving in the long run. Random thoughts for meetings, lectures and workshops can immediately be recorded on personal computer. It helps us prepare well in advance saving our time and anguish at the last minute.

Computers generate heat, light, sound and other types of known and unknown radiations.

They create a huge amount of rajas energy. Computer screens symbolise life and activity, which create and attract the active prana. Computer room shall be fitted with sufficient electric points so that no loose wires are visible. Great rajas energy of computer room can be balanced with a tamasic colour scheme such as blue or grey. Lush green potted plants also help to redress the balance. Prefer understated lighting in the computer room.

It is said that continuous use of computers can cause health problems including deterioration of eyesight, epilepsy, headache, stress, impotency, radiation risk to unborn babies, lowered immunity to diseases and Repetitive Strain Injury (RSI). Most of these ill-effects arise due to the wrong way of using a computer and not because of the computer itself.

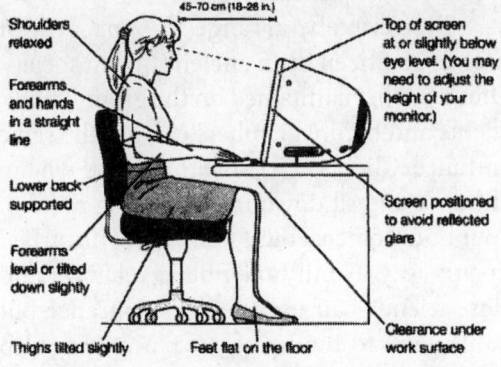

Fig 5.22 (b): Right Placement of Computer

We are likely to suffer from a health problem if we sit in one position all day long. Frequent users (over one hour a day continuously) must take regular breaks. Many countries have now legally limited the number of safe working hours for computer work. One must use a suitable revolving chair and working table. Sit in a proper position. Lot of natural light and fresh air helps a lot. Proper ventilation helps in reduction of harmful electro-smog. Work on a less bright monitor screen. Screen filters may also help to some extent. Get your eyes tested after regular intervals. Wear glasses with Anti Reflective coating (ARC), if necessary.

Wherever possible, use a laptop in preference to other computer. Cathode ray tubes are major cause of above discussed problems. Laptops do not have these tubes. Wear natural fibres such as cotton while working on the computer. They do not create static electricity.

Home Office

First business places all over the world were generally the front portions of businessmen's houses. In multi-storey buildings, usually ground floor was meant for business purposes. Industrial revolution led to separate places for businesses. Large scale production required separate factories, markets, super markets, commercial plazas, super stores and super specialty malls.

Complete bifurcation of residential and commercial activities in the past years has also led to new problems in the big cities. These problems are the space scarcity, traffic jams, difficult transportation, increased pollution, longer distances between home and workplace, vulnerability to road accidents, tensions, anxieties and many more.

However, many professionals and retired people work from their home. It is now being said that traditional large office buildings will become more and more of a rarity in future. Large organisations are getting smaller in many cases. Increasing number of people will be running their own businesses from smaller office premises or from homes. More and more employees will be home based. Electronic equipments – such as computers and laptops, internet, tele-conferencing, video-conferencing, e-mail, fax, phones, mobiles and a large range of latest Apps will help them to link up with their head office. Companies may increase the use of hot desking in near future.

Working from home has many definite advantages. Two main reasons of running the business from home, rather than from an outside office, are financial reasons and family commitments. It is normally far cheaper to work from home rather than rent or buy an office somewhere else. You will save the rent or loan repayments and travelling expenses to and from work. You need not spend time travelling to work. Consequently, you will gain two to three hours of extra time each day. You are also able to juggle, looking after your children or the dependent elderly relatives.

In ancient India, a person residing in his own house and earning in his own village was considered to enjoy *rajayoga* (combination of enjoying royal position with power and extraordinary lucky). In Vedic Astrology, fourth *bhava* (house) of the horoscope signifies residence. Any affliction to this house may lead one to undesired foreign travels and staying in a far off land. Home is more comfortable and more convenient for work. You can work early in the morning, you can work late at night, you can work a longer day without travelling times, you are free to work in your dressing gown, pyjamas, bermudas, *lungi* or in T-shirt. You are always 'on the spot' to deal with any problem that arise in your working or home life both.

There are certain disadvantages in working from home too. Work can interfere with home life. You are never entirely away from your business. Temptation may be to keep working without any break. You can also spend too much time working on the weekends as it is too easily accessible. Because of your constant availability, people may call you even at odd times. You may be interrupted during your meals by phone calls or door bell. In such cases, you can take the help of an answering machine or an assistant.

There are other practical disadvantages of working from home too. Your home may not have sufficient accommodation. Local authorities and/or your proprietor may not permit you to run a business from home. Your property deeds may prohibit the running of a business. The location of your home may be unsuitable for the business purposes. Conversely, you may be tempted not to work at all. Watching television or playing computer games might seem more attractive to you.

Creating a productive workspace, without affecting a home or apartment's prana, is a unique challenge. If your customers visit you in your home office, it should be located near the front entrance. Home office at the back of your house is not auspicious. Your clients will have to walk right through the house to reach you. It will be very inconvenient for them. The family privacy will also get disturbed. It will be still better if there is a separate entry for your clients and family members.

Alternatively, arrange the space floor wise as practiced in an ancient Indian society. Office can be maintained on the ground floor; clients and family members can use the same entrance. Clients can come through the main entrance and sit down in the waiting room of your home office. Your family is not disturbed in this way. Family members, relatives and close friends can use the same entrance but go upstairs to the living area. You may also provide a separate staircase leading directly to the upper floors, if possible. But it shall also be kept in mind that a completely separate side or back entry gives lesser control on the family affairs as well.

Avoid using bedroom as your home office. Each space needs a different type of energy. A bedroom requires calming tamasic energy, while the office requires active rajasic energy. They do not mix here harmoniously. Mix the two and you may snooze while working or ruminate on work while lying in bed. Use your creativity to effectively divide the office and the bedroom. One option is to construct a thin wall. This wall of veil will create a separate office. A curtain, screen or an accordion-style sliding door may be chosen as another option. However, a bedroom may be used cleverly as a home office as shown here in Figure 5.24.

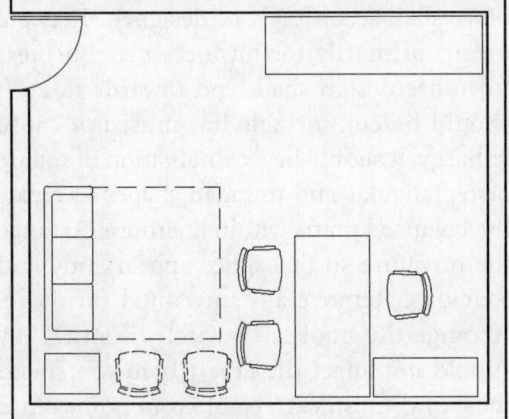

Fig 5.23: Bedroom cum Home Office

Move the office to a corner of the living room, if so possible. Home offices are better when located in a living room than in a bedroom. Mark its boundaries clearly. Otherwise, office work might create a cramped and cluttered look in the living room. Generation of bad energies is the direct result. A thin wall, screen or curtains are helpful here. Home office too near the main entrance, if used for serious study or writing or single handed work, is not good. You will be constantly disturbed by family guests. In such cases, separate library or office should be in a secluded quiet area of the house.

Study and work must go on without any interruption. The space for home office should be clearly marked. When you are working inside it, you are working to earn money, name, fame, power or position. Once you leave it after finishing your day's work, you are no longer at work. When you close the door behind you, you symbolically leave your work behind.

Your home office should preferably face south-east, east or south directions. These directions receive maximum daylight. East receives the earliest sunrays; south-east receives warm sunrays, while rays received by south are very hot. However, if home office is to be used more as a study than as a consultation chamber, north-east or north sector is better. These are the cool *sattvic* directions of knowledge. A regular shape office like square or rectangular is better than that of an irregular shape. An L-shape room can be symbolically converted into two separate rectangular areas. Use one of these areas for placing your desk and entertain your guests in the other.

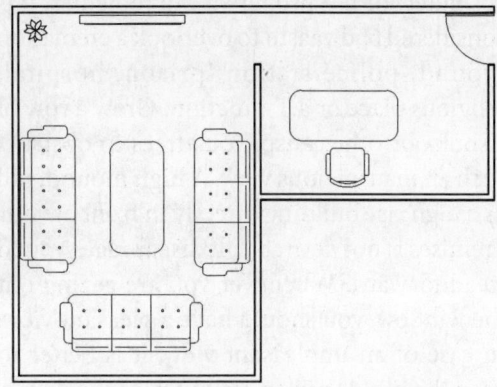

Fig 5.24: Arranging an L-Shape Room

Home office is mainly meant for rajasic and sometimes sattvic activities. There is no place for tamasis activities here. Therefore, you need to encourage larger amount of prana here. Increased prana increases your activities, creativity and thinking power. Increased activities increase the likelihood of success. An excellent way to encourage the prana of home office is making the availability of sufficient natural light. It gives a positive work environment. If good natural light is absent, provide the artificial light.

Strong lights, glaring or shimmering lights create negative energy. Glare can also come in through the doors, windows and ventilators. Arrange the amount of light with properly located sunshades, awnings, curtains and blinds. Avoid harsh lights or direct glare on your work. Try to shield your eyes from the harsh light. You can also use coloured or photo-chromatic spectacles. It is better to have windows beside your desk, rather than behind you. A window behind you makes you lacking in solid support. A window on the left hand side gives more of the useful natural light.

Thoroughly check your home office for any vedha caused by the neighbouring houses, telephone or electric lines, roads, trees, an electric transformer, or a large dustbin. Anything else can also be the probable cause of a deadly vedha. Eliminate these vedhas absolutely or use proper vaastu remedies. It is considered bad vaastu to overlook a cremation ground, police station, prison, hospital, religious place or a T-junction. Grow a row of Ashoka or other auspicious trees to obstruct such an inauspicious view. A high mound, hill or a high rise building directly in front of your premises is not desirable. It discourages you to tread forward. Whenever you are gazing out the window, you should have a pleasant view. In case of an unpleasant view, it is better to keep the blinds pulled for much of the day.

Arrange your home office according to the position of *Vaastu Purush*. The most important thing here is the placement of your desk. Place it in a commanding position. You should be able to see anyone coming in the room. Sit with your back supported by a solid wall. People sitting with their backs to an open door get frustrated. Apply the detailed principles about the working table as discussed earlier. These principles apply equally well even if you never get to meet any of your customers.

Your desk in the south-east, south or east sector keeps you active and alert. Energies of north-east and north are conducive for creative writing. If you are working on an ancient scripture, west direction is the best. Place your computer, telephone and fax machine in the active and easily approachable areas. If you are not getting enough business calls, keep your phone in the rajas area of air (NW) or fire (SE). Properly advertise your phone numbers. You can also energise your phone by keeping a globe, pyramid or Shri Yantra made of good quality crystal next to your phone instrument.

Furniture and furnishings in the home office shall accordingly be designed. They are meant primarily for business use. Business furniture design shall tend towards rajas. It should be comfortable but must not cause lethargy. It should be a combination of square or rectangular and rounded shapes to create the balanced prana within the room. Arrange the furniture so that office appears tidy and spacious. Remove any unwanted furniture. Arrange the bookcases wisely, if any. They should not affect the area where you spend most of your time. Decorate your home office in a mix of formal and casual styles. Neat and uncluttered space makes it an ideal place for doing efficient work.

The colour scheme of your office should reflect your personal and helping elements, your aims and type of business. If your element is fire, use different shades of red, orange and yellow in your colour scheme. The colours used in jewellery showrooms are usually pink and golden. Pink represents good health while golden colour represents money – the two most vital life necessities.

Avoid any clutter in your home office. Clutter pulls your spirits downwards. It constantly distracts your mind, constricts the available prana and gives negative feelings of lack, limitation and loss. Clear out the clutter and you will feel your spirits rising. You will also feel more focussed, more creative and more energetic.

You will achieve much better results when you work on a clear desk than when working on a cramped desk surrounded by clutter. A cluttered desk distracts your attention. Best performance in any task needs 100% concentration. Keep your writing table clear of extra papers and files every evening before heading home. This is good for security reasons too.

When you are using part of a room as your study or workplace, determine the most important activity at a time and arrange the room accordingly. You can use a room for writing a book during the day and to sleep in at night. Place the bed in the south-west corner. This corner, full of tamasic energy of inactivity, is best for sleeping purpose. Place an office desk in the most commanding position in the room. Use a decorative screen to make the bed symbolically disappear during the day or simply keep your back towards the bed while studying or working. These simple adjustments can change the emphasis of the bedroom from passive sleeping to active working. You will soon realise that your career is thriving.

Everybody is not lucky enough to have a separate room just for work or study. I myself used part of my bedroom as my study and part of it as my workplace for around fifteen year (see Figure 5.26). The study table was along the east wall. While sitting on the chair, my back remained towards the bed, the seat of tamas. A slight turn of head towards the door gave pleasant view of healthy potted plants kept just outside it. South-east entrance supplied lot of active natural light throughout the day. This is a practical example how you can apply principles of vaastu shastra even on a small living area.

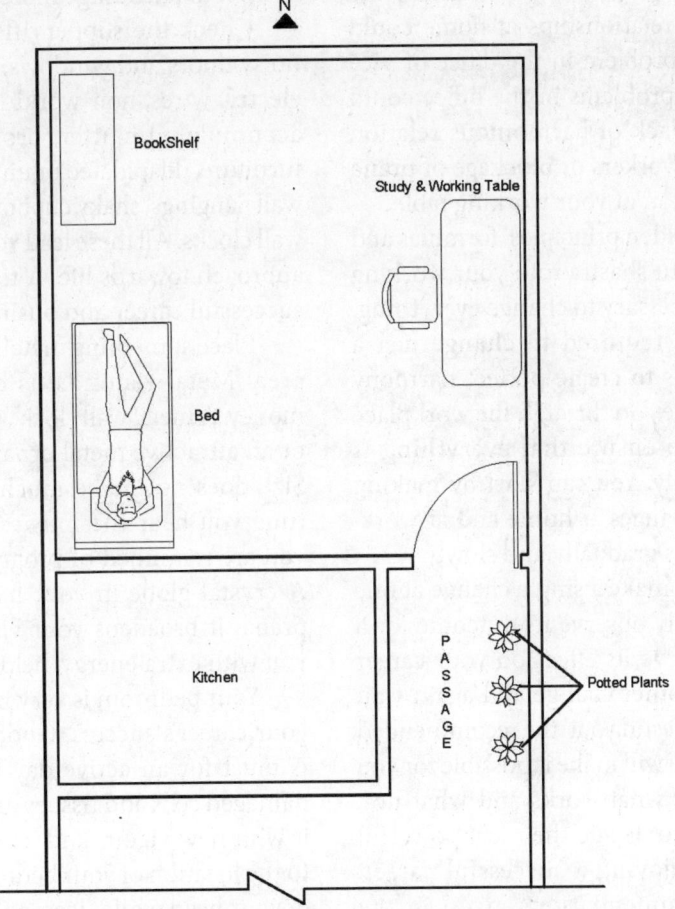

Fig 5.25: Bedroom cum Study Arrangement

An office having an airy and clean feel, a peaceful view and an ergonomic desk can be considered a nice office. Dark and windowless rooms with stale air are not conducive to study or work. Clutter free clean rooms, receiving plenty of natural light and fresh air, are necessary to support the thought process. Place a large picture of mountains, a lake or river or Mother Nature on the wall facing your eyes or towards your active hand side. They are believed to foster creativity and motivation.

Vaastu in Career Building

The principles of vaastu shastra, used creatively in the home and office, can greatly contribute in career success. The energies of home and workplace are not independent of each other. Something wrong with one will affect the other. Unhappy relationships at home could be because of a problem in the office or vice versa. Likewise, problems in the office could be caused by a lack of harmonious relation between the co-workers or blockage of prana due to bad position of your working table.

Try all the golden principles, formulas and methods of vaastu shastra into your working lives. It is not necessary to change everything. Mostly, you are required to change just a handful of things to create perfect harmony in your workplace. Go through the workplace in a set order to ensure that everything is evaluated properly. You can start by making certain minor changes at home and at work. Make the changes gradually and slowly.

It is better to make a single change at one time and faithfully observe its outcome for a few weeks. Observe its effect on your career before trying another change and again wait for a few weeks. 'Testing out' the recommended changes over time will make it possible for you to observe freely what works and what not. You will be able to decide the most powerful methods. For enjoying a successful career, follow the recommendations given in the following paragraphs and success shall quickly follow.

Examining the home

The process of your career enhancement starts from your home itself. There should not be any vedha affecting the front door. Well lit entrance area encourages the prana inside. Activate your living area, study table and working desk. Pay proper attention to the kitchen and dining area. According to Ayurveda, our diet and food deeply influences our physical, mental and spiritual state of health. It directly influences the quality and efficiency of our work. Make sure that kitchen and dining areas receive enough light. Natural light is the best. Leave no dark corners. If necessary, increase the amount of light to encourage more prana in.

Check the slippery floor and stair-case, noisy doors and windows, leaking taps, loose electric wires, non-working electric switches, accumulated clutter, broken or unpainted furniture, dilapidated or unpainted walls, tilted wall hangings, shaky cupboards and unmoving wall clocks. All these lead you to a lackadaisical approach towards life. A tidy home leads to a successful career and business life.

Place something metallic in your working area. Metal reminds us of coins and thus money. A metal wall clock with musical sounds or an attractive metal ornament is good here. Size does not make much difference. Every time you hear the musical sound or see it, you are reminded of progress in your career. A crystal globe in your home office attracts prana. It broadens your vision and provides you with extra energy, helping in your career.

Your bedroom is very important factor in your career's success. Good and sound sleep is must for an active day life. It repairs the damaged cells and tissues of our body and fills it with new vigour and vitality. Pay attention to the location of your bedroom and direction of your head while sleeping. Place your bed in

Workplace Vaastu

a safe, secure and private area which is full of tamasic energy at night. It should, at the same time, be preferably farthest from the main entrance. The most favourable directions for taking rest are south-west, south and west sectors. If these sectors are not available for your bedroom, position your bed in the south-west area of your room. Align it so that your head points towards south while sleeping. This position allows the pranic energy to flow into your body even as you sleep, thereby attracting success to flow towards you.

Arrange bed in such a position so that you are able to see anyone coming into the room without moving your head more than half a right angle. If you sleep with your back towards the door, you symbolically encourage people to work against you behind your back. Do not sleep with your head or feet directly opposite the door. If you do, all your future progress will stagnate and perish. If your bed is against a wall having a large opening like a door or window, do not sleep with your back towards this wall.

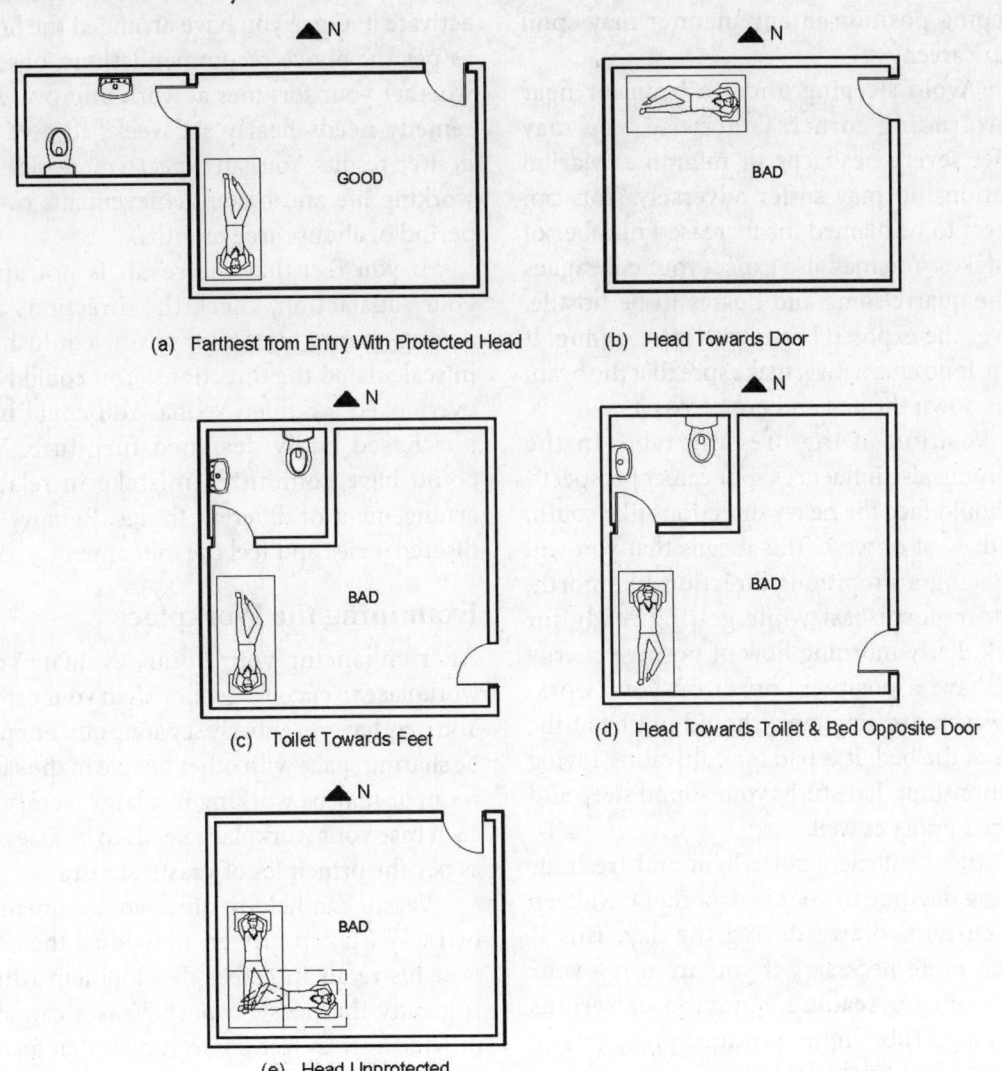

Fig 5.26: **Arranging a Bedroom**

In modern days, many bedrooms are designed to have an attached bathroom cum toilet. Do not sleep facing such an adjoining toilet or bathroom. You will lie directly in the path of ill fated energy coming from the toilet. You will breathe in negative energy all night along and hence encounter several problems in your life. The energy from the toilet is too powerfully tamasic. Ruled by Rahu and negative Saturn, this tamasic energy weakens your rajasic energy. Rajasic energy is so vital for success in career. Please remember, negative sleeping position in any manner may spoil your career.

Avoid sleeping under a beam or near a protruding corner. Otherwise, you may suffer severe headache or migraine. Marital relationship may suffer adversely. You can expect to be blamed for increased number of mistakes. You may also expect your colleagues to be quarrelsome and bosses to be hostile. Cover the exposed beam with false ceiling. If there is no alternative, make sure that the beam runs down the bed and not across it.

Position of the dressing table in the bedroom also influences your career prospects. It should face the heavy directions like south, south-west or west. This means that you will be facing a propitious direction like north, east or north-east while getting ready for work. Early morning flow of positive energy will have a positive impact on your work. However, dressing table should not be at the foot of the bed. It is bad for cultivating loving relationships. It disturbs your sound sleep and overall prana as well.

Allow sufficient solar light and fresh air during daytime in your bedroom. Don't keep the curtains drawn during the day. This is much more necessary if you are using your bedroom for reading, studying or serious working. Tube lights produce great rajasic energy. Use a bright lighted table lamp on your study table, if you read or work here at night. It creates a sattvic effect. Sit facing your best direction in order to achieve success in the career, wherever possible.

Place something on the wall opposite the working table that reminds you of your career and wealth. You can also place an object made of your element near your working table. For example, a potted plant of dark green colour represents earth element.

Locate your desk in the active sector of your home, or study,. You can also keep here papers related to your career. Use a large crystal or metallic object on the desk to activate it. Once you have arranged the home as per the above recommendations, observe whether your fortunes at work improve. Any remedy needs nearly six weeks to give the desired results. You can expect a more pleasant working life and better achievements over a period of about three months.

If you feel that the result is not up to your satisfaction, check the directions and arrangements once more. You could have miscalculated the directions. You could have overlooked a hidden vedha. You could have purchased badly designed furniture. You could have committed mistake in relative arrangement of different things. Remove the discrepancies and feel the outcome.

Examining the Workplace

After enhancing your home, evaluate your workplace to encourage success in your career. You may have an entirely separate office or may be sharing space with other people in the same room or may be working in a large factory. In each case your workplace needs to be assessed as per the principles of vaastu shastra.

Vaastu can help in office environment in two ways. It can give an individual the edge over his rivals in career development which is greatly the rajasic aspect. Vaastu can also provide a stress free environment that fosters harmonious working relationships, improves job satisfaction and develops personal career. This is mainly the sattvic aspect.

The building shall gain support, either from the nearby high rise land or from the neighbouring buildings. It should mix comfortably with the surrounding buildings. For instance, a small building surrounded by sky-scrapers is not auspicious. People working in such a building feel constricted and restricted. Feelings of oppression and depression overpower them.

One of the prime aims of any businessman is to make money. Water reminds us of money. It is the most precious gift of mother earth after oxygen rich air. An inwardly flowing water fountain or a pond, especially lotus or fishpond or gently flowing water in front of your building, shall bring financial benefits. These water bodies need to be looked after properly. Dirty water creates negative prana which can harm the business.

Room at the end of a long straight hallway suffers from *marga vedha*. This vedha needs to be remedied. A healthy plant or a mirror on the outside of the door of such a room may rectify this vedha (see Figure 5.9).

Carefully evaluate the front entrance of your workplace. Any vedha to the front door needs to be properly remedied. The door should be of a suitable size. Its size should nearly be equal to the size of other doors inside the building. Too large a door allows your wealth to escape. Too small a door constricts the amount of prana coming in. The door should open fully. The entrance should be well lit. It should be kept clean and tidy. Approximately seventy-five% of your business prana comes in through the main entrance while the rest comes in through the other door and windows.

A solid door in the workplace (without any clientele) is better than glass panelled doors. It provides greater privacy and ensures that you will be more productive. Some executives like to sit in an office fitted with glass doors. They are able to see what everyone is doing. However, it lessens an executive's privacy and work efficiency too. Also, employees like to be trusted. A glass door sends a psychological message that people are not trusted.

The location and direction of doors and entrances greatly influences an individual's fortunes. Check that the front entrance faces one of your lucky directions. To enhance your career fortune, use this entrance daily. If the main entrance is not in your best direction, see if there is another entrance. Try to use the entrance that corresponds to your lucky directions, whenever you enter or leave the office premises. Companies also have birth dates and thus certain auspicious direction. These directions can differ from that of the chairman or CMD. Remember, the main entrance of office building may not be individually auspicious for the present head of the organisation, though it may be auspicious for the company as a whole.

Place your working table in an auspicious area. Never sit with your back towards the door, passage or a large open window. It is more important to sit in a commanding position than to face a positive direction. You should be able to see people coming in and going out. Direct physical and psychological effects rule supreme. Mystical effects come afterwards only. The size of your desk reflects your status in the corporation. The working area should be of sufficient size. The desk should be of rectangular shape with curved corners or slightly curved in shape. An L-shaped desk causes vedha.

Protect your workspace from any vedha. An overhead beam acts like a vedha. Working directly under an exposed beam may cause continual headache. The prana should flow smoothly around the premises. Dark corners or accumulated clutter affects good prana. Dripping taps, slippery floors or anything else working badly erodes away your good fortune. Sticking doors, hard to open windows or jammed ventilators cause frustration. They create negative energies and affect your career prospects badly.

Activate your working area. It should be well lit to attract the beneficial prana. It should appear cheerful and energising. For instance, place an image of Goddess Lakshami dropping gold coins from her hands. You may place a small metal box containing few coins on your desk or its upper drawer. Alternatively, use something gold or white in colour to represent metal. Golden and white metals represent money. These help you progress in your career. Progress in you career means that you will steadily reap the increasing rewards. It does not happen on its own.

It is good to display something that relates to your personality. Display personal photographs, ornaments or such other related things. Personalising your workspace makes you feel at home and relaxed. You will consequently be happier and more productive in a vaastu friendly environment.

Finally take a slow walk around your working area. See it with a stranger's eyes. Feel intuitively if everything in the room is in balance? If you feel happy, it means your workplace is in perfect harmony and balance. If you do not feel comfortable, make further changes.

One shall always remember that vaastu shastra is not a magic. It does not do everything for you instantly. It mainly helps in creating a positive environment around you. Consequently, you are able to work efficiently and apply your creativity to the fullest extent. This positive environment makes it easier to get along with our co-workers. God has created everyone 'unique' in this world in one or other way. You are constantly required to make an effort to get along with the disagreeable people. Vaastu shastra helps you to work diligently to the best of your ability, increasing your luck and career prospects.

Chapter 6
Applied Vaastu of the Masses

यो यमर्थं प्रार्थयते तदर्थं चेहते क्रमात्।
अवश्यं स तमाप्नोति न चेदर्धान्निवर्तते॥

Whoever wishes for whatsoever and perseveres in its acquisition, surely succeeds in getting them, provided he does not (get tired and) stops short midway.

Yogavaashistha, 2.4.12

Principles of vaastu, along with the residence, may equally be applied to all the places related with the masses. These places may include not only the religious, industrial, commercial, and public buildings but all other types of constructions. I am discussing here only some peculiar areas of mass appeal. Once gone through the earlier chapters and these pages conscientiously, intelligent readers would be able to apply the vaastu principles to each and every type of vaastu listed below.

The list includes religious places of all faith, yoga and meditation centres, gyms, industries, workshops, five star hotels, holiday homes, picnic spots, fun parks, resorts and lodges, theatres and cinema halls, water and entertainment parks, water sports, boat clubs, beaches, fashion industry, beauty parlours, moving sets or pandals (for holy discourses, film shooting, dance and drama shows, marriage ceremonies, political rallies etc), banks, petrol pumps, consultancy services, executive clubs, stadiums, guest houses, auditoriums, banquet halls, memorials, parade grounds, and trusts. Case studies regarding some particular areas have also been discussed in chapter nine.

Temples

Knowledge and application of vaastu shastra is must for construction, maintenance and successful operation of temples. Many ancient as well as modern temples constructed as per the established norms of vaastu shastra are still famous among millions of devotees. People have deep faith in these places as they consider these places potent. People make secret vows at these places and find that their vows are fulfilled.

According to the ancient Indian tradition, planets and gods' idols are closely related. A planet is called 'graha' in Sanskrit which literally means; 'to catch hold of' or 'that which receives'. Idol is called 'vigraha' in Sanskrit which means; 'that which transmits power received from graha'. Planets ruling the eight directions transmit power to the relevant gods situated in their relevant directions.

Vaastumandanam (1.89) recommends riverside, confluence of rivers, teertha (a holy place for bathing in a river or a water tank), siddhashrama (an accomplished hermitage) or the mountain top as ideal places for location of temple. These places are thought to fulfill the

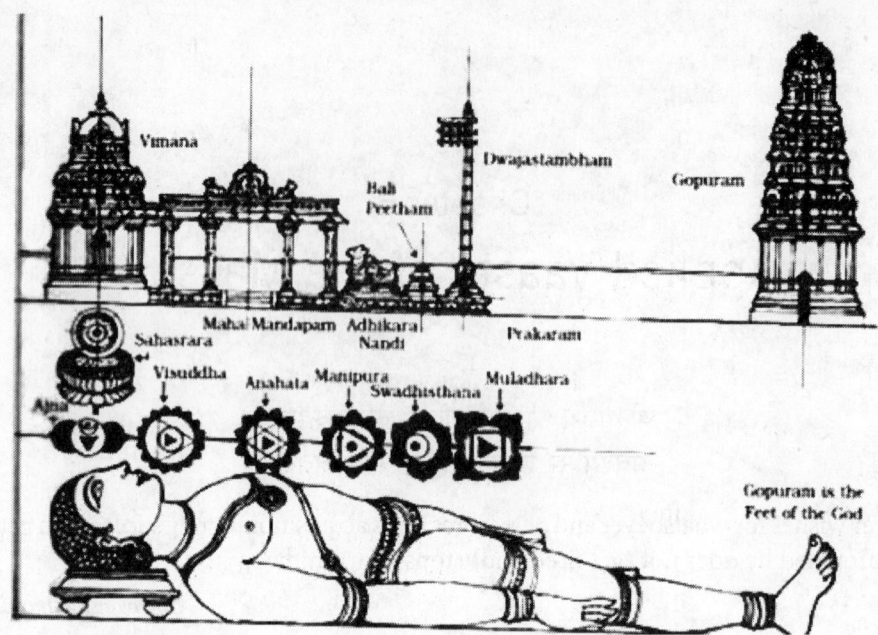

Fig 6.1: Temple as the "Body of the Deity in the Lying Position"

vaastu requirements automatically to a large extent, without any consideration of directions. Shilpa Ratnakar (2.76) also considers these places fit for construction of a temple.

The sea, a perennial river, fresh water lake or a fresh water pond - particularly in the north or east of the temple - is considered auspicious. Jyotirlinga temple in Rameshwaram, Vivekanand Memorial in Kanyakumari and Hanuman Mandir at Yamuna Bazar in Delhi are some of the examples. Places situated on mountains or a tall hill, where the population is quite thin, are also good choices for a temple. The austerity of the god is easily maintained here. Some of the striking examples are the Kedarnath, Badrinath, Amarnatha, Hemkund Sahib, Kailash-Mansarovar, Tirupati Balaji, and Jakhoo Mandir in Simla.

As per the temple vaastu, the shadow of temple should not fall on other buildings. Also, no building of any other type should be situated in front of the temple. These conditions get fulfilled when temple is situated on a hill or a mountain. Easily approachable god yields least or no results in the long run. A temple in the vicinity is usually not recognized by the locals.

Mayamatam describes three types of temple buildings (as well as Linga): naagara, dravida and vesara. The square or rectangular building is called naagara, the hexagonal or octagonal one (whether regular or elongated) is called dravida and the circular, elliptical or epsidal one is called vesara. According to Kamikagama (I.45.136), naagara temples are located to north, north-east or north-west of a town, dravida temples to south, south-east or south-west and vesara temples to east or west.

Maansaar (Chapter 19) classifies buildings into sthanaka, asana and shayana which are also called respectively samchita, asamchita and apasamchita. In the sthanaka class, measurement of the height is considered, in the asana the breadth and in the shayana the length. In the sthanaka, asana and shayana buildings the idol is respectively in erect, sitting and recumbent posture.

Another classification in Maansaar refers to the shape. Buildings are classed as purusha (masculine) when they are equiangular or circular, and as feminine when they are rectangular. Male deities are installed in masculine temples, and female deities in feminine temples. However, images of the latter can also be placed in masculine temples.

Plot meant for a temple should be exactly square or made so with due rectification. Its land should slope towards the northeast or east. The four geographic cardinal directions should be parallel to the plot, not in the corners. A compound wall should be constructed around the temple complex to maintain its sanctity.

Four boundary gates as well as entrance gates to the main temple building are considered very auspicious. One single boundary gate is best in the east. Single gate towards the south or west is not considered auspicious. Two gates are best, when in the east and north. The main entrance gate should be taller of all the other gates and should be extraordinarily decorated.

For construction of temples, 64 square vaastu mandal should be used. Maansaar (Chapters 20-32) describe the location of divine images with which the walls are decorated. Gate houses (gopura) are built in front of each of the five courts into which the whole temple compound is divided. Different courts (Prakara) should be constructed for bali (offerings), parivara (attendant deities), shobha (beauty) and rakshana (defence). At the eight cardinal points of the innermost or the first court, the temples of a group of eight deities are built.

Mayamatam (Chapters 19 to 25) describe temples and their annexes. There are four series of possible dimensions for one storeyed temples, starting from three or four cubits and increasing successively by two units (up to nine or ten cubits). Their height may be ten sevenths their width or one a half, one and three quarters or twice it. These four

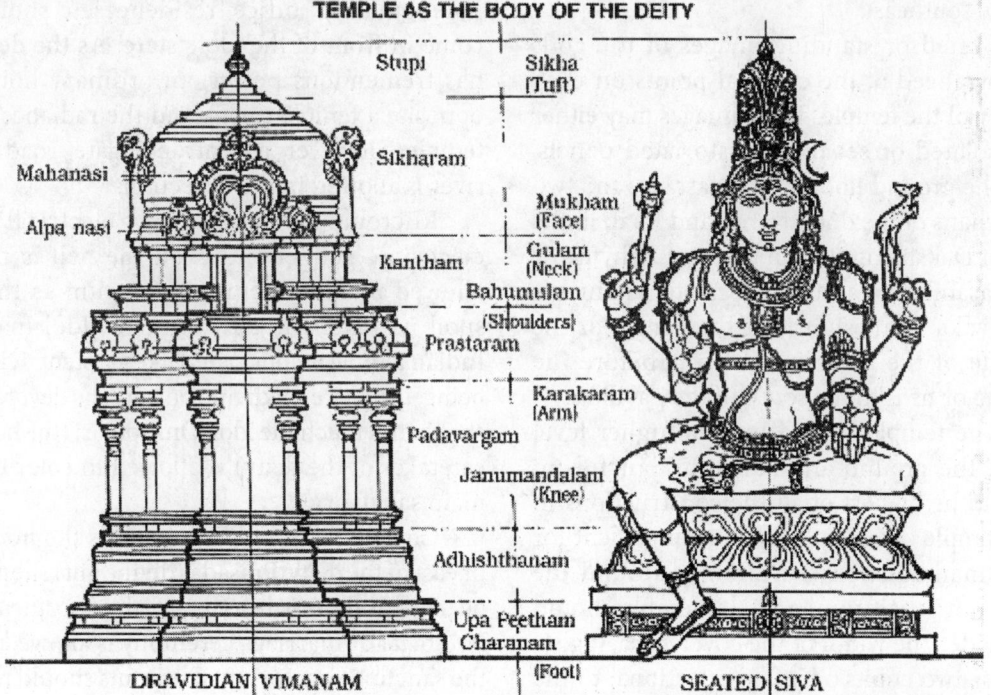

Fig 6.2: Temple as the "Body of the Deity in the Sitting Position"

dimensions are called shantika, paushtika, jayada and adbhuta. Plan of one storeyed temple may be square, circular, rectangular, elliptic, apsidal, hexagonal or octagonal. The plan of the roof may be same or different from that of the building.

According to Mayamatam (26.16a); "For gods the chamber is in the middle of the main building, for men it is at the side". This appears to be the main difference between the divine and human dwelling houses. In a temple, the chamber of the god is to be at the centre while in human houses that chamber is always placed off-centre, in one of the side parts of the main building.

Dividing the temple complex in four equal parts (2 X 2), main temple building with sabha mandap should be in the southwest. Different stories and anecdotes about the different deities should seriously be taken into consideration. Godowns, shops and rest-houses should be in the northwest. Water tank should be in the northeast. Kitchen and dining room should be in the southeast.

Seated or standing images of the gods are arranged at the cardinal points on each storey of the temple. These images may either be isolated or set up in historiated panels. On the ground floor, in the east, are the two guardians of the door, Nandi and Kaal; in the south Dakshinamurti, in the west Achyuta or Lingasambhuta and in the north Pitamaha. Vinayaka (Ganesha) is at the centre of the façade of the pavilion which is before the shrine or he is to the south of the pavilion.

The temple should be at a higher level from the ground and Sanctum Sanctorum should be highest of all the constructions in the temple complex. Proper arrangement for circumambulation (Parikrama) around the sanctum sanctorum, and the temple should be made. The width of the covered passage is one or two cubits or it is proportional to the dimensions of the temple. The thickness of the walls of the pavilion and covered passage is equal to that of the walls of the shrine or is three quarters or half that width. The possible widths for the sanctum (house of the embryo or matrix) calculated from the width of the temple are one third to one half.

There should be a window to the east of the sanctuary so that sunrays fall directly on the idol in the morning. There should be no room towards the backside of deity. No door has been provided towards the backside of the main idol in Akshardham temple in New Delhi.

The door is situated in the middle of the façade wall of the temple. The height of the door is nine tenths, eight ninths or seven eighths that of the pillars and its width is half its height. The line of sight of the idol of main deity should be trained on the seventh part, when front door is divided in nine equal parts. It means there should not be any dwar vedha (door obstruction) towards the face of idol.

Also, no obstruction in the form of a tree, pole, building, office, residence etc should come in front of the idol's stare. As the deity has tremendous power, an ordinary house opposite a temple can't stand the radiance of temple. However, an entrance gate, road or river is allowed in this direction.

Microphone, speaker, any electrical or electronic gadget and even the bell is not allowed in the sanctum sanctorum as they spoil its magnetic environment. Idol in an Indian temple is considered like a potent living being, the bearer of divine power. The devotees should not touch the idol. Only pujari (the holy caretaker of the deity) is allowed to enter the main sanctuary.

Charity pot should be towards the north or east of the deity. Prasada (divine gift) should be towards the northeast or north of northeast. No social or marriage ceremony is allowed in the sanctum sanctorum. Coconuts should not be broken here.

The pavilion in front of the shrine (Mukha-mandapa) is built in front of the door of the main temple (which contains the sanctum, garbhagriha). The mandapa is so called because it protects (pati) the manda that is 'the decoration' (Mayamatam, 25.26a).It appears as a nave where are accomplished several rites which cannot be enacted in the sanctum due to its exiguity. Its width is same as the shrine or three quarters or half of that width. If there is a covered passage (linking pavilion and temple) and a porch, the pavilion is then the same width as the temple.

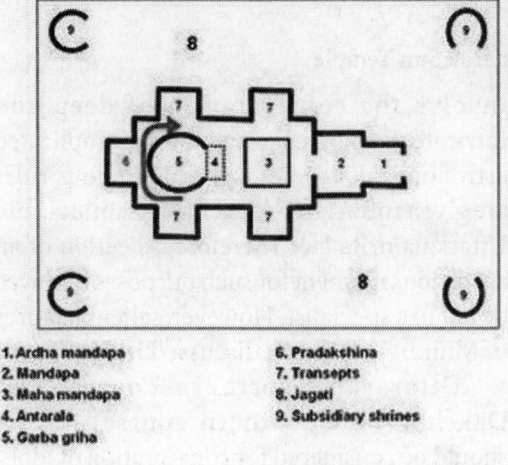

1. Ardha mandapa
2. Mandapa
3. Maha mandapa
4. Antarala
5. Garba griha
6. Pradakshina
7. Transepts
8. Jagati
9. Subsidiary shrines

Fig 6.3: Plan of the Kandariya Mahadeva Temple

The pavilion is provided with an even number of pillars arranged symmetrically. The colour of walls, flooring and pillars should be white, yellow, golden yellow, light saffron, or light pink.

In front of Vrishbha, half way from the temple, is the place for the flag mast (dhwaja) with the trident in front of it. All three, beginning with vrisha, are inside the enclosure and to the left on the way from gateway to temple (Mayamatam, 23.82-83a). The flag mast in front of the altar is to be in proportion to the temple. Outside the main shrine, vijaya-stambha (victory tower) should be situated towards the left side of the idol. Deep-stambha (light post), and hom-kund (sacred fire place) and agni-kund (fire place) should be in the southeast area.

The building for preparation of cooked oblations is built in the south-east corner against the wall of the maryadi enclosure. The treasury between this corner and the eastern gateway, whilst the pavilion for ablutions is on Yama's square where too is the pavilion for flowers. The pavilion for the god's weapons should be close to the south-west corner whilst the dormitories are to be at the squares of Varuna and Vayu (Mayamatam, 23.83b-85).

The pavilion for religious discourse is at Soma's square, the stepped well at that of Isha and the well encompasses that of Aapvatsa. The pavilion for musical instrument is between the north-east and the eastern gateway (Mayamatam, 23.86-87a).

The house of the head priest, the stepped well, the well, the garden and the pond may each be placed in any position as may the matha and the dining hall. The matha is often a school with students' lodging attached to the temple. It may also be used as a dharmashala for pilgrims or wandering ascetics (Mayamatam, 23.92). however, priest and other caretakers' family should live outside the temple premises.

There are images of bulls along the entire length of the top of the enclosure walls. The houses of courtesans are to the east and at a distance from the flag mast of the goddess equal to three, four or five times the width of the main temple. The place for masseuses is on both sides of it. All around outside the enclosure are the habitations of the servants of the temple. These houses may otherwise be to the east. The hermitage of the master (head of matha) is in the south or in the east but opens to the south (Mayamatam, 23.94b-97a).

All buildings intended for gods and ascetics may be built in brick, stone or wood (Mayamatam, 25.186b). The trees suitable for

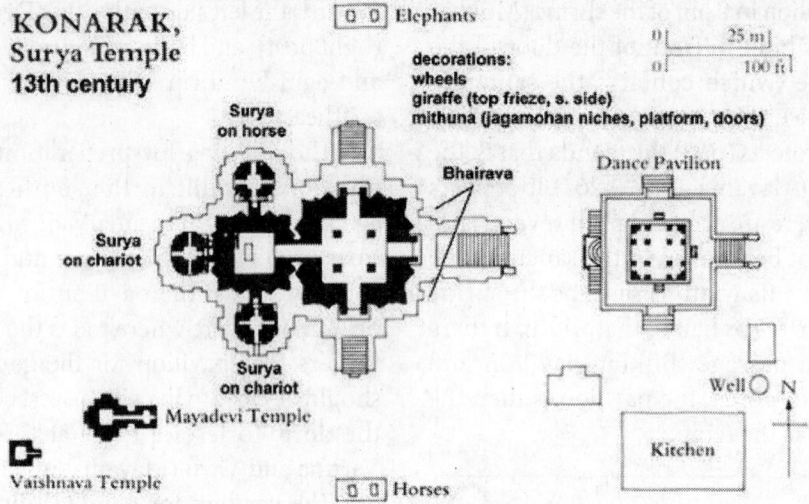

Fig 6.4: Plan of the Konarak Sun Temple

the making of pillars are Khadira, khaadira, vahni, nimbi, saala, silindrak, pishita, tinduka, rajadana, homa, and madhuka. Their wood may be used for all constructions intended for gods, Brahmin and kings (Mayamatam, 25.182-182).

Drinking water is best in the northeast while bathrooms are best in the east. Arrangement for removing and keeping shoes as well as for washing hands and feet should be in the southeast or northwest, outside of the path of circumambulation. Parking of public vehicles, toilets, urinals, and dustbins should be outside of the temple premises.

Fountains and lotus ponds are best in the east direction. Grow holy trees and plants like basil, peepal, vata (bargad), bel, nimba, kadamba, ashoka, parijata, coconut, banana, champa, jasmine, mango, jackfruit, gular, shirisha, etc in the open space surrounding the temple.

For construction and installation of the deity's idol, auspicious time (Muhurta) should be chosen for the intended auspicious results. When starting time is not auspicious, donors face financial problems or devotees don't visit the temple regularly. The temple is abandoned in the long run. Building temples and installing deities (prana pratishtha) involve the consideration of deep and intricate astrological principles. Complicated astronomical, astrological and religious rules are given in such works as Brihatsamhita, and Uttarkalmrita etc. Therefore, selection of an auspicious moment for such purposes may well be left to a specialist. However, salient features of Muhurta are being discussed here.

Uttarayan (Northern course) and Dakshinayan (Southern course) of Sun should be considered for consecration of idols. Hot tempered gods like Narsimha, Durga, Kali and Bhairava should be consecrated during Dakshinayan while gods of calm temperament like Narayana, Hanumana, Krishna and Lakshami should be consecrated during Uttarayana. It is auspicious to establish and consecrate Shivalinga in the month of Sharavana, Goddess Durga (and other forms of Shakti) in Ashvin, and Lord Vishnu in Margshirsha.

The lunar month of Magha should be avoided. The ceremony is to be avoided when Moon, Jupiter and Venus are debilitated, combust, placed in enemy's sign or defeated in planetary war. The ceremony should be avoided at the end of an Ayana, end of a year, end of a lunar day and end of an asterism. Days on which halos round the Sun and the Moon are visible should also be avoided. Days of malefic planets should be avoided for consecrating the idols of the calm temperament gods.

All odd lunar days (except the 9th) including the 2nd, 6th and 10th are favourable. Moon should be transiting Rohini, Mrigasira, Punarvasu, Pushya, Uttaraphalguni, Hasta, Swati, Uttarashadha or Uttarabhadra constellation. The Ascendant must be a fixed sign. A dual sign may also be selected for a female Deity. Movable signs should always be rejected. The Ascendant should not be conjoined by the luminaries or malefics or otherwise the town concerned will be destroyed. No malefic should occupy the 7th house. There should be no planet in the 8th house.

Personal prayers at home should be offered in the north-east or east direction. Main thing at home that helps in prayers is the nectar like radiations coming from the north-east and east. The deity's idol in front of you is not charged and is only symbolic. That's why restriction of one hasta (45 cm) height of deity's symbol has been imposed at home. On the other side, in the temple, it is the power of deity that enriches us. Temple is the abode of deity and thus the most prominent direction ie southwest, south or west is reserved for him or her. Deity receives new life energy when facing east or northeast. The devotee in the temple, standing before the god, is secondary. Unless deity is potent enough to fulfill the desires of the devotees, there is no use of entering the temple!

Institutions of Learning

Ancient Indian society had gurukuls (abode of teacher) which were located in the forest, away from the urban areas. A guru is one who teaches the ultimate knowledge, knowing which nothing remains to know. Early boarding schools in India - particularly in hill stations like Mussoorie, Nainital, Simla etc - were also established on gurukul pattern away from the thick human habitation. In the modern cities like Delhi, most of the schools don't even have a playground for students. Young students abound in rajas energy that needs to be spent in a constructive manner. Otherwise this energy finds outlet in destructive ways like playing video games, late night parties, rash driving, drugs and violence.

Educational institutes should be located in peaceful green areas where students can enjoy deep learning with peace of mind. These should preferably be away from the maddening city crowd. Their construction and operation should encourage all-round development of the students. Classrooms should be large-sized with sufficiently big size windows. These should provide neat and clean environment, big playgrounds and gardens.

Institutions of learning conforming to the vaastu principles perform much better. Educational institutions should be towards the east of any locality. Land of a school, college or other similar educational institution should have more open areas towards the north and east directions. More open space towards north and east can also be achieved by leaving broader setbacks towards these directions. Morning shift schools are better than evening shift schools. Slope of plot should be towards north, east or north-east direction. The school plot should be of a regular shape, preferably square or rectangular.

Classrooms should invariably receive sunlight from the east direction during the summer season and from the south during the winters. Morning time sunrays are like medicine in disguise, providing vitality and broadening the horizon of students. Afternoon sunrays should be avoided. If morning time sunrays are amrita (nectar), afternoon rays are halahal (poison). Administrative block should be near to the entry, preferably in the eastern zone of the plot. This power position enables controlling authority to administer school in an efficient manner.

Skyscrapers

A skyscraper is generally defined as a building taller than 150 metres. In Delhi, garden bungalows are considered the height of aspirational living and lower floors fetch a premium in residential multi-storeys. Builders and developers, sensing the scarcity of land that is likely to confront the National Capital Region (NCR) in the near future, are focussing their attention on high-rises and skyscrapers. With demand for service and luxurious apartments set to go up in future, present real estate projects are mainly focussed on mixed land use and vertical developments.

Sky-scrapers become life-threatening during an earthquake. High-rise buildings swing like pendulum when the earthquake strikes. Delhiites prefer to live close to the ground despite the fact that top floors of multi-storeyed buildings are more convenient. Lower floors command a higher price in Delhi unlike Mumbai where the higher you live, the better it is! Delhiites prefer to remain ground footed for the psychological reasons too. These reasons have been shaped by various historical, geographical and infrastructure reasons like water, electricity and problems of elevator on the upper floors.

When there is no electricity during the summers, it is difficult to bear the heat with the blowing hot dry winds. Terrible water problem and mosquito menace is also severe on the upper floors. People prefer open areas in the front, direct access to the road, and minimal dependence on the elevator. There is added fear of earthquake in the high rise. However, according to some experts, "It is not the earthquake that kills people, but the faulty design and construction of buildings". In an earthquake prone area like Delhi you may remain as safe in a high rise as in a low rise if the construction adheres to the safety norms. The height of building has nothing to do with its seismic safety. It is the technology and design of the building that matters.

Japan and California region in USA, both of which are high earthquake-sensitive areas, abound in high-rise structures and multi-storeyed apartments. In Japan, developers put springs in building foundations. It ensures that the building moves like a monolithic structure during a high intensity earthquake, minimizing casualties. Statistics show that for almost all types of construction, additional cost of making a building seismically safe is merely 4 percent.

Delhi Development Authority (DDA) has prescribed a height of 15 m for houses built on individual plots and local shopping centres, 26 m for community centres, 33 m for group housings, and 37 m for government offices and district centres. There is a serious demand to remove these restrictions. Builders are showing their readiness to take adequate measures like providing power backup, facilities management services, and taking care of other aspects to make life more comfortable and pleasurable on the top.

All over the world including Mumbai, prices of housing units in multi-storeyed decrease as one comes down the floors. The plus points of apartments on higher level are a better view, ample sunlight, more cross ventilation and lots of fresh air. One does not hear the chatters of morning walkers on the upper floors. A few people living on the ground and first floors put grills on their windows for safety purposes. But you are not worried about somebody climbing in through the windows when living on higher floors in a high rise building.

But case of Delhi and its surrounding areas is the reverse. North Indians still want to be close to the ground. One of the major reasons is the geography and climate. Unlike the coastal areas, there is a lot of dust on the upper levels in Delhi and surrounding areas. You don't have so much dust in Mumbai. All you get in Mumbai is humid air. In the NCR region, polluting gases go up and hang in the air at night at a height of 20 to 30 feet and above. The concentration of oxygen also diminishes as we go higher. Doctors advise asthma patients to live on lower floors. Chest congestion, high blood pressure, heart problems, vertigo, and sinus problems are other ailments that may occur if you live on upper floors. Ground floors are still sought after; particularly by older people.

A strong aspirational culture and the brand-building needs of developers have greatly influenced the recent real estate developments in the NCR. Designer condominiums, shopping malls and world-class commercial complexes are now part of every developer's blueprint. Though it costs more to build vertically, upbeat cosmopolitan urban youth want homes for 'total' living as they see homes as a sanctuary. They demand the best quality and durability. They are willing to splurge on luxury, convenience and entertainment.

After the success of high-rises in Mumbai and other metropolitan cities, NCR is now ready for tall buildings. High-rise projects with 300 metres height and 80 floors are being planned in Noida, Gurgaon and Delhi. Developers are providing health clubs, helipads, sky-bridges, swimming and infinity pools, gymnasiums and spa facilities. These projects are claimed to be digitally controlled. Some are claimed to be self-sustaining green projects that will take care of the energy and water conservation. South-east and north-west of the plot can be used to provide facilities like family shopping centre, cafeteria, lobbies, crèche, play school and a primary school. Central tower may have a waiting lounge, lobbies, cafeteria, and high-end shopping areas.

Apartment Living

Statistically, Delhi is still very much the city of independent houses rather than flats. Around 74 per cent Delhiites live in independent houses and only 15 per cent in flats. The sprawling bungalows which were once the hallmark of the city are now limited mainly to Lutyens' Delhi. Around 53 per cent families are living in a home that measure less than 450 square feet. At least 62 per cent Delhiites own the places they live in and 35 per cent have hired dwelling units. The percentage of Delhi's population residing in joint housing environments is on the increase as pressure on the land mounts.

Traditionally, Indian urban living followed the mixed use pattern, in which the ground floor had shops and the upper floors had residences. Apartments have gained immense popularity in urban India since ninety's. The typical Indian dream of single-family home on an owned plot of land is passé for a large number of the urban middle class. Rising cost of land and changing perceptions of lifestyle are driving people towards the fancy of condominium living.

Apartment living is becoming more popular with growing percentage of double-income families in urban areas and an emphasis on hassle-free and secure living. People seek homes that make them part of a community, where they can combine privacy with advantages of a self-contained neighborhood. Two kinds of people are mainly attracted to apartment living. The first is upper end person who has had exposure to western lifestyle and is willing to pay for value-added services. The second is budget client who goes in for a basic apartment.

Apartment living has become popular in the Indian metros fuelled by a keen desire for home ownership, relative affordability of apartments over plotted single family homes, and easier availability of home loans. The large homestead has also become difficult to maintain with family units becoming smaller and more people working out of the home. Additional amenities and hassle-free lifestyle are the main attractions of these new apartments. The community life and proximity of other similar families that creates an atmosphere of security is an added advantage of apartments.

Common spaces in housing societies act as special spaces where children can play and adults can interact socially. These modern condominiums are providing all the necessary amenities like better roads, parking, 24-hour power back-up, and modern security systems. Now community facilities for recreation, child care and sports, landscaped open spaces and centralized payment systems are also becoming the common features.

Apartments built on stilts are dangerous. Stilted building designs are the first to fail during an earthquake. There should be clear segregation of pedestrian and vehicular traffic areas. A separate parking lot or basement parking with direct entry from and exit on the existing road may ensure the same. In this way, rest of the complex becomes completely free of vehicular traffic where pedestrians can walk and children can play around freely. Trees and plants can liberally be planted around the complex, leaving the built portion. About 80 per cent open area can also help in effective rainwater harvesting. Other provisions to improve the quality of a housing society are: a terrace girdling each of the upper floors, fire safety, security, basement dedicated parking, energy efficiency, balcony attached to every room and direct sunlight in all the rooms.

Apart from the direction criterion, choice of a flat also depends on cost, availability, legal clarity, space aesthetics, neighbors, structural parameters, and earthquake resistance functionality. If you want a home where living is a joy then do utilize the services of a competent vaastu expert and pay him his due. Constructing a home is once-in-a-lifetime investment. You will barter away a lifetime of pleasurable living by scrimping on the vaastu expert's fee. Vaastu friendly design not only contributes to the joy of living, it also results in substantial savings in construction through proper utilization of space and materials. I am discussing here the design features one should look for while buying a house within a group housing complex and safeguards while living.

Fig 6.5: Apartments with an Undulating Exterior

An undulating exterior (façade) gives each apartment a view of the main road outside the complex. It adds to the feeling of openness within each apartment. A huge central court of the entire complex offers space to children and adults to play or to lounge around. It moderates the temperature within the complex. When each apartment is provided with doors, windows and ventilators, air from outside of the complex can move freely into the apartment and then into the central court or in the opposite direction. Apartments remain cool in this way resulting in substantial savings in the electricity bills.

Entire complex should be built in such a way that all the rooms in an apartment receive adequate natural light. Microbes can't grow in the lighted areas, promoting healthy living. Corridors provided on each floor overlooking the central court are good. Parents and grandparents can sit here comfortably and watch their children playing in the central court. These wide corridors also promote socialization which is so missing in most apartment complexes. People can meet their neighbors in these corridors while entering or exiting their homes. Corridors on each floor running along the entire length of the complex also prove good during emergency. In case of fire, if you can't exit from one staircase, you can run to the other safer part of the building and exit using another staircase.

Internal walls within the apartments should not be load bearing. If internal walls can be dismantled easily, the owner can alter the inner configuration at will. Thus people will be able to alter the size and number of rooms as per their own requirements. Projected balconies are dangerous to some extent, particularly during earthquakes and during overloading. They shall be supported by beams or walls, which make them more resistant to earthquake. Vertical passages - through which the drain pipes, water pipes etc run - should be easily accessible from virtually every apartment. Repair work becomes easy with their easy accessibility.

The housing complex can be centrally air-conditioned through a very cost-effective method. In this method, cool air of the basement is utilized. The air in the basement remains at about 25 degree centigrade during the hottest months. This air can be drawn up through shafts using blowers. This draught of air will hit the walls of apartments, thereby keeping them cool.

A building shrinks and expands throughout its life. Get your housing society building checked from time to time. Caulking around windows, doors, chimney, foundation and other common leakage points is mandatory every year. Get a civil engineer to inspect the building thoroughly every ten years. Paint the walls regularly as it provides protection as well as decoration to the walls. You need to get the exteriors painted every five years and the interiors every three years. Install a water level sensor to save water and electricity and to prevent overflowing of water. This water can seep into the structure, especially if the terrace is not clean. Lay white tiles at the bottom of your tank so that you can see deterioration in the surface or in the water.

Maintenance charges impose heavy burden on flat owners in a housing society. In lieu of the paid maintenance charges, you get services like security, housekeeping, gardening, lift, power back-up, painting and white-washing and civil repairs in the common areas of the society. As a thumb rule, maintenance charges are inversely proportional to the quality of materials used in construction, and directly proportional to the age of the building. The older it gets, the greater the expenses on repairs and upkeep. Maintenance charges are also directly proportional to the size of initial investment. These charges further increase when flat is situated within premises that offer cutting-edge facilities like club, gym, swimming pool, internet den and the like.

Penthouses

Till recently, the top floors of houses were dismissed as barsaatis in and around Delhi. Now, termed as penthouses, these are seen as status symbols of the rich and the famous. They are emerging as a hot option for high-end salaried couples, NRI's, diplomats, and expatriates. Basically, a penthouse is a top floor apartment of around 6,000 to 7,000 square feet that offers a panoramic view of the outdoors. The quality of construction, amenities and specifications provided are all luxurious and high grades. These apartments are claimed to be a "life-long affair with luxury" that offer value for money in terms of luxury features and space.

The buyers are on the lookout for factors like good location, layout plans of the apartments and high-end specifications. Penthouses are being provided with Italian marble floors, shower cubicles, Jacuzzis, saunas besides swimming pools. Lots of granite and

Italian marble is thrown in to lend the homes an aesthetic look. Huge glass panels lend the apartments an ethereal look. The ambience is such that it gives owner the feel of a five-star deluxe suite. Builders are also providing facilities like wireless Internet connectivity, piped natural gas supply, gyms, clubs and helipads.

In an instance, every penthouse is being provided with a private elevator, garden on the private terraces, and private car parking with the objective to make the owner feel good. The projects claim to have a quake-resistant structure, fully furnished apartments with 100 percent power back up, 24 hour filtered water supply, air-conditioned rooms, modular kitchens, CCTV surveillance system, Jacuzzis, saunas, gym, swimming pools, club facilities, tennis courts, eco-friendly water management and waste management systems.

Principles of vaastu shastra are equally helpful here - during construction itself as well as while purchasing an already built up penthouse. There should be open space all around it, at least one ninth of the respective side. Whole of the layout plan of construction and individual rooms should be nearly square, length never exceeding twice the width. Too much glass on the exterior walls causes problems regarding safety, security, privacy and solid backing. Western and southern walls should invariably be solid with small windows, though wider openings in the south are good in winters. More glass can be used in northern and eastern walls. Swimming pool is auspicious in the east, small garden in the Bhrish square (east of southeastern), gym in the south-east, and servant's quarter in the north-west. Master bedroom should be in the south-west, farthest from the main entry and one should sleep keeping his head towards the south.

Parking Norms

Parking space must be provided for vehicles of both residents and guests for multi-storeys and apartments. It should be planned well ahead of construction. Vaastu classics recommend vehicle parking towards left of the door while going out. Here are some vaastu tips regarding the parking:

Never park vehicle in the north-east and south-west directions. The place for vehicle parking is north-west or south-east. Heavy vehicles can be parked in the south direction.

Portico or porch is best in the north or east of the north-east. Roof of the porch area should be 2 to 3 feet lower than the roof of ground floor of the main building. Ground or floor sloping towards north or east is considered best.

The engine side of the parked vehicle should be towards the cool directions ie north, north-east or east to avoid its overheating.

Northern or eastern part of the basement can also be used as parking space.

Parking area should always be kept clean and free from congestion. Roof and walls of the parking area should be separate from the main building.

Gates of Townships

Gateways have always been a signature of a city. Traditionally, gates have marked the points of control. The architecture of gates not only symbolizes the financial and intellectual powers but also cultural status of the community. Delhi's walled city of Shahjahanabad still boasts of its Ajmeri Gate, Delhi Gate, Mori Gate, Lahori Gate and many more. An entrance affords the first impression and should therefore be imposing. Developers open the gates to sell dreams on barren pieces of land. Construction of an imposing and hi-tech entrance gate to a futuristic township is the ongoing trend.

Generally four aspects are attached to a gateway – security, branding, ambience and character of a township. A gateway is like a corporate symbol. They are suggestive of the beginning of a project and are instrumental in creating an aura around it. They are the starting or entrance point and thus serve as demarcation of the city. The façade of a gateway suggests of a secure, private and exclusive conclave.

Developers spend their time, money, and efforts on the gateways which often cost over a crore. This money can be called well spent as these gateways act as a tool to generate excitement, and brand recall. They also function as a reassurance to the potential buyers. Townships of some renowned developers have standardized gates. When a prospective buyer visits the site, this piece of hi-tech modern architecture offers him an image of a wonderful lifestyle, something tangible.

Pre-Fabricated Structures

Pre-fabricated structures are deemed as temporary constructions as per the local building bye laws. They were traditionally used in India by the army for building barracks at high altitudes where brick and mortar construction was not possible. Rapid increase in the requirement for additional space in urban India, alongside scarcity of time, has again popularized the pre-fabricated structures. These are being used primarily for building an extra room such as children's room, store-room, office room, servant's room or bathroom on the terrace or for expanding a floor.

Pre-fabricated structures can be set up quickly, even in a day, without requiring any special tools or machines. They are also flexible structures and can be moved or dismantled easily, if so required. The life span of a pre-fabricated structure has increased with newer material entering the market. Now these structures are as long lasting as brick and mortar constructions. Thermal comfort level in a pre-fabricated structure is as good as in a brick masonry structure. These structures also enable cleaner and faster construction with minimum wastage.

Doors, windows and ventilators of pre-fabricated structures can be made of steel, aluminum or PVC. The roofs can be made of pre-coated steel sheets, aluminum sheets, corrugated galvanized iron (CGI) sheets, fiber reinforced plastic (FRP) sheets or asbestos cement sheets. Pre-fabricated structure should ideally have a false ceiling for better insulation.

Service Apartments

Service apartment is a new concept in India. It is a home away from home with the frills of a luxury hotel at a fraction of the cost. Service apartments work only for a stay of more than seven days whereas hotels can duplicate and work well for both long and short stays. Service apartments are rapidly taking root for two reasons – the presence of growth drivers (a corporate base, manufacturing or service sector) and absence of the cold perfection of a hotel. Their demand will emanate from corporate interested in upcoming information technology (IT) parks. Foreigners also prefer service apartments for privacy reasons.

Service apartments are meant to provide comfort of home combined with the business-like efficiency of a hotel. Rooms are bigger than the hotels, giving a feeling of openness. They offer perfect alternative to hotels for business travelers, holidayers and visitors. They provide an exceptionally flexible and cost-effective way of living while travelling. Service apartments are now largely the preferred accommodation option for IT and corporate professionals as their stay is usually assignment based.

Most service apartments are usually furnished to a very high standard. Their size could range from a studio to a five bedroom set equipped with a kitchen and a lounge.

Some have their dining rooms too. Everything required for daily living in a service apartment is either already provided or is available on demand which could include television, air-conditioning, kitchen with all the works, an office desk with telephone and internet connectivity. You can ask for locker facility to keep your valuables safe. Domestic help is available who will not only handle the kitchen but will also bring necessary things for you from the market.

Other facilities on offer may include an informal lounge-cum-bar in the central atrium designed like a side-walk café, a health club and a swimming pool on the rooftop. The health-club features a fitness center, a Jacuzzi and a steam room. Along with the kitchenette facilities in each apartment, guests also have other dining options within the building. Conference rooms located at the ground level cater to the business and entertainment needs of the guests. Other facilities may include an in-house convenience store, round-the-clock security, uninterrupted power supply, a 24-hours concierge, daily housekeeping and an in-house laundry service.

Several service apartment formats are in vogue, all geared to satisfy the needs of the discerning business traveler. Most recognized format is the stand-alone development. These are built as apartment complexes for purpose of being leased as service apartments. Mixed use development is another popular format. It incorporates serviced apartments in the larger commercial developments including offices and retail spaces. These apartments will most likely have the ground floor reserved for retail, first floor for restaurants and upper floors for service apartments.

New service apartment projects are featuring modern state-of-the-art facilities such as a business centre, spa, health club and personalized valet service. Builders are ready to experiment with all sorts of models for service apartments such as apartments being part of a hotel, mall and even studio service apartments. Business centres are being developed near the service apartments. These are being used for conferencing, holding meetings and training programmes. Service apartments are also being booked for marriage and honeymoon purposes.

The prime factor in determining the rental values of service apartments is their location. Rents also vary depending upon quality of construction, furnishing, interior fit-outs and services provided in the apartment.

Service apartments should be planned keeping in mind the general principles of vaastu shastra and specific principles of business vaastu. Once the broad guidelines are followed and layout is finalized, the inner layout of each and every service apartment should be designed like home vaastu.

Agriculture Vaastu

The main requirements of agriculture are of course the fertile soil, proper irrigation, guarding the crop, availability of timely rains or irrigation water; heat; air and light at the proper time, and wise use of fertilizers and insecticides. However, principles of vaastu can also be applied for choosing a particular type of soil/field for growing particular type of crops/vegetables/fruits/medicines, getting increased output, and more benefits with least disturbances. For example, a low lying marshy land may be good for fisheries and not for agricultural crops. Likewise, a land receiving sunrays in abundance will be good for the crop of sunflower, not for the other delicate type flowers.

All trees and plants - including the grains, vegetables, fruits and the medicinal plants – increase in size and volume mainly at night. Therefore, moonlight is must for their growth. That's why Moon has been called "Aushadheesh" ie "Lord of medicines". In the presence of sunlight, green leafy plants participate in the process of photosynthesis and prepare their food, and emit oxygen and water vapours. Vegetables grown in the greenhouses are not as rich in vitamins and minerals as their natural counterparts. Vegetables and fruits receiving abundant solar and lunar radiations also taste sweeter.

Crops requiring maximum amount of solar heat and light give best output when south is open. Crops requiring cool environment without direct sunlight deliver best results with open north. Crops requiring neither too hot nor too cold temperature but with lot of direct sunlight give most production with open southeast. Crops requiring normal temperature with least direct sunlight give most production with open northwest.

The fields should preferably be regular in shape. Too much angular sides/corners or cuttings/extent ions in the sides leads to its incomplete use or involves extra running cost. The well or tube-well should be installed at the highest level of the field so that water can flow easily to the remotest part by the force of gravity. If otherwise, lot of extra electrical or diesel power will be required.

Fish pond and white water lily (kumud) pond are good in the north direction. Fish pond needs protection in the form of thin wires above the pond from the birds of prey. Lotus pond is best in the east direction. Floriculture gives best results in the east of southeast direction. Mushroom production is best in the north of northeast. Bee keeping is best in the square of Bhrish. Honey gets its start as flower nectar which is available abundantly in this square of Kamadeva. A nursery is best in the east or the southeast.

Vaastu of Farmhouses / Holiday Homes / Resorts

Farmhouses provide a welcome relief to the people who are forced to live in the big metropolitan cities. These pollution free oases are used as weekend resort and an ideal getaway from the stresses and strains of maddening city life. Small but gracious and elegant farmhouses in style can be developed on well developed agricultural land starting with a quarter of an acre. For attracting the clients, right location is most important.

Landscaping with hills, hillocks, mountains, earthen mounds or big rocks towards the heavy direction are best. Otherwise, a rock garden with water cascade or a waterfall can be designed in the southwest. Land sloping towards the northeast, east or north direction is ideal. Water bodies like river, lake, pond, rivulet, spring or waterfall is best towards the light directions. A water pond above the ground level may be provided in the western part, if so required.

Parks with small flowering plants are good towards the north and east. Grow fruit bearing trees in all the directions as per their requirement of sunlight and heat. Large ornamental trees and timber producing trees are good in the south, southwest and west directions. Medicinal plants mainly need positive sunlight or moonlight.

The main building should be in the south, west or southwest of the plot with entry from the east or north. Cottages in the scattered form are good in all the directions, provided they have some form of support in the form of a hedge, boundary wall, mound and the like. North-south orientation of rooms and protection of east-west walls from the summer sunrays diminishes the requirement of air conditioning to a large extent.

Parking is best in the northwest or the southeast. Well or boring for drinking water should be towards the north, east or northeast of the construction. Water used for irrigation and horticulture work may be arranged in the west, the direction of God Varun. Electric supply and electrically operated equipments and appliances are best in the southeast.

The Wi-Fi Lounge and Games Room should be in the north or east. Here, guests can unwind, have fun or catch up on some e-mails.

The room may have a fireplace (in its southeast or south), a billiard table or TT table (in its northwest or southeast), a diverse selection of books (in its east or west) and complimentary Wi-Fi access (in its north). It can be filled with charming trinkets and treasures.

A multi-cuisine restaurant or kitchen, as well as a kitchen garden, are best in the southeast. Main dining room should be towards its west ie between the southeast and south. However, breakfast is best served in the east, lunch in the south and dinner in the west. Barbecue to prepare delicious grilles food should be in the southeast for the daytime and in the northwest for the evening time. A bar is best in between the north and northeast of the building or the bar room. Granary should be in the northwest.

Children's play areas and green lawn should be towards the north or east of the farmhouse. It should be a safe area equipped with outdoor toys, swings and a slide for making their holidays to be really unforgettable. Wave and slide pools, Water Park, Aqua Park and artificial waterfalls are good in the north and northeast. The swimming pool with a sunbathing area fully equipped with sun umbrellas, pool chairs, sun beds and an outdoor shower should be in the east.

Golf course is best towards the north and east. Lawn tennis, badminton and squash courts should be towards the northwest. Indoor games, including the Table Tennis, are good in the northwest or southeast. Gym cum health club should be in the southeast with massage parlour, sauna, tread mill, roll on, muscle toners and beauty aids. Fitness centre or exercise room should be open for entry of fresh air. South direction is best for practicing boxing, martial arts and other violent games. Chess, carom, playing cards and similar light games are best in the north.

Yoga and meditation hall is best in the northeast or east. The best place for 'Spa' is the northeast sector, particularly the square of Parjanya, Jayant, Aditi, Aap, or Aapvatsa. Spa literally means; "a mineral spring considered having health-giving properties". Northeast sector makes water like nectar. A well-maintained library is best in the west, the direction of Saturn.

Tamed animals such as cows, buffalos, goats, sheep, horses, camels, dogs and cats should be kept towards the northwest or southeast of the residential premises, outside the main building. Poultry farm is also good in these directions. Its east-west axis should be more than the north-south axis. In this way, it will receive maximum amount of heat during winters. East and west façade should be protected during summers. Fish pond is best in the cool north direction.

Animal's house should not touch the main building. Animal's mouth should be towards the north while eating fodder. Any path passing through the animal's house or presence of a nearby well leads to destruction of animal wealth.

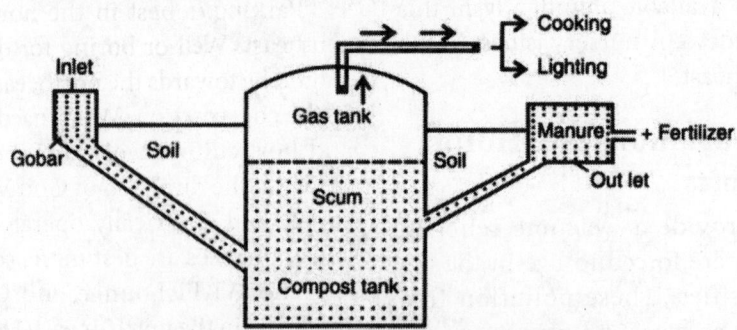

Fig 6.6: Working of the Gobar Gas Plant

Pit for preparing manure and compost should be dug in the west or southwest. Bio-gas or gobar gas plant should be in the southwest, the direction of Rahu. Rahu governs disintegration, degeneration and dissolution. Bio-gas is produced from cattle dung in a bio-gas plant, commonly known as gobar gas plant, through a process called digestion.

Hotel and Restaurant Vaastu

Hotel vaastu also includes restaurants, boarding and lodging houses, guest houses, motels, fast food plazas, and party lawns. These are normally a blend of commercial and residential activities. People visit or assemble here, stay, eat, and do their work or business. The construction of hotels and clubs should be more open and airy as a large number of people visit there. Large size windows help in keeping healthy environment.

The regular shape plot, easily approachable by the city or town dwellers, should be strategically located. Apply the vaastu principles regarding the open areas and slope of land. For a star category hotel, plot should be fairly big for horizontal expansion in future. Future vertical expansion should be kept in mind while designing the foundation. Follow the vaastu rules for providing boundary gates and entrance gates. Being a public building, main gate may be provided in the middle.

Bore well, underground water tank, sump etc are good towards the north / east of the northeast, swimming pool in the east, lawns and fountains in the north and/or east, a small temple in the northeast, idol of Lord Ganesha towards the right side of front entrance (while entering from outside).

Reception counter should be on the ground floor, near to the entrance. The reception staff should sit with a protected back, facing the auspicious direction. Cellars in the north and east may safely be used for car parking. In a centralized AC building, central AC plant should be in the northwest. AC's in the individual rooms should be fitted towards the north side for avoiding overheating.

Boilers, diesel generators, transformers, control panels, capacitors invertors and similar equipments should be installed towards the southeast, preferably separate from the main building. Elevators and staircases, though best in the rajasi areas, should be provided wherever so required.

Main kitchen should be on the ground floor in the southeast direction. Kitchen store is considered best towards the west or northwest of the kitchen. Area beyond the kitchen in the paishach-sthan should be vacant so that kitchen receives good amount of light and ventilation. General purpose dining rooms and banquet hall are good on the ground floor. However, in a star category hotel, east and southeast are the best direction for serving breakfast, south and southwest for serving lunch and west and northwest for serving the dinner.

Kitchens of theme based specialty restaurants can be on the upper floors, preferably in the southeast of the respective level. The main granary should be in the northwest of the premises/store area. All the electrical equipments like ovens, grinders, mixers and juicers are good in the southeastern part of kitchen.

GM / MD / owner office should be on the first floor, in the private southwest area. Office on the upper floors reduces one's stronghold on the management. Executive centres, conference rooms, office chambers should be provided on the upper floors. Shopping arcades should be on the ground floor, preferably in the southeast or northwest. Money exchanger, on the ground floor, is best in the north or northeast.

Guest rooms, suites should be on the upper floors. Balcony in the north and east is good throughout the year while balcony in the south provides sunrays during winters. In a room; bed should be in the southwest, south or west, farthest from the room entry. Bed's head side should never be towards north. No mirror should be fitted in front of the bed. Wardrobe should be in the north of northwest. TV is good in the southeast or northwest. Room heater is good in the south. Toilet should be in the west or south of the southwest, away from the entry. Mirror and wash basin should be on the north or east wall.

Restaurants

Pay special attention on getting the vaastu of kitchen right. Restaurants having orange and yellow colours – being the colours of ripe fruits, vegetables and grains - tend to do well. Soft red colour is equally auspicious. All these colours complement the natural fire element of the restaurant business. Well-lit restaurants have great power to pull in the customers. Light is a part of the fire element, the other part being the heat. Dimly lit restaurants seldom do well.

However, natural light is the best for eating food. Lot of oxygen is present in the environment till sunset as the green plants emit oxygen through the process of photosynthesis. Oxygen is vital for digestion of food. Probably it was the main reason that Lord Mahaveer, the last teerthankar of Jainism, prohibited dinner after sunset. Ayurveda also recommends consumption of food during night as abdominal fire (jathragni) becomes weak in the absence of sunlight.

Good quality wall mirrors in the restaurants symbolize the doubling of customers. It is auspicious for restaurants to display large figurines depicting a full tummy and happiness. Chotiwala restaurant in Rishikesh utilizes the services of a full time model, big tummy male wearing beautiful makeup, seated at the entrance. Indian restaurants usually display a large statue (sometimes life size) of Lord Ganesha with a bowl full of laddoos (sweet balls) in front of him. His seated posture with earth like big round stomach, according to a foreign author, represents a well-fed baniya (Indian business class)!

Liquor Bars and Gambling

A bar is different from a restaurant. It belongs to the water element. In such cases, hot colours and bright lights would be unsuitable. Instead, black and dark blue will be the most suitable colours. Hence, it is preferable that bars and such like other establishments are dimly lit. However, since liquor contains certain percentage of alcohol which causes lethargy and reduces our alertness, consuming liquor is a tamasi activity. Tamasi activities are best in the south-west. Some of the other tamasi activities are gambling, killing animals and selling meat, fishing, prostitution, animal training and law enforcing.

Vaastumandanam and Rajavallabha recommend southwest for "distillers and vendors of spirituous liquors, including the prostitutes and people of the lowest castes (meaning people involved in lowest type of activities)". Samaranganasutradhara recommends southwest for "people involved in rearing and killing pig; sheep and deer, fishermen, manufacturers of sharp smelling (hard) liquor, boatmen, horse-trainers and other animal trainers, law-enforcement officials". Vaastumandanam also recommends the square of Nirriti for gambling room.

It means bars and/or liquor shops should be in the southwest of any market or shopping complex, hotel, restaurant or party lawn. However, liquor should be stored in between the north and northeast of the bar. Vishwakarmaprakash (2.98a) recommends the area between north and northeast for keeping medicines. Liquor stored here will become rich in medicinal value to some extent. Liquor, particularly wine and its other delicate forms, may get deteriorated when stored in the southwest.

Shopping Malls

A large number of malls are coming up in the suburbs of metro cities where land is available in plenty. Rising income levels and attitudinal changes among young consumers drive the shift towards organized retailing in the country. Time has become a constraint in the modern hectic life of metropolitan cities. Leisure and pleasure within a limited time period hold great attraction for families. Shopping malls have evolved as one stop shopping paradise for consumers. The idea of shopping-cum-entertainment has become an excuse to enter these premises.

Most of the malls are multi-level, enclosed, and air-conditioned premises with multiplexes and food courts. Malls are complete destination, catering to all age groups where whole of the family can spend an entire day. The other key components of a modern mall cum multiplex may be starred hotel, banquet hall, water cum amusement park, convention centre, hotel rooms, food court, amphitheatre, fountains, club, and many more. Malls are also ready to fulfill the demand for well-run service apartments. Information technology (IT), ITes, BPO, bio-technology, manufacturing, consulting and financial services, infrastructure and telecom sectors are generating demand for service apartments. Visitors for medical tourism also require service apartments next to large hospitals.

With so many similar players in the market, malls are struggling to make money unless they have something different to offer. Experts feel that the future of malls lies in exclusivity. Therefore to stand out in the crowd, builders are coming out with ambitious projects with specialty concept malls like auto mall, interior mall, celebration mall, jewellery mall, and hotel-in-a-mall etc. The concept of "hotel-in-a-mall" came up in Dubai and Thailand. It is now fast gaining ground in India. The shopping mall is developed in tandem with a hotel. The hoteliers have the advantage of being present at a premium location at relatively lower cost. Also they have assured footfalls even on leaner days.

Mall culture in India is not all welcome and has been heavily criticized for different reasons. Malls have been termed as the secular cathedrals, and the temples of steel and glass. Critics of mall culture consider shopping malls as huge, bright and train-station sized buildings which are filled with shops and activities that try and seduce the visitors into buying things that they don't really need. Malls are the wicked temples of consumerism, all clustered under one roof.

The shop fronts, fancy restaurants and pointless commodities have an aesthetic appeal that has its own place in this pluralistic world. The mall is less of a shopping arcade but more of a place away from the rest of the city inside the city. The intimacy of the local store gets lost in the mall. A person is alone among the crowds' here. A mall is a perfect venue for aimless walking, and pointless watching. People can sit down inside an environment that has a perpetual festival air about it without there being a festival.

The conversion of visitors to customers is much higher in a shop as compared to what it is in a mall. When a mall opens, there is a definite effect on the sale in nearby shops for one or two months. That is actually the honeymoon period for mall. But the conversion of visitors to customers is very low. After that, people start going back to the retailers. It has been found that only 15 to 20 per cent of visitors actually end up purchasing something in malls whereas in stand-alone stores 40 to 60 per cent do so.

The decline in sales figures in traditional markets due to the emergence of a mall is nearly 20 per cent. However, a new, high-end shopping complex in or around a market boosts the total footfall of the market as lot of people come to have a dekko at the mall. This, in turn, jacks up their sales. The markets are still retaining their stronghold as no mall can cater to all the requirements of a customer. Malls can't offer "variety"

In the present scenario, mall mania seems to be gradually coming to an end. In the recent years, many mall projects across the country have changed plans midway. Malls are partly being converted into commercial or office space and info-tech hubs which are more in demand. Some of the other reasons for end of mall mania are: over-optimistic estimation of the demand for malls, bad location, flooding of mall space in locations where there are too many players, poor turnover due to high rates, non-attraction of local audience to brands, consumers with mall fatigue, people's preference to shops in specific areas, demand for office space by IT and ITES industries, extremely tardy mall management as the mall is run as a real estate property not as a retail venture and such other factors.

High operation costs, lease and maintenance rates, competition and shrinking profits are forcing retailers to shut shops in many of the malls in and around Delhi and other cities in India. Maintenance cost for the retailer can be reduced if fixed expenditure is cut down while constructing the huge mall. Principles of vaastu shastra and good modern practices of mall management could help in reduction of construction and maintenance costs.

Location of a mall plays vital role in the success of stores located in it. Mall should not be located in a remote area. Its visibility will suffer here resulting in low sales. Mall should be easily accessible by public transportation. The mall should not be situated near an established market. Here it will face tough competition from the street side shops. Though the crowd will step into the mall to enjoy its ambience and air-conditioned air, they will prefer their shopping from the outside shops that are less expensive with good quality.

Vaastu Shastra stresses on the surroundings and soil investigation before selecting the piece of land. Pay attention to the location, surroundings, transportation, vegetation and habitation. Get the soil analysis done and then take advantage of the available technologies to bring down the construction cost. Though initially capital cost of technology might be high, running cost of the mall would be less. Provide shade to the surroundings of mall area by planting trees as per the tenets of vaastu. Insulate the walls and the roof. Cost of air-conditioning gets reduced in this way, thereby reducing the common area maintenance charges.

The design of mall should be simple. According to Leonardo Da Vinci, "Simplicity is the ultimate sophistication". Ideally, a mall should not be designed as a high rise building. The elevation should blend with the surrounding environment. Sloping roofs, archways and walkways add architectural beauty. Today's air-conditioned environment is making them redundant. Security guards as well as the visitors should be able to have a complete view of the mall from different locations on various storeys. Such a type of planning helps in the movement of shoppers from one point to another. It also helps in creating interest in some particular product or outlet.

Front side of the mall should have open spaces with flowerbeds, green lawns, lotus pond, fountains and other water bodies. Fresh environment will ensure proper movement of prana to every nook and corner of the building. A water body at the entrance area is particularly important, enhancing inside the mall. Take care to create open areas within the mall which will create an overall good impression of space. It can be achieved by having a central atrium and a sky-light, the modern version of classical *brahamsthan*. It can reduce power consumption by 10 to 70 per cent during the daytime.

Vaastu shastra recommends entrances in all the possible directions. For any shopping area, southeast or east entrance is best throughout the year, north during the summers, and south during the winters. West is the least preferred direction. There should not be any dwara vedha (obstruction to entrance) to the mall. It should have easy entry and exit from a main road or highway.

Mix the mall landscape with the retails. Most of the malls are inward like a fort which block out the outside world. All the shops in the mall are normally aligned to face the atrium (brahamsthan). Such a system is inauspicious. It puts maximum load on air-conditioning and power system. Go for multiple layer landscaping – at the lower ground level, at the ground level and at the food court level. We can have a lot of cool air filtering in through waterfalls and other artificial water bodies. Consequently, the load on heating gets reduced and ambient temperature is maintained.

Install a Building Management System (BMS). This system helps in controlling illumination. The mall gets lit up only when the sun goes down. BMS is an automatic process and saves a lot of power fuel. Its function is the same with air-conditioning where it automatically modulates temperature. BMS is also useful in terms of safety, security and fire-fighting systems.

Introduce rain-harvesting system and recycle the used water. Use cisterns that do not waste water unnecessarily. Introduce the waterless urinals. Save power by running the escalators on the economy mode. With these small methods, running cost can be cut down to around 30 to 40 percent. This saving can then be passed to the retailer who rents space in the mall.

The most striking feature of the high-rise commercial properties including malls is the liberal use of glass. It is being used extensively owing to the market demand for contemporary looking structures. Demand for glass-clad buildings has gone up with the influx of MNC's in India as they want their offices to conform to international standards of architecture. One advantage of glass building is that it allows you to use daylight as the source of lighting. Though the glass was prevalent even in the Gothic period, today one sees an intelligent synthesis of art, nature and technology. Glass is a versatile material which while enclosing space expands it visually.

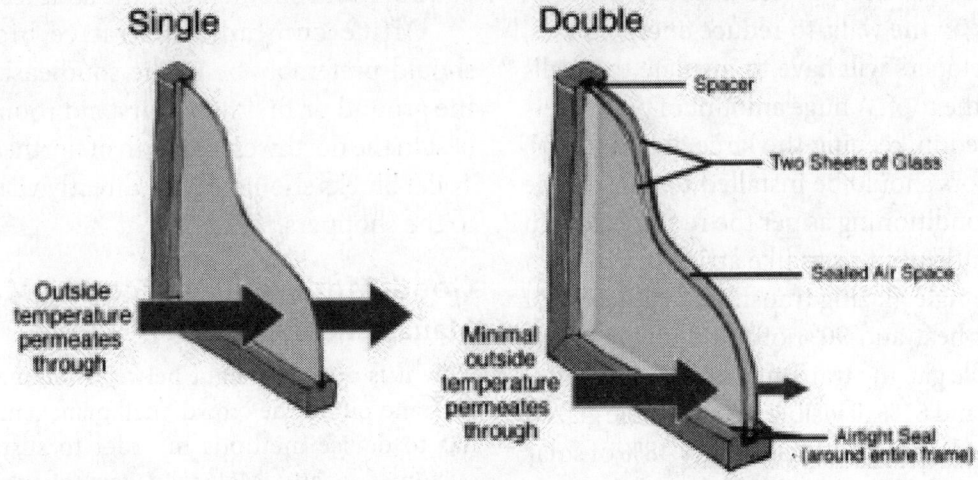

Fig 6.7: Single versus Double Glazed Glass

Mall's walls should be solid - at least in the southwest and west directions. Glass may be used in the light directions only. Glass facades result in loss of prana or positive energy. Vaastu is extension of our body while façade is the face. Our face, which has seven major openings, is never covered fully. It is completely covered only when a culprit is put to gallows. Bureau of Energy Efficiency (BEE), which works under the Bureau of Indian Standards (BIS), has prepared an Energy Conservation Building Code for builders who use 500 KW or more power in their buildings. The objective is to conserve power and maintain the ecological balance. This new code restricts developers from using too much glass on walls.

Glass exposes buildings to sun and increases the power spent on air-conditioning. The building would remain comparatively cooler when the use of glass is minimum on its outer walls (envelop). Now any building can have only 40 per cent of glass on the outer walls. Builders will be required to use a double layer of glass on the walls to reduce energy losses. Developers will have to insulate the walls and the roof. A huge amount of power gets wasted in keeping the large atriums cool. Sensors should be installed to control the air conditioning as per the requirement in the little used areas like atriums.

Single glazing transmits inside 86% of solar heat and 90% of visible light, while double glazing transmits only 76% of solar heat and 81% of visible light. Double glazed (tinted) transmits inside only 48% of solar heat and 69% of visible light, while triple glazing transmits 50% of solar heat and 65% of visible light.

Adequate parking space, underground and regular, in the mall is a must. It is particularly so for the malls situated on highways and far-off places from the cities. Lack of parking space deters visitors from visiting again. Provision for parking is best at the ground floor or a place receiving ample amount of natural light. Parking charges should be nominal, in accordance with the prevailing rates in the nearby areas.

Food courts are best at the ground floor with sitting in the open atrium. Specialty restaurants with limited clientele could be on the upper floors. The footfall decreases as we rise higher. AC plant could be in the cool north or northwest direction. Overhead water storage could be in the west. Water meant for drinking and cooking should be stored in underground tank in the northeast, leaving the northeast-southwest axis. Uninterrupted power supply is the pre-requirement for a centralized air-conditioned mall. Electrical control room should be in the southeast.

Office cum administrative block should preferably be in the southeast on the ground or first floor. First aid room is best in the northwest or north of northeast. Toilet blocks should not be directly visible to the shoppers.

Good Modern Practices of Mall Management

Now it is a mutual fight between the malls. To stand out in the crowd, mall management has to devise methods in order to sustain customer loyalty. Mall management means getting crowds into the mall, increasing the conversion of footfall into the potential buyers, treating the crowd in terms of deals and also to keep the tenants happy.

Apply the time, place and person factors. For any mall to be successful in the long run, it has to be specifically tailored to the specific zonal needs of the market it operates in. A mall should identify the segments it wants to cater to. It can't be all things at all times and for all people. Thus the positioning of any mall should be very clear. For example, depending on a specific need and demand, a mall could be successful as a hypermarket, neighboring outlet, convenience facility, a large format variety mall or a very specialized high-end mall.

Management should go for the right tenant mix. The most crucial factor is to have a popular anchor so that it gets identified with the mall and is able to attract huge crowds. Large sized malls can have more number of major anchors. Choice of the anchor tenant defines the mall's character. It should be wisely chosen.

A shopping mall must have an overall competitive advantage that can be leveraged to achieve long-term sustainability. The essential and influencing factors in a mall are flexibility for innovation, re-leasing, re-configuration and expansion.

The mall shall also cater to the local needs in order to sustain itself in the long run, failing which it becomes just a high end shopping facility. Its client base is consequently restricted to quite an extent. The retail mix must also match the requirement pattern of the area populace. Follow the principle of 'demand and supply', at least in the beginning.

Having high traffic or having the right kind of traffic that constitutes your clientele is two different things. You can expect large crowds and office executives even on working days if the mall is located in a busy commercial district. Contrarily, weekdays may not be very fruitful if mall is located in an isolated area.

The mall management should seriously look into the customer's complaints with an open mind and resolve them at the earliest. Such a practice brings good name.

Retail Store in a Mall

In a well-designed store, customers feel that they have got better value for their money. They also want to repeat the experience. A retail store can convey subliminal messages to customers through the layout and design of the store and the manner in which wares are displayed. While choosing your retail store in a mall, avoid the dead-end spots. These are the spaces located in the end of a corridor and starting or ending points of the stair-cases, lifts, and escalators. The design of the store should not draw attention away from the merchandise.

The ambience in which the merchandise is displayed should be such that the merchandise stands out and speaks for itself. This makes it easier for the customers to make a purchase decision. For example, façade of the store should convey to the customer what products are sold in the store; whether it is premium or low-end store; the ambience and standard of service shopper can expect; the likely price range and so on.

Retail designers and visual merchandisers should first try to get the passer-by to enter the store. Once inside, they should try to keep him inside the store for a longer time. Lastly, they should try to help the client make wiser purchase decisions. White lighting is better suited to a contemporary and stylish store. Yellow light being warm is better suited to a homely and comfortable ambience.

A retailer can use the 'Tree of Refuge Theory' for getting business. According to this theory, people feel safer under objects of low height and curved shape; say a tree or a cave. Thus a retailer can make the customer feel more comfortable in his store by providing a low and curved ceiling.

According to 'Theory of speed-lines', shape of a space or of an object speeds up the visual or physical movement in a certain direction. For example, if we look at Qutub Minar, our eyes automatically travel towards its pinnacle. That's why we tend to read a script written in italic faster than one written in bold or plain text. Retails' designers use speed-lines to get customers walk farther inside the store.

According to the 'Theory of opulent spaces', people take up much less space in posh places where they are not very comfortable. They will sit upright and speak softly in such places. This human psychology can be used by the retailers to make the customers feel either comfortable or awe-struck.

Markets and Shopping Complexes

Market should not only be a place for just shopping but a place where you can hang out with friends and chill. A market with reduced footfall should be redesigned and be given a complete face lift. It should be made pedestrian friendly with segregation of parking. Now it has been internationally proven that segregation of parking and upgrading market environment makes visitors feel happy and de-stressed. Its striking features can be a raised walkway, a small amphitheatre and unified signage for all emporia. Selective sculptures could also be used for beautification.

Revive the old concept of town squares or plazas. These places were at the heart of the cities. These were the place for outdoor meeting and living where one went to hear news, buy food, talk politics, or simply watch the world go by.

There should not be any parking chaos, distracting traffic sounds and unpleasant ambience. Traffic sound and other noises can be muffled by a centrally placed fountain and water cascades. The inner roads should particularly be freed from haphazardly parked cars and be converted into walking plazas made of non-skid earthen coloured tiles. Market should be landscaped and greened, segregating it from the road traffic. A sloping buffer green can be created by filling earth around the market and grassing it.

Automated sprinklers and drip irrigation should be used for watering the plants and grass. Rainwater should be harvested. Grills or fences around the market give it a 'walled-in' look which is not good for growth of business. Low seating arrangement in the locally available building material can be created along the edges of the greenery. Ramps make the market disabled friendly.

Modern lighting concept may be used. At night, the market place should be well lit with ambience lighting and fancy fountains. Cut the glare by using diffused lighting techniques. The fountain which changes from mist to single jet and multi-jet, by turns, and the water cascades can be lit from within so that only the effect is visible. The light under the large trees can be firmly cemented into the earth. Lights can also be tucked away under the seating area and the steps to give diffused yet well lit look. Large RCC pipes should be provided under walkways for inserting cables without breaking walkways.

In any shopping complex, common staircase and common space around the complex is generally neglected. These common spaces belong to everybody. Badly-kept common spaces result in decreased footfall. In the long run, such areas are grabbed by illegal, anti-social, and unethical activities. Dark and dank premises cause sickness amongst the workers working there.

It is better to shop in the morning when we feel fresh and energized. Night is not good for shopping as evil reins during this time. A kind of malignance prevails at darkness that encourages crime and other illegal activities. Many people are seen drunk at night. Single women avoid travelling at night. 'Good morning' generally means starting a new day in a happy mood while 'good night' means enjoying a sound sleep. There is no wishing of any work at night.

In India, shopper is the king and he wants comfort more than anything else. He tries to avoid an overcrowded market in favour of an organized one or will opt for internet shopping. Terrible overcrowding of any market leads to lowered gains for the shop-owners. Any market starts dying when it becomes inaccessible, when it runs out of parking space. Shopping becomes a herculean task due to huge number of street vendors sitting on the roads, footpaths and outside the shops. They occupy every nook and corner of the road and also stand around when having no place to sit.

Overcrowding is causing slow death to Chandni Chowk, Karol Bagh, Kamla Market, Lajpat Nagar Market and many more local markets in Delhi. Shoppers normally want easy accessibility, sufficient parking space and peaceful environment which they don't get in such an overcrowded market.

Shaded verandahs outside the shops allow the prospective buyer to shop for longer duration without needing to step out into the sun. Verandahs are a boon in a hot country like India. Connaught Place in New Delhi has a wide verandah running in front of its every block giving it a classical ambience. Verandahs encourage window shopping in any shopping centre. Most of the showrooms in CP in New Delhi are now showing their products with price tags in the showcases. Any new buyer, without prior knowledge of the quality and price of the articles, hesitates to directly step into a shop.

A verandah acts like a middle ground between the road and the shops. Shoppers love to walk leisurely in these verandahs. Today's window shopper is tomorrow's prospective purchaser. When these verandahs are choked by the street-sellers, the richer buyers start drifting away to more accessible shopping areas with better parking facilities. Internet shopping is also the easiest available option. A well-maintained park or fountain in the centre of market works as its brahamsthan which is vital for its well-being.

Real Estate

Development of the real estate, as well as business of buying and selling houses and apartments, is ruled by the earth element. Your element is earth if you are an architect, civil engineer or contractor. Therefore, you should try to activate the earth sector of your office. Locate people important to your business in the southwest sector. Activate the earth element in this sector with natural quartz crystals, clay flower pots, carvings of marble or other forms of stone. Use natural earth colours for tiles, roof coverings and other forms.

Money Transactions and Gold Loans

People whose business involves dealing with cash, money and gold eg banking, insurance, money-changing, money-transfer, gold loan etc are governed by the water element. The colour of water is glass (crystal clear), blue (colour of deep water, blue in the solar spectrum is governed by Jupiter which is the planet of growth), orange (governed by Moon in the solar spectrum, which also governs water), indigo (governed by Venus in the solar spectrum, which also governs water and riches).

Such companies will do well if they incorporate these colours into their décor or logo. Their business premises should be softly lit. Strong lights represent the fire element. The décor should include paintings with a watery theme. Flowing water will encourage your client to keep his money in flow. Such a painting should be placed in the northern or northeast sector of the office. Because metallic coins represent money, metallic bells are an excellent enhancement. Water element also governs trading, shipping and travel industry.

However; precious gems, platinum, gold, silver and other precious metals are governed by the earth element. Jupiter, the planet of expansion, rules gold which is the base and criterion of any currency. Such people and companies will do well if they incorporate bright metallic colours into their décor or logo.

Gems and Jewellery

Gems and Jewellery business is governed by the earth element. The precious metals like gold, platinum and silver – being the refined form of earth - are good in the southeast or east (gold), and northwest (silver). Activate the relevant sector with the décor that include painting with an earthy theme. Install a beautifully decorated idol of Goddess Lakshami or Radha Krishna. Use gold or silver coins inscribed with Lakshami and Ganesha to give a boost to your business. Jaisalmer yellow marble flooring would be ideal for your business. Other examples of such earth related businesses are mining, engineering, car assembling, machinery and equipments.

Wood Working

Some of the wood related businesses are farming, horticulture, forestry, paper manufacturing, gardening, lumber merchants, furniture makers, and sawmills. The direction of green wood is east (Sun) and southeast (Venus) while processed wood is governed by southwest (Rahu) and west (Saturn). Activate the east or southeast sector by placing a well-maintained live or artificial plant. Southwest of west may be activated by placing a beautiful piece of art carved from an auspicious wood. As water helps in the growth of trees and plants, it is therefore the complementary element.

Call Centres

Call centre industry is called the "poster child" of new Indian economy. Being a growing industry, it has enough job opportunities. The best aspect about call centres is that they give an opportunity to young people, fresh out of college. They provide good work environment with well planned facilities like cafeteria, gym and play rooms.

The call centres work through work stations at the basic level. Each work station has a phone and a computer. The computer has various information that a caller might need plus Frequently Asked Questions (FAQs). In case the query is beyond the FAQs, the floor supervisor helps. Call centres are witnessing phenomenal growth at 55 per cent in the NCR which is more than the national average of 45 per cent. There are around 90 to 95 call centres in the NCR employing more than 55,000 employees directly and around 1.6 lakh indirectly (security, travel etc).

The negative side of call centre working is that it demands lifestyle changes. Normal working hours are the best. Odd hours' working upsets the biological body-clock impacting workers' physical and psychological health. Complete change in the body-clock can trigger varied side effects including sleep disorders. Weight loss due to "drastically changed" lifestyle is common and leads to exhaustion. Graduates and even undergraduates join call centres lured by the promise of some easy money. There are no great career prospects at the end of couple of years in call centres. And if the call centre boom goes bust, future of youngster will be in darkness.

Salary is based on performance here and pay gets cut if set target is not achieved. There is an abysmally high rate of attrition in the call centre industry. Many are unable to take the hours and changes in the lifestyle for very long. Many lose their real identity and assume an artificial identity they are required to work under. The growth of an individual and his emotions are greatly hampered. The skills like learning to talk with a different accent are superficial and are not of much use in other jobs. No life is left after doing night shifts.

However, principles of commercial and office vaastu can be applied to the design, layout and operation of call centres to lessen their ill effects to a large extent. These principles have already been explained at length.

Hospital Vaastu

Modern life is not at all normal. The disadvantages of modern civilization are many including the pollution of air; water and food by chemicals and radiations, pollution of our minds by noise and unnecessary information, pollution of our humanness by mechanization and pressure of deadlines and pollution of our emotions by loneliness and breakdown of the family. We experience avoidable as well as unavoidable stresses daily. These stresses accumulate within us and sicken us. These traumas produce in us a host of degenerative diseases. Modern hospitals are required to provide preventive and curative health care to the people, but only temporarily alleviate the degenerative conditions caused by our environment. This alleviation is also fraught with peril.

It has been found that some human beings live long and healthy in the remote parts of the world which are still devoid of the modern technological advancement. Main factors responsible for their longevity are the nectar of pure water, pure air and pure food, hard work and the lovely support of their family and friends. Modern man has tried to use the scientific knowledge to control the environment than living in harmony with it. Vedic sciences believe that Earth behaves like a living organism. All the natural forces eg wind, fire, air, earth, and the like are the living, conscious beings.

Anything entering our body can exert three possible effects on it: it can act as food and nourishes it, it can act as medicine and balances it or it can act as poison and disturbs it. The hot dosha 'pitta' tends to create the extra heat in the internal environment. Vata and kapha tend to produce more cold, vata causing a dry cold and kapha, a wet cold. A pitta person often feels hot. Such a person usually hates hot climates and loves cold environment. A vata person hates to be cold and generally loves heat. Kapha people generally enjoy the changes in the seasons. It stimulates their systems.

Indications regarding the health issues have also been given while discussing the forty-five demi-gods and goddesses. Readers are advised to deeply go through the relevant pages. Classical vaastu principles, after due modifications, can be applied for design, construction and management of hospitals. We find some recommendations regarding health issues in the classical text Vishwakarmaprakash (2.97-100):

"The person - desirous of enjoying kingly position - shall keep place for weeping in between the west and the north-west, place for sexual activities in between the north and the north-west, storage of medicines in between the north and north-east and lying-in chamber (child's delivery room) shall be in the south-west.

Place for expectant mother is especially meant during the ninth month of pregnancy, and immediately after the delivery. The person enjoying a kingly position shall get it constructed in advance. Temporary place for child's delivery, if so required, shall be constructed on an auspicious day of the first half of the ninth month of pregnancy. It should be well-decorated and the expectant mother shall be made to enter it on an auspicious day in the bright lunar half of the month".

In the modern context, weeping place means the place for psychiatric treatment.

Thus, in a hospital, Psychiatry department or psychiatrist's chamber shall be located in between the west and the north-west directions.

Place recommended for sexual activity in between the north and north-west was meant for conception. This sector can be best utilized by the fertility clinics in the modern era. This area is governed by Naag, which also mean "kind of coitus or sexual intercourse". Nagas (snakes) are linked with fertility in the Indian and many other ancient cultures. They are also said to carry the elixir of life and immortality (medicine).

Storage of medicines is recommended in between the north and north-east. So this sector is the best place for location of blood bank, medical store, chemist shop, refrigerator storing life-saving drugs, and eatables consumed for curative and medicinal purposes.

Maternity chamber (lying-in chamber) has been recommended in the south-west. Thus this sector is best for maternity ward in a modern hospital.

According to the vaastu classic *Mayamatam* (26.214); "Women's apartment is in the farther or back portions of the first or second enclosure. Maternity chamber (lying-in chamber / sutika-griha) is on the square of Nirriti as are the latrines. The women's house may also extend from the square of Pavana to that of Indu (Moon)".

Such lying-in rooms are rare in the modern homes. However, the 'Maternity Ward' which is equivalent of the lying-in chamber in a hospital, can be kept in the south-west direction. During the classical era, about one month before the delivery, the expectant mother was ushered in the light and airy maternity room in the east facing south-west corner of the house. It was done while following all the traditional rituals and playing the auspicious music. She would live there quietly meditating on her child and remain there for around two weeks after the delivery. Before, during and after the delivery, the father-to-be would generally be busy with the performance of protective rituals. The period of ritual impurity ended about two weeks after the birth. At this time, emergence of mother and child from the lying-in room would occasion a big feast.

The planning of hospital begins with locating a proper site. Hospital shall not be too near the residential area. It would be still better if it located outside the city or in the institutional area. Hospital site should preferably be selected near the main roads for easy accessibility. Plots with roads towards the north, north-east, or east should be preferred. When road is towards west or south, arrange the plot according to the tenets of vaastu. Keep more set back towards the east and north and provide main entry in the north-east. Orient the building according to the cardinal directions.

Hospital land and building falls under the *brahmana* category. The aim of a *brahmana* is to know the *Brahm*, to be one with Brahm. The principal word for health in Sanskrit is 'svastha'. It is combination of 'svayam' and 'sthita', means 'established in oneself'. Thus a healthy person means a person who has established himself in Him-Self, who is completely happy with himself, who has become one with his body, mind and soul.

Mayamatam recommends that a brahmana plot should be square in shape with length equal to width. In a square, all the five great elements of nature – space, air, fire, water and earth – are well balanced. The existing soil should be white in colour with an auspicious odour of clarified butter. The flavor of soil should be sweet. Holy and medicinal trees and plants eg peepal, mango, tulsi, neem, banana, arjun, ashoka etc should flourish here. Such a north sloping land bestows peace, comforts and spiritual elevation. East sloping land is equally good for hospital.

Sufficient *paishach sthan* shall be left open to the sky all around the hospital building, not less than one ninth of the relevant side. It is must for provision of essential services as well as to facilitate the movement of traffic, trolleys, stretchers and ambulances. The great vaastu classic *Maansaar* has spoken of different heights related to the breadth of building. These are Shantik (height = width), Paushtik (height = 1.25 times the width), Jayada (height = 1.5 times the width), Sarvakamika or Dhanada (height = 1.75 times the width), and Adbhuta (height = twice the width). Hospitals are best when all the activities are confined to the ground floor. Upper floors require round the clock availability of electricity for movement of lifts and escalators. Additional manpower required for such activities results in extra consumption of energy and increased cost of treatment.

The plot should be procured at an auspicious time. After procuring the plot, shalya shodhan (removing the inauspicious deposits) should be done. All the defects, discrepancies and irregularities should be rectified. A compound wall should be constructed to ward off the ill effects of the surrounding plots.

The main building should be constructed in the south-west area. With the rising needs, other smaller blocks can be constructed in this order; in the south, west, south-east, north-west, north or east (or vice versa), and north-east sectors. South-west shall be the first option for construction and north-east the last. There should not be any construction on the six vulnerable points of the Vaastu Purush: head, face, mid-point of the right and left chest, heart and the navel. Paishach-sthan and braham-sthan of each and every block shall always be kept open to the sky.

Compound gates should be in the east of north-east (G1), south of south-east (G2), west of north-west (G3) and north of north-east (G4). These points are considered the exalted zones of any plot. In this way, a vehicle entering the plot from one compound gate can exit the gate opposite to it without changing the direction of vehicle carrying patients.

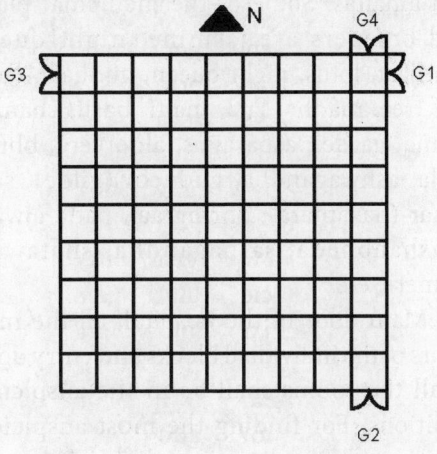

G1 & G3 , G2 & G4 Directly Opposite

Fig 6.8: Location of Boundary Gates

Healthy medicinal, flowery or green leafy trees and plants giving auspicious odours shall be planted alongside the boundary wall: inside and if possible, outside too. They act as a buffer between the hospital and the outside environment. Trees trap the dust particles, prevent noise and smoke pollution, increase the oxygen level, decrease the temperature, reduce the dryness, increase the moisture and provide privacy to the patients as well as to the surrounding inhabitants.

Thorny, milk-emitting, fruit bearing and foul smelling trees in and around the building are not considered auspicious as per vaastu. The shape of trees and plants shall not be frightening. Round, pyramid -shaped, and umbrella shaped trees and plants and good looking healthy creepers are considered good vaastu. All the dead, diseased and haphazard shaped plants shall be removed. Healthy plants with shining leaves and blooming flowers create positive energy and spread positive message of health and well-being.

Some of the auspicious or medicinal trees are peepal, neem, arjuna, bael (bilva), haridra, baheda, amla, sandalwood, bamboo, banana, teak, ashoka, gulmohar, mulberry, kadamba, putrajiva, shirisha, deodar, mulberry, and amaltas. Some of the medicinal plants and creepers are jasmine, night queen, paarijaat, lotus, night queen, gudhala, curry leaf tree, madhvi lata, malti, basil, champa, henna, garden asparagus, aloe vera, bhumi amla, ashwagandha, guduchi (giloe), sada bahar (nayantara), bhringraaj, patta ajwain, paashanbheda, sarpagandha, shatawari, turmeric etc.

Main door of the hospital, all the main doors of the individual blocks and entry doors of all the rooms shall be in the auspicious positions. For finding the most auspicious position in any direction, divide it in nine equal parts. Standing inside the room, fourth part from the left is the most auspicious position for a door. Door can also be placed in the middle of any cardinal direction. North, north-east and east entrances are preferred. Ishan oriented hospital becomes famous for early recovery of patients within a short span of time. North direction is good in scorching summers. Western and southern entrance shall always be avoided in north Indian planes. Southern entrance, receiving sufficient solar heat, is good in cold hilly areas. South direction shall be used in the plain areas in winters only.

Varahmihir, in his classical text Brihatsamhita (53.71-75), has elaborately given result of placement of main door in all the 32 squares on the outer periphery. These should seriously be considered while planning main door and secondary doors for the hospital. Results of doors placed on any of the 32 demi-gods are given here in a tabular form.

Table 6.1: Thirty-Two Squares, Demi-Gods and Results of Placements of Doors

S No	God Name	Result of Placement of Main Door (Brihatsamhita, 53.71-75)
1	Vahni	Fear from fire
2	Parjanya	Birth of daughters
3	Jayant	Abundant wealth
4	Mahendra	Favour from the King
5	Aaditya	Angry nature
6	Satya	Untruthful
7	Bhrish	Cruelty
8	Antariksh	Theft
9	Maarut	Less number of children
10	Poosha	Slavery
11	Vitath	Meanness
12	Grihakshat	Food, drinks & children in abundance
13	Yam	Fierceness

14	Gandharv	Thanklessness
15	Bhringraaj	Poverty
16	Mrig	Destruction of children and power
17	Pitar	Sorrow about children
18	Dauvaarik	Increase in enemies
19	Sugreev	Gain of wealth & children
20	Pushpdant	Gain of wealth, property and sons
21	Varun	Wealth and property
22	Asur	Danger from the king
23	Shosh	Loss of wealth
24	Paapyakshama	Disease
25	Rog	Death and confinement
26	Naag	Increase of enemies
27	Mukhya	Gain of child & wealth
28	Bhallaat	Gain of all the virtues & wealth
29	Som	Gain of children and wealth
30	Charak	Enmity with children
31	Aditi	Problem with females
32	Diti	Poverty

Vaastu Purusha's body parts lying in different positions may indicate the directions, sectors and squares related to the treatment of relevant body parts / organs / systems. There is a popular saying in Ayurveda, "To enjoy a sound health, one should keep his feet warm, the stomach soft and the head cool". The head of Vaastu Purush is in the coolest area northeast while his feet are in the hottest zone southwest. His navel point Brahamsthana shall be kept soft by keeping it kachcha. The earth here shall not be compacted and shall naturally be able to absorb the rain water. No constructions are allowed here.

These forty-five demi-gods and goddesses are offered different eatables as *Bali* (offerings) during the Vaastu Poojan (worshipping the Vaastu God). Offerings to all the 45 demi-gods, as available in chapter 8 of Mayamatam and Vishvakarmaprakasha (5.117-132) are given in Table 6.2. Type of eatable may indicate the type of activity related to that particular square or squares. For example, squares offered non-vegetarian food are good for cruel activities like surgery. On the contrary, squares offered the vegetarian food are good for healing, recovery and rejuvenation.

Table 6.2: Forty-Five Squares, Relevant Body Parts of Vaastu Purush, and Offerings

S No	Name of Door	Body Part of Vaastu Purush (Brihat-samhita, 53.51-54)	Offerings (Mayamatam, chapter 8)	Offerings (Vishvakarma-prakash, 5.117-132)
1	Ish or Ishan or Shikhi	Head	Rice and ghee	Ghee and cooked food grains
2	Parjanya	Right eye	Rice, ghee and lotus (makhana)	Ghee and cooked food grains with lotus-seed
3	Jayanta or Aindra or Jaya	Right ear	Fresh butter and flowers	Lamb's quarters plant (bathua) and curd
4	Indra or Mahendra or Pakshashan or Kulishayudh	Right chest (neck)	Entrails and flowers	Panch-ratna (five gems) and nutritious food
5	Surya or Bhaskara	Shoulder	Honey and onions	Kusha (type of grass), fried cake (pua) prepared from red wheat and gur (raw sugar) and sattu (multi-grain drink)
6	Satya or Satyak	Right arm	Honey	Ghee and cooked wheat
7	Bhrish or Bhrsh	Right arm	Fresh butter	Cooked fish and rice
8	Antariksh or Gagan or Akash	Right arm	Beans and orpiment	Poori (deep fried bread) and bird's meat
9	Agni or Anila or Vahni (Anala, Jwalan)	Right arm	Milk, ghee and tagara powder	Sattu
10	Pushan	Right arm	Vegetables and milk	Laja (roasted paddy)
11	Vitath	Right side	Cooked kanku	Boiled black grams
12	Brihatkshat or Brihatkshati or Grihatkshat or Rakshash	Right side	Intoxicating juice	Grains with honey
13	Yama	Right thigh	Vegetables and boiled rice	Raw meat

14	Gandharv	Right knee	Pure perfume	Sweet smelling cooked rice
15	Bhringraja	Right shank	Sea fish	Tongue of ram or he goat
16	Mrsa or Mrish (Mrig)	Right buttock	Rice with fish	Cooked barley grain
17	Pitar or Nirriti	Feet	Sesame oil cake	Cooked black or blue barley of longish size
18	Dauvarik	Left buttock	Sesame seeds	Khichri (rice and pulse cooked together)
19	Sugriva	Left shank	Cake	Darbha grass (dant-kaashth) and flour prepared from urad pulse
20	Pushpadant or Kusumdant	Left knee	Flowers and water	Cooked barley grain
21	Varuna or Jaladhip	Left thigh	Rice and milk	Watery or marshy animals
22	Asura	Left side	Blood	Liquor
23	Shosha	Left side	Rice and sesame	Ghee and rice
24	Papayakshama or Rog	Left arm	Dried fish	Goh (Iguana) meat
25	Rog or Vayu	Left arm	Fat and orpiment	Ghee and rice
26	Naag or Ahi or Ahirbudhnya	Left arm	Wine and roasted rice	Fruits, flowers and naagkesar (an Indian flower)
27	Mukhya	Left arm	Flour, curd and ghee	Ghee and wheat
28	Bhallata	Left arm	Cooked rice with molasses	Cooked Moong pulse and rice
29	Soma (Kuber)	Left shoulder	Milk rice	Kheer (milk and rice cooked together) and ghee
30	Mrga or Mriga or Bhujaga (Shail)	Left chest (neck)	Dried meat	Nutritious food grain
31	Aditi	Left ear	Cake	Poori (deep fried Indian bread)
32	Diti or Uditi	Left eye	Sesame rice	Kachori (deep fried Indian bread with spices)

33	Apah or Aapa	Face	Lotus, flesh of shellfish and tortoise	Milk
34	Aapavatsa	Chest	Lotus, flesh of shellfish and tortoise	Curd
35	Aryama or Aaryaka or Aarya	Breast	Cake of fruits, cooked beans, sesame seeds	rice boiled in milk (kheer) with gur
36	Savita or Savitra	Right hand	Roasted rice	Food prepared from kusha and its seeds
37	Saavitra	Right hand	Perfumed water	Pua (fried cake prepared from gur (raw sugar) and wheat flour) or maalpua (fried cake prepared from wheat flour)
38	Vivasvan or Vivasvat	Right side of the stomach	Curd	Red sandal and rice boiled in milk (kheer)
39	Indra or Shakra	Genital organ	Goat's fat and crushed beans	Ghee, haritaal (yellow orpiment) and cooked rice
40	Indrajaya or Jaya or Indraraja	Genital organ	Goat's fat and crushed beans	Laddoo, pepper, ghee and sandal
41	Mitra	Left side of the stomach	Doorva grass	Ghee and cooked rice
42	Rudra	Left hand	Meat and fat	Gur and rice boiled in milk (kheer)
43	Rudrajaya or Rudraraja or Rudradas or Rajayakshama	Left hand	Meat and fat	Raw meat and honey
44	Bhudhara or Prithvidhara or Mahidhara or Amitaujas	Left breast	Milk	Meat and Kooshmaand (kind of pumpkin)
45	Brahma or Vidhi	Heart	Perfumes, garlands, incense, milk, honey, ghee, rice boiled in milk, roasted rice	Panchgavya (cow's milk, cow's curd, cow's ghee, cow's urine and cow dung), cooked barley, black til (sesame seed), rice and curd

Mayamatam (chapter 8) also recommends bali (offerings) to demi-goddesses of corners. It recommends bali of wine and roasted rice for Charaki (governing northeast), salt for Vidarika or Vidari (governing southeast), cake of flour, grated coconut and sugar for Pootana (governing southwest) and bean water for Paap-rakshashi (governing north-west).

A small temple can be constructed in the north-east of the hospital plot, a peaceful area away from the main entry. Boring for drinking water or underground water tank shall be towards the north or east of north-east, leaving the area covered by the north-east axis of building and the plot. Overhead water tank is best in the west direction of Varun, the lord of oceans. Bathrooms without toilet are said to be good in the east; "*Poorvasyam snanamandiram*" (Vishwakarma-prakash 2.94).

Parking space for visitors should be in the north and east side of set-backs all around the building (paishach sthan), preferably towards north-west or south-east. The basement can also be used for parking purposes. Staircases and lifts are very active areas of any vaastu. These should be away from the operation theatre (OT) and patient wards. Persons' movement should not disturb the patients taking rest in the wards. Silent generator, transformer, inverter, electric main connection and operating system shall be installed in the south-east direction, preferably outside the main building.

South-east of the building is not good for layout of the general wards. It is best utilized as an administrative block. Rajas energy of the south-east keeps the workers active throughout the day. This direction is the mid-point of light zone, moderately hot and moderately cold. South-east zone can also be utilized as kitchen, pantry and canteen area. Small pantry can also be arranged in the west direction. Dining room should be in the west of any block or in the west of the canteen area; "*Bhojanam pashchimayam*" (Brihad-vaastu-mala-prayoga).

Registration, reception, out patients department (OPD), billing etc can be in the north-west or alternatively in the south-east. These are the rajas directions: north-west is full of the rajas of air while south-east is full of the rajas of fire. Billing can also be done in the north, the direction of Mercury. Mercury governs calculations and Kuber governs money. Waiting room should be provided adjacent to the reception area.

Doctor's consultation chambers shall be in or near to the rajas areas, preferably towards the north or east directions. Doctor's seat should be in the south-east, preferably farthest from the entry of his room. South-east is the active rajas area. His back and inactive hand side should be protected with a solid wall or a piece of heavy and stable furniture. There should be more open areas in the front as well as towards his active hand side. Examination table can be placed in the south-west corner. Dark, bright and dull colours should be avoided in the consultation chamber. Pink, sky blue, light green, greenish yellow and yellowish green are good colours for consultation chambers.

No sign of death should directly be visible to the visitors in the hospital premises. Only positive life images depicting the serenity of life, beauty of nature, and joy of living are allowed here. All the pictures, paintings and sculptures shall convey a positive message of life, health, peace, recovery and the jovial spirit.

Hospitals usually go for unnecessary medical tests. Medical tests should not be performed unless the expected benefits exceed the expected risks. Along with benefits of medical tests, their negative side includes over-diagnosis, missed diagnosis, and risks from the test, such as exposure to ionizing radiation from the X-rays or potential infection after a blood draw. It has been found that at present roughly one fourth of the patients entering a hospital develop an iatrogenic disease, a disease caused by the medical procedures. According to a study, death rates actually decreased in 1973 in Israel and in 1976 in Los Angeles and Bogota when doctors went on strike. Modern medicine is forgetting the Hippocratic dictum 'first do no harm' to the patient.

Vaastu can be of great help in medical diagnosis. Test laboratories using poisonous drugs, strong chemicals and nuclear medicines should be established in the west of south-west. This is equivalent to the eighth house of the horoscope in the north Indian system of Vedic Astrology. Poisonous body wastes like stool, urine and cancerous growth can be tested here. Test labs using *ayurvedic* medicines, lifesaving drugs and mild chemicals are best in the north of northeast. East is equivalent to the first house of the horoscope in the north Indian system of Vedic Astrology. Blood and saliva samples can be tested here. South-east sector is good for radiological tests. Likewise, energy of north-west can be best utilized for psychiatric and respiration related diagnostic tests.

Residential quarters for doctors, nurses and hospital staff should be separated from the hospital area by a boundary wall with the provision of easy access to the hospital premises in an emergency. Backside of the hospital area, preferably south-west, south or west side should be reserved for this purpose. Hostel for junior staff should preferably be in the north-west or south-east of the hospital premises. These directions are full of the rajas energy of air or fire. Red colour should never be used as wall colour in the hospital premises. Blue, light green, light pink and white colours are full of medicinal value.

World Health Organization (WHO) has accepted hospital's symbol as capital 'H' written in white on a bluish background of square shape. White is a mixture of all the seven colours of solar spectrum while cool blue colour is governed by Jupiter, the planet of growth and expansion. Pink is directly related to the condition of perfect health. The word 'Patient' literally means the person who has to keep patience, till he or she recovers. This great spiritual quality of patience is bestowed by a benefic Jupiter. Any disease bounds us like Saturn; while forces of auspicious Jupiter expand us physically, socially, monetarily, mentally and spiritually.

Fig 6.9: The Symbol of Hospital

A protective, dirt free and aseptic place is required as the operation theatre. Main operation theatre (OT) should be in the south-west, the most protective, calm, serene, and private place. Minor or major surgery is must at the time of birth of a human child. At least a sharp instrument like new shaving blade is required to severe the umbilical cord connecting the child with the mother. For child birth, vaastu texts recommend south-west area. It is the direction of Rahu, the significator of shattered, dilapidated, broken or damaged body, body wastes, poison and poisonous drugs used in anesthesia. Here child gets separated from its mother's body.

Rahu also governs dim light or shadow based electronic equipment used widely in modern surgery e.g. endoscope, laparoscope, video monitors, endo-video-cameras and fiber-optic cables. Minor operation theatre can be located in south-west of the respective department. Green colour scheme should be used in the OT as it helps to maintain the patient's blood pressure normal. Green is a neutral colour, neither too hot nor too cold. It is soothing to the eyes as well.

Intensive care units (ICU) should be adjacent to the operation theatre ie towards the west or south of south-west. Patient wards should be in the west and south sectors of the hospital area. While lying, head of patients should be towards the south, may be towards the east or west but shall never be towards the north. Blue or green colour scheme should be used for the hot climate. Red colour in the form of clothes, bed sheets and blankets can be used during the cold weather or for the patients suffering from cold. The general ward, where patients are soon to be discharged, should be in the rajas areas ie north-west or the south-east.

Main sterilization unit of the hospital should be planned between the south and south-east. Vaastu texts recommend this direction for storage of clarified butter. This direction receives sufficient heat to kill the harmful germs. Sterilization units of different departments should also be designed between the south and south-east of their respective blocks. Emergency sterilization in the OT itself should be done in between its south and south-east.

All the waste water generated in the hospital falls in the sewage category. Sewage cannot be used directly for any purpose like gardening or washing. This waste water should immediately be removed from the premises through the covered pipes and drains. Toilets should be towards the south and west of south-west, leaving the north-east – south-west axis. Area adjacent to the north-west can also be utilized for this purpose. Toilets and urinals should never be directly opposite to the main entrance or the entrance of any ward or room. These must always be arranged in the secured corners.

Medical solid waste treatment plant or incinerator should be installed in the south-west, outside the main hospital premises. This place can also be used as temporary dunghill or garbage dumping yard for the medical waste.

Washing of patients' drapes, bed sheets, aprons, curtains and other clothes should be done in the north-west, the rajas area of air. It should be done outside the main hospital building.

Mortuary should be towards the south-west of the main hospital building, preferably with a separate entry. Rahu – planetary lord of this direction – rules over the skeletons, burial grounds, graveyards and crematoriums. Mortuary should not be visible to the patients and their family members. It should be constructed as per the principles of out-houses (upagraham).

Today's premier hospitals increasingly resemble five-star hotels. They don't smell like hospitals. Large-dimension vitrified tiles, or granite are used as flooring material in most of them. Combination of laminated wood and steel is used for walls and partitions. The top end suites for patients boast of a sitting room and a kitchen. A dietician decides the patient's diet based on his medical condition and his cultural background. The walls of patients' rooms are being done in bright colours.

Large windows that offer a good view have become mandatory. Venetian blinds are also chosen in colours and materials that provide a sense of well-being. Earlier the pipes through which life-saving gases are supplied were usually exposed. Now architects provide a POP wall that keeps these ungainly pipes out of sight. Designers try to use materials that will be able to withstand a lot of traffic. That's why the sidewalls of lifts are now made up of stainless steel as it can easily be cleaned when get soiled.

While designing a hospital, the first thing to take into consideration is the kind of hospital. Whether it is going to be a super-specialty hospital, a multi-specialty hospital or a general hospital that will treat all diseases but won't deal with highly complicated cases? The architect should pay attention to the load the hospital will be called upon to handle ie number of outdoor patients (OPD), number of in-patients, size of the casualty department etc. He must know whether it will be a single-storeyed, low level, or multi-storeyed structure.

Architect should pay a lot of attention to ensure that once the patient arrives at the hospital, the route taken to transfer him to the treatment area is as short as possible. He should keep in mind which department should be located next to which one for optimal functionality and best flow of traffic. The lifts should be big enough to accommodate stretchers. They shouldn't be too fast as this could cause discomfort to the patients. The corridor width should be at least 2.4 metres so that stretchers, which are about 1.8 metres long, can easily be manoeuvred around. Basic layout map of the building is produced when all these factors are taken into consideration.

Toilet's floors should not have any drop in level. A gentle slope should lead to the shower area, where a depression is required. Toilet walls must have handrails to offer support to the patients. This will help the patient to manoeuvre his wheel chair into the right position. The toilets can be fitted with call bells that sound an alarm at the nurse's station in case of an emergency. If the patient rooms or toilets get locked from inside, they could be easily opened from the outside. Patient's medicines stored in the nursing station should be kept in separate lockers to avoid the danger of mix-up.

The critical areas should have anti-static and bacteria free flooring. At most of the premier hospitals, operation theatres are modular units made from prefabricated, joint-less stainless steel. Air handling units in operation theatres and critical care units keep impurity level in the air below 0.01 micron level.

Patients just feel good to be in a vaastu-friendly hospital building. Appolo hospital group, the single largest private healthcare provider in India, has built hospitals at Colombo; Sri Lanka, Ahmedabad; Gujarat and Dhaka; Bangladesh to vaastu principles. Good vaastu design always responds well to a tropical climate by keeping a lot of open space and air-circulation as top priorities.

The state-of-the-art medical facility at Dhaka has been built according to the principles of vaastu shastra, the Indian art of placement that predates feng shui. The stainless steel and glass façade of the building and its tidy landscaping look normal. The plan for the main entry and its soaring wing like roof are marked with the element Air. Building's boiler plant is marked Fire. The bulk of building's mass is in a corner of the property marked Earth. A water tank is situated in an area called the water quadrant. Although vaastu is a Hindu tradition, around 88 percent of Bangladeshis are Muslim. This means you can't orient the toilets toward Mecca, nor you should aim the patients' feet toward the west. The hospital entrance is elevated so that it seems like people are entering on a higher level.

Factory Vaastu

Modern mega factories were non-existent in the classical era. Our physical activities are seen from the tenth house in the horoscope. As tenth house corresponds with the south direction, all the heavy industrial activities may be considered good in the south direction. It is also the direction receiving maximum heat throughout the year in the northern hemisphere. Solar heat is vital for any industrial activity. Likewise, food processing industries may be considered the extended version of home kitchen which is considered best in the southeast.

Though layout for different industrial activities will differ a lot as the production processes are entirely different, the underlying principles of factory vaastu should always be kept in mind. These principles have been discussed at length in first three chapters where industrial activities have been related with the nine planets, ten directional lords, forty-five demi gods and goddesses, five great elements, and three gunas.

The headquarters or head office of the factory and the residential premises should not be located at the very same place. Supply of required manpower and raw material, and transportation through rail/road/ship/air is a must. Vaastu must also be synthesized with the latest available technology, ergonomics, robotics, computer aided design; operation and management, study of time and motion etc.

A list of industrial activities is given in Table....which is only indicative. For a specific activity, the relevant direction(s) should invariably be open so that natural solar radiation which is rich in quality helping that particular type of activity can enter the premises. For example, a chemical plant for its proper functioning requires direct sunlight from the south throughout the year. A food processing unit will flourish well while receiving sunrays from the southeast.

Table 6.3: Industries and Mandatory Open Directions

S No	Industry	Open Direction(s)	Logic
1	Chemical	South	Mars governs chemicals
2	Steel	South and west	Saturn governs steel and Mars governs its extraction process
3	Cement	South and west	Saturn governs cement as building material and Mars governs its formation as a chemical
4	Textile / cloth mills	North	Mercury governs our skin (the natural cloth of body)
5	Electronics	Southwest	Rahu governs electronics
6	Marble / granite / stone cutting and polishing	Southwest	Rahu and Nirriti govern the dead/mutilated body
7	Food processing	Southeast	Venus governs the taste sense and Agni helps in proper cooking
8	Malt production for breweries and pharmaceuticals	South	Mars governs alcohol
9	Truck manufacturing	South and southwest	Mars governs heavy machines and Rahu governs wheels
10	Garment export unit	Southeast or northwest	Venus governs stitched clothes while Vayu governs exports
11	Assembling of electronic gadgets eg TV, computer etc.	Southeast	Proper light available here with the beauty of Venus
12	Vehicle workshops	Northwest	Moon is the fastest moving planet (we need vehicles to move fast)
13	Edible oil mills	South of southeast	Venus and Mars combined help in extraction of oil with proper nutrition value
14	Flour mills	East of southeast	Venus and Sun combined help in grinding of grains with proper nutrition value (due to less heat generated)

15	Bakery	Southeast	Venus governs the taste sense and Agni helps in proper cooking
16	Saw mills	Southwest	Rahu and Nirriti govern the dead/mutilated body
17	Metallurgy	South and West	Mars governs production and purification process while Saturn governs the raw form of metals
18	Water bottling plant	Northeast or north	Jupiter governs nectar while Mercury is neither too hot nor too cold
19	Publishing house	North	Mercury rules bookish knowledge
20	Electronic items for entertainment industry	Southeast and northwest	Venus and Moon are sensual planets

A stinking environment in the surrounding is not welcome. There is no future for a factory in a stinking neighborhood. We Indians usually emphasize the internal environment at the expense of the external. Hindu philosophy is to look inside rather than outside. But a slum area in the surrounding can stink up our space and destroy our peace. Stink is related to the earth element. It can destroy your health, wealth and even this precious life.

The plot meant for a factory should preferably be rectangular. Otherwise make it so with the help to trees and plants, dividing it in regular shape sections or through regular shape construction. The east-west axis should be longer than the north-south axis for maximum exposure to sunrays. Much undulating land is not good. The bearing capacity of soil should be good to safely bear the load of heavy structure and machinery.

Sufficient surface or ground water should be available round the year for the industrial processes. Boring for drinking water should be in the north or east of the northeast. Water used in the industrial process (except water used for drinking and cooking) can safely be stored in the west.

Proper fencing of the land is must for safety and to avoid encroachment. Solid compound wall, with proper arrangement of cross ventilation (eg honeycomb construction), is preferable to avoid any inauspicious happening. Provide compound gates as per the norms of vaastu shastra. Industrial shed should not abet your neighbor in any direction.

One should be able to have a walk around the factory. Paishach Sthan should never be encroached in the form of a canteen, guard room, urinal, toilet, garage, storeroom, workshop, storage of raw material and the like. Central place of the building as well as of the individual work-stations should be kept vacant.

The face of factory should preferably be towards the east. Paint the factory in white or blue from the outside. The ceiling lights admitted through the north provide a cooling effect. Depending on the type of production, other specific directions should also have openings in the form of big windows and ventilators.

Machinery should be arranged as per the heaviness of directions – heaviest in the southwest, heavy in the south and west, moderate in the southeast and northwest, and light in the north and east. Northeast and brahamsthan should not be loaded with any machinery. Furnace is best in the south but oven in the food factory should be in the south-east.

Heavy raw material should be stacked in the south-west, west and/or south, separate from the working area. Semi-processed material should be kept in the south and/or west. Storage of finished goods, packaging and dispatching is best done in the northwest / east / southeast. Products ready for delivery could be in the north-west as it is a wind-buffeted direction. Nothing remains here for long. Delivery could also be from the north or east of the premises.

Electric motors, generators, transformers, ovens, switch-gears, capacitors, control panels, smoke chimneys and other equipments requiring / generating lesser amount of heat should be installed in the southeast. Boilers, oil filled or electric furnaces and other equipments requiring / generating greater amount of heat should be installed in the south.

East or southeast is good for computers and its technical staff. Accounts section is good in the north of the admin block. The cash-chest of any organization, invisible to the common workers, should be in the south-west with its door towards the north. Provide large windows towards the north and east of the administrative block. For arrangement of office furniture, follow the earlier explained rules.

West or south area can be used as an administrative block. It can also be arranged on the first floor. Factory owner shall ideally occupy the south or west room and face north or east. North attracts money while east improves the quality of work bringing name and fame. Directors and heads of departments are also best in the south or west, towards the right and left of the head, as per their importance in the administration. Marketing and sales section of any industry should be in the north-west. It is the direction of air which signifies movement.

In a multi-storey building, staircase is best in the northwest or the southeast. Weigh bridges should be in the open, towards the north or east of the premises. Heavy vehicles eg cranes, trucks, trolleys etc may be parked in the south or southwest. Light commercial vehicles should be parked in the north or east directions.

There should be proper availability of natural light and air. Sufficient light and colours encourage prana in the factory. Attractive appearance of factory encourages more prana, which increases the morale and contentment of workers. Proper maintenance of ideal working temperature has a huge effect on the quality and quantity of the produced work.

A well-maintained small temple or place for offering prayers for the workers should be in the northeast or in the centre (if too large area) of the premises. Always keep the brahamsthan level as neither any digging and nor any rise is allowed here. Labour rooms should be in the northwest. A well maintained staff canteen is best in the southeast, with an attached dining hall towards its west. Toilets should be in the northwest, or west / south of southwest. Time office should be near the entry itself. Security cabin is best towards the right, while entering or leaving the premises. It is still better if it falls in the northwest or southeast sector.

Factory owners in India pay very little importance to their work areas. Quality of work or products suffers due to unclean environment of factory or working area. Any factory may be considered the projection of home's kitchen, the most active zone which is used for production of food items throughout the day. In Indian tradition, it is considered inauspicious to enter the kitchen without taking bath or wearing dirty clothes. Unless a working environment is neat and clean, well-lit, airy and uncluttered like a kitchen, it won't deliver the desired quality of the product.

The factory workers should be clean and well-clad. Soiled clothes of employees bring down efficiency as well as quality of the products. Good quality products can't be produced in a dirty and ill-lit factory. Pay proper attention to the space element. More openings in the east ensure quality products while open north ensures wealth. Remove all the clutter (kabaar). Toilets should be in good shape and be cleaned on regular basis.

In the garment export units and the similar industries, working in huge halls brings better results than working in separate cubicles. Making several small cubicles for different tasks means ruining the space as well as vision of the workers. Space around us is no good if we can't see it.

Each and every vaastu, including the factories, should be a part of the nature. Workers should be able to enjoy the natural light and air, outside scenery of trees and plants and also the open sky to some extent. If you have a lot of space around the factory premises, grow flowers and other ornamental plants. These plants can change a dumb and drab environment in a vibrant and living one. The beautiful environment will also boost worker's productivity in the long run. Lawns with big avenue trees should be in the heavy directions while tender plants and fountains should be towards the light directions.

One of the major side effects of an industrial unit is pollution which may be due to air, noise, water, earth, heat or contracted space. Too much noise or too quiet an environment is equally bad. Use sound-proofing techniques to reduce the noise pollution. Otherwise, the staff may complain of headaches and the daily presence may reduce.

Only completely ready products should be shown to the prospective clients. While showing garments to the buyers which are ready to be exported, snipping off the extra threads from the same gives poor impression. All the things, including the time, should be well organized. Mismanagement consumes much of our precious time. One should be punctual in the delivery of one's promises as well as the products. Chaos in factory premises or in time management results in a chaotic life.

Now-a-days, so called vaastu experts are suggesting a number of shortcut methods for rectifying the vaastu doshas (defects). Most of these methods are the inventions of vaastu practitioners, based on their whims and fancies. Some have been developed keeping in mind the people's psychology, their impractical expectations, their greed and impulsive nature. Most of these remedies don't enjoy the sanction of classical vaastu texts. The only way to win the battle against any vaastu dosha (fault) is to structurally remove that dosha.

Each element is related to a specific direction. Harmonize the five elements in the industry ie space, air, fire, water and earth. Otherwise, sickness may strike an industrial unit. For example, fire and water are inimical to each other. Fire rules the south-east and water rules the north-east. If fire related activity like a furnace or boiler is installed in the north-east, it will bring misfortune. Likewise, a huge underground water tank in the south-east will invite unfortunate consequences. An out of order south-east can lead to disputes and agitation.

Likewise, industrial activities can also be categorized as sattvic, rajasi and tamasi activities. Sattvic activities - like production of medicines, scents and water purification - are best in the sattvic zone of north-east. Rajasic activities like food processing plants and vehicle workshops are best in the rajasi zones of south-east and north-west. Tamasic activities like processing of dead trees ie timber, quarried stones, animal leather and bio-waste plants are best in the tamasi zone of south-west.

Provision for fire-fighting, first-aid, drinking water, crèche, restrooms, rooms for changing dress, pollution control measures, water treatment and effluent treatment measures are mandatory as per the prevalent laws of the land. Industries running successfully should be expanded according to the principles of vaaastu shastra. Some practical cases of factory vaastu have been discusses in chapter nine.

Monasteries (Viharshala)

Mayamatam (26.200-202) explains construction of monasteries meant for residence of ascetics. According to it, a monastery is to be built like a temple. The length of the main building is triple the dimension chosen for the width. Other buildings are added to it lengthwise, whose length is initially chosen as double the width until the total length of monastery is twenty-two times the chosen width. There are then eleven buildings in all. Thus the edifice appears to be an elongated one made out of eleven oblong main buildings, one of them being bigger and perhaps located in the middle.

Each main building has a porch on its front façade and is decorated with square and elongated outwork constructions, and with false dormer windows. There is a verandah at the back; or each main building has two gables and resembles a garbhakoot. It has one, two, three or more storeys. There are various projecting elements on the front and behind.

Chapter 7
Modern Perspective of Vaastu

कलिः शयानो भवति सञ्जिहानस्तु द्वापरः।
उत्तिष्ठन् त्रेता भवति कृतं संपद्यते चरन्॥
चरैवेति। चरैवेति॥

A person is in *kali* (*yuga*) when sleeping (unconscious), in *dvapar* (*yuga*) when woke up (regaining consciousness), in *treta* (*yuga*) when stands up and in *krita* (*yuga*) when starts walking. Keep going! Keep going!!

Aitreya Brahmana

Modern Architect's view about vaastu is based on strong scientific principles, climatic conditions and human behaviour. There is no place for mystical vaastu recommendations in modern architecture. Location of plot and various rooms in the house are based on pragmatic fundamentals like the direction of sunrise with respect to the plot, and the direction of wind. In the old days, the wise learned people had to "mystify" these principles. They had to make it sound like real bad luck would fall upon the house owner in case he did not follow these principles.

According to the modern architect, best location for your bedroom is the south side as it gets the best winter sun and very little of the summer sun. Therefore, ideally your plot should face north because then public areas like drawing and dining are in the front. The west side is the hottest and therefore, it needs to be most insulated. Its driveway should be towards the east so that the morning sunrays enter into the house. The hot west side will have another plot adjoining it, with the neighbor's house insulating your wall because their driveway will be on the other side (i.e. their west side) as per the building bye-laws. Architects normally put toilets and stores on the west side to further insulate the house against heat. West side windows should be small while the other three cardinal directions can have large windows.

If you have a sufficiently big plot, leave setbacks (vacant spaces) all around the building and in the middle. In this way, it is possible to have a wraparound garden from the front to the back. Create a central atrium in the middle of the house. You can only construct on 50 percent of the ground and need to leave an open area in between. So it is possible to create a lawn in the middle of your house, which is also good vaastu wise. An empty space in the middle is not only scientific, but also brings good luck as claimed in vaastu shastra. It is termed brahamsthan which should be left open to the sky.

Magnetic Declination

Magnetic declination or variation is the angle on the horizontal plane between magnetic north (the direction the north end of a compass needle points, corresponding to the direction of the Earth's magnetic field lines) and true north (the direction along a meridian towards the geographic North Pole). Magnetic declination varies both from place to place and with the passage of time. By convention, declination is positive when magnetic north is east of true north, and negative when it is to the west. The lowercase Greek letter δ (delta) is frequently used as the symbol for magnetic declination.

Fig 7.1: Example of magnetic declination showing a compass needle with a "positive" (or "easterly") variation from geographic north. N_g is geographic or true north, N_m is magnetic north, and δ is magnetic declination.

The magnetic declination in a given area may (most likely will) change slowly over time, possibly as little as 2 to 2.5 degrees every hundred years or so, depending upon how far from the magnetic poles it is. For a location closer to the pole like Ivujivik, the declination may change by 1 degree every three years. A rough estimate of the local declination (within a few degrees) can be determined from a general isogonic chart of the world or a continent, such as that illustrated in figure 7.2. *Isogonic lines* shown in this chart are the lines on the earth's surface along which the declination has the same constant value and lines along which the declination is zero are called *agonic lines*.

To work with both true and magnetic bearings, the user of a simple compass needs to make simple calculations that take into account the local magnetic declination. The example below shows how you would convert a magnetic bearing (one taken in the field using a non-adjustable compass) to a true bearing (one that you could plot on a map) by *adding* the magnetic declination.

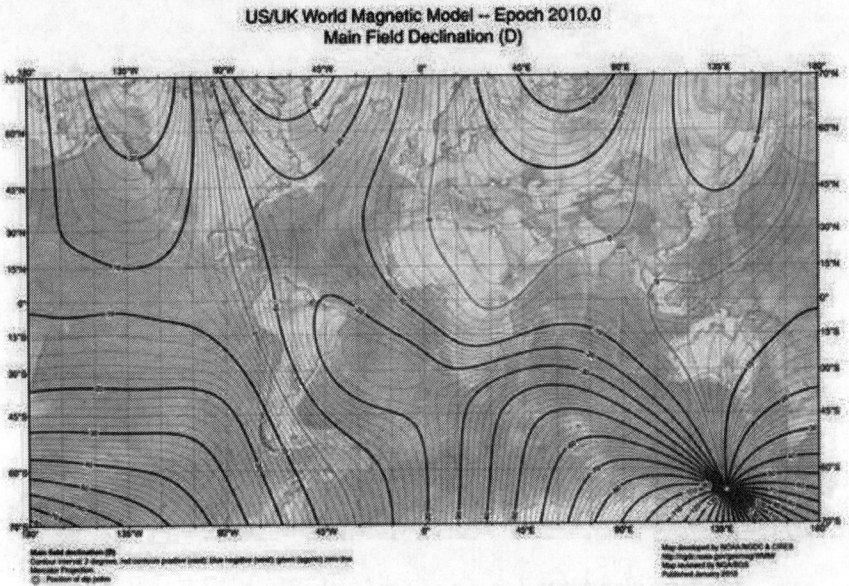

Fig 7.2: Isogonic Chart of the World

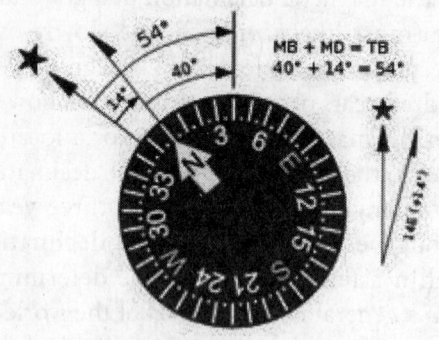

Fig 7.3: Converting a Magnetic Bearing to a True Bearing

In this example, the declination is 14°E (+14°) as the compass points to a "north" 14 degrees to the East of true North. To obtain a true bearing, add 14 degrees to the bearing shown by the compass: 40°+ (+14°) = 54°.

If, instead, the declination was 14°W (-14°), we would still "add" it to the magnetic bearing to obtain the true bearing: 40°+ (-14°) = 26°.

The opposite procedure is used in converting a true bearing to a magnetic bearing. With a local declination of 14°E, a true bearing (perhaps taken from a map) of 54° is converted to a magnetic bearing (for use in the field) by *subtracting* the declination: 54° - (+14°) = 40°. If, instead, the declination was 14°W (-14°), we would still "subtract" it from the true bearing to obtain the magnetic bearing: 26°- (-14°) = 40°.

Sun-Responsive Design

Sun path means the apparent significant seasonal and hourly positional changes of the sun (and length of daylight) as the earth rotates and orbits around the sun. The relative position of the sun is a major factor in the heat gain of buildings and in the performance of solar energy systems. Specific knowledge of sun path and climatic conditions is essential for economic decisions about orientation, landscaping and summer shading of buildings.

Sun paths at any latitude and any time of the year can be determined from basic geometry. The Earth's axis of rotation tilts about 23.5 degrees, relative to the plane of earth's solar system orbit around the sun. As the earth orbits the sun, this creates the 47 degree peak-to-peak solar altitude angle difference, and the hemisphere-specific difference between summer and winter.

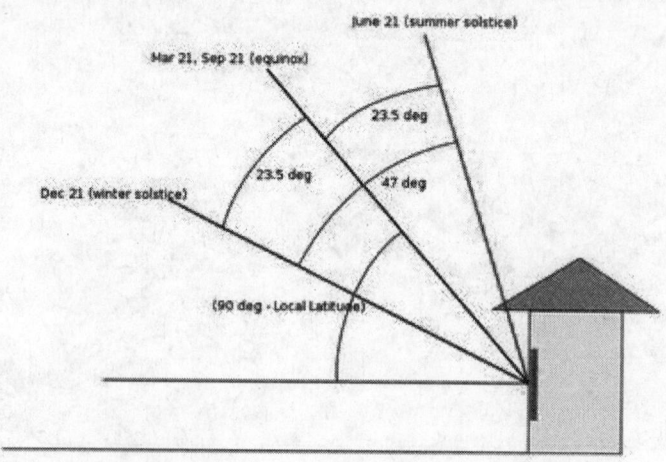

Fig 7.4: Solar Altitude over a Year for the Latitude of Delhi

Except for the poles, the sun rises due east and sets due west everywhere around the world during the equinoxes (March 20/21 and September 22/23). In the Northern Hemisphere, the equinox sun peaks in the southern half (about halfway up from the horizon at mid latitude) of the sky, while in the Southern Hemisphere, that sun peaks in the northern half of the sky.

When facing the equator, the sun appears to move from left to right in the Northern Hemisphere and from right to left in the Southern Hemisphere. The "equator side" of a building is south in the Northern Hemisphere, and north in the Southern Hemisphere, where the peak summer solstice solar altitude occurs on December 21.

In the moderate latitudes (between the circles and tropics, where most humans live), the length of the day, solar altitude and azimuth vary from one day to the next and from season to season. The difference between the length of a long summer day and a short winter day increases as one moves farther away from the equator.

On the northern hemisphere, both rise and set positions are displaced towards the north in summer, and towards the south for the winter track. Accordingly, sun lighted area on 21 June and 21 December at 30^0 North latitude is shown in figure 7.5.

On the southern hemisphere, both rise and set positions are displaced towards the south in summer, and towards the north for the winter track. Accordingly, sun lighted area on 21 June and 21 December at 30^0 South latitude is shown in figure 7.6.

In the Northern Hemisphere, the winter sun (December, January, February) rises in the south-east, peaks out at a low angle in the

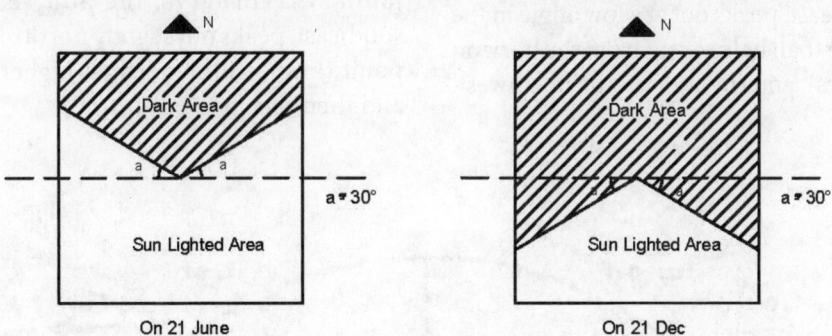

Fig 7.5: Sun lighted Area on 21 June and 21 Dec at 30^0 North Latitude

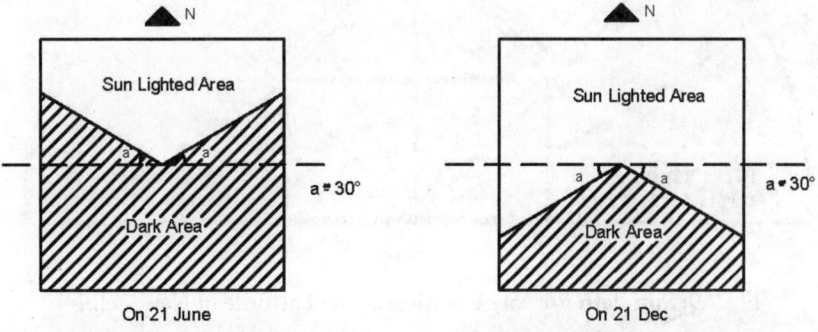

Fig 7.6: Sun lighted area on 21 June and 21 Dec at 30^0 South latitude

south (more than halfway up from the horizon in the tropics), and then sets in the southwest. It is on the south (equator) side of the house all day long. Vertical south-facing (equator side) window is excellent for capturing solar thermal energy.

There, the north-facing window would let in plenty of solar thermal energy to the house.

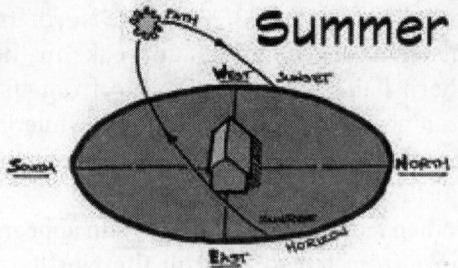

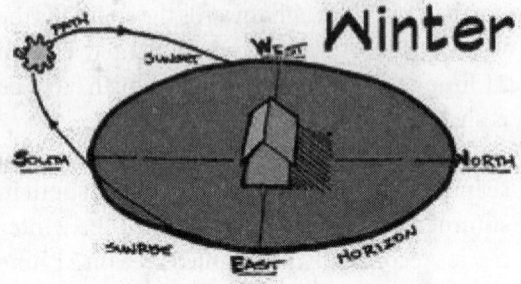

Fig 7.8: Sun's Path during Peak Summers in the Northern Hemisphere

Fig 7.7: Sun's Path during Peak Winters in the Northern Hemisphere

For comparison, the winter sun in the Southern Hemisphere (June, July, August) rises in the northeast, peaks out at a low angle in the north (more than halfway up from the horizon in the tropics), and then sets in the northwest.

In the Northern Hemisphere in summer (June, July, August), the Sun rises in the northeast, peaks out slightly south of overhead point (lower in the south at higher latitude), and then sets in the northwest, whereas in the Southern Hemisphere in summer (December, January, February), the Sun rises in the southeast, peaks out slightly north of overhead point (lower in the north at higher latitude), and then sets in the southwest.

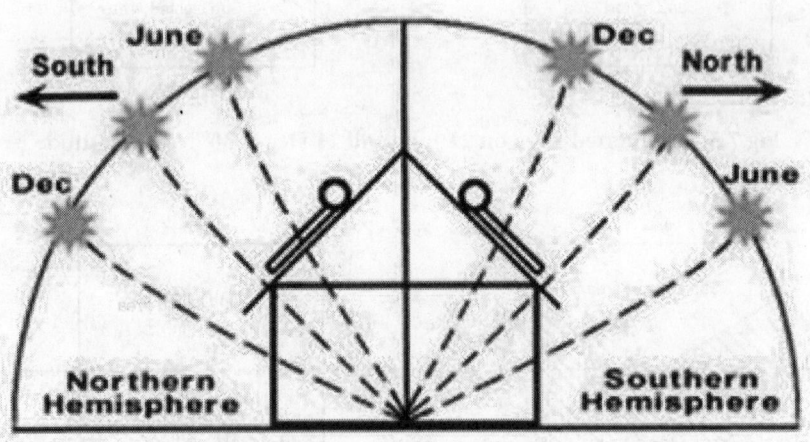

Fig 7.9: Sun Path for Any Location at the Latitude of New Delhi

The horizontal projections of the movement of Sun are called **sun path diagrams,** because the curves represent the sun paths on the 21st day of each month. Only seven sun paths are needed to represent all the 12 months because of the annual solar symmetry. The sun makes the same path across the sky dome on the 21st days of January and November, of February and October, of March and September, of April and August, and of May and July. Only the June 21 and Dec. 21 sun paths represent one day each. The altitude (vertical angle) and azimuth (horizontal angle) lines are also projected as concentric circles and radial lines respectively.

The major goal of sun-responsive design is to collect the sunrays in winters while rejecting the same in summers. To understand solar geometry in relation to building design, it will be assumed that the sun revolves around the building site as we see every day that the sun rises in the eastern sky and sets in the western sky. The sun path diagram shown in figure 7.10 is the horizontal projection of the sky dome shown for 32 degrees north latitude.

The sun path diagrams clearly show that the summer sun spends the whole morning in the eastern sky, the noon hours high overhead and the afternoon in the western sky. A simple latitude-dependent equator-side overhang can easily be designed to block 100 percent of the direct solar gain from entering vertical equator-facing windows on the hottest days of the year. Roll-down exterior shade screens, interior translucent / opaque window quilts,

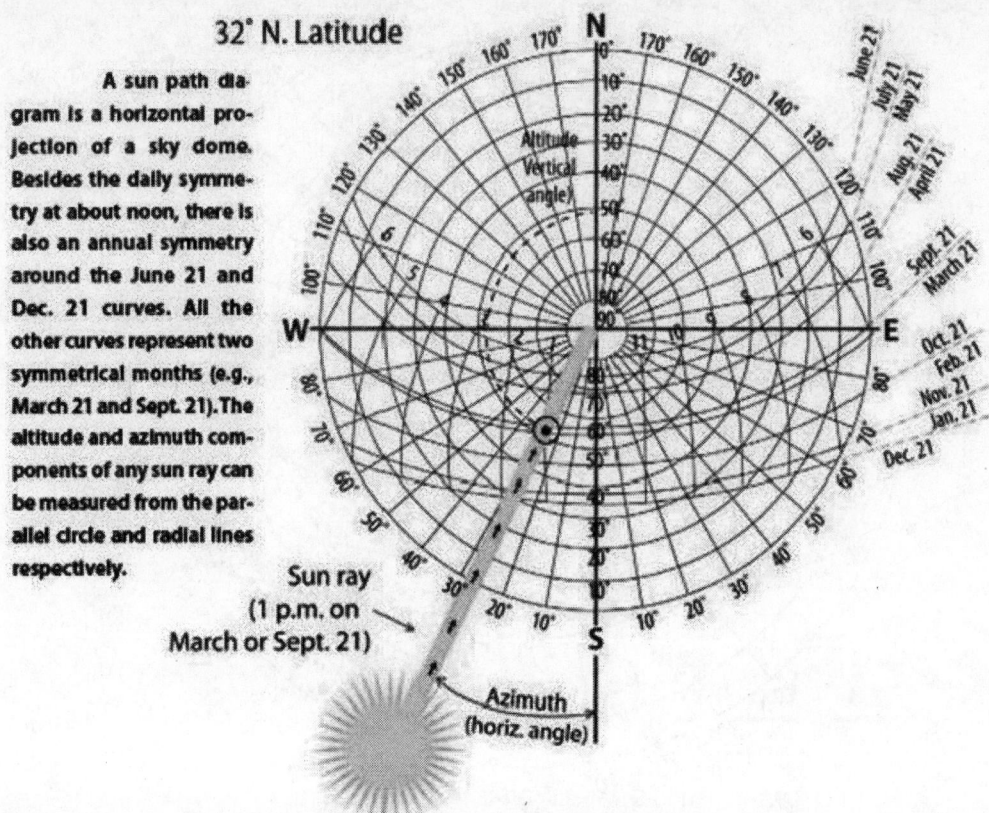

Fig. 7.10 : Sun Path Diagram at 32 Degree North Latitude

drapes, shutters, movable trellises etc can be used for hourly, daily or seasonal sun and heat transfer control (without any active electrical air conditioning).

Further, buildings must be designed to respond to the thermal year, not the solar year. Although Earth receives most solar heating on June 21, it is hottest in July/August. Because of the Earth's mass, it takes time for the Earth to heat up after the previous winter. Similarly, the Earth receives least solar heating on Dec. 21, but the coldest months are January and February, because it takes time for the Earth to cool down after the previous summer's heating. Thus, it is important to understand that although sun angles and the solar heating effect of the solar year are symmetrical about the insolation peak and low points of June 21 and Dec. 21 respectively, the resultant heating and cooling requirements of the thermal year do not correspond with these dates.

Because the thermal year is out of phase with the solar year, two sun path diagrams are necessary to show the relationship between the solar and thermal year. The diagram (for June 21–Dec. 21) shows the over-heated period ending on Sept. 21, and the diagram (for Dec. 21–June 21) shows the under-heated period ending on March 21. These diagrams also show how the hottest and coldest times are about one-and-a-half months after the days we get the most and least solar heating.

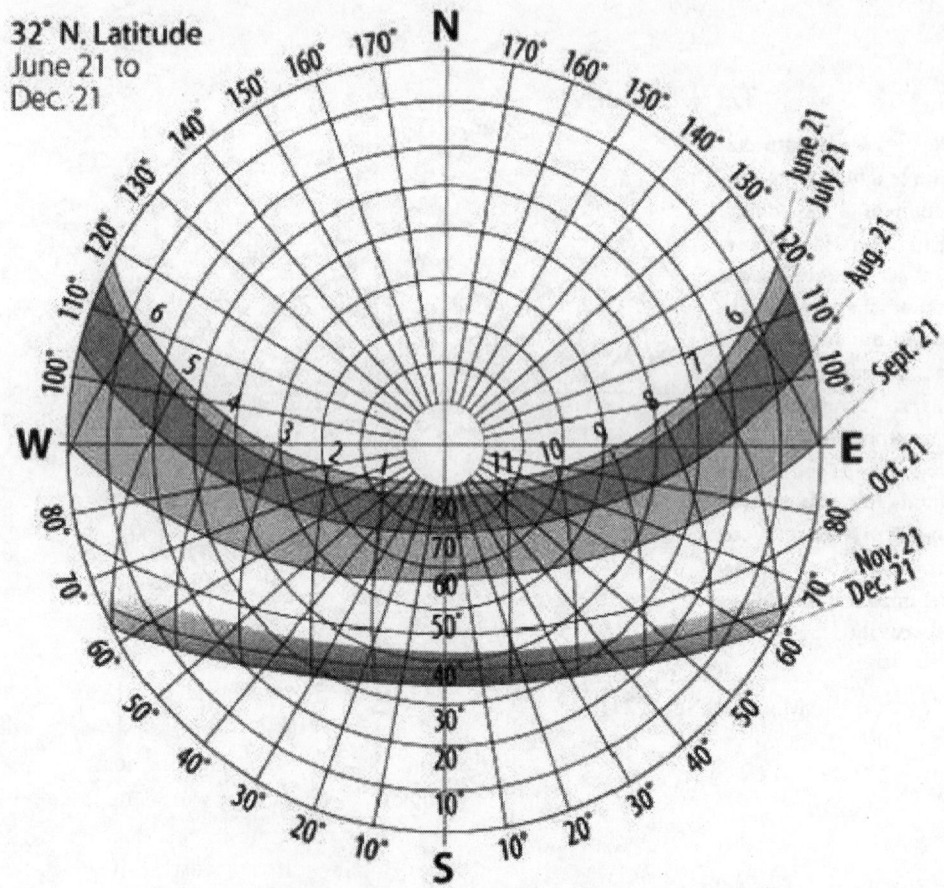

Fig 7.11: Sun's Path During June 21 to Dec 21 at 32° N Latitude

Modern Perspective of Vaastu

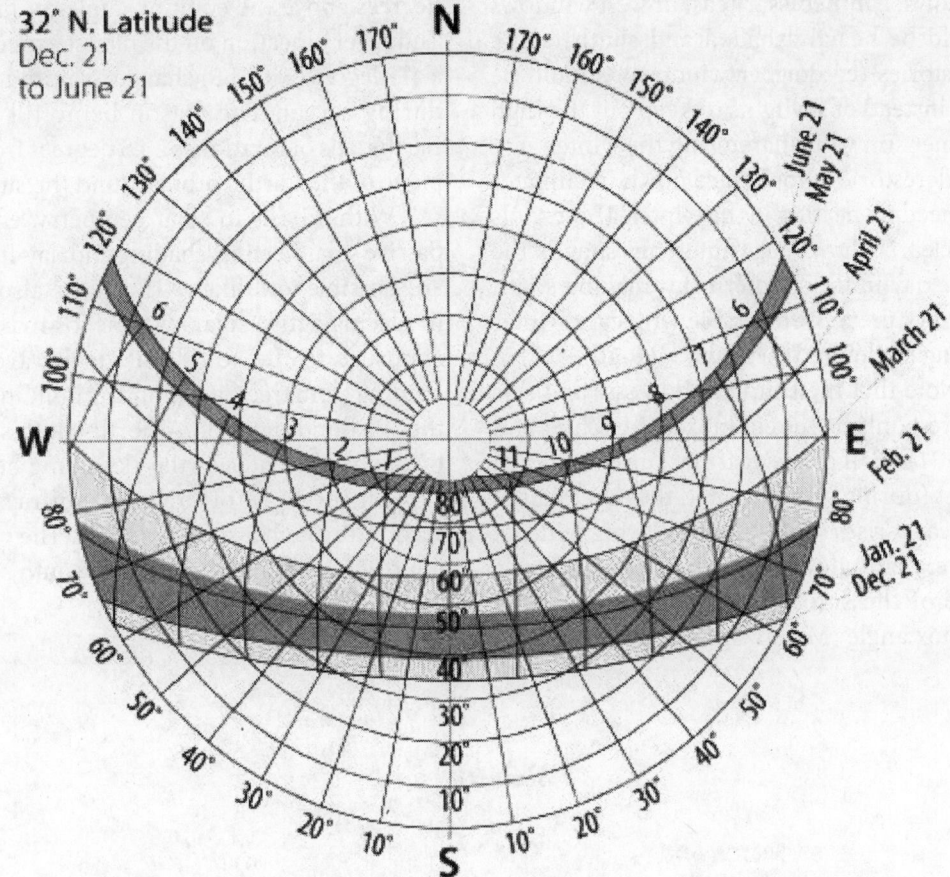

Fig 7.12: Sun's Path During Dec 21 to June 21 at 32° N Latitude

For this example, climate in which end of the over-heated period is about Sept. 21 and end of the under-heated period is about March 21, has been used. A somewhat colder climate would have the end of overheated period (summer) around Aug. 21 and the end of under-heated period (winter) around April 21 as sun makes the same path across the sky on both Aug. 21 and April 21.

Because the sun makes the same path across the sky on March 21 and Sept. 21, a fixed overhang can't let the sun enter a window on March 21 and keep it out on Sept. 21 as the sun angles are the same. As with the climate where we want full shade until Sept. 21 and full sun exposure until March 21, overhangs need to be able to change from full shading to full sun exposure in one day.

Unfortunately, fixed overhangs are unable to meet this goal. Since the daily changes in sun angles are small, it takes many months for a fixed overhang to go from full shading to full solar exposure. Consequently, there are many hot months when a fixed overhang does not shade sufficiently and many cold months when much of the valuable sunshine is blocked. Movable shutters, shades, shade screens, or window quilts can accommodate day-to-day and hour-to-hour solar gain and insulation requirements.

As a result, sun-responsive design should minimize east windows, skylights and west windows. Any necessary east or west windows should be heavily shaded and south-facing clerestories (eg dormer windows) should be used instead of skylights to keep out the high summer sun while harvesting the winter sun. The clerestories should face north in climates that need no heating in the winter. These tools also clearly show that winter sun spends the whole day in the southern sky, making south windows the most desirable wherever winter heating is required (see figure 7.9-10).

Note that the sun rises due east and sets due west only on the equinoxes (March 21 and Sept. 21). Half of the year the sun rises north of east (during summer), and the other half of the year it rises south of east (during winter). At every latitude at noon, the Dec. 21 altitude angle of the sun is 23.5 degrees below the equinox angle (March and Sept. 21) and 23.5 degrees above the equinox angle on June 21. Thus every location on the planet experiences a 47-degree (2 x 23.5) change in altitude angle during a year. The reason being tilt of the Earth's axis of rotation is 23.5 degrees from the plane of the Earth's orbit around the sun.

With a basis in solar geometry, effective passive solar heating, shading and day-lighting are possible and likely. This basis also helps in placing active solar systems for maximum exposure to the southern sun by avoiding shading from trees, neighboring buildings and the site building itself. A north-south section through the center of the sky dome helps to explain the logic of drawing sun rays on a section through a south window. The view in figure 7.13 is similar to a north-south section through a south-facing window.

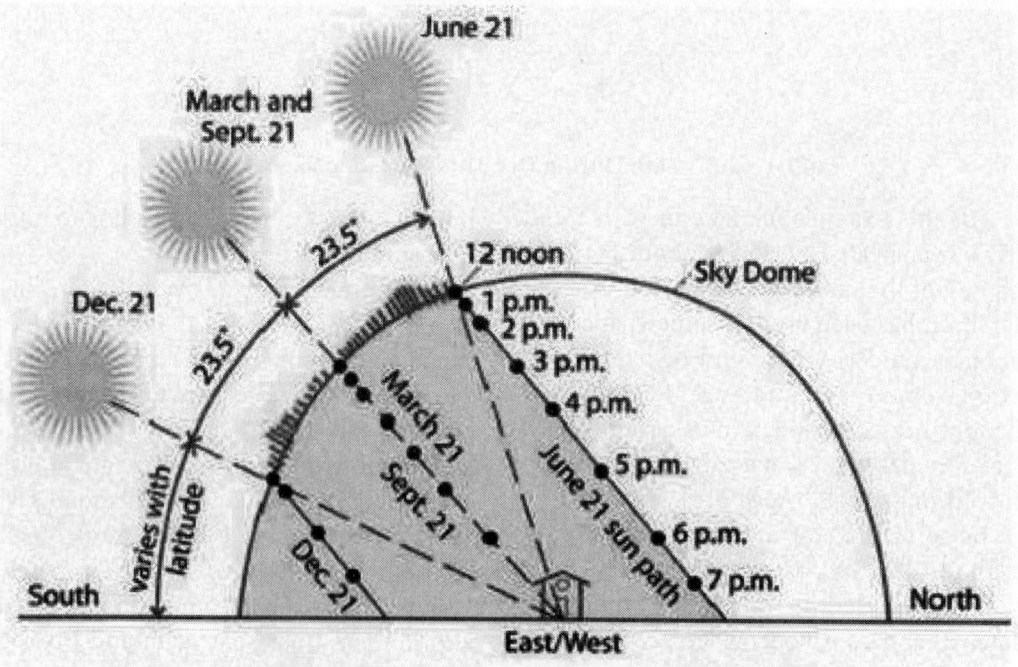

Fig 7.13: Sunray's Position during Different Times of the Year

Modern Perspective of Vaastu

Careful arrangement of rooms completes the passive solar design. A common recommendation for residential dwellings is to place living areas facing solar noon and sleeping quarters on the opposite side.

Building Orientation

Orientation of any building determines the amount of radiation it receives. Variations of solar radiation intensities on a horizontal surface and the vertical walls of different orientations are shown (see figure 7.14) in graphical form at the latitude of New Delhi (28.65 degree N).

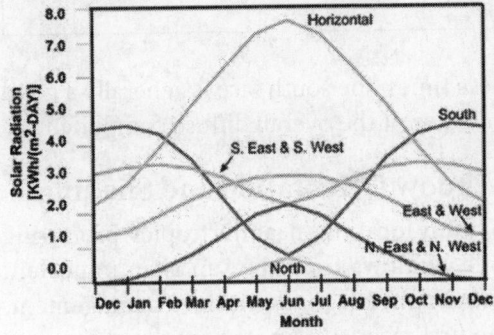

Fig 7.14: Solar Radiation in Various Directions

Accordingly, heat gained in June (hottest month) and December (coldest month) by the walls of eight directions in a nine sector vaastu are shown in figure 7.13. Heat received by the horizontal surfaces in June and December is around 7.7 Kwh/(m²-Day) and 2.2 Kwh/(m²-Day) respectively.

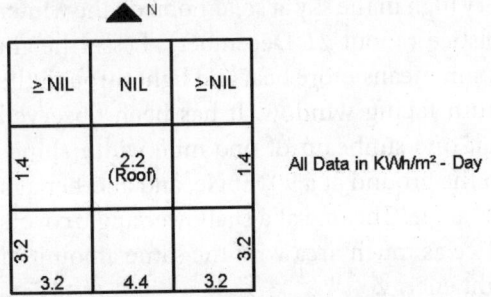

Fig 7.15 (a): Heat Gain in Dec by the Outer Walls and Roof

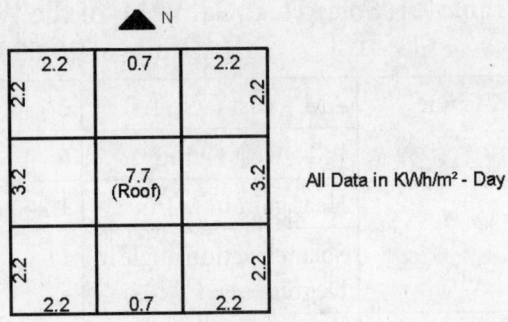

Fig 7.15 (b): Heat Gain in June by the Outer Walls and Roof

In most equatorial and tropical locations, but especially near the equator, the horizontal surface receives the greatest intensity. At the higher latitude, the wall facing the equator receives the next highest intensity in winter (when the sun is low) but it receives very little in summer. In the equatorial location, north and south walls receive the least intensity and that only for short periods of the year. East and west facing walls receive the second highest intensities in the equatorial location and consistently large intensities even at the higher latitude.

In the equatorial location, if solar heat gain is to be avoided, the main windows should face north or south. At the higher latitude, an orientation away from the equator would receive the least sunshine, but here it may be desirable to have some solar heat gain in winter, when the sun is low. So, an orientation towards the equator may be preferable. In both locations, only minor openings of unimportant rooms should be placed on the east and west side. Solar heat gain on the west side can be particularly troublesome as its maximum intensity coincides with the hottest part of the day. Solar heat gains per square metre of the wall area of the east and west facades at the latitude of 28.65 degree N (New Delhi) are given in Table 7.1.

Table 7.1: Solar Heat Gain / M² of the Wall Area of the East and West Facades at the Latitude of 28.65 Degree N (New Delhi)

21 June	AM – east facing	6	7	8	9	10	11	12
	PM - west facing	6	5	4	3	2	1	-
	Heat gain in MJ/m²	1.24	2.2	2.4	2.2	1.66	0.94	0.5
	Solar elevation angle in Degree	11	23	36	49	63	76	85
21 Dec	AM – east facing	6	7	8	9	10	11	12
	PM - west facing	6	5	4	3	2	1	-
	Heat gain in MJ/m²	0	0.12	1.84	2.02	1.56	0.78	0.29
	Solar elevation angle in Degree	0	1	13	23	31	37	39

It can be seen from this table that significant heat gain occurs between 0600 hrs to 1000 hrs on east walls, and between 1400 hrs to 1800 hrs on west walls when the sun is lower in the sky. Thus, east and west windows are the sources of solar heat gain and should therefore be either eliminated or reduced in size. It is also advised to place unconditioned spaces (garages, closets and other buffer places) in the east and west sides. Orientation for taking advantage of breezes in warm and humid climate and for prevention of hot winds in hot and dry climates is important but not as critical as orientation for solar heat control.

In summer, much more radiation falls on the horizontal surface than on the north face. This is because the sun is much higher in the sky, so that the angle of incidence favours the horizontal surface. The incident radiation on the east face in the morning and the west face in the evening is much greater than that on the north face during the middle of the day. The south face peaks in the morning and in the evening. This is because the sun rises and sets slightly south of east and west, providing a small direct component at these times. Outside these times, the south face is generally a good indicator of the overall diffuse component.

Window Orientation and Shading

In sunny locations near the tropics, protecting your windows from the sun is an important component of good window management. The first step is to know how the sun moves through the sky and to orient the building and place the windows in it so as to minimize direct solar admission through your windows.

In the northern hemisphere in summer, the sun rises north of due east and sets north of due west, climbing rather high in the sky at solar noon on the summer solstice (about 21 June). In the winter the sun rises south of due east and sets south of due west, climbing not very high in the sky at solar noon on the winter solstice (about 21 December). Lesser height of sun means more heat and light through the south facing window. It has been observed that one sunbeam of one mile width shines on the ground at a 90° angle, and another at a 30° angle. The one at a shallower angle covers twice as much area with the same amount of light energy.

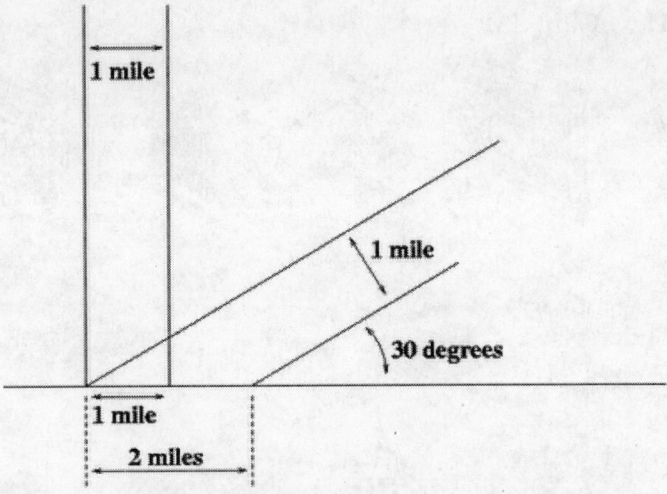

Fig 7.16: Effect of the Sunbeam Angle

Thus it is easy to protect south-facing windows with a roof overhang for all but the lowest winter sun. In climates with cool or cold winters, it might be desirable to allow some solar radiation into south-facing windows. So don't make your roof overhang too wide in such cases. However, it might be best in hot climates to make the overhang wide enough to block the midday winter sun year round.

North-facing windows hardly need any shading, since the only time the sun impinges on them is early in the morning or late in the afternoon in summer. At those times, the angle of incidence is so great that much of the radiation is reflected from the glass or blocked by the walls on either side of the window, especially if the window is recessed somewhat into the wall.

The biggest problems with solar heat gain and the glare which direct sun entry can produce are experienced with the windows facing east and west. The sun can be low enough in the sky in the middle of the morning and afternoon and only a very wide overhang can be effective. In such cases it is best to block the sun outside, before it reaches the glass, using tress, awnings, shutters, or other shading methods (see figure 7.17).

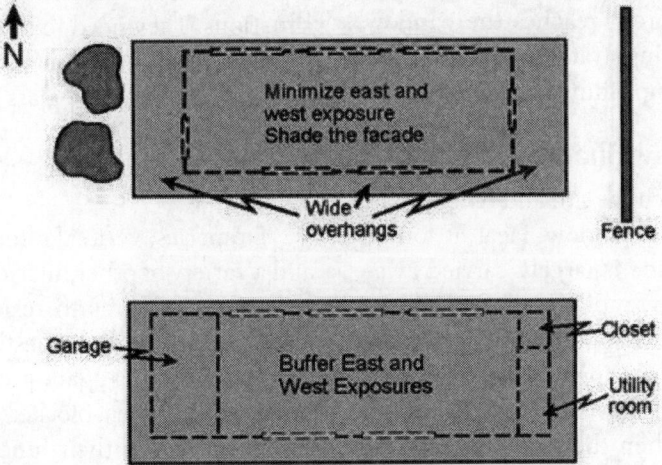

Fig 7.17: Protecting Eastern and Western Sides (Externally and Internally)

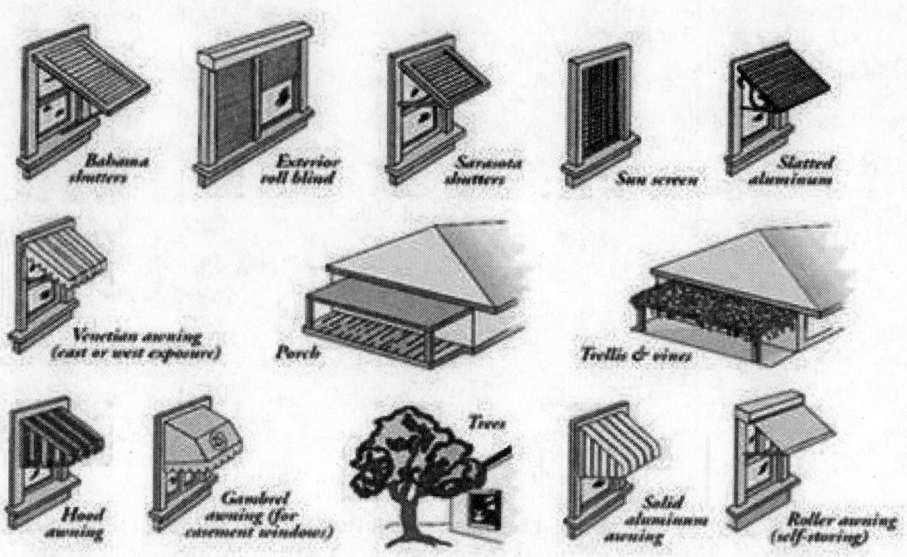

Fig 7.18: Variety of Shading Strategies

Another alternative, illustrated in the drawing, is to reduce the glazed areas in the building facing the east and west directions and/or to place unoccupied or non air conditioned spaces on the east and west sides of the building, to serve as buffering or insulating zones (see figure 7.17).

Both interior and exterior shade options can be used to protect windows not otherwise shaded from the sun. In general it is best to block the sun before it reaches the window. The variety of shading strategies shown below is effective at accomplishing that goal.

Exterior Window Shading

Exterior shades catch the sun and reflect some of it away from the window. Heat absorbed by the exterior shade is largely carried away from the window by radiation and air borne convection currents. For otherwise un-shaded east-facing windows, operable shades are a real advantage, because they can be lowered in the morning when the sun is rising, yet raised when the sun is on the other side of the building, thereby affording unobstructed views to the east. The same is true of west-facing windows in the afternoon. Some exterior shades serve a secondary window protection function. They can be lowered to fully cover the window and protect it from wind-blown debris or other consequences of adverse weather.

Interior Window Shading Strategy

Interior shades can also be effective in some situations. They need to be brightly reflecting toward the outside, so that solar radiation admitted through the glass is reflected by the shade back out through the window. Thus little of the sun's radiant heat can remain inside the building.

Draperies, vertical blinds, roll up shades, and a variety of other interior attachments are common additions to residential windows. They are used more for aesthetics and privacy than for solar heat gain prevention, but they can be effective heat blockers just the same. The key to success in their function is their *solar reflectance* on the window-facing side. You can have any colour and pattern you want for the room-side of the shade, but it should be quite bright on the other side. White or near-white is best.

Interior shades are more effective at reflecting solar radiation if the glazing system they cover is highly transparent, but they will reflect whatever beam radiation they receive back toward the window. Some of that radiation will transmit through the window and therefore not enter the room as heat gain.

An important advantage of interior shades is that they are operable. They can be opened or closed or partially open, to suit your needs and the degree of solar radiation incident on the window. For instance, with west-facing windows you can have your shades wide open for maximal view and daylight illumination in the morning, when the sun is on the East side of the building, and close them in the afternoon when the sun shines strongly on the window during the hottest part of the day. If you are not installing new windows, or replacing old ones, and your interior shades are inadequate, you may like to consider adding applied window films.

Sunlight

Sunlight is believed to have anti-carcinogenic properties. The 'sunshine vitamin' helps prevent multiple deadly diseases including cancer. Although we get some Vitamin D from foods such as fatty fish, milk and eggs, around 90 per cent of it is generated in the skin by ultraviolet light from the sun. Researchers of Melbourne Pathology have found that non-availability of proper sunlight is a major cause of Type II diabetes as such patients lack sufficient amount of Vitamin D. Inadequate amount of sunlight and Vitamin D also causes cancer.

American researchers have found that sun's 'medium wave ultraviolet (UVB)' light reduces danger of lung cancer. Rate of lung cancer have been found more in the countries which are away from the equator as these places receive lesser amount of UVB light. Researchers at the University of Toronto have suggested that women who spend an average of three hours a day in the sunshine can reduce the risk of developing breast cancer by half. Laboratory tests suggest that breast cells are capable of converting vitamin D obtained from sunlight to a hormone that has anti-cancer properties.

Hygiene and comfort can be provided in our homes by ensuring adequate daylight. Daylight, in addition to saving energy, also improves productivity and health in schools, offices and any other workplaces. Natural sunlight leads to balanced physical and mental development of a person. It can cure diseases like obesity, arthritis, and osteoporosis. Person enjoying natural sunlight remains safe from Parkinson disease.

According to a report 'andhere se beemari, roshni se ilaaj', published in the Hindi daily "Navbharat Times" on 4th September 2006, sunlight is medicine itself while darkness causes diseases. Professor George C Bernard working in the Neurology Department of Jefferson Medical College Philadelphia in USA has conducted a deep study regarding the role of light in influencing the nature and temperament of the human beings. He presented his report in the International Lighting Technology Conference.

According to him, people working in shifts for a longer time or working in call centres in odd hours, may easily be affected by Seasonal Affective Disorder (SAD) leading to depression. SAD is prevalent in areas receiving lesser amount of sunlight. Sunlight influences our way of thinking, thinking capacity itself and also our mood. He further advises that while designing our homes and offices, we should keep in mind that the incoming sunlight should be comfortable and soothing to our eyes. Its extra heat should be absorbed by the building as more than 80 percent of people around the world work in the buildings.

Good day-lighting allows electric lights to be dimmed or turned off completely during the day. The benefits of daylight are substantially diluted when employees inadvertently turn on the lights or forget to turn them off when there is adequate daylight. It should be ensured that the incoming daylight works with other building systems as HVAC and electric lighting and not against them. To reap the benefits of day-lighting, investment in appropriate window systems, shading and electric lighting control is a must.

The amount of daylight received by any premises depends on the position and intensity of sun, cloud cover, shading from the nearby trees, and other surrounding buildings. The doors, windows, ventilators and skylights shall specifically be designed to capture daylight. Windows provide visual relief, connection with nature, time orientation, possibility of ventilation and emergency outlet. Windows can be supplemented with top lights, separating view window from the daylight aperture.

There are three sources of daylight: direct sun or sky components, exterior reflected components, and the internal reflected components. Exterior reflected components are mainly ground surface, pavements, adjacent buildings, wide window sills and objects. Once the daylight enters the room; the surrounding walls, floor surface and the ceiling act as light reflectors. Daylight can also be made to bounce around the room and reduce the extreme brightness contrast by using high reflectance paints or surfaces in the ceiling. High reflectance paints and tiles with reflectance value of 90 or more are easily available in the market.

Different elements contribute to the generation of diffused light in the following manner: ceiling (more than 80 percent), walls (50 to 70 percent), floors (20 to 40 percent) and furnishings (25 to 45 percent). Daylight can be troublesome if it is not handled sensitively or designed properly. It can cause glare. It may also increase the consumption of energy in the building, even in the worst possible times especially during the summers. Daylight is designed in such a way so that it allows in just the right amount of light and doesn't increase the load on air-conditioning.

In order to distribute daylight properly; the quality approaches like glazing and shading systems, daylight harvesting instruments and devices like light shelves and solar sensors need to be considered. A room with higher ceiling compared to its depth gives deeper penetration of daylight whether from side lighting windows, or from top lighting, skylights and clerestories. Deeper penetration and even illumination in a room can also be achieved by increasing the window height.

The higher the top of the window above the floor level, the deeper the light penetrates into the room. Larger the window size relative to the floor area, higher is the day light factor (DF). The overall quality and quantity of daylight within a room is affected by reflectance of internal wall surfaces and relative contrast at the windows. To reduce the peak daylight contributions, high performance skylight designs incorporate reflectors or prismatic lenses.

We can learn much about various aspects of the daylight from the historical buildings. These buildings have wider openings on the interior walls and reduced openings on the exterior walls. Diagonal walls erected for privacy in front of the doors and windows also help in avoiding the glare. Higher levels of ceilings create a pool of reflected and diffused light. Aesthetically pleasing jaali work in marble or sandstone has been used in most of the traditional buildings with Persian origin including the Taj Mahal as well as in the havelis of Rajasthan.

Jaali work was used to filter daylight as per the need of particular space. These openings are well designed to cut off the harsh sun on the one side and make maximum use of the daylight for the interior spaces on the other side. These jaali windows are particularly important when sunrays fall directly on the light coloured white marble floor, while walls and the sheen of light become glare. Modern buildings can make use of the shading devices to help keep flexibility in lighting needs.

Skylights and roof lights fixed or operable can be used. The courtyard admits, absorbs and reflects the daylight according to its proportions and surface colours. Light coloured surfaces diffuse daylight to the surrounding arcades and spaces. A substantial amount of reflected light is cast onto walls and ceilings of the arcade when the courtyard floor is very light in colour.

Atrium (Light Well)

Fig 7.19: An Atrium in a Mall

The atrium or light well is a core lighting technique used commonly in modern multi-storeyed buildings. Atrium, which is open or semi covered from the top, can be called the modern version of classical brahamsthan. Light wells are generally constructed with their height to width ratio of 2:1. The centre of the building is opened up with a glazed element at the top. The centre receives diffused light from the atrium whilst the outer perimeter is lit with windows.

Skylights

Skylights and roof windows can provide interior building spaces with the warmth and brightness of natural daylight. Versatile engineering thermoplastics have been introduced as polycarbonate sheets which can be used for glazing and covering skylights. These sheets can optimize the light coming through a building's skylight and thus control the heat too. Polycarbonate sheets can be used to create a variety of designs.

Plastic glazing is usually inexpensive and less liable to break than most other glazing materials. Acrylics and polycarbonates are the most commonly used materials in this type of skylight. Acrylics cost less but are weaker than polycarbonates. Though polycarbonates offer high impact resistance, some get yellow with age. Their surfaces scratch easily; they become brittle and get discoloured over time. Many plastics allow the entry of ultraviolet (UV) rays in, unless their glazing is coated with a special film. This may cause the furnishings to fade.

Glass skylights are generally more expensive and much harder. These are durable than plastic and does not discolour. Glass used for skylights must have the safety tag. Skylights are often made with tempered glass on the exterior and a laminated pane on the interior. It gives maximum impact resistance protecting occupants from the falling shards of glass.

Some skylights can be thrown open for ventilation while others are fixed. Larger skylights that can be used as doors are sometimes called 'roof windows'. These are always located within a few feet of the door. A building ventilated through a skylight opening releases hot air that gets accumulated near the ceiling. Skylights usually open outwards at the bottom, some more than others. Some units vent through a small hinged panel. They may be opened manually with a pole, chain or crank.

Location of a skylight is of primary consideration to maximize the natural lighting and passive solar heating potential. North facing skylights on the roof allow sunlight to filter in keeping the room cool. Skylights on the east facing roofs provide maximum sunlight and solar heat in the morning. West facing skylights allow sunlight in the evening to filter in. South facing skylights allow the sunlight to filter in throughout the day making the room too hot in summers. It can be prevented by installing the light in the shade of deciduous (leaf shedding) trees. You may also add a movable shading device like louvers, shades or awnings on inside or outside of the skylight. A solar control film with a solar heat gain rating can also be used.

The tilt or slope of the skylight also influences room temperature to a large extent. A low slope admits relatively more solar heat in summers and less in the winters, exactly opposite of the desired result.

Clerestory window

It is a vertical glazing which is located high on an interior wall. A south facing clerestory produces higher daylight illumination than the north facing one. East and west facing clerestories have potential for high heat gains. Wherever possible, diffusing material should be used to provide even distribution of light while avoiding the glare. Roof lights with a minimum of 10 percent of the floor area can lit up the area sufficiently when any building space is more than six metres away from the nearest window. Hence, these are particularly useful in big size workshops and factories.

Awnings

Awnings are modern version of sunshades. In Vedic Astrology, Rahu governs shade and therefore awnings too. Awnings are high rated shading devices because they block the direct sunlight. Forty percent of unwanted heat enters through the windows. Excessive heat can be blocked out by using awnings. You can cut off heat before it enters your home through windows. An awning creates an elegant atmosphere when you entertain in the evening. It can create a pleasant indoor climate. Awnings can be retracted for the sun in cold winters when extra heat is welcome.

Fig 7.20: An Elegantly Designed Door Awning

Awnings can dramatically enhance the appearance of your home or any other premise. Aesthetically, an awning mounted at an angle of 45 degrees is pleasing to the eye. It also lowers the bills incurred on air-conditioning. Awnings can lower the indoor temperatures by as much as 15 degrees and reduce sunlight with its glare by as much as 94 percent. They can reduce the heat entering the house by as much as 80 percent. The AC cooling becomes up to 15 percent more effective. Fabric awnings block up to 77 percent of the sun's direct heat, lowering the interior temperature between 8 to 15 degrees.

You can expand your outdoor living space and add value to your home without extra construction by using awnings. Your furniture and carpets are protected from fading. Awnings add beauty to any façade as they are available in a galaxy of fabrics in most enchanting colour combinations which brighten up the entire exterior space. Canvas awnings stop the heat on the outside of your building without obstructing the view. They are usually made of fabric, attached above the window, extended outward and down. A light coloured awning also reflects the sunlight. Different types of awnings are available for terraces and windows. Tunnel awnings are also available for Porsche.

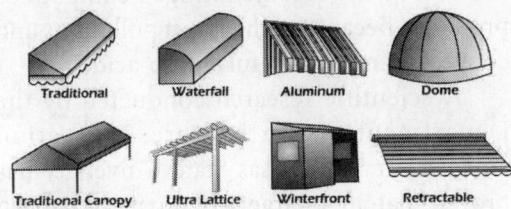

Fig 7.21: Different Shapes of Awnings

Motorized retractable awnings combine beauty with functionality. You can control light and shade at the touch of a button. You may cool any deck, patio, terrace or balcony on demand. It can retract against the façade of your home when sun shading is not required. It will be out of the way when you want it to be on a cloudy day or at dusk allowing light to enter the room. These awnings come with wall switch. The electric motors are fully contained within the roller tube of a retractable awning. It provides a clean and concealed installation that blends right into the lines of your home. They can count on their automatic sun and wind sensors when home owner is away. You can control it from any location inside your home or outside with a hand held transmitter. You can move from sun to shade by merely pressing a transmitter button.

Artificial Lights

Artificial lights can successfully be used in business to attract Goddess Lakshami. Hongkong attracts a large number of tourists; four times of its own population on an average. Its tourism industry was devastated in 2003 due to the worldwide diseases like SARS pneumonia and bird flu. To attract the tourists again, Hongkong administration started a grand laser show named 'symphony of lights' on 18th January 2004 which popularized it as 'city of thousand lights'. Every night, thousands of lights scattered throughout the city dance at 8 pm, through a computer guided programme.

Thus Hongkong celebrates Diwali on every night. These dancing lights have attracted back the tourists on a large scale. Also, Hongkong has branches of USA based Disneyland and London based 'Madam Tussad wax museum'. It organizes events on such a large scale for the tourists that it is also being called the 'events capital of the world'.

Colours

Colours not only define our mood and emotions, they also reflect our personality and image. We call someone who is gloomy as being in the "blue", while "red" denotes activity and anger. North facing home receives diffused cool light in an indirect manner. Warm colours like red, orange and dark yellow are good in such places. East facing areas in the home are good if painted with green or blue colour. South receives maximum light and heat of sun throughout the day. Hence it should be painted in cool colours like indigo and blue. West is the direction of setting sun. White, off white and other light colours are good here. Research conducted at Washington State University suggests that people in rooms with a lot of greenery can tolerate more physical pain than others. Orange is known as the most irritating colour to the eyes. It gets noticed in a stack of mail or in a crowd of vehicles.

Trees and Plants

Trees symbolize life, progress and fortune. They signify independence and a strong will to survive. Planting Ashoka trees helps in avoiding the natural calamities, anxiousness and other unfavorable circumstances. Any religious place, cremation ground or a hospital located in front of the house is not considered auspicious. Planting a row of auspicious trees in front of the house can rectify this defect. Giant trees near the windows prevent sun's rays from entering. Absence of sunlight in the house or office can cause diseases. The house owner or worker is more likely to struggle for progress in life.

A report was published in the Hindi daily "Navbharat Times" on 13th October 2008 regarding a study conducted by the Texas State University which revealed that office employees feel more satisfied and happy in a green and open environment. It concluded that company management can increase the satisfaction level of employees just by changing the office environment towards the greener side. People working in offices having open windows and green plants were mostly found satisfied with their work. A greener and better environment at office was also found helpful in improving their quality of life.

According to the Japanese scientists, plants not only brighten your room but they also absorb toxic gases present there. Researchers used genetically engineered plants that can absorb formaldehyde, a pungent chemical compound used as adhesive in building materials and furnishings. Formaldehyde is considered a major factor in what is known as sick building syndrome - headaches, dizziness and other health problems triggered by improper ventilation and chemical substances in the home.

Prefer keeping healthy and selected auspicious potted plants in your room if illnesses are common in the family. Scientists expect these plants to absorb the chemical formaldehyde steadily, along with carbon dioxide for photosynthesis. These plants have two kinds of genes imported from micro-organisms known as methylotrophs which use formaldehyde for their growth.

Trees and plants not only reduce the environmental pollution but they also destroy harmful substances produced by the pollution. The study conducted in this regard by Paul Shepstone and his associates of Perdue university of America has been published in the Geographical Research Letters. Trees can imbibe Organic Nitrate through their leaves and can convert it into nitrogen. It means trees can absorb the organic nitrogen compounds produced because of the forest pollutants and convert them into useful amino-acids.

A scientific research conducted by the Department of Horticulture, Recreation and Forestry of Kansas State University has proved that after surgery of a patient, a deep connection with nature and greenery not only reduces tensions but also helps in avoiding pains. Plants and flowers have very positive effect on the patients recovering from stomach surgery like appendicitis. Patients recovering in rooms having healthy plants required lesser amount of pain killers. Their BP and heart rate also remained normal. It means a greener environment is must in the hospitals for the patients recovering from surgery. Patients should also get involved with the plants by watering and caring them. Gardening itself is a medicine in disguise.

Ecology can be regulated as per the requirements of architecture. Eco-architecture is being used for a long time in America, Australia and Israel to adjust the size and shape of plants and their branches. The science of regulating the tree size is called 'aerial rule development'. The stem of some special species of plants doesn't become hard when they are grown in the air rather than in the soil and water. In this technique, roots are grown in the desired shape with the help of a metal frame rather than moulding the branches. Trees can be converted into useful structures with the help of this technique. Later on, these trees are used for different purposes including the furniture.

Technical experts of Tel Aviv University and a company named Plantware are working on the possibility of growing such trees and plants whose shapes can be adjusted according to the requirements of a developing city. The purpose is to use trees for erecting a bus stop or developing a structure on the playground without putting much labour on the shape and size of trees. In future, this technique may help in construction of complete home in an eco-friendly manner. An architect of MIT has developed such a house where not only the green design has been used but the complete home behaves as a live eco-system like a tree. The basic framework of this house has been developed based on the 'pleating technique' used in horticulture.

Israeli scientists have found that medicine prepared from the essence of tomato is very helpful in curing high blood pressure. It also reduces dangers related to prostate cancer and heart diseases. Indian scientists have found that in Indian condition, mustard oil is far superior for heart than any other oil. Linolenic acid found in the mustard oil works as an anti-cancer agent. It has been considered even better than the olive oil in some matters. We should prefer using mustard oil without processing it.

In case of space scarcity, you may choose to keep a terrarium or bottle garden. It looks beautiful like an aquarium. It is specially designed for those houses which lack sufficient space for lawn or even a balcony garden. Terrarium is a mini environment where plants can be kept healthy in scanty space. Its size may vary from a two litre capacity bottle to a fish tank of three gallon capacity. It could be open or closed at the top. Brandy glasses, big bottles, fish tanks and ceramic bowls can be used for this purpose. Terrarium designed on a particular theme looks like a planned decorative piece, not just a lump of plants. Some good ideas can be desert theme, rainforest theme and magical theme. Terrariums should properly be taken care of like the indoor plants. Availability of natural light and water should be ensured.

Trees should be carefully planned and planted in streets and open spaces to take advantage of shade as well as sunshine without obstructing the smooth flow of natural wind. Trees have great ability to abate glare and provide cool or warm pockets in the developed areas. Some trees shed leaves in winter while retaining thick foliage in summer. Such trees are very useful by allowing sun during winter and blocking it effectively in summer, particularly where building is exposed to sunrays towards south and west.

Energy Efficient Design

Generally houses are not designed to be energy efficient. We should look for energy efficient design while planning to purchase or construct or relocate to a new house. The aim of energy management is to contain or reduce energy costs through conservation or substitution. Conservation involves reducing the waste and improving the efficiency of energy use. Energy substitution involves replacing expensive and scarce fuels with the cheaper and more readily available ones.

Typical household electricity consumption pattern is lighting (20-30%), air-conditioners during summers (50-75%), water heating during winters (30-40%), room heating during winters (30-50%), well-designed refrigerators (10%), television (5%) and irons and other miscellaneous gadgets (less than 5-15%). This percentage of consumption share mainly depends on lifestyle, family size and number of hours for which each item is utilized.

A properly designed house should provide ample sunlight during the daytime. The energy consumption during daytime should be zero. Energy requirements for cooling (air-conditioning) and heating can also be reduced drastically by using proper construction material and fixing of windows in the right directions. Solar energy can also be harnessed for multiple uses.

People are using some form of energy when they turn on a switch, use any machinery or turn on the ignition. People usually use remote to switch off the electric and electronic gadgets but it is not really switched off. It rather goes in the standby mode. Your electricity bill can increase at least 25 percent if you keep your TV, computer, set top box, printer and other such gadgets on the standby mode rather than completely switching them off. Digital electricity meters installed in Delhi record even the slightest load consumption.

Zero watt electric bulbs available in the market are actually of 12 watts. It means they consume 12 watt electricity when switched on. Electricity consumed by a mosquito repellent is 10 watts. Mobile charger takes 5 watts load, voltage stabilizer 25 watts and UPS inverter 40 watts. A compact audio system consumes 27 watts of electricity when on the standby mode. Likewise DVD player (including CD and VCD) consumes 12 watts, microwave oven 6 watts, cable set top box 25 watts, inkjet printer 5 watts and TV 22 watts when switched off but kept on the standby mode. Make it a habit to switch off these gadgets manually, when not in use.

Ensure that lamps are off when not in use. Clean the light fixtures periodically as some light is lost through dirt deposits on lights.

Ensure that there is no leakage through doors and windows in air-conditioned areas. It saves a substantial amount of energy over the long run.

Energy consumption can be reduced up to 30 percent with the installation of lighting controls like photo sensors, timers and dimmers.

Use sunlight as it provides excellent colour rendering. It is often preferred by employees and it comes free. Studies suggest that employee productivity is better in natural lighting than in the artificial lights. However, it can be a nuisance without glare control. Workers working near windows, when provided a manual dimmer, can save up to one third of energy just be dimming lights down to the level they want.

Choose proper colour and surface finish for obtaining maximum reflection or absorption of heat energy. Requirement of AC in summers can be reduced by using properly designed fans and humidity controllers. To reduce the energy consumption, look for experts and ask for an energy audit of your facility.

Use public transport or walk on foot at least twice a week. Work from home, if possible. Pool a car with your friends or colleagues. Prefer a train than a plane.

Consume regional and seasonal grains, fruits and vegetables as far as possible. Go green as far as possible and prefer the organic items. It saves huge amount of energy used in transportation and shipping industry and thereby reduces pollution.

Solar Geysers

Hot water is required for domestic, commercial and industrial purposes. Among the non-conventional methods of water heating, solar water heating system is the most techno-economically feasible solution. Earth receives about 150 billion megawatts of solar energy per second which is around 16,000 times the

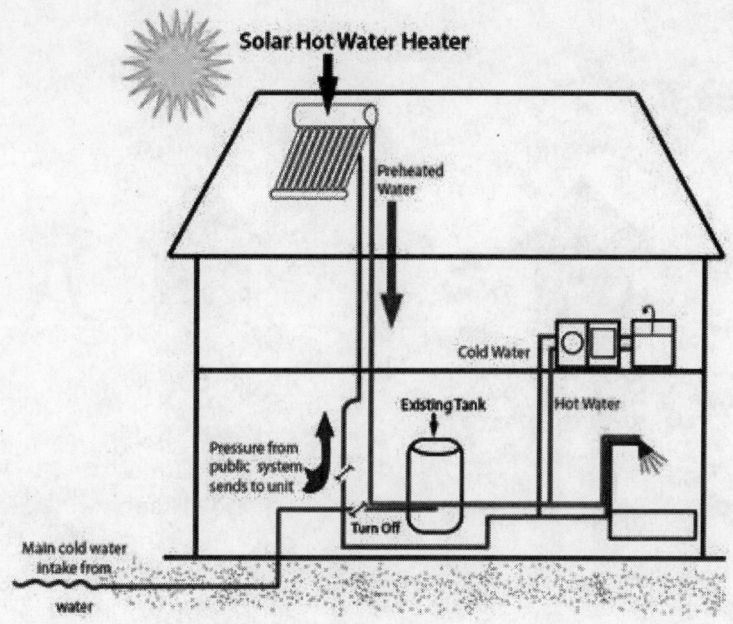

Fig 7.22: Working of the Solar Geyser

global energy consumption. Basic requirement for solar water heating system is the availability of unobstructed solar radiation and provision to adjust the inclination of the collector to receive maximum solar radiation. Solar energy is widely available in India as we have about 325 clear sunny days. South direction receives maximum solar radiation throughout the year.

Hot water produced by the solar heating system during the day is stored in an insulated storage tank. Thus water heated during the previous day remains hot and can be used in the next morning. This system prevents pollution, protects against inflation in the fuel costs, and saves against the possible reduction in peak electricity load. If solar water heating system is used in the present conditions for year round use, it could pay back in 2-3 years against electricity, in 3-5 years against oil and in 4-6 years against coal. However, this system may not produce sufficient hot water during monsoons and cloudy days. Thus electrical back up is required during these days.

Solar water heating system can easily be adopted in hospitals and nursing homes, hotels, lodges and guest houses, hostels of schools and colleges, training centres, barracks of armed forces; paramilitary forces and police, and individual residential buildings having more than 150 square metre plinth area.

Geothermal Energy

Geothermal system cuts heating and cooling costs by 60 percent. In this process, non-polluting water-glycol solution is pumped around 150 feet (50 m) deep into the bedrock. Geothermal heat pumps use the stable ground temperature for heating and cooling the home. According to the experts, geothermal systems can save 30 to 70 percent on home heating and 20 to 50 percent on home cooling costs over the conventional systems. But the initial installation costs are very high.

A geothermal heat exchanger system consists of indoor heat pump equipment, a ground loop and a flow center to connect

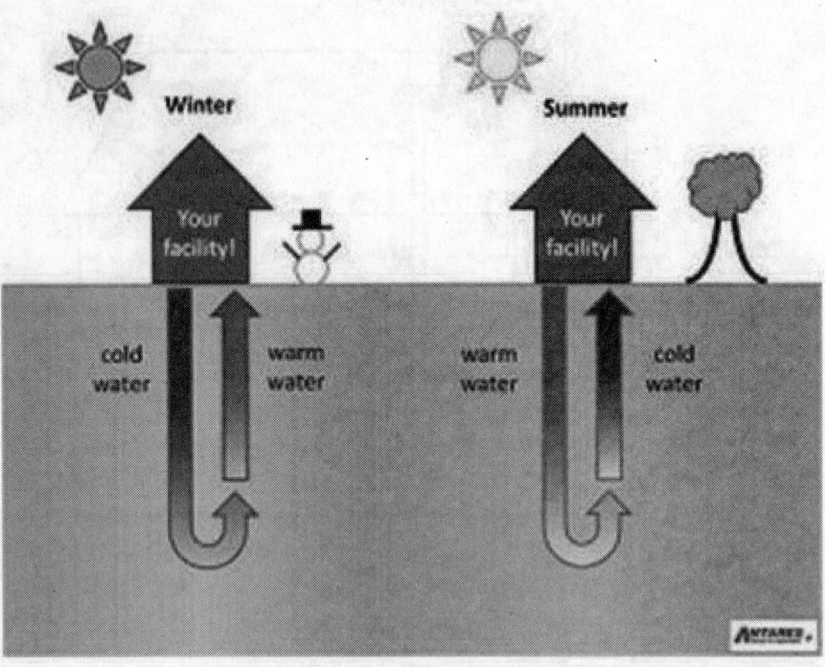

Fig 7.23: Geothermal Heat Exchanger System

the indoor and outdoor equipment. The ground loop geothermal system uses constant temperature of the ground or water several feet underground. Pipes are buried to a depth below the freezing line where the ground temperature is constant. The pump circulates temperature sensitive fluid through the ground loop, which stays 50 to 60 degrees year-round. In winters, warm fluid carries heat into the house. In summers, cool fluid draws heat out of the house.

Before adopting this system, one needs a home energy audit to determine size of the system needed. This process may result in energy efficient gains. A certified contractor experienced with geothermal installations is required. Determine the land area available for underground pipes. When area is ample, a backhoe can be used for horizontal loops in shallow trenches. In case of limited area, a drilling rig is used for deeper vertical loops.

Natural Methods of Cooling

Incorporating solar heating and natural cooling in the building is the need of present time. Cooling in buildings is much more than just fixing a cooler or an AC. One shall use a variety of passive solar and evaporative cooling techniques to bring the temperature down. You can switch on to alternative cooling techniques to limit the electricity bills.

Blazing sun can be used to cool your house. Solar air-conditioners have replaced the conventional devices at Solar Energy Centre in Gurugram (earlier Gurgaon). The cooling effect is maximum on the hottest day. This air-conditioner works by capturing solar radiation which generates pressurized hot water. The heat from this water further generates chilled water which is circulated through a fan coil unit.

Building having 'passive solar' architecture further contributes to the cooling effect.

'Passive solar' is the use of sun's energy to heat or cool the living spaces. A terrace garden cools down the building's roof. Vertical shafts fixed with evaporators, insulated walls and enough number of trees around the building keeps it cool during the summers. White tiles can be fixed on the terrace of the building which will radiate sun's heat; thereby keeping it cool. Terrace surface can be covered with a layer of pebbles and water on it can be sprinkled to keep the interior cool. Using evaporative coolers is also a good option.

Usually 70 to 80 percent reduction in energy consumption can be achieved by applying these techniques. These features have successfully been applied in the buildings like The American Institute, Teri Retreat, ITC Centre of Excellence in Gurugram and other buildings in Delhi and Noida.

Modern cities also create a 'heat island'. The concrete pavements, black-top pucca roads, walls painted with coal tar and rooftops in cities absorb sun's heat during the day time and create a heat island. They in turn warm the air blowing over them, resulting in the increase of city's temperature to around 5 degrees Fahrenheit above those in the surrounding suburbs.

"Cool Roof" Techniques

In most of the region called Indo-Gangetic plains, inside of a building becomes hotter than the outside during summers, major reason being the heated roof. The maximum heat load of a building comes through its roof. The roof absorbs around 60 to 70 per cent of the heat of sun's rays falling on it. In an already constructed flat roof, you may go for a cool roof.

"Cool roofs" concept was introduced by the building and construction industry in the USA after the Californian energy crises. A cool roof is one where the slab structure is sprayed with a special bright white liquid that reflects back most of the heat of the sunrays. This white liquid has high solar reflectance and high thermal emittance. Reflectance is the solar energy reflected away from the surface. Emittance is the percentage of energy a material radiates away after it has been absorbed. A cool roof doesn't warm beyond 40 to 50 degree centigrade.

Sloping or dome shaped roofs generally keep a building cooler. These shapes have frequently been used in the religious structures throughout the world.

Use mud-fuska and inverted kulhars (small clay pots used for drinking tea) on the roof top. The air-pockets developed in these kulhars help in keeping the house cool during the summers as air is a bad conductor of heat.

Paint the rooftop with white colour. An ordinary white wash of the roof surface can be done periodically to retain the reflectance properties. It will keep the interior cool in the same way the white shirt keeps us cool during summers. In this way, inside temperature of the house can be reduced up to 33 percent. Clay tiles of white colour could also be laid out over the roof to increase the roof's reflectance.

Roof cooling devices based on the principle of evaporative cooling can also be used. In this technique, cooling mats are laid over the roof. An electronically controlled spray mechanism operates intermittently over the mats using very little electricity. The water evaporates due to sunrays falling on it and roof surface stays cool.

A roof shading device in the form of a canvas cover can also be used. The white canvas cover should be placed close to the roof during daytime. It should be rolled up at night to allow further cooling. Inverted earthen pots can also be used. They shade the roof and increase the surface area for emission through radiation. But using this method, you won't be able to use the roof for any other purpose during the summers.

If you are living on the top storey, you can create a terrace garden. Plants and creepers provide green cover to the roof. Evaporation from their leaves lowers the ambient temperature. Water stored in the open on the roof and in roof ponds act as a heat sink and takes away heat from the surface. Right choice and effective application of any of these methods may keep your home several degrees cooler.

Water Conservation

The most important facet of water conservation is to use water in a judicious manner in our daily lives. Water should be stored in the areas where there is a mismatch between supply and demand. Store the rainwater in an underground tank to use it for the rest of the year. No water is qualitatively better than this water.

Locate the hot water system and bathrooms, laundry and kitchen as close to one another as possible while planning the home. Initial cost of plumbing gets reduced in this manner. It also saves water and energy by reducing the need to flush out too much cold water from hot water taps. Farther the bathroom from the heating system, more quantity of cold water in the pipe is required to be discharged before the hot water begins to flow. Insulating the hot water pipes also saves power.

Check the leaking taps, valves, pipes and dishwasher hoses. One leaking tap can waste more than 50 to 75 litre of water a day. Each drop of this water has consumed a large amount of energy in the form of its filtration, purification and transportation to your home. Further energy is consumed by the booster pumps and water purifiers at home. Install water efficient taps to cut the water usage. Once you have finished using a tap, shut it tightly to avoid leakage. Replace the washer as soon as a tap begins to leak.

Don't keep the water tap open while shaving or brushing the teeth. Use a water mug instead. Taps with electronic sensors may be used in public places for avoiding wastage of water.

Thaw the frozen foods by taking them out of the freezer much before you begin cooking. Don't thaw them under the running water. Wash fruits and vegetables in a small bucket of water instead of washing under the running water. This water can be used for watering the plants. Use water discarded by ACs, ROs and such other gadgets in gardening, floor cleaning and car washing.

Use dishwasher and washing machine only when you have a full load. It not only saves the precious water and energy but also reduces the amount of detergent entering the sewerage system. Regularly clean the lint filter in your washing machine. Go for phosphate-free, eco-friendly detergents and cleaning products. Rinse your dishes in a plugged sink rather than under a running tap. Use a sink strainer.

Avoid rinsing your razor under a running tap. It wastes a lot of water. Use a water mug instead. Don't leave the tap running while brushing your teeth. Wet your toothbrush in the beginning and use a glass of water to rinse your mouth at the end.

Recycle the waste water. More than 80 percent of water used in industrialized countries is recycled water. Available technologies enable 90 percent of water and process by-products to be recycled. These are cost-effective systems that manage both water and waste, conserving water while controlling pollution. Sullage (grey water from kitchens and bath-rooms) recycle systems are ideal for residential colonies as well as hotels, hospitals and large institutions. Sullage is treated and recycled for toilet flushing and gardening, reducing fresh water requirement by 60 percent. It makes more water available for drinking, bathing and laundry.

Packaged sewage treatment plants are also available for treating and purifying sewage. After disinfection, the water can be used for toilet flushing, gardening and irrigation or to recharge the ground water. It is ideal for installation by housing complexes, townships, hotels, military and police camps, parks, clubs and service stations. The system requires very little maintenance and operating costs.

Rainwater Harvesting (RWH)

Use of water across the globe has increased six-fold over the last century which is more than twice the population growth rate. With one-seventh of the world's population, India needs to address the issue of rainwater harvesting on a war footing. The water level is sharply going down. Rain water is precious and needs to be saved. It reaches us free of cost, is sweet, pure and full of minerals. Saving each raindrop and using is for our own benefit is imperative as it is not inexhaustible. It is the social responsibility of every individual to undertake rainwater harvesting.

There is an acute shortage of water in Delhi during the summer months. The common man, government authorities and developers are not making necessary arrangements for rainwater harvesting. We can fight the shortage of water if necessary arrangement for rainwater harvesting is in place. At present, Delhi requires around 850 million gallons of water daily whereas the supply is only 650 million gallons. Only 50 percent of the rainwater harvested could help in bridging the demand-supply gap in Delhi. The best design for any premises is where the land absorbs each and every drop of rainwater falling over it.

The method through which rainwater is saved to recharge the underground aquifers or stored for later use is known as rain water harvesting (RWH). In RWH all the rainwater that falls on the roof, balconies, chajjas and open areas of the building is collected and channelized into the ground through pipes or drains at a depth of around 2 metres below the existing ground level. Rainwater may be taken to a soak-pit where it percolates back into the soil and recharges it, or into a collection tank where it can pass through various sand filters. It is stored in tanks for reuse or recharge.

Though the term 'Rainwater Harvesting' has recently been coined, our forefathers used to save rainwater through generations. In the olden days'; *kunds, johads, talabs, vavs*, and *baolis* were built to save water though the threat of water scarcity was unimaginable in those days. Vaastu shastra ensures it by leaving brahamsthan and paishachsthan kachcha (porous). The age-old Indian tradition of water management was broadly built on two principles:

1. Rainwater harvesting had primacy over the river water or groundwater harvesting.
2. Community and household management had primacy over the state supply of water. So, every household had to collect the rainwater. Every drop was harvested.

Rainwater harvesting not only help in raising the ground water level but also mitigates the ill-effects of drought. It may also achieve drought proofing. Rainwater harvesting reduces the runoff which chokes the storm water drains. The flooding of roads is also reduced substantially. The quality of water improves, and soil erosion is reduced. The best thing is that energy required to lift the ground water per well is saved to the extent of 0.40 KWh per metre of rise in the water level.

Physical Work

According to a report of World Health Organization (WHO), in India 55 percent deaths up to 2020 will be caused by diseases which can easily be avoided with little care. These diseases are mainly heart problem, diabetes, high blood pressure, asthma and obesity which arise due to the modern inactive lifestyle. Around 60 to 85 percent of world's adult population is suffering from these lifestyle diseases. WHO has recommended changing the lifestyle and at least half an hour exercise on daily basis. We should learn the importance of physical work and improve our lifestyle. Car, lift, air-conditioner, washing machine, TV, Internet and the like make our life comfortable but also take away our precious health.

It has been found that behavior modification is the key to preventing heart attacks. Genetic predisposition increases risk of heart attacks just by 10 to 20 percent. It's primarily the poor lifestyle that adds layers of risks. The main risk factors are diabetes, high triglycerides, high cholesterol, high blood pressure, obesity and smoking. A study made at All India Institute of Medical Sciences (AIIMS), New Delhi shows that Indians have high bad cholesterol, low good cholesterol and high triglycerides, all of which can be altered by eating healthy food, losing weight and exercising. Smoking is the biggest cause of sudden cardiac deaths. Quitting smoking halves the risk of heart attacks.

Sleep Patterns

Some wise man has said, "Sleep is the most selfish thing you can do". A report "men sleep better alone" was published in the newspaper "The Hindustan Times" on 20 July 2006. According to this report, a new study featured in the New Scientist Magazine has found that sharing a bed with a woman could temporarily saddle man's brain and make him stupid the next day. However, the women sleep deeply and are more refreshed than the men. The findings suggest that if a man has an important day ahead, he is best advised to head off to the spare room rather than sharing the marital bed. Historically, we have never been meant to sleep in the same bed as each other. It is a bizarre thing to do.

Previous studies have shown that 70 million Americans are sleep-deprived, contributing to increased accidents, worsening health and lower test scores. The common sense notion is that creativity and problem solving is directly linked to adequate sleep. Scientists at the University of Luebeck in Germany have demonstrated that our sleeping brains continue working on problems that baffle us during the day and the right answer may come more easily after eight hours of rest. It provides a valuable reminder for overtired workers and students that sleep is often the best medicine.

Everybody feels refreshed following a good night's sleep. German experiment reveals that sleep can help to turn yesterday's problem into today's solution. Scientists found that volunteers taking a simple math test were three times more likely than sleep-deprived participants to figure out a hidden rule for converting the numbers into the right answer if they had eight hours of sleep. The results support bio-chemical studies of the brain that indicate memories are restructured before they are stored.

A lack of sleep can make people grumpy is hardly news. We all know implicitly the link between bad sleep the night before and bad mood the next day. Researcher Walker and his colleagues at Harvard Medical School have found that a few nights without sleep can not only make people tired and emotional, but may actually put the brain into a primitive "fight or flight" state. Without two full days sleep, brain was unable to put emotional experiences into context and produce controlled, appropriate responses.

Study Timings

In the Indian tradition, best time for study is the time before sunrise and sunset. It means around 4 to 6 AM in the morning and 4 to 6 PM in the evening. It is said that morning time study of 2 hours is equivalent to four to six hours of study during the odd hours. Our mind is completely at peace during this time. Brain secretes a neuro-chemical called endorphin that makes us feel happy and helps in memorizing any event easily. Endorphin is mainly responsible for our happiness and freshness in the morning. Whatever is studied is perfectly committed to memory and can easily be reproduced in the examinations.

Study is a creative act, governed by Lord Brahma. While studying, always keep in mind the five headed Lord Brahma. In the morning, mind is completely fresh after the night time sleep. Deep sleep eradicates our daytime happenings, tensions and anxieties through dreams. Pituitary gland is most active during the morning hours. It is the master gland which controls all the other glands. Brain also secretes hormones such as melatonin and serotonin in somewhat larger proportion in the morning which helps in concentration. Excessive physical work results in deposition of lactic acid in our muscles, leading to lethargy and non-concentration in studies.

Professor Russell Foster, a neuro-scientist of Oxford University, is an expert in how the brain functions. He is the head of circadian neuro-science, the study of how the daily routine affects the brain. His studies reveal that the time at which children become fully awake gets progressively later as they get older. Pupils at secondary school should start their classes in the afternoon because it is 'cruel' to make them turn up in the morning. Morning time classes can result in more errors, poor memory, reduced motivation and depression. Youngsters would achieve more if they are allowed to lie in and defer lessons until later in the day.

According to Professor Russell Foster, grumpy teenagers follow different sleep patterns from adults, making them more alert in the afternoon than in the morning. Switching to late start times results in improved success in exams and reduced rates of truancy and depression. Allowing them to lie-in would improve performance in key subjects. It is cruel to impose a cultural pattern on teenagers that makes them underachieve. Most school regimes force teenagers to function at a time of day that is suboptimal. Many university students are exposed to considerable dangers from sleep deprivation.

Sick Building Syndrome (SBS)

If at the end of a day you feel more run down than you should, probably you have been afflicted by the Sick Building Syndrome (SBS). Sick Building Syndrome can be described a situation in which the building occupants experience acute health problems or discomfort which appears to be linked to the time spent inside that building. The complaints may even be localized to a particular room or zone or may be widespread throughout the building. However, the occupants are not able to pinpoint a specific illness or cause. Many employees in the office also suffer from the SBS, symptoms of which may include lethargy, fatigue, headache, nausea etc.

The main causes of SBS are: improper Indoor Air Quality (IAQ), poor ventilation, lack of air movement, air-borne pollution, excessive humidity, biological contamination and uncomfortable level of temperature. Up to 30 per cent of buildings have lesser or severe problems related to IAQ. Poor indoor air quality can impact health, comfort and productivity of office workers. Sometimes indoor environment can have pollutant levels much higher than those found outside. The features like a good ventilation system, adequate power back up, proper drainage and good security arrangements are a necessity in both residential and commercial complexes.

Outside air enters and leaves a house by infiltration, natural ventilation and also by mechanical ventilation. The rate at which the outside fresh air replaces the inside stale air is called the "air exchange rate" (AER). The pollutant level increases when AER is lesser than the required rate. Immediate effects of indoor air pollution are usually short-term and treatable. Symptoms of asthma, hypersensitivity, pneumonitis and humidifier fever may show up. To determine odours in your home, step outside in the fresh air for a few minutes. Now re-enter the home and note whether the odours are noticeable.

An individual needs at least 15 cubic feet of air per minute in the open. However, this requirement is higher in closed spaces. In workplaces, hospitals, hotels and smoking lounges, it is respectively 20, 25, 30 and 60 cubic feet per minute per person. A person's daily exposure to air pollutants comes mostly through inhalation of indoor air. It is because the amount of time spent indoors is larger and generally there is higher pollution level within. The main victims of indoor pollution in any residence are the people who spend most of their time indoor. They include house-wives, infants and the elderly, those suffering from heart and lung diseases, asthma patients and persons who are extremely sensitive to the chemicals.

Air-conditioned rooms could contain carbondioxide (CO_2) gas up to 700 parts per million (PPT) though it is only 320 PPM in the open. Usually there are changes in the usage of building space at the time of design and at present. Buildings after construction undergo renovation and remodeling of interior spaces. Normally, mechanical systems of ventilation are not modified to compensate for the physical changes to the occupied space. Hence, airflow patterns may get altered creating pockets of thermal discomfort and indoor quality problems.

The air-conditioning and ventilation duct in a building accumulate sizable deposits of fine particles and other contaminants over the years. Combined with temperature and moist atmosphere within the ventilation system, these deposits often yield bacterial colonies. It may even cause physical discomfort by degrading the quality of air one breathes indoors. It can also result in variety of allergy related problems including skin rashes, frequent cough and cold, asthma and other multiple diseases.

Some of the moisture condensed by the AC system may splash on the interior insulation and some may be left standing at the bottom of the pan. This moisture may support the growth of micro-organisms. Therefore, use proper drain pipes for taking the moisture out and repair the damaged pipes. Outdoor sources like radon, pesticides and outdoor air pollutants can also pollute the air inside your home. Sources of indoor air pollution within any home may be:

- Combustible sources like oil, gas, kerosene, coal, wood and tobacco products.
- Building materials and furnishings like asbestos containing insulation, wet or damp carpets, and furniture or cabinetry made of certain pressed wood products.
- Products for household cleaning and maintenance, personal care or hobbies.
- Central heating and cooling systems and humidification devices etc.

Building materials, furnishings and household products like air fresheners release pollutants on a regular basis. Some pollutants are released intermittently based on peculiar activities. These may be smoking, using malfunctioning stoves / furnaces / space heaters, solvents used in cleaning and hobby activities, paint strippers used in decorating, cleaning products and pesticides used in housekeeping.

We can reduce energy consumption for heating and cooling by sealing the building tightly. But it also leads to stale air being circulated and re-circulated inside. Pollutants in the form of dust, bacteria, viruses, mould, fungus, mildew, and poisonous gases circulate inside the building. As the occupants walk in and out of the building, dust from the shoes, hair, skin, clothes and the household articles gets added to the air inside a building.

The philosophy of space usage has also changed over the last few decades. Now organizations mostly go for the open floor designs as opposed to the private spaces more prevalent in the past. It has resulted in higher occupancy density within a given space. Today's typical schools and offices also use equipments that generate heat and emit pollutants.

As buildings become sick mainly due to indoor air pollution, one should prevent or minimize the release of indoor pollutants. Chemical products like cleaning agents, paints and glues should be used outdoors whenever possible. Whenever used indoors, carefully follow the directions on the label and provide lots of ventilation in the initial stages. Stop smoking indoors as it has certain toxic pollutants. Some types of plywood and particle boards and many other products emit significant amount of formaldehyde and other gaseous pollutants. These must be avoided if possible. Get the new carpets and furniture aired before taking delivery or usage. It can also be done in your open courtyard or garage. Store the solvents properly. Frequent house-cleaning removes dust and moulds and helps you maintain good indoor air quality.

One of the effective ways of maintaining good indoor air quality is to provide adequate ventilation, though it may not completely remove all the pollutants. A room with no outlet will not have enough air circulating inside, as shown in figure 7.21(a). The ideal combination for optimising cross ventilation is to provide inlet at a lower level and outlet at a higher level, as shown in figure 7.21(b). Downward louvres help to drive the incoming fresh air towards the floor, providing circulation in a larger volume of the room, as shown in figure 7.21 (c). The chhajja uses the same principle as the downward louvres and deflects the air inside the building to enhance ventilation, as shown in figure 7.21 (d).

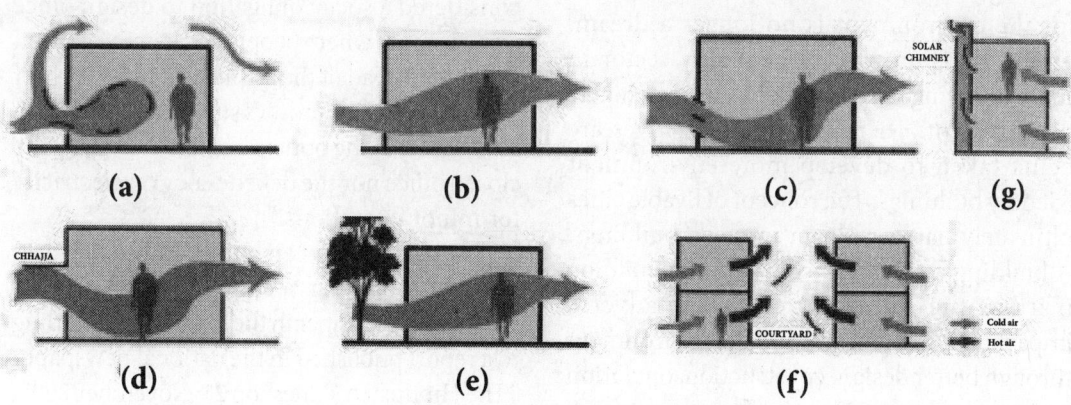

Fig 7.24: Working of the Natural Ventilation

Trees and other landscaping features should be suitably placed so that they do not obstruct the air flow, as shown in figure 7.21 (e). A courtyard (classical Braham-sthan) enhances air circulation through principle of stack effect (air movement driven by buoyancy). Air heats up and starts rising when it passes through the interiors. The courtyard allows this air to escape, as shown in figure 7.21 (f). The solar chimney enhances the stack effect and sucks out the exhaust warm air from the rooms. Consequently, cool air from the outside rushes in to take place of the warm air, thereby increasing natural ventilation, as shown in figure 7.21 (g).

To increase the level of ventilation, open windows and doors whenever the weather permits. It is mandatory to open these openings when using products or engaging in activities that generate pollutants. Kitchen and toilet exhaust fans should be properly vented to the outdoors. They are very effective at removing pollutants generated during cooking or passing stools.

Green buildings or Intelligent Buildings (Automation within commercial buildings)

Making your home or workplace and caring for the environment is no longer a dream. Tremendous growth in the reality sector in India is posing major challenge to sustainable development. Therefore, new initiatives are being taken to develop more environment friendly buildings. The concept of livable cities ultimately narrows down to green buildings. A building can be termed as a green building if it has the ability to reduce the adverse impact on human health and the environment through better design, construction, operation and maintenance. Non-profit organizations and corporate world is now going for green buildings which are eco-friendly and energy efficient.

First intelligent building in India was the CMC House in Mumbai. Tata Research Centre at Pune and ITC building in Gurugram are also intelligent buildings. Some of the eco-friendly buildings in Delhi are India Habitat Centre (IHC) at Lodhi Road, Tata Energy and Resource Institute's (TERI) university in Vasant Kunj, Science and Environment building in Tughlaqabad Institutional Area, World Headquarter of NGO "Development Alternatives" (DA), IFC headquarter, American Express Bank, and SCOPE.

In a green building, arrangements are made so that the bulbs switch off automatically sensing the outside light, tap water stops flowing as soon as you withdraw your hands. The garden drip irrigation system waters plants according to their needs. Solar panels, fuel cells, and wind turbines are installed in the building to lower the carbon emissions. Electric bulbs consuming lesser amount of electricity are used, have an eye on the electric bills and only energy efficient electrical gadgets are purchased.

The design and construction material used in a green building ensures least consumption of electricity and water. Green building provides healthier living environment than any other contemporary building. It is now considered a social obligation to design office in such a way where people work in the natural sunlight instead of the artificial light. Instead of air conditioner, windows supply the cool fresh air. Neither is the oppressiveness caused by the closed office nor the dependency on electricity for minor operations.

A house in a green building costs 10 to 20 per cent more than a conventional home but would prove cheaper in the long run. According to a report published in the national newspaper "The Hindustan Times" on 2nd November 2007, The Energy and Research Institute (TERI) has designed a new rating system 'GRIHA' for the construction of residential and commercial

Modern Perspective of Vaastu

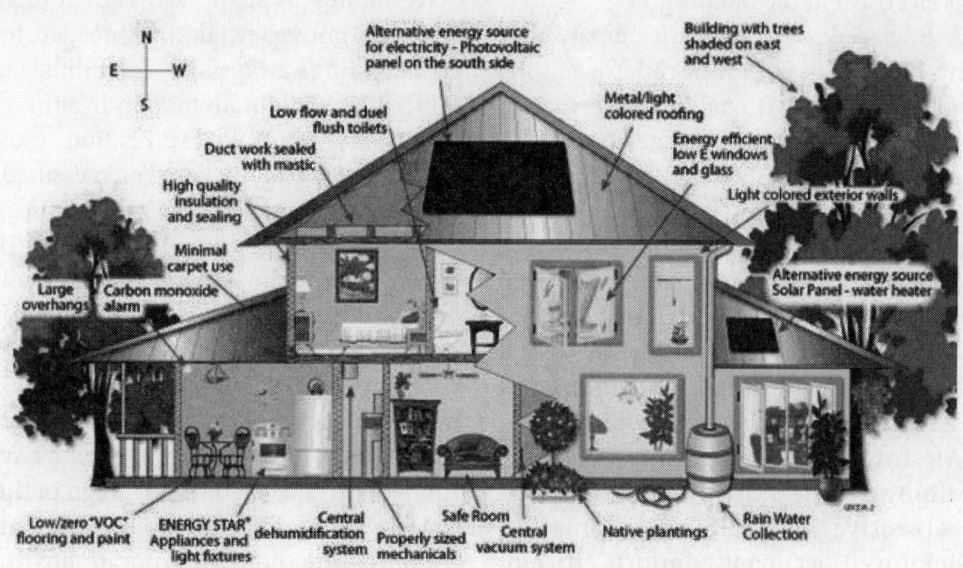

Fig 7.25: Essentials of the Green Building

buildings that would help reduce Green House Gas emission. This system takes into account provisions of the National Building Code 2005 and the Energy Conservation Building Code 2007.

Under the new building code, a building can get 1 star to 5 stars rating. To apply for green rating, the qualifying mark is 50. With score of 50-61 points, you get 1 star. Building will get an additional star for each additional 10 points. Hence building with 91-100 points will get 5 stars. The points are given on 32 parameters which are further divided into 6 sub-groups:

1. **Energy**: A 40% reduction in energy consumption means a 5 star rating. Energy consumption is reduced by way of better lighting, shades and visual conditions.

2. **Environment**: Reduced destruction of natural areas, habitats, bio-diversity and soil erosion through better site planning.

3. **Air and water quality**: Reduced carbon emission.

4. **Water**: Reduced consumption and generation by way of re-cycling, re-use and water harvesting.

5. **User-friendliness**: Building enough parking spaces, minimizing the use of polluting measures and using fly ash or hollow bricks.

6. **Image and marketability**: A green building should look better than a conventional building.

The term *building automation system* refers to any automatic centralized electrical control system that is used to control a building's heating, ventilation and air conditioning (HVAC), lighting and other systems through a building management system (BMS) or building automation system (BAS). A building controlled by a BAS is often referred to as an "intelligent building", "smart building", or a "smart home" if it is a residence. Building automation includes monitoring and control of the mechanical, security, fire and flood safety, lighting (especially emergency lighting), humidity control and ventilation systems in a building. Modern BAS can control everything that is electrical in the building.

A BAS reduces building energy and maintenance costs compared to a non-controlled building. It enables the owner to maximize his return on real estate investment. Its direct result is that it fetches higher capital value and rental returns. It can help you cut budget, personnel and problems. Almost all multi-storey green buildings are designed to accommodate a BAS for the energy, air and water conservation characteristics. Most commercial, institutional, and industrial buildings built after 2000 include a BAS.

An intelligent building combines technology with skillful management. The objectives of building automation are; improved occupant comfort, efficient operation of building systems, reduction in energy consumption and operating costs, and improving the life cycle of utilities. It helps to maintain optimum temperature within the building, thus creating a decent ambience. BAS also enables precise control of temperature and humidity in the air-conditioned area, thus avoiding under or over-cooling. BAS also reduces energy consumption by properly controlling the HVAC process, without compromising on comfort levels inside the building.

BAS core functionality keeps building climate within a specified range, provides light to the rooms based on an occupancy schedule. Lighting can be turned on, off, or dimmed with a building automation or lighting control system based on the time of day, or on occupancy sensor, photo sensors and timers. One typical example is to turn the lights on in a space for half an hour only since the last motion was sensed. A photocell placed outside a building can sense darkness, and the time of day, and modulate lights in outer offices and the parking lot.

In this system, most air handlers mix the inner and outside air. So, less temperature / humidity conditioning is needed. This can save money by using less chilled or heated water. Some external air is needed to keep the building's air healthy. To optimize energy efficiency while maintaining healthy indoor air quality, controlled ventilation adjusts the amount of outside air based on measured levels of occupancy. Often chilled water is used to cool the building's air and equipment. The hot water system supplies heat to the building's air-handling unit. All modern building automation systems have alarm capabilities.

Room automation is a subset of building automation and with a similar purpose. It is the consolidation of one or more systems under centralized control, though in this case in one room only. Most common example of room automation is corporate boardroom, presentation suites, and lecture halls, where operation of large number of devices that define the room function (such as video-conferencing equipment, video projectors, lighting control systems, public address systems etc) would make manual operation of the room very complex. It is common for room automation systems to employ a touch-screen as the primary way of controlling each operation.

Three things are most important in intelligent buildings: energy conservation, communication and security. The systems and practices which form an indispensable part of green buildings are rainwater harvesting system, creating a garden on the terrace to prevent the formation of heat islands, proper landscaping to prevent the soil erosion and maximizing the use of renewable energy sources such as photovoltaic cells.

These buildings are aimed at zero emissions and 100% carbon neutrality. For conservation of energy, natural light and air is harnessed to the maximum possible extent. Use of solar power is preferred instead of the conventional sources of energy. Intelligent buildings are fixed with window panes which allow the sunlight but don't allow the heat in. Reflectors are installed to admit sunlight inside in desired quantity. A central computer monitors the sunrays falling on different areas and accordingly opens or closes the venetian blinds.

When sunrays fall on room's window, its' venetian blinds gradually open automatically to admit sunlight in the room. Room's lights are automatically switched off after receiving sufficient sunlight. When room temperature becomes comfortable, the AC gets switched off automatically. The windows automatically open when a cool breeze blows at night so that the room becomes cool and AC is not required in the morning. This system saves 25 to 45 percent of electricity.

In green buildings, AC's are fitted with such gadgets that make it Chloro Fluoro Carbon (CFC) free. CFC gases are considered most dangerous to the ozone layer of earth's atmosphere. Building is fitted with Carbon-dioxide sensors. White and other light colours are used to increase the natural light. Artificial light is not used during the daytime. During the dark hours CFL and T-5 lamps with less voltage but more light are used. Sensors are fitted in the rooms and in the toilet where tube lights, fans, ACs and coolers are switched off automatically within 2 minutes of leaving the space. A gadget called variable frequency drive (VFD) is fixed which decreases the speed of pumps, motors and ACs in accordance with their load. Only eco-friendly paints and carpets are used.

Though an intelligent building is 12 to 15 percent more expensive than the other commercial buildings but it ultimately leads to 20 to 30 percent saving in energy and 30 to 50 percent saving in water. According to the estimates, green buildings reduce negative impact on the environment up to 40 percent. A green building depends on clean and renewable solar energy. Therefore it has much lower air conditioning bills. Green buildings make optimum use of natural light and are well attuned to the seasonal rhythms. They use water efficiently by treating it and then recycling it. These buildings can easily be adapted to new uses, can easily be dismantled and can be re-constructed for new usage.

Conventional design and construction methods produce buildings that have a negative impact on the environment as well as on the occupant's health and productivity. These buildings are expensive to operate. They contribute to excessive resource consumption, waste generation and pollution. Green building protects and restores the local air, water, soil, flora and fauna supporting pedestrians, bicycles, mass transit and other alternatives to fossil fuelled vehicles.

Some of the benefits of green buildings are: 30 to 40 percent reduction in the operation cost, improved occupant performance, green corporate image, improved health and safety of the occupants, enhanced occupant comfort, improved performance of the occupants, imbibing best operational practices from day one, incorporating the latest techniques and technologies resulting in reduced impact of the building construction and operations on the air, water, landfills and non-renewable energy resources.

Around 30 percent less embodied energy is required to construct the building by low energy natural materials like mud, fly ash blocks and timber (for doors and windows) instead of burnt bricks, concrete and steel. Only 25 percent of external wall are glazed, and aluminum or PVC are not at all used. Most of the material used is local, thus involving minimum transportation. Highly efficient use of materials can reduce waste to less than 5 percent.

Around 15 percent recycled materials are used in green buildings. Mud from old building is used to make new compressed earth blocks. Industrial wastes such as fly ash and stone dust is also used in construction.

30 percent less steel and cement is required. Shallow domes with fly ash blocks require no steel reinforcement. Short span reinforced cement concrete frame is preferred for basic infrastructure. Ferro cement channels of 25 mm thick are used instead of 150 mm thick slabs. Minimal cement plastering is done.

Around 40 percent less operational energy is required in green buildings. Indoor temperature ranges from 18 degrees (in winter) to 28 degrees (in summers), minimizing the energy consumption. It maximizes natural lighting and ventilation to minimize the heat gain. The innovative 'hybrid' air conditioning system minimizes the use of energy and water.

Rainwater harvesting, recycling the waste water for use in toilets and gardens, treatment of surplus waste water before recharging the ground water are pre-requirements of a green building. The aim is to recycle 100 percent waste water. Green buildings use non-toxic materials, paints and finishes which greatly enhances the indoor air quality. Green buildings easily blend with the adjacent constructions and the landscape. These are designed to elevate the human spirit and are a magnificent celebration of space.

In a greenhouse, construction time is nearly half as compared to a conventional house. Extra cost incurred on construction is recovered within 3 to 4 years as electricity and maintenance cost is cut by 40 percent. It does not produce construction waste as most of the matter is recyclable. Rainwater harvesting on one acre of land may save 75,000 litres of water. Residential energy accounts for 16 percent of all greenhouse gas emissions. Some tips for an energy efficient home are given below:

1. Proper orientation of building helps in saving energy. Light from the north does not allow the heat to penetrate into the building. Daylight can be harnessed by the design features like skylights, light shelves and the use of glass bricks which become the source of diffused light. Adequate shading of windows reduces direct heat gain. Fine distribution of light can be achieved within the room if small slit openings are kept on the east and west faces and are filled with glass bricks.

2. Height of the basement should ideally be four feet above the surrounding ground level. But where its ceiling height is below the ground level, light pits may be constructed all around the basement and windows be fixed to get natural light directly to the basement rooms. It can also be achieved through the use of reflecting glasses, the same principle which is used in the design of a periscope.

3. Full advantage of the direction of wind should be taken. For this purpose, inlet openings should face the prevalent wind direction. To increase the wind's flow rate, inlet openings should be located at lower level on the windward side and on higher level on the leeward side. Always have windows in the adjacent walls as the prevailing wind direction does change.

4. Inlet openings should be well distributed along the length of building. In case only one wall of the room is exposed to the outside, it is good to provide two small windows than to provide one large window. For adequate air flow, inlet openings should have an area of 20 to 30 percent of the floor area. Windows larger than the requirement invite extra heat in the room.

5. Double skin brick wall with 25 mm air cavity (cavity walls or hollow walls) and double glazed glass of low thermal capacity minimizes heat ingress into the building envelope.

6. Roof top gardens help in keeping the house cool.

7. Some of the simple practicable methods to keep the house cool during scorching

summers are the light coloured cotton curtains, natural heat blocks (trees and plants, greenery, creepers, indoor plants), shades on windows, CFL bulbs, no use of table lamp but using wall or ceiling lights, opening curtains and windows in the evening, cotton bed sheets, and light coloured pillow covers.

8. Some methods of passive air conditioning in the house are the use of air ducts, wind louvers, and thermal chimneys to vent hot air from the house.

9. Passive heating and cooling measures like Trombe Wall, solarium or solar house on south walls save energy to a large extent.

10. Geothermal system cuts heating and cooling costs by 60 percent. In this process, non-polluting water-glycol solution is pumped around 150 feet (50 metre) deep into the bedrock.

11. Fit an air-duct around 20 to 30 feet into the ground. It keeps your building naturally warm during winters.

12. For multi-storeyed buildings constructed side by side, light is not sufficiently available in the lower storeys. Assisted light can be obtained here by the windows designed especially for reflected light.

13. Double glazed window glasses allow light to enter into the house but not the heat. Use tinted glass which absorbs least amount of heat and radiates the rest back to the environment. Cover windows with cardboard, tin or aluminum foil. Use louvers which cut off the summer heat but allow the much needed sunlight during winters.

14. Triple pane windows reduce ultraviolet rays during the day; provide almost three times the insulation of conventional windows.

15. Seal the windows and doors with natural materials to control heat, air and moisture leakage.

16. Keep the window panes clean. It will admit more amount of natural light.

17. Compact fluorescent light bulbs (CFL) are around 10 times costlier than the conventional incandescent bulbs. A CFL bulb of 10, 12 or 15 watts gives light like a 40 watt tube light, using around a quarter of the electricity only. A CFL also contains 5-10 mg of liquid mercury, a toxic metal. CFL's therefore require careful competent handling for their safe disposal.

18. To derive maximum brightness, place lamps such that light reflects off at least two walls.

19. Use energy efficient ACs only as they save up to 30 percent electricity. Install AC in the cold directions ie north, northwest or northeast. If you live on the top floor, don't switch on the fan while AC is working. Fan pushes the hot air downwards which increases load on AC. Put the AC on power saving mode and save the electricity bill. Set your air conditioner at 25 degree Celsius.

20. Keep the refrigerator away from any source of heat like a gas stove and washer. Ensure that your fridge door's gasket is sticky enough and in shipshape. To check it, close the fridge door on a piece of paper. If you can pull out the paper easily, get the seal replaced immediately.

21. Go for solar geyser as it uses the perennial heat of sun. It automatically gets connected to the power grid when it's cloudy.

22. Use window frames made of certified wood from Malaysia. The wood is certified because a new tree is planted every time a mature one is cut down. Using certified woods help in reducing the depletion of forests.

23. Go for locally available natural building materials. Some building materials with renewable resources are composite woods, woolen and coir carpets and linoleum flooring. Use materials with high recyclable value. It reduces the impact resulting from extraction and processing of new materials. Ceramic tiles have high recyclable contents (20 to 30 per cent) after fly ash blocks. Fly ash bricks or special mud bricks help keep inside of the house cool.

24. Use eco-paints. They should not contain any solvents or chemicals. Green-seal certified paints are available in the market. Paint your roof with white colour. White colour reflects all the colours making your home cooler by around 4 degrees. Roof tiles can be painted with reflective paints that help to keep the heat away.

25. Harvest the rainwater by making it flow into the specially constructed pits which then go into the earth. It is then recycled for use. Driveways, sidewalks and streets laid with porous concrete blocks let rainwater soak into the ground.

26. Adopt 100 per cent waste water recycling. Waste water enters the tank and solids settle; blower splashes water onto grid, bacteria digests waste and clean water is produced.

27. Go for drip irrigation instead of the traditional systems. It is based on a computerized system which senses and waters plants accordingly resulting in saving the precious water.

28. To save water, instead of bath take shower or use a bucket. Wash a full load of clothes in the washing machine.

29. Keep the car in the garage and use the public transport whenever feasible. Transport accounts for more than a fifth of carbon-dioxide emissions. Re-use the newspaper to cover books or to line the shelves.

30. Switch off the PC when you log it off for more than 30 minutes. You may save more than half the power it consumes.

31. Use organic waste as bio-fertilizer in your kitchen garden.

32. Solar panels on roof back oriented towards south generate electric power. Roof made of stone-coated recycled aluminum and zinc doesn't trap extra heat.

33. Worldwide, only 0.4 percent of the total consumption of energy is received from the solar energy. A Dutch company has developed an instrument to harness the solar energy from the roads which get heated during the daytime. This company is using heat of solar rays falling on a 180 metre long road and on the small parking area for heating the four storey buildings in the vicinity. It is a completely a new technology, utilizing sunrays to the maximum possible extent.

34. The buildings should be disabled friendly.

35. Premise should be earthquake resistant.

City and Town Planning

Cities built according to the principles of vaastu shastra bring happiness and prosperity to their residents. Jaipur, Chandigarh, Bangalore and Jamshedpur are some of the cities that have been built on the principles of vaastu shastra and feng shui. Railway stations, picture halls, schools, temples, palaces, hotels and industries all have their own different auspicious directions. Locating these buildings in the appropriate direction can help their inmates achieve their goals in life.

A conference on new architecture and urbanism was organized in the recent years by International Network for Traditional Building, Architecture and Urbanism (INTBAU) in association with the Nabha Foundation. In this conference, architects and planners warned India against adopting the "monstrous and inhuman" architecture of glass towers and skyscrapers. Instead, it should evolve new architecture based on diverse traditional practices that have held good for centuries. We have to go back to our past to create cities of our future. INTABU was founded to counteract the notion that tradition and modernity in architecture are opposed to each other. It is dedicated to promoting a humane urban environment.

Acclaimed urban theorist Leon Krier who carried out the Poundbury village project in Dorchester in United Kingdom for Prince Charles said that vertically growing cities will become unlivable when there is no uranium to power turbines or fossil fuels for vehicles. Only those buildings and settlements will endure that follow traditional ideas and allow human activities to be carried out in an aesthetic and pleasant way. The way out is to create attractive alternatives so that people themselves can accept the good and reject the bad. Big glass towers with shanties below indicate a collapse of social and community structure that in turn leads to increased violence. No building should be more than three-storey high, the height that people can climb comfortably.

India is fortunate enough in having a large resource pool of traditional crafts-persons that can help to provide the strategy for our future buildings. We have to evolve modern architecture from our own traditions instead of westernizing. The liberal capitalism typified by glass and glitz is a threat to the traditional Indian architecture. Builders have developed high rise buildings in haphazard manner. These buildings neither have the proper fast speed lifts, advanced climate control system and fire fighting system nor the modern security system.

Modern town planners, architects and builders are using glass on a large scale. The popularity of glass is in fact a classic case of a product dictating architectural styles. Builders and architects in India usually ignore the reasons behind the extensive use of the all-pervasive glass facades in the western world. Natural sunlight is rare in the western world where primary reason for using more glass in buildings is to trap maximum sunlight. Sun shines all year round in India and its climate is already too hot. An unhindered exposure to more scorching heat is not desirable. What is required is more shade to improve energy efficiency. In glass-clad high-rises where the beaming sun enters the room and the dissipation of heat is almost negligible, air-conditioning becomes unavoidable and even mandatory.

A report "modern cities make us fat" was published in the national daily, 'The Hindustan Times" on 22 January 2007. It reveals that the problem of "obesogenic" or fat-making environment is also deeply rooted in faulty building designs. People's behaviour gets changed with the change in building designs. Our public spaces like our cities, suburbs and shopping centres are enforcing a culture that consumes energy without spending it, encouraging inactivity and poor eating habits. Using the stairs is not seen as normal. In most of the modern buildings, crowded lifts and empty staircases are a regular feature. Stairwells are usually hidden away like dirty secrets in too many modern office blocks. The focal point when one enters tends to be the lift.

Architects and town planners can also tackle the obesity problem by designing buildings that encourage exercise. Exercise can happen during the course of the day itself ie during shopping, commuting and walking the dog. Town planners shall maximize the potential for casual exercise by incorporating cycle paths and pedestrian areas in their designs. Parks and other green areas encourage people to exercise. People are more likely to leave the car behind if a shop is within walking distance. Even a signpost to the stairs is a step in the right direction.

In some cases; existing offices, estates and shopping centres can be retrofitted to make them more exercise-friendly. High density town planning is also an invitation to get off the sofa. Local shops and facilities are mixed up together in the dense urban environment. People tend to use those more. A lot more walking is involved, just because of the inconvenience of driving.

On the contrary, low-density housing leaves the resident with few options. You invariably need a car if you want to get anywhere as these places usually have no local shops or facilities. Connectivity is the king when designing an exercise-friendly environment. In poorly designed housing estates, people have extreme indoor lifestyles where children play indoors or they are taken by car to friend's homes. They can enjoy an outdoor lifestyle as soon as they have an environment where they can enjoy being outside.

A research conducted in USA in 2003 shows that adults in low-density, car-dependent housing weighed more, walked less and were more likely to be obese. Each additional hour spent in a car per day is associated with a 6 percent increase in the likelihood of obesity.

According to a news report, new bungalows may go the traditional way in New Delhi's Lutyens' zone. The central government had asked the Delhi Urban Arts Commission (DUAC) to look into the possibility of adding more bungalows in the Lutyens' zone of New Delhi. The DUAC chairman Charles Correa suggested that the new bungalows that are contemporary in design could have stairs leading upto a 'barsaati', terraces and courtyards that are basic features in the traditional North Indian style homes. The new homes will have separate living area for the family, an office area and service area that will have garage for four vehicles and servant's quarters with its own courtyard. Gardens and driveways will be an integral part of the design.

Planning, Designing and Construction of Buildings

Three fundamental factors which contribute to the safety of a building are: (1) Design, (2) Construction and execution, and (3) Maintenance and management. All these three factors are inter-related which cannot address the goal of a safe built environment in isolation. Design of a building should incorporate safety against earthquake, fire, floods, lightening and such other disasters. An often overlooked issue is the design of crime free spaces. Designers should avoid creating spaces which are difficult to watch over and which can easily become breeding grounds or soft targets for the anti-social elements. Public spaces which can easily be monitored or controlled can greatly reduce the chances of misuse.

A building should be constructed with the same professional acumen as it was designed with. One should not try to unnecessarily cut on costs and ignore the value of professional services. A building can serve its purpose successfully only when it is under the constant supervision of professional experts. The vital components regarding maintenance and management of modern contemporary buildings are: lifts, air-conditioning, back-up power, fire alarms and fire fighting systems, electronically operated entrance gates, electronic identification of authorized building users and visitors, regular building maintenance and repairs, and overall safety and security of the facility.

Functional Homes

The building should be constructed around a courtyard (brahamsthan) or shaft (diminutive form of brahamsthan) for proper ventilation of different rooms, kitchen and toilets. This courtyard should be designed so that it has large glazings with lots of plants to give light and airy feel. This courtyard could also be used to promote cross ventilation.

South facing home has the advantage of receiving much larger solar radiation during winter than in summer. A small sunshade for openings on the south façade can cut off direct solar penetration during summer and allow it during winter. South wall receives the least solar radiation during summer in northern India. South façade causes greater thermal discomfort and visual glare due to the incidence of ground reflected radiation on the human body from a southerly sun. Suitable non-reflective and absorptive surfaces like grassy lawns should be developed in front of the south façade to minimize this reflected heat.

On the western façade, due to higher air temperature in the afternoon, the heat flow indoors is further augmented by the incidence of solar radiation. This heat can be minimized by reducing the western façade or by providing thermal insulation on the exterior. Western façade should have deep verandahs / canopies / chhajjas, creepers, plants etc. to protect the inhabitants from the blazing summer sun. To minimize heat intake into the house, west side openings should also be kept to a minimum.

In a west facing house, insulate the front wall by creating a cavity wall of four-and-a-half inches each, with foam concrete in between. Make the western and eastern walls thick; say around 12 inches or more. For heat insulation purpose, mud mortar is far better than cement mortar. Mud is bad conductor of heat and is chemically inert when compared to cement. Keep the ceiling height to around 13 to 14 feet. Your roof should also be insulated with at least 4 inches thick foam concrete. Inverted "kulhads" of 5 inches height (used for drinking lassi in walled area of old Delhi) can also be used for this purpose.

If you have more openings in the east and west of your home, close the unnecessary ones. Otherwise prefer planting trees in these directions. Cover the windows and doors with bamboo chik curtains. Using khus curtains is also an agreeable option. Khus not only keeps the interior cool but its fragrance also calms down the worst of hotheads. Use glass reflectors in the house having big windows. A glass reflector is a glass with a metallic look that doesn't allow sunlight to enter the building.

For home cooling purpose, central air cooling ducts can be provided into the masonry of the house. You need to create vertical shafts in the brickwork, with openings in the slabs to allow vertical shafts to reach the roof so that a desert cooler can be installed on the roof. The brick shafts are also very economical.

Cellars

The basement can actually be put to good use with a little effort and creativity. One must ensure adequate light and ventilation by arranging windows, doors and ventilators in the right way. You may also go for a sunken patio that leads directly to the basement. Basement can also be converted into a mini party hall as many motels, banquet halls and farm houses are doing in Delhi on a large scale. A home office can be run in the basement. In the Master Plan of Delhi 2021, Union Ministry of Urban Development has allowed commercial activities in basements situated on wide roads.

Selected professionals have also been allowed to work from the basement and out of rented residential premises. These professionals include doctors, advocates, town planners, architects, engineers, interior designers, chartered accountants, IT professionals and management consultants, company secretaries, cost and work accountants, media professionals, and documentary makers. There is a growing breed of professionals operating from home just like it happen world over under the concept of Small Office Home Office (SOHO). These professional's offices cause very little nuisance as they invite very few footfalls.

A basement can be used as a home gymnasium if it has plenty of fresh air and light. Otherwise, the health benefits from the workout will be nullified or reduced by the unhealthy atmosphere. If basement is spacious enough, you can use it as a mini concert area with a raised platform in one corner and durries on the floor for the audience. Religious functions, group chantings or bhajans can be held here. Basement can also be used for conducting hobby courses, including tuitions and coaching classes.

A basement can be turned into a children's play area with one wall having cartoon characters. Colourful floor mats can be spread with arrangement of plenty of toys and toy racks. Children will love the dedicated space to store their toys and games. It can also be a separate space for teenagers where they can play games, paint, draw or do the countless other things. Any adult can also use a basement as a secluded and private area for painting, designing or other creative activity. Basement can also be turned into a library with a study.

Building Materials

The futuristic exteriors of the newly constructed buildings in the NCR region with their glittering glass facades are climatically unsuitable. Particularly, western and eastern side of the buildings clad in glass not only results in increased energy consumption but also puts huge load on their maintenance. In an effort to ape the west, little is being done to use those building materials that suit our climatic conditions. Factors other than the façade of a building are being put on hold.

Let's take the example of India Habitat Centre building which is one of the best examples of a modern office building in the capital. Its energy efficient construction has created a benchmark in a number of ways. Everything – ranging from the presence of huge courtyards with lots of greenery to the materials used eg bricks, Kota stone and white marble for the flooring – is suited to our climate.

Construction in the NCR is mainly carried out in three ways which include Reinforced Cement Concrete (RCC) frame structures, load bearing structures and a few other alternative methods. RCC frame structures are most common around the world. Load-bearing structures are common in India. They consist of load bearing brick or stone walls on which the RCC slab or roof can rest. Other materials like terracotta tiles, stone, glass and aluminium panels are widely used for the outer treatment.

Choice of building materials generally depends on their cost and availability. Presence of the right people ie labour is also important. For example, Rajasthani labour is skilled in stone crafting but very few of them do the RCC work. Time consideration also influences the choice of building material. More the time one takes, more the cost climbs. Commercial constructions tend to use more reflective glass and aluminium cladding these days.

India is home to a diverse climatic conditions leading to the presence of various methods of construction in different climatic zones. The most appropriate building materials for any place are the ones that belong to the area. For example, stone and bricks are appropriate for Delhi and Rajasthan, wood in Gujarat and hilly regions and bamboo in the northeastern states. With industrialization, cement and RCC have become predominant building materials in India. Because of the tremendous heat for most part of the year in the northern plains including Delhi, we should prefer earthy materials like bricks, terracotta tiles and stones from Dholpur, Agra and Jaisalmer.

Planning also plays a great role. In case of improper design, even these materials will not help create a structure suited to our climatic conditions. Cavity walls, recessed windows, and higher ceilings reduce heat penetration inside the house. Brick, wood and hollow concrete blocks are suitable as they do not conduct heat. Metallic surfaces and glass are not suitable. They have to be treated and used carefully. Low-cost, environment-friendly materials need to be promoted as they are more suited to Indian conditions. But limited availability and traditional mindsets restrict the use of these materials.

Glass as Building Material

Architectural glass has been popularly used in facades and windows for a long time. Now due to its high flexural stiffness, glass has found its way to doors, stair treads, balustrades, walkways, bridges and floorings. Glass domes, glass beams, glass fins and glass columns are finding regular use in buildings. Architectural glass is becoming a preferred choice as it has a tough interlayer that is 100 times stiffer and five times stronger than the traditional safety glass. Today doubts about the fragility of glass are gradually being replaced by an acceptance of its structural potential.

Glass is being said the 'material of the millennium'. It is now being manufactured in different forms: clear, extra clear, tinted (coloured) and reflective. Now glass can be bent, toughened, heat strengthened, laminated (making it bullet-proof), insulated (so that it transmits very little sound), coated, painted, etched, and acid washed.

The major advantages of using glass are cited as sophisticated high-tech appearance, zero maintenance, weather resistance and transparency. Glass industry experts claim that opaque, soft-coat and hard-coat glass cuts down sound transmissions by as much as 10 decibel points.

This quality makes it a preferred material for entertainment venues, medical clinics and counseling rooms. Studies reveal that less noise means less stress. As glass tends to reduce the unwanted noise, people become more creative, productive and healthier in a clam environment. Though brick and stone walls are solid and stronger, glass has emerged as a viable alternative. As it is lighter than brick, it causes lesser injury to the occupants in case of natural disasters. In case of fire, it is easier to break glass and evacuate the occupants.

Glass is being called a healthy and hygienic material being easy to clean and maintain it. Its non-porous and inert surface does not support growth of mould, mildew and bacteria. Therefore, it is ideal for the healthcare, hospitality and home segments. Glass chambers take care of the green house effect by reflecting the infrared rays that build up heat though it also needs adequate ventilation. Thanks to different types of coatings, glass-clad buildings are able to meet the most stringent thermal insulation requirements. A high performance glass façade can improve access to daylight, offers better indoor air quality and also provides greater energy efficiency.

Some companies claim to manufacture a whole range of glass, spanning from sound proof glass, and tampered glass to burglar proof glass. Burglar proof glass or laminated glass is bullet proof glass. Laminated safety or sentry glass has good tactical resistance, is burglar proof and scratch resistant. It can bear specified wind loads and can meet structural requirements with low mechanical strain under other loads. It has outstanding post-breakage resistance to creep and collapse after quakes.

Glass security laminate offers your building protection against bomb explosion. This safety and security laminate makes glass resistant to bombs and bullets but they don't reduce the visual clarity. The installation process is simple and can be completed within a short period of time. They can be fitted without too many people getting to know.

Malls, most of which have facades that use glass extensively, are now installing these laminates. Normally PVB glass is used in these malls which can't withstand a bomb explosion or a seismic tremor. Laminated glass can also be used in place of iron grills. Food-processing plants are installing these laminates. People are also getting these installed in the car windows as one out of every ten car theft take place by smashing the window.

The area very close to the airport has a very high level of noise in Delhi. At times, high vibrations shatter the window panes. The best bet is to use vacuum glass which is quite sound-proof and offers thermal insulation. Vacuum glass is essentially two pieces of glass with an air gap in between, held together by a polysulphide frame. The air is then extracted to create a vacuum. An ordinary window pane breaking is just bad workmanship in fixing the glass. If the glass is left loose in the beading, it will vibrate with sound waves and may break. Ordinary glass will not break if it has been fixed with proper putty to prevent rattling.

Though private residential properties still don't use much glass because of its high cost and requirements of privacy, safety and security; glass is being increasingly used in the builder's flats. Unfortunately a majority of high rise buildings in India are using glass leading to increased monotony in the urban landscape. In an attempt to acquire the best corporate image, companies are constructing super-structures, most of them with glass facades. It has also given rise to millions of square feet of environmentally deficient space. The increasing use of glass has also triggered debate on the desirability of adopting this western architectural element into the Indian tropical conditions. Here, it is often seen as a conspicuous energy consumption symbol which is unsuitable for hot and humid climes.

Glass needs to be used sensibly, sparingly and judiciously like every new material. This is not the right thing to do as a human being could not easily relate to and be comfortable with glass. Glass exteriors can lead to a greenhouse effect, trapping heat within the building. The heat generated by the electronic and electrical equipments including computers results in extra load on the air-conditioners resulting in increased power consumption and hefty bills.

It is necessary to orient buildings so as to minimize the solar radiation. This can be done with the wise provision of courtyards and verandahs. The traditional elements like *jaalis* and screens over glass surfaces can also be used to create an aesthetic and environment-friendly look.

Scientists are now looking at smart glazing's that respond to exterior conditions and can equally control the entry of daylight as well as the amount of solar heat gain. The most promising of such technologies is electro-chromatic glazing, where the glass undergoes a reversible change in optical property when exposed to light. It will behave like a photo-chromatic glass, becoming darker when exposed to sunlight thereby keeping the interiors cool.

Wooden Flooring

In the National Capital Region (NCR), wooden floors are now common in the master bedroom, living room, study and the kid's room. More and more commercial establishments like restaurants, coffee shops and upmarket stores are now installing them. One of the good reasons for their popularity is aesthetics. They look beautiful and impart a natural feel to your interiors. They also offer hygiene besides aesthetics. They are especially suitable for households having young children who spend a lot of time on the floor. Wooden floors are easy to maintain. All they require is regular wiping and they continue to look good for years.

Wooden floors are also easy to install. You can lay these floors over existing floors with tongue and groove mechanism and hence need no adhesive for fixing them. An entire 3-bedroom flat can be done up in one to two days. When you are shifting from one house to another, you can take apart your wooden floor along with you without causing any damage to the floor or to the house. Wooden floors are normally made up of individual boards. If some part of the floor gets damaged, you are required to replace one or two boards only.

Wooden floors are generally of two categories: real wooden floors and laminate floors. Real wooden floors are made up of real wood while laminate floors are made up of high density fiber boards. It is better to use planks with the larger width in bigger rooms. Using the narrower planks in a smaller room creates a sense of space. Wooden floor needs more care in comparison to a tile floor. Water accumulated on the wooden floor for a considerable length of time may damage it. The heels of your shoes also produce lot of noise on it.

Contemporary Workplace Design

It is the workplace where our hard work gets translated to success. It's inappropriate design, construction, furnishings, decoration or placement of equipments can prove havoc to one's business or career. The office should be lean and mean, and minimalist as per the modern perspective. It should be stripped of the extra frills that traditional Indian offices were so fond of having, for example the Plaster of Paris cornice, the beveled glass and the inlay flooring. More emphasis should be on creating a comfortable, no-nonsense office that is conducive to transact business in a way that the employees feel comfortable.

GE, Microsoft and such other multinational corporations now prefer lighter colours. They use a lot of metallic trims, a lot of glass to give a very airy, transparent feel and the work stations fitted in just so. Now some of the pastel shades are giving way to colour on walls, upholstery and accessories. The concept of paperless office is gradually making its mark. Offices are getting even more lean and mean and are beginning to look much tidier. Internet has further changed the way business is transacted. E-mails, Video-conferencing, WhatsApp and other similar facilities have reduced commuting and thereby traffic on the roads.

The actual practice of office work generally lags behind the technology and the new practices of work technology makes possible. Design of the workplace must be dictated by the business objectives. The modern workspace shall be designed to offer maximum flexibility. A certain space in the office may have to be closed and private one day and open and collaborative the next. One should be able to change from an open environment to a private one and back to open.

Work has now become more knowledge-intensive, collaborative and immediate. Now savvy facility directors are focusing on creating a high performance workplace that will boost employee productivity. Now the focus is on the nature of work people do, not on the space they occupy. Thanks to modern technology and high level of connectivity, work is no longer so place dependent. Hence, today's workplace needs round the clock connectivity, along with the appropriate combination of space, protocols, technology and tools. To ensure high productivity, six integrated performance systems must function well.

First of these is the air quality system which deals with the health, safety and comfort related concerns of the employees by providing ventilation, filtration and humidity control. Second is the thermal control system which must provide individualized control to the workers. It must allow them to respond to their constantly changing need for more heating or cooling. A system with control in the hand of employees works much better than a complaint-driven system. Third is the connectivity for voice, data and power systems. It poses one of the biggest challenges in creating an adaptable workplace which requires both wireless and wired connectivity. Provision for access to infrastructure should be in such a manner so that ongoing operations are not disturbed.

Fourth performance system in any adaptable workplace is lighting which must adjust for individual and group tasks. Adaptable lighting requires distribution of controls. In order to maximize the energy efficiency, design should also take advantage of the available natural light. Fifth performance system is an adaptable interior. Manufactured components allowing maximum adaptability are increasingly being installed in the office interiors. Previously isolated systems are being integrated which shall lead to greater adaptability. Sixth performance system is the building shell which should be so designed that it projects the right image of the enterprise housed within.

Include fun in the office. It removes tension. A happy environment at the workplace enhances employee's courage, reduces their tensions, keeps them healthy and helps in encouraging the team work. According to the findings of neuro-sciences, neuro-chemicals released during our laughter reduce our anger, depression and tensions on the one side and increase creativity on the other side. Employees should laugh together on creative jokes, not on each other. Sweet and soft language reduces our tensions.

Ergonomically Designed Office Furniture

Office is a place for business and office furniture is a serious business. Set-up of any office may include desks, office seating, workstations, conference room furniture, training room furniture, reception units, cupboards, filing cabinets, multi-drawer cabinets, lockers, sofa sets, bookcases and chairman's desk with plush leather chair. Productivity can be enhanced by selecting the right furniture. Ergonomics is playing a major role in the design of office interiors. An ergonomically designed chair has comfort, stability and looks. These are designed so that an employee can sit in comfort and discharge his duties for eight hours at a stretch.

The primary work spaces are the office desks which are typically made of wood, laminate or metal. Wood is considered the best material for solid look. As it requires careful handling and maintenance, most of the desks today are made of laminate which has a plastic finish applied to a wooden core. Laminate is available in a wide array of patterns, from wood-grain to colour finishes. Most of the imported range comes in MDF (medium density fiber).

Fig 7.26: An Ergonomically Designed Chair

Office chairs are equipped with a variety of mechanisms based on the ergonomic principles. Most chairs are equipped with a hydraulic system that provides height adjustment options according to the user's comfort. Only multi-purpose and visitor chairs are cantilevered. Fabric chairs are more preferable than the PU (polyurethane, a synthetic resin) chairs. Steel furniture is also getting popular because of its sleek look and durability. The core range comprises of completely knocked down, powder coated steel products. Knocked down furniture is advantageous in case of relocation as the pieces can be reassembled within a few hours.

The prime factors people take into account while buying office furniture are comfort, look, style, durability, maintenance and price. Currently in vogue is the modular, sleek furniture that gives office an uncluttered look and makes it a congenial place for work.

Earthquake Resistance of Buildings

Buildings are perhaps the most significant symbol of human development. Their safety is to be thought of in right earnest. Delhi, the capital city of India, spreads across 1450 km² area with a Population Density (people per sq. km of land area) of 11,297 (as per 2011 census). Because of the alluvial cover of Indo-Gangetic plains, even the distant earthquakes are felt quite strongly. A rise of one magnitude on the Richter scale translates into a 30 times stronger earthquake. An earthquake changes its direction up to 10,000 times in a few seconds, enough to make a multi-storey fall

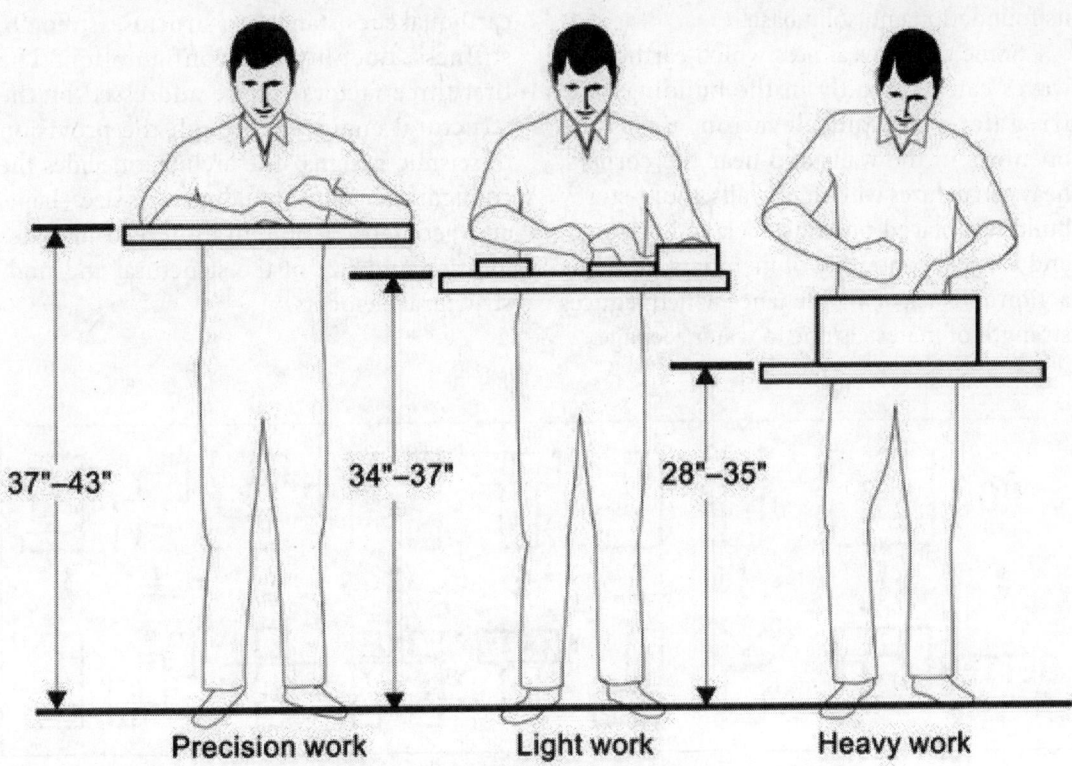

Fig 7.27: Ergonomics of the Working Table in the Standing Mode

like a pack of cards. Poor workmanship and poor quality of construction material will have adverse effects everywhere in Delhi during such a disaster.

Delhi and NCR area falls in high seismic zone IV. Central Building Research Institute (CBRI) has found that Trans-Yamuna, Old Delhi walled city and Dwarka areas are likely to suffer maximum damage in case of an earthquake in Delhi. Trans Yamuna area has loose soil. In case of an earthquake, groundwater will mix with this soil weakening the building structure leading to its collapse. Majority of the buildings are old and dilapidated in the walled city. They flout safe building norms and are located in the congested areas. In most of the Dwarka area, entire ground floors have been converted into the parking lot. Pillars (stilts) have been constructed on the ground floor to support the building which ultimately weakens its foundation and solid base.

Some of the weakness which earthquake waves catch instantly in the buildings are: irregular plan and elevation, excessive openings in the walls and near the corners, heavy structures with thick walls, multi-storey buildings placed on stilts, lack of horizontal and vertical continuity of members for a box action and lack of maintenance which reduces strength of materials due to water seepage.

Main causes of damage in reinforced concrete buildings are poor detailing at critical points of structural elements, beam column joints, negligible transverse reinforcement and poor concrete quality. Non-structural components like cladding, ceiling and partitions etc can cause significant damage and thus require proper anchorage. Mud houses are required to develop resistance for diagonal cracks leading to overall collapse of certain walls. Low strength masonry walls require resistance for corner failure and failure at openings.

Fifty-nine percent of the Indian Territory, which includes all metropolitan cities, is prone to seismic risk. Architects and engineers are being seen as guardians of life and property in case of earthquakes. They are required to prefer disaster resistant design and construction of buildings. Essentially, four factors affect the earthquake resistance of a structure: strength, stiffness, ductility and configuration. The first three factors can be addressed by the structural engineer through the provision of seismic designs. The architect decides the configuration of the building ie its size, shape, and geometry. Configuration also includes location and size of the structural and non-structural elements.

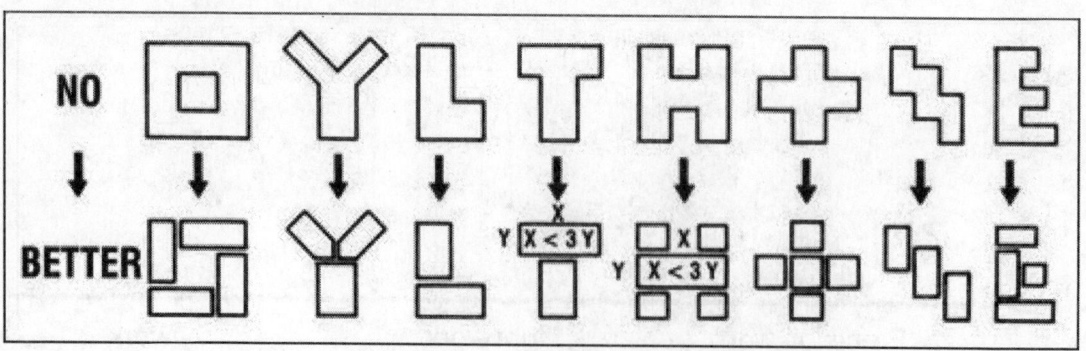

Fig 7.28: Modifying Shapes for Better Earthquake Resistance

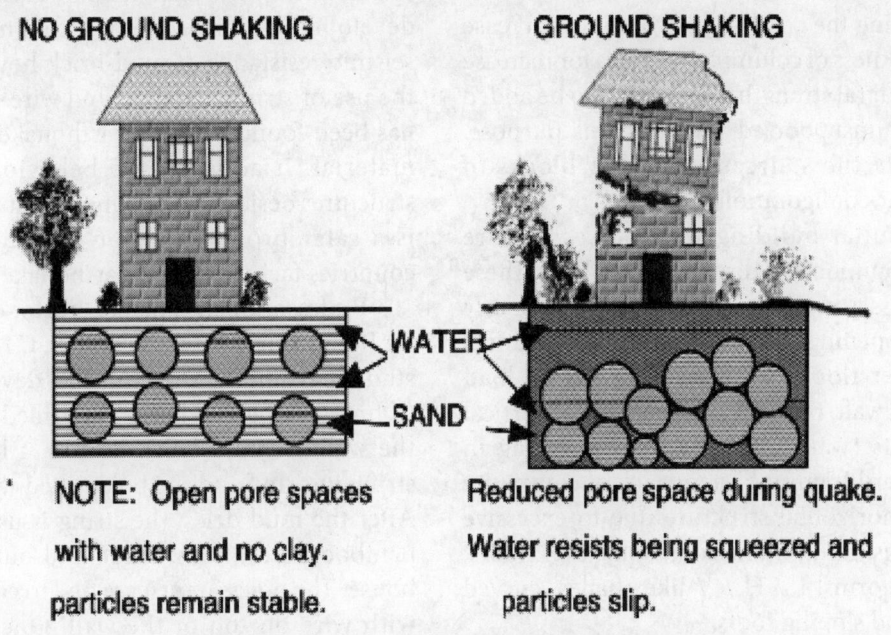

Fig 7.29: Role of Ground Stability in Earthquake Resistance

The architect is required to conceive a stable shape with elements that are properly knitted together. The most stable are the convex forms where a line between any two points within the structure passes through the mass of the building itself. Structural elements that form a tight box are stable. Simplicity is the ultimate sophistication. Thus the size and placement of openings is critical in earthquake resistant design. Contrarily, alphabet-shaped configurations are unstable. Buildings on stilts shall strictly be avoided. Construction materials should be as light as possible.

All types of buildings in an earthquake prone area should have strong footings and bands around the building to hold it together. Soil below the foundation should be stable. That's why construction on the river zones or sides of lakes is prohibited because of the porous soil. Additional reinforcement should be provided in the columns. Horizontal bands of reinforcement in concrete (or wooden logs) after every 4 feet height of wall induces box action in masonry buildings. 'Through stones', which are stones covering the full thickness of walls, help in uniform distribution of loads. Ring beam is an essential component of earthquake resistance. It ties together all the walls at plinth, sill, lintel and roof level. It could be of timber or concrete in low strength masonry walls. It integrates all the building elements to behave in unison against the vibrations of seismic forces.

Some of the characteristic features of earthquake resistant buildings are ductility, deformability and redundancy. 'Ductility' is the capability to undergo sway under vibrations. 'Deformability' is the virtue by which certain parts can assimilate stress without permanent deformation. 'Redundancy' is designing alternate load paths so that the building gets more time before collapsing.

Structural system of stronger column and weak beam design is recommended to save a building from complete collapse. Weak beams under extreme stress develop cracks dissipating some amount of seismic energy and saving the crushing of columns. Increase the thickness of columns and walls for increase in the lateral strength. Piers can also be added to long unsupported walls for this purpose. Separate the staircase block or blocks of irregular configuration.

Peculiar building weaknesses require expert opinion and dexterous handling. These weaknesses may include large and irregularly placed openings, lack of continuity of columns to upper floors, absence of shear or load bearing wall, random arrangement of vertical elements (walls and columns) resulting in haphazard framing system, lack of continuity in the horizontal structure due to excessive openings, multi-plane roof, split-level floors, special forms, L / H / V like shapes, curved walls and sloping roofs.

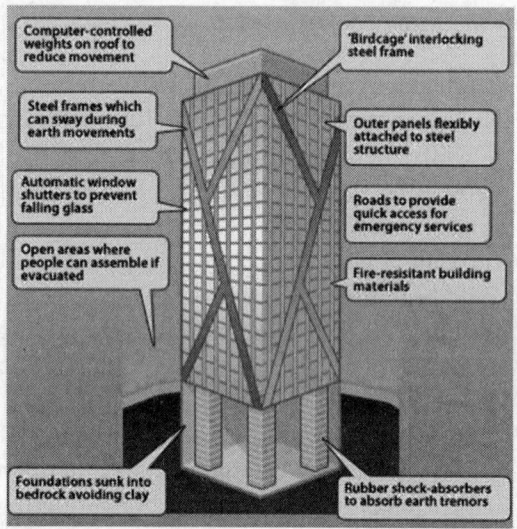

Fig 7.30: Structural Provisions for Earthquake Resistance

In India, around 40 percent of houses are made of plastered mud or mud-blocks. Such houses are kachcha (temporary) and are much vulnerable. The traditional construction methods of Assam, Kashmir or Kutch have something wise, equipped to face the ravages of time. A group of scientists at the University of Technology in Sydney (UTS), Australia has developed a simple method for improving seismic resistance of mud-brick houses with the use of string, bamboo and wire. Bamboo has been found to be an earthquake friendly material. It adds ductile behavior to low structures besides being light weight. Bamboo is a safer proposition for the developing countries facing massive earthquake risk.

Professor Bijan Samali, Director of Centre for Built Infrastructure Research, UTS and his student Dominic Dowling has developed a technique whereby holes are drilled through the walls of mud-brick houses, a length of string inserted and the holes filled with mud. After the mud dries, the string is used to tie bamboo poles, both inside and outside the house. The poles in turn are tied to each other with wire on top of the wall. Once all the wires are securely fastened and the bamboo poles are connected to the beam at the top of the wall, the bamboo is held tight against the wall. The bamboo and wire ensure that the string is not subjected to severe stresses. With this technique, initial cracking of the house was delayed and its collapse prevented, even during the highest intensity simulations. The reinforced house gives people a greater chance to escape their mud-brick homes during a large earthquake.

Precautions before, during and after an earthquake

Earthquake comes without warning. Collapse of buildings and panic causes great deal of casualties. A bit of self-control and steps mentioned here could prove life.

1. Don't stay in any damaged building. Get it repaired at the earliest. Keep monitoring the existing load bearing capacity of the structure.

2. Check the irregular basic configuration of your building with the help of your architect as they are likely to get additional

stress due to eccentricities. Separation of complex plan shapes into structurally independent units is considered better. The vertical structures like columns and load bearing walls should have continuity from foundation till upper floors.

3. Take care of the projected balconies and roof top water tanks for their proper anchorage to the main structures. Properly anchor the non-structural buildings as they fall apart easily under the influence of earthquake forces.

4. The wall openings should not be more than 20 percent of the load bearing wall area. Openings should also be located symmetrically, away from the corners and topped with a lintel (RCC, stone or wood).

5. Masonry buildings can be made more ductile by putting iron dowels vertically at the corners and horizontally at a distance of 1.2 metre.

6. Lightness of material and lower centre of gravity shall be ensured for better performance in seismic tremors.

7. Keep shear walls or load bearing walls for both axes of the building.

8. Free standing walls, chimneys and towers pose greater risk during the seismic tremors. Their slenderness ratio (free height to base ratio) should be kept optimally low.

9. Always be prepared mentally for such disasters.

10. Store emergency supplies like water, food, first aid, torch, cash etc.

11. Immediately turn off the gas and all electrical appliances.

12. Take shelter under a sturdy table or desk for protection.

13. Open the door quickly to secure exit as it may get deformed due to earthquake forces.

14. Stay calm and avoid rushing out of your house when living on a higher storey where immediate evacuation is not possible.

15. When outside, protect your head from the falling objects. Try to take refuse in an open ground or a safe building.

16. Evacuate on foot rather than by car and carry only what you really need.

17. Follow instructions of the staff when caught in a mall or theatre.

18. When on road, park your vehicle to the left and give way to the ambulances and fire brigade vehicles.

Retrofitting

We all wish to strengthen our buildings and make our houses quake resistant. One can certainly ensure that a structure is earthquake resistant to a considerable extent. Retrofitting is a method implemented to reinforce the structure post construction. The first step of retrofitting is to identify susceptibility of the building toward earthquakes. The next step is retrofitting. Retrofitting involves certain modifications like doing away with unnecessary open spaces that make the building weak. The emphasis is on tying all the beams together so that the entire building shakes like a monolithic structure and the load is equally distributed on all the columns. The building is more damage prone if the pillars shake individually.

Seismic retrofitting can limit the damage if not completely avoiding them. If the seismic loads are less than the building's strength, it may cause damage but not the collapse. However, there can be two possibilities when loads exceed the available strength. If the building is brittle, it will collapse. But if it is ductile, localized area of structural damage will prevent collapse.

Seismic retrofitting is based on visualization of initial forces developed in a structure during earthquake, planning a simple and direct path for transfer of the forces to the ground, and maintaining the integrity and stiffness for energy dissipating characteristics. Concept of seismic strengthening has mainly two aspects:

(a) Restoration of lost strength to pre-earthquake levels

(b) Upgrade the strength of building for future earthquake for total collapse prevention and major (or total) damage prevention

First step of retrofitting is to identify and eliminate weaknesses in the structure. Weaknesses could be from excessive openings, lack of uniformity of load bearing walls or columns, concentration of stress due to asymmetrical forms and composition, long unsupported walls and cantilevers leading to inadequate lateral strength.

Building should never block natural drainage of the site as strength of foundation gets affected by soil erosion. Retrofitting of an existing foundation could not be possible without expert consultation. A concrete apron of 4 to 5 inch thick should be provided around the building to prevent penetration of water to the foundation. It is also necessary to provide foundation beam connecting the isolated column footings.

Archaeological Survey of India (ASI) has placed glass pieces on the ground near Qutab Minar to check tremors' impact. Grouting of Qutab Minar has also been carried out twice in the past few decades. "Grouting" is a process in which dead mortar near the Minar is sucked out and the fresh one is injected to keep the foundation strong.

It is good to reduce the building mass. Hollow bricks can be used in new buildings for this purpose. Retrofitting may include removal of upper floors for reduction of mass and closing certain openings which are critically located to disturb the continuity of strength in all the members.

Fire Safety

A building should be well equipped to facilitate quick and easy exit in case of emergency. Egress has become a crucial issue because of very large occupancies, limited floor spaces and increasing heights of tall buildings. The ability of occupants to leave safely during fire is a major concern. In tall buildings people trapped in areas above the site of disaster have no options for escape particularly where fire stairs are used. Rescue from above is dangerous and time consuming. Building codes have fixed a high level of design and fire rating, alarms and communication systems, suppression technologies and evacuation plans. Following points are crucial in fire safety:

1. When a fire does break out, it should effectively be managed. Potential heat sources in a building should be separate from the potential fuels. Once the fire breaks out, main factors that influence the control of combustion process are: fuel load, interior finish of the room, air-supply and size, shape and construction of the room.

2. Fire can be controlled by construction in the form of barriers like walls, partitions, floors and separate building spaces. Barriers prevent fire from spreading. Fire can also be extinguished by fire extinguishers, ventilation and adequate water supply.

3. Keep the common corridors and staircases clear of any obstructions. Clear spaces will allow people to exit quickly in case of fire.

4. Never use basement for any purpose other than what is permissible. Lack of ventilation here in case of a fire may turn them into death trap.

5. Don't misuse the fire-fighting water tanks or leave them remaining empty. Keep the access to these tanks clear of any blockage in case of emergency.

6. Wet riser system is provided to check the spread of fire before the arrival of fire brigade. Keep this system damage free as its good maintenance ensures your safety.
7. Train yourself in the proper operation of first-aid hose reel (which is provided at each floor level) and fire extinguishers. Acquaint yourself with the layout of escape routes, staircases, refuse areas, location of fire alarms and call points.
8. Never use electric panel or meter room as storage or dumping area as these are potential fire hazards.
9. Refuse areas or fire shelter are built at different levels in high rise buildings to provide shelter in case of fire. Never enclose or misuse these areas.
10. In case of fire, don't use lift as it may fail trapping the people inside. Prefer using the staircase instead.
11. Don't leave electrical appliances unattended. Use one socket for one electrical appliance only. Switch them off after use, and remove the plug from the socket. Don't overload the electrical circuits. This may result in short-circuit and a fire. Switch off the 'main switch' when you are leaving home for a long period.
12. In the event of fire, don't switch off the electric supply of the entire building. If you do so, all the fire protection and fire-fighting systems installed in the building will stop functioning.
13. Keep your LPG stove or burner on a non-combustible raised platform. Turn off the gas cylinder valve and burner when gas stove is not in use. Ventilate the entire room if LPG cylinder or PNG connection is leaking. Don't operate the electrical switches at this point of time.

No one single measure guarantees protection against a fire. A combination of active and passive protection measures offer the best protection. A balanced fire protection design blends the systems eg alarms with fire fighting gadgets like fire sprinklers. Passive measures like using the fire resistant building materials, compartmentalization, pressurized stairways, fire-rated floors, walls and doors etc also help in stopping the fire. Passive fire protection systems confine the smoke and flames to one part only, thereby making the outbreak more manageable. Built-in fire resistant construction helps to separate buildings from one another and also to separate the different usage areas.

Termite Problem

Termites or white ants are a group of insects that are helpful in the forest environment or in an open land situation as they recycle natural material using their unique ability to degrade cellulose-based material. But it is unfortunate that termite is one of our worst enemies as damage likely to be caused by termite is huge. The damage caused by termites in USA has been found to be more than the combined damage caused by fire, storms and earthquakes.

Termites attack both cellulosic and non-cellulosic materials. The first thing that termites access in their foraging activity is wooden interiors. It makes the wooden furniture hollow from inside without any notice. They also damage materials of organic origin with cellulose base. Termites also damage rubber, leather, plastic, neoprene and lead coating used for covering underground cables.

Termites enter the building through the wood buried in the ground or by means of mud shelter tubes constructed over unprotected foundations. Termites can be detected if you see soil lining on the walls and flooring. Powder falling from wooden furniture may also indicate its presence. Inspect the wooden furniture and other articles from time to time.

Be alert when paint on the walls and windows is found peeled off or when lines made of soil are seen on the walls.

Termite multiplies easily in damp and dark areas. Keep your building and surroundings damp proof to avoid termite problem. Purchase only termite resistant wooden furniture. Make proper arrangement for ventilation of your building. Don't allow the water to get accumulated near the foundation. Remove the heaps of wood, paper and other garbage from the surroundings.

Termite control is more critical in low income housing, as earth built houses or houses built with low-cost material are more prone to termite attacks. Even high cost housing undertaken without the appropriate pest prevention measures is susceptible. Chemical barriers are becoming the only reliable means of controlling termite problem. The chemical barrier pre-construction anti-termite treatment has been well-established for more than half a century now. It is successfully practiced in many countries.

Now-a-days both pre-construction and post-construction termite treatment are available. Pest control companies are providing these specialized services. Different termite control solutions are also available in the market. Use only the authorized termite resistant chemicals while construction. Obtain a certificate from the builder that termite resistant measures have been taken during the pre-construction itself. Termiticide should not be allowed to contaminate the wells or springs, which serve as source of drinking water.

Noise Pollution

Owners of more than 90 lakh vehicles in Delhi constantly honk to find a way on the congested city roads. Cars in the colony keep people awake at night. Fancy reverse horns are a sheer torture for the people. All night one or the other car screams to tell us that it is backing up. Some others' burglar alarm goes off even if someone rests on it. Vehicles with their pressure horns and reverse horns are said to be the biggest sources of noise pollution in Delhi.

Fig 7.31: Some Sources of Noise Pollution

Huge diesel generators that make malls dazzle and multiplexes thunder are giving sleepless nights to the residents of nearby residential areas. These generator sets and their cooling towers make so much noise that people have to keep their windows shut for almost whole of the day. The generators continue spewing venom. Diesel-run generator sets are the prime culprits. Petrol and kerosene ones are also bad. The worst are the cheap Chinese models that meet no standards of noise level limits.

Noise pollution from loudspeakers gets deafening, particularly during the elections and political rallies, religious celebrations and marriages. Small factories and commercial units operating illegally in the residential areas make it unbearable for the residents with the drilling, hammering and vibration of machinery.

Frequent night long religious functions make the decibel level rise in the vicinity. People get irritated, their BP shoots up and may fall ill if it continues. As per the norms, nights should be quieter than the days. However, airport remains open all night long in Delhi. People living in the vicinity can't sleep or study at night as frequent flights shatter the calm. Colonies under the 'flight path' like Vasant Vihar, Dwarka and JNU have a jumbo jet plane mercilessly treading over their sleep every few minutes.

Noise pollution is leading to all types of deafness, irritability, heart ailments and stress. Noise damages your hearing, interferes in communication, causes annoyance, reduces efficiency, disturbs sleep, brings anxiety, and invites stress and high blood pressure. Some of the frequently observed physiological effects of noise pollution are; increased hormone production from thyroid, higher heart rate, and increased secretion of adrenaline leading to dilated eye pupils and constriction of blood vessels. Delhi traffic police is the worst sufferer of noise and air pollution at traffic intersections.

If you hear constantly a humming or ringing sound, immediately consult an ENT specialist. There is an urgent need to have strict noise norms for all spheres and implement them effectively. Till now, only some unsuccessful efforts have been made to curb only the loudspeakers and crackers. Recently, Supreme Court has completely banned sale and purchase of crackers in Delhi and NCR. Central Pollution Control Board (CPCB) is considering issuing Noise under Control (NUC) certificates for vehicles.

Based on a study conducted by researchers at Newcastle University, a report was published in the national daily "The Times of India" on 15th October 2012 regarding pleasant and harsh sounds. The study revealed that the sound of a woman screaming is among the top 10 unpleasant sounds for humans, while that of applause or a laughing baby is among the most pleasant. The top three unpleasant sounds in a list of 74 are the sound of a knife on a bottle, fork on a glass and chalk on a blackboard. A baby crying or an electrical drill also figures in the list of unpleasant sounds. The cracking of thunder or the sound of flowing water is among the least unpleasant.

Electrosmog

Most of the people today are well conversant with the outer pollutants of our environment bur are unaware of the invisible pollution present inside our living spaces. We are constantly falling prey to an invisible smoke present in our homes and workplaces. Neither can we see it nor can we smell it. Scientists have termed it 'electrosmog' which is produced by electronic gadgets like mobile phones, TV and computer screens, refrigerators and microwave ovens. It is called a silent killer and causes many serious diseases including cancer. Washing machines, vacuum cleaners and dish washers generate low frequency radiations while mobile phones, TV and computer screens and microwave ovens generate high frequency radiation. Higher the frequency of radiations, higher the bad influences.

An electro-magnetic field develops around these electronic gadgets during their operation. This electro-magnetic field causes headache, disturbed concentration, allergy and reduced immunity. We should be constantly vigilant about it. Small children should not be allowed to play with such gadgets. Keep your phone call as short as possible. Rooms should have proper cross ventilation. Don't use any such gadget in your bedroom.

Facilities Management (FM)

Comfort and a good lifestyle are increasingly becoming important to the urban population. Buyers now prefer homes that have facilities like landscaped gardens, health spa, high-tech elevators, swimming pool and parking spaces. They also desire arrangements for professional maintenance and upkeep of the property. Professionally managed properties fetch a good return even after 10 years of their construction.

Facilities management (FM) companies are striking good deals for maintaining such premises. FM is a novel concept and is gaining acceptance as it is critical to maintaining and enhancing asset value of the property. The term FM means a process of coordinating the physical workplace with the people and work of an organization. Outsourcing support functions to a FM company generates quality services and also cuts costs drastically. Costs are fixed and accountability is clear.

The primary function of FM is to plan, establish and maintain a work environment that effectively supports the goals and objectives of the organization. For this purpose, FM incorporates skills from various fields like business management, architecture, engineering, real estate and human resources. These FM companies are providing large range of facilities in residential complexes, commercial buildings, shopping malls and educational institutions.

FM companies do it all, from repairing a leaking tap to conducting annual general meetings of the housing society. Their functions include HVAC, electrical, plumbing, security, data and communications cabling, maintenance of building structures and interiors including maintenance of facade, maintenance of furniture and equipment, maintenance of ground, landscaping, gardening, site improvement, administrative jobs, waste management, pest control and also housekeeping services.

The coordination and integration skills of a facility manager appear like that of an orchestra conductor. A facility manager is expected to manage all the building systems discussed above. He is expected to serve as a Project Manager (PM) for coordination from planning stage till completion. He is also required to ensure round the clock safe, reliable, and code & procedure compliant operations.

Chapter 8
Diminutive Vaastu

कर्मणा मनसा वाचा यदभीक्ष्णं निषेवते।
तदेवापहरत्येनं तस्मात् कल्याणमाचरेत्।।

That which a person pursues in word, deed and thought, wins him for its own. Therefore, one should always seek that which is for his good.

Mahabharata, Udyogaparva 7.42

The tenets of vaastu shastra are meant to protect us from the atrocities of nature and not from the gifts of nature itself. It is rare to find nice homes with unhappy people or happy people in rotten homes. Abraham Lincoln had once remarked, "First we shape our buildings and then our buildings shape us". Vaastu friendly homes help the families to develop a wholesome attitude towards life. On the contrary, living in the cramped ill-lit homes also cramps our view of the world.

We are not able to see life in its true perspective if our rooms are not ventilated and well-lit. Family members should not feel restricted or constricted in the home. A home should promote movement. It should be uncluttered. Dark areas, ill-ventilated rooms, and heavy furniture suck our positive energy. You may enhance the prosperity of your business by activating the element with which it is associated. Any business may be equated with a planet, a directional lord, a demi-god(dess), one or more of the five great elements, triguna, heavy or light load, and amount of light and heat required.

Here, in this chapter, I am briefly discussing the varied aspects of vaastu. Intelligent readers may use this information for further enriching their minds. Some aspects, though discussed at length in the earlier chapters, have been added to provide the additional knowledge regarding the classical, modern, personal or practical view.

History of Vaastu

The Yukatan Peninsula in the Mexican territory of Central America contains some Hindu monuments. The Maya manuscript book records the migration of the clans to America. The chief one of the clan 'Maya' is stated in the great Indian epic Mahabharat to have built a wonderful audience hall for the king Yudhishthira. The British museum guide to the Maudsley Collection of Maya Sculptures further confirms the building activities of Maya clan in America.

Vaastu and its Four Types (Maansaar)

The place where men and gods reside is called vaastu (dwelling or habitation). It is divided in four classes:

1. Dhara or ground
2. Harmya or building
3. Yaan or conveyance
4. Paryanka or seats

Of these four, ground is the principal one, for nothing can be built without the ground as a support. Harmya includes prasada, mandapa, sabha, shala, prapa and ranga. Yaan includes syandana, shivika and ratha. Paryanka includes panjara, manchali, mancha, kakashta, phalakasana and bala paryanka

Origin of Vaastu (Maansaar)

Vaastu shastra (science of architecture) has come down from Shiva, Brahma and Vishnu; through Indra, Brihaspati, Narada and all other sages. From the four faces of Brahma originated in order the heavenly architect Vishvakarman, Maya, Tvashtar and Manu. Their four sons are respectively called Sthapati, Sutra-grahin, Vardhaki and Sutra-dhara or Takshaka. These four evidently represent the progenitors of the four classes of the terrestrial artists.

Sthapati is highest in rank; he is the chief architect or master builder. Sutragrahin is the draughtsman or the designer. He is the guru of vardhaki (painter) and takshaka; while vardhaki is the instructor of takshaka. Sthapati must be well versed in all sciences (shastras). He must know the vedas and must have qualifications of a supreme director (acharya). Sutragrahin should also know the Vedas and the shastras. He must be an expert draughtsman (rekhagya). Vardhaki too should have a general knowledge of the Vedas. But the object of his special duty is painting (chitra-karman). Sutra-dhara or takshaka must be an expert in his own work of joinery or carpentry.

Sources of Vaastu (Maansaar)

(1) Classical texts of vaastu

Maansaar, Mayamata Shilpa Shastra of Gannamacharya, Amshumad-Bheda of Kashyapa, Vishvakarma (shilpa / shilpa shastra / prakasha / vaastu shastra) or Vishvakarmiya Shilpa, Aagastya or Aagastya-Sakaladhikara, Sanat Kumar Vaastu Shastra, Shilpa Shastra of Mandana or Rajavallabha Mandana or Sutradhara Mandana or Bhupati Vallabha, Silparatna of Srikumara, Samrangana Sutradhara of king Bhojadeva, Shilpa Samgraha, Puranas: Vishnu-dharmottara, Agni, Garuda, Matsya, Bhavishya, Brahmanda, Agamas: Kamikagama, Suprabhedagama, Vaikhanasagama, Natya shastra of Bharata, Sangita-Makranda of Narada, Sangita-Ratnakara of Nihsanka-Sharngdeva, Nirukta of Yaska, Amarkosha, Brihatsamhita of Varahmihira

(2) Other sources of Vaastu

Vastu vidya ed. Ganapati Shastri, Bimbamana, Manu-Samhita, Shatapatha Brahmana, Aitareya Brahmana, Chhandogaya Upanishada, Shulva Sutra of Baudhayana, Shilpa-Ratna

(3) Miscellaneous treatises on vaastu

Arthshastra of Kautilya, Shukraniti, Harshacharita, Rajatarangini of Kalhana, Ramayana & Mahabharata, Garga Samhita, Surya Siddhanta, Siddhanta Shiromani, Lilavati, Poetical works of Magha, Kalidasa, and Bhavbhuti, Shisupalavadha (dwarka city described), Vikramorvashiya, Meghaduta, Uttara Ramacharita, Mrichchhkatikam

Pada-Vinyaas or Site Plan (Maansaar)

A building should preferably face east or Northeast, and never the southeast. Reasons have not been discussed. After selecting site for constructing a village, town or building there on, the ground is divided into different number of squares. 32 kinds of such schemes are distinguished by as many different designations. The whole scheme has been arranged in such a manner that in each case the number of partitions represents the square of the serial number. The eighth plot, for instance, which is called 'chandita', comprises a division into 64 squares. The ninth plot, called paramshayika, is divided into 81 squares. Each of these squares is assigned to its presiding deity. Some deities are lords of more than one square.

Lord of the central square is always Brahma. Charaki, Vidari, Putana and Paparakshashi are the presiding deities of corners beyond ishana, agneya, nairritya & vayavya respectively. Finally, vaastu purusha, who is described as hump backed and of crooked shape, is said to occupy the whole of vaastu. Bali is offered to different deities. These offerings consist of milk in its various forms, butter, rice, sesame, parched grain (laja), honey, sweets, incense, lamps, flowers and fruits. Modaka is offered to sugriva, blood to asura, dried meat to mriga, dried fish to roga and sea-fish to bhringraja. The four corner demonesses also receive their share. For example, rakshasi receives meat of goats mixed with blood.

Foundation (Maansaar)

The foundation is excavated in the ground best suited for a structure to the depth of a man's height with uplifted arms. Bottom of the pit thus excavated must reach rock or water. Best soil for receiving foundation is rock, gravel or closely pressed sandy earth.

Graam-Lakshan-Vidhaan or Villages (Maansaar)

There is not much difference between a village, a town and a fort. All the fortified places are intended for the residence of people. A town is the extension of a village. A fort is in many cases nothing more than a fortified town. A fort is principally meant for the purpose of defense, while a village or a town is mainly intended for habitation. Villages are divided into eight classes according to their shape. These are dandaka, sarvato-bhadra, nandyavarta, padmaka, swastika, prastara, kaarmuka, and chatur-mukha.

Each village is surrounded by a wall made of brick or stone. Beyond this wall there is a ditch broad and deep enough to cause serious obstruction in the event of an attack on the village. There are generally four main gates at the middle of the four sides, and as many at the four corners. Inside the wall, there is a large street running all around the village. There are two other large streets, each of which connects two opposite main gates. They intersect each other at the centre of the village, where a temple or a hall is generally built for the meeting of the villagers. The village is thus divided into four main blocks.

Each block is further subdivided into many blocks by streets which are always straight and ran from one end to the other of a main block. The two main streets crossing at the centre have houses and footpaths on one side of the street. The ground floor of these houses on the main streets consists of shops. The street, which runs round the village, also has houses and footpaths only on one side. These houses are mainly public buildings, such as schools, libraries, guest-houses etc. All other streets generally have residential buildings on both sides.

The houses, high or low, are always uniform in make. Drains (jala-dwara or water passage) follow the slope of the ground. Tanks and ponds are dug in all the inhabited parts. These are located where they can conveniently be reached by a large number of inhabitants. Temples for public worship as well as the public commons, gardens and parks are similarly located. People of the same caste or profession are generally housed in the same quarter. The best quarters are generally reserved for the brahmins and the architects. The inhabitation of the chandalas, as well as the places for cremation, is located beyond the outside wall, particularly in vayavya. Temples of fearful deities, such as Chamunda, are also located outside the wall.

Nagar-Vidhaan or Towns (Maansaar)

A town is a large village. Dimensions of the town unit vary from 100 X 200 dandas to 7200 X 14400 dandas ('danda' or pole measured four cubit (hasta) or approximately six feet). A town may be situated from east to west or from north to south according to the position it occupies. There should be one to twelve large streets in the town. It should be built near a river or a mountain. It should have facilities for trade and commerce with the foreigners (dvipantara-vartin). Like a village, it should have walls, ditches and gates, drains, parks, commons, shops, exchanges, temples, guest-houses, colleges etc. For military defense purposes, the towns are generally well fortified. Towns are divided into eight classes: rajadhani nagara, kevala nagara, pura, nagari, kheta, kharvata, kubjaka and pattana. The distinction between them is slight. The city called pattana is a big commercial port which is situated on the bank of the sea or a river and is always engaged in exchange and commerce with foreigners; especially dealing in jewels, silk, perfumes etc imported from other countries (dvipantara).

Forts (Maansaar)

Forts are first divided into eight classes, called shivira, vahini-mukfia, sthaniya, dronaka, samviddha or vardhaka, kolaka, nigama, and skandhavara. These forts are further divided according to their position. They are known as giri durga (mountain fort), vana durga (forest fort), jala durga (water fort), ratha durga (chariot fort), deva durga (divine fort), panka durga (marsh fort), and mishra durga (mixed fort). Mountain fort is further sub divided into three classes: built on the top of the mountain, in the valley, or on the mountain slope. All these forts are surrounded with strong walls and ditches. The wall is made of brick, stone and similar materials. It is at least 12 cubits in height and at least 6 cubits thick at the base. It is provided with sufficient watch towers

Bhumi-Lamba-Vidhaan or Height of Buildings (Maansaar)

Maansaar and kamikagama deal with the measurement of length, breadth and height of buildings of one to twelve storeys. Various building shapes may be square, rectangular, round, octagonal or oval. Buildings of all kinds, such as the vimana (temple), harmya (palace), gopura (gate-house), shala (storeyed mansion), mandapa (pavilion), and the veshman (residential houses generally) should have one of these five shapes. The proportion between height and width is expressed by five technical names; shantika, paushtika, parshnika (jayada), sarva-kamika (dhanada) and adbhuta. When the height of a building or idol is equal to its width, it is called shantika. Paushtika height is 1.25 times the width, parshnika or jayada height is 1.5 times the width, sarvakamika height is 1.75 times the width and adbhuta height is twice the width.

Shantika and paushtika heights are prescribed for the large type of measurement, parshnika or jayada for the intermediate type & sarvakamika and adbhuta for the small type. According to kamikagama, width of a 12 storeyed building is 70 cubits and the height 100 cubits. The number of storeys allowed are according to the social status of their occupants – five to seven storeyed palace for a chakravartin while one to three storeyed residence for yuvaraja or samanta-pramukha.

Building Materials (Maansaar)

Four kinds of building materials are distinctly mentioned: stone, brick, wood and iron. Though buildings are made of one, two, three or all the four of these materials, preference is given to the use of one material only. Building made of one material only is called "shuddha", when made of two materials is called "mishra", and "samkirna" when made of three or more materials.

Classifications of Buildings (Maansaar)

Buildings are again divided into four classes: jaati, chhanda, vikalpa or samkalpa, and abhasa. Here these are considered with regard to their measurement. Jaati, chhanda, vikalpa, and abhasa are respectively measured in the cubit of 24, 25, 26 and 27 angulas.

The Dwelling Houses (Maansaar)

The breadth of a house is said to be of five kinds, from 2-3 dandas to 10-11 dandas, the increment being by two dandas. The length may be equal to twice the breadth. Houses are stated to be built in a village, town, pattan, grove or hermitage, near a hill or mountain or on the bank of a river. Braham-sthan is stated to be unfit for a residential building. Temple of the family god is generally built in this part. The karagara (jail) is located in a rather out-of-the-way place, such as the bhrish or antariksha square.

Ratha-Lakshan-Vidhaan or Cars and Chariots (Maansaar)

Cars and chariots are constructed for the ceremonial and ordinary use of gods, brahmins and kings, as well as for war and other purposes. The wheels and other parts of cars, their shapes, their measurements, their ornamentations and moulding are described. Wheel is always circular, made of timber from particular trees. A lofty structure is raised, on a double support (called adhara and upadhara), resting on the axle. It is provided with balconies (bhadra) and is profusely decorated. It may have as many as nine storeys, the height of each upper storey being smaller than the lower one.

Square cars are called nagara, octagonal ones dravida, circular ones vesara, hexagonal ones andhra, and the oval ones kaalinga. A fighting car has three wheels, the car for mock fighting has four wheels, for ordinary festivals (nityotsava) has five wheels, for special festivals (mahotsava) may have 6, 7, 8, 9, or 10 wheels. In the same manner number of vedis (platforms) vary according to the special purpose for which a car is to be used.

These cars should be decorated with peacocks' feathers, chowries, torana, little bells, bright mirrors, fans and garlands. There should be carved images of various deities, particularly on the upper part of the structure. Basement is adorned with representations of lions, elephants and crocodiles, with foliated ornamentation and with figures of dancers, bhutas and yakshas.

Shayan-Vidhaan or (Couches) (Maansaar)

Couches are meant for the use of deities and human beings. They are of two types - baal paryanka (small) and paryanka (large). Width of baal-paryanka may vary from 11 to 25 angulas, the increment being by 2 angulas, thus making 8 varieties. Width of paryanka may vary from 21 to 37 angulas, the increment being by 2 angulas, thus making 9 varieties.

They are generally furnished with four legs to which castors are attached so that they may easily be moved from one place to another. Legs of royal couches should be decorated with lions. Couches are generally rectangular. Swings suspended from four chains are said to be used by gods and upper castes. Wood of certain trees is used for making seats and couches. Special kind of timber is recommended for the legs

Rangashala Vaastu (Maansaar)

Natya-Shastra of Bharata describes in great detail the stage proper and the auditorium. The audience house admits of three varieties: the circular or semi-circular, quadrangular and triangular pavilions. A similar account of the stage proper is also given. On the two sides of it, an entabulature is raised over four pillars.

Green rooms are made at the back and on the sides. The platform or the theatre proper is erected at the front, on a level higher than the auditorium. Two of these three types of theatres have been referred to in the Vishnudharmottara Purana. Sangeet-makaranda of Narada supplies an account of an unspecified type of stage and auditorium. Sangeet-ratnakara of Nihsanka-Sharngadeva describes auditorium alone.

The Measurements (Maansaar)

An angula is of 6, 7 or 8 yava. Four different kinds of hasta (24 to 27 angulas) are used, based on specific purpose:

1. Yaan (conveyances) and Shayan (couches) = 24 angula
2. Vimaan (storeys) = 25 angula
3. Buildings = 26 angula
4. Villages = 27 angula

The presiding deity of the hasta and danda (four hastas) is Vishnu, and that of rajju (eight dandas) is Vasuki, the king of serpents.

Linear measurement is divided into six kinds

1. Maan, is the measurement of height from the foot to the top of the head
2. Pramaan, is the measurement of breadth
3. Parimaan, is the measurement of width or circumference (paritah)
4. Lamba-maan, is the measurement by the plumb lines or the lines drawn perpendicularly through different parts of the body, the mana or the measurement of height being taken by the surface of the body.
5. Unmaan, is the measurement of thickness (nimna) or diameter.
6. Upamaan, is the measurement of interspace (antara), such as that between the two feet of an image.

The primary measurements (adimaan) refers to comparative measurements and is divided into nine kinds. The height of an image is determined by comparing it with the: (1) Breadth of the main temple (2) Height of the adytum (garbha-griha) (3) Length of the door (4) Measurement of the basement (5) Cubit (6) Taal (7) Angula (8) Height of the worshipper, and (9) Height of the riding animal.

Each of the measurements is again divided into nine kinds. Under (1), (2), (3) and (4), the proportions naturally vary on various occasions.

Angula, equivalent to 3/4 ", is perhaps the earliest unit of measurement. There are 3 kinds of angula: manangula, matrangula, and dehalabdhangula. Manangula, which is equal to 8 barley corns, is meant to be the unit proper. matrangula is the measure taken by the middle finger of the master who makes an image of the building. Dehalabdhangula is the measure equal to one of the equal parts into which the whole height of a statue is divided for sculptural measurements.

The tala-mana is a sculptural measure. The length of face (tala) is taken as the unit of measurement. Tala is the distance between the tips of the fully stretched thumb and middle finger. Ten tala measures are mentioned in manasara which means that the whole length of an image is ten times the face. In the nine tala system, the whole length would be nine times the face, and so on. Alternatively, the whole length is also divided into 124, 120 or 116 equal parts.

The height of an image may be equal to the full height of its worshipper. It may extend upto his hair limit on the forehead, eye line, nose-tip, chin, arm-limit to the shoulder, breast, heart, navel and sex organ. The height of the riding animal is compared with the height of the main idol in the same manner

Marcus Vitruvius Pollio (Maansaar)

Vitruvius is the name of a roman architect. In a sense, all European architecture is based on his treatise, which seems to have been composed in 25 BC. It was first printed in Rome in or around 1486 AD. The measures necessarily used in all buildings and other works are derived from the members of the human body, as the digit, the palm, the foot and the cubit.

Symmetry and proportion are as necessary to the beauty of a building as to that of a well formed human figure. Nature has fashioned the face from the chin to the top of the forehead (or to the roots of the hair), a tenth part of the height of the whole body. From the chin to the crown of the head is an eighth part of the whole height. The navel is naturally placed in the centre of the human body.

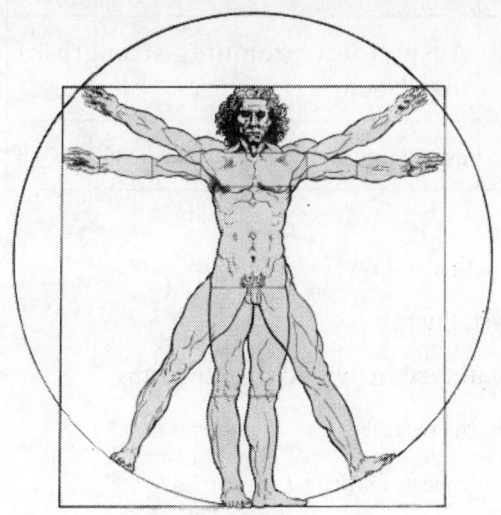

Fig 8.1: Vitruvian Man

If, in a man lying with his face upwards and his hands and feet extended, a circle be described from his navel as the centre, it will touch his fingers and toes. The human body may also be similarly placed in a square (see figure 8.1). Measuring from the feet to the crown of the head, and then across the arms fully extended, we find the latter measure equal to the former. The lines at right angles to each other, enclosing the figure, will form a square.

Marma-Sthanas or Vulnerable Points (Brihatsamhita, 53.57, 58, 63-65)

The meeting points of the longer diagonals (vamsha) and the exact middle points of the squares should be considered as marmas. Vamsha also stands for minor lines connecting a few pairs of squares in addition to the two main diagonals, there are four minor ones called rajjus. These six bring about nine points of intersections. A wise architect ought not to hurt these (BS, 53.57).

Should these marmas be hurt by dirty materials like unclean utensils, nails, pillars, pegs, shalya, heavy things like stones etc, they would cause trouble to the owner of the building in the corresponding limbs of his body. The limb of a man correspond to those of the house god or vaastu purush (BS, 53.58).

The nine points of intersection of the lines connecting Shikhin and Pitar, Jayant and Bhringraaj, Aditi and Sugreev, Agni and Vayu, Bhrsh and Mukhya, and Vitath and Shosh are the ati-marma sthanas. The measurement of ati-marma part is an eighth part of a square (pada). Already mentioned 6 diagonal lines are called vamsha(s). East-west and north-south lines are called shira(s). Breadth of a diagonal (vamsha) is as many digits as the number of cubits each square measures. Breadth of shira is 1.5 times the vamsha (BS, 53.63-65).

Shalya (Brihatsamhita, 53.59-62)

If, at the time of query, owner of the house scratches a limb, corresponding limb of vastu purush has shalya (affliction or hurt), or if at the time of offering oblations to the deities at the sacrifice (connected with the construction of the house), there is some evil omen (such as sneezing, spitting, leaving apana vayu, weeping, howling, uttering inauspicious words etc), or unnatural behaviour of the fire (sudden sparks, crackling sound, bad odour etc), that particular limb of the vaastu purush occupied by the relevant deity (to whom oblations are offered), should have shalya.

Table 8.1: Type of Shalya and its Result

S No	Type of shalya	Result
1	Wood	Loss of memory
2	Bone	Fear of disease, bad for cattles
3	Iron	Trouble from weapons
4	Skull or hair	Death
5	Charcoal	Fear of thieves
6	Ashes	Constant danger from fire
7	Metals (except gold and silver)	Highly dangerous
8	Husk or chaff	Obstructs influx of wealth
9	Gold, silver, gems (including in marma-sthanas)	Auspicious, promotes strength of foundation
10	Ivory (except at marma-sthanas)	auspicious

Directions

South and southwest directions are dustbins of the house. Thus, a store room is best suited in these directions. The west side of the house is ideal for students, children and minors. Rahu rules south-west as dikpala and west direction as the demi-god Asura. Rahu governs in-laws, electricity, hidden enemies, black magic and witchcraft, shades and shadows, and also legal disputes. South-west and west side of the workplace should ideally be kept for the unknown visitors, controversial guests and unverified servants. The east side should house the talented young children, innocent people in general, yoga and meditation rooms and silent places apart from dwellings of pets. Nine zones and their most prominent activities may be tabulated as under.

Northeast: Power

East: Energy

Southeast: Activity, changing forms

South: Death

Southwest: Darkness, heaviness

West: Laziness

Northwest: Movement

North: Money

Brahamsthan: Spiritual

Five Elements

Major functions of the five elements, relevant finger in the hand and their mutual relationship is given here in a tabular form.

Table 8.2: Five Elements and their Mutual Relationship

Element (Tattwa)	Function	Related Finger	Fast Friend	Neutral	Enemy
Earth	Creation	Ring	Water	Fire	Air
Water	Growth	Little	Earth	Air	Fire
Fire	Burning	Thumb	Air	Earth	Water
Air	Communication	Index	Fire	Water	Earth
Space	Blessedness	Middle			

Simplicity of Design

Our properties should be simple like our body. While constructing or purchasing any property, focus on what you want out of it? What is the real purpose of moving? Don't start reveling about how this place will impress people or making them envious. Deviated intentions lead to overspending on the space, construction, interior design, furniture and furnishings. Simplicity is graceful, natural needs are elegant, not the infinite wishes. Elaborate designs are meant for public buildings, not for residential premises. Vaastu prescribes secular architecture for homes, offices, shops and factories. For temples, it prescribes religious architecture.

Overhead water tank, antenna, air vent pipe, advertisement board, flag etc – upper level of all these fixtures and fastenings should be same.

Electric conductor is must for high rise buildings of 45 feet and above.

Synchronicity with Surroundings

Surrounding environment and our neibourhood are very important. Any empty plot of land in the north or east of your premises is good but must be neat and clean. Generally such vacant plots are used as garbage dumping grounds by the neighbouring people. A depression in the southwest of the premises increases the bad effects of demon goddess Nirriti. Infrared radiations, which are radioactive in nature, get accumulated in the premises leading to ill-luck.

Success is the progressive realization of your dreams and desires in life. The features of a building indeed affect fortunes of its residents, including their lifestyle. The environment around the building also affects the homes and offices within. If the building's energy is damaged, then the inhabitants may not get success despite hard work. When a big building stands detached from other smaller buildings on the same road, then the inmates of the former will live in isolation from the rest of the community. A house with a completely different style and elevation from that of its neighbouring houses will not be a very happy house. Mainly doors, chimneys and porches make up the façade of any building.

To generate positive energy, design and planning of your home and office must be in sync with that of the neighbourhood. Strict building bye laws help preserve the positive energy of these areas leading to happy and prosperous lives of the residents. Prana of any locality dissipates when different types of houses and buildings develop here and there without any sense of symmetry or uniformity. Community life is often found missing in such areas. The World Trade Centre in USA was not quite in sync with the other neighbouring buildings in the area. These twin towers were much taller than the surrounding buildings. This factor was one of the reasons to their untimely destruction.

A huge building may come up in future blocking sunrays to your premises, particularly in the east. Here comes the role of changing dashas (time periods) of planets. It is better to sell out such a workplace or house and shift to a vaastu friendly location.

A holy structure like a temple or a gurudwara coming up near your residence will destroy your happiness. It is wise to get out before the temple is made. Your property's value goes down as a holy structure rises up in the surrounding. The road outside the home is forever clogged with vehicles of worshippers. Music plays in odd hours.

Every big business house shall be built independent of the surrounding buildings. It should not touch another on the side. Outside road level raised higher the floor level of the business premises over the years is an unfortunate development. Higher road level towards the northern, eastern and particularly front sides of the business premises is particularly inauspicious. Higher elevation of road causes the premises to look sunken. The sales get dwindled and the footfall goes down.

In such a case, raise the level of business premises so that it is around two to three feet higher than the existing road level. Sometimes rising roads on the southern and western side (not in the front of course) of the residential premises may prove lucky.

Openings

One shall be able to walk around his building. People's wealth is generally proportionate to the openness of their house. More the number of sides open around the house, more the riches. Even the size of personal car also increases as the open sides of the house increases in the metropolitan cities like Delhi.

Entrance

Classical vaastu recommends that there should be no obstruction like rock, boulder, or huge tree blocking the home entrance. A flyover near the entrance is a huge mass of steel and concrete that weighs us down.

Entrance to any premises shall not be too narrow. Steps leading to it should not be too steep. Reaching the main door should be a comfortable process. Gradually ascending steps lessen the probability of slipping and consequent accidents. A southwestern entrance in the residence spells financial ruin.

Door

According to Mayamatam (26.16-17); "In a house with one single main building, it may be to the east, south, west or north and is appropriate for all classes. However, it may be to the south or the west when it is for human beings only. All these positions are in relation to the centre of the site".

Arrangement of doors for all purposes is described in Mayamatam (26.26); "In a single main building house, length of the main building is to be divided into nine parts. Then a point is marked at five points from the right hand extremity and another at three parts from the left one. The access door is placed in between them in such a way that it is farther from the right end than from the left. So the door is to be off-centre when used for ordinary people. In a house intended for men, the door must simply be to the left of the median line of the building".

Female Goddesses

Taking information from "Mayamatam" of the different forms of female Goddesses, only two deities are connected with snakes and skulls. One is Chamunda, also identified as Kali. She is the concept of total destruction of enemies. Mounted on a corpse, she holds the skull and has a cobra in place of a breast band. The second image of Mother Goddess that has connection with snakes is that of Katyayani. She holds a noose in the form of a snake and wears a breast band made of snakes. Mounted on lion and dressed in lion skin, she is particularly known for removing marriage-hurdles and in getting a happy married life. Her worship starting from the Full moon of Dec- Jan was done by young girls during Lord Krishna's times.

There is another type of Mother Goddess principle called as the Sapta Mata – the seven mothers. According to Mayamatam, they are Brahmi, Maheshwari, Kaumari, Vaishnavi, Varahi, Indrani and Kali. Each one of them had a symbolism and related paraphernalia. Among them Kaumari or Kumari holds the key to the antiquity of Mother Goddess worship. Mayamatam describes her as having a cock and spear and mounted on a peacock. These are the accessories of Lord Skanda, also known as Kumar, the son of Shiva and Parvathi. The literary tradition of the olden Tamil Sangam (sunken) lands is that all these three once lived there.

This makes Kumari of Sapta-Mata as the mother of Kumar or Skanda. She is none other than Shakti or Parvati, the female consort of Shiva. The location of Kumari was in the Indian Ocean. After it was submerged, her image has been consecrated at the tip of South India (at Kanya Kumari) facing the ocean where she once had her abode. People from different parts of India go to this place to worship Kumari for release from the sin of adultery. The Tamil epic Manimegalai contains a reference to a woman from Varanasi who went to Kumari and worshipped her as a propitiation for the adultery committed by her.

By the location of Kumari in the South Seas, it is deduced that she and all her coterie in the Sapta-Mata group must have existed in the lands that are now submerged in the Indian Ocean. These seven mothers must have been the earliest group of Mother Goddesses, which however got separated in the course of time and worshipped as separate entities nowadays. There are of course olden temples with Sapta Mata and even Ashta Mata (eight mothers). Mayamatam says that Sapta-Mata must be consecrated at a great distance from the village. The Indus tablet of seven women seems to be about the Sapta-Matas.

Jyeshtha Devi (Alakshmi or Sheetala Mata)

A French author Pierre Sonnerat mentions an ancient goddess Moudevi (also 'Mahadevi and "Bhoudevi"), the 'goddess of discord and misery'. She is the one riding a donkey, and carrying a crow banner, the one not particularly 'beautiful'. He explains how 'Churning of Sea' produced three goddesses - Saraswati (claimed by Brahma), Lakshami (claimed by Vishnu) and Moudevi (unclaimed). Moudevi has also been called the second wife of Vishnu.

A book called 'Roles and Rituals for Hindu women' by Julia Leslie (1992) mentions in details a goddess named Jyeshtha, who in Tamil is often called Kakkaikkodiyal (crow-bannered). Crow is considered the bringer of bad luck and famine. She is the one who rides a donkey (*Khararudh*a) and often carries a broom. According to the Linga Purana, Jyeshtha was the first one born from *Saagar Manthan* and married off to a hermit who couldn't control her unreligious beliefs that make her feel at ease among "the false mendicant (bhksubimba), the naked Jain monk (ksapanka), and the Buddhist (bauddha)."

Fig 8.2: Khararudha Crow Bannered Jyeshtha Devi

Jyestha ie 'Elder' is the representative goddess of 'Misfortune'. She was the second thing after poison that came out of the sea during its churning, and found herself unwanted as she is inauspicious. According to another story, she is in fact Mohini (the female seductress form of Vishnu), who saves the Amrit (elixir) from Asuras (demons). According to some other traditions, Jyestha was taken-in by Eshwara (Shiva).

These words "Jyestha" and "Eshwara" become "Jyestheshwar" in their combined form which is again a name of Shiva. It is believed that the Shiva temple atop the Shankaracharya Hill in Srinagar (Kashmir) was originally dedicated to a form of Shiva known as Jyesthesvara. An ancient goddess temple called Zeethyaar is also located somewhere between the hills of Shankaracharya and Mughal Garden of Chasma Shahi. This Shrine at Zeethyaar is dedicated to Zeestha Devi, a form of Parvati.

Aurel Stein, in notes to his translation of Kalhana's Rajatarangini, mentions 'Zeethyaar' as the spot of a Shiva temple dedicated to Jyesthesvara (the name of the lingam present there) and the spot for holy Tirtha of Jyether. According to the Mytho-folklore (based on *Jyestha-mahatmya*), Shiva liberated Jyetha (ie Parvati) from the Daityas (demons) at this particular spot and on marrying her took the name Jyesthesa. This picturesque spot surrounded by hills has a spring dedicated to Zeestha Devi. Here also the story of her origin mentions the churning of the sea. Meat (particularly goat liver) offerings are still the norm of this temple.

Jyeshta Devi was the first born before Lakshami, when the sea was churned. She was supposed to be ugly and obese. Taking cue from iconography described in the 'Mayamatam', the book by Maya on the science of building which covers the science of iconography of the ancient deities, this image of the female Goddess has pendulous lips, prominent nose and fallen breasts and stomach. She is seated on a throne. This image is consecrated in the outskirts of the dwellings – in places where evil and dirt are seen. This deity is kept in neglected places, in the temples too. People can remain safe in beautiful, clean and happy surroundings by worshipping this deity.

Fig 8.3: Jyeshta Devi in Kailasanatha temple, Kancheepuram

In some parts of India, particularly in the north, she is identified as Sitla or Sheetala who also carries a broom and rides a donkey. Sheetala is the goddess of measles or smallpox. She is also called Harita / Hariti - 'the green one' - the goddess of smallpox from Gandhara Art of Kushan Dynasty, the demon goddess of 500 children who was reformed by Lord Buddha.

Shayan Vaastu (Vaastu of Rest and Sleep)

Bedroom in our home is just like the sanctum sanctorum (garbha griha) of the temple. Our bedroom should also be small like the sanctum sanctorum of the temple.

One can enjoy deep sleep at night; only when he get sufficient physical work during the day. A rickshaw puller can easily sleep on his rickshaw in the shade on a scorching summer noon. On the contrary, most of the intellectual people have over-worked minds while their bodies are under-worked. The car culture has resulted in people not walking at all.

TV in the bedroom is the main cause of disharmony among the newly married couples. It destroys mutual communication while shifting attention towards the social issues.

According to vaastu, space below the bed should be empty. Even the utensils, slippers or sweeping material is not allowed under the bed. Ideally, lower side of the bed (palang or charpoy) itself was designed with minor openings for air-circulation. For this purpose, *nevaar* made of cotton threads or string made of plant fiber was used traditionally. Box-beds without the provision of air gaps on the lower side are thus inauspicious. Mattresses, woolens, boxes and other things stored inside the box-bed drain of our energy in the same manner as a basement does to a family living just above it.

Bunk-beds are not comfortable for children. Sleeping on the upper levels of bunk-bed is equally uncomfortable like sleeping on an upper berth of a moving train. Child on the top of a bunk-bed runs the danger of falling off the ladder taking him down when he gets up in the middle of the night to go to the wash room.

Sleeping in a north-eastern bedroom is like people sitting in the first row of the cinema hall. A drawing room is best in the northeast. Spending some time here every day is beneficial, but spending most of the time can be damaging. Living in the northeastern sector makes one lose interest in the daily activities of the home. One will immerse himself in his own life because in the northeast one gets so much from nature that he forgets about everything else. A person's position also gets weakened while occupying a northeast room.

Sleeping in the bedroom located in the southeast corner invites involvement in litigations and extra-marital affairs. Friction develops between the couple occupying it. People using this bedroom become angry and volatile and ready to explode anytime. This fire-zone heats up your body and temperament.

Fire of the southeast is best for a kitchen and heat generating objects like a generator or any other electrical machinery. But bedroom in the southeast leads to multiple problems including separation of ways of the husband and wife. Remember southeast is the home of agni-deva (fire-God)! Kitchen under a bedroom may make a person hot-tempered. A fire burning on the lower floor right below your bed can inflame your mind.

Anyone occupying southwest of the premises becomes powerful and can't be controlled easily. A person occupying southwest acquires the power of earth's solid land mass. The oldest couple shall occupy the south-west, south or west directions otherwise they can be easily influenced by the younger generation in a negative way. Their worth shall decrease with the passage of time. Contrarily, a newly-wed couple occupying the southwest begins to dominate the family.

Sleeping in the northwest corner destabilizes the occupant. Person living here is not able to stabilize. A newly married sister-in-law occupying the northwest may eventually leave her husband. Northwestern room is best for an unmarried daughter. Her chances of getting married are maximized here. Northwestern room doesn't allow its user to dig roots.

Sleeping with head pointing towards the north leads to negative thinking, pessimism, hallucinations and can be a cause for ruin. We are most vulnerable to heart attacks at night. Sleeping with head towards the north accelerates it.

Retirement

Retired people can be equated with the setting sun. A village home, a peaceful hillside location, or a house in the outskirts of the city, which is away from its maddening hustle and bustle, is best for spending one's life in peace. Retired people should occupy a bedroom situated farthest from the house entry; preferably in the southwest, west, or south sector of the home during night. However, during the daytime, lighted and airy areas like east and north in the front side are good for the old family members.

Phone Etiquette

Any type of phone should be towards your right or left side, preferably towards the south-east, or north-west side. The battery charging points should never be towards the back side. Phone should always be kept away from water. Use it to the minimum possible extent. Switch it off while taking rest. Don't ever keep it in your left side pocket of shirt, near the heart.

Interiors

Unpainted walls, patches of dropped plaster on the wall, cobwebs hanging from the ceiling, creaking doors, slippery floors and foul-smelling rooms – all these indicate that the premises is under the evil influence of Rahu. Any building is the projection of its inhabitant. Just remember; how you feel without taking your daily bath, not brushing your teeth regularly, without a shave or while wearing soiled clothes?

Do not keep a watch which is not running properly. A watch is linked with time and the planet Saturn. Broken chairs, shaky tables, flat tyres, clutter, and unused articles bring bad luck.

Mirrors

Mirrors can enhance energy of any business space. They increase the natural light by reflecting it and symbolically double the available space when placed on a single wall from top to bottom.

Wall Paintings

Wall paintings which depict depressing scenes are not auspicious. Looking repeatedly on such a painting may become a cause of depression in the long run. Any piece of art works like a thought provoking mechanism. Thoughts result in action. Steady actions result in habit, habit ripens as character and character makes our destiny. Whatever we think so shall we become. Depressing pictures make us less cheerful and energetic.

Furniture

Carved furniture is not good in North India from practical point of view. It is impossible to keep the home dust free in north India's scorching summers. You are not able to remove dust that settles on the minutely carved inner spaces. Furniture with plain surfaces is a good vaastu choice as it can easily be dusted. When we close windows to shut out dust, we also block the natural wind and light. It is like closing your nose completely to avoid the air having dust particles.

Straight lines with the rounded corners are evergreen, not the zigzag furniture.

The size of furniture should also suit the needs and position of the person using it.

In vaastu shastra, sitting is related to the earth element. Chairs meant for sitting should be solid like earth. Thus the revolving chairs are not suitable for sitting for long hours.

Vaastu is essentially the study and practice of our connection with the nature. We are deeply connected with the other human beings, animals, birds, trees and plants. Any furniture made from the natural material looks better and feels better than made from an artificial material. Wood is considered an evergreen construction material because it once had life. It was a part of some tree or plant. The same logic applies on the cotton and silk clothes. They look and feel better than the synthetic clothes as we get cotton from a plant. Vaastu considers that even stone and earth has prana till these are dug out from the earth and processed.

Don't go for a revolving chair if you need concentration on a particular point, subject or piece of work. A plain chair is good for such a condition. A revolving chair slides forward, leans back, half-turns one way, then the other. It makes a user fidgety. Revolving chairs are good for mature persons who are required to deal with multiple tasks at the very same time. A revolving chair is like a driver's seat that has to take care of his and other's vehicles, pedestrians and road conditions simultaneously. Driver's seats are designed accordingly.

The size of your home plays a major part in furniture selection. Minimalistic furniture usually fits well into small apartments. On the other hand, people with sprawling villas should go for classical style furniture. Age of the buyer and family background also determine the choice. Those above 45 tend to prefer classical furniture. However, younger buyers tend to be more adventurous and like to experiment with contemporary and neo-classical styles. One must avoid going in for ultra-modern furniture as it may not be in vogue after a few years.

Structure of the family and its modern or contemporary outlook also determine the choice. Classical furniture is best suitable for a conservative family. Large sized families shall prefer Indian furniture that can withstand rough use. Size of the room also determines the choice. Large and ornate looking furniture can make a small room appear even more cramped.

Now people want styling, design and neat contours that only imported furniture can offer. But imported furniture can't be customized. If you want a wardrobe that fits snugly into an odd-shaped niche in your home, it is better to go to a local furniture manufacturer. He will produce a built-to-size product for you. Also low-end variety imported furniture is less durable than Indian furniture. Indians tend to regard furniture as a lifetime purchase and want it to be robust. Contrarily, people in the west don't keep their furniture beyond a few years. In furniture like the sofa, it is difficult to tell which type of wood has been used below the foam and the fabric. It is better off buying Indian furniture from the nearby dealer of Indian furniture whose goods come with a guarantee.

Lighting

Good lighting is that which uses less power and doesn't pinch the eyes. It should neither be too bright nor too dim. Keep in mind the wall colour, texture, size of lamp and bulb fixture while selecting the right light.

Cover the windows with curtains or coloured glass. You will receive only the desired amount of light. To adjust the amount of natural light, you can also opt for a slit window.

If you want to use light as a piece of decoration, lamp holders decorated with glass, beats, pearls, stones and paper work will work well.

If shadow of an object is desired, keep the light behind the object.

Use concealed lights to get a soft look. These lights look beautiful in the bedroom.

Fluorescent lights are good to highlight an architectural design or a piece of art.

Any antique piece, wood finishing showpiece and stone showpiece in the drawing room can be made to look impressive with the use of white and yellow lights. Balance the white and yellow lights. Milky white light is good for peace of mind while yellow light is good for keeping us energetic.

Lamp's light colour matching with the room colour gives a mesmerizing look.

Experiment with the decorative table lamp, floor lamp or a chandelier which can decorate any room. You may use lamps with antique looks having base of wood, copper, brass, glass or marble.

You may use lamps and sculptures made of paper in your living space. They make it a romantic and warm place. Use floor lamp or corner lamp for romantic mood.

Place a ceiling lamp as well as a bedside table lamp in the children's room.

Use direct light on study and computer table.

Lights reflecting shadows pinching to the eyes, and which are too bright or too dim are not comfortable for the room.

Use general light in the kitchen. Properly light the top of counter for availability of sufficient light during working.

Use chandelier made of wood or steel above the dining table. Don't go for crystal here.

Orient multiple lights on a painting or a statue to highlight it.

Use dim light in the TV room as watching TV in the dark is harmful. You won't be able to watch TV properly in the light of a high watt power bulb.

Make it sure to have an adjustable pull chain in the hanging light. The brightness of light can be controlled as per one's mood.

Summer Interiors

- Keep the home closed so that the inner coolness doesn't get leaked. It also keeps the outer heat and humidity away. Open windows and curtains at night for cross ventilation of air.

- When humidity level is high during summers, keep the fan of air-conditioner on 'low' level. Replace the filters on monthly basis. Use a desert cooler instead of an AC, if possible. Install ceiling mounted pedal fans. They keep the air in circulation making you feel cool.

- Switch off unnecessary lights to avoid the heat generated by them.

- Wash the floor at least twice a week with fresh water as it keeps the floor cool.

- Introduce the crisp smell of fresh flowers into your room. A vase of fresh flowers is the fastest way to add colour, vitality and fragrance to your interiors.

- Replace the old bed sheets and bed covers. Cotton sheets in bright and fresh cool colours will keep your bed cool on hot summer nights.

- Roll up all the rugs, throws, cushions and curtains. Replace heavy rugs with cool-coloured cotton durries. Strategically placed colourful cushions on furniture add life to any room. Use sheer curtains and sheer table-cloths in the summer. Prefer plain, embroidered or printed sheer materials.

- Rework your accessories and artifacts. Replace heavy objects and try to create a lighter ambience. The sparkle of your silver artifacts lends a luminous splendour to the interiors. Bring them out. Lampshades, artifacts, vases, pots and sculptures add colour and texture to your room.

- Painting just one wall in different colour becomes the focal point of your living room. A niche is the perfect space for adding extra colour. You can go for a subtle colour in a shade darker than the shading on the other walls.

- Position your table or chair near the window. It will allow you to enjoy the colours and fragrances outdoors.
- Pieces of art add colour, texture, theme, style and depth to any space. If you have large walls or high ceilings, use large framed pieces of art rather than tiny objects that would get lost. Arrange small pieces of art on an appropriately sized smaller space or wall. Arrange similar prints in one formation.
- Place a large mirror on a bare, boring wall. The mirror will reflect colour from around the room and will add light to the space. Choose an interesting frame for it. Hang the mirror in such a manner so that it reflects light back into the room and lights up the dark corners. It can also be used to reflect a wonderful view if you have one.
- Summers are more prone to fire hazards. Fireproof textiles should be preferred in the buildings as textiles play a major role in spreading fire. Some points to keep in mind to help your home resist a fire are: using Class A roof coverings, tree branches at least 2 meters away from the house to minimize the brush that can ignite nearby trees, thicker boards, fences made of non-combustible materials, dual pane windows, tempered glasses, no obstruction to the fire ladder etc.

Greenery

The greenery of a park facing your premise is life-giving. In the densely populated areas of Delhi, first or second floor is normally the better-lit and airier than the ground floor. Ground floor is generally dwarfed by the tall building coming up next door. Due to boundary wall and parked cars, ground floor doesn't receive the required natural light and air circulation.

Grow leafy trees towards the east, south and west sides to break the summer heat. Fruit bearing, spiky, milky, cacti, gum-oozing and large holy trees like peepal are not good near the premises. Cactus plant leaves don't change for weeks together. Thus they have a kind of deadness about them. Vaastu is a way of living with the ever changing environment. Vaastu favours trees having a visible life cycle – they shed the old leaves and grow them again, bear flowers and fruits and so on.

Television (TV) versus Music

Switching on the TV distracts us a lot. Listening to music, particularly the soothing classical music doesn't distract us from our work. Rather, soothing music can improve concentration in many cases. Many students study with music playing while preparing for their examinations. Departmental stores, shopping malls, exhibition grounds, large showrooms and the like also play soft music. On the contrary, playing TV in a shop is not good for your business. Customers start watching it rather than making a purchase.

Television is a curse of society. Most of our energy is lost through our eyes. That's why there are so many techniques in Yoga Shastra which are practiced with closed eyes. TV is a source of light when switched on. Watching TV is like staring directly at the light bulb. TV is worst in comparison to the cinema hall where the source of light is towards the backside of movie-watchers. What we see at the screen is the reflected light only. TV also triggers fighting in any home as everyone wants to see his favourite channel. Opting for individual TV sets jeopardizes the family unity and mutual communications.

A person watching TV is immersed in other's lives rather than living his own life to the fullest. People are watching cricket or other games rather than playing themselves. We should not neglect our own work. We can't live other's life. Everyone is unique in this world. These cricketers and other sportsperson are not neglecting their daily work of net practice, training, batting, bowling, and fielding to improve their stamina. Similarly one should concentrate on his own work.

Water Vaastu

Water is integrally linked with prosperity. Water from springs, rivers, wells and hand-pumps is cooler in summers than water stored in the over-head water tanks. For getting cool water during the summers, overhead water tank should be made of brick work or reinforced cement concrete using water proof cement. White colour on its periphery does not attract heat. Overhead plastic tanks can be insulated by wrapping a layer of thermocol around them as well as on their roof.

Auspicious Trees

Trees suitable for the shafts of pillars are: purusha, khadira, saala, madhuka, champak, shimshapa, arjuna, ajakarni, kshirini, padma, chandana, pishita, dhanvana, pindi, simha, rajadana, shami, and tilaka. Equally suitable are nimbi, aasana, shirisha, ska, kaala, katphala, timisa, likucha, panasa, saptaparnaka, bhauma, and gavakshi (Mayamatam, 15.64-76a). However, bamboo is suitable for everyone, as are the palm tree and the coconut tree, the kramuka, reeds and the ketaki (Mayamatam, 25.185b-186a).

Brahamsthan

Villagers congregate at the centre-point of the village. It is called chaupal, the brahamsthan of the village vaastu. As long as the villagers come to meet at the chaupal, a village stays fine. Troubles begin when they start meeting in the corners. When factions are formed, frictions start creeping in. Similar is the case of an individual home. A wisely arranged central point of the home cements the inhabitants together.

The central courtyard or brahamsthan serves as a common meeting point for the family. Brahamstan of any space shall ideally be open to the sky and unoccupied. Covering it will be disastrous as harmony of the place gets destroyed. It may invite a series of setbacks, accidents, ailments, fights and lack of mental peace. In a home, brahamsthan may hold fire only on two occasions: when a havan is organized and when the daughter of the home gets married.

Modern architects usually prefer shafts instead of braham-sthana and paishach-sthan due to space crunch in the modern mega cities. Shafts in any building are the smaller version of brahamsthan. Shafts are required to admit light and to provide cross-ventilation into homes which are joined on one side to the walls of an adjacent home. Ideally, size and number of shafts shall increase with the increased number of storeys but practically it is not so. It is a general practice in residents of housing societies in Delhi to cover the common shaft area which may cause havoc in the long run.

Our kitchen, bathroom and bedroom are expanding in size in the modern times; mainly on the cost of brahamsthan which has been replaced by small shafts or dark and narrow corridors. Connaught Place can be termed as the brahamsthan of New Delhi developed by Edwin Lutyens. An open brahamsthan connects every construction to the infinite space and thus it can be termed as the soul of any premises.

The brahamsthan of the complete home as well as of the individual rooms should be completely empty of any furniture or other heavy objects. Covering brahamsthan means denying entry of positive energies and emptying the existing ones. It also stirs up disunity among the family members. A depression here drains the positive energy.

Basements

Basements are not good in general. A person feels entombed when he goes below the existing ground level. Basements receive little natural light and fresh air. A basement can be the biggest feeder of negative thoughts when used for daily activities like studying, communicating, cooking and working. Basement used as an office or an entertainment area with a home theatre and a dance floor with strobe lights is unnecessary. A home is to live, study, work and sleep.

Staircases

Staircase shall run clockwise with an uneven number of steps. A staircase right at the entrance makes the person to imagine that vast problems confront him. It needs extra energy and effort to ascend a staircase!

Art of Living the Vaastu Way

We should live in tune with nature. There should be a balance in our life. Success at work should not come at the cost of family harmony, love and care. Studies should not be pursued at the expense of physical health.

Vaastu is like a well-designed road in good condition. It provides an ideal condition for all sorts of vehicles running on it. But an extraordinarily designed vehicle will perform better on it than an inferior one. Life can be equated with a car which is considered good when running smoothly. Sudden acceleration or application of brake on a car leading to jerks is not welcomed in driving. The switchover should be gradual. Likewise, working non-stop from Monday to Saturday and then thinking of taking complete rest on the seventh day doesn't work. Sun doesn't rise or set suddenly. It is a gradual process, passing through many phases. That's why it is beautiful to see a rising and setting sun.

Maintain balance in your life. There is no importance of the weekend in nature or in vaastu. For nature, all the seven days of the week are the same. We Indians have blindly copied this disease of the western society. According to Bible, God rested on Sunday as he felt tired after six day's creation work. According to Hindu scriptures, this universe is the outcome of Brahma's leela (playful act). Weekend holiday is required only when we overwork during the so-called working days. Daily exercise, work, rest and family get-together are the right vaastu way of living.

Celebrating special days, including the birthday, is a city culture. Villagers and small town people in India mostly enjoy each and every day of their life like a special day. Rest and work shall go together in life. Day is meant for work while night is meant for rest. Living in tune with nature doesn't require any special celebrations. According to Christian theology, God will decide people's karma's on the judgment day after the resurrection of the dead. Hindu theology, on the other hand, believes that our karmas (deeds) are the cause of immediate results, leading to new birth. Such a long wait for deciding one's karmas as described in Christianity doesn't exist in classical Indian religions.

Vaastu allocates unique spaces for unique activities. Spirituality teaches us to live in the present moment. Multi-tasking or doing several things at the same time is the best recipe for disaster. Such people are burning candle from both the ends and thus need to slow down. If you are constantly disturbed by the family members in your home office, you immediately need to shift to a nearby office which is separate from your residence.

One should separate his home life from the business life. A separate mobile phone can be used for taking business calls and that too only during the business hours, say nine to nine during the day time. When you work, concentrate only on your work. When you play, concentrate on playing. Too many things at the same time shall lead to exhaustion. It is better to keep TV, computer and phone out of your bedroom for enjoying a deep sleep.

Vaastu is all about time, place, person and activity. We are bound to perform a particular activity at the particular time and place. One should get up before sunrise and see the sunrise before starting exercise, yoga or any other work. Vaastu goes with the daily stages of sun. It equates our morning with childhood, midday with adulthood, evening with middle age and night with death. Waking up every morning is a temporary re-birth and going to sleep at night is a temporary death. The simplest rule is to work during the day and sleep at night.

Every action has its specific time and specific place. A person in a three piece suit enjoying sunshine on the sea beach will look odd. And we can't think wearing beach-wear in a corporate meeting. Dining table is not meant for studying and bed is not meant for eating food. A home - particularly the bed room - is meant for developing the emotional relationships, not for discussing the office problems. Husband and wife shall divide their work clearly so that work being handled by the one has nothing to do with the other. It will also be an ideal condition if work lives of husband and wife are different altogether.

One should not do office work at home and vice versa. When a person brings his office to the home or his home to his office, neither can be focused. Westerners follow this principle instinctively, without even knowing the word vaastu. They work hard during the five working days and enjoy family life in the weekends. Their focused behavior leads them to progress. In fact, some organizations pay the workers on weekly basis. The inner and outer space of residential premises and workplaces is entirely different. A home is a peaceful and private area while a business place is open to all.

Office life is hectic and full of tensions while home life should have peace and quietness. That's why the best vaastu friendly houses are not situated on busy roads. They are best in the peaceful interiors of any colony. The space of your office and home stands apart. Sitting in the drawing room wearing a tie or working in office in kurta pyjama is violation of the space element. Soothing music, say classical instrumental music, expands our space. It doesn't disrupt our concentration.

If you want to have a sense of togetherness in the family, never go for arranging too much separate facilities for the inhabitants. Though personal washroom, toilet, wardrobe, TV, bedroom, kitchen and dining room seem to be part of rich, luxurious and comfortable life in the beginning, they prove detrimental to the family unity in the long run. Vaastu emphasizes on common meeting points like drawing room, dining table or the TV room.

For a close knit family, entrance and exit of the home should preferably be one and one only. When there are separate entrances for separate sub-units in the same family, anybody can enter or exit from his unit without awareness of the other family members. This is a very bad situation for the family unity. Ideally, family members ought to know who is coming in or going out. One common entrance ensures the same in the perfect manner.

Night culture is anti-vaastu. Never party in the evening. Nights are meant for sleep, not for dancing in the discotheque and drinking liquor in the pub. Once it gets dark, one should head for his bedroom. Entire animal kingdom sleeps at night barring nocturnal creatures likes owls. Call centers face the problem of high attrition rate. Their night time workers quit within months as they easily get worn out.

Any premises, if required, shall be divided floor-wise. Ideally, one floor should not be shared by two owners. Going for width wise or length wise division of small size premises is an inauspicious move.

It is foolish to close windows for want of privacy or security. Open all the windows, balconies and ventilators on the daily basis, at least for three hours in the morning. South side windows, when opened during the midday in winters, admit the necessary heat rich in vitamins. A closed building gets inhabited by the ghosts.

Changing the Home

Change your home if it is not worth living or its surroundings have deteriorated to the extreme. Some of the outer causes for change may be a high rise coming up and blocking the sunrays towards the auspicious directions, commercialization of the locality, increased traffic, noise pollution, smoke, blocked drains and sewers, insanitary condition, increased road levels towards the north and east sides causing your premises to sink, religious construction in the neighbourhood, nearby presence of school or doctor's clinic, and shrinking parking space.

Domestic Help

You can easily retain your full time domestic servant by following the simple vaastu rules. Servants also need their private space; sufficient enough to meet their needs. If you are unable to provide space to your servants, space element of your house gets imbalanced. Servant's room should be naturally lighted during the day time. There should be at least one window and one ventilator for proper cross-ventilation of fresh air. The walls and its roof shall be sufficiently thick to ward away the heated sunrays.

Servants also need respect and appreciation for their work. We must keep in mind that in the good old days' domestic servant in the kitchen was called *Maharaj* (the great king)! He was treated just like a family member. Servant's room is best in the northwest or southeast of the main building. Separated from the main building, it can be designed as an outhouse. It can also be provided on the rooftop in earlier mentioned rajasic directions. If sufficient space is not available in your house, it is better to arrange a rented room for servants in the vicinity.

Offices

In the past times, offices were usually a part of the homes of merchants and businessmen. From the start of 18th century, more and more offices started moving into various kinds of commercial premises. During the 19th century, offices began to be more departmentalized. Offices gradually developed in size and complexity to accommodate the growing number of employees working in them.

The design of the office should be such that really caters for the people working in it. Now specialized office blocks are constructed in sky scraping buildings. Sky scrapers, though destroy the surrounding landscape, are becoming a necessity in the modern mega cities. The time tested golden principles of Vaastu Shastra can also be used (though in somewhat modified form) in these modern offices for the welfare and safety of office workers. These principles ensure satisfactory working conditions. In this way, offices become comfortable and pleasant places to work in. Now men and women of different status work together respecting each others' status in the office hierarchy.

The office can be a private or public sector office. The key functions of an office are information and communication. The office will work successfully if the information is handled properly. On the contrary, the office will run badly if the staff fails to communicate properly. Bad communication results in the loss of valuable information, time and money.

In this technological age, we are getting used to working with machines of every shape, size and purpose. Many older people have an inherent hatred of new things. We should treat these machines not as foes, but as our friends. What is needed is a moderating approach towards these machines. Of course, excess of everything is bad. Adequate training gives necessary confidence to operate these machines. Remember, a machine is only as good as its operator.

Manager of an office is like a plane's pilot. He should be able to motivate and support his staff. If he himself looks and acts in a negative way, the staff will also do the same. On the other side, if manager shows a positive and dedicated attitude in all his works, the staff is also likely to respond in the same manner.

A successful manager should use these key words in his thought, speech and action: hard working, approachable, dedicated, helpful, positive, conscientious, reliable, loyal, organized, well-groomed, diplomatic, sympathetic, cheerful, experienced, tactful, smart, firm, friendly, efficient etc. A good and successful manager shows initiative, sets new trends, listens attentively, achieves the set goals, delegates the duties, establishes a good rapport, motivates the people, communicates effectively, possesses the required skills and works well under pressure.

Start your business in the premises only after getting due permission from the local planning, building or development authority. In this way, you appease Lord Ganesha, the lord of obstacles. Office premises in the office blocks generally don't require any permission. Change of land use, fully or partially, may normally require proper permission from the local authorities. Adhere to the local building bye laws. Otherwise, a disastrous situation may arise after the business is up and running.

The symbolic arrows in a building should point upwards, not downwards or sideways. Upward arrows symbolically give an upward lift to your building and the business. Downward arrows, on the other side, represent daggers thrusting in the building. The building should not, as far as possible, cause any vedha to the neighbouring buildings. It turns your neighbours hostile towards you. Vaastu believes in the principle of "live and let live". Whatever we sow, so shall we reap. Rounding off corners of a high-rise building is a friendly gesture. It ensures that buildings do not create killing vedha for their neighbours. Sharp edges of multi-storey buildings are like poisonous arrows. These edges, when directed towards the main entrance of another building, bring misfortune for it. Consequently, it invites retaliation.

Stairways, escalators and elevators are the blood veins of any business. Health of a business depends on its quick service and easy access. Easy access allows for good flow of energy in the form of customers. Align the staircases and escalators to draw prana into the building from an auspicious direction.

Two large stone or metal lions, one on each side of the entrance, guard the door. They must be placed in this position at an auspicious time.

Bookcases with open shelves are not good. Use doors to hide the shelves from people's view. The recommended dimensions of a bookcase are 5'6" high and 18" deep. Full length storage cupboards help to keep the office free of clutter. A large proportion of storage in the reading room may overwhelm the study table.

Roads and flyovers with flowing traffic are like rivers. A curve of a flyover bending towards a building represents a blade or a scythe cutting into it. It brings inauspicious energies in the building. A road that encircles and embraces the building gives protection. It generates protective energy flows. A good example is the Connaught Place, situated in the heart of New Delhi. An open park opposite the main entrance of any building enhances the positive vaastu effect.

Water represents wealth. Fresh flowing water energizes the office environment and brings prosperity. Activate the wealth of your office by introducing a water feature into the area; say an aquarium. Live fishes symbolize growth. A small revolving fountain represents continuous turnover.

Sometimes, minor but well planned alteration like increased lighting or display of potted plants, can greatly increase customer turnover in a restaurant.

The desk of manager shall never be under a beam. Vibrations of tensile forces, generated from the beam's underside, hinders in clear thinking and decision-making. Well organized uncluttered desk leads to clear thinking and reduces stress.

A person's efficiency at work depends on a number of factors; some within and some beyond his control. Usually, one is free to organize his personal workspace according to the principles of vaastu shastra. It supports him and enables him to work efficiently. One may not always be able to change the layout, furniture, furnishings and lighting on his own. In such an uncomfortable situation, one must try to influence the decision making process so as to achieve a balanced and harmonious environment. This will support the benefit of workers as well as the company.

Offices without any natural light prevent creativity. In such a situation, use mirrors, bright lights, false windows, and landscape pictures. They give an illusion of spaciousness.

A reception area - receiving plenty of natural light – looks attractive. Potted plants placed inside the reception area give a sense of relaxation to the guests and customers. It is good to provide drinking water here for the staff and visitors. The reception area in a restaurant enables customers to relax while they wait for their table.

A central place for meetings and discussions ensures that ideas come from all the directions.

Everyone wants to decorate his office according to his own sweet will. Pastel colors are generally considered the best. Red carpets and black or brown walls do not encourage positive thinking. A few well chosen pictures, decorative plants and attractive pastel wall and carpet coloring may create an attractive working place.

Equip your office with a personal computer and printer, telephone, fax machine and photocopier. Be careful while choosing computer equipment. Memory needed to run the modern sophisticated programs is increasing every day. Always go for a computer with a bigger memory than your present need.

Low barriers give a view of the whole office and do not confine people into their own space.

A large plant or a low screen towards the back side of your chair supports it.

Glass paneled manager's office allows no privacy.

A round edged table is ideal for meetings and prevents passers-by knocking into it.

The energy should circulate freely in the brahamsthan ie centre of the office. It should be kept tidy through an efficient storage system.

Staff welfare

Keep your staff happy and you will be well on your way to a happy future. Everyone's work has its own importance. Pay due attention to the health and safety of workers, even if it results in lower profits. Labour laws also lay down minimum requirements for first aid and safety, lighting, heating, washing facilities and minimum space required for each worker to work in. Treat your cleaners decently and not as members of an inferior society. Ideally, an office should contain a first aid kit including plasters, bandages and dressings. At least one member of your staff should be trained in first aid course.

An attractive staff kitchen or restaurant does wonders for office morale. South-east, east, west and northwest are the favourite areas for kitchens. It must be kept clean and tidy. Good ventilation is must to ensure that the air is fresh at all times.

Expanding your office

Don't expand your office unless you are sure the time is right. Many small businesses work very well until they are made bigger. They go under with more staff and more overheads. Make sure it does not happen to your business. Don't rush for expansion, change in a planned way rather. Expansion also means upheaval. The office has to be moved physically to larger premises which may upset the staff. Though expanding a business is exciting, it can be fraught with worries and problems.

Take your time and tread carefully after due research. Notify your customers and suppliers of your office move. Send out letters in advance stating when and where you are moving to, clearly mentioning the days when the office will be closed altogether.

Stability

Entrance to any business premises should not be shaky and moving. It should be firm, solid and good looking. The surface on which we are studying, working or sleeping should be solid and non-shaky. We need something solid beneath our feet. Our bed, our chair, our study or working table should not shake, creek or wobble. Our weight rests on the floor, bed, chair or foot wears. Our boots, shoes and slippers should also be in a good and stable condition. These seemingly trivial things matter a lot in the long run. Any problem with these things brings instability in life in one or the other manner. It may result in a shaky health, inconstant income, and unstable emotional or business relations.

Cleanliness

Clean your business premises on daily basis to increase prosperity. It removes undesirable energy from the premises and restores harmony. Thoughts, spoken words and actions of people working or visiting there leave residue that builds on walls and corners. It results in energy blockages. People feel lighter, more confident, more positive, and more energetic and have a clear vision about their lives after cleaning the occupied premise. Anyone who feels stuck in his life would benefit from a sacred space cleaning. Goods for sales shall be kept in the wind-buffeted northwest. Wind's volatility will ensure that they do not remain there for long.

Vaastu Friendly Workplace

The layout, design and colour scheme of your office must synchronize with the type of your business activity. A vaastu-friendly office promotes good interpersonal relationships and helps to create a good rhythm and pace of work. Such an office promotes clear thinking and efficient management. It helps in creating an amicable environment and a stress-free workspace. It can help maximize profit and give a fillip to your carrier. It is imperative to create the right kind of ambience at the workplace that will help us deal with the cut-throat competition, long work hours and also help reduce health problems like cardiac arrest, high BP, diabetes etc.

Reception area makes the first impression on the visitor. It colours his expectations about the company. The reception should be nice looking, spacious and well-lit with natural light, if possible. Flowers and plants make this area vibrant. Soothing, harmonious and melodious sounds in the reception area attract wealth and prosperity. An aquarium in the north or north-east of the reception area brings good luck.

Within the office, keep more open space towards the north and east. Desk should be made of good quality wood. Avoid iron and plastic tables. The desk should not face a wall. It should preferably be in the south-west sector of the room. Occupy the south or west of south-west. This position will strengthen your grip and position and will help you in stabilizing your business. A window or any other opening behind your back is highly inauspicious. You will lack confidence while making decisions.

Sit on a solid four-legged heavy wooden chair with back, head and hand rest. Such a chair supports our *Mooladhar Chakra* (The Root Chakra) located at the base of our spine. This chakra governs the earth element which is directly related to our survival, stability and material prosperity.

The ideal workplace for a professional is his office from where he controls and oversees the entire range of his operations. Today's highly competitive environment has compelled most people to keep a small office at home. At your home office, you can create a stimulating personalized ambience. The home office is best in the south-east sector. It is the sector of wealth and prosperity.

A small fountain in the north-east is also auspicious. Filing cabinets and cupboards are good in the west, south-west and south. Current files are good in the north-west. Computer and related accessories are good in the south-east for their long life and smooth working. Keep the planner, diary, calculator and forecaster in the north-east or east side of the desk. Keep fresh flowers in the east, north-east or north area. Cheque book and financial planner should be placed on the safe west side. Keep the awards received in the past on the east, south-east or south wall.

Use colours that are refreshing and rejuvenating. Good colour combinations create positive impact on the mind and body. Neutral colours include earth colours such as sand, shell, coral, pearl and stone which create a sense of peace and well-being. They cultivate quite conversation with family and friends and dispel loneliness. Light green, light blue, yellow, and white colours are considered nurturing or healing colours. Green colour helps us in adjusting in a particular environment. White, black and grey colours promote stability. Sharp, witty and unique colours convey the message that owner has a high level of engagement.

Good lighting is crucial for effective work. Good lighting makes a design come alive. Mixing the lighting colour with wall colour can create interesting effects. High contrasts should be avoided to reduce the eye-strain and fatigue. Area wise and even desk wise selective switching and control can help restrict usage and operating costs of lighting.

Home Office

Thanks to the high cost of commercial spaces and long distance between home and office, new concept of home office is gaining ground in the Metros. Professionals have been allowed to work from the basement of their residences in the posh colonies. It results in the availability of more time and less traffic on the roads. Time saved in commuting can be devoted to other constructive activities.

Office at home should be carefully designed with functional, well-planned spaces. When you have to work for long hours, office is the room where you can relax and shut out the world. Ground floor is the ideal place for your home office. The southern direction governs our business and career. It is equivalent to the *karma sthan* (tenth house / bhava) in the North Indian system of horoscope casting. Other auspicious directions are the southeast and front portion of the residence.

You may display a figure of galloping red horse on the southern wall of your workplace to reap profits as horse signifies power and speed. You may even go for painting the southern wall in red colour in a cold climate. Otherwise, use curtains of red colour or place a red object like a vase or red flowers in the south direction. To boost your career prospects, hang a beautiful painting or photo of large mountains, rocky hills, and big trees with dashes of red in the south. For getting power and position, upholster your chair in a red coloured fabric. You may also prefer to keep a red coloured object on your working table.

Career

A lot of people are unhappy with their jobs because they are incompatible with their personalities. Our career and overall happiness are moulded by the kind of home we live in. Vaastu of our home is more important than the vaastu of our workplace. A person spends around one third of his life in his bedroom, one third in the home outside the bedroom and rest one third outside the home. Moreover, we have more freedom to arrange our space at home as per vaastu in comparison to the space at our workplace.

A vaastu friendly comfortable home is more cheerful to our lives than an inviting and comfortable workplace. Thus home should become a more comfortable place to live in. A home protects us from the atrocities of nature. It should be deeply connected to the Mother Nature – the soothing sunrays and gently flowing air reaching every nook and corner and outside scenery of naturally growing green trees and plants. No one can think of living in the open under the scorching sunrays or torrential rains.

Our residence is the foundation, the root cause of our career. An ideal home should be open from all the sides to reap the auspicious energies of Mother Nature. Delhi's most powerful and the wealthiest people live in bungalows situated on central Delhi roads like Amrita Shergill Marg, Aurangjeb Road, Ashoka Road, or Janpath. A house connected to the other house on one of its side is like a man whose one hand is hand-cuffed to the hand of another man. Open east is must for quality life. Living in too crowded area is detrimental to our creativity and adventurous spirit in the long run.

Web Vaastu

Loss in your business or a slow going business may be due to its badly designed website. A website of any business is made up of five great elements (panch-mahabhootas). Layout of the website denotes the earth element. Square and rectangular shapes are related to the earth element. Its text is governed by water, backend or html construction by the air element, colours by the fire element and URL or domain name by the space element.

Libraries and Museums

Libraries and museums have collection of rare books and articles. A small or medium size library should be oriented towards east. West direction of a specified place is best for big size public libraries and museums. These should be so arranged that they don't get spoiled. Books or articles should be stored / displayed in termite proof and damp proof almirahs / showcases. Stone, iron, glass and cement concrete almirahs should thus be preferred.

Hospitals

Avoid south, west and south-west entrances for a hospital. Otherwise, the hospital will gain notoriety and evil aura for illegal treatments eg abortion, treating criminals, organ trade and end up in closure due to financial losses or bad reputation. In a hospital; reception, registration and billing can be in the north of north-west. The doctor's consultation chamber should be in the north or east. Doctor's seat is best in the south. Patient should sit towards the left hand side of doctor. Patient's examination table should be in the south, west or south-west side of the consultation chamber. Dunghill, garbage dumping point and incinerator are best in the south-west of the hospital plot, separate from the main building. Sterilization unit is best in the south-east. Miniature or emergency sterilization for operation purposes may be kept in the south-east of the relevant operation theatre (OT).

Vaastu in Muslim Architecture

Muslims also have an instinctive awareness of directions throughout the world. Mosques are built in such a manner so that the worshippers always face the holy Mecca which is towards the west in India. All the historical seven cities of Delhi were built towards the south and west of river Yamuna. Qutub Minar was built towards the south-western part of Delhi during the reign of Qutub-ud-din. High rising and heavy constructions are considered best in the south-west as per vaastu shastra.

It is said that Mughal emperor Humayun used to wear clothes matching the planet of the day. He also organized government departments based on four elements. These were: fire (army), air (stable, kitchen and wardrobe), water (canals and wine cellar) and earth (land and buildings, agriculture). The minister-in-charge of the department had to wear the colour suited to the department.

In Agra, Red Fort and Taj Mahal were respectively built towards the west and south of river Yamuna. These locations are according to the principles of vaastu which recommends that a perennial source of water should be towards the north or east of the city, fort, palace or any other construction. Mughal emperor Shah Jehan preferred south of river Yamuna for building Red Fort of Delhi.

Vaastu plays a great role in the beauty and popularity of Taj Mahal. Taj Mahal is built on a parcel of land to the south of the walled city of Agra. River Yamuna flows towards its north direction from west to the east. The length, width and height of Taj are the same. Vaastu shastra considers such buildings the most stable ones. Square, octagonal and circular shapes have freely been used in the main building. These shapes are considered auspicious in vaastu shastra of the masses. Central focus of the entire Taj Mahal complex is the tomb. It is a large white marble structure standing on a square plinth and consists of a symmetrical building with an arch-shaped doorway topped by a large circular dome and finial. The four guest rooms on its four sides give it an octagonal shape.

Astro-Vaastu

Astronomy is the study of cause of movement of heavenly bodies. Astrology is the study of the effect of these heavenly bodies (particularly of our solar system) on us. Vaastu is primarily the study of the effect of earth on us which is right under our feet. Astrology mainly stresses on time and thus has the concept of kaal purush (time personified). Vaastu, on the other side, stresses on place or space and thus has the concept of vaastu purush (space personified).

The face of kaal purush is upward (time being more dynamic than space) while the face of vaastu purush is downward (space being more inactive when compared with time). Astrology has the concept of dasha (planetary time periods) while vaastu has the concept of disha (the directions). Thus astrology and vaastu, combined together, decide the dasha and disha (time and place) of any person. Effect of all the planets of the solar system are considered in Astrology while the effect of earth is taken in vaastu shastra. If 50 percent of human destiny is guided by combinations of planets seen from the horoscope, rest of 50 percent depends on vaastu.

A person generally seeks advice of vaastu expert when he is under the influence of Jupiter in his horoscope, when major or sub-period of the planet connected with the 10th or 5th houses is running and sub-period of planet related to the 4th house is to come.

Benefic (yoga-karaka) Rahu in one's horoscope gives good results regarding the south-west to a large extent. Likewise other planets can be related to their particular directions in vaastu.

Dynamic Vaastu

Intimidating railway tracks, foot over-bridges and flyovers can be dangerous to any vaastu. Their bad effects increase when situated towards the entrance or towards the north and east directions of the premises. They damage vaastu of nearby residential as well as commercial premises. They bring ill-luck to the construction as well as to its inhabitants. A flyover coming up near your house years after its construction will ultimately result in bad vaastu though primarily the house was constructed in accordance with the tenets of vaastu. This is the dynamic aspect of the karmas as described in Vedic Astrology.

A house owner is being constantly ruled by good and bad dashas (planetary periods). We must remember that Astrology is mainly concerned with dashas while vaastu is related to dishas (directions) which work together. Vaastu of any place tend to change with the changing time. It may become better or worse depending on fate of the owner. Any business premise overshadowed by a flyover is under the malefic influence of shadow planet Rahu. Rahu is the planet of disintegration, destruction and devastation. No one will like to stare at huge concrete pillars of the flyover all the day.

Ayadi Formulae (Mayamatam, 26.206-211)

Calculate the width and length of the proposed building in hasta. Hasta measures around one and a half feet. Multiply the width by three and divide the product obtained by eight. The remainder corresponds to one of the eight elements of the 'matrice' series, which are standard (flag), cloud, lion, dog, bull, donkey, elephant and crow. Amongst these, standard, lion, bull and elephant bring success, the others being inauspicious.

Multiply the width by eight and divide the product obtained by twenty-seven. The remainder corresponds to one of the asterisms, the first of which is Ashwini. It is by way of this remainder that zodiac signs favourable to the building are determined.

Multiply the length by eight and divide the product obtained by twelve. The remainder is called riches. Multiply the length by nine and divide the product obtained by ten. The remainder is called debt. To be auspicious, the gain must be greater than the debt.

Multiply the perimeter by nine and divide the product obtained by thirty. The remainder will correspond to one of the thirty lunar days. There is a conjunction of solar and lunar days – Sunday being the first. The asterism and this conjunction must correspond to the conjunctions: amrita, vara and siddhi and not to any other.

That house is auspicious whose asterism corresponds to that of the birth of its owner. This indication applies to constructions intended for men. If the building is destined for the immortals then that which is auspicious for the builder is so for the building.

Muhoorta (Auspicious Time) for starting a business

Major and sub-period of the person starting the business should be auspicious.

All Tithis (lunar dates) except Rikta (4, 9, 14 of bright and dark half) are good. All weekdays except Tuesday are good.

All Dhruva (Fixed) nakshatras (Uttaraphalguni, Uttarashadha, Uttarabhadrapada, Rohini), all Mridu (Gentle) nakshatras (Mrigashira, Revati, Chitra,

Anuradha), all Laghu (Short) nakshatras (Hasta, Ashwini, Pushya, and Abhijit) and Vishakha are considered auspicious at the time of starting a business. Moon shall be transiting in either of these nakshatra at the stipulated time.

All ascendants except the Aquarius are considered good. At the time of starting business, benefic planets should be posited in 2nd, 10th and 11th houses and malefic planets in 3rd and 6th houses. There should be no malefic planets in the 8th & 12th houses. It is most auspicious if Moon and/or Venus are also posited in the ascendant.

Auspicious Days for Business Travel

Thursday and Friday are best for travel. Sunday, Monday and Wednesday are medium while Tuesday and Saturday should be avoided. Also, use auspicious days for business travel towards a particular direction. Vedic Astrology considers that journey towards a particular direction is auspicious only on particular day(s) of the week. Journey made towards a particular direction on inauspicious days is called vaar-shoola and brings misfortune.

Avoid Monday and Saturday for journey towards the East, Monday and Thursday for journey towards the Southeast, Thursday for Southward journey, Sunday and Friday for journey towards the Southwest and the West, Tuesday for Northwest, Tuesday and Wednesday for North and Saturday and Wednesday for Northeast direction. The direction shall be considered from the place of starting the journey. These are summarized in Table 8.3.

Trees and Plants as Remedy

Plants are living entity and have a more radiant flow of pranic energy. Growing plenty of plants in a building will create a more fresh and alive atmosphere. They help move the pranic energy and avoid stagnation in front of internal corners. Plants calm down swirling pranic energy in external or protruding corners. They slow down fast moving pranic energy in a long corridor.

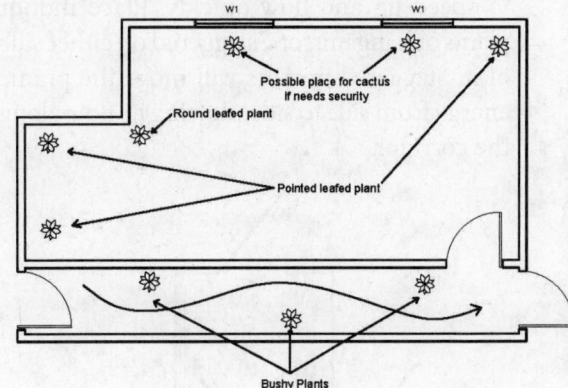

Fig 8.4: Locating Different Plants for Creating Different Effect

Different types of plants create a different effect. Plants with pointed leaves tend to help move pranic energy more quickly. These plants are more rajas and well-suited to internal corners where the aim is to reduce stagnation. Plants with rounded floppy leaves are more tamasic and are effective when placed in front of an external or protruding corner. They tend to calm the flow of pranic energy. Bushy plants help slow the flow of fast moving pranic energy and work well in the long corridors or near doors. Cactus plants are considered too

Table 8.3: Inauspicious Days for Travelling in Different Dirctions

Direction	East	South-east	South	South-west	West	North-west	North	North-east
Days to be avoided	Mon, Sat	Mon, Thurs	Thurs	Sun, Fri	Sun, Fri	Tue	Tue, Wed	Wed, Sat

prickly for the interior of a building. However, they can help deter burglars when placed on a window sill.

Mirrors as Remedy

Pranic energy behaves in a similar way to light. Thus, mirrors can be used to change the direction of the flow of pranic energy in the same way as a mirror reflects light.

Along a long corridor, pranic energy tends to speed up and flow quickly. Place indoor plants or hang mirrors, staggered on either side of it. Staggered mirrors will move the pranic energy from side to side, slowing its flow along the corridor.

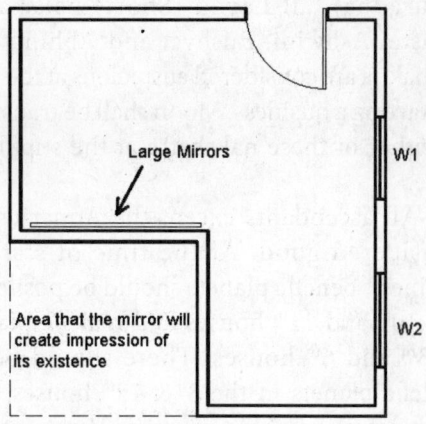

Fig 8.6: Using Mirrors for Extending the Missing Area

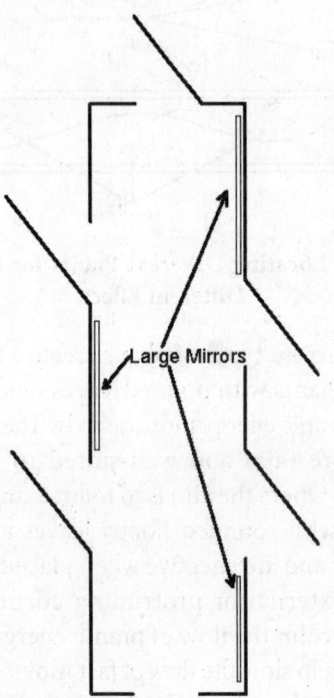

Fig. 8.5: Mirrors Staggered on Either Side of a Long Corridor

Large mirrors can also be used to give the impression that a room extends into a missing area. Looking at the mirror while standing in the room will create the illusion that space facing the mirror exists behind it.

Mirrors need to be large enough, and positioned so that the reflection does not cut off the top of any of the occupant's heads. Other objects having shiny, reflective surface will have a similar effect like mirrors.

Building at the Top of a T-Junction

Vehicles approaching such a building direct the flow of negative energy towards it. The occupants of the building are in the path of a funnel of fast-moving negative energy and will feel unsettled. They can't really relax in this building and will want to go out a lot. The solution is to slow down and subdue the flow of negative energy, as well as to deflect some of this negative energy in another direction.

Grow a hedge and bushes in the front garden for this purpose as shown in the figure 3.8. As the negative energy directed by the road and traffic passes through the hedge, it has a similar effect as water passing through a sponge. Negative energy from the road meets a resistance and begins to move more slowly. Another way to change the direction of this negative energy is to position a round, convex mirror or shiny plaque on the outside wall facing the road that points towards the building.

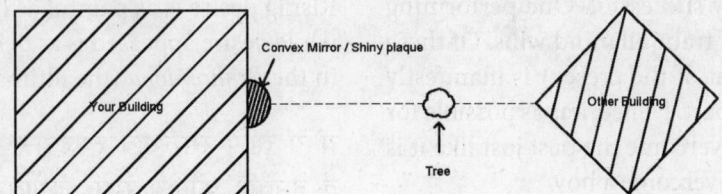

Fig 8.7: Avoiding Kona (Corner) Vedha by Provision of a Tree and Convex Mirror

Kona Vedha (Cutting Corner)

Any protruding corner will make the passing pranic energy swirl. This can be disorientating to people immersed in this swirling pranic energy. It may occur inside an L-shaped room (see figure 5.4), or the corner of another building may be pointing towards your building.

The simple remedy is to grow a plant in front of this type of corner. A tree or bush would be suitable outside and a small potted plant inside, as the case may be. A convex mirror or shiny plaque on the outside of your building facing the protruding corner of another building will reflect and spread out some of the cutting pranic energy.

Classical views on earning, human karmas, destiny, and desires

वसामि नित्यं सुभगे प्रगल्भे दक्षे नरे कर्मणि वर्तमाने।
अक्रोधने देवपरे कृतज्ञे जितेन्द्रिये नित्यमुदीर्णसत्त्वे॥

Mahabharata, Anushashan Parva 11.6
(Sree said) I always reside with him that is eloquent, active, attentive to business, free from wrath, given to the worship of the deities, endowed with gratitude, has his passions under complete control, and is high minded in everything.

यात्रामात्र प्रसिद्ध्यर्थं स्वै: कर्मभिरगर्हितें:।
अक्लेशेन शरीरस्य कुर्वीत धनसंचय:॥

One should accumulate money only as a means for the present life, as per his position, while indulging in unquestionable (good) deeds, without causing any unnecessary distress to the body.

दिवसेनैव तत्कुर्यात् येन रात्रौ सुखं वसेत्।
यावज्जीवं च तत्कुर्याद् येन प्रेत्य सुखं वसेत्॥

One should indulge in such deeds during the daytime by which he gets a carefree sweet sleep during the night. He should do such deeds in his lifetime by which he lives delightfully in the life to come.

गते शोको न कर्त्तव्यो भविष्यनैव चिन्तयेत्।
वर्तमानेन कालेन प्रवर्त्तन्ते विचक्षणा:॥

Grieve not for the past, worry not for the future, now is the moment to act, for the wise doer.

दैवे पुरुषकारे च लोकोऽयं सम्प्रतिष्ठित:।
तत्र दैवं तु विधिना कालयुक्तेन लभ्यते॥

Mahabharata, Adiparva
Worldly affairs rest firmly on the destiny and human efforts. Destiny succeeds here only because of the timely efforts.

ऐहिक: प्राक्तनं हन्ति प्राक्तनोऽद्यतनं बलात्।
सर्वदा पुरुषस्पन्दस्तत्रानुद्वेगवाञ्जयी॥
द्वयोरद्यतनस्यैव प्रत्यक्षाद्बलिता भवेत्।
दैवं जेतुं यतो यत्नैर्बालो यूनेव शक्यते॥

Yogavaashistha, 2.6.18-19
Present deeds destroy those of the past life, and those of the past life can destroy the effect of present deeds, but the exertions of a man

are undoubtedly successful. One performing his deeds with a tranquil mind wins. Of these two powers, that of the present is manifestly superior to the past. Hence, it is as possible for the present to overcome the past just like it is for an adult to overcome a boy.

इच्छोदयो यथा दु:खमिच्छाशान्तिर्यथा सुखम्।
तथा न नरके नापि ब्रह्मलोकेऽनुभूयते।।
Yogavaashistha, 6(2).36.24

Rising desire is as painful as living in the hell while desire appeased is as delightful as living in the *Brahamloka* (the ultimate heaven).

यं यं वापि स्मरन्भावं त्यजत्यन्ते कलेवरम्।
तं तमेवैति कौन्तेय सदा तद्भावभावित:।।
Shrimadbhagwadgeeta, 8.6

One attains whatever state (of being) one thinks about at the last when relinquishing the body, being ever absorbed in the thought thereof.

Chapter 9
Case Studies

उद्योगिनं पुरुषसिंहमुपैति लक्ष्मीर्दैवं हि दैवमिति कापुरुषा वदन्ति।
दैवं निहत्य कुरु पौरुषमात्मशक्त्या यत्ने कृते यदि न सिद्ध्यति कोऽत्र दोष: ॥

Only the lion (like) person who makes (constant) efforts gets *Lakshmi* (wealth). Cowards (only) depend upon destiny. One must throw away (the concept of) destiny and make all his possible efforts. It is not one's fault if work is not accomplished inspite of the efforts!

Panchtantra, 1.217

During the past twenty years, while teaching vaastu and writing books, I have been giving vaastu consultancy to hundreds of people for residential, commercial and industrial purposes. Some people contact me before starting the construction process, some during or after the completion and some for vaastu analysis of their existing house or business premises for rectification of vaastu defects.

There may be many stages in vaastu consultancy, ranging from the selection of plot to identification and removal of vaastu defects arising at later stage due to inner or outer changes. We may divide consultancy in seven stages:

1. Selection of plot in a particular locality.
2. Rectification of plot to remove the vaastu discrepancies.
3. Vaastu friendly design and construction of the space and the building.
4. Arrangement of furniture and furnishings.
5. Entry at an auspicious time.
6. A vaastu friendly living / working.
7. Identification and removal of vaastu defects arising at later stage.

The earlier a client approaches a vaastu expert, the better. In such cases, vaastu expert has more freedom to apply the rules of this ancient wisdom. In the same way, an already constructed building or premises can be chosen, changed and arranged to a certain extent as per the norms of vaastu. As the present work is related to business, I have chosen some cases of distinctly varied nature, related to the different types of vaastu.

These cases are being discussed here so that the readers can have a fair idea of peculiar requirements of different businesses. Vaastu analysis of one single case may require five to ten pages. I have deliberately avoided mentioning the unimportant and repeated details of these cases. Only most important unique points, which are helpful for further learning and gaining deep knowledge of vaastu, have been discussed in details. The identity of clients has not been revealed for want of privacy.

Readers are advised to first go for the general principles of vaastu shastra - residential and commercial both - before giving a study to these cases. These cases should not be applied in the same manner to all the similar cases. Always apply the Desh (place), Kaal (time) and Paatra (person) facors. A vaastu expert acts like a doctor of sick buildings. Each single building should be diagnosed thoroughly before suggesting medication. Medicine is necessary only when building is ill and not always. Sometimes only the time of the owner might be running very bad!

1. Publishing House in Sector 63, NOIDA, Uttar Pradesh

This publishing house is renowned in India for children's comic books, magazines of common interest and books having mass appeal. The owner wanted a vaastu friendly business cum residential complex on a pre-owned plot facing west. The most auspicious direction for publishing, printing and stationary work is north, the direction of Mercury. Mercury governs reading, writing and acquired intelligence.

This west facing plot was so arranged that it became north facing. The driveway was kept towards the north with less offsets towards the south. Sufficient open space was kept in the east direction too. Being the front, more open space was required in the west as per the building bye-laws norms of Noida. So, west was made heavy by a well designed stepped lawn in the front sloping towards east and Ashoka trees outside the boundary wall. In the constructed area also; west was protected through the provision of a lift, staircase and a godown.

The ground floor will be used for sorting, cutting, binding and dispatching the books. MD's room was designed in the south-west direction of first floor, the direction of power and stability. Design and editorial staff will be on the first floor. It will provide them the required privacy and quiet environment for unleashing their creativity.

The second floor was designed for residential purposes which the owner intended to use in future. Brahamsthan was kept open to the sky but keeping in mind the security,

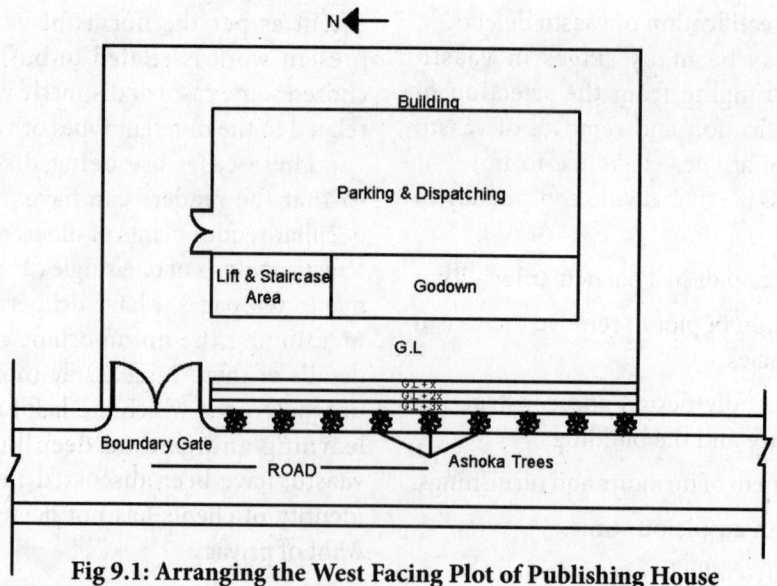

Fig 9.1: Arranging the West Facing Plot of Publishing House

rains and dust storms, a transparent dome of good architectural beauty was provided with due provision for the circulation of fresh air.

The owner is now happier than ever before. He has started a new monthly magazine on vaastu and jyotish with sale in thousands. His monthly magazine on yoga is selling like hot cakes in many Indian languages including English.

2. Footwear Factory in Narela Industrial Area

The owner was in the business of manufacturing footwear parts. He was facing problems like low turnover and parties' denial to collect their finished goods. The factory was on the first floor; it was north facing with big windows in the west direction. South and east were closed. An area, having openings in the north and west only, makes one unstable like air. The person wants to run the business for short term quick gains, but not for long term stable and constant income.

South-east invites heatless solar light. Light is equivalent to money in a business. Closed south and east direction are not good for business purposes. The beneficially moulded energies coming from the south are good for physical activities. South is the area of our physical activities (karma bhava), equivalent to the tenth house in the astrological chart.

Brahamsthan, the middlemost area of the factory, was full of chippings and striplings. An occupied brahamsthan stops circulation of prana to every nook and corner of the working area. A machine towards the eastern wall was always out of order. It was too close to the wall in a dark area. A machine should be installed so that the workers are able to work upon it from any side without any hindrance. There should be proper provision of light, preferably the natural light, in the working area.

The office was in a shabby condition. Owner's desk was in the south-west direction. A bed was in the south-east direction. A bed is not good in the factory office. Sleeping is too tamasic while industrial production is too rajasic. When bed is visible while sitting on the working table, person is less likely to take interest in his factory work. The working table, in this case, is best in the south-east. It will be farthest from the main entry as well as a commanding and energy giving position.

The desk was shaky on the slightest touch. Unstable desk means instability in business. The person won't be interested to sit and work. Moreover, there was a heap of broken bricks due to some half finished repair work. Clutter or garbage stops the entry of wealth goddess Lakshmi. The repair work once started should be finished at the earliest. Half finished jobs bring bad name to the business. New opportunities stop coming. The chair of owner was shabby, unmatched with the height of desk and with an unwashed towel on the back. Chair shall always be well dressed and

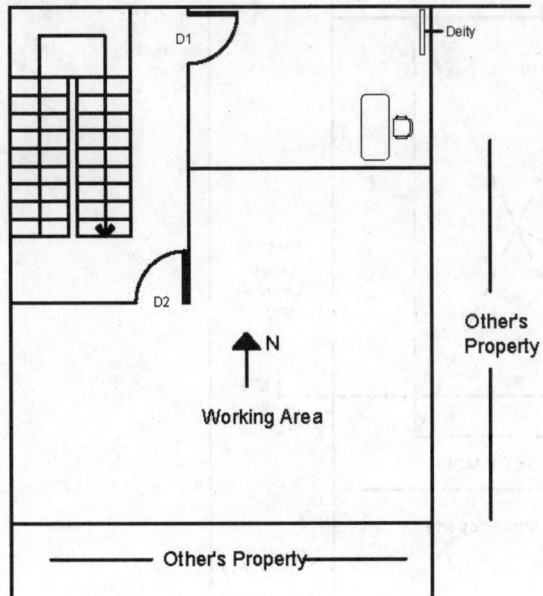

Fig 9.2: Plan of the Footwear Factory

in proportion to one's position and size of the desk. Its furnishing should always be neat and clean.

The deity, whom the owner worshipped, was in the north-east direction but was seated too high. Owner was using a stool to reach the deity to offer his daily prayers. This is a very bad situation. One shall have an easy access to his deity. Otherwise, everything will seem far from reach and one will have to depend on the mediators to accomplish all the jobs.

The finished but undelivered goods were advised to be kept in the north-west direction, near to the door D2. The air element of this direction helps delivery of goods at the earliest. After acting on my suggestions, owner was able to get rid of the undelivered goods. He and his workers are feeling better in the changed environment. More offers are pouring in.

3. Electronic Parts Manufacturing Unit at Okhla, Delhi

The owner of this factory was manufacturing electronic parts for multinational companies. These parts were further used in electronic goods. Though the owner has earned a good name in this field at an early age of 35 years; he was suffering from multiple physical diseases. Moreover, workers did not want to stay for long.

The vaastu of this factory is very interesting. There is a natural steep ground slope in this area. The ground floor in the present unit while entering from the south-west becomes the basement when the same is accessed from the north-east. This ground floor counted from the south-west side is completely closed in the north-east because of earth and road. South-east side was also closed because of the adjoining unit.

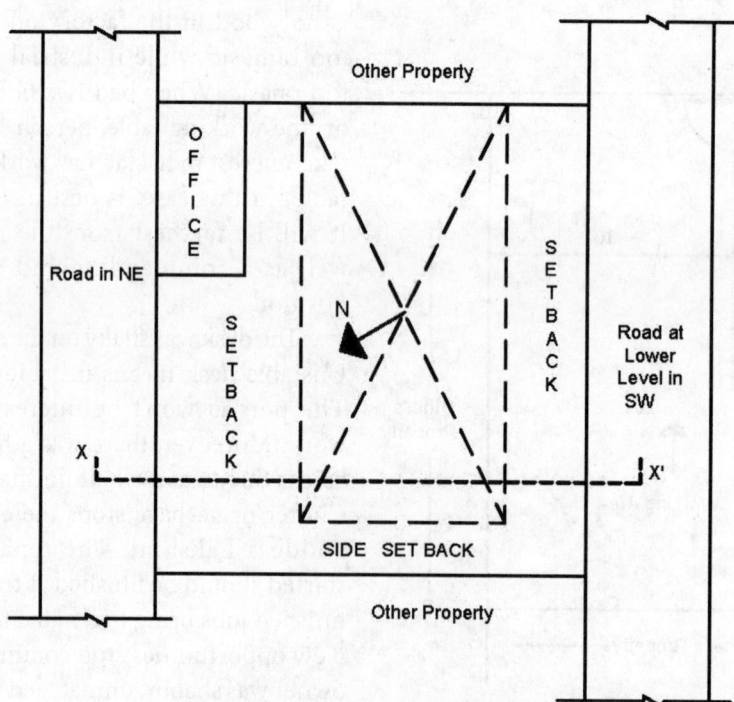

Fig 9.3: Plan of the Electronic Parts Manufacturing Unit

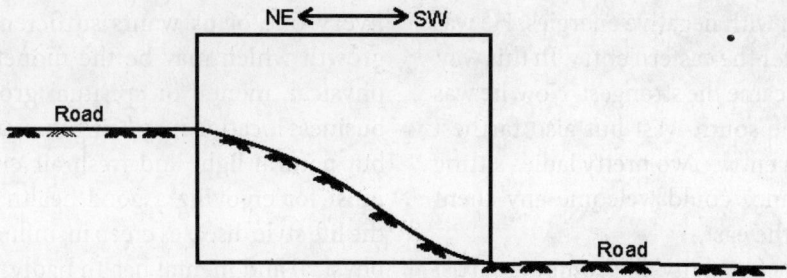

Fig 9.4: Section Plan of the Unit along X-X¹

Driveway was in the north-west. There was a big iron leaf gate (at the ground floor level of backside) in the south-west, which was kept closed. Owners and the workers were using the north-east gate for entering the premises and going downwards in the main working area where heavy machines were installed. Rear gate was used only for bringing in or taking out machines and the heavy material.

Iron leaf gate in the south-west was absorbing sun's poisonous infrared radiations. An electronic goods manufacturing unit does not need so much of heat. Here, this side wall should be a cavity wall or a wall of at least one foot thick. This door should be as small as possible, preferably made of wood. Double doors are the best. Wood does not allow the outside heat in.

There were ventilators towards the north-east as well as towards the south-west in the working area. These should always be kept open. Fixing two exhausts fans - one in the north-east and other in the south-west - in a zigzag manner can further increase their efficiency. Fresh air should be drawn in from the north-east and expelled out from the south-west.

The owner was using a specially prepared cabin in this area (basement from the entry) for keeping a close vigil on his workers. The cabin was a glass house with blinds on the three sides. It helped him to keep a vigil on his workers by just using the tip of his fingers. Virtually, he was using this grave like place for sitting for a long period of five to six hours a day. The award came in the form of increased blood pressure, diabetes and anxiety. Isn't it foolish to go for such a cabin in the modern world of CCTV!

He was advised to sit on the first floor in an already built office. It was towards the left side of the ground floor when entering from the north-east. Close circuit TV's can be installed for keeping an eye on the ongoing activities in the factory premises. It needs meager amount of money for such arrangement, but the benefits are thousand fold.

4. Advertising Agency in Chandni Chowk, Delhi

I came in contact with the owner of this agency in concern with our courses' advertisement in the newspapers. His was a small office on the first floor of a big old building in Fatehpuri. It was east-west oriented with entry from both the sides. He was using mostly the western side for coming in and going out. West side is good for study and research till late hours but is not good for health purposes. The owner was occupying a seat in the south-west, but nearest to the entry. This is not a strong position for the head. The workers, three in all, were sitting towards his backside. The owner was suffering from indigestion and severe skin problem.

The office floor level was also around two feet lower than the outer floor level of the premises. Using west as the main entry was filling this area with negative energies. He was advised to prefer the eastern entry. In this way, his position became the strongest. Now, he was not only in the south-west but also farthest from the main entry. Two pretty ladies sitting near the entrance could welcome any client coming from the east.

Due to space scarcity, the computer artist responsible for designing the advertisements was sitting on an artificially created wooden mezzanine floor. It was hardly five feet high and he had to bend forward to save his head striking the ceiling. Consequently, no artist was happy working here. No one wants such a cramped working space where he is not even free to stand upright on his own two feet!

The owner took serious action on my suggestions. Years back, he has purchased new premises in the same building and has shifted his computer designer there. Computer artist is also happy working there in a 14 feet high room with lot of extra space in the surroundings. Every one of us wants sufficient space for growth which may be the monetary, social, physical, mental or spiritual growth. Good business location may bring monetary success but natural light and fresh air circulation is must for enjoying a good health. Otherwise the life style diseases creep in, influencing one's physical and mental health badly. Bad health, in turn, reduces one's earning capacity.

5. A Public School in Gurgaon

It was a CBSE recognized senior secondary public school, run by husband and wife together. Their son and daughter-in-law were also running a middle school on Gurgaon-Rewari highway. Plan of this school was prepared years back by an architect Mr Vinod Gupta who had deep interest in the ancient wisdom of vaastu shastra. Later he joined our Institute for detailed study of vaastu shastra in a scientific manner.

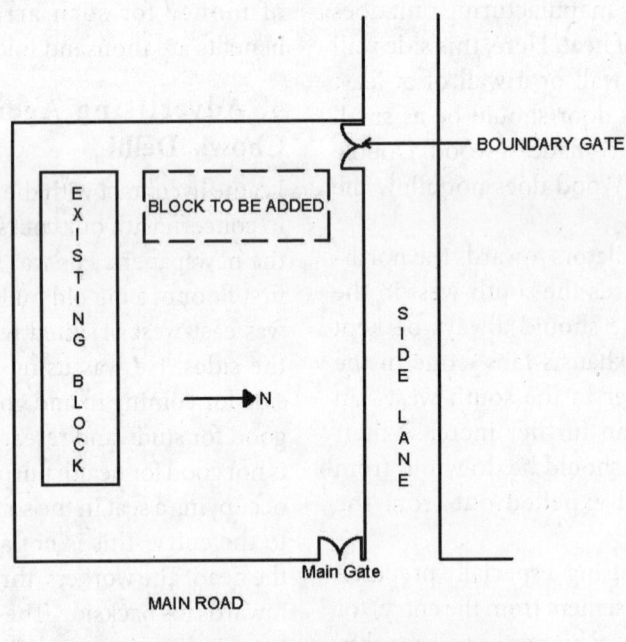

Fig 9.5: Plan of the Public School

The present school designed by him had flourished so much that the owners purchased a newer one. School plot was of a regular rectangular shape with main road towards east and small road towards the north. Other good vaastu points of this school were:

1. Building was in the south direction with lot of open space in the north direction. North orientation is best for general educational institutes.
2. There was open space all around the building. It helps in cross ventilation and arrival of natural sunlight.
3. The boundary gate was in the east of northeast, the ideal position. While entering from this gate, wide open ground gives a very good overall impression of the school.
4. Another boundary gate was in the northwest, opening in the side lane.

Presently, the owners wanted to add one more block to the existing one. While adding a new block, following vaastu principles should strictly be adhered to:

1. It should be of square or rectangular shape where length is not more than thrice the width.
2. It should stand independent of the existing blocks. If connection is inevitable, provide the expansion gaps at least as per the norms of civil engineering.
3. The block should be in the south-west, south or west direction so that more open space is available towards the north-east, north or east direction.
4. It should be farthest from the main entry. Classrooms away from the entry point help in creating a quiet environment, which is must for studies.

The main stress in an educational institute is the classroom where knowledge is imparted to the students. The main vaastu points in its design are:

1. The blackboard should be on the north or east wall. With this arrangement, students will face an auspicious direction. The stage for the teacher should not be too high. Simple rectangular shape in plan, 6" to 8" high platform is okay for teacher's visibility.
2. Door (D1) should never be towards the blackboard side. Otherwise, all the students get disturbed whenever a latecomer enters in. A door is best towards the left (D2) or back (D3) of the sitting students. A separate door (D4) can be provided exclusively for the teacher's movement. For school students or where greater control of the teacher is required, door D2 / D3 can be kept closed.
3. More number of windows should be towards the north and east directions. South side windows are useful in winters. Windows opening towards the corridors disturb student's attention.

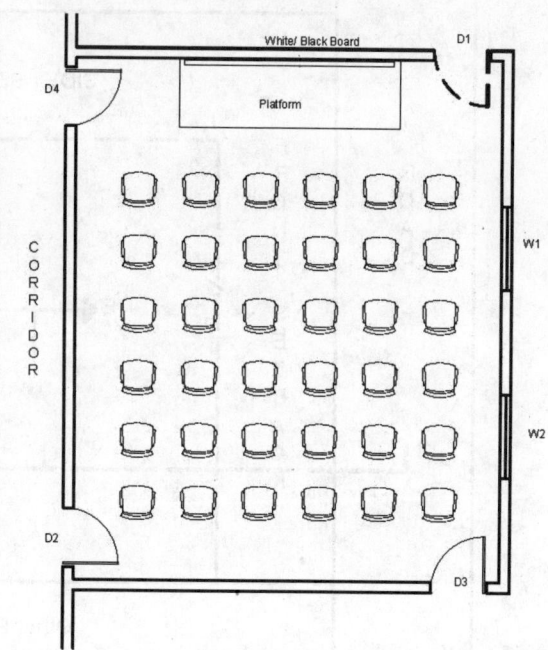

Fig 9.6: Arrangement of an Ideal Classroom

Other important vaastu consideration in a school is student's facing while offering morning prayers. For it, North facing is best though it requires a somewhat higher stage in the north direction. East facing is problematic during summers when sunrays become unbearable during the early morning hours.

6. Wheat Flour Mill in Bawana Industrial Area, Delhi

The owner contacted me for a vaastu friendly design of his flour mill on a DSIDC plot. It was an east facing plot. East is ruled by sun. Sun also rules wheat. Wheat crop needs early summer heat of sun for its ripening. So, open east and south-east are best for a flour mill.

According to the DSIDC norms, offsets in the front and back portion were compulsory. Also basement was allowed only in a small portion of the plot area. Most of the owners also tend to cover 100% plot area as the basement. They are usually reluctant to leave offsets as open areas. They think it wastage of their precious space.

As evident from the plan, most of the mills are closed from the three sides. In such a situation, if basement is provided in the full area, exhaust will be available only in the front east direction in the present case. The basement will behave like a cave. It may lead to increased health problems, accidents, bad quality of the product (here wheat flour), unhealthy working conditions and decreased efficiency of workers.

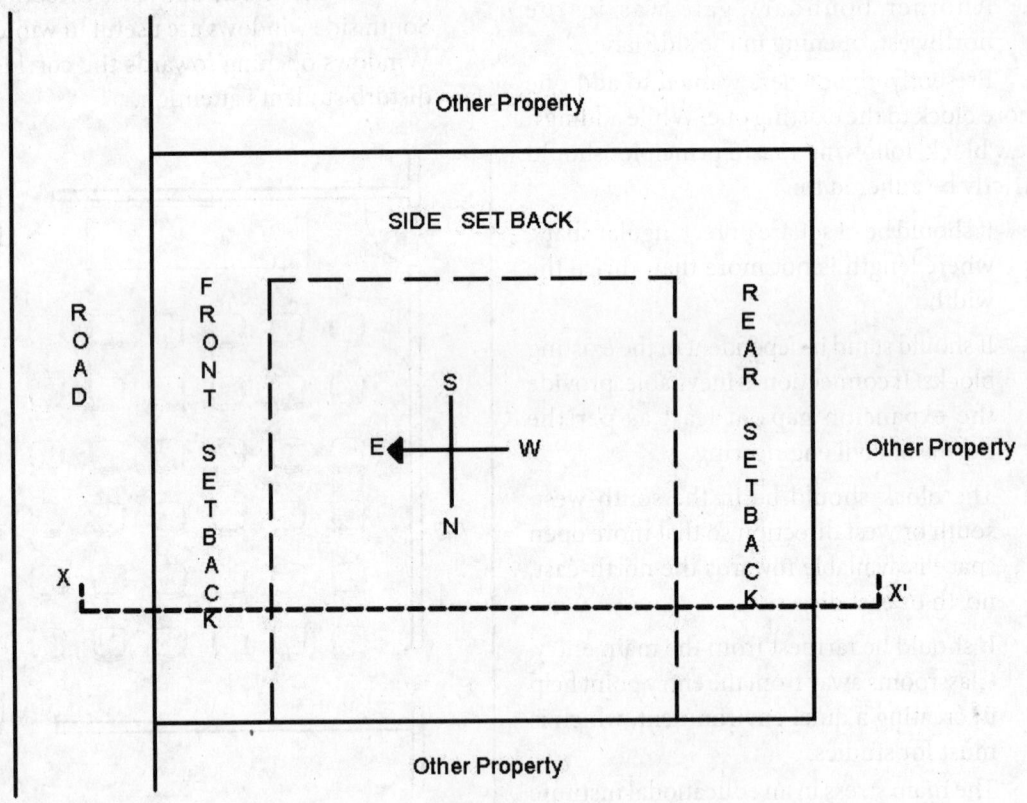

Fig 9.7: Flour Mill with the Location Plan

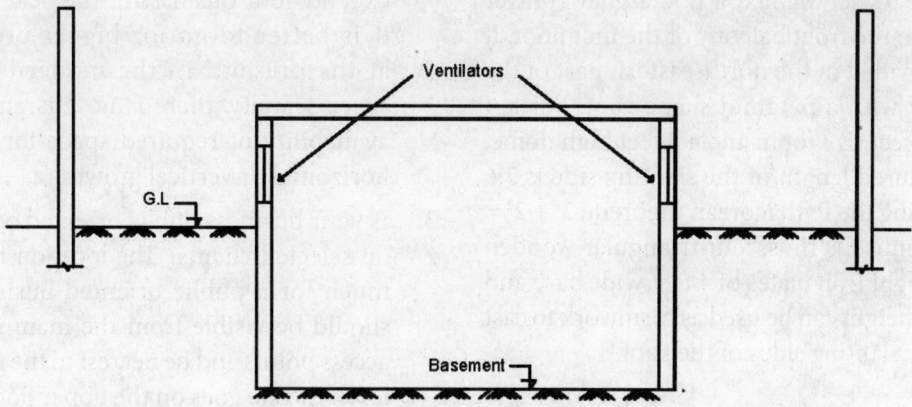

Fig 9.8: Provision of Ventilators in the Set Back Areas (X-X Section)

Offsets on all the four sides of the basement area are best. They help in giving natural light and cross ventilation. Ventilators are must at least on the two opposite sides. Presence of natural light and fresh air not only increases the worker's efficiency but also reduces the electricity bill. Chances of any disaster get lessened.

Provision was also made to leave the 3' x 3' middlemost area of the construction open to the sky, which the owner reluctantly agreed.

After completion of the structure, when I visited the site in the morning on another day, there was virtually no need of any artificial light. Each and every corner of the finished structure was clearly visible with the naked eyes. That vaastu is best where we don't need any artificial light from sunrise to sunset for our day to day working. Basements too become useful when the principles of classical vaastu are adhered to.

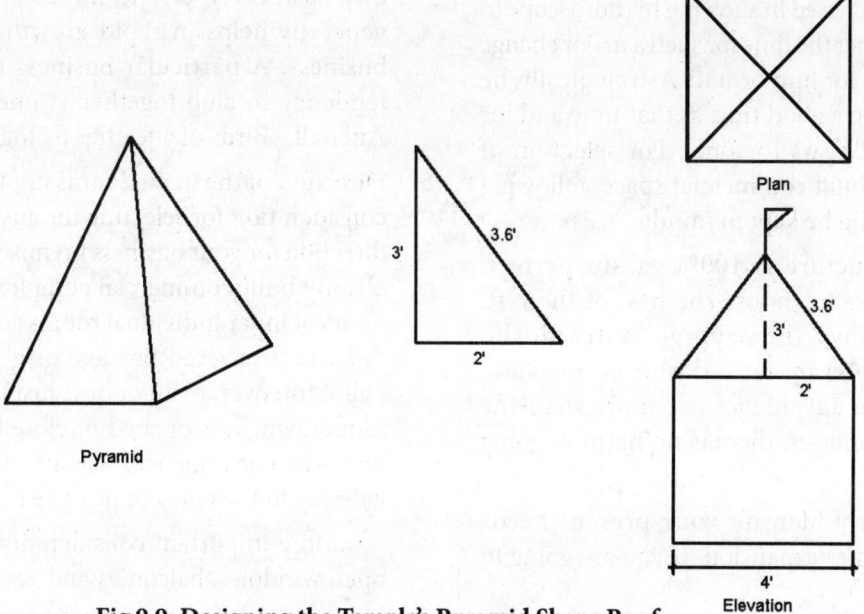

Fig 9.9: Designing the Temple's Pyramid Shape Roof

The owner wanted a pooja ghar (prayer room) in the front balcony of the first floor. It was provided in the north-eastern part of the balcony with a pyramid shape roof. For a 4 feet x 4 feet size room and a 3 feet high dome, the required length of the slanting side is 3.6 feet (using the Pythagorean theorem; $3^2 + 2^2 =$ Hyponenuse^2). Thus, four triangular wooden or wrought iron plates of 4 feet wide base and 3.6 feet height can be used as formwork to cast the four slanting sides of the roof.

7. Selection of Commercial Space for Renowned Plywood Company in Netaji Subhash Place, Pitampura, New Delhi

The owner of this company had read my book, "Unfolding the veil of Mystery, Vaastu: The art & science of living", published by Sterling Publishers Pvt. Ltd. He was running his business successfully from Asaf Ali Road, New Delhi and now wanted to shift it to the newly developed Netaji Subhash Place. It is a rapidly growing commercial area and was just a stone's throw distance from his residence.

The owner had already selected some premises and wanted me to select the best out of them as per the vaastu recommendations. He was also interested in showing his horoscope to know whether the time for such a major change is favorable for him or not? Astrologically, he was running a good time at that time and for a couple of years to come. For selection of an already built commercial space, following points should be kept in mind:

1. No structure is 100% vaastu perfect. We have to choose the best of the rest. So, follow the saying; "Yatra dosho gunadhikyam tatra dosho na vartatey" (Where advantages are more than the disadvantages, there is no harm in going for it).

2. Honestly identify your present needs and future expansion. If you are going to expand your business in the near future, it is better to go for bigger premises at the present. In the modern age of space scarcity, there is no guarantee for availability of required space for future horizontal or vertical growth.

3. Is your business public oriented or based on selected clients? The location matters much for a public oriented business. It should be visible from the main roads / access points and be nearest to the ground level. As one goes on the upper floors, the number of clientele reduces. In a high-rise building, everyone visits the ground floor but selected people reach the upper ones.

   Some people are claustrophobic and try to stay away from the lifts. They will not try the staircase too to reach your office on the tenth floor. Moreover, asthmatic people feel bad on upper floors. Upper floors can safely be chosen if you deal only with a selected number of known clients or you run business only on phone or Internet.

4. Like increases like. Select a business premises where people are already of your own business type. A healthy competition generally helps in rapid growth of any business. A particular business has the tendency to club together at one place. After all, "Birds of a feather fly together."

5. Direction of the main door is not the sole consideration for selecting the auspicious direction for your business premises. In an already built commercial complex, main doors of inner individual rooms generally open in a covered passage or a central hall. Moreover, main door is just like our mouth, which is opened or closed as per our own convenience. It is not the sole gateway to the entry of positive energies.

   More important consideration is the open windows, balconies and ventilators in the auspicious directions ie south-east, east and north. South of south-east is the door to entry of Lakshami, the wealth goddess. Go for that area which has more openings towards the auspicious directions than towards the south-west, west and south directions.

6. The premises should be of sufficient height, preferably 12 feet or more. The shape should be square or rectangular with no protruding or cut corners. You can easily arrange the full space in a regular shaped working area. Even one square inch floor area shall not go waste.

7. Easy and economical - preferably free parking facility - attracts more clients.

8. Three Star Hotel on Haridwar Rishikesh Highway

The owner, a Bengali lady was in the business of foreign exchange and restaurants. She had purchased this hotel from a Delhi based businessman and got franchise of a renowned USA based hotel company. After the worldwide popularity of Baba Ramdev and his ashram in Haridwar, hotel industry has a bright future there. The present hotel was running in loss in the hands of its previous owner. The lady approached me through one of my students, a lady painter. She wanted a thorough vaastu analysis and my expert comments.

The main entry of the building was in the corner, towards one side of the lobby. For public buildings, entry should preferably be in the middle and should be of sufficiently big size to facilitate the entry of two-three persons at the same time. The reception was on the first floor! It should preferably be on the ground floor, at the right side of the entry itself. Otherwise, the prana of a newcomer gets disturbed. At least, someone should be present there to properly guide the customer.

One of the main problems in this hotel was the staircase. It was turning anti clockwise. Such a staircase invites accidents and unhappiness of its users. There were big looking glasses on each landing in the beginning and end of each flight. The lady had consulted some vaastu expert in the past and provided these on his suggestion. But these were of no use. It was a sheer wastage of money. In an anti clockwise turning staircase, the railing is generally towards our left hand side that requires extra labour while ascending. The grip of our left hand is not as strong as of the right hand.

To distract one's attention from this uncomfortable situation, a looking glass (mirror) right in front - in the end of the flight, at the landing - can be fitted. A person's attention gets diverted towards his image in the mirror, his movement and body gestures. But if one is not able to see even the tip of his head, why to erect such a costly mirror! When image is not visible in the mirror while ascending, it is better to install a beautiful attractive painting or a piece of art, or an aquarium or simply a well maintained decorative plant. These can be placed covering the full landing width, just opposite the flight or in the corner.

The second main problem was in the arrangement of rooms. The hotel was using blue and yellow colour schemes irrespective of the specific directions. Main doors of all the rooms were towards south-west or north-east, opening in a covered passage. There was no question of entry of natural light and sufficient air from this side. Every room had a big balcony. The rooms facing the south-west had balcony in the north-east and vice versa. In such a situation, rooms having balcony towards the north-east will remain cool during the summers. On the other side, rooms having balcony in the south-west side will be uncomfortable during the summers, though most sought after during the winters. The effect of main door will be negligible because of the covered passage. Following suggestions were given regarding the arrangement of the rooms:

1. Use cold colors; ie blue and green, in rooms having balcony towards the south-west and hot colors; ie red and yellow in the rooms having balcony towards the north-east. In this way, the balance of hot and cold is achieved.
2. Keep the bed at least three inches away from the wall. It should be farthest from the door. There should be solid walls towards the head and the left hand side (or the passive side) while sleeping.
3. Remove the mirrors placed right in front of the beds. It disturbs the sleep. It may be placed on the side walls, preferably on the east or the north wall.
4. Side tables' uppermost drawer was fitted with electrical switches. The person occupying the room should not be able to open it without a key, which may otherwise cause accidents.
5. Provide cover to the TV placed on a low cupboard just opposite the bed so that the person can cover it as per his own convenience while going to sleep at night. TV screen acts like a translucent mirror. An open screen sends electromagnetic radiations that can cause disturbance in enjoying a sound sleep.

The owner, a devotee of Mother Goddess Kali, had renovated an existing old temple in the hotel premises. The goddess was facing east and the entry was from both the south and east sides. The south entry is not recommended here. One should reach the goddess from the front and not from the side. However, southern opening is good for receiving radiations for the hot tempered Goddess. In a temple meant for a god or goddess, direction of the deity is important, not the direction of any devotee.

But in the pooja ghar in your house, your face should be towards an auspicious direction. The deity here is just a means not the end in itself. Prana-pratishtha (charging or energizing) of the idol of deity is not done in the house, though it is must in a temple meant for a particular deity. In the temple, the deity is considered a live divine being with manifested powers.

9. Gems and Jewellery showroom in the main market of sector 18, NOIDA

The owner called me after reading my book, "Vaastu: The art and science of living." He had purchased an already existing jewellery showroom in a commercial mall in sector 18, NOIDA. The renovation work was in full swing. He wanted me to arrange it as per the accepted norms of vaastu shastra. Whether his wife - a highly educated lady - will be able to run it successfully? What would be the lucky name for the business?

The showroom was on the first floor, facing the south-west. There was a wide passage towards the front side. The open well in the middle of the mall was closed in the upward direction for facilitating the centralized air-conditioning. There was no point of entry of the malefic infrared radiations from the main door (situated in south-west) in the present showroom.

The first problem was the closed north-east. It was the back portion of this showroom that was open to the sky. There was a big window in this direction that the owner wanted to close for getting maximum benefit of centralized air conditioning. This is like cutting one's own limbs. North-east is the gateway to amrita like solar rays. It is the prime source of cool light and air. Closing it means closing the eyes, nose, ears and mouth of the vaastu purush - the personified form of your business space. It is like cutting the head of your business. No air conditioning can equalize the energies entering from the north-east.

All types of people enter an air-conditioned mall, accompanied with dust and sweat. They cough and sneeze and leave their body micro-organisms which go on circulating in the whole of the building. Its ill effects are seen afterwards in the form of worker's low efficiency, disturbed BP, asthmatic tendencies and decreased immunity to fight diseases.

The second problem was his insistence to renovate the existing toilet on the mezzanine floor in the backside ie in the north-east. His logic was that everyone in the mall had his or her private toilet. There was a well-maintained common toilet on the same floor, hardly ten metres away from this showroom. In such a situation, it can't be called wise to go for your personal toilet when one square feet area costs you in thousands. This toilet was disturbing the regular shape of the floor area too.

Vaastu does not recommend toilet as an inevitable part of the main construction. Avoid it if you can. For how long you use it in a day! Your space is more precious. It can be used for other better purposes. Sterling Publishers Pvt Ltd, publisher of my first vaastu book, is a well known name in the field of quality books publishing. The MD does not have a private bathroom. He uses the same meant for the staff and the visitors. It not only makes him near to his employees but also helps in better maintenance of such usually unattended areas.

The third problem was the desks meant for showing jewellery. The plan shape of table is given in the figure 9.10. This shape helps the salesman to sit for long hours. He or she can thrust his or her body inside the table. The table, in turn, hugs him and brings him closer to the customers. But the customer's side of the desk represents a cutter's edge. The customer won't be able to stay here for long. This shape spins away the prospective customers. Consequently, the business will decrease. The customer side of the desk should be straight with rounded corners.

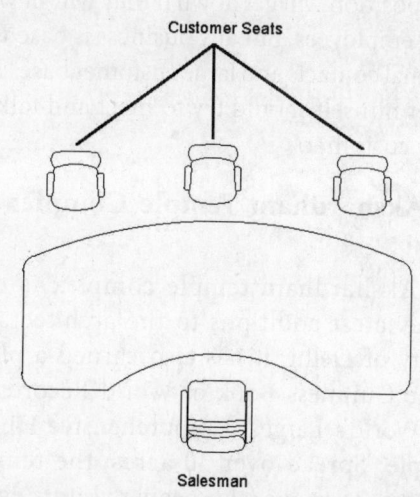

Fig 9.10: Shape of the Salesman's Table (Plan)

Colour of the walls was light green. It is not the most suitable colour for a gems and jewellery showroom. Green represents unripe grains. Grains, when ripe, turn golden yellow. The best colour shades for a jewellery showroom are golden, bright yellow, light orange and silvery white. Jewellers normally use soft pink paper for wrapping the ornaments!

A jewellery showroom should be a bright and cheerful place, full of lights and mirrors. Such a place leads lady shoppers to the other world of their dreams. The shop girls should be exquisitely dressed and groomed. Offer drinking water, tea, coffee or lassi to the shoppers. Every customer shall be treated like a prince or a princess.

Jewellery business is built mainly on human relationships. A shop is the place of business seeking to attract as many shoppers as possible. Owner should never get cut-off from his own shop, shop-girls and other employees. It is a common mistake which flourishing shopkeepers make when they get rich. Such newly-rich shopkeepers enclose themselves in a cabin in the backside of the premises and think themselves as CEO's. They think that their position will get down if they will sit with other employees. But any business is based on personal contacts and large customer base. The owner himself should try to meet and talk to every customer.

10. Akshardham Temple Complex in Delhi

The Akshardham temple complex is one of the latest additions to the architectural beauty of Delhi. It has also earned a place in the Guinness Book of World Records as the 'World's Largest Comprehensive Hindu Temple'. Spread over 30 acres, the temple now gets over one lakh people visitors every week. Consecrated on November 6, 2005 by Pramukh Swami Narayanswaroopdas of temple trust Bochasanwasi Sri Akshar Purushottam Swaminarayan Sanstha (BAPS), the temple has 234 ornately carved pillars, nine domes and 20 quadrangular shikhars.

This ornately hand crafted temple was conceptualized by consultant Veerendra Sompura and his team based on the principles of Vaastu Shilpa Shastra. Sompura are a known traditional tribe of temple builders. Around 7,000 artisans from Rajasthan, Orissa and Bengal carried out the intricate carvings on the walls. No steel has been used in its construction as it leads to corrosion due to harsh weather conditions which in turn leads to reduced life of the structure.

Institute of Mystique Sciences (Regd) conducted a vaastu visit to the Akshardham temple for vaastu students. A temple should preferably be in the north-east or east part of the city. Akshardham temple (though the authorities claim it a monument of Swami Narayana) is in the eastern part of Delhi, on the other side of river Yamuna. Again, a perennial source of fresh water is considered best in the east or north side of a temple. River Yamuna is towards its western side (also back side), which is not a good position.

Fig 9.11: Front View of Akshardham Temple at Delhi

Probably due to this vaastu dosha (defect), Akshardham temple has been mired in controversy right from the planning stage. Environmentalists hugely protested against such a large structure on the Yamuna riverbed which was then a no-construction zone. Akshardham complex is also facing grave seepage problem. The main monument, the lake around its three sides leaving the eastern side and the musical fountain had been closed from time to time for major repairs. Termite control is a major concern.

There is a wide road and a flyover towards the front east side, which of course, is like a modern river. It helps in incessant flow of devotees and tourists. There is a large parking area in the north-east, separated from the main premises. The entry is from the north-east. These are ideal vaastu conditions. The main monument is highest than all the other buildings and situated in the west of south-west.

The main door is exactly in the middle and east facing seated idol of Swami Narayana is visible from far away. This monument has three doors, one in each cardinal direction, leaving the west direction. The western door is only symbolic when seen from inside. Thus the back of main deity has been protected with a solid wall. The main entry for the visitors is from the eastern door, symbolic western door is completely closed, southern door is half closed and northern door is kept open.

Other gods and goddesses surround the main garbha griha (sanctum sanctorum), which enshrines the idol of seated Swami Narayana. The height of main garbha griha is more than the surrounding ones. Mostly circular and octagonal shapes have been used. Octagonal shape is considered very auspicious in public related vaastu. It gives a sense of all the eight directions and appears soothing to the eyes as well.

In a regular geometric shape, sum of all the angles can be found by using the formula $(2n - 4) \times 90°$, where 'n' is number of sides. So, in an octagon, the sum of all the eight inner angles will be, $(2 \times 8 - 4) \times 90° = 1080°$, and one angle $= 1080°/8 = 135°$. The nearer the inner angle to $180°$, the better are the results. Octagonal shape has freely been used in most of the buildings of Akshardham premises, including the musical fountains.

A religious place should be constructed on a large open space. Sufficient set back should be provided around it so that devotees can enjoy peace of mind, away from the city crowd. Akshardham temple fulfills these vaastu conditions. The main problem lies with the film hall where a 40 minutes film show, based on the complete life of Neelakantha (who was later called Swami Narayana) is conducted. In a fray to provide the biggest screen, proper attention has not been paid to the sitting arrangement. The full screen is not visible from all the seats. Irregular shape of the hall, too steep a slope and gaps in the end of rows of seats may invite accidents at any time.

A movie projector, which is an opto-mechanical device, displays motion picture film by projecting it onto a screen. This projection should be from the south-west, the direction of Rahu. All seats in the cinema hall should thus be oriented towards the screen in the north-east, the direction of amrita. Rahu is considered a shadowy planet in Vedic Astrology and governs photography and film shows. This shadow, coming from the poisonous direction south-west, gives an amrita like effect when reflected back from the north-east. The shapes of hall, balcony and box should be regular. Constantly changing width and number of seats create confusion. They may invite ill happenings. In the long run, people try to stay away from such places.

11. Vaastu of Shakuntalam Theatre in Pragati Maidan, New Delhi

Mayamatam (29.32b-33a) describes vaastu of theatres; "There is a building in the shape of a niche (a recess in a wall) or nest on the square of Gandharva. It has a stage and is suitable for the dance. It may be a vimanamandira, a shala or a harmya". In Bharata's Natyashastra, the theatre is said to be shaped like a 'mountain cave'.

This is a theatre cum film hall situated in the exhibition grounds of Pragati Maidan, New Delhi. All around it are lush green lawns. People can enjoy nature and soothing instrumental music while waiting for their turn. It is used as a theatre during the exhibition time in November every year. Innumerable artists of national and international fame have performed here from time to time. Millions of people have enjoyed their performance. Rest of the time, it is used as a film hall. Tastefully selected movies are screened at an easily affordable price. Delhi's well-educated cultured people prefer to visit this theatre.

The screen is towards the east, means the people will sit facing east for the full show. It is a good direction. The slope of floor is so smooth. It does not frighten anyone. There are two doors on each side for entry and exit purposes. The environment is very healthy. No one is allowed to smoke. Dim lights are generally on during the shows which help to avoid any untoward incidents. People can find their path in and out easily. Complete darkness, while watching a movie or television, is not good. It puts unnecessary stress on our eyes.

There is a water cooler inside the premises and one need not purchase the drinking water from the canteen. Eatables and hot & soft drinks can be purchased from the canteen at an affordable market price. Eatables are not allowed inside the hall. According to the Indian tradition, free drinking water shall be offered to the guests. You will find here one month's full programme in advance of the forthcoming films. In this way, the people remain attached in future.

12. Vaastu of a Bank of India branch in Delhi

Banks are the financial institutions, ruled by Kuber; the lord of accumulated wealth. His direction ie north is thus best for designing a general bank. Main principles of bank vaastu are enumerated as under:

1. North orientation is best for attracting people's money for long term deposits. More offsets should be left in the north direction. The employees should also sit facing north.

2. Entry of a bank shall not be restricted. It is a common practice in the nationalized banks in Delhi to keep the door half shut with two chains in the open portion for security purposes - one below and another above the head. It not only discourages the entry of bad elements but also encourages an honest visitor to keep away. The entry should be unrestricted, without any hindrance to the head, feet and the two arms. A new visitor is a prospective customer.

   The security can be ensured through other means like CCTV's, metal detector etc. Think of a shopkeeper who keeps his shop's door shut for fear of shoplifting! Will anyone be able to enter his shop? Though an open door tempts a saint but with a well-guarded unobstructed door saint remains a saint, while a rogue won't ever be tempted to do the wrong.

3. Eastern openings are good for investment in the safe areas. Constant gains are assured through the east. If south openings are more, the bank tries to get quick gains through its investment that may lead it into dangerous situations. West facing bank may fall a prey to investments in illegal, anti social and unethical activities. If the vaastu is good otherwise, the bank will invest in research-oriented activities like higher studies.

4. The cash transactions should be in the north, east or the north-east. Money flows like water. Water direction ie north-east is best for the transaction of money. It should not be too near to the bank's entry. A person standing at the entry should not be able to see the cash transaction counter.

5. The guard should be able to keep an eye on the whole working area. The manager should be able to control the staff through direct visibility or through a CCTV.

6. Strong room should be in the south-west and away from the main entry. It is the direction of our forefathers. Things kept in the south-west remain safe, secure and stable. No one should have a direct approach to this area.

This bank is running well and has a good name in the area. It is east facing, the direction of health and creativity. Northern area is open for movement of visitors. The door is in the east of north-east. Heavy cash transaction is made in the north of north-west direction. It is far away from the main door and not visible from the outside. Most of the staff is sitting facing north, the direction of Kuber. North orientation is best in a bank or any financial institution.

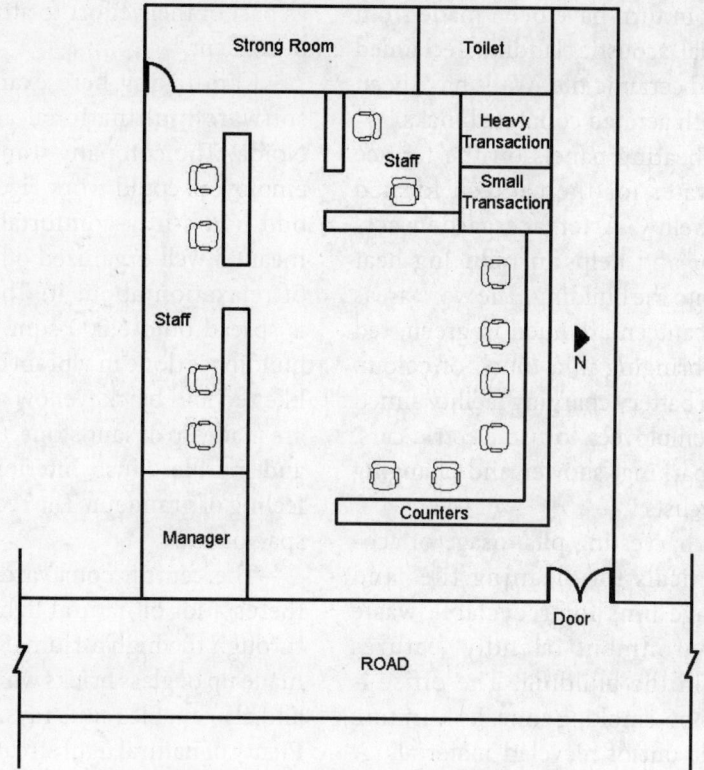

Fig 9.12: Space Arrangement inside the Bank

Manager is sitting in the south-east, the active rajasi direction. His transparent cabin gives transparency in work and enables him to control the office while sitting comfortably on his seat. The strong room is in the south-west, the ideal direction for safety, security and stability. Common visitors won't be able to have a look of it. Toilet is in the north-west, separated from the main premises.

13. Green Office of an Indian Software Company at Gurugram

This office in Gurugram has extensively used green power. It is a platinum rated green building which saves 40 to 45 percent power in comparison to others. Glass facades, colourful emblems, geometric designs, well-manicured front lawns and heavy security are the common features to the shining corporate offices. Shaped like a semi-circle, the reception has double glazed glass panels on either sides with chic black leather sofas placed in a semi-circle and the reception counter in the middle. A corridor on the first floor looks down upon the reception below.

Shaped like a semi-circle, the façade of this office sports double-glazed glass panels that use high efficiency glass that lets natural light come in and thus reduces the load on air-conditioning. Energy consumption is also reduced with the help of lamps that adjust the luminosity according to the outside light. They have also been fitted with an occupant sensor that automatically switches off when there is no one in the room. Light-shelves have been used for increasing natural lighting in the building.

The building is built in a circle around a small uncovered courtyard. The courtyard has a nicely landscaped green area with a fountain in the middle. All the offices and the glass lift look out into the courtyard, imparting a soothing feeling. The building is made of fly-ash bricks that in turn have been made from recycled material, acoustic cladding, reclaimed wood, glass and ceramic tile. Walls have been constructed with aerated concrete blocks.

The solar heating panels on the terrace provide hot water for the canteen located on the floor below. A terrace garden acts as an insulator and helps in reducing heat transmission into the building. The work areas as well as the canteen are hued in green, red and orange – bringing in a touch of colour. The office has a battery charging facility aimed at prompting employees to use electric cars. There is also parking, shower and changing facilities for cyclists.

Rainwater harvesting pits, usage of eco-friendly chemicals for cleaning tiles and separate storage bins for recyclable waste are other environment friendly features incorporated in the building. The office is designated as a no-smoking zone. Its furniture has been made out of recycled materials. A sewage treatment plant recycles the waste water which is used in cooling towers, for flushing and irrigation of the green areas.

14. Office of Multinational Software Company

The quality of infrastructure is closely correlated to the performance. If your employees are constantly worried about power cuts, too much noise, too many people, too much cold or hot within, some of their energies then get diverted by these avoidable issues. If you provide a world-class infrastructure, you can also expect people to perform at that level.

Be an altruistic employer. Employees perform better if you offer them good salaries and optimum working conditions. Employee productivity and companys' bottom-line will improve if you provide them with good facilities. Some companies in the highly competitive sectors like software are offering their employees good office architecture, plush interiors and an unparalleled range of facilities as part of their effort to attract and retain the best talent.

I am taking here example of renowned software multinational at Electronic City, Noida. The company wanted a place where employees could work rigorously even at the odd hours in a comfortable atmosphere. It meant a well organized office that had an air of relaxation about it. The square building is spread onto 6,000 sqm. The façade of the building is done in vibrant contrasting colours like red and black, yellow and blue. The walls are made up of sandstone, the floors of granite and marble. Plush interiors only add to the feeling of grandeur. The reception area is very spacious.

The central courtyard is large, airy and there's a lot of natural light streaming into it through the high atrium. Skywards is a dome made up of glass bricks which act as insulators and also enables sun's rays to penetrate easily. Plenty of natural light streaming into the office through the atrium also helps in conserving energy.

On all the four sides of the central courtyard, there are open halls where programmers work in the natural light. The office workspace is divided into 12 clusters which look like small rooms unto themselves. All the cabins and workstations are spacious with more than 300 square feet space per employee in the building (more than 17 feet x 17 feet). They are not only spacious, but have also been designed in an eclectic way. The employees sit on ergonomic chairs. The wooden furniture is all Burma teak. Colours on all the upper floors where people work are more muted but elegant when compared to the vibrant colours of façade.

Each cluster on the floor has a modern seating area for relaxation. The upper floors have a small balcony like the chhatris in the erstwhile royal palaces that overlook the lobby below. When programmers get drained, they stand by the railings and drive away their fatigue watching the play of water and light from the fountain. These balconies have a small seating area with a table for the employees. Here they can unwind and get to know each other in between their hectic work schedules.

At one end of the central courtyard is a fountain that cascades from the ground floor to the basement. The sound of water imparts a soothing effect. Stairs on either side of the waterfall wind their way down into a café that has partly wooden and partly marble flooring. Cafeteria is done up with bright yellows and red. Furniture used in the cafeteria is all polished wood and gleaming steel. The lounge is furnished with rattan sofas. Coffee machine in the corner is the same one that a top coffee chain uses.

An indoor games room has been provided to play games like table-tennis as well as for company gatherings. Employees are regularly called together to celebrate birthdays and company events, to recognize and reward the individuals, and to hold quizzes and tournaments. A whole lot of things are done here to release the inner positive energy and create a culture of fun. A lawn tennis court for the mentally weird programmers has also been provided outside this room.

15. Government Buildings at Bhopal and Delhi

Madhya Pradesh State Assembly building has been in news from time to time because of its bad vaastu. One dozen of its members fell to untimely death within a span of five years of its operation since August 5, 1996. Employees working here are also said to be facing varied difficulties. The deaths have prompted some political leaders to claim the Assembly building is jinxed, exudes "negative energy", or violates principles of vaastu shastra — directional prescriptions for buildings scripted in ancient India.

It was designed by the renowned architect Charles Correa with a cost of around 70 crores. The building suffers from "faulty construction and layout". There are three main entrances: for citizens to the south-west; legislators to the north-west; and VIPs to the south-east. The history of this Assembly building is not good. The Bhopal gas tragedy took place in 1984, when the construction started. Four years after shifting to this building, Madhya Pradesh was bifurcated (with the formation of Chhattisgarh). Senior political leaders are also planning a range of spiritual methods, including yagyas and vaastu corrections to ward off the effects.

Certain bungalows in New Delhi, situated on Pandit Pant Marg, BD Marg and Talkatora Road have been lying vacant for a long time and are used only for hosting functions. It is because they do not conform to vaastu. Bungalow at 33, Shamnath Marg has gained the reputation of being jinxed. Four politicians have stayed there, but not a single one was able to complete his full term in office while staying there. No minister or bureaucrat has ever willfully opted for this spacious house.

It is a 14-corner building which is bound to bring negative influences. It has four bedrooms, a huge drawing room, several servant quarters, two garages, one store-room and a spacious guard room. Entry of this bungalow is from north-west, the direction of air which does not allow any occupant to permanently settle down. A fountain in the south-west corner, the direction of demon Rahu and demoness Nirriti, adds to its woes. Anti-clockwise spiral staircase suggests a downfall in one's career.

दुर्जनः सज्जनो भूयात् सज्जनः शान्तिमाप्नुयात्।
शान्तो मुच्येत बन्धेभ्यो मुक्तश्चान्यान् विमोचयेत्॥

May the wicked become good, may the good realize peace, may the peaceful be released from all bondage, and may the released redeem others.

Reference Books and Other Sources

1. **Vedas:** Rig, Yajus, Atharva, Krishna Yajurveda
2. **Upanishadas:** Kena, Katha, Chhaandogya, Garuda, Brihadaranyaka,
3. **Brahmanas:** Shatapatha, Taittiriya, Aitreya,
4. Taittiriya Samhita
5. Taittiriya Aranyaka
6. **Puranas:** Shiva, Padma, Agni, Vishnu, Vayu, Brahamvaivartta, Brahmanda, Harivamsha, Matsya, Bhaagavat, Devi Bhaagvat, Vishnudharmottara, Garuda, Vaaman, Skanda
7. Ramayana of Valmiki
8. Mahabharata of Vedavyasa
9. Shrimadbhagvad Geeta (Sanskrit – Hindi), Geeta Press, Gorakhpur
10. Yoga Vasistha Maharamayana of Valmiki, English Translation by Vihari Lala Mitra (1891), edited by Thomas L. Palotas (2013), Handloom Publishing, Shivabalayogi Seva Foundation, Tucson, Arizona U.S.A.
11. Vishnu Sahasranama (Commentary of Adi Shankaracharya)
12. Yoga Sutra of Paatanjali
13. Dharma Sutra of Baudhayana
14. Ayurveda
15. Charak Samhita of Acharya Charak
16. Manu Smriti
17. Nirukta of Yaska
18. Kamikagama
19. Naatya Shastra of Bharata
20. Sangeet Makranda of Narada
21. Sangeet-Ratnakara of Nihsanka-Sharngadeva
22. Meghaduta of Kalidasa
23. Katha Saritsagara
24. Vetala Panchvimshati
25. Mrichchhkatikam of Shudraka
26. Mantra Mahodadhi
27. Prasanna Kumar Acharya: Manasara Series 1 and 2, Low price Publications, Delhi
28. Mayamatam Treatise of Housing, Architecture and Iconography, edited and translated by Bruno Dagens, vol. I & II, Indira Gandhi National Centre for the Arts, New Delhi and Motilal Banarsidass Publishers Pvt. Ltd., Delhi, Reprint 2000.
29. Ram Raz: Essay on the Architecture of the Hindus, Isha Books, New Delhi, Reprint 2013
30. Jin Purush Ashok Padam: Vaastu Reinventing The Architecture Of Fulfillment, Management Publishing Company
31. Richard Craze: Vaastu the Indian spiritual alternative to feng shui, Carlton Books Limiited, 2001, London
32. Jonathan Dee: An Introduction To Vaastu the Hindu tradition of arranging your home to improve health and wellbeing, Silverdale Books, 2002, Devon, England
33. Jami Lin: The Practical Feng Shui Architecture Landscape Decoration Healthy Body Healthy Home Healthy Spirit, B. Jain Publishers (P) Ltd., 2000
34. Simon Brown: Thorsons Principles Of Feng Shui
35. Lillian Too: The Complete Illustrated Guide To Feng Shui, Harper Collins Publishers, London
36. Richard Webster: Feng Shui For Home, Health & Harmony, New Delhi
37. Richard Webster: Feng Shui For Workplace, Health & Harmony, New Delhi
38. R. Venketesh: Feng Shui The User's Manual, the avenue press, Chennai, 1998
39. Gill Hale: The Practical Encyclopedia Of Feng Shui, Hermes House, USA
40. The Universal History of Numbers From Prehistory to the Invention of the Computer by Georges Ifrah, The Harvill Press, London, 1998
41. M M Goyal: Handbook of Building Construction, Amrindrea Consultancy (P) Ltc., Revised Edition, 2004
42. Osho: Gita Darshan (Chapter 9-10)
43. Robert E. Svoboda: Ayurveda life, Health and Longevity, Penguin Books 1993
44. Lal Kitab
45. K. K. Joshi: Muhurta Traditional and Modern, Sagar Publications, New Delhi, 2003
46. The Hindustan Times (Daily Newspaper)
47. The Times of India (Daily Newspaper)
48. Navbharat Times (Hindi Daily Newspaper)
49. Google Wikipedia, the free encyclopedia "https://en.wikipedia.org/" on different Gods and demi-gods, images, terms and topics
50. Hindupedia, the Hindu Encyclopedia "www.hindupedia.com/en" on different Gods and demi-gods, images, terms and topics
51. Google Online Sanskrit English Dictionary for Spoken Sanskrit "spokensanskrit.de/" for translation of Sanskrit terms available in Classical texts of Vaastu

Hindi books

52. "योगवाशिष्ठ और उनके सिद्धान्त" द्वारा भीखनलाल आत्रेय, तारा प्रिंटिंग वर्क्स, बनारस, 1957
53. "वास्तुमण्डनम्" अनुवादक-श्रीकृष्ण 'जुगनू' चौखम्बा सुरभारती प्रकाशन, वाराणसी 2009.
54. समराङ्गणसूत्रधार (भाग 1 व 2), सम्पादक एवं अनुवादक डॉ. श्रीकृष्ण 'जुगनू' एवं प्रो. भँवर शर्मा, चौखम्बा संस्कृत सीरीज ऑफिस, वाराणसी, 2011
55. अपराजितपृच्छा (भाग 1 व 2), सम्पादक एवं अनुवादक डॉ. श्रीकृष्ण 'जुगनू' एवं प्रो. भँवर शर्मा, परिमल पब्लिकेशन्स दिल्ली, 2011.
56. कौटिलीय अर्थशास्त्रम्, सम्पादक- वाचस्पति गैरोला, चौखम्बा विद्याभवन, वाराणसी, 2013.
57. अमरकोष: भाषा टीका, सम्पादक श्रीमन्नालाल 'अभिमन्यु' एम.ए. चौखम्बा विद्याभवन, वाराणसी 2012.
58. श्रीविश्वविजय पञ्चागम् सन् 2015-16, सम्पादक - Er. श्री सुधाकर शर्मा त्रिवेदी सोलन, हिमाचल प्रदेश।

...